Special Edition Using XML

David Gulbransen

que®

201 W. 103rd Street

Indianapolis, Indiana 46290

SPECIAL EDITION USING XML

International Standard Book Number: 0-7897-2748-x

Library of Congress Catalog Card Number: 2002103037

Printed in the United States of America

First Printing: June 2002

04 03 02 01 4 3 2 1

Trademarks

All terms mentioned in this book that are known to be trademarks or service marks have been appropriately capitalized. Que Publishing cannot attest to the accuracy of this information. Use of a term in this book should not be regarded as affecting the validity of any trademark or service mark.

Warning and Disclaimer

Every effort has been made to make this book as complete and as accurate as possible, but no warranty or fitness is implied. The information provided is on an "as is" basis. The authors and the publisher shall have neither liability nor responsibility to any person or entity with respect to any loss or damages arising from the information contained in this book.

Associate Publisher
Candy Hall

Acquisitions Editor
Todd Green

Development Editors
Sean Dixon
Alan Moffet

Managing Editor
Thomas Hayes

Project Editor
Sheila Schroeder

Copy Editors
Maribeth Echard
Rhonda Tinch-Mize

Indexer
Kelly Castell

Proofreader
Plan-It Publishing

Technical Editor
Alan Moffet

Team Coordinator
Sharry Gregory

Interior Designer
Ruth Harvey

Cover Designers
Dan Armstrong
Ruth Harvey

Page Layout
Michelle Mitchell

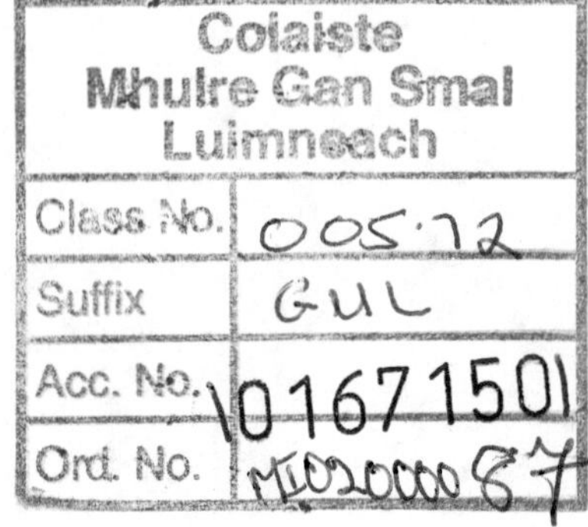

Contents at a Glance

Table of Contents

About the Author

David Gulbransen has been employed as an information systems professional for more than eight years. He began his career with the Indiana University Departmental Support Lab as an analyst/manager, overseeing a consulting group responsible for advising university departments on technology deployment. After an appointment as the computing support specialist for the School of Fine Arts, David left for a position as the manager of information systems at Dimension X, a Java tools development company. While there, he grew the information systems environment from a small Unix-based shop, to a shared Unix-NT environment serving customers as diverse as Fox Television, MCA Records, Intel, and Sun Microsystems. Upon the purchase of Dimension X in 1997 by Microsoft, David co-founded Vervet Logic, a software development company developing XML and Web tools for new media development. He is currently a freelance consultant specializing in XML and Web development. Some of his other titles include *Creating Web Applets with Java*, *The Netscape Server Survival Guide*, *Special Edition Using Dynamic HTML*, and *The Complete Idiot's Guide to XML*. David holds a B.A. in Computer Science and Theatre from Indiana University.

Kynn Bartlett is an instructor, consultant, and author from Southern California. He designed his first Web site in 1994, and founded Idyll Mountain Internet in 1995 with his wife Liz. Kynn's personal mission is to increase the accessibility and usability of the World Wide Web for all users, including people with disabilities. As an active board member of the HTML Writers Guild, he led the growth of the organization to more than 100,000 members and founded the Guild's Accessible Web Authoring Resources and Education Center. Kynn teaches online courses through the HWG/IWA eClasses program, contributes articles to the International Center for Disability Resources on the Internet, and has worked on revolutionary Web accessibility software at Edapta and Reef. His fields of interest include HTML/XHTML, XML, XSLT, CC/PP and CSS, and he is an active participant in the World Wide Web Consortium's Web Accessibility Initiative working groups.

Earl Bingham has been a programmer since the age of 10 with the original Atari 400. Since that time, he has been a pioneer of experience designing and implementing enterprise distributed applications. He has led development in emerging technologies such as XML and large-scale, enterprise applications. He currently works at leading the initiative to further the product suite of XMLCities, a startup that has built leading content capturing software. Earl has written articles for technical magazines and has submitted a number of patents in the area of peer-to-peer computing.

Alexander Kachur graduated from one of the renowned Moscow Universities—the University of Aerospace Technology—and he has a master's degree in Computer Science.

Since he started his professional career, Alexander has been involved in Information Security, e-/m-Commerce, and Digital Rights Management. He led and participated in interesting projects in Moscow, New York, and Dublin including the B2-level Security System for Windows-based corporal networks, which is now used by many Russian banks and government organizations and e-/m-commerce systems for the Bank of Ireland, German HypoVereinsbank, and Irish mobile operator Eircell. At the moment, he is a software architect with the Dublin-based company Altamedius Ltd.—a European leader in e-/m-Commerce software development.

Alexander has been working with Pearson Technology Group for five years. This is his second book. In 1999, he was coauthor of Que's *Microsoft Windows 2000 Security Handbook*. For several years, he has tech edited a great deal of books on EJB, Java, DCOM, and so on.

He can be reached at `askel@usa.net`. Comments and questions are welcome.

Kenrick Rawlings is the cofounder of Vervet Logic, a leading XML tools development company. He has coauthored several technology books including *Creating Web Applets with Java* and *Special Edition Using Dynamic HTML*, and he has been a contributing author to many other books.

Andrew Watt is an independent consultant and author with an interest and expertise in XML technologies including SVG. He is author of *Designing SVG Web Graphics* (New Riders) and *XPath Essentials* (Wiley), and he was a contributing author on Que's *XHTML, XML and Java 2 Platinum Edition*. He has also coauthored or been a contributing author on *Professional XSL*, *Professional XML 2nd Edition*, and *Professional XML Meta Data* (Wrox Press), as well as *XML Schema Essentials* (Wiley) and *Sams Teach Yourself JavaScript in 21 Days* (Sams).

Dedication

David Gulbransen

To Kristyna, for her love, encouragement, and understanding.

Alexander Kachur

This work is dedicated to my beloved wife Elena, who has always encouraged and inspired me.

Acknowledgments

This title would not have been possible without the assistance of a great many people: Todd Green, Sean Dixon, Candy Hall, Alan Moffet, Maureen McDaniel, Sheila Schroeder, Alex Kachur, Andrew H. Watt, Kynn Bartlett, Ken Rawlings, Charles Mohnike, Earl Bingham, and all the folks at Que who worked so hard on this title. I'd also like to thank my family, Anne, David, Mary Anne, Matt, and Kristyna, as well as friends who tolerated me during the pressure of deadlines: Kim, Dusty, Kate, Mikey, Stef, and Ken.

We Want to Hear from You!

As the reader of this book, *you* are our most important critic and commentator. We value your opinion and want to know what we're doing right, what we could do better, what areas you'd like to see us publish in, and any other words of wisdom you're willing to pass our way.

As an executive editor for Que, I welcome your comments. You can email or write me directly to let me know what you did or didn't like about this book—as well as what we can do to make our books better.

Please note that I cannot help you with technical problems related to the *topic* of this book. We do have a User Services group, however, where I will forward specific technical questions related to the book.

When you write, please be sure to include this book's title and author as well as your name, email address, and phone number. I will carefully review your comments and share them with the author and editors who worked on the book.

Email: `feedback@quepublishing.com`

Mail: Candy Hall
Que
201 West 103rd Street
Indianapolis, IN 46290 USA

For more information about this book or another Que title, visit our Web site at `www.quepublishing.com`. Type the ISBN (excluding hyphens) or the title of the book in the Search field to find the page you're looking for.

INTRODUCTION

To assemble one single title that deals with all the possibilities and potential of XML is nearly an impossible task. The problem stems from the fact that XML is more than just a single technology based on a single Recommendation from the W3C. What started as a very simple means to allow people to develop their own markup languages has quickly grown into more than a dozen interrelated and interconnected technologies, all of which, in some form or another, could be termed XML.

At the core of the whirlwind of XML activity is the XML 1.0 Recommendation, which started a giant snowball of technology when it was introduced as a formal Recommendation in 1998. XML started with the goal of simplifying SGML for use on the Web, with the idea that 80% of the problems people were facing required a solution simpler than SGML, and for the remaining 20%, SGML would still be around. Now, however, there is so much confusion surrounding the issue of what is XML and what isn't that it seems as though that goal of simplicity may have been eclipsed.

At the heart, however, XML remains a simple technology. If you want to start developing your own markup language, there is painfully little that you need to learn about XML in order to get started. The more you want to **do** with that language, however, the more you will become immersed in all the Recommendations and Working Groups that are developing technologies that "extend" the power of XML.

This doesn't even begin to address the issue of technologies that are now maturing that have been written using XML. These languages, or XML vocabularies, were written following the XML 1.0 Recommendation's guidelines, and, as such, they could be considered XML technologies as well, even though they aren't XML in the purest sense of the word.

So, what is the result of all this activity? People are still confused about what XML is and what it is not, and how all of these new Recommendations fit together to create a cohesive technology that you can actually use to solve your IS problems.

As I mentioned before, to cover all of these topics in depth would either be impossible or result in a book that required its own fleet of trucks to transport. To master all the technologies of XML and those related to XML would require diligent study of Herculean proportions. However, chances are more than great that you don't need to learn all the XML technologies to do what you need to do. The odds are that you can accomplish your goals with one or two, or perhaps a handful of these technologies at the most.

The result is that you don't need a book that will allow you to master all the XML technologies. What you need is a book that presents all the XML technologies, with a competent level of technical detail, so that you can make informed decisions about the XML technologies that are right for you, and even get started building solutions using those technologies. Then, as you become more and more experienced in an area, such as XPath, you can build on the knowledge we have imparted here by turning to more advanced, expert resources that focus on the one specific technology you are using.

With this title, we're going to start by making sure you have a firm grasp on the fundamentals of pure XML. In Part I, we'll look at the basics of XML syntax, how to author and work with well-formed XML and valid XML. We'll look at Document Type Definitions and authoring XML Schemas to create your own valid XML documents and XML vocabularies.

In Part II, we will move on to working with the display of XML. We'll talk about how XML can be used with CSS and current browser technology. And then we will address how XML will be displayed (and is being displayed) with cutting-edge technology such as Extensible Stylesheets and XSL Transformations.

In Part III, we will look at some XML location technologies. These are technologies that can help you navigate and organize the data in your XML documents—technologies such as XPath, XPointer, and linking with XLink.

In Part IV, we will take a look at programming with XML, giving you a glimpse inside working with the Document Object Model, or the Simple API for XML. We'll also take a look at using XML with some hot programming environments such as Sun's Java and Microsoft's .NET. We will also look at XML and Perl, one of the most popular scripting languages on the Net.

In Part V, we'll look at some real-world XML technologies, such as working with XML and databases. We'll take a look at existing databases and XML native databases to see how you can best manage your XML documents. We'll also look at Document Repositories designed for managing large-scale documents with XML. And, finally, we'll look at how new technologies, such as XQuery, make it easier to find information in your XML documents.

Finally, in Part VI, we will examine some XML-related technologies and vocabularies. We will take a look at how wireless technology and XML are working together with the Wireless Markup Language (WML). We'll look at how XML is impacting Web graphics with Scalable Vector Graphics (SVG). The Synchronized Multimedia Integration Language (SMIL) will change the face of animation and presentations with XML. And we'll take a look at the future of the Web and HTML with the W3C's adoption of XTHML.

We will also take a look at how XForms will change the way we gather and use data, and how the Resource Description Framework (RDF) is being used to help organize and categorize all the information currently flooding the Web. Finally, we will take a look at the future of where XML and the World Wide Web are headed with initiatives such as the Semantic Web.

The goal here is to present you with a number of XML technologies so that you are aware of the choices you have available as you start to work on your own projects—and to give you enough technical information to make informed choices and start work on your projects right away. From there, you will be confident in the decisions you've made, and be ready to turn to more advanced resources to become an expert in the technologies on which you've finally decided. In the meantime, enjoy learning about all the exciting possibilities XML has to offer.

PART I

XML Fundamentals

CHAPTER 1

The XML Jigsaw Puzzle

In this chapter

by David Gulbransen

XML AND THE W3C

The Extensible Markup Language, or XML, is another in a set of technologies from the World Wide Web Consortium (W3C) that is changing the way we share and exchange information via networked computers. XML is a technology that was developed with the World Wide Web in mind, as a mechanism for structuring data for multiple uses, while still keeping that data in a format that would be friendly for exchange via the Web. The result of the W3C working group's efforts came to fruition in February 1998 with the publication of the XML 1.0 Recommendation. Since then, XML has evolved from that single Recommendation into a host of Recommendations, all interrelated and based on the basic tenants of XML. In this chapter, we are going to take a look at how all of these various XML-based technologies fit together to form the big picture for XML, and why that makes XML and the XML family of Recommendations such a powerful set of technologies.

THE GOALS OF XML

The main goal of XML was to bring the ability to author structured markup languages to the masses, via the World Wide Web. The technology to create your own markup languages already existed in the form of the Standard Generalized Markup Language, or SGML. However, for many applications, the complexity of SGML was too much, and frightened away many potential users. XML was created to provide a subset of what SGML could provide, allowing developers to create their own markup languages (or XML vocabularies) without all the complexity in SGML. For those users who need advanced features, SGML is still around and useful.

One of the best documents explaining XML succinctly is "XML in 10 Points," published by the W3C and written by Bert Bos. You can read that document in its entirety at the W3C site (`http://www.w3.org/XML/1999/XML-in-10-points`); however, here are the main points:

- XML is for structuring data—XML documents reflect the structure of the data that they contain. For example, if the document were a book, it might contain `<section>` elements, which would in turn contain `<chapter>` elements, and so on.
- XML looks a bit like HTML—XML uses tags, both start and end tags, which contain the data in the document and "mark up" the document structure.
- XML leads HTML to XHTML—The HTML language of the Web is currently being rewritten to comply with XML. The result will be an XHTML that is case sensitive, and requires all tags to be properly nested and closed.
- XML is text, but isn't meant to be read—Although XML is verbose, and it is all ASCII text, XML is still designed primarily to be used by automated systems, not necessarily read by humans.
- XML is verbose by design—XML is not designed to be compact; tags can be as long as you would like them to be, in order to make sense. Text is also not the most compact form for storing documents; however, this helps keep XML portable and readable by humans.

- XML is a family of technologies—The core of XML is the XML 1.0 Recommendation. However, there are a number of other technologies that contribute to the usefulness of XML. These technologies include the Extensible Stylesheet Language, XML Namespaces, and XML Schemas. In addition, there are XML vocabularies such as Scalable Vector Graphics, which are markup languages written using XML.
- XML is new, but not that new—Although XML is relatively new, and subject to much hype, it is based on SGML which is a very well-established technology.
- XML is modular—Using XML, you can define vocabularies that are designed to be reused. By creating DTDs or XML Schemas, you can create sets of documents that are all based on common vocabularies. Similarly, using XML Namespaces, you can publish and share those vocabularies without conflicts.
- XML is the basis for RDF and the Semantic Web—RDF, or the Resource Description Framework, and the Semantic Web are both initiatives of the W3C to help refine the way information is organized on the Web. XML is the basis of these technologies, and will help organize the information on the Web, making it easier for users to find and access the information they need.
- XML is license free, platform independent, and well supported—XML is not owned by any corporation, nor is it controlled by a corporation. It is a publication of the W3C, and as such, it can be used freely by anyone. And although some may have issues with the W3C process, or what ends up in the final Recommendations, the bottom line is that it makes XML a fairly open standard.

The W3C has put a great deal of effort into the development of XML and the XML family of technologies. A quick perusal of the W3C site reveals the level of commitment to XML by the W3C, and the ever-growing XML family. And because XML is text based, and an open recommendation from the W3C, you are not locked into any one vendor's XML solutions; anyone is free to develop solutions using XML, as long as they adhere to the guidelines of the Recommendation.

Note

What is a Recommendation?

Unlike an officially sanctioned standards body, such as the International Standards Organization (ISO), the W3C is not an official standards organization. The W3C simply publishes "Recommendations," which are not binding in any way. Simply put, they are a set of guidelines, published and copyrighted by the W3C.

The power of these "Recommendations" comes from the fact that people treat them as standards by consensus, and the fact that you can't claim compliance with a Recommendation and not be in compliance without violating the copyrights. Many people are surprised that the W3C has no official status, but many more are shocked to learn that the W3C is not a democracy at all. Although "Recommendations" might be authored by a working group, nothing becomes a final "Recommendation" until signed off by the W3C Director, Tim Berners-Lee.

So, although there are no requirements to follow "standards" released by the W3C as Recommendations, the major players in the Web, such as Netscape and Microsoft, have all agreed to support the W3C.

MANY TECHNOLOGIES CONTRIBUTE TO THE POWER OF XML

As we mentioned earlier, XML is not simply one Recommendation and one technology. This can be a bit confusing to people who are new to XML and are looking for a single, simple language that they can use, such as Visual Basic. For example, it is possible to use XML, the core 1.0 Recommendation version of XML, to create well-formed XML documents for use in a variety of computing applications. These XML documents could be used as a standard file format for storing application documents, or they could be used as configuration files for a server, and so on.

However, if you wanted to use XML as a file format for storing information, and then publishing that information in print, on CD-ROM, and on the World Wide Web, you would need to make use of some other technologies that are not specifically XML, but might be based on XML, or be supplementary to XML. For example, you might have an XML document that you want to display on the Web; however, XML documents do not contain any information about display formatting. To transform the XML data into HTML or XHTML for displaying it on the Web, you might need to use a style sheet, such as the Extensible Stylesheet Language (XSL).

You might also need to specify exactly how XML files are to be structured, using a set of rules such as a Document Type Definition (DTD). DTDs are an integral part of creating valid XML, but they are actually not formally defined anywhere.

Note

XML can come in two varieties: well formed and valid. Well-formed XML means that the XML is written in the proper format, and that it complies with all the rules for XML as set forth in the XML 1.0 Recommendation. Valid XML means that the XML document has been validated against a rule set, or schema, such as a Document Type Definition or an XML Schema. XML cannot be considered "valid" unless it has a DTD or schema, and the document meets the constraints set out in that schema.

DTDs are a holdover from SGML, maintained for compatibility reasons. The syntax used for the declarations in DTDs is defined as a part of the XML 1.0 Recommendation.

DTDs are useful—without them or another type of schema, it is impossible to verify that an XML file is structured properly within the rules the author had in mind. But DTDs are not required in order to use XML. In fact, that is how many of the following technologies could be described: They extend XML and are supplementary; however, none of them are required. Still, they can be very handy in saving you time and effort when working with XML. It's a good idea to familiarize yourself with these technologies and their uses, so that you can save yourself development time and effort in the long run.

XML 1.0

When people talk about XML, they are generally referring to the Extensible Markup Language as defined in the XML 1.0 Recommendation published by the W3C. This Recommendation defines the basic structures of XML, such as

- Elements
- Attributes
- Entities
- Notations
- CDATA sections
- PCData Sections
- Comments

This includes defining the conventions for names, case sensitivity, start tags, end tags, and so on. Everything you need to work with well-formed XML is contained within this one Recommendation.

With well-formed XML, you could develop a document format to be used with a specific application. You could develop a document format for exchanging data between two applications, between vendors and suppliers, customers and vendors, and so on. Virtually any type of document that contains data can be constructed using simple, straightforward, well-formed XML. Here's a short example of a well-formed XML document:

```
<document>
<title>Introducing XML</title>
<byline>John Doe</byline>
<body>Learning about XML is not complicated…</body>
</document>
```

All the elements have both start and end tags, and all the tags are properly nested; therefore, it meets the basic requirements of an XML document. However, if you want to go one step further, and actually make sure that the structure of the document adheres to some rules, you can author a Document Type Definition (DTD) and use that with your XML documents to create validated XML. Validation allows you to check each XML document against the rules set for violations, which helps you make sure that all of your documents are formatted correctly and helps you ensure data integrity.

All the information you need to author DTDs, from Element Type Declarations to Attribute List Declarations, are outlined in the XML 1.0 Recommendation. However, DTDs do have a different syntax from XML, which confuses many XML newcomers.

So, even though DTDs might seem as though they are a supplementary technology (because, in a way, they are), they are still part of the XML 1.0 Recommendation. We will take a closer look at DTDs and authoring them in Chapter 4, "Structuring XML Documents with DTDs."

XML-Related Recommendations

Building on the foundation established with the XML 1.0 Recommendation, there are also a number of W3C Recommendations that are very closely related to the core XML technology. In this category, the Recommendations define some technologies that are designed specifically to add functionality to XML 1.0. In fact, these could be part of the 1.0 Recommendation, although that would complicate it needlessly. These technologies all have some common features:

- They are all W3C Recommendations.
- They are all related to well-formed or valid XML.
- They are structural Recommendations.

These technologies include XML Namespaces and XML Schemas, both of which are designed to address shortcomings within the XML 1.0 Recommendation. Let's take a closer look at these Recommendations now.

Namespaces

XML allows developers to create their own markup languages, for use in a variety of applications. However, there is nothing to stop two developers from developing markup languages that have similar tags, but with different structure or meaning. If both of these developers were using their markup languages internally only, this might not be a problem. But what if these developers start sharing their vocabularies with their clients, vendors, and the general public? The result could be confusion about what tag means what, and in what context.

For example, let's say both developers want to keep track of customer names, a very common piece of information to store. Developer One designs a `<name>` element that looks like this:

```
<name>
<first>John</first>
<last>Doe</last>
</name>
```

Developer Two, however, prefers to use a `<name>` element with no children:

```
<name>John Doe</name>
```

Both are perfectly valid uses of XML, and both might have advantages over the other. That doesn't really matter in this example. What does matter, however, is that we now have two `<name>` elements that store similar data, but in different ways.

For example, what happens if a vendor is working with both organizations? How do they know which name format to use when? That is where namespaces come in handy. They allow you to create elements as being a part of a specific namespace. This means that when they are used, the parser is aware that they belong to a namespace, and if a similar element is used, but it belongs to a different namespace, there is no conflict.

Namespaces make use of a special attribute called *xmlns* that allows you to define a prefix and the namespace URI. For example, here's a simple document with two namespaces, vendor and supplier:

```
<?xml version="1.0"?>
<customers
        xmlns:vendor="http://www.vendor.com"
        xmlns:supplier="http://www.supplier.com">
<vendor:name>John Dough</vendor:name>
<supplier:name>
<first>Jane</first>
<last>Doe</last>
</supplier:name>
</customers>
```

As you can see, we have two name elements; however, one is in the http://www.vendor.com namespace, and the other is in the http://www.supplier.com namespace. We will discuss namespaces and using them with XML in greater detail in Chapter 6, "Avoiding XML Confusion with XML Namespaces."

XML SCHEMAS

We've talked briefly about the concept of well-formed versus valid XML (and we will discuss this in more detail in later chapters as well). So, you should understand that in order to be considered valid, the XML document needs to either have a DTD or an XML Schema.

As we mentioned earlier, there is no formal Recommendation that deals explicitly with Document Type Definitions. Instead, the mechanics of DTDs are addressed directly in the XML 1.0 Recommendation as they are needed. Because of this, if you wanted to learn the mechanics of DTDs (which we will in Chapter 4), you would turn to the XML 1.0 Recommendation.

However, there is another mechanism for providing the rules set, or schema, for an XML document: XML Schemas. XML Schemas represent a formal schema language for defining the structure of XML documents.

The XML Schema specification deals with some of the shortcomings of DTDs, such as the lack of robust data structures, and also abandons the cryptic syntax of DTDs for an easier-to-use XML-based syntax. That doesn't mean that XML Schemas are necessarily simple; in fact, they can be very complex and powerful. We'll take a closer look at XML Schemas in Chapter 5, "Defining XML Document Structures with XML Schemas."

In fact, there are actually three separate parts to the Recommendation for XML Schemas:

- XML Schema Part 0: Primer
- XML Schema Part 1: Structures
- XML Schema Part 2: Datatypes

The first part, Part 0, is a tutorial designed to familiarize developers with the XML Schema syntax and use. The second part, Part 1, deals with the logical structures of XML Schema, and the syntax used for authoring schemas. Finally, Part 2 deals with data structures. Data structures are an important step for XML, because with DTDs there are no mechanisms for specifying data structures within a document. However, XML Schema brings the power and complexity of data structures to XML.

XML FAMILY

The XML 1.0 Recommendation, XML Namespaces, and XML Schema Recommendations all deal directly with the structure of XML documents. However, there are also a number of W3C Recommendations that deal with various aspects of XML that are not necessarily related to the structure of an XML document, but provide mechanisms for implementing XML in practical solutions. These recommendations are related to the display or navigation of XML documents. Let's take a closer look at these technologies and their uses.

XSL

XML documents are simply text, and therefore they are readable by humans. However, that is not the general intent of XML. XML files are text primarily because nearly any type of application can access ASCII text files. However, XML files are really designed for automatic processing. But XML files do not contain information about how they should be displayed. XML documents are designed for structure, not presentation. To aid in the presentation of XML, a stylesheet language was designed with XML in mind: the Extensible Stylesheet Language (XSL).

XSL was designed to be used specifically with XML. As a stylesheet language, it is similar to Cascading Style Sheets (CSS), although there are some significant differences. Both use a different syntax even though XSL shares many formatting objects with CSS. CSS has also been around much longer than XSL, so support for CSS is better in most browsers. In fact, CSS can be used with XML, as we will discuss in Chapter 7, "Using XML with Existing Stylesheet Technologies (CSS)." This can be a good way to get XML documents displayed using current browser technologies. However, XML and XSL support is advancing rapidly, and browsers will soon support XSL natively.

XSL uses an XML syntax to specify how elements within an XML document should be displayed. For example, take our earlier simple XML document:

```
<document>
 <title>Introducing XML</title>
 <byline>John Doe</byline>
 <body>Learning about XML is not complicated…</body>
</document>
```

If we wanted to display the title of the document in italic, we could use an XSL sheet that looks something like this:

```
<xsl:template match="title">
 <fo:block font-style="italic">
  <xsl:apply-templates/>
 </fo:block>
</xsl:template>
```

When the stylesheet and XML document are processed by an XSL-capable parser, the result will be a document displayed with the title in italic. Currently, you can use several different processors to render XSL/XML documents into PDFs; support for popular browsers such as Internet Explorer and Netscape is still being developed.

If you look closely at the XSL example, you will notice that it makes use of namespaces, with the "xsl:" and "fo:" prefixes. The "fo" namespace prefix denotes that the element is an XSL Formatting Object element. Formatting Objects are display objects that have properties that can be manipulated for presentation. The XSL Recommendation itself deals with the structure of the XSL stylesheet, and with the Formatting Objects. We will address Formatting Objects in greater detail in Chapter 10, "The Nuts and Bolts of XSL: Formatting Objects."

However, there is another component to XSL, which is the Recommendation that allows the XML document to be transformed by the stylesheet. This is XSL Transformations, or XSLT.

XSLT

XSLT is a technology that allows developers to author a stylesheet which when processed, will result in the elements and attributes of an XML document being transformed into another format. For example, by using XSLT it is possible to transform an XML element:

```
<byline>John Doe</byline>
```

into an HTML tag set:

```
<b>John Doe</b>
```

XSLT does this by allowing you to select individual elements and attributes using XPath, which is yet another XML-related Recommendation. XPath enables you to specify the location of elements or attributes. The `match` and `select` components of the stylesheet actually use XPath to specify the XML element or attribute being selected. Using XSLT, you can then manipulate the selected component.

For example, you can combine HTML within an XSLT stylesheet to display information from the XML document within an HTML document. This simple stylesheet:

```
<?xml version="1.0"?>

<xsl:stylesheet version="1.0"
     xmlns:xsl="http://www.w3.org/1999/XSL/Transform">

 <xsl:template match="/">
  <html>
   <head>
    <title>
```

```
      <xsl:apply-templates select="/document/title"/>
     </title>
    </head>
    <body>
     <b><xsl:apply-templates select="/document/byline"/></b>
     <p>
     <xsl:apply-templates select="/document/body"/>
    </body>
   </html>
  </xsl:template>
 </xsl:stylesheet>
```

when applied to our simple XML document, will result in the following HTML document:

```
<html>
 <head>
  <title>
   Introducing XML
  </title>
 </head>
 <body>
  John Doe
  <p>
  Learning about XML is not complicated…
 </body>
</html>
```

This type of exercise shows just how interdependent solutions are on the various components of XML. Here we start with an XML document, and then by using XSLT in conjunction with XPath, we end up with HTML. XSL and XSLT are powerful technologies, and we will discuss them in greater detail later in Chapter 8, "The New Wave of Stylesheets: XSL," and Chapter 9, "Transforming XML Data into Other Formats with XSLT."

XPath/XPointer

Many of the XML technologies presented in this book build on another XML technology in some way. For example, with XSL, XPath is used to specify the location of components. In fact, XPath is a Recommendation that was developed specifically for locating components within an XML document.

For example, let's say we had an XML document describing the books in a library:

```
<library>
<book>
<title>First Book</title>
<author>John Doe</author>
</book>
<book>
<title>Second Book</title>
<author>Jane Doe</author>
</book>
</library>
```

Of course, in this simple example, it's not hard to locate one book in the document. However, what if we had thousands of books? And we wanted two books by specific authors in order to display them on the Web? We could match those authors and create the HTML using XSLT; however, that does involve using XPath to specify the location of our elements.

XPath provides a variety of ways for us to specify the location of elements. For example, if we wanted to select all of the `<book>` elements in the library, we could use

```
library::*
```

which selects all the children of the `<library>` element. We could also select each book by its position in the document, for example, selecting the first book in the library, or the last book. And XPath is not limited to elements—attributes can be specified by location as well.

The details and syntax of XPath are covered in Chapter 11, "Locating Components in XML Documents with XPath." But XPath doesn't just stop there. In fact, XPath is the basis for another locator technology called *XPointer*.

XPointer is a Recommendation that allows developers to easily refer to and locate XML document fragments. This is very useful for several types of applications, including the ability to have multiple authors working on a single large XML document, or making extremely large XML documents more manageable for editing purposes. XPointer enables you to specify points and ranges within your XML documents, which can then be treated as "mini" documents in their own right. Chapter 12, "Extending the Power of XPath with XPointer," deals with the specifics of XPointer in greater detail.

XLINK/XINCLUDE/XBASE

One of the most powerful aspects of information on the World Wide Web is the ability to link together documents of interest. Publishing documents in an easily accessed forum is useful, but the ability to click on a hypertext link in one document and then be taken to another relevant document is powerful. Therefore, a linking mechanism for XML documents naturally increases the power of XML.

The XLink and XBase Recommendations are both used to specify information about linking XML documents together. Linking in XML is more complicated than in HTML, because there are more types of links available to developers. For example, here is a simple link from one XML document to another, which functions much like a link in HTML would:

```
<employees
  xmlns:xlink=http://www.w3.org/1999/xlink
  xlink:type="simple"
  xlink:href="employees.xml">
List of Current Employees
</employees>
```

Here we have an element called `employees` which serves as a simple link to the `employees.xml` document. As you can see, the syntax looks somewhat similar to HTML, but there is more information. That is because XML Linking actually allows for different types of links, including a single link that points to multiple documents, or a bidirectional link that flows between two documents. This makes XML Linking very flexible, and provides levels of tying together documents that are not possible with HTML.

There are also applications where simply linking between documents might not be ideal, and you might want to build a large XML document from a set of smaller documents. For that purpose, there is the XInclude Recommendation, which provides the means to include sets of XML documents into a single document structure.

The specifics and syntax of XLink and XInclude are discussed in Chapter 13, "Linking Information: XLink, XBase, and XInclude."

PROGRAMMING AND MODELING

XML documents by themselves are simply text files, and similar to word processing documents sitting on a hard drive, they don't really do anything. What makes XML documents useful is when the data they contain is read by an application, and then the application makes use of that data.

Because XML is such a flexible data format, there are a number of different mechanisms that can be employed to work with XML in a number of different programming languages, ranging from scripting languages, such as Perl, to more complex languages, such as C++.

DOM

At the heart of documents on the World Wide Web, including both HTML and XML is the Document Object Model, or DOM. The DOM is an effort by the W3C to develop a set of standards for interacting with documents. The goal is to provide an interface that is not dependent on any specific computing platform or programming language, or owned by any commercial interest.

XML and structured documents like XML are trees, and the DOM is essentially an API (Application Programming Interface) for manipulating the document tree.

Note

The tree structure is one commonly found in application development in many different programming languages. The idea is that the structure of the document resembles that of a tree, with each item in the document related to another through a series of branches, and each individual element, or node, in the tree similar to a leaf.

Rather than an API based on user events (such as clicking a mouse), the DOM is based on the structure of the document itself.

If you are not a programmer, intimate familiarity with the DOM is not necessary. It's always a good idea to have a basic understanding of the DOM, however, because many decisions about implementing and developing with XML will be impacted by it, which is why we've covered the DOM in more detail in Chapter 14, "XML and the Document Object Model."

SAX

Although some applications, such as XML editors, are a natural fit for working with the Document Object Model, other applications are better served by an event-driven API. While powerful and intuitive, working with the DOM also involves greater overhead (larger parsers, more memory consumption, and so on) which might not be appropriate for all applications. That's where the Simple API for XML, or SAX comes into play.

SAX is an event-driven API, which means that rather than working with the document structure as a whole, SAX allows you to deal with specific parts of a document as the document is parsed. This allows for some very lightweight components. Again, an intimate familiarity with SAX is not necessary to work with XML; however, being aware of how SAX is used can be important when making decisions about how to structure your total XML solutions. SAX is covered in Chapter 15, "Parsing XML Based on Events."

Java and .NET

There are tools for working with XML in a wide variety of programming languages, and it would simply be impossible to cover them all. However, there are two languages that are a very natural fit for XML, and have a number of resources available to allow programmersto work easily with XML: Java and .NET.

Java and XML are a good fit, because Java provides a mechanism for platform-independent application development, and XML documents are also platform independent. There are also a number of resources, such as XML parsers, already written in Java, which can save you time and effort to avoid reinventing the wheel. Java can be used with XML on both the server side and the client side, allowing you to build anything from a generic XML editor to a highly customized inventory application with XML. Working with XML and Java is covered in Chapter 16, "Working with XML and Java."

One up-and-coming technology that is being positioned as a challenger to Java is Microsoft's .NET initiative. .NET is actually a set of technologies, not just a programming language, designed to make portable application development robust and easy. One advantage to working with .NET is that .NET has been designed with XML in mind as a supplementary technology. Because of Microsoft's long-standing involvement in XML, the .NET set of technologies is making its debut with a number of XML-based features already incorporated. Chapter 17, "Working with XML and .NET," deals with how .NET and XML work together and can provide a solution for developing your own XML tools.

Scripting

Not all work with XML involves advanced programming languages. Because XML files are just text files, a great deal can be done with XML just by using scripting languages, and no scripting language is more famous for dealing with text than Perl.

Perl offers a means for working with XML server side on a variety of platforms, from Unix to Windows. Perl is widely supported, and there are a number of XML tools already written in Perl that you can use to create your own custom solutions. As Perl continues to be developed into a more and more advanced scripting language, you can actually use Perl to build some very complicated XML solutions.

XML and Data

In broad terms, there are really two applications for XML: documents and data. The difference between the two is not always cut and dried, but in general, documents fall along the lines of traditional documents: books, articles, journals, and so on. Data applications of XML encompass a wide variety of uses, such as storing data for application configuration files, inventory information, or any other application where you might have traditionally used a database to store that information.

Although we always talk about XML in terms of "documents," those "documents" might reflect the content of an actual document, or they might reflect a more data-centric content model. Because of this range of applications for XML, there are tools for working with XML and databases, and tools for working with larger-scale XML documents, such as document repositories.

Databases

Many organizations are faced with some troubling questions when they begin to look into new technologies such as XML. One such question arises when organizations with a significant investment in database technologies look at XML and wonder whether they will be able to utilize XML with the database solutions they have in place.

The bad news is that database technology and XML are not always a good fit, depending very much on vendor-specific databases. However, the good news is that the majority of database vendors, from Sybase to Oracle to IBM, are incorporating XML support into their products, and some have already released XML-compatible products. As XML matures, database support promises to mature with it.

In addition to the more traditional relational databases being retooled to accommodate XML, there are also a number of specialty databases on the market designed to work specifically with XML. These XML databases offer some advanced features, such as the capability to assemble XML documents based on document fragments, which are not necessarily found in traditional relational databases.

The bottom line is that there are a number of different solutions available for working with databases, which are covered in Chapter 18, "XML and Databases." From working with your existing database implementations to building new XML-centric database solutions, XML and databases are a natural fit that will continue to develop.

DOCUMENT REPOSITORIES

On the document side of XML, traditional relational databases can be more of a burden than a solution. For large documents, such as technical manuals, dictionaries, encyclopedias, operational manuals, and so on, traditional databases simply are not designed to handle extremely large chunks of text. And because XML documents are simply large chunks of text, these databases fall short in features and performance.

However, because the document industry has been working with SGML for more than a decade, there are a number of tools called *document repositories*, which are designed specifically for maintaining large documents or sets of documents. And because these tools are based in SGML, most have rapidly adapted to XML and are available for use now.

Document repositories can be viewed as specialized databases, designed to work with large documents. They often have special features, such as the capability to enable users to edit only a part of a document, and then integrate that part into the whole. These types of features can be valuable if your organization needs document, rather than data, management. Chapter 19, "XML and Document Repositories," addresses some of the issues with document repositories and looks at a couple of vendors' implementations.

XQUERY

Working with a database for any length of time will teach you two valuable lessons—first, that proper design of your database structure (the schema) is essential, and second, that the best data in the world is useless without proper queries.

Because XML documents are now being stored in relational databases, object databases, document repositories, and as simple flat files, the W3C wanted to create a common query language which would enable users to create queries that would work across all these different kinds of data applications. One way to look at XQuery is as an XML-specific SQL.

The advantage to XQuery for XML is that XQuery is being designed specifically for XML, with the structure of XML documents in mind. So, queries with XQuery on XML documents will be optimized to work with XML.

XQuery contains a number of expressions—path expressions, sequence expressions, comparison expressions—which, in conjunction with XPath, allow you to locate data within an XML document. For example, we could use an XQuery to build a table of contents from a `book.xml` document by creating a query for the chapter titles:

```
<contents>
 {
 filter(document("book.xml")//
   (chapter | chapter/title | chapter/title/text())
 }
</contents>
```

The query makes use of XPath expressions to locate specific elements within the document, demonstrating how many XML technologies work together. XQuery is covered in detail in Chapter 20, "Querying Documents Using XQuery."

THE RELATED TECHNOLOGIES

So far, we have looked at a number of technologies that are all directly related to the XML Recommendation or extend XML in some way. However, there is another category of XML technologies called *XML vocabularies*. These are individual markup languages that have been written using XML 1.0.

XML vocabularies can be treated just like any other XML document, because they are well-formed (and in many cases, valid) XML. When you are developing XML documents, what you are really doing is developing your own XML vocabularies. However, there may already be an existing XML vocabulary that will meet your needs.

Note

XML vocabularies are also sometimes referred to as *XML applications*. To avoid confusion, we've tried to use the term *vocabulary* whenever possible; however, in other sources, you may hear these markup languages referred to as *XML Applications*, and you should not confuse them with something such as an XML editor for Windows, which is an "application" in the more traditional sense.

There are literally hundreds of XML vocabularies in existence and more being developed every day. Some of these vocabularies are being developed privately for use within a specific organization. And some are being developed publicly for anyone to use. The vocabularies we have chosen to cover here are vocabularies that are being developed in conjunction with the W3C, and either are, or will likely become, W3C Recommendations.

XHTML

One of the XML vocabularies that will have the greatest impact on the World Wide Web is *XHTML*, which stands for *XML HTML*. XHTML is simply HTML, rewritten to comply with the rules for being well-formed XML.

The reasoning behind this move is that XHTML will allow XML applications to read and treat HTML as if it were just another XML document. Currently, HTML violates enough rules of XML that parsing HTML documents in XML applications is not easy. Also, the standardization on an XML-based version of HTML will mean that browsers can easily support both XML and HTML, which will benefit everyone.

XHTML doesn't look all that different from HTML. Here's a simple sample document:

```
<?xml version="1.0" encoding="UTF-8"?>
<!DOCTYPE html
     PUBLIC "-//W3C//DTD XHTML 1.0 Strict//EN"
    "http://www.w3.org/TR/xhtml1/DTD/xhtml1-strict.dtd">
<html xmlns="http://www.w3.org/1999/xhtml" xml:lang="en" lang="en">
 <head>
  <title>A Sample XHTML Document</title>
 </head>
 <body>
```

```
  <p>This is a simple XHTML Document.</p>
 </body>
</html>
```

The major difference is the inclusion of the XML prologue information, but other than that, the tags in the document should be familiar to you from HTML. One critical difference is that unlike HTML, XHTML is case sensitive, and all the tags have to appear in lower case. That is because XML is case sensitive, so `<body>` and `<BODY>` are not the same tag. Additionally, as you can see from the `<p>` and `</p>` tags in the previous example, XHTML requires that all tags be properly closed and nested; HTML does not.

The differences between HTML and XHTML are discussed in Chapter 21, "The Future of the Web: XHTML." Additionally, there is a Recommendation that deals with forms. The XForms Recommendation, covered in Chapter 25, "Using XML to Create Forms: XForms," deals with using XML to create forms for the Web and beyond.

WML

Wireless devices have become a very hot commodity, and with the future development of wireless technologies such as BlueTooth and G3 cellular services, the demand for wireless communications is on the rise.

To make wireless communication easier between devices, and to serve documents to wireless devices, there is an XML-based vocabulary in use (and in ongoing development) designed specifically for wireless: the Wireless Markup Language (WML).

WML exists to allow developers to build applications that streamline the transmission of data between wireless devices. Being XML based, WML is easy to learn and use, and is flexible as well. WML is covered in more detail in Chapter 22, "XML and Wireless Technologies: WML."

SVG

Plain-text documents are great, but realistically the Web pages that we visit are usually a combination of text and graphics. The same holds true for documents we see in print. Even business memos and Word documents are being spiced up more and more with graphics.

However, dealing with a mix of graphics formats has always been problematic. Take .gif and .jpg graphics for the Web. Originally, Web browsers did not support .jpgs. Then when there was a scare about Unisys charging royalties for the use of .gifs, many people switched to .jpgs as their standard format. The bottom line, though, is that binary graphic images are large, even when compressed, and they take much more time to download than text. Additionally, if you have a logo that you want to use on your site, and you want a large version for the title page, but a smaller version for other pages, you have to create two separate graphic files, increasing download time further.

That's where Scalable Vector Graphics (SVG) come into play. A vector graphic is a graphic that is defined by the geometry of the image, not as a bitmap. Therefore, vector formats aren't really good for photos, but they are fantastic for line art or illustrations such as logos.

For example, drawing applications such as Adobe Illustrator or Macromedia FreeHand work in vector formats.

SVG is an XML-based specification for creating graphics, which could be used on the Web or in print. SVG enables these graphics to be created in a text file, based on the geometry of the graphic. Here's a simple example that draws a gray rectangle with a red border:

```
<?xml version="1.0"?>
<!DOCTYPE svg PUBLIC "-//W3C//DTD SVG 20010904//EN"
  "http://www.w3.org/TR/2001/REC-SVG-20010904/DTD/svg10.dtd">
<svg width="12cm" height="4cm" viewBox="0 0 1200 400"
     xmlns="http://www.w3.org/2000/svg">

<rect x="100" y="100" width="400" height="200"
  fill="gray" stroke="red" stroke-width="10"  />
</svg>
```

The advantage to SVG files is that they are much smaller than the same file would be as a .gif or .jpg, and if you want to use the image multiple times on one page, you need to load the SVG file only once; it can then be scaled, rotated, and displayed as many times on one page as necessary. SVG is a very promising XML application for the Web, and it is covered in detail in Chapter 23, "Scalable Vector Graphics."

SMIL

Another aspect of the Web that has become quite popular is multimedia files, such as Flash/Shockwave animations or presentations. The development of multimedia on the Web has not gone unnoticed at the W3C, and thus the Synchronized Multimedia Integration Language (SMIL) has been developed.

SMIL is an XML-based language that allows developers to create multimedia presentations in an XML-based language. It allows features similar to that of PowerPoint or Flash, such as animated graphics, sounds, and the ability to interact with the presentation on some level (such as following links).

SMIL is based in XML, which makes it more portable than proprietary multimedia formats, and it is designed to work with other XML-based vocabularies as well, such as SVG. Chapter 24, "XML and Multimedia: SMIL—The Synchronized Multimedia Integration Language," takes a closer look at SMIL and what is possible with this XML vocabulary.

RDF

One of the biggest problems facing the World Wide Web is growth. As the current number of Web sites continues to grow, organizing and processing information on the Web is becoming more and more time consuming. One of the mechanisms being developed by the W3C to help manage the automated processing of information on the Web is the Resource Description Framework (RDF).

RDF is primarily an XML-based format for expressing metadata about information on the Web. Metadata is data about data; for example, a table of contents in a book might be considered metadata because it describes the contents of each chapter in the book.

RDF's goal is to create an XML-based model for describing information on the Web so that various resources can be described in a consistent manner, theoretically making it easier to classify, catalog, and locate information on the Web. The RDF syntax and uses are described in more detail in Chapter 26, "Future Directions and Technologies."

ROADMAP

This entire chapter serves as a roadmap for you to explore XML and all the various components you can use to create XML-based solutions. Hopefully, you now have a better understanding of how all of these various Recommendations and technologies are all related to XML, and how they fit together as part of the XML jigsaw puzzle to create a full picture of how XML could be used within your organization.

Now that you have a general, basic understanding of what each of these technologies does and how they fit together, let's take a look at each of these technologies in greater detail.

CHAPTER 2

THE BASICS OF XML

In this chapter

by David Gulbransen

OVERVIEW OF XML

With XML often being held up as such a revolutionary new technology, one common mistake is to assume that XML is a complicated technology. However, when examining the core of the XML 1.0 Recommendation, XML is actually a very simple technology, and it is from that simplicity that XML gains its power.

Although XML has evolved into a family of technologies (which is the focus of this entire book), the core XML 1.0 Recommendation itself is not overly complicated, by design. The idea has always been to create a minimal set of rules that can be followed to allow for maximum flexibility and compatibility.

The Extensible Markup Language has its roots in some older structured markup technology, which has been around since long before the World Wide Web: SGML. The Standard Generalized Markup Language (SGML) is an international standard (ISO 8879:1986(E)) and the parent of XML. SGML has some impressive progeny; in addition to XML, SGML is also the parent language of HTML.

BRIEF HISTORY

HTML is one of the enabling technologies of the World Wide Web, but it was not conjured out of nothing. When Tim Berners-Lee created HTML, he used SGML as the parent technology. HTML was written using SGML, just as the next generation of HTML, called XHTML, will be written using XML.

Over time, as the Web has become commercialized and mass popularity has set in, the limitations of what can be accomplished with HTML has been pushed to the limits. The result has been a deluge of "enabling" technologies from JavaScript to VBScript to Flash. All of these are designed to bring added functionality to the Web, but they don't do much to increase the sharing of data, or the ability to better organize information; that is where the functionality of XML comes in.

XML was conceived to bring structured documents to the Web more easily. Although SGML has been used for a number of years in document management, many of the features of SGML aren't necessary for managing data in a Web context, and the complexity of SGML has deterred many users from using the technology. With SGML's problems in mind, the W3C formed a working committee to adopt SGML specifically for use with the World Wide Web. The goal was to create a meta-language which could be created to provide structured markup to documents, while still being simple enough to adopt and implement that it would gain in popularity where SGML had failed.

Note

The differences between SGML and XML are highlighted in a note published by the W3C, which can be found at: `http://www.w3.org/TR/NOTE-sgml-xml-971215`.

XML IS A SIMPLE TECHNOLOGY

XML is the Extensible Markup Language, as defined in the XML 1.0 Recommendation published by the W3C. The Recommendation is now in the Second Edition, which exists to correct some simple clerical errors in the first edition—nothing substantive has been changed that would necessitate a new version number.

MARKUP

At the core, XML is not really a language per se—it is really a meta-language. That is, you don't author documents directly in XML as you might with HTML, but instead you use the rules of XML, which are called XML Vocabularies, to develop your own markup language.

For example, with HTML you might have something that looks like this:

```
<B>Webster</B><BR>
<I>123 Fake Street</I>
<I>Chicago, IL 60611</I>
```

Although this might produce a nice-looking address, the HTML only instructs the browser about how the address should be formatted. For example, the HTML indicates that "Webster" should be **bold** but what does "Webster" mean? It could be a family name or it could be a company. Using XML, we might have

```
<company>Webster</company>
<address>123 Fake Street</address>
<city>Chicago</city>
<state>IL</state>
<zip>60611</zip>
```

or, we might have

```
<name>Webster</name>
<address>123 Fake Street</address>
<city>Chicago</city>
<state>IL</state>
<zip>60611</zip>
```

With each of these examples, we have a clear idea of what the data actually represents. The tags are human readable, and they give us some information about the text between them. HTML is a markup language, used to mark up how information is to be displayed. XML also allows you to mark up documents, but for structure, not for display.

STRUCTURED DATA

The advantage of XML over HTML lies in the structure that XML provides documents. As in the previous address example, XML allows you to create your own tags (or more correctly, elements) that reveal information about the meaning of the data. However XML documents are also structured in a different sense; the elements in an XML document are related to one another by their position in the document itself.

In HTML, there are really two types of tags—some that must be closed and some that do not need a closing tag. For example, with the <B> tag, you always need to use a </B> tag in order to denote the end of the bold formatting. However, if you want to start a new paragraph, you can use the <P> tag, but you don't need to use a </P> tag at all.

Note

Elements in XML are required to have end-tags, but there is a shorthand for combining start and end-tags into one tag with elements that do not have any content. This is called an "Empty Element" which can be denoted with one tag which is a combination of the start and end tags. For example:

```
<company></company>
```

can become

```
<company/>
```

to indicate that there is no content within the element.

In addition to this, elements have to be properly nested within XML. For example:

```
<company><address>123 Fake St.</company></address>
```

is not a valid piece of XML code because the <address> element is not properly nested within the <company> element. To be properly nested, the preceding example would be

```
<company><address>123 Fake St.</address></company>
```

In an XML document, all the elements within a document must be properly nested, and all elements are contained within a "root element," which contains the entire document.

As the documents you work with become more complicated, XML will aid with the structuring even more. For example, if we were working with a newspaper document, it might look something like this:

```
<newspaper>
 <section>
  <page>
   <article>
   <headline>XML 8 Announced</headline>
   <byline>Jan Doe</byline>
   <body>The W5C today announced...</body>
   </article>
   <ad>
   <client>Crazy Ed's Cars</client>
   <size>1/4 page</size>
   <run>2 weeks</run>
   </ad>
  </page>
 </section>
</newspaper>
```

From this, you can see that the structure of the document reflects the structure of the newspaper: The newspaper contains sections, which in turn have pages, and on each page are articles and advertisements.

TREES AND RELATIONSHIPS

As you can see from the preceding example, XML documents are structured as trees, and there are relationships that exist between the elements in an XML document. For example, with these elements:

```
<newspaper>
 <section>
</section>
</newspaper>
```

the `<newspaper>` element is the **parent** of the `<section>` element, and the `<section>` element is the **child** of the `<newspaper>` element. This parent-child relationship extends through all the elements in an XML document. Elements nested another level down would be grandchildren, and so forth. You can think of it in the same terms as a family tree.

These relationships become very important as you move into more advanced areas of XML, as you will use these relationships for navigating and locating information within the XML tree with technologies such as XPath.

ELEMENTS

The bulk of actual data in your XML documents will be in the form of elements. Elements are tag pairs, which are case sensitive, consisting of both a start tag, and an end tag. The name of the element itself is called the **element type**, whereas within a document, when the element occurs it is referred to as an instance of the element.

START AND END TAG FORMAT

Each XML element begins with a start tag, which is the element type, contained within less-than and greater-than symbols:

```
<example>
```

In this case, we have the start tag for an "example" element. The end tag takes a similar form; however, the element type is prefixed by a slash:

```
</example>
```

the slash denotes that this is the end tag, signifying the end of the element.

The complete element would be as follows:

```
<example>An Example Element</example>
```

The element type here is "example"; however, the *element* itself is actually the entire string, with the start tag, content, and end tag all together. The text contained between the tags is called the *element content*. Elements can have several different types of content:

- PCData (text)—When elements have PCData or text content, they do not contain any child elements, only text as in the previous example. The "PCData" stands for "Parsed Character Data," which is simply data that is read by the XML parser.
- Element—If an element has only child elements as its content:

  ```
  <example><child>Some text...</child></example>
  ```

  then the element is said to have **element content.**
- Mixed—If an element has both text and element content:

  ```
  <example>Text and <bold>emphasized</bold> text.</example>
  ```

  then the element is said to have **mixed content**.

All elements in an XML document must have both a start tag and an end tag. Also, XML is case sensitive, so both the start and end tags must match exactly. For example, the following are **not** valid elements:

```
<example></EXAMPLE>
<Example></example>
```

This is one major difference between XML and HTML, so if you are coming from a Web background, be sure to pay special attention to this.

Empty Tags

There are instances where you might have an element that is empty, or does not contain any text or child elements. If this is the case, you can write the element with both start and end tags:

```
<empty></empty>
```

However, there is also a shorthand that can be used for elements that do not have any content:

```
<empty/>
```

Here, the slash is present, but because the element has no content, there is only a single tag, with the slash after the element type. This is a convenient way to quickly represent empty elements and cut down clutter in your documents.

Attributes

Not all data in XML documents is stored in element content. Some information may be stored in attributes. Attributes are simply a means for associating named values with elements. You've probably already seen attributes in HTML. For example:

```
<img src="myimage.gif">
```

In the preceding `img` tag, the `src` specification is an attribute.

Attributes are placed in the start-tag of the element, separated with a space. The content of the attribute is enclosed in quotation marks, either single or double, and an element can have any number of attributes, so long as each attribute name is unique.

Here are some examples of attributes:

```
<shirt size="medium"/>
<pants size="30">Bell Bottoms</pants>
```

As you can see, attributes can be used with empty elements or elements with text or mixed content as well.

2

We will take a closer look at using both elements and attributes in Chapter 3, "XML Building Blocks: Elements and Attributes," but you now know enough about both of them to start writing simple XML documents. So, now let's look at the structure of the XML document itself.

XML DOCUMENT STRUCTURE

XML documents are text documents, which are commonly denoted as XML documents by use of the .xml extension. There are no restrictions on the length of the XML document; however, at a certain point, a document that is too long may become difficult to navigate or use in conjunction with XML software.

Now let's take a look at some of the physical constructs of XML documents.

THE XML DECLARATION

Every XML document should begin with the XML Declaration, which takes the following form:

```
<?xml version="1.0" encoding="UTF-8" standalone="yes"?>
```

The XML declaration always starts with the "`<?xml`" and always ends with "`?>`". Additionally, there are three attributes that are also used in the XML Declaration:

- `version`—The `version` attribute is required, and it is used to alert the XML processor to the version of XML which was used to author this particular XML document. Currently, the only acceptable version is "1.0."
- `encoding`—The `encoding` attribute is used to specify the character set that is used for encoding the document. You can use any Unicode character set here, and the default value is "UTF-8." This attribute is not required.
- `standalone`—The `standalone` attribute is used to denote whether or not the document requires a DTD in order to be processed. If the value is "No" then the XML Processor will assume that the document needs a DTD, and if there is not one, it will cause an error. This attribute (or declaration) is not required, and the default value is "Yes."

Technically, the XML Declaration is not required by the 1.0 Recommendation (this aids in working with document fragments); however, good XML style and form dictate that every XML document should have an XML declaration.

THE XML PROLOG

The XML Prolog consists of least two parts—the XML Declaration which we have just discussed, and a DOCTYPE Declaration. The DOCTYPE Declaration is used to associate an internal set of declarations with the document, or to link the XML document to an external DTD file for validation. The XML Prolog is not required to work with well-formed XML; however, to work with valid XML you will need to use the DOCTYPE declaration.

For now, we will address well-formed XML, so it's not necessary to deal with DOCTYPE Declarations. However, we will discuss DOCTYPE declarations again in Chapter 4, "Structuring XML Documents with DTDs," when we learn about DTDs.

THE ROOT ELEMENT

In accordance with the XML 1.0 Recommendation, all XML documents will contain one, and only one, element which contains all the other elements in a document. That element is called the *root* element, and every XML document must have one.

For example, in this XML document:

```
<?xml version="1.0"?>
<book>
<chapter>One</chapter>
<chapter>Two</chapter>
<chapter>Three</chapter>
</book>
```

The `<book>` element is the root element. The following document would **not** be considered a well-formed XML document because it does not have a root element:

```
<?xml version="1.0"?>
<article>
<headline>Dinosaurs Extinct</headline>
<body>Some text...</body>
</article>
<article>
<headline>Water Found Potable</headline>
<body>Some text...</body>
</article>
```

Because there is not one element that contains all the other elements in this document as its children (or grandchildren, and so forth), this is **not** a well-formed XML document, and an XML processor would generate an error if it tried to read it.

AN XML DOCUMENT EXAMPLE

With the basics of XML at our disposal, it is now possible to create an XML document that is well formed, and can be used in a variety of applications.

In this example, we're going to create a simple XML document for a technical journal. This journal XML document will contain some elements that describe the cover, a table of contents, the journal articles themselves, and an index. Obviously, we could go into a very fine level of detail here, and as you learn more about XML, hopefully you will see ways in which you could extend this exercise. However, for this example, we're going to try to limit the document to what we've covered so far.

First, we need to start our XML document with the XML declaration and the root element:

```
<?xml version="1.0"?>
<journal>
</journal>
```

The XML declaration contains the mandatory `version` attribute, but because we are not going to do anything with special character sets or with validation, we can leave out the `encoding` and `standalone` attributes. By not specifying them, the default values will be used.

Next, we will create the element for the cover of our journal, and call it `<cover>`. The cover of our journal will contain a photograph and a few slugs, or teasers, that call attention to the articles in the journal.

Here we have the opportunity to make use of an attribute as well as the element. Our cover contains only one photograph, so we could use an attribute to specify what photo would appear there. The result looks something like this:

```
<cover art="photo.jpg">
 <slug>Learn the Secrets of XML</slug>
</cover>
```

The `cover` element has an `art` attribute, which is used to specify the cover art. The `cover` element has element content; that is, it contains another element, which is called `slug` which contains the text for the slug, or teaser, that will appear on the cover as well. The `slug` element contains PCData content, which is just text.

Next, we want to create the element for the table of contents. We'll call this element `contents` and like the `cover` element, it will have element content, in the form of a `title` element. The `title` element will contain text that is the title of the article, as it would appear in the table of contents. The other piece of information we need in the table of contents is the page number on which the article appears.

We could use an element to store the page number information; however, because the article will have only one starting page, and that page is descriptive of the article, we can also use an attribute to store the page number, which is what we have done here with the `page` attribute:

```
<contents>
 <title page="3">Authoring XML Documents</title>
</contents>
```

Now with the cover of our journal taken care of, and the table of contents squared away as well, we are ready to move on to the articles in the journal. For the articles, we're going to use a number of elements to describe the article:

- `article`—This element will contain the child elements which contain the data for the article and its author.
- `headline`—This element is the headline of the article.
- `byline`—The byline for the author of the article.
- `body`—The text of the article.

The resulting XML code looks like this:

```
<article>
 <headline>Authoring XML Documents</headline>
 <byline>Joe Smith</byline>
 <body>So you want to work with XML...</body>
</article>
```

Finally, we want to create an index to track references to technologies within the article. The `index` element will be used to store each reference that will appear in the index, and it will contain child elements for each `reference`. That `reference` element will also need to have a page number associated with it, so we can once again make use of a `page` attribute to track the page number of the reference. The resulting XML code is as follows:

```
<index>
  <reference page="4">XML Prolog</reference>
</index>
```

When we bring all of these code snippets together into a final XML document, the resulting well-formed XML document is shown in Listing 2.1.

Listing 2.1 A Complete Well-Formed XML Document

```
<?xml version="1.0"?>
<journal>
 <cover art="photo.jpg">
  <slug>Learn the Secrets of XML</slug>
  <slug>XSLT Transforms the Web</slug>
  <slug>Namespaces and Why You Need Them</slug>
 </cover>
 <contents>
  <title page="3">Authoring XML Documents</title>
  <title page="6">Transforming the Web with XSLT</title>
  <title page="9">What's in a Namespace?</title>
  <title page="12">Graphics and XML with SVG</title>
 </contents>
 <article>
  <headline>Authoring XML Documents</headline>
  <byline>Joe Smith</byline>
  <body>So you want to work with XML...</body>
 </article>
 <article>
  <headline>Transforming the Web with XSLT</headline>
  <byline>Jane Doe</byline>
  <body>XML can easily be turned into HTML...</body>
 </article>
 <article>
```

Listing 2.1 continued

```
  <headline>What's in a Namespace?</headline>
  <byline>Jane Jones</byline>
  <body>When is an name not a name...</body>
 </article>
 <article>
  <headline>Graphics and XML with SVG</headline>
  <byline>Sally Smith</byline>
  <body>Drawing on the Web with SVG...</body>
 </article>
 <index>
  <reference page="4">XML Prolog</reference>
  <reference page="8">apply-templates</reference>
  <reference page="11">xmlns</reference>
  <reference page="15">SVG</reference>
 </index>
</journal>
```


This document is a complete XML document, ready to be used in any number of applications. We could now write a stylesheet using XSLT and XSL-FO, which could be used to create a PDF version of our journal based on this very XML document.

As you can see, it is very easy to create XML documents from scratch with the knowledge that you currently have. In the next chapter, we will look at the details behind elements and attributes that will give you a few more rules and things to consider when authoring your documents. But after that, you will have well-formed XML under control. And many applications that utilize XML do not need more than well-formed XML.

After that, we will move on to valid XML, which involves working with DTDs or XML Schema to create a set of rules that describe how your XML documents have to be structured. Validation is a powerful tool, and it can be used to ensure XML will function correctly when used with other technologies.

Additional Resources

There are a number of very good additional resources available on the Web for learning about XML. Here are a few of the best ones to consult:

- XML 1.0 Recommendation (`http://www.w3.org/TR/REC-xml`)—The XML 1.0 Recommendation (Second Edition) from the W3C is the final word on XML. If you have a question about a technical aspect of XML, this should be the first source you consult.
- Annotated XML Recommendation (`http://www.xml.com/axml/testaxml.htm`)—The Annotated XML Recommendation is an excellent resource for making sense of the sometimes difficult-to-read XML Recommendation. Written by Tim Bray (one of the XML 1.0 Editors), the Annotated XML Recommendation provides some clarification on confusing areas of the Rec, and offers some historical tidbits as well.

- XML-DEV (`xml-dev@xml.org`)—The XML-DEV mailing list is a good resource for developers actively working with XML. Discussion ranges from Recommendation debates to practical tips. To subscribe, send an e-mail to the address with "subscribe" in the body of the message.
- `comp.text.xml`—The `comp.text.xml` USENET Newsgroup can also be a great resource for interacting with other XML developers.
- The XML FAQ (`http://www.ucc.ie/xml/`)—The XML Frequently Asked Questions can address some issues such as why XML is structured the way it is, and when it might be appropriate to use XML as a solution.
- XML.com (`http://www.xml.com`)—XML.com is a commercial Web site dedicated to tracking and reporting on XML and XML-related issues. The site covers not only XML 1.0, but also any and all related activities and can be a great source of tutorials, articles, and general XML information.
- XML.org (`http://www.xml.org`)—XML.org is another commercial site, billing itself as the industry portal for XML. The site features the XML Cover Pages, which is Robin Cover's news column tracking developments in SGML/XML.

Also, additional resources for all aspects of XML and the topics covered in this book are located in the Appendixes.

ROADMAP

From here, we will take a look at the specifics of dealing with Elements and Attributes in Chapter 3. We'll look at how they are named, when they are used, how they are declared, and how to create a well-formed XML document. This will lead into creating valid XML documents with technologies such as Document Type Definitions, which are covered in Chapter 4. DTDs are one mechanism for creating valid XML documents. Another mechanism for creating valid documents is XML Schemas, which we will cover in Chapter 5, "Defining XML Document Structures with XML Schemas."

Because XML documents can either be well formed or valid, DTDs and XML Schemas relate directly to the use of XML, and should be technologies you are familiar with before you begin authoring your own XML vocabularies.

CHAPTER 3

XML Building Blocks: Elements and Attributes

In this chapter

by *David Gulbransen*

XML ELEMENTS

Much like HTML, XML is a markup language with documents composed of tags that "mark up" the data in a document. A typical XML document will contain a large number of these tags, start and end tags, with data contained within the tags. For example, if we were looking at the representation of a name in XML, we might have

```
<name>John Doe</name>
```

Here we have two tags—the start tag `<name>` and the end tag `</name>`. Tags are a very important part of XML. They are what you use to mark the beginning and ending of elements in your XML documents. The two tags, taken together along with the content between them, constitute an XML element.

We would actually refer to the element by the element type, which is synonymous with the name used in the start/end tag pair. In the previous example, we have a `name` element, the content of which happens to be the name `John Doe`.

Elements are referred to by their names, or element types. However, the actual element instance is both tags and the element's content nested between the tags. Elements can have text content, which is called *Parsed Character Data*, or *PCDATA*, or they can have other elements as their content. For example, we might alter the `name` element to contain more information:

```
<name>
 <first>John</first>
 <last>Doe</last>
</name>
```

Now we have three elements—a `name` element, which has as its content the `first` element and the `last` element. The `first` and `last` elements contain PCDATA, which represents the actual name of the person being stored in the name element.

Elements in XML must be composed of both start and end tags (with one exception for empty elements, which we will discuss later). This is one way in which XML differs significantly from HTML. For example, in HTML, there are a number of tags that can be used without end tags, such as `<P>`, `<HR>`, or `<BR>`.

With XML, each start tag contains the name of the element type, and each end tag contains the name of the element type as well, preceded by a `/` to denote that it is an end tag. The start and end tags must match exactly—for example, the following tags do not match:

```
<name>John Doe</NAME>
```

Unlike HTML, XML is case sensitive, so start and end tags must match in case as well. You might be surprised at how strict XML seems as compared to HTML; however, this does help keep your documents consistent and readable.

Note

Current versions of HTML do allow some tags without end tags, and HTML is also not case sensitive. However, in an effort to promote compatibility and extensibility, the W3C is in the process of rewriting the HTML Recommendation using XML, and the result is XHTML. XHTML requires all tags to be properly closed, and introduces case sensitivity to HTML. There are some other differences as well; the specifics of XHTML are covered later in Chapter 21, "The Future of the Web: XHTML."

Shorthand for Empty Elements

There are times when you might have an element in your document that does not contain any data. For example, in a contact document, you might have an element for cellular phone numbers:

```
<cellular>312-555-1212</cellular>
```

This is fine, assuming that your contact has a cellular phone. However, if they do not, then you might have a document with some empty `<cellular>` elements:

```
<cellular></cellular>
```

These empty elements can be written as shown, with a start and end tag; however, there is also a shorthand which can be used for empty elements:

```
<cellular/>
```

By including the `/` character at the end of the tag, an XML processor will know that the element is empty. Use of the empty element form can reduce clutter in your documents, and also save time when authoring.

Generic Identifiers

All specifications are concerned with semantics, and XML is no exception. In the case of elements, the semantic game is played with the terms we use to refer to elements within a document.

As we mentioned before, an element is actually the entire instance in an XML document, including the start tag, content, and end tag. However, we refer to elements by the moniker in the tag, or the element type. For example:

```
<name>Stella Ryan</name>
```

Here, the element is the `<name>` tag, followed by the `Stella Ryan` name, and the `</name>` tag. This is the element instance. The element type in this case is name, which is also called the *generic identifier*. This is how elements are commonly referenced. For example, in talking about this element, we would simply refer to it as the *name* element.

SOME RULES FOR NAMING ELEMENTS

XML is designed to allow you to be descriptive with element names, in keeping with the idea that XML should be readable. Allowing you to use descriptive names also contributes to the structure of the XML document, enabling you to use element names that are descriptive of their content and relationships to other elements. This is why we use names such as `phone` and `cellular` for elements as opposed to `drexel`. There is nothing in the XML Recommendation to stop us from using `<drexel>` as an element for cellular phone numbers. But it wouldn't be the most descriptive name we could use, and wouldn't help anyone derive meaning from our document.

At the same time, you don't want to get carried away, and overuse the capability to name an element. Calling the phone element `mobile-phone-number-for-employee` would be a bit verbose. Imagine trying to read a document with

```
<mobile-phone-number-for-employee>328-233-1231</mobile-phone-number-for-employee>
```

That would be quite a chore. Although brevity is not an essential aspect of XML, common sense does dictate that element names should be as concise as possible without detracting from descriptiveness.

ELEMENT NAMING CONVENTIONS

The XML Recommendation defines some rules that must be followed to produce a valid XML name. These rules for naming do not apply solely to element names, but any XML component that requires a valid XML name.

The XML Recommendation says that a name must begin with a letter or one of a few punctuation characters, followed by letters, digits, hyphens, underscores, or colons.

This means that you are therefore limited in what characters you can use in an element name in XML. In fact, you can include only the following characters other than letters in a name:

- .

  The period may be used in an element name—for example, `<first.name>` is a valid element type.

- -

  A hyphen may also be used in element names. You can use it to separate or hyphenate, as in `<first-name>`.

- _

  Underscores are commonly used in variable names in many programming languages and they can be useful in XML as well. Because you can't have spaces in element names, the underscore is commonly used in place of a space—for example, `<first_name>`.

- :

  The colon is a valid character to be used in XML names; however, it is also a special character that is reserved for use with XML Namespaces. Therefore, you should refrain from using the colon in your names (unless you are using a Namespace). Namespaces are discussed in greater detail in Chapter 6, "Avoiding XML Confusion with XML Namespaces."

There are a number of other characters that you might be tempted to use in names, such as the `%` sign or `&`; however, these characters cannot be used in XML names. Also, names in XML may not contain spaces.

Note

Keep in mind that XML is designed to be an internationally compatible technology. So, just because a character isn't a letter in the English alphabet doesn't mean that you can't use it. If the character is a valid letter, such as an á, an é, an ö, or another diacritical mark, then it is valid in XML. However, you really want to avoid special symbols such as the dollar sign or pound sign.

3

Additionally, XML names must begin with letters. XML names may contain digits, however they may not begin with them. So, any of the following names would be **valid** XML names:

- `<contact4sales>`—Digits are acceptable within an element name.
- `<home-phone>`—Hyphens are fine after letters as well.
- `<señor>`—Accents and diacritics are acceptable.

The following are **not** valid XML names:

- `<2do>`—Names must not begin with a digit.
- `<-name>`—Names cannot start with special characters such as a hyphen or period.
- `<x+2=4>`—Names cannot contain special characters other than the period, hyphen, underscore, and colon.

In addition to these naming rules, XML names cannot start with `XML`, `xml`, `XmL`, `xMl`, or any variation of the letter `X`, followed by the letter `M`, followed by the letter `L`. The `xml` designation is reserved for special features of XML that might be implemented in future versions. The only people who can create names using `xml` are the W3C.

Caution

XML is case sensitive; however there is no established convention for using uppercase, lowercase, or mixed-case. You may encounter documents that contain names that are all uppercase, which increases readability by clearly delineating between markup and content. Other documents may use mixed case to correspond to existing data, such as programming language conventions. You should always make sure to check the XML vocabulary guidelines for the application you are using. For example, XHTML makes use of all lowercase names.

STORING THE DATA IN XML

XML documents contain data that is stored in elements or attributes (which we will discuss later). This data is in the form of characters, and any valid Unicode character is also a valid character in XML. For example, all 26 letters of the English alphabet are characters, as are all the digits 0-9. All 33 characters of the Cyrillic alphabet are also valid characters.

The text in an XML document can be divided into two groups: character data and markup. Markup consists of the tags and syntax of XML components, whereas character data makes up the information stored in the document. In the example

```
<book>
<title ISBN="0000-0000-0000">Using XML</title>
</book>
```

the element tags and the attribute name are all considered markup, whereas the character data consists of the "0000-0000-0000" of the attribute value and the Using XML content of the title element. Character data in an XML document is divided into two types: Parsed Character Data (PCDATA) and Character Data (CDATA).

PARSED CHARACTER DATA

XML documents are read and processed by a specific piece of software called an *XML parser*. When a document is processed by the XML parser, each character in the document is read, or parsed, in order to create a representation of the data.

Any text that gets read by the parser is *Parsed Character Data*, or *PCDATA*. This is important because you will see the term *PCDATA* pop up all over. Element content is considered either other elements or PCDATA. Attribute values are considered PCDATA.

By definition, PCDATA is parsed, which means that the parser looks at each of the characters and tries to determine their meaning. For example, if the parser encounters a < then it knows that the characters that follow represent an element instance. When the parser encounters a /, it knows that it has encountered an end tag.

Because PCDATA is parsed, it cannot contain <, >, and / characters, as these characters have special meaning in markup. For example:

```
<math>
If you want to denote one number is smaller than another,
you can use the < less-than sign
</math>
```

This element will cause an error, because the parser will interpret the < as the start of a new element. If you want to include these characters, you will need to use the equivalent entity—for example, <, to represent a less-than sign.

Bypassing Parsing with CDATA

There are times when you may want to include data in your document that contains markup, but which you do not want to be parsed. For example, if you were authoring a tutorial on HTML, and storing it in an XML file, you might have the following:

```
<instruction>
Titles can be <I>italicized</I> using the <I> tag.
</instruction>
```

This instruction element could be used in an XML document as is; however, it would cause an error because the parser would assume that <I> was a new element. To denote that the content should not be parsed, you can utilize a CDATA Section.

CDATA Sections can occur anywhere character data can occur. They are used to escape blocks of text containing characters that would otherwise be recognized as markup. CDATA Sections begin with the string <![CDATA[and end with the string]]>.

What that means is that you can enclose information inside these CDATA markers and that text will be ignored by the parser. So, let's take another look at our example:

```
<instruction>
<!CDATA[Titles can be <I>italicized</I> using the <I> tag. ]]>
</instruction>
```

Now the XML parser will completely ignore whatever text follows the <!CDATA[tag until it encounters the]]> tag. This allows you to include any type of data in that section you would like.

Keep in mind, though, that nothing inside a CDATA Section is parsed. Therefore, if you were to include entities, they would not be parsed. So, <I> would remain <I> if it were contained inside a CDATA section.

A CDATA Section can be used anywhere PCDATA occurs—as element content, and so on. However, attribute values are always parsed unless they are specified as CDATA in a DTD or Schema. So, you cannot include a CDATA Section in an attribute value.

Note

Some users of XML have raised the idea of including text-encoded binary data into CDATA Sections. Because the text in a CDATA Section isn't parsed, this seems like an okay idea. However, to do so, you would need to ensure that the encoding did not include]]>. With XML Schemas, there are a number of binary datatypes that are a much better mechanism for including binary data as element content.

By default, the text content of XML documents is PCDATA, and you will not encounter the PCDATA keyword until we discuss valid XML with DTDs and Schemas. However, CDATA sections that can be used in well-formed XML do escape large sections of text, as well as be used in DTDs and Schemas. We will discuss the use of DTDs and valid XML later in Chapter 4, "Structuring XML Documents with DTDs," and XML Schemas in Chapter 5, "Defining XML Document Structures with XML Schemas."

ATTRIBUTES

Elements are the most fundamental component of an XML document; all XML documents have at least one element, the root element. However, there is also another fundamental mechanism for XML documents, which allows associating name/value pairs with elements: attributes.

Attributes should already be familiar to you from HTML:

```
<IMG SRC="logo.gif" BORDER="0">
```

The `IMG` tag makes use of many attributes, including the `SRC` attribute, which is used to associate the location of the image, and the `BORDER` attribute, which specifies the width of the image border.

ATTRIBUTES SUPPLEMENT ELEMENTS

Attributes are best utilized to store data that might not be important to the document structurally, but increase the informational value of an element. For example, in a document describing photographic equipment, we might have a `camera` element. For the `camera` element, it might make sense to have an attribute called `format` with values such as `APS` or `35mm`. That's an attribute that relates to the element; it makes sense. However, you probably wouldn't want to have an attribute called `phone`, unless it's a very unusual camera.

WHEN TO USE ATTRIBUTES

It would be possible to create an entire document using nothing but elements. After all, you can use elements to mark up any kind of data. For example, we could describe a camera using only elements:

```
<camera>
 <manufacturer>Nikon</ manufacturer>
 <model>D1</model>
 <lens>28mm</lens>
 <format>35mm</format>
</camera>
```

There is nothing wrong with this approach. In fact, often elements are more flexible than attributes, and can be easier to alter. However, we could also structure this XML using attributes:

```
<camera manufacturer="Nikon" model="D1" lens="28mm" format="35mm">
</camera>
```

With an example of this level of simplicity, there isn't really a huge impact in the differences between using elements versus attributes. However, some types of information naturally have a clearer structure. For example, look at this description of a family:

```
<family>
 <parent>John Doe</parent>
 <parent>Jane Doe</parent>
 <son>Timmy Doe</son>
```

```
 <daughter>Sally Doe</daughter>
</family>
```

The grouping of the family members within a family element makes some structural sense, but we could take it even further:

```
<family>
 <parents>
  <father>John Doe</father>
  <mother>Jane Doe</mother>
 </parents>
 <children>
  <son>Timmy Doe</son>
  <daughter>Sally Doe</daughter>
 </children>
</family>
```

This makes the relationships a little clearer, but we are still element centric. Now, what if we wanted to add some information about each family member, such as age? One way might be to add elements:

```
<family>
 <parents>
  <father>
   John Doe
   <age>39</age>
  </father>
  <mother>Jane Doe</mother>
 </parents>
 <children>
  <son>Timmy Doe</son>
  <daughter>Sally Doe</daughter>
 </children>
</family>
```

However, this clutters our tree structure somewhat. We might instead use an `age` attribute:

```
<family>
 <parents>
  <father age="39">John Doe</father>
  <mother age="37">Jane Doe</mother>
 </parents>
 <children>
  <son age="10">Timmy Doe</son>
  <daughter age="8">Sally Doe</daughter>
 </children>
</family>
```

Now, we have the age information associated with each element, but without adding unnecessary elements, and keeping the information streamlined.

There really are no right and wrong answers when it comes to choosing when to use elements versus attributes. The best course of action is to take a close look at the data you are describing and to see whether you spot a natural breakdown in the data itself. Barring that, it is mostly a matter of personal preference.

Classifying Attributes: Attribute Types

Attributes can be classified based on the kind of information that they contain. When you define an attribute in XML, you are really defining the attribute type, or the kind of information that the attribute may legally contain to describe an element. Attributes can be one of three different types: strings, tokenized types, or enumerations.

In the interest of compatibility and to create rules for validation (which we will discuss later in this chapter), there are a number of different types of attributes. Attributes consist of predefined datatypes that can be assigned to your attributes when you are working with a Document Type Definition or an XML Schema.

For example, one attribute type is `ID`, which is an identifier for the element, a unique identifier. What this allows you to do is to refer to an element by its `ID`, rather than the tag name. An ID attribute can be used to provide a unique identifier for a specific instance of an element, whereas the element name might refer to multiple instances of an element within a single document. If you are working with a DTD or an XML Schema, you can declare your attributes to be an ID type.

Why is this useful? We could have a document describing the parts of a camera:

```
<camera>
<part ID="body">Nikon F4</part>
<part ID="lens">28mm</part>
<part ID="flash">Speedflash 50</part>
</camera>
```

Each of the part elements refers to a part of the camera, but what if we wanted to refer to just the lens for the camera? We could not refer to the part element, because there are several parts to the camera. Instead, with the `ID` attribute, we can reference the appropriate part by `ID`. This becomes even more useful for documents with large amounts of similar data, such as a catalog:

```
<catalog>
<part number="09339">Hyrdolic Pump</part>
<part number="33881">Flange Gasket</part>
<part number="33291">Flexi-hose</part>
</catalog>
```

Tip

Because you can have attributes of different types, sometimes you might want to have the type of the attribute explicitly in the name of the type. For example, we could have named our attribute "number_ID" to indicate that the attribute was a number. If you are working with attributes that are just text (CData), this probably isn't necessary, but for IDs or IDREFs it can come in handy.

Here we have a listing of parts that might not even be related to one another, other than as part of the same catalog. Although the usefulness of this type of attribute is readily apparent, the value of some other attribute types might not seem so straightforward.

Note

Attribute names do not necessarily reflect the datatype of the attribute. For example, the `number` attribute used in the catalog example could still be an `ID` attribute, even if it is not called `ID`.

Attribute types are associated with a specific datatype only if you are working with valid XML, including a DTD or an XML Schema. Otherwise, XML parsers do not differentiate between the types of information in attribute content.

Taking advantage of most of the different types of attributes requires that you use a DTD or XML Schema with your document. However, you can still use attributes in an XML document that is only well-formed. We'll talk more about using attributes with DTD later in Chapter 4 and with XML Schemas in Chapter 5. However, now let's get acquainted with the different types of attributes that you will have at your disposal, so you can start thinking about them as you work with XML.

ID

The first type, and arguably one of the most useful, is the `ID` attribute type. You've already seen an example of how an `ID` attribute can be used to help classify parts. The basic idea of an `ID` is to provide a unique identifier for each instance of an element type in a document.

This is important, because the nature of classifying information leads to multiple instances of elements. If you had an XML document describing the holdings of a library, you would probably have a `book` element, and there would likely be many instances of the `book` element. There might be hundreds, if not thousands, of `<book>` entries in your document. Although you might have child elements that would help narrow your searches, such as `<title>` or `<author>`, you could use an `ID` attribute to provide a unique identifier, that could then be referenced by other attributes or elements. The unique `ID` attribute might be the call number of the book, for example, which would allow you to quickly locate the correct `book` element that you were looking for.

This is a very important concept as XML usage becomes ubiquitous. Providing unique, internal identifiers can be a great mechanism for linking to specific elements within a document.

There aren't too many rules to follow when creating `ID` attributes:

- The attribute name has to be a valid name. That is, like element names, it cannot begin with `xml` and so on.
- The value of each attribute with an `ID` type must be unique.

IDREF AND IDREFS

The next attribute type we're going to discuss goes hand-in-hand with the `ID` attribute type: `IDREF`. An `IDREF` attribute is a reference to an `ID` attribute. `IDREFS` refers to more than one `IDREF`.

What good is a reference to an `ID`? Well, for starters it can be a great way to organize and classify information. Let's look at an example. Suppose we work for a company that sells cameras and lenses. We want to have a document that lists the parts of each item we sell, which might look like this:

```
<catalog>
 <product type="film-camera">
  <part>Nikon F4 Body</part>
  <part>28mm Lens</part>
 </product>
 <product type="digital-camera">
  <part>Nikon D1 Body</part>
  <part>28mm Lens</part>
 </product>
</catalog>
```

Here we have two products, with an `ID` attribute called `TYPE` which lets us differentiate between our different types of cameras.

However, in this example, each camera shares a common part, the 28mm Lens. The lens in question is actually the same part, but we might sometimes need to be specific with respect to which camera the lens in question belongs. For example, we might want to alter the filter that shipped with the lens depending on whether it was for the film or the digital version of the camera.

There are several ways we could do this. We could create new elements such as `<digital-lens>` and `<film-lens>`; however, it really is the same lens, so instead, we can create an `ID` and an `IDREF` to link the two elements together. Our modified document might look like this:

```
<catalog>
 <product name="F4" type="film-camera">
  <part model="F4">Nikon F4 Body</part>
  <part model="F4">28mm Lens</part>
 </product>
 <product name="D1"type="digital-camera">
  <part model="D1">Nikon D1 Body</part>
  <part model="D1">28mm Lens</part>
 </product>
</catalog>
```

Now each of our elements has an ID attribute called `name` that is used to uniquely identify each product. We then can use an `IDREF` attribute—in this case, `model`—to refer to the `name` attribute of the appropriate product. Keep in mind that these types would all be declared in our DTD or XML Schema. Being able to refer to the specific product by a unique name can help ensure that future items that need to be linked to a model can also be linked correctly—for example, if we added a section for filters, we have the model number associated with the lens, so we could ship filters based on the model of camera.

Although, in this case, the relationship is clear because of the document structure, we might have a separate file that looks like this:

```
<catalog>
 <product model="F4" type="lens">28mm</product>
 <product model="F4" type="lens">35mm</product>
 <product model="F4" type="lens">50mm</product>
 <product model="F4" type="lens">70mm</product>
 <product model="D1" type="lens">28mm</product>
 <product model="D1" type="lens">35mm</product>
 <product model="D1" type="lens">50mm</product>
 <product model="D1" type="lens">70mm</product>
</catalog>
```

Here, we still have references to the `ID` attributes, even though the relationship of the lens is not clear from the structure. In fact, we can group together elements to many different `ID`s, by using the attribute type `IDREFS`, which is just more than one `IDREF`:

```
<catalog>
 <product model="F4 D1" type="lens">28mm</product>
 <product model="F4 D1" type="lens">35mm</product>
 <product model="F4 D1" type="lens">50mm</product>
 <product model="F4 D1" type="lens">70mm</product>
</catalog>
```

Now you will notice that our attribute for the shared lens reads `<product model="F4 D1">`. You can use the `IDREFS` type to reference multiple `ID`s, each one separated by a space.

To make effective use of these datatypes for attributes, you will need to use a DTD. The reason for this is simply because without a DTD, all attributes look the same to a parser. There is no way for an XML parser to know whether the attribute is an ID or not unless that datatype is specified in the DTD. We'll talk more about how you define attributes in the DTD later in Chapter 4.

ENUMERATED ATTRIBUTES

One of the most useful types of attributes that can be defined in XML is enumerated attributes. These attributes allow you to define a list of values for the attribute, and allow users to select the value from that list. It's a way you can create multiple-choice attributes.

This is useful for a number of different applications. For example, let's say that you were defining an XML document for a clothing catalog. You might have XML that looked something like this:

```
<catalog>
 <item>
  <shirt>Men's T-Shirt</shirt>
 </item>
 <item>
  <shirt>Women's Blouse</shirt>
```

```
 </item>
</catalog>
```

It would certainly make sense to have an option for specifying the size of the garments that are available. One way might be to offer a choice from a list of available sizes—for example, `Small`, `Medium`, `Large`, and `Extra-Large`.

We can add a `size` attribute to the `<shirt>` element:

```
<shirt size="Large">Women's Blouse</shirt>
```

This attribute allows us to specify the size of an item. However, as it is currently defined, the value of the size attribute could be literally any value. To limit the choice of the value to "`Small`," "`Medium`," "`Large`," or "`Extra-Large`," we need to make the attribute an enumerated type.

An attribute type of enumeration means that the value for the attribute must be chosen from a list of attribute values defined in the DTD or XML Schema. Just like other attribute values, the enumerated values have to meet the constraints for attribute content (that is, no < symbols). And you can't use enumerated attributes without a DTD or an XML Schema, because without the rule specifying what the choices are, there is no way for the XML application to know ahead of time what you want them to be.

ATTRIBUTE RULES

Attribute type names are subject to the same naming rules and conventions as elements. The names are case sensitive, so `NAME` and `name` are not the same:

- Attribute names cannot contain spaces. An attribute could be called `FirstName` but not `First Name`.
- Attribute names must begin with a letter (or the underscore). So, `Four11` would be an acceptable attribute, whereas `411` would not.
- Attribute values must be enclosed in quotation marks.
- An element may have only one attribute of a given name.
- Attribute content may not contain <, >, or `&`.

Although attribute content must be contained in quotation marks, you can nest quotation marks within attribute content. To nest quotations, you simply use double quotation marks and single quotation marks, in either order:

```
<NAME First="John 'Stinky'" Last="Doe"/>
```

or

```
<NAME First='John "Stinky"' Last="Doe"/>
```

As long as the quotation marks are properly nested, the order in which you use single versus double quotation marks does not matter.

Well-Formedness Rules

XML documents must be well formed in order to be considered XML. The XML 1.0 Recommendation spells out some conditions that must be met for a document to be considered well formed. These conditions are called well-formedness constraints, and if the document fails to meet these constraints, it is not an XML document.

This can lead to some confusion when working with XML, as you may have a document which seems to be perfect XML, yet it will not load into your XML application. That is because if the well-formedness constraints are not met, XML parsers cannot properly load the document. This is very contrary to the behavior of most Web browsers, which are very forgiving of errors in HTML.

It would be impossible to enumerate each of the well-formedness constraints in the XML 1.0 Recommendation without delving into minutia that are not really very germane to creating XML documents. For example, if a document uses element names that are forbidden, such as `<411>`, then the document is not well formed. However, we've already discussed this rule in the context of naming your elements, so rehashing each of these details here would be tedious.

The important aspects of well-formedness can be boiled down into a few rules that should always be followed, and significantly lower your chances of creating a malformed XML document:

1. All element and attribute names must follow the conventions for XML naming, as outlined previously (that is, not starting with a digit, and so on).
2. Elements must be properly nested.
3. Every start tag must have an end tag, or take the form of the empty element.
4. All tags must properly match case.
5. A well-formed document must have one, and only one, root element that contains all the other elements in the XML document.
6. All entities must be properly referenced.

If you follow these rules, chances are your XML documents will be well formed.

Well-Formedness and Entities

An entity is just a way of using shorthand in XML. Entities can also be found in HTML. For example:

```
&copy;
```

is an entity that represents the copyright © symbol.

The syntax for most entities is

```
&entityname;
```

Entities can be used to replace long strings, or to represent symbols that you cannot include legally in an XML document. For example, let's say that you wanted to include a less-than symbol:

```
<equation>2 is less-than 7</equation>
```

You could not legally say

```
<equation>2 < 7</equation>
```

This violates the well-formedness constraints because it includes the < symbol that signifies the beginning of a tag. Fortunately, entities provide a way to reference this without actually including the symbol: `<`. An entity exists for the greater-than symbol as well: `>`.

There are a number of entities that are predefined for XML, so using these entities in your document does not violate any rules for well-formedness:

- `&`

  This entity is used to represent the ampersand symbol `&`.

- `<`

  The less-than entity is used to represent the less-than sign <, which is also the beginning sign of any tag. Because it denotes the beginning of a tag, if you want to show a tag in text, or use the less-than symbol, you should use the `<` entity.

- `>`

  The greater-than entity is similar to that of the less-than entity. You would use it to represent the greater-than symbol > in the content portion of an element.

- `'`

  The apostrophe entity is used to represent an apostrophe `'` or a single quotation mark.

- `"`

  This entity is used to represent a quotation mark: `"`.

You should note that although these entities are found in HTML, some entities found in HTML such as `©` are not present in XML. Any other entities that are used in your document would need to be defined by you in a DTD or XML Schema in order for the document to comply with well-formedness.

There are actually two ways that you can define entities. You can use an entity declaration in an external DTD, or you can also declare entities in the internal DTD subset, self-contained within your document. We will discuss Document Type Definitions, both internal and external, in more detail in Chapter 4.

A well-formed document does not have to have a DTD associated with it to be well formed. As long as the document is structured correctly, it can be considered well formed. For many documents, there is no need for a DTD or Schema. By enforcing well-formedness, XML enables you to create flexible documents that might serve your needs without adding a level of complexity with a Document Type Definition (DTD) or XML Schema.

CREATING A WELL-FORMED XML DOCUMENT

Let's take a look at the creation of a well-formed XML document. In this example, we will create a simple document for keeping track of appointments.

First, we could create this document using only elements. Here are the elements we're going to use in the document:

- `appointments`—This element will serve as the root element of the document, containing all the other elements in the document.
- `event`—The `event` element will contain the information about each individual appointment.
- `date`—A child of the `event` element, this is the date of the event.
- `start-time`—A child of the `event` element, this is the starting time for the appointment.
- `end-time`—A child element of the `event` element, this is the ending time for the appointment.
- `type`—Also a child of `event`, the type of appointment, such as a meeting, doctor's appointment, and so on.
- `title`—A child of `event`, a title for the appointment.
- `description`—A child of `event`, the description of the appointment.
- `location`—A child of `event`, the location of the appointment.
- `reminder`—A child of `event`, this element is used to define a reminder (instant message or e-mail) for the event.
- `status`—A child of `reminder`, the status of whether or not a reminder should be sent.
- `interval`—A child of `reminder`, the interval of time before the event when a reminder should be sent.
- `method`—A child of `reminder`, the method by which the reminder should be sent.

We can create the XML document using only these elements. All XML documents should begin with the XML declaration. The XML declaration takes the following form:

```
<?xml version="1.0" encoding="UTF-8" standalone="yes" ?>
```

The declaration has three attributes:

- `version`—The `version` attribute specifies the version of XML that was used to author the document. The `version` attribute is required.
- `encoding`—The `encoding` attribute is used to specify the character set that the document utilizes. The attribute is not required, but if it is not specified, the parser will assume the default value of "`UTF-8`," which is the standard 8-bit Unicode encoding.

3

- `standalone`—The `standalone` attribute is optional, and is used to indicate whether the document is self-contained (standalone="`yes`") or whether it requires a DTD/Schema (standalone="`no`"). In our example, we won't be using a DTD or XML Schema—our document will be self-contained, so the attribute value will be "`yes`."

The XML declaration is not required in order for the XML document to be considered well formed; however, there are very few instances when you should not use the XML declaration. Unless you have a specific reason not to (such as working with a document fragment), you should always use it.

The `appointments` element is the root element of the document, and will contain the remaining elements. When we populate the document with the elements with the proper relationships, here is the result:

```
<?xml version="1.0" encoding="UTF-8" standalone="yes" ?>
<appointments>
 <event>
  <date>03-05-02</date>
  <start-time>09:00</start-time>
  <end-time>10:00</end-time>
  <type>Meeting</type>
  <title>Staff Meeting</title>
  <description>Weekly staff meeting.</description>
  <location>Conference Room</location>
  <reminder>
   <status>yes</status>
   <interval>1-day</interval>
   <method>e-mail</method>
  </reminder>
 </event>
</appointments>
```

This is a well-formed XML document, which does describe appointments adequately. However, you will notice that the document does not make any use of attributes, and there are a couple of places where it might be easier to use attributes to describe our data.

For example, we could easily describe some of the factual information regarding the event, such as the date and times, as attributes. If we start with the `event` element

```
<event>
  <date></date>
  <start-time></start-time>
  <end-time></end-time>
</event>
```

we can easily rework this structure to make use of attributes. The result is an `event` element with three attributes:

```
<event date="" start-time="" end-time="">
```

We can do something similar with the `reminder` element. We start with the element-only structure:

```
<reminder>
 <status></status>
 <interval></interval>
 <method></method>
</reminder>
```

And change the child elements into attributes as well:

```
<reminder status="" interval="" method=""/>
```

Although both structures work, the use of the attributes helps streamline the data and results in a cleaner-looking document:

```
<?xml version="1.0" encoding="UTF-8" standalone="yes" ?>
 <appointments>
  <event date="" start-time="" end-time="">
  <type></type>
  <title></title>
  <description></description>
  <location></location>
  <reminder status="" interval="" method=""/>
 </event>
</appointments>
```


In the content of the attributes is primarily a limited set of data; with the date, we will keep a standard format "MM-DD-YY" and the start time and end times will be in 24-hour time format. Later, when we discuss XML Schemas and datatypes, we could easily make these attributes date/time datatypes, which would mean that if the content of the attribute weren't properly formatted, the document would be invalid. Because here we are concerned only with well-formedness, that capability isn't as crucial.

However, data that is always of a limited type is often appropriate for attributes. For example, the "status" of the reminder is a boolean, either a yes or a no. Booleans are a perfect application for attributes because they explicitly modify the state of an element.

Again, there are no clear-cut rules for when to use attributes and when to use elements. You have to use a combination of consensus among the other developers you are working with and your own personal preferences. But as you can see from this example, there are often as many ways to structure an XML document as there are to write a sentence. Let your applications dictate how you structure your documents.

Now, if we take our document and populate it with some data, we get the results shown in Listing 3.1.

LISTING 3.1 A COMPLETE, WELL-FORMED XML DOCUMENT WITH DATA

```
<?xml version="1.0" encoding="UTF-8" standalone="yes" ?>
<appointments>
 <event date="03-05-02" start-time="09:00" end-time="10:00">
  <type>Meeting</type>
  <title>Staff Meeting</title>
  <description>Weekly staff meeting</description>
  <location>Conference Room</location>
```

LISTING 3.1 CONTINUED

```
  <reminder status="no"/>
 </event>

 <event date="03-06-02" start-time="14:00" end-time="15:00">
  <type>Interview</type>
  <title>Developer Interview</title>
  <description>Interview new developer candidate.</description>
  <location>Office</location>
  <reminder status="yes" interval="15-min" method="ICQ"/>
 </event>

 <event date="03-15-02" start-time="13:45" end-time="15:00">
  <type>Dentist</type>
  <title>Root Canal</title>
  <description>Root canal on lower left molar.</description>
  <location>Dr. Scrivello's Office</location>
  <reminder status="yes" interval="1-day" method="e-mail"/>
 </event>
</appointments>
```

This is a simple document, but it does utilize all the concepts outlined here. The element and attribute names meet the naming requirements, the elements are properly nested, with proper start and end tags. The document contains a single root element, `appointments`, and there are no errors in the content that would cause parsing problems, such as a < symbol. Yet, this document could be used by a calendar application to store information about appointments. That is the power of XML: Documents do not have to be overly complicated in order to be useful.

THE BASICS OF VALIDATION

There is another concept in XML that is just as important, if not more so, than well-formedness: validation. The idea behind validation is to create a document with defined structure and rules for how the content is to be organized. Then, by checking the document against the set of rules, the document can be declared valid or an error can be generated, indicating where the document is incorrectly formatted or structured.

The document that establishes the set of rules is called a *schema*, with a lowercase *s*. The terminology here can become somewhat confusing, because a schema in the generic sense is just a set of rules that define the structure. However, with XML, there are two common types of schemas that are used to support validation: Document Type Definitions (DTDs) and XML Schemas.

Within both DTDs and XML Schemas, you can establish rules for what elements and attributes may be used in your XML documents, as well as define other resources, such as declaring any entities to be used in your documents.

After the schema (in the form of a DTD or XML Schema) is written, the schema is then linked to your XML document. In the case of a DTD, this is accomplished with a

DOCTYPE declaration in the document. When the document is read by a parser that supports validation, or a validating parser, the document is checked against the rules contained in the DTD. If the document fails to comply with the rules, then an error is generated. If the document complies with the rules in the DTD, then it is valid. A similar mechanism is employed to link an XML Schema with a document, and the result of validation is the same: A document that meets the validity constraints is valid. The specifics of DTDs are discussed at length in Chapter 4 and the specifics of XML Schemas are discussed in Chapter 5.

Validating an XML document provides many benefits. Validation can provide a mechanism for enforcing data integrity. It can be a method for expediting searching or indexing. It can also help manage large documents or collaborative documents that might be broken into chunks for editing purposes.

All of these issues, and many more, make validation one of the more powerful tools of XML.

DOCUMENT TYPE DEFINITIONS: A GLIMPSE

One common mechanism for validating XML documents is the Document Type Definition. An XML document is valid if it has an associated document type declaration and if the document complies with the constraints expressed in it.

The document type declaration is the statement in your XML file that points to the location of the DTD. For example:

```
<?xml version="1.0" ?>
<!DOCTYPE document SYSTEM "example.dtd">
<document></document>
```

Here we have a document called `document`, which is linked by the document type declaration to the example.dtd file. This means that to be valid, the document would need to match all the rules established in that DTD.

Likewise, the document type declaration can also include the rules itself, rather than pointing to an external DTD:

```
<?xml version="1.0" ?>
<!DOCTYPE document [
   <!ENTITY legal "This document is confidential.">
   <!-- More rules would be included here -->
 ]>
<document>
 &legal;
</document>
```

In this case, you would include the same rules in this form as you would have in the external DTD. This can be very useful for keeping your files linked to the rules, or for including a few simple entity declarations. There are advantages to including your declarations in the internal DOCTYPE, or in pointing to an external DTD. We will discuss those issues more in Chapter 4.

XML SCHEMAS: A GLIMPSE

Document Type Definitions are actually a holdover from SGML, and as such, there have been many critics of DTDs with respect to XML. The first problem with DTDs is that they use their own special syntax, which is not very intuitive to many authors. The second problem is that DTDs themselves are not well-formed XML. Finally, DTDs do not provide a mechanism for defining complex datatypes, which limits some of the potential of XML.

In response to the limitations of DTDs, the W3C has developed a schema mechanism that is specific to XML: XML Schemas. XML Schemas use a (somewhat) more intuitive syntax, and are actually XML documents themselves. This makes it easier for XML developers to integrate XML Schema support into applications.

Additionally, XML Schemas provide a means for defining datatypes for elements and attributes. Datatypes allow you to restrict the content of elements and attributes to specific types of data, such as a digit, a date, or a string. This is a very powerful new aspect of schemas that was not possible with DTDs. We will discuss XML Schemas and datatypes at length in Chapter 5.

XML Schemas are also external files, which are linked to XML documents through a couple of special attributes:

```
<?xml version="1.0" ?>
<document
  xmlns:xsi="http://www.w3.org/2001/XMLSchema-instance"
  xsi:noNamespaceSchemaLocation="example.xsd">
</document>
```

The first attribute is the `xmlns:xsi`, which defines the namespace for the `xsi:noNamespaceSchemaLocation` attribute, which is actually used to point to the location of the schema.

XML Schemas can also be included within an XML document by making use of namespaces (which are discussed in detail in Chapter 6). Because XML Schemas are XML, they can be included directly in the document:

```
<?xml version="1.0" ?>
<document
  xmlns:xsi="http://www.w3.org/2001/XMLSchema-instance">

 <xs:schema xmlns:xs="http://www.w3.org/2001/XMLSchema">
  <xs:element name="title" type="xs:string"/>
  <!-- More schema rules defined here -->
 </xs:schema>

 <title>My Document</title>
</document>
```

We will discuss the mechanisms for writing and including XML Schemas in your XML documents in greater detail in Chapter 5; however, you should keep XML Schemas in mind for validation. XML Schemas are easier to author and offer more power and flexibility than DTDs. However, because DTDs are essentially a part of XML 1.0, in which Schemas are a separate Recommendation, there may be more application support for DTDs until Schema usage becomes more widespread.

Another point to keep in mind: Validation is not necessary. Well-formed XML can be used in many applications without any problems whatsoever. However, validation can be a valuable tool, and it is important to consider this idea of validation. If you are using XML as a data format then validation can really be an important asset. By using a DTD or Schema for validation, you can enforce your markup language's rules for others authoring XML instance documents.

Validation can also be used to make sure that users do not corrupt the data being stored in your XML files. This is perhaps the most important reason for validation: It enables you to enforce some degree of data integrity.

How Do Applications Use XML?

XML files by themselves are just as Word documents are by themselves—without an application in which to open and manipulate the contents of the file, there is not much point.

Using the data in an XML document requires applications that are capable of handling XML, such as browsers for viewing and displaying XML, and data-processing applications that can read XML files as well. The software component responsible for reading the XML document and building a representation of the document that can be accessed by other parts of an application is called an *XML parser*.

For example, consider a very simple XML document:

```
<?xml version="1.0" ?>
<contact>
 <name>Jane Doe</name>
 <address>123 Fake Street</address>
 <phone>312-555-1212</phone>
</contact>
```

One of the benefits of XML is that the documents are, for the most part, human readable. When we read the preceding example, we know that the name element represents a person's name, the address element represents an address, and so on. However, to a piece of software, these elements have no semantic meaning; software cannot reason or surmise the content of elements from the element name, barring some significant advances in artificial intelligence.

So, to actually use the information in a software application, you need to create code that reads each character until it encounters a less-than symbol, <. That signals that a tag is about to start. Then, each character that follows can be read as the name of the element, until a greater-than symbol > is encountered. After a > is hit, that signifies the end of the start tag to the program.

From there, each character that follows is part of the element's content—that is, until it hits a less-than symbol, followed by a slash, </, which signifies the end tag. The whole process

also needs to repeat all the way through the file, "parsing" the file into tag pairs and their content, and keeping track of the relationships of the tag pairs. Oh yeah, it also has to deal with entities, attributes, comments, and so on. Now, you need to do this type of parsing each time you are reading in an XML file. This is the job of the XML parser.

An XML parser is an XML processor that reads in the file, and does the job we've just described, and, in fact, more. XML parsers also assist in finding errors in the XML file, and helping build data structures for storing the XML information in your applications.

Now, even if you are not a programmer, knowing that your XML documents are really written for the parser will help you understand why some of the well-formedness constraints exist. Also, you may be developing custom applications for XML where you will need to make decisions about what parsers to use.

NON-VALIDATING PARSERS

The first category of parsers is known as *non-validating* parsers. These are parsers that deal only with well-formed XML files, and they don't do anything with Document Type Definitions or XML Schemas. They do, however, work to enforce well-formedness, and help you add the ability to process XML files to your applications. The advantage of using non-validating parsers in your applications is that you gain XML compatibility, but you don't take on the overhead of validation. This tends to lead to lightweight parsers that process XML files very quickly, but at the expense of validation.

An example of a non-validating parser:

- XP and `expat`—From James Clark. XP is an XML parser written in Java, whereas `expat` is a non-validating parser written in C. See `http://www.jclark.com/xml/expat.html`.

Non-validating parsers will report errors in your files as well; however, keep in mind that even non-validating parsers are not required by the XML 1.0 Recommendation to read non–well-formed XML documents. Also, if you need your data to be validated against a DTD or XML Schema, you need to turn to a validating parser.

VALIDATING PARSERS

A validating parser does all the things that a non-validating parser does. A validating parser reads in XML files, and checks them for errors of well-formedness. A validating parser can also help you build appropriate data structures. But a validating parser goes a step beyond.

In addition to reading the XML file and parsing it, a validating parser also reads in the DTD or Schema that is associated with your XML file. This allows the parser to check and make sure that the XML file conforms to the rules established in the DTD/Schema. Many parsers will also report errors in the DTD or Schema itself, which can be an incredible benefit, especially if you aren't feeling all that comfortable with DTD/Schema authoring.

Some examples of validating XML Parsers include

- MSXML—From Microsoft, this is a C++ validating parser. See `http://www.microsoft.com/xml`.
- Xerces—From the Apache XML Project, this is a Java-based, open-source validating XML parser. See `http://xml.apache.org`.

In addition to these parsers, there are also parsers from Sun, Oracle, and a number of other vendors. Each one is designed with certain performance characteristics, and it pays to shop around when looking for a parser. Keep in mind also that at the time of this writing, XML Schemas are a relatively new technology, and therefore they are not supported by a large number of parsers. This will undoubtedly change as the technology matures.

For many authors, this is all you will ever need to know about XML parsers and their use. For developers who need to learn more, specifics of parser implementations are covered in Chapter 16, "Working with XML and Java," and in Chapter 17, "Working with XML and .NET."

An Overview of XML Tools

As XML begins to mature as a technology, the software available that supports XML is beginning to mature as well. There is still a long way to go before XML software reaches the maturity level of applications found in MS Office. However, some of the tools presented here can be very useful XML applications.

- Internet Explorer (`http://www.microsoft.com/windows/ie/default.asp`)

  Current versions of Internet Explorer support the viewing and validation of XML documents; however, the support is not robust. In the current version, 6.0, Internet Explorer does not fully support XSL or the validation of XML documents against XML Schemas. However, the support in IE is much more robust than the support found in Netscape Navigator.
- Amaya (`http://www.w3.org/Amaya/`)

  Amaya is the reference implementation browser and editor from the W3C. Although not as polished as some commercial software, this editor/browser is designed to support the W3C standards fully, and it can be used to test your XML documents.
- XML Spy (`http://www.xmlspy.com/`)

  XML Spy is a complete XML Integrated Development environment. It supports the authoring of XML documents, as well as validation against DTDs and some support for XSL. If you are engaged in complex XML development, XML Spy could be a good choice.
- XML Pro (`http://www.vervet.com`)

  XML Pro is an editor that supports full validation, and features a tree-interface geared toward using XML with data applications. XML Pro does not support advanced features such as XSL, but can be a good choice for simple, lightweight projects.

- XMetal (`http://www.xmetal.com`)

  XMetal is a complete XML editor that features a more word-processor–like interface for editing XML documents. XMetal is a very powerful editor, including support for SGML, so it is not for everyone. However, if you have the need for a full-featured editor with support for advanced technologies such as SGML, it is a good choice.

- Excelon Stylus Studio (`http://www.stylusstudio.com/`)

  Stylus Studio is an XML development environment that includes full-featured XML, XSLT, and Java editors, and the capability to graphically create Schema documents, execute XPath Queries, and debug XSLT stylesheets. Stylus Studio is another very powerful tool that can help with many aspects of XML development.

This is by no means a comprehensive list of all the software available that supports XML. These applications are just a starting point for editing and displaying documents with XML. As we discuss other XML topics and related technologies in later chapters, we will mention appropriate software packages in the text. Additionally, a complete list of XML software resources can be found in Appendix D.

ROADMAP

The information contained in this chapter describes the core of XML as a technology. A familiarity with elements and attributes is essential for understanding the remaining technologies in this book.

In these roadmap sections, we intend to give you some insight into how the technology presented in the chapter relates to the other technologies presented in this book, and other technologies you might encounter as you continue to explore XML. However, with the focus on XML 1.0, the information you've just seen applies to any technology related to XML.

As we begin to look at DTDs and XML Schemas, you will need to have an understanding of XML 1.0, because both DTDs and Schemas are used to author the rules that you will use to validate your XML documents.

Namespaces play a vital part in XML 1.0, in enabling you to create your own XML vocabularies, and helping to avoid incompatibilities with other XML vocabularies you might also be using.

The stylesheet technologies presented with CSS, XSL, and XSLT are all related to enabling you to display the contents of your XML files with some level of graphic design. Additionally, XSL and XSLT are actually technologies written in XML themselves, so understanding XML 1.0, relates directly to understanding how to write your own XSL and XSLT Stylesheets.

The linking and locating technologies of XPath, XLink, XBase, and XInclude were all created to add functionality to XML, which was not provided in the XML 1.0 Recommendation. As your XML projects become more complex, you will want to make use of these technologies to accomplish all of your development goals with XML. The same holds true of XQuery, which is a technology designed to assist you with searching your XML documents.

Finally, there are the XML vocabularies:

- XHTML—A rewrite of HTML with XML well-formedness constraints in mind.
- WML—The Wireless Markup Language uses XML to create a language for increasing Web browsing and communication over wireless technologies.
- SVG—The Scalable Vector Graphics language uses XML as a base for defining a new, vector-based graphic language for the Web.
- SMIL—Synchronized Multimedia Integration Language is another XML vocabulary designed to bring new levels of multimedia authoring and integration to the Web.
- RDF—Resource Description Framework is an XML vocabulary designed to catalog and describe Web resources to help manage the wealth of information available online.
- XForms—An XML-based method for describing forms designed to move beyond the current capabilities of HTML forms.

At the core of all these technologies is the well-formed and valid XML as defined in the XML 1.0 Recommendation. A mastery of elements and attributes will open the door to dozens of exciting new technologies that will change the way you develop for the World Wide Web.

Additional Resources

Additional information regarding core XML as defined in the XML 1.0 Recommendation can be found in the following locations:

- W3C XML Homepage (`http://www.w3.org/XML/`)

  This site is the official W3C homepage for XML activity. It contains links to the official Recommendation, as well as papers and other resources for XML developers.
- Extensible Markup Language (XML) Recommendation (`http://www.w3.org/TR/REC-xml`)

  This is the location of the official XML 1.0 Recommendation.
- The Annotated XML Recommendation (`http://www.xml.com/pub/a/axml/axmlintro.html`)

  This guide, authored by one of the editors of the 1.0 Recommendation, Tim Bray, is an excellent tool for helping understand the details of the Recommendation, as well as learning about why some choices were made in the development of XML.

- Webmonkey XML Tutorial (`http://hotwired.lycos.com/webmonkey/98/41/index1a.html?tw=authoring`)

  The Webmonkey tutorial provides a guide to learning XML geared toward Web authors and those who are very familiar with HTML.

- A Technical Introduction to XML (`http://www.xml.com/pub/a/98/10/guide0.html`)

  This guide from XML.com also serves as technical introduction to XML for Web-centric developers.

CHAPTER 4

Structuring XML Documents with DTDs

In this chapter

by David Gulbransen

Well-Formed and Valid XML

In the first few chapters of this book, we have covered the various components that make up XML documents, such as elements and attributes. We've also taken a look at how those components come together to construct well-formed XML documents. You should now be familiar enough with the basics of XML to create your own well-formed XML documents without many problems, and now you should also be ready to move on to the next level of XML—valid XML documents.

Well-formed XML documents are appropriate for many applications; however, there are some instances where well-formed XML does not offer enough power to provide a good solution. In cases where entities are needed, or where you want to enforce specific rules about the document structure, well-formed XML does not suffice.

For example, if you had an XML document describing some inventory items:

```
<?xml version="1.0"?>
<inventory>
 <item>
  <description>Coffee Mug</description>
  <sku>9842392</sku>
 </item>
</inventory>
```

you could use this document as a well-formed document. However, it might be useful to place some restrictions on the document. For example, you might want to insist that every `inventory` element was required to have both a `description` element and `sku` element. That would ensure that items in your inventory .xml file were described adequately. You could not accomplish this with well-formed XML. The XML Parser reading the XML document would have no way of knowing that you had placed these constraints on the document. That is where validation comes in. With a validating parser, you can use a Document Type Definition (or some other schema, such as XML Schemas) to describe the rules that the document must follow to be considered a valid document. When the validating parser reads the XML file, it also reads the DTD, and then it checks the file to make sure it follows those rules written in the DTD. If it does, the document is considered valid. If the document does not meet the validation requirements then the parser will return an error.

Using a DTD to create valid XML offers several advantages over using just well-formed XML. With valid XML and DTDs you can

- Specify the types of child elements and content that an element instance in your document must have.
- Specify the order and number of times elements may occur within a document.
- Specify attributes for elements and force those attributes to be required.
- Specify the default value for the content of an attribute.
- Limit attribute values to a predefined list of choices.
- Create entities, or shorthand, that can be used to represent special characters or strings within your XML documents.

Making use of a DTD allows you much greater control over the content of the final XML instance document. Using DTDs can help authors create documents that are structured properly with respect to how your data is organized.

Validation is a powerful XML tool, and should be considered when it is important for your XML documents to be structured according to specific rules.

DOCUMENT TYPE DEFINITION BASICS

Like XML, Document Type Definitions are text, and therefore can be theoretically read by humans. DTDs can either be saved as separate files from the XML instance documents they describe or they can be saved as an internal subset of the document itself. We'll discuss this mechanism for internal versus external DTDs later in the chapter. Now let's take a look at some basic information about DTDs.

DTDs ARE A TYPE OF SCHEMA

In the generic sense of the word, a *schema* is a set of information that describes the structure of another set of information. You could think of a schema as a set of rules, or a grammar for describing some kind of structured data. Schemas aren't just used with XML—databases have schemas too, which describe how data is stored in the database, and how the various data relate to one another.

DTDs are a type of schema for describing the data structure of an XML document. There are other types of schemas that can be used with XML, such as XML Schemas, which are actually written in XML. We will discuss these in greater detail in Chapter 5, "Defining XML Document Structures with XML Schemas." It can be confusing sometimes because the XML Schema is a specific type of schema, and DTDs are schemas, too. But the end result is the same—both are grammars for describing the contents of an XML document that can be used by a validating parser to check an XML instance document for validity.

DERIVED FROM SGML

Document Type Definitions are not a new technology. They are actually a holdover from the days of SGML, and because XML was derived from SGML, DTDs came along with the package. There are a number of differences between DTDs in SGML and DTDs in XML, which are not really important to discuss here. If you are coming from an SGML background and have DTDs that you need to convert to XML, you might consult "Converting an SGML DTD to XML" by Norman Walsh.

The important thing to realize is that DTDs were not designed specifically for XML, and therefore although some of the syntax and structures of DTDs might seem very convoluted, they are the result of adapting the SGML technology for XML.

DTDs Use a Different Syntax from XML

The first thing that you will notice about DTDs is that they use a completely different syntax from XML. DTDs do not contain start tags and end tags, per se. DTDs have their own syntax, and **DTDs are not well-formed XML**. This is a critical difference between DTDs and XML Schemas, which are written using XML and are themselves well-formed XML documents. Let's take a look at a simple DTD:

```
<!-- A Simple DTD -->
<!ELEMENT inventory (item+)>
<!ELEMENT item (description, sku)>
<!ELEMENT description (#PCDATA)>
<!ELEMENT sku (#PCDATA)>
```

At first glance, it might seem as though this is similar to XML because you see < and > symbols. However, a close inspection would reveal that these are not actually tags, they have no starting tag or ending tag, and they do not have attributes. DTDs use an entirely new syntax, which is not XML. We will discuss this syntax in greater detail later in the chapter as we discuss element declarations and attribute declarations.

DTD Components

The DTD can be either a separate file, or as a header included with your XML document. Within the DTD itself is a series of rules that can be used for the following:

- Defining what elements are legal to use in the XML document.
- Specifying the number of legal occurrences of an element.
- Defining what elements are children and parents of other elements.
- Defining what attributes each element may or may not have.
- Defining any enumerations for attribute content.
- Defining Entities.
- Defining Notations.
- Enforcing a document structure to ensure data integrity.

This covers the basic things you can do with a DTD. If you think about how you can combine these ideas in one document, it's easy to see how DTDs could become very complex very quickly.

Why Use a DTD?

We've already discussed that you might want to make use of a DTD to enforce rules in an XML document. That is the generic case for using a DTD. Here are some specific instances in which you may want to use a DTD to create valid XML documents.

USING A PREDEFINED MARKUP LANGUAGE

Let's say you are using the Chemical Markup Language (CML) to define some molecular structures in an XML document. The CML is a markup language that has been defined to make it easy to exchange chemical data among chemists. Therefore, it's important that they all utilize the language in the same way. If authors were to apply the CML in different ways, they would not be able to ensure that everyone's CML documents were compatible or made sense. So, this is a perfect time to use a DTD.

Anytime you are using an XML vocabulary that is based on a Web standard or industry standard, it's a good idea to use a DTD to ensure compatibility. Now, the upside of using existing DTDs is that you don't have to write them. In the case of using a standard DTD, you will most likely just be using the DTD to validate the content of your documents.

CONSISTENCY

Let's say that you are writing a document to catalog books in a library. You might want to make sure that each of the XML entries for books is in the same format. Chances are you will use some standard method of cataloging, such as the Dewey Decimal System. You could rely on your talents and attention for detail to make sure each record is complete and accurate. However, that leaves you open to potential problems. After all, even the most diligent author sometimes makes mistakes.

By using a simple DTD that outlines what elements and attributes must be used in your XML records, you can make sure that every one of your records is completed correctly, without having to worry about paying strict attention to each record you author. If they're filled out incorrectly, the record won't validate, and then you can correct the problem before proceeding.

COLLABORATIVE AUTHORING

The problem of consistency or data integrity is also a concern when working in a collaborative environment. Because you cannot always rely on everyone to be as data savvy and conscious as you, DTDs and validation offer a method for making sure that everyone is entering the data in their XML documents in the same way, and that their data is good after it is entered into the document. This can be a real lifesaver if you are entering huge amounts of data. Imagine having a workgroup entering thousands of records. If they aren't all good, tracking down the bad data could easily consume more time than authoring a simple DTD.

HIGHLY STRUCTURED DOCUMENTS

Some documents are built to be flexible, and some are not. If you are building an XML document-based CD catalog for your record collection, you might not care too much about data integrity or structure. But if you are building a part description for an engineering project, data integrity is a much more important issue.

For highly structured or very data-intensive applications, DTDs can help force users to be complete in their documents, and they can help make sure the documents are structured logically and usefully.

As you can see, there are several instances in which DTDs can be very helpful, if not necessary. And the examples we've provided here are by no means all the reasons you might want to use a DTD. The best gauge of when to use a DTD or not will be your own judgment, based on what you need from your documents and what you feel you can accomplish in the DTD.

DTD STRUCTURES

There are basically four physical constructs that can be used in a DTD to create the rules that are used for an XML document, and there are two pieces that can be used internally in the DTD. Those components are

- Element Declarations
- Attribute Declarations
- Notation Declarations
- Entity Declarations
- Parameter Entity Declarations
- Comments

So, now let's look more closely at each one of these components and what function each one of them serves.

ELEMENT DECLARATIONS

The element declaration is the mechanism that is used inside a DTD to define the elements that may occur in an XML document. The element declaration can be used to specify that an element may contain other elements, that it may contain anything, or that it must be empty.

The real power of the element declaration comes from the idea that you can actually define the relationships between the elements in your documents using the declaration. The element declaration is flexible enough to allow you to define what parent elements may contain what child elements, and also the number of times those elements may occur in a document.

ATTRIBUTE-LIST DECLARATIONS

Attribute-list declarations are the way that you define attributes for your elements inside the DTD. The attribute-list declaration allows you to list all the attributes for a given element, and to provide specific information about each of the attributes.

You can specify the type of data that attributes can contain. You can also specify whether an attribute is optional or required. You can even use a special feature called *enumerated attributes* to provide users multiple-choice attribute content in the XML document.

NOTATION DECLARATIONS

Notations are an interesting feature of XML and DTDs, but they are not especially common. The basic idea behind a notation is that XML is not really designed to contain binary data, but binary data can be useful.

For example, what about GIFs or JPEGs? They are both binary data formats that are commonly used on the Web. So, if XML is designed to be used with the Web, it might make sense to include a way to utilize binary formats like these.

This can be done through notations. A notation is simply a way to annotate some information in your XML document that might not be familiar to the parser. For example, if you have some data in your document that is not XML (such as an unparsed entity), the XML parser will not know what to do with that data. An annotation simply allows you to provide a note to the parser saying, "Hey, here's what this information is."

ENTITY DECLARATIONS

Entities are a type of shorthand. You define the contents of the entity, and the text that will represent the entity in the XML document. After the entity is defined in the DTD, you can then use it in the XML anytime you want, as often as you want.

Entities are one of the most confusing aspects of DTDs to many users, and they come in several different forms. There are entities that are self-contained within the document, which are internal entities. There are entities that are defined in an external document, or external entities, and there are entities that are built in to XML, a number of character entities. We will discuss the major types of entities in greater detail later as well, but for now, just think of entities as a method of shorthand, or representing special symbols within an XML document.

PARAMETER ENTITY DECLARATIONS

Although entities are designed to be shortcuts that are used in your XML documents, there is also a type of entity designed to be used as a shortcut in your DTDs. These entities are called *parameter entities*.

Parameter entities are of no use outside the DTD. They have their own syntax separate from standard entities, and they are really designed to be used to make your life in the DTD a little easier.

For example, let's say that you had several different elements, all of which were going to have similar attributes. You might have an inventory XML document, for example, with several different elements, all of which might have attributes such as `Price` or `SKU`. Using a parameter entity, you could define a parameter entity, called "*Common_Attributes*," and use that in the ATTLIST declaration. This would save you from having to type the attributes over and over; but, more importantly, it would enable you to make universal changes to the attributes by changing one location in the DTD.

COMMENTS

Comments are an essential part of any DTD, as they can help communicate what you were doing to whoever is reading your DTD. This is particularly important in a Document Type Definition, because they are often shared with other XML authors.

For example, if you were writing a DTD for your company to use in a memo format, comments in the DTD would help any potential authors understand the rules that you established for writing XML documents based on your DTD. Not only that, but well-placed comments can also help you understand what you were writing as well. Sometimes a comment can really help jog your memory if it has been a while since you had revised a particular DTD.

DTDS AND XML DOCUMENTS

Writing the DTD is a very fine and noble endeavor; however, it's a complete waste of time if you don't link the DTD somehow to your XML document.

The linking of the two documents actually occurs in the XML document, not in the DTD. This is because most XML-based languages have only one DTD. That DTD is used by many different documents, so specifying the link in the DTD would become difficult to manage.

Instead, the link is created in the XML document through the DOCTYPE declaration. The DOCTYPE declaration is actually pretty flexible in that it enables you either to specify a reference to an external file that contains the DTD, or actually to include the DTD within the XML document itself, inside the DOCTYPE declaration.

The advantage of including the DTD internally in the XML file is that the document is then self-contained, and can be transferred as one single file rather than two. This ensures that if you share your XML document with someone, the document can still be validated even if the DTD somehow gets lost in the shuffle. However, an internal DTD set cannot be linked to other documents or easily shared with other users, so specifying an internal DTD limits the usefulness of the DTD for use with multiple documents.

There is, however, another solution. You can actually use both an internal and external DTD. The internal DTD can actually override rules in the external DTD, which can be very useful if you are using a shared DTD as the basis for validation of your document but want to have some additional customizations.

DON'T REINVENT THE WHEEL

Anytime you decide that you need to use validated XML, the first step you might want to take is to look for other people or organizations that might be doing similar work. There may already be a DTD that has been written by another company or trade organization that suits your needs. This can be especially important if you are working on a project for something that is industry specific. For example, if you were working on a DTD for the healthcare industry, it would be a good idea to check with trade groups to make sure you are not duplicating a massive effort.

ELEMENT DECLARATIONS IN DTDS

With an understanding of what valid XML is, and why we might want to take advantage of it, it's time to take a look at the physical constructs that make up a DTD. Let's go back to our first simple DTD example:

```
<!-- A Simple DTD -->
<!ELEMENT inventory (item+)>
<!ELEMENT item (description, sku)>
<!ELEMENT description (#PCDATA)>
<!ELEMENT sku (#PCDATA)>
```

This example is actually a complete and valid DTD. You will notice that unlike with XML, there is no prolog or any formal structure that identifies this as a DTD. We have added a comment line that identifies it, but there are no formal requirements or headers for DTDs.

The DTD itself will consist of a series of declarations, and the first declaration we're going to take a look at is the `ELEMENT` type declaration.

THE ELEMENT DECLARATION

To create a formal definition of our elements in the DTD, we can actually use a mechanism defined in the XML 1.0 Recommendation called the *element type declaration*. An element type declaration is just a syntax for formally describing what an element-type is, and what type of data it can contain. The specification of what an element may contain is called the element's *content model*. We'll discuss some different types of content models you might design in the next section.

An element type declaration takes the following basic format:

```
<!ELEMENT name     (content-model)>
```

The `<!ELEMENT` portion of the declaration never changes.

It is case sensitive, and must appear exactly as you see it here for it to be recognized by an XML parser. On the surface, it might look like a tag, but it is not, and there is no closing tag associated with the element declaration at all. Also, you must start a new declaration for each element, even if they share the same type of content model. For example, if we have a DTD describing contact information for attendees of a seminar, we might have some address elements which all contain text. We still have to define each element with a separate element declaration, even though these elements will share a similar content model.

The *name* refers to the element type, which is sometimes called the *general identifier*. This is the same name that will appear in the start tag and end tags, and it must adhere to all the rules for creating a valid XML name, as we discussed in Chapter 3, "XML Building Blocks: Elements and Attributes."

So, let's say that you wanted to create an element called `<NAME>` that could just contain text. You would use the following:

```
<!ELEMENT name    (#PCDATA)>
```

Now you could use that element like so:

```
<name>John Doe</name>
```

and it would be considered "valid". The `#PCDATA` keyword used in the content model stands for *"Parsed Character Data"* which is another way of saying, "text, but text that will be read by the parser, so it can't have any greater-than or less-than symbols in it." Because the preceding element we wrote has only text content, it is valid. However, if we were to use

```
<name><first>John</first></name>
```

it would not be valid because the element declaration for `name` makes no mention of the `first` element.

The first part of the declaration, the `<!ELEMENT` *`name`*, is very simple. However, the content model can get pretty complex. In the content-model section of the element type declaration, you can specify a number of different options. Here are a few:

- Element Contents

  You can specify that the element is to contain another element, or element content:

  ```
  <!ELEMENT     my_element     (child_element)>
  ```

  There are also some special syntaxes for specifying how many of a given child element the parent may contain. However, if the element is simply named, with no other symbols, it must appear once and only once. We'll cover the other options later.

- PCDATA

  You can also specify that the element contains text:

  ```
  <!ELEMENT     my_element     (#PCDATA)>
  ```

  This declaration simply means that the element may contain text data, and that the data it contains will be parsed by the XML application reading the file. This means that the element may not contain tags or any other kind of XML markup, or it will cause an error.

- ANY

  If you specify that an element may contain `ANY`:

  ```
  <!ELEMENT     my_element  ANY>
  ```

  then the element can literally contain anything: other elements, in any number, and text.

- `EMPTY`

  If you specify that an element is empty:

  ```
  <!ELEMENT      my_element      EMPTY>
  ```

  then the element may not contain any other elements or text. This might not seem very useful, but remember the element can still have attributes, which can be used to store information as well.

Using these in combination with one another can become quite complex. However, you now have an idea of just how specific you can be when you are constructing your documents. And when you use these rules to establish what your XML documents are supposed to look like, a document will not be valid unless it follows all of these declarations.

So, let's take a look at what each one of these declarations might look like.

Let's say we were going to have an element called `name`, as in our previous example, but that it could contain two more elements, `first` and `last`. We want only the `first` and `last` elements to be able to have text. So, our element declarations look like this:

```
<!ELEMENT name (first, last)>
<!ELEMENT first (#PCDATA)>
<!ELEMENT last (#PCDATA)>
```

This now makes it legal, or valid, for us to use the following XML:

```
<name>
<first>John</first>
<last>Doe</last>
</name>
```

4

The first declaration:

```
<!ELEMENT name (first, last)>
```

defines the `name` element, and says that it must contain one `first` and one `last` element. We could use some special symbols if we wanted to specify that the `name` element could contain more than one `first` or `last` element, but if we just list the names separated by commas as we have done here, the children must be one, and only one, of the specified elements, and in the order listed.

Now, let's take a look at a simple XML document that we could use for our seminar attendee contact data:

```
<?xml version="1.0"?>
<seminar>
 <attendee reg="2992">
  <name>
   <first>John</first>
   <last>Doe</last>
  </name>
  <title>CTO</title>
  <company>Initech</company>
  <address>
   <street>123 Ontario</street>
```

```
    <city>Indianapolis</city>
    <state>IN</state>
    <zip>46206</zip>
  </address>
  <phone type="office">1-800-555-1222</phone>
  <phone type="fax">1-800-555-1212</phone>
  <email>jdoe@initech.com</email>
 </attendee>
</seminar>
```

Here we have a number of elements that can be used to store information, some of which also have attribute information. We'll discuss the attributes and their declarations a little later in the chapter. For now, let's concentrate on the element declarations:

```
<!ELEMENT seminar (attendee*)>

<!ELEMENT attendee (name, title?, company?, address, phone+, email*)>

<!ELEMENT name (first, last)>
<!ELEMENT address (street, city, state, zip)>

<!ELEMENT first (#PCDATA)>
<!ELEMENT last (#PCDATA)>
<!ELEMENT title (#PCDATA)>
<!ELEMENT company (#PCDATA)>
<!ELEMENT street (#PCDATA)>
<!ELEMENT city (#PCDATA)>
<!ELEMENT state (#PCDATA)>
<!ELEMENT zip (#PCDATA)>
<!ELEMENT phone (#PCDATA)>
<!ELEMENT email (#PCDATA)>
```

We have a number of element declarations, some of which will look familiar, and some of which contain some new symbols. Let's step through them and see what is happening.

The first Element Type Declaration sets up the root element, `seminar`, which will have an element content model:

```
<!ELEMENT seminar (attendee*)>
```

This element declaration defines our root `seminar` element and lets us know that the root element is going to have any number of `attendee` elements as its children. The asterisk that appears after the `attendee` element in the content model is one of those special symbols we mentioned, which is used to denote how often a child element may occur. For example, if we look at the declaration for the `attendee` element, we see a number of symbols used in the content model:

```
<!ELEMENT attendee (name, title?, company?, address, phone+, email*)>
```

Each of these symbols, `?` `+`, and `*`, has a special meaning when appended to the end of an element name in the content model. Table 4.1 is a summary of the symbols and their meanings.

TABLE 4.1 THE SYMBOLS USED TO DETERMINE ELEMENT OCCURRENCE IN ELEMENT DECLARATIONS

Symbol	Meaning
None	If no symbol follows an element name, the element must appear once and only once.
?	A question mark means that the element may not be used at all, or that it may appear only once.
+	A plus sign means that the element must occur at least once, but it may be used more than once.
*	An asterisk means that the element may not be used at all, or it may be used any number of times.

So, from the declaration:

```
<!ELEMENT attendee (name, title?, company?, address, phone+, email*)>
```

we can see that our `attendee` element is going to have the following content:

- Exactly one `name` element.
- The `title` element will be used only once, or not at all.
- The `company` element will be used only once, or not at all.
- Exactly one `address element.`
- At least one `phone` element, up to an unlimited amount.
- An unlimited amount, including zero, of `email` elements.

Now it should be clear how useful a DTD can be for restricting data in an XML document. For example, we want there to be exactly one name given for each attendee, and we want to make sure we have at least one phone contact for the attendee. However, all attendees might not have an email address, whereas some might have several. The DTD gives us the power to put this information into rules, so now we know our XML document will have the structure and information we want.

Now we need to define the rest of the elements that we're going to use in the DTD:

```
<!ELEMENT name (first, last)>
<!ELEMENT address (street, city, state, zip)>
```

We have two more elements, `name` and `address`, that are going to have element content. That element content is pretty straightforward, with each element occurring exactly once.

There are other ways we could structure this data, however. For example, if we wanted to group some elements together in the content model and provide choices, we could easily do that as well. For example, with our address element, suppose we were gathering address information for statistical purposes only. Then we might want people to provide a city/state pair, or a ZIP Code, but not necessarily both:

```
<!ELEMENT address ((city, state) | zip))>
```

We would start by grouping the `city` and `state` elements together:

```
(city, state)
```

so they could be treated as one unit. Then, we could use the `|` to denote "or" in the content model, and build the content model as we would with single elements. The result is a model that enables us to use `city` and `state` elements *or* a `zip` element, but not both.

Finally, we have a number of elements that simply have text content models, and are very simple element declarations:

```
<!ELEMENT first (#PCDATA)>
<!ELEMENT last (#PCDATA)>
<!ELEMENT title (#PCDATA)>
<!ELEMENT company (#PCDATA)>
<!ELEMENT street (#PCDATA)>
<!ELEMENT city (#PCDATA)>
<!ELEMENT state (#PCDATA)>
<!ELEMENT zip (#PCDATA)>
<!ELEMENT phone (#PCDATA)>
<!ELEMENT email (#PCDATA)>
```

That is how you formally define your elements. It can really be that simple, if all you require for your documents is a straightforward, simple structure. DTDs can be simple, yet by combining all of these simple little syntaxes, you can actually create some very complex structures, with a great deal of flexibility.

ELEMENT CONTENT BASICS

The idea of element content is a pretty simple one, but also pretty important. Remember in Chapter 3 when we talked about what an element *is*, we mentioned that an element is more than just its name. An element's name is just the element type. The actual element consists of the start tag bearing its name, the end tag bearing that same name, and everything in between. The information between those tags is the content, and how that content is structured is the content model.

Just to keep things extensible and to lend structure to your documents, elements can have a few different types of content as we discussed earlier. They can have "element content" or "mixed content," which can also be thought of as "text/PCDATA" content.

ELEMENT CONTENT

Remember when we talked about well-formedness and validity, we talked about proper nesting. For example, if you have a document that looks like this:

```
<note>
<author>John Doe<day></author>Monday/day>
</note>
```

it is not well formed because the `day` element begins before the `author` element has properly ended. So, to be well formed, it would need to be

```
<note>
<author>John Doe</author>
<day>Monday</day>
</note>
```

with all the tags properly nested. If you look at this well-formed example, you will notice that the `note` element really contains only other elements. The name of the author is the content of the `author` element. The `day` element contains the day. From the perspective of the `note` element, it looks like this:

```
<author></author>
<day></day>
```

So, the `note` element can really contain only an `author` element and a `day` element. When an element contains only other elements, we call the content of that element *"element-content."* It simply means that its content is limited to that of other elements, no PCDATA (or text not contained within an element).

MIXED CONTENT

Just as the preceding `note` element contains only other elements, the `author` and the `day` elements contain only text. If an element contains only text, there really isn't any special designation given the content model (although it's sometimes referred to as *"text"* or *"PCDATA"* content), it just falls under the guise of mixed content.

An element is considered to have "mixed content" when elements of that type may contain character data, optionally interspersed with child elements. Practically, that means you can mix it up when defining the content model for mixed content.

An element that has a mixed content model may contain both other elements and character data. For example, the following is a mixed content model:

```
<note>
This is the text of a note by <author>John Doe</author>.
The note was composed on <day>Monday</day>.
</note>
```

In this case, the `note` element still contains both the `author` and the `day` elements, but now it also contains some general text that comprises the body of the note. This mixing of elements and text is a mixed content model.

An element that has a mixed content model can contain other elements and it can contain text, both parsed character data (PCDATA) and character data (CDATA). Parsed character data is text that is read by the parser and interpreted, whereas CDATA is ignored and just treated as a blob of text.

So, what does all this stuff about content models actually mean in your XML documents? Well, when we are talking about well-formed documents, without a Document Type Definition (DTD), they don't mean much. They are simply two different ways of looking at the structure of your document. However, when discussing validated documents, content models really begin to take on meaning.

When you are creating a DTD to validate your XML documents against, you are really creating the structure of the document before the document actually has any content. Because of that, you will want to spend a lot of time thinking about how you want your data organized and your document structured, and this is when the content models will become much more important. Content models aren't just important when working with DTDs. They are important when working with any type of schema and XML, from DTDs to XML Schemas as well.

Attribute Declarations

In addition to elements, other fundamental building blocks of XML are attributes. One way to think of attributes is to imagine that elements function as nouns, and attributes are adjectives. Attributes can be used to store information that describes or modifies the information contained within an element. For example:

```
<phone type="office">1-800-555-1222</phone>
```

Here we have a `phone` element, which has the actual phone number as its content. However, without the `type` attribute, we wouldn't know whether this was a home phone, office phone, mobile phone, fax, or so on.

In this way, attributes can be very useful in XML documents, and in DTDs, attributes are declared in a manner similar to elements, using an `ATTLIST` declaration.

ATTLIST Declaration

An `ATTLIST` declaration is the physical structure in a DTD used to declare an attribute, and link it to an individual element. Because elements can have more than one attribute, the declaration is called an *attribute list declaration* because you can actually use it to declare more than one attribute for the same element.

`ATTLIST` declarations take the following form:

```
<!ATTLIST element
  name     TYPE     KEYWORD>
```

The *element* is the name of the element (which must be previously declared) for which you are defining this attribute list. The *name* is the actual name of the attribute itself. The *TYPE* refers to the type of attribute that you are declaring, which we will talk about more later, and the *KEYWORD* is a keyword that denotes how the attribute is to function.

Attribute Types

There are a number of different types of attributes that you can declare for use with an element. The type of attribute actually refers to the type of data that an attribute contains. The vast majority of your attributes will be CDATA, or character data, which simply means that the attribute values will be treated as text. However, there are a few more types you can choose from:

- ID—An ID type refers to an attribute, which is functioning as a unique ID for an element. This type will limit the acceptable value of an attribute to be a unique string for each instance of the element.
- IDREF and IDREFS—If you have declared an ID type attribute for an element, you can also use IDREF and IDREFS, which are references to the ID or group of IDs.
- ENTITY and ENTITIES—ENTITY and ENTITIES allow you to specify that an attribute has an entity or entities as its value.
- NMTOKEN and NMTOKENS—NMTOKEN and NMTOKENS allow you to specify that an attribute has a Name Token or Name Tokens as its value.

Attributes with ENITITY or NMTOKEN values are actually pretty rare, so we won't discuss them in much detail here. However, ID attributes are more common, so let's take a look at how we might use an ID attribute.

Let's say that we had an employee file, and we wanted to have an employee ID that was unique to each employee, such as a Social Security number. We could have something that looked like this:

```
<employee soc="123-00-1234">John Doe</employee>
```

Now, if we were building a DTD to describe this structure, we would have the following element and attribute declarations:

```
<!ELEMENT employee (#PCDATA)>
<!ATTLIST employee
   soc      ID       #REQUIRED>
```

This establishes our employee element, and creates the soc attribute that is functioning as an ID. Because the soc attribute is an ID, we could not have two employees with the same soc value, or the document would not be valid. ID types allow you to establish that a unique value is required for the item.

Now, say we had another element, elsewhere in the document, called payroll and we wanted a way to link the payroll element back to the original employee. Here we could use an IDREF:

```
<!ELEMENT payroll (#PCDATA)>
<!ATTLIST payroll
   soc      IDREF    #REQUIRED>
```

Now, our payroll element would also have a soc attribute, but rather than serving as an ID, it would actually be treated as a reference back to the ID associated with the employee.

This type of unique ID and referencing mechanism might be somewhat familiar to you if you have worked with databases. The structures in DTDs are nowhere nearly as sophisticated as keys and unique keys in a database; however, they can be very useful. XML Schemas, however, actually add some datatypes specifically designed for mimicking the behavior of keys in databases.

IMPLIED VERSUS REQUIRED

In the last few examples, you may have noticed that we have made use of the keyword `#REQUIRED`, which as you may have guessed, means that the attribute is required. If you use the `#REQUIRED` keyword with your `ATTLIST` declaration, when the element is used in an instance document, that attribute will be required to be used as well. If you would like an attribute to be optional, you would use the `#IMPLIED` keyword. For example:

```
<!ELEMENT employee (#PCDATA)>
<!ATTLIST employee
  soc     ID      #REQUIRED
  dob     CDATA   #IMPLIED>
```

Here we have the `soc` attribute for the `employee` element, which is required, but we have added a `dob` attribute for the Data of Birth, which is optional. This means we could have either

```
<employee soc="123-00-1234" dob="1-29-67">John Doe</employee>
<employee soc=""789-00-1234">Jane Doe</employee>
```

Both elements have the required `soc` attribute, but only the first element uses the optional `dob` attribute.

So, turning back to our DTD example, our seminar attendees each have a registration number, and we want that attribute to be associated with the `attendee` element:

```
<!ATTLIST attendee
  reg     ID      #REQUIRED>
```

Now we have an attribute called `reg` for the attendee element, which is required, and which will also serve as a unique identifier for each attendee.

FIXED

The final keyword that can be used with attribute declarations is `#FIXED` which can be used to declare an attribute that will always have a fixed value. For example:

```
<!ELEMENT employee (#PCDATA)>
<!ATTLIST employee
        tax       CDATA   #FIXED "US">
```

This creates an attribute called *`tax`*, which will always have a fixed value of `"US"` for a company withholding U.S. payroll taxes. Having a fixed value does not mean that the attribute is required, just that it is assumed to have a fixed value. Because this information is stored in the DTD, when the XML document is read by a parser, the attribute will be assigned the `FIXED` value, present or not. For example, the following two elements are equivalent:

```
<employee>John Doe</employee>
<employee tax="US">John Doe</employee>
```

Even though the attribute is not present on the first element, a parser would still have read the fixed value as `"US"`.

Fixed attributes can be very useful for including information in XML documents that you always want present, and do not want users to be able to change, because the value is set in the DTD, not the document.

ENUMERATIONS

One of the nicest features of working with a DTD regarding attributes is the capability to specify an enumeration for the value of an attribute. An enumeration is simply a fixed list of choices for the value from which the author of the XML document must choose in order to select a correct attribute value. Enumerations are very common in computing applications, such as with pull-down menus in forms on the Web.

For example, let's say that with our seminar attendee, we want to get a phone number, but we are really interested in only an office, mobile, or fax number. So, we want to be able to specify the type of phone number collected with the `phone` element, using an attribute. But we want to limit the values of that attribute as well:

```
<!ATTLIST phone
  type (office | mobile | fax) "office">
```

This creates a `type` attribute, which is an enumeration. The choices for the value of the attribute are limited to the choices placed in the parentheses as shown, separated by the "`|`" symbol for "or." Finally, the default value of the attribute is specified after the choices in quotation marks—in this case, our default value is `"office"`.

Enumerations can be a great way to put flexibility into your XML documents, while still exerting some control over the value of the attributes, and you will find that appropriate places for enumerations pop up all the time.

4

ENTITY DECLARATIONS

Entities are simply a method of shorthand for including information in an XML document which is either repeated often or specialized characters.

For example, let's say that we were working on a set of legal documents, and we wanted to include a disclaimer in those documents, and we wanted to repeat it many times (at the top and bottom of each page, for example). We could insert the entire disclaimer word-for-word multiple times in the document, or we could use an entity.

When entities appear in an XML instance document, they look like this:

```
<element>&entity;</element>
```

The ampersand `&` denotes that the text is an entity, and the semicolon `;` denotes the end of the entity. The *entity* represents the name of the entity, as defined in the document type definition. For example, if we declared an entity called `disclaimer` in a DTD:

```
<!ENTITY disclaimer "This document is for internal use only.">
```

we could use it in our document like this:

```
<contract>
&disclaimer;
</contract>
```

When an XML parser reads this document, it would substitute the `&disclaimer;` with the text in the DTD. So, to the XML parser, the document would look like this:

```
<contract>
This document is for internal use only.
</contract>
```

The value of the entity is called the *substitution text* because it is substituted for the entity when the document is parsed.

If you have worked with HTML, you have seen entities before. For example, if you wanted to put a less-than symbol in an HTML document, you would have to use `<` to do so; otherwise, an error would be generated by the extra < in the code. XML also has a number of built-in entities that can be used to represent special symbols so that you can include them in your XML documents without causing any errors. Here are the entities that are built into XML:

- `<`—The less-than symbol, or < symbol.
- `>`—The greater-than symbol, or > symbol.
- `&`—The ampersand, or & symbol.
- `'`—An apostrophe, or '.
- `"`—A double quotation mark, or ".

These entities are predefined for XML, so they can be used in your documents without any special declarations.

INTERNAL VERSUS EXTERNAL ENTITIES

Entities come in a variety of flavors, parameter entities, parsed and unparsed entities, and internal and external entities.

Parsed entities are all entities that can be read by the parser and then have the substitution text inserted by the parser. Unparsed entities are entities that have data that the parser can't read, such as binary data, which is where notations become involved (we'll talk more about notations later in this chapter).

Parameter entities are a special type of entity that can be used only in the DTD—we'll describe this in the next section.

Finally, there are internal and external entities. Internal entities are entities that are defined within the Document Type Definition. These entities are declared using the `ENTITY` declaration in the DTD and the value of the entity is described as a string of text.

An External entity is also declared in the DTD; however, instead of using a string to define the substitution value, the `SYSTEM` keyword is used to point the parser to an external file that defines the entity. This external file can be an .xml file or another .dtd file, but the important aspect is that it is not included in the content of the original DTD.

ENTITY SYNTAX

Now, let's take a look at the syntax we would use to declare our entities in the DTD. The first type of entity is the easiest to declare, and that is an Internal Parsed entity:

```
<!ENTITY name "Value">
```

The *name* is the name of the entity, and the *value* is the value of the entity's substitution string. For example, if we wanted to define an entity called `rights` for a copyright statement, we would use

```
<!ENTITY rights "Copyright 2002">
```

To use this entity in our XML document, we would use

```
&rights;
```

To define a similar entity, but as an External entity, with the definition of the entity out on the Web, we would use

```
<!ENTITY name SYSTEM "URI">
```

The *name* is the same as the name in our other declaration, but now we have a `SYSTEM` keyword, which lets the parser know we are going to an outside resource, which is defined by a `URI`. So, to define our entity now, we would use

```
<!ENTITY rights SYSTEM "http://www.myserver.com/rights">
```

The entity would then have the value as defined in that external document on our server. Finally, we have the unparsed entity, which takes the following form:

```
<!ENTITY name SYSTEM "URI" NDATA notation>
```

We could use this type of entity to declare an entity that represented a `gif` for our company logo—for example:

```
<!ENTITY logo SYSTEM "http://www.myserver.com/logo.gif" NDATA gif>
```

For this to not cause an error, though, we would need to declare the `gif` notation we've used with the `NDATA` keyword. Notations are discussed later in this chapter.

PARAMETER ENTITIES

The final type of entity is a special type called a *parameter entity*. Parameter entities differ from regular entities (which are also known as General Entities) because **they can be used only inside the DTD.** Parameter entities have no meaning inside the XML document—they are simply a way for you to group data within a DTD for the sake of convenience.

For example, let's say that we have a catalog with a number of clothing items, as elements, such as `shirt`, `pants`, `skirt`, and so on. Now, each one of these elements is going to have the same attributes, so we could type all the attributes in by hand, or we could use a parameter entity.

Parameter entities are declared in the DTD, similar to regular entities, with one important difference:

```
<!ENTITY % name "Value">
```

You will notice there is a percent sign `%` inserted between the `ENTITY` keyword and the *`name`*. That is what denotes this as a parameter entity. Parameter entities are used in the document with

```
%name;
```

Also, parameter entities must be defined before they are used in the DTD, so they are usually defined at the top of the DTD.

So, let's take a look at our sample DTD:

```
<!ENTITY % common "
   size (small | medium | large) 'medium'
   color (red | blue | green | black | white) "'white'
   price   CDATA   #REQUIRED">

<!ELEMENT shirt (#PCDATA)>
<!ELEMENT pants (#PCDATA)>
<!ELEMENT skirt (#PCDATA)>

<!ATTLIST shirt
   %common;>

<!ATTLIST pants
   %common;>

<!ATTLIST skirt
   %common;>
```

The first step is to define a parameter entity, which is actually the definition of our common attributes for each element:

```
<!ENTITY % common "
   size (small | medium | large) 'medium'
   color (red | blue | green | black | white) 'white'
   price   CDATA   #REQUIRED">
```

Then, we declare the elements themselves, followed by the `ATTLIST` declarations, which is where we use the parameter entity:

```
<!ATTLIST shirt
   %common;>
```

When the XML parser reads this, the entity is substituted, and the parser reads the `ATTLIST` as

```
<!ATTLIST shirt
   size (small | medium | large) 'medium'
   color (red | blue | green | black | white) 'white'
   price   CDATA   #REQUIRED>
```

and so on for the other elements' `ATTLIST`s as well. As you can see, this saves a lot of typing of redundant information, which is exactly what parameter entities are useful for.

NOTATIONS AND PROCESSING INSTRUCTIONS

Two features of XML that are holdovers from SGML and very rarely used are Notations and Processing Instructions. We will cover them briefly here, but they are both specialized enough that should you have the need to use either of them extensively you should consult either the XML 1.0 Recommendation or a text that deals exclusively with advanced XML development. Chances are you'll never use notation or processing instructions; but if you do that, you are coming from an SGML background and are already familiar with their use.

NOTATIONS

The word *notation* means a note or an annotation. It's a means of communicating additional information. That's really what a notation is in XML, as well—it is a means for an XML parser, reading the XML file, to pass additional information along to the program that will be using the XML file.

4

Notations come in handy when you want to include binary data with your XML documents. For example, if you wanted to include a GIF in your XML document, you couldn't just cut and paste the GIF into a text file. Instead, you would need to point to the GIF somehow. You can actually include a reference to the external graphic, either as an attribute or an entity.

Note

XML Schemas actually provide two datatypes specifically for this purpose. If you are going to be working with large amounts of binary data often, XML Schemas would be a better choice for validating your XML documents than DTDs.

However, even if you do include a reference to the binary data, how does the application know what to do with the information? Well, you can point it to helpful information using a Notation.

ATTRIBUTES AND ENTITIES

The idea of a notation is quite simple; sometimes it is necessary to explain the meaning of data in an attribute or entity. That can be done through a notation.

For example, let's say that you wanted to include a GIF image in an XML file, such as a company logo. You could include the URL to the file in an attribute:

```
<image source="http://www.mysite.com/myimage.gif">
```

That is perfectly legal, and, in fact, a common way to reference files, through an external reference. However, to the XML processor reading the file, the filename itself is no more than a string of text. It does not know that the string of text actually refers to an image, and specifically to a GIF image.

In fact, the XML Parser is not even required to know what the data means; after all, it is just processing text. However, it might be nice if the parser could pass along specific information about referenced files to outside applications that could in turn deal with the data. That is what Notations enable us to do.

So, with a Notation declaration, we could say

```
<!NOTATION gif  SYSTEM "gif">
```

This defines a notation for `"gif"`, and that in turn can be used to define a Notation Attribute Type, which would represent a GIF image. First, we define the notation:

```
<!NOTATION gif SYSTEM "gif">
```

Second, we define the attribute type:

```
<!ATTLIST image
                    source CDATA #REQUIREDtype NOTATION (gif) #REQUIRED>
```

Now we are free to use the notation in our XML attribute:

```
<image type="gif" source="http://www.mysite.com/myimage.gif" >
```

Of course, using a notation really isn't something you would do in well-formed XML. It does require that you define the notation and attributes in a DTD.

The notation is declared in the DTD by using the notation declaration, which takes the form

```
<!NOTATION name SYSTEM "notation information">
```

The name of the notation is what you use in the `ATTLIST` declaration, or in the entity declaration. The notation information is the information that will be passed along to the application dealing with the binary data format. It could be a simple keyword, such as the "gif" in our example. However, it could be a URL or some other type of description.

Because the XML parser isn't actually dealing with the binary data, XML doesn't really care what type of data it is. As long as it has a notation to pass along, it's perfectly happy. So, if you are using a notation in your document, it's important to make sure that the application that is going to use your XML document can adequately handle the notation.

Notations can also be used with entities. Making use of an unparsed entity is another way in which you might include a piece of binary data in your XML file. Let's revisit the example of including a company logo in your document. One easy way to do this would be to include the notation and entity declarations in an internal DTD, assuming you didn't have any other need for validation.

Let's say that we have two versions of the company logo, one as a GIF and another as a JPEG. First, we would start with the notation declarations:

```
<!NOTATION gif SYSTEM "gif">
<!NOTATION jpeg SYSTEM "jpeg">
```

Now that the notations of `"GIF"` and `"JPEG"` have been declared, it is possible to declare entities for the logos themselves:

```
<!ENTITY logo-gif SYSTEM "images/company-logo.gif" NDATA gif>
<!ENTITY logo-jpeg SYSTEM "images/company-logo.jpg" NDATA jpeg>
```

Now you have two entities that can be used for the logos. If we put these declarations into an XML document, in the internal DTD:

```
<?xml version="1.0" ?>
<!DOCTYPE document [
   <!NOTATION gif SYSTEM "gif">
   <!NOTATION jpeg SYSTEM "jpeg">
         <!ENTITY logo-gif SYSTEM "images/company-logo.gif" NDATA gif>
         <!ENTITY logo-jpeg SYSTEM "images/company-logo.jpg" NDATA jpeg>
]>
```

you are now ready to use the entities in that document:

```
<?xml version="1.0" ?>
<!DOCTYPE document [
   <!NOTATION gif SYSTEM "gif">
   <!NOTATION jpeg SYSTEM "jpeg">
<!ENTITY logo-gif SYSTEM "images/company-logo.gif" NDATA gif>
<!ENTITY logo-jpeg SYSTEM "images/company-logo.jpg" NDATA jpeg>
<!ELEMENT document ANY>
]>

<document>
Welcome to our company!
&logo-gif;
</document>
```

The notation information would be passed by the parser to the application, and assuming that the application was properly set up to deal with the notation, your company logo would be inserted.

PROCESSING INSTRUCTIONS

Because we have been talking so much about including data from external sources, and dealing with new types of information, such as images, Processing Instructions are the natural next step.

An XML parser actually does very little with the XML code in your documents. In fact, it's not required to do much by design; one of the goals of the authors of the specification was to make it easy for programmers to create XML parsers.

The problem with limiting what functionality the XML parser (or processor) must perform is that it limits your ability to include different types of data into your XML documents. With Notations and Entities, we've seen how you can include different types of information in your documents, such as images.

Processing Instructions (PIs) enable you to pass additional information on to the applications using your XML, beyond the XML Parser. In spite of what the name might imply, Processing Instructions are not used by the XML parser to process image (or other types of) data. Instead, Processing Instructions are used to tell the XML parser what external applications are to be utilized to deal with data of a certain type, or specific instructions for the processor related to the document at hand.

What happens is that when the XML parser is reading your XML document, and it encounters a PI, it simply hands that information off to the application the parser is part of. The parser is under no obligation to do anything else with it. If the application doesn't know what to do with the information, that's not the parser's problem. That's why if you are going to use PIs, you should make sure that you are using them correctly according to your specific application.

Processing Instructions are not a part of the document's character data. That's why the parser doesn't care about them. However, XML processors are required to pass the PI along to the application, according to the XML 1.0 Recommendation. PIs all take the following form:

```
<?TARGET instruction ?>
```

The *target* is analogous to the name of the Processing Instruction, and is used to identify what application the instruction belongs to. Usually, you will want to use a notation for the target, so that there is some mechanism for associating a specific application to the PI. The only thing you can't use as a target is any form of the letters *xml*, as these are reserved for use by the W3C. In fact, you've already used a processing instruction with many of the examples we've used in this book:

```
<?xml version="1.0" ?>
```

The XML declaration is in the form of a Processing Instruction. The target indicates that the instruction applies to `xml`, and the information provided is the version of XML we are using. That's an example of how XML uses the reserved keyword `xml` for its own uses.

Another example of a processing instruction might be for processing GIFs. If we have a notation for GIFs defined that specifies a GIF as a notation type, we could pass specific parameters to the application reading the file for GIFs, such as the following:

```
<?GIF scale="50%">
```

indicating how images are to be scaled. Of course, our PI would need to reflect instructions our application could understand. And that varies from application to application, so we can't give you any specific examples here.

Processing Instructions can come in very handy as a way of defining how XML is processed, and they are one of the mechanisms that can be used to take XML from the world of theoretical markup into practical markup. They are one of the ways in which XML is extensible, but in practice, they are used rarely. So, if you start working with XML and it's a long time before you encounter one, don't worry about it. Just keep PIs and their syntax in mind, so that if the need to use one does arise, you will remember why and how.

COMMENTS

Although we've mentioned comments briefly before, we're mentioning them one last time here in detail to make sure you understand their usage, and to make a point about working with code in documents and DTDs.

Both XML files and Document Type Definitions may contain comments, which are simply pieces of text that are completely ignored by the XML parser, so they can contain just about anything you want to put in them.

Contents in XML take the form

```
<!-- Comment -->
```

The comment must begin with the `<!--` string, and it must end with the `-->` string. Here's an example of a comment:

```
        <!--  This is my XML document. -->
```

If we had

```
    <!- This is not a valid comment -->
```

or

```
    <!-- This is also not a valid comment ->
```

it would not be a valid comment. Similarly, you cannot use the string `--` anywhere in a comment except the end. So, the following is **not** a valid comment, because it contains the `--` string:

```
<!-- This is -- not -- a valid comment -->
```

It is very good style to adequately comment your DTDs and XML code. That's because XML and DTDs are both meant to be shared, and it might not always be obvious to an outside party why you designed something in a certain way.

INTERNAL VERSUS EXTERNAL DTD

Document Type Definitions can be incorporated into your XML documents in one of two ways: internally or externally.

As we've discussed in earlier chapters, the first line in your XML document should be the XML declaration

```
<?xml version="1.0" ?>
```

Although this is not a formal requirement of XML, and XML is not required to contain this prolog, it is good form and a good authoring habit to always include it.

The next section that should follow the XML declaration, if you are authoring valid XML, is what is called the *Document Type Declaration*, and it takes the following form:

```
<!DOCTYPE name     SYSTEM uri>
```

`name` and `uri` conform to the rules for naming and URIs. This Document Type Declaration is what is used to point to the DTD that is associated with an XML document, or to contain the data for an internal DTD set. Let's look at the following two examples:

```
<!-- An XML File for Human Resources -->
<?xml version="1.0" ?>
<!DOCTYPE employees SYSTEM "hr.dtd">
<employees>A bunch of data about our staff.</employees>


<!-- An XML File for Parking Tickets -->
<?xml version="1.0" ?>
<!DOCTYPE tickets SYSTEM "http://www.mycity.gov/parking.dtd">
<tickets>Parking Ticket Info</tickets>
```

Note

The *name* in the DOCTYPE declaration must match the root element of your document *exactly*. The case and form must match precisely, or the document validation will fail.

In both of these examples, we use the DOCTYPE declaration to point an XML parser to the location of the DTD. As you can see from the previous examples, we can point either to a file on the local filesystem or to a file that is out on the Web somewhere. This is how we implement an external DTD in our XML files.

Caution

The Document Type Declaration must appear in your XML documents before the first element. The best way to ensure this is to always follow the XML Declaration with your document type declaration, thus avoiding possible conflicts.

We can also include our DTD inside the XML document, in an internal DTD set. To do this, you would still use the DOCTYPE declaration—you would just then include the contents of the DTD:

```
<!-- An XML File for Human Resources -->

<!DOCTYPE employees [
```

```
   <!ELEMENT employees (#PCDATA)>
]>

<employees>A bunch of data about our staff.</employees>
```

Here we have just included the contents of our DTD file in with the XML, setting it apart with brackets []. Because the DTD information is contained within the XML document, this is an Internal DTD. The declarations that are contained inside an Internal DTD are exactly the same as those in an External DTD, so there is no difference when writing the DTD content itself.

There are advantages and disadvantages of both internal and external DTDs. They both have their places, and how you utilize them will depend on the application.

For example, internal DTDs enable you to keep the entire document and DTD in one file. This makes transporting it over the Net a little easier. It is also easier to make revisions to the DTD this way; however, then the internal DTD has to be recopied into any other XML documents it applies to, which can be problematic.

External DTDs enable you to maintain a single DTD, and then apply it to an unlimited number of documents. Because both files (the DTD and the XML) are usually pretty small, most authors tend to stick to using an external DTD for most applications, and using internal DTDs to do only very simple tasks, such as defining an entity or two.

There is also the issue of reconciling Internal and External DTDs. For example, a document can have both an external DTD specified, and then have some definitions contained in an internal DTD as well. In this case, the contents of the two DTDs are combined; however, if there are any conflicting declarations, the declarations from the internal DTD subset will be used over those in the external DTD. This can be exploited as a feature, for example, if you want to make slight modifications to an existing DTD for your own uses; however, if you are using an external and internal DTD, you should do so with considerable caution.

A VALID XML EXAMPLE: CONSTRUCTING THE DTD

Now that we have seen all the components that can be used to construct a DTD, let's take a look at an example from scratch.

In this example, we're going to create a simple DTD for use with a newspaper. Our newspaper is going to contain information about the `edition`, such as the `paper` name, the `publisher`, and some copyright information. Then, the newspaper will contain `sections`, a minimum of one, which will in turn contain `articles` and `ads`.

Each `article` must contain a `headline` and a `body`, and may additionally contain a `subhead`, a `lead`, and some `notes`. Each `article` must also have an attribute for the `author`, and may have attributes for the `editor`, the `date`, and the `edition`.

Each `ad` will contain the ad copy, and attributes for the `author`, as well as optional attributes for the `editor`, `date`, and `edition`.

The first step in constructing our DTD will be to define some entities that we will use for identification purposes, such as the newspaper title, publisher, and so on. These can be used in each paper document, as entities to save input time:

```
<!ENTITY paper "DTD Times">
<!ENTITY publisher "DTD Press">
<!ENTITY rights "Copyright 2002 DTD Press">
```

Next, because we know that both our articles and ads are going to share a common set of attributes, we can use a parameter entity to define those attributes for use later:

```
<!-- Define a Parameter Entity for Attributes -->
<!ENTITY % info "
  author CDATA #REQUIRED
  editor CDATA #IMPLIED
  date CDATA #IMPLIED
  edition CDATA #IMPLIED">
```

Now we're ready to declare the `newspaper` element, which must contain an `edition` element, and must contain at least one `section` element, but may contain more, so we use the + symbol:

```
<!ELEMENT newspaper (edition, section+)>
```

The declaration for the `edition` is simple because the edition element will contain only text:

```
<!ELEMENT edition (#PCDATA)>
```

Every `section` must contain at least one `article` and at least one `ad`, so we can use the + again to define the content model for the section:

```
<!ELEMENT section (article+, ad+)>
```

Now we're ready to declare the `article` element, which must contain a `headline`, followed by an optional `subhead`, `byline`, `lead`, and then one and only one `body`, which can be followed by any number of `notes`:

```
<!ELEMENT article (headline, subhead?, byline?, lead?, body, notes*)>
```

With the element declared, we can then declare the attributes for the `article` element, which, if you recall, we have established a parameter entity to make use of:

```
<!ATTLIST article
  %info;>
```

Finally, the remaining article elements are simply `PCDATA` content models:

```
<!ELEMENT headline (#PCDATA)>
<!ELEMENT subhead (#PCDATA)>
<!ELEMENT byline (#PCDATA)>
<!ELEMENT lead (#PCDATA)>
<!ELEMENT body (#PCDATA)>
<!ELEMENT notes (#PCDATA)>
```

The last task to our DTD is declaring the `ad` element and its attributes, where once again we can make use of our parameter entity:

```
<!ELEMENT ad (#PCDATA)>
<!ATTLIST ad
  %info;>
```

When we bring all of these declarations together with comments, we have a complete DTD, which defines the structure for a simple newspaper document. The resulting DTD is shown in Listing 4.1.

Listing 4.1 A Sample DTD for Validation of a Newspaper XML Instance Document

```
<!--   A Sample Newspaper Article DTD  -->

<!ENTITY paper "DTD Times">
<!ENTITY publisher "DTD Press">
<!ENTITY rights "Copyright 2002 DTD Press">

<!-- Define a Parameter Entity for Attributes -->
<!ENTITY % info "
  author CDATA #REQUIRED
  editor CDATA #IMPLIED
  date CDATA #IMPLIED
  edition CDATA #IMPLIED">

<!-- Define the Root Element -->
<!ELEMENT newspaper (edition, section+)>

<!-- Define the Edition -->
<!ELEMENT edition (#PCDATA)>


<!-- Define the Section -->
<!ELEMENT section (article+, ad+)>

<!-- Define an Article -->
<!ELEMENT article (headline, subhead?, byline?, lead?, body, notes*)>
<!ATTLIST article
  %info;>

<!ELEMENT headline (#PCDATA)>
<!ELEMENT subhead (#PCDATA)>
<!ELEMENT byline (#PCDATA)>
<!ELEMENT lead (#PCDATA)>
<!ELEMENT body (#PCDATA)>
<!ELEMENT notes (#PCDATA)>

<!-- Define an Ad -->
<!ELEMENT ad (#PCDATA)>
<!ATTLIST ad
  %info;>
```

With this DTD, it is now possible to author XML documents that can be validated against it, to make sure that the `Newspaper` documents follow the proper format. An example of a valid document is shown in Listing 4.2.

LISTING 4.2 A VALID XML DOCUMENT BASED ON THE newspaper.dtd

```
<?xml version="1.0"?>
<!DOCTYPE newspaper SYSTEM "newspaper.dtd">

<newspaper>
 <edition>
 Early
 &paper;
 &publisher;
 &rights;
 </edition>
 <section>
  <article author="Jane Doe" editor="John Public" date="02-23-02">
   <headline>DTDs Made Easy</headline>
   <byline>Jane Doe</byline>
   <lead>Have DTDs got you down?</lead>
   <body>Let's look at a DTD...</body>
   <notes>None</notes>
  </article>
  <ad author="Jim Frink" edition="Early">
  Crazy Jim's House of DTDs
  </ad>
 </section>
</newspaper>
```

ADDITIONAL RESOURCES

There are a number of places on the Web where you can go to do research on schemas and DTDs. These are sites that might have a DTD that already does what you are looking for, or that may contain links to industry standards. There are also a few software packages that allow you to edit and work with DTDs:

- BizTalk (`http://www.biztalk.org`)—BizTalk is a Microsoft-led initiative to facilitate businesses in utilizing XML and other standards. Although it is a Microsoft-based site, there are still some good resources here, especially those related to business XML formats.
- OASIS XML.org (`http://www.xml.org`)—OASIS is the Organization for the Advancement of Structured Information Standards, and it is an industry group composed of more than 150 members who have an interest in promoting information standards. The XML.org site also contains general information, in addition to a repository for DTDs and other schemas.
- XML.com (`http://www.xml.com/`)—XML.com is an industry trade site that tracks news and information related to XML in general. It is a good resource for many types of XML-related information.
- Near and Far Designer (`http://www.opentext.com/near_and_far/`)—Near and Far Designer is a GUI tool for designing Document Type Definitions for XML. It enables you to develop a DTD using a graphical interface, rather than code, and then export the DTD for use with your XML documents.

- TurboXML (`http://www.tibco.com/products/extensibility/solutions/turbo_xml.html`)—TurboXML is another graphical DTD editor, with support for other schema formats as well. TurboXML also features an integrated XML editor to enable you to work with DTDs and XML instance documents.
- `http://www.xml.org/xml/registry.jsp`—This is the DTD/Schema repository for xml.org, which is an XML-specific portal. This particular link will take you to their page for Schemas (both DTDs and XML Schemas) which you can either browse by category or search.
- `http://www.oasis-open.org/cover/xml.html#applications`—Robin Cover's site also contains a list of DTD/Schema initiatives, broken down by industry or organization. This is just a lump sum list, so searching it isn't the easiest, but it can be a valuable resource.
- `http://www.schema.net`—Schema.net is another site which has a repository of XML-related Schemas, including DTDs and XML Schemas. You can also browse them by category or search for specific types of schemas.

ROADMAP

This chapter brings you up to speed on creating valid XML in addition to well-formed XML, and introduces some of the concepts associated with XML and validation as well. Many of the terms and concepts in this chapter also apply to working with other types of valid XML—using XML Schemas, for example—to create valid XML documents.

In Chapter 5, we will move on to discussing XML Schemas as a mechanism for validation. There are also a number of alternative schemas, and we will touch briefly on the two most popular: RELAX NG and Schematron.

After you have a solid grip on well-formed and valid XML, you are really ready to hit the open road with respect to XML. All the XML vocabularies that are discussed later in this title are simple instances of valid XML, with DTDs associated with the languages to make sure you are authoring them properly—nothing more. That's how XML is extended and why having a good grasp on the fundamentals of XML is so important in moving forward to work with more advanced technologies.

CHAPTER 5

Defining XML Document Structures with XML Schemas

In this chapter

by David Gulbransen

XML SCHEMAS ARE A TYPE OF SCHEMA

XML Schemas offer an alternative to describing an XML grammar using DTDs. They do not "replace" DTDs, nor do XML Schemas necessarily make DTDs obsolete. DTDs are simple, and they are established technology. There are times when in the interest of expedience and compatibility, it would make sense to use a DTD.

Both tools are useful for describing XML documents. If backward compatibility is an issue, DTDs might be a wiser choice. But if you need some of the features XML Schemas offer, such as datatypes, then the choice will be made for you. It's simply a question of using the right tool for the job.

From the XML Schema Requirements Note published by the W3C, the goals of the XML Schema Recommendation state that XML Schemas should be

- More expressive than XML DTDs
- Expressed in XML
- Self-describing
- Usable by a wide variety of applications that employ XML
- Straightforwardly usable on the Internet
- Optimized for interoperability
- Simple enough to implement with modest design and runtime resources
- Coordinated with relevant W3C specs (XML Information Set, Links, Namespaces, Pointers, Style, and Syntax, as well as DOM, HTML, and RDF Schema)

Now, let's take a look at what schemas have to offer.

SCHEMAS GO BEYOND DTDS

The Document Type Definition is a great way to express XML grammar. However, there are some limitations to the functionality that can be achieved with a DTD. DTDs don't allow inheritance or scoping. And DTDs don't allow for datatyping. These are features that can be very useful in XML design, and thus Schemas are designed to include these types of functionality.

SCHEMAS ARE XML

One of the biggest advantages of working with XML Schemas is that XML Schemas are actually XML documents themselves. Unlike DTDs, XML Schemas follow the structure of a well-formed XML document.

Let's look at a very simple XML Schema:

```
<?xml version="1.0" encoding="utf-8" ?>
 <xs:schema xmlns:xs="http://www.w3.org/2001/XMLSchema">
 <xs:element name="Name" type="xs:string"/>
</xs:schema>
```

Now, this is a very simple XML Schema that defines an element called `name` that is a string. That's all it does, which isn't very useful in itself.

However, take a closer look at the Schema. Notice that it starts with an XML declaration:

```
<?xml version="1.0" encoding="utf-8" ?>
```

This is the same declaration that starts any XML document. It lets an application know that the document is an XML document and that it is based on the 1.0 XML Recommendation, and uses the UTF-8 character encoding set. This declaration should already be familiar to you from well-formed XML documents. It is used with XML Schemas because ***XML Schemas are well-formed XML documents.***

This is a very important feature of XML Schemas because it allows any application that is already XML aware to process XML Schemas. Because they are XML, the same parser can parse schemas as well as XML documents. Unlike DTDs, which have their own complicated syntax, XML Schemas are based on well-formed XML and make extensive use of Namespaces to define elements, attributes, datatypes, and so on. This makes it much easier for software developers to incorporate schema support into their applications.

In fact, if you look at the next line in the sample Schema, it is a Namespace declaration:

```
<xs:schema xmlns:xs="http://www.w3.org/2001/XMLSchema">
```

This is also important, as it provides a mechanism for scoping and versioning, which we will discuss later.

Finally, this defines the "`xs`" Namespace and points back to the XML in which we get to the meat of the Schema, the actual element declaration:

```
<xs:element name="name" type="xs:string"/>
```

The declaration makes use of our Schema namespace, and it uses attributes to provide information about the element we are defining. We will discuss namespaces in greater detail in Chapter 6. Here we define an element called `name` and we also go on to specify that it is a string. That `type` attribute is a critical component of XML Schemas, as it is what allows us to do datatyping.

5

SCHEMAS ARE FAR REACHING

Because XML Schemas are written using XML, that allows Schemas to be adopted quickly and easily by applications already using XML. This helps Schemas meet the requirements of the Working Group that Schemas be "usable by a wide variety of applications that employ XML; and straightforwardly usable on the Internet." Because XML is text based, it is easily transferable via common Internet file transfer methods, such as FTP and HTTP. This means that accessing XML files, and therefore XML Schemas, is as simple as mailing an attachment or visiting a Web page.

In fact, Schemas are "optimized for interoperability" in this way because they are recursive, self-describing documents. By employing XML as the language of Schemas (unlike DTDs, which have their own complex syntax), Schemas are already optimized to work with other XML-based applications.

SCHEMAS ALLOW DATATYPING

Of course, the fact that XML Schemas are actually XML is significant. But the main reason people are looking to XML Schemas is for datatyping.

Datatypes allow you to specify that a piece of information has to be in a specific data format. For example, a `string` type is a concatenation of characters. An `integer` would need to be a whole digit, such as 1, 2, 3, and so on.

Datatypes are a very powerful mechanism for placing constraints on your XML documents. We'll discuss datatypes in much greater detail later in this chapter.

XML SCHEMAS COMPARED TO DTDS

As we saw in Chapter 4, "Structuring XML Documents with DTDs," Document Type Definitions can either be internal or external sets of declarations and definitions that describe the XML document structure.

Document Type Definitions are a holdover from the days of SGML. However, DTDs when used with XML are more limited in what can be accomplished than with SGML. DTDs basically provide a mechanism for specifying elements, attributes, entities, and notations. Now, that does not mean that DTDs are not useful. In fact, there are many applications of XML in which DTDs are exceptionally powerful.

But there are many applications in which DTDs fall short, and many users find that authoring XML Schemas is simpler than authoring DTDs because Schemas are XML, and the syntax feels more natural than DTDs.

ELEMENT DECLARATIONS IN XML SCHEMAS

In Chapter 4, we learned about XML declarations in Document Type definitions. Physical structures, such as element declarations and attribute declarations, are defined in the first part of the XML Schema Recommendation: Structures. In XML Schemas, element declarations take a different form:

```
<xs:element name="address" type="xs:string"/>
```

This is a basic element declaration in XML Schema. The declaration uses the `element` type, which has a number of attributes that manipulate properties of the element. In the preceding declaration, there is a `name` attribute, which is used to specify the name of the element type being declared. There is also a `type` attribute, which is how you specify the datatype associated with an element using XML Schema. You don't have to specify a datatype; however, this is one of the more powerful aspects of XML Schemas, and we will discuss datatypes in greater detail later in this chapter.

You can also specify the scope of declarations, based on where they appear in the XML Schema itself. Elements can be scoped globally, which means that they can then be referenced anywhere in the schema, or they can be scoped locally, which limits them to being used within a specific content model.

VALID <element> ATTRIBUTES

The element declaration in an XML Schema takes the form of the `<element>` tag. That tag forms the start of any element declaration in your schema. The `<element>` declaration can accept a number of attributes, each one designed to manipulate one or more of the properties that make up an element declaration. The attributes that can be used with an `<element>` declaration include (but are not limited to)

- `default`
- `fixed`
- `id`
- `maxOccurs`
- `minOccurs`
- `name`
- `nillable`
- `ref`
- `substitutionGroup`
- `type`

Now let's take a look at each of these attributes and the possible values for each one, so we can see how element declarations are structured .

name

The `name` attribute. is used to specify the name for each instance of the element in an XML instance document. For example, if we have

```
<xs:element name="address"/>
```

this would declare an element called `<address>`, which we could use in an XML document.

The form of the name is an XML Namespace NCName, which essentially conforms to the XML naming standard we discussed earlier. Valid names must begin with a letter, and may not begin with a combination of "XML." The colon ":" is reserved for namespace use, and the underscore "_" is a valid character.

Note

An NCName is simply a name that meets the requirements of XML naming, without the colon prefix for namespaces.

default

The `default` attribute allows you to specify a string as the default value for an element. So, if we wanted to declare a copyright element, we could use

```
<element name="copyright" default="Copyright 2001"/>
```

which would create an element called `<copyright>`, which, if no other content were specified, would have a default value of `Copyright 2001`, looking like this:

```
<copyright>Copyright 2001</copyright>
```

Specifying a default value can be quite useful for ensuring that vital elements in your document contain data, regardless of whether the document author neglects to include a value for a specific element.

fixed

The `fixed` attribute allows you to specify a string that will be the fixed value of an element. So, for example, if you declared

```
<xs:element name="info" fixed="For information call 411"/>
```

then all of your `<info>` elements would be required to have a value of `For information call 411`:

```
<info>For information call 411<info/>
```

Fixed elements are one way to include information that you want to be a part of the instance document, but which you do not want the author to have the power to alter.

id

The `id` attribute allows you to specify an ID for the element, which as an ID in a DTD, serves as a unique identifier for the element. The `id` attribute actually accepts a value that is an `id` datatype, as specified in the XML Schemas: Datatypes Recommendation. The `id` is a unique identifier for the element.

maxOccurs

If you remember from Chapter 4, when we were looking at a DTD, the syntax made use of `+`, `*`, and `?` to denote how often an element could occur in a content model. Schemas do away with this cryptic system, and instead make use of the `maxOccurs` and `minOccurs` attributes.

The `maxOccurs` attribute specifies the number of times an element may appear in the document (or in the content model). It accepts the value of a non-negative integer or "unbounded," which means that the element may occur any number of times. The default value is "`1`." So, if we wanted to specify that a `<part>` element could occur up to 3 times, we would say

```
<element name="part" maxOccurs="3"/>
```

As you can see, this provides us with a great deal more flexibility than the previous `+`, `?`, or `*`.

minOccurs

The `minOccurs` attribute goes hand in hand with the `maxOccurs`. It is used to specify the minimum number of times an element may occur. The default value for `minOccurs` is also "`1`." So, let's say we were declaring an element called `"features"` for a clothing catalog, and we wanted to specify that each listing had to list at least two features of an item, but no more than 6:

```
<element name="features" minOccurs="2" maxOccurs="6"/>
```

As you can see, using the `minOccurs` and `maxOccurs` attributes together provides a great deal of flexibility in the content model for your document.

nillable

The `nillable` attribute is a Boolean that accepts the values of "true" or "false." The default value is false. The `nillable` attribute is used to specify whether or not an element is nillable—that is, whether it can be set to the `xsi:nil` type, which is used to denote an `EMPTY` element.

ref

The `ref` attribute is used to refer to a reference to a global element that has already been declared. In other words, if you want to reuse an element that has already been declared in the document, you can use a `ref` attribute to do so:

```
<xs:schema>
 <xs:element name="full_name" type="xs:string"/>
 <xs:element name="supervisor">
  <xs:complexType>
   <xs:element ref="full_name" />
  </xs:complexType>
 </xs:element>
 <xs:element name="employee">
  <xs:complexType>
   <xs:element ref="full_name" />
  </xs:complexType>
 </ xs:element>
</xs:schema>
```

In this example, the `<full_name>` element is declared, and then it is referenced using the `ref` attribute inside the declarations for the `<supervisor>` and `<employee>` elements. It is very important to note here that the original element, `<full_name>`, is declared with a global scope. That is accomplished by not declaring the element within the content model of any other elements. To use `ref` to reference an element, the element being referenced must be either globally scoped or in the same local scope as the `ref` attribute itself. It is also important to note that a `ref` attribute may not be used within a global element declaration.

5

Note

The issue of scope is an important one to consider when you are authoring your schemas. When an element is scoped globally, as in the example in this section, that means you can use the reference in multiple content models by using the `ref` attribute. It's important to note, though, that you can't specify cardinality of globally declared elements. In other words, you can't use the `minOccurs` or `maxOccurs` attributes. That's because the global declaration doesn't create any instances of the element–that is done by the reference, and therefore the cardinality is specified in the reference.

When you declare an element locally, or within the content model itself, you would specify the cardinality with the element declaration. However, because the element would be scoped locally, you cannot then use the element elsewhere in your document by reference.

So, you could not legally do

```
<xs:schema>
<xs:element name="full_name" type="xs:string"/>
<xs:element ref="full_name" type="xs:string"/>
</xs:schema>
```

because this would represent a `ref` used on a global element declaration .

`substitutionGroup`

The `substitutionGroup` attribute is used to create a grouping of elements that can be used *somewhat* interchangeably. Substitution groups themselves are composed of a "head element," which is a globally scoped (it must be globally scoped) element that serves as the element in the schema for which members of the Substitution group may be substituted. Members of the Substitution group do not have to be globally scoped, but they must be of the same type (or a derived type) as the head element. We will take a look at some Substitution groups later in the chapter. Substitution groups are used in a similar manner to parameter entities in DTDs.

`type`

The `type` attribute also accepts a namespace-qualified name (with the "`xs:`" prefix) as its value, and the value refers to the datatype of the element, which can be from the XML Schemas: Datatypes specification, or can be from another namespace as well.

There are many different datatypes that can be used in conjunction with your elements, and we will discuss datatypes in greater detail later in this chapter.

CONTENT MODELS

Although there are some times when an empty element is useful in a document, most elements are not empty. Elements can have content that is of a simple, straightforward type, such as a string or a number, or they can have a mixture of text and other elements.

When an element contains only a value, and no other elements, we say that it has *simple* content. If an element is a parent element that contains only other elements as children then the element has *element* content. And, finally, when an element contains a mixture of data and other elements, we say it has *mixed* content.

There are some confusing terminologies used with XML Schemas. For example, we have `simpleContent` and `simpleType`. We also have `complexContent` and `complexType`. Although on the surface these components are similar, they do have different uses and applications. When it comes to defining straightforward content models, we should look to `simpleContent` and `complexContent`. Both `simpleType` and `complexType` are useful if we want to create specific element content types that can then be referenced or used again later.

The `<element>` declaration itself may contain any of the following:

- <annotation>
- <simpleType>
- <complexType>

An annotation is simply used to provide comments and other information to the document author or an automated processing mechanism.

Annotations function similarly to comments; however, they provide some mechanisms for more extended information. For example, an annotation has two child elements, documentation and appinfo. Here's an example of how an annotation is structured:

```
<xs:annotation>
 <xs:documentation>
   Annotations function similarly to comments...
 </xs:documentation>
</xs:annotation>
```

The use of the documentation element allows you to build annotations into your schemas that could then be automatically read to create documentation for the schema. The appinfo element can be used to pass information to an application reading the schema. Keep in mind, however, that XML Processors are not required to do anything with annotations.

The <simpleType> element is used to specify content that is based on built-in or derived simple types. Complex types are a little more flexible, and may be either restrictions or expansions of existing simple or complex types.

For example, let's say that you want to create an element that represents temperature. Because temperature can be expressed as a decimal representation, you could use the "decimal" type to create a new <temperature> element. However, if you also wanted to include an attribute that specified whether the temperature was centigrade or Fahrenheit, you would need to use a complex type.

5

When dealing with simple or complex types, Schemas provide a way to add to or take away from a type. Extensions and restrictions are two ways in which you can create new types based on an existing type. As the terms would suggest, an extension *extends* an existing type by adding more information, and a restriction *restricts* an existing type by placing more constraints on the type. We'll take a closer look at both extensions and restrictions later in the chapter.

The most straightforward element content models, however, simply use the existing datatypes that are built in to the XML Schemas Recommendation. These datatypes include (but are not limited to) string, decimal, date, Boolean, and time.

When using one of those built-in datatypes, and content that is simply data—that is, if the element does not contain any child elements or any kind of mixed content—you can simply use a standalone element declaration. Let's look at some examples:

```
<xs:element name="quantity" type="xs:integer"/>
```

This declaration would create an element called `<quantity>`, which could have an integer as its value. For example:

```
<quantity>5</quantity>
```

We could also use a similar declaration with the `decimal` type, to declare an element called `temperature`, which would be a decimalization

```
<xs:element name="temperature" type="xs:decimal"/>
```

which would declare

```
<temperature>98.6</temperature>
```

We can also make use of data structures that help standardize formats for commonly used data, such as the "`date`" datatype:

```
<xs:element name="holiday" type="xs:date"/>
```

The `date` datatype takes the form `YYYY-MM-DD`, so if we wanted to represent the U.S. holiday of July 4th, it would look like this:

```
<holiday>2001-07-04</holiday>
```

A Boolean type is useful for elements that will contain a value of either true or false. The value can be represented using "`true`" or "`1`" for a true value, *or* "`false`" or "`0`" for a false value:

```
<xs:element name="attendance" type="xs:boolean"/>
```

which we could then use to indicate attendance—for example, an employee's presence at a meeting:

```
<attendance>true</attendance>
```

Finally, we could use a string datatype to declare an element that is character data:

```
<xs:element name="title" type="xs:string"/>
```

that would allow the following elements:

```
<title>SE Using XML Schemas</title>
<title>Inside XML 3.5</title>
```

Now, these are by no means all the data types that can be used. In fact, we could easily spend hundreds of pages discussing all the available datatypes. However, with the knowledge that you can use these types, we can start creating element declarations, and the most basic declarations (as we have seen) take the form:

```
<element name="element name" type="some_datatype"/>
```

This works well for elements that have very simple content. However, in many cases, we need to represent elements that have more complex content, such as content that is another element, or content that is a mixture of data and other elements. So, let's take a look at some other content models and the element declarations that accompany them.

<simpleType>

The <simpleType> element allows you to create an element with a content model that is still simple content—that is, content that contains only data and not child elements or mixed content. However, it provides a new level of flexibility: the ability to place restrictions on the existing datatype.

Why is this useful? Well, one example might be declaring an element for inventory. Let's say that you have an inventory item, and you want to create an <inventory> element to represent that inventory. However, because you order the item by the gross, there will never be more than 144 of the item in your inventory, and there can be as few as 0 items in stock. We can use the <simpleType> to declare this kind of element:

```
<xs:element name="inventory">
 <xs:simpleType>
  <xs:restriction base="xs:integer">
   <xs:minInclusive value="0"/>
   <xs:maxInclusive value="144"/>
  </xs:restriction>
 </xs:simpleType>
</xs:element>
```

This will declare an element called <inventory>, which can legally have a value of 0 or any integer up to 144.

The <simpleType> element may contain only a restriction, a list, or a union. Therefore, if you need to extend an existing datatype, you cannot use a <simpleType>.

Additionally, the <simpleType> element does accept some attributes including

- id—This serves as an ID for the type.
- name—A name for the type.

5

A nice side effect of the ability to create and name a simple type is that you can reuse the type in other declarations. For example, let's define a simple type called currency and declare an element called price:

```
<xs:simpleType name="currency">
 <xs:restriction base="xs:decimal">
  <xs:fractionDigits value="2"/>
 </xs:restriction>
</xs:simpleType>

<xs:element name="price" type="currency"/>
```

Now we have an element called <price>, which can contain a decimal value with two fraction digits. We limited the fraction digits to two decimal places using the value attribute, which is a facet of the fractionDigits. Facets are properties of datatypes that can be manipulated in order to change the characteristics of the type. So, any of the following values would be valid:

```
1.00
10.99
19.95
```

Now, because we have given our new `<simpleType>` a name "`currency`," you will notice that we did not nest the `<simpleType>` declaration for the currency type within the currency element declaration.

That was deliberate, because if we nested the `<simpleType>` within the element declaration, it would be locally scoped. By declaring the `<simpleType>` first, and then using that type with our element declaration, we now have a globally scoped type called `currency`, which we could use with another element:

```
<xs:element name="total" type="currency"/>
```

The power to reuse types that you define is one of the greatest flexibilities of schemas.

LIST

New simple types can be derived by `list`, which allows you to create a type that has a value set that consists of a list of acceptable values, rather than just one.

For example, if you wanted to create an element called `<color>` that could have values of "Red", "Blue," "Green," or "Black," and so on, you could use the following declaration:

```
<xs:element name="color" type="xs:string"></xs:element>
```

But with that declaration, `<color>` could have only one value at a time. If an item were multicolored, we couldn't list all the colors unless we change the declaration to a new type: a list:

```
<xs:element name="color">
 <xs:simpleType>
  <xs:list itemType=" xs:string">
   <xs:restriction>
    <xs:minLength value="1"/>
    <xs:maxLength value="5"/>
   </xs:restriction>
  </xs:list>
 </xs:simpleType>
</xs:element>
```

Here, because the simple type includes a `<list>` with `itemType` defined as `string` the values for the `<color>` element could consist of a list of strings. The `minLength` and `maxLength` values do not refer to the lengths of the string, but rather the length of the list.

For example:

```
<color>Red Green Blue</color>
```

would be an acceptable list. However, this would **not** be

```
<color>Red Green Blue Black Orange Red Purple Brown</color>
```

This list is not valid, because it contains 8 list items, which is more than the `maxLength` of 5.

Lists can be useful for creating elements or attributes for which you want to be able to assign multiple values.

Union

A union is simply a means for joining two simple types together. The benefit of a union is that when you declare an element or an attribute with a union, the value of that element or attribute can be a part of the value set of either simple types used in the union.

For example, if we wanted to create an attribute for the size of the writing tip on a pen, we might want the size to be able to be expressed as a name, such as "Extra Fine" or as a decimal, such as ".05". So, we could start with defining a simple type for listing the size by name:

```
<xs:simpleType>
 <xs:restriction base="xs:string">
  <xs:enumeration value="ExtraFine"/>
  <xs:enumeration value="Fine"/>
  <xs:enumeration value="Medium"/>
  <xs:enumeration value="Large"/>
 </xs:restriction>
</xs:simpleType>
```

This would create a type with the value set "ExtraFine, Fine, Medium, Large." Now, we could define another type, called "decimal," which has a value set between .01 and .99:

```
<xs:simpleType>
 <xs:restriction base="xs:decimal">
   <xs:minInclusive vale=".01">
   <xs:maxExclusive value="1.00"/>
  <xs:fractionDigits value="2"/>
 </xs:restriction>
</xs:simpleType>
```

To combine these two value sets, so that they could be used with an attribute called "size," we would use a <union> to create a new simple type that was a union of our two types:

```
<xs:attribute name="size">
 <xs:simpleType>
  <xs:union>
   <xs:simpleType>
    <xs:restriction base="xs:string">
     <xs:enumeration value="ExtraFine"/>
     <xs:enumeration value="Fine"/>
     <xs:enumeration value="Medium"/>
     <xs:enumeration value="Large"/>
    </xs:restriction>
   </xs:simpleType>
   <xs:simpleType>
    <xs:restriction base="xs:decimal">
     <xs:minInclusive value="1"/>
     <xs:fractionDigits value="2"/>
    </xs:restriction>
   </xs:simpleType>
  </xs:union>
 </xs:simpleType>
</xs:attribute>
```

We could then declare an element that uses our new attribute:

```
<xs:element name="Pen">
 <xs:complexType>
```

```
  <xs:compexContent>
   <xs:attribute ref="size"/>
  <xs:complextContent>
 <xs:complexType>
</xs:element>
```

And because the attribute consists of a union between our two simple types, either of the following would be legal values for the "size" attribute:

```
<Pen size=".05"/>
<Pen size="ExtraFine"/>
```

<complexType>

Because XML Schemas have a `<simpleType>`, it follows that they also have a `<complexType>`. A complex type is used for developing element content, which is either element content or which has mixed content of both elements and data.

The representation of `<complexType>` is similar to the other components we have seen. It has a number of attributes that contribute to the ability to customize the `<complexType>` element:

- `id`—A unique id for the complex type.
- `mixed`—A Boolean accepting "true" or "false" with a default value of `false`. A value of `true` is used to represent a complexType that has mixed content—that is, both data and child elements.
- `name`—A name for the complex type, which can be referenced by element declarations, extensions, restrictions, and so on.

By using the `<complexType>` element with these attributes, you can create some very complicated content models for your elements, and, in fact, you can go one step further and define the `complexType` globally so that it can be used with more than one element.

The `<complexType>` element has a number of valid children, including

- `<simpleContent>`
- `<complexContent>`
- `<all>`
- `<group>`
- `<sequence>`

So, now let's take a look at these subcomponents and see how they modify and define a `<complexType>`.

<simpleContent>

The `<simpleContent>` element is used to provide element content that is only character data, and does not contain any child elements. For example, if we wanted to declare an element called `<address>`, which could contain only the street address of someone or something, we could use `simpleContent` to do so.

The <simpleContent> element has only one attribute id, which can be used to provide a unique identifier for the <simpleContent> element itself.

The content of the <simpleContent> element, however, must either be an extension or a restriction. That is, the element being declared must be an extension or restriction of a built-in or derived datatype.

Let's look at an example. Say we are going to declare an element called <title> and we want it to contain only a text string. Well, because the XML Schemas: Data Structures provide a string type already, we can make our element an extension of the string type. So, our element declaration would look like this:

```
<element name="title">
  <complexType>
  <simpleContent>
    <extension base="xs:string"/>
  </simpleContent>
  </complexType>
</element>
```

Keep in mind that the simpleContent element is the means to extend a simpleType to a complexType because a simpleContent element can contain an extension whereas a simpleType cannot.

An extension uses the base attribute to specify the datatype the extension is based on, and then you may also specify additional attributes. In this case, because we simply want an element that is a string and contains only character data, we don't need to deal with attributes at all.

That leaves us with a very simple element declaration, for <title>, which may contain a string as its value.

Similarly, we could also use a restriction to define our simple content. For example, if we wanted to create an element for quantity, which was limited to a dozen, we could use the following:

```
<element name="quantity">
 <simpleContent>
  <restriction base="positiveInteger">
   <maxInclusive value="12"/>
  </restriction>
 </simpleContent>
</element>
```

This creates a <quantity> element, which may have a positive integer, up to and including "12" as its value.

That is all there is to creating simple content, and there are many instances in which you will want to use simple content. But for many elements, you will want the content to be other elements, or a mixture of elements and character data.

5

<complexContent>

Of course, if we have simpleType and complexType, it makes sense that because we have simpleContent, we can also have complexContent. If the content is not simpleContent then it's complexContent, but practically speaking, complex content is content that includes elements, either in an element content model or in a mixed content model.

The <complexContent> element may contain both restrictions and extensions, which gives it more flexibility than simpleContent. So, now let's look at the content models we can use complexContent to define.

ELEMENT CONTENT

When an element contains only other elements, that is called *element content*. An example of an element with element content might be an <address> element, which would contain <street>, <city>, <state>, and <zip> elements:

```
<?xml version="1.0"?>
<xs:schema xmlns:xs="http://www.w3.org/2001/XMLSchema">
<xs:element name="address">
  <xs:complexType>
    <xs:sequence>
    <xs:element name="street" type="xs:string"/>
    <xs:element name="city" type="xs:string"/>
    <xs:element name="state" type="xs:string"/>
    <xs:element name="zip" type="xs:string"/>
    </xs:sequence>
  </xs:complexType>
</xs:element>
</xs:schema>
```

This would create content of

```
<?xml version="1.0"?>
<address xsi:noNamespaceSchemaLocation="address.xsd"
xmlns:xsi="http://www.w3.org/2001/XMLSchema-instance">
<street> 1000 North Milwaukee</street>
<city>Chicago</city>
<state>IL</state>
<zip>60622</zip>
</address>
```

As you can see, all the data in the value of the <address> element is actually data inside other elements.

When defining element content locally, as in the preceding example, we can do so simply by using a complexType, without using complexContent at all. This is using an inline anonymous complexType, and simpleType can be used in this manner as well.

However, once again, if we want to provide flexibility, we can instead declare our complex type independent of the element declaration.

Let's look at another example. In this example, we want to end up with a customer element that contains the name of a contact and the contact's company. For the contact, we want to have a first name and a last name. So, we can start by declaring a complex type called full_name, which will be composed of our <first_name> and <last_name> elements:

```
<xs:complexType name="full_name">
  <xs:sequence>
  <xs:element name="first_name" type="xs:string"/>
  <xs:element name="last_name" type="xs:string"/>
  </xs:sequence>
</xs:complexType>
```

Now we can declare our <contact> element:

```
<xs:element name="contact" type="full_name"/>
```

Next, we need to build our <customer> element, which will have element content, composed of a <contact> element and a <company> element. If we want that company name to now become part of our <customer> element, we can do that with <complexContent>:

```
<xs:element name="customer">
  <xs:complexContent>
    <xs:extension base="full_name">
      <xs:sequence>
        <xs:element name="company" type="xs:string"/>
       </xs:sequence>
    </xs:extension>
  </xs:complexContent>
</xs:element>
<customer>
  <first_name>David</first_name>
  <last_name>Gulbransen</last_name>
  <company>ABC Company</company>
</customer>
<xs:element name="customer">
  <xs:complexType>
    <xs:sequence>
      <xs:element name="contact" type="full_name">
      <xs:element name="company" type="xs:string"/>
    </xs:sequence>
  <xs:complexType>
</xs:element>
<xs:complexType name="full_name">
  <xs:sequence>
    <xs:element name="first_name" type="xs:string"/>
    <xs:element name="last_name" type="xs:string"/>
  </xs:sequence>
</xs:complexType>

<xs:complexType name="customerType">
  <xs:complexContent>
    <xs:extension base="xs:anyType">
      <xs:sequence>
        <xs:element name="contact" type="full_name"/>
        <xs:element name="company" type="xs:string"/>
      </xs:sequence>
    </xs:extension>
  </xs:complexContent>
</xs:complexType>

<xs:element name="customer" type="customerType"/>
```

Now we have a <customer> element that has complexContent. Because it is based on an extension of the <full_name> element, the <customer> content will include the <first_name> and <last_name> elements from the full_name type. Then, the full_name type is extended with a sequence to add the <company> element to the complexContent for the <customer> element. The end result is an element called *<customer>*, which takes the following form:

```
<customer>

  <first_name>David</first_name>
  <last_name>Gulbransen</last_name>

  <company>Vervet Logic</company>
</customer>
```

Tip

When working with large documents that have a number of user-defined types, keeping track of the type can be a chore. One way to address this issue is to include a keyword, such as "Class," "Union," or "List" in the name of the type, which allows you to easily determine how the type should be used. For another resource regarding schema design and naming conventions, visit http://www.hr-xml.org/resources/SchemaDesignGuidelines-1_0-20010712.pdf.

As you can see, XML Schemas provide a great deal of flexibility. In fact, there are often multiple ways to build any given component. How you construct your components will vary depending on how you need to reuse your data and make it available to other structures in the schema.

MIXED CONTENT

A *mixed* content model is when an element has both data and child elements as its value. For example, let's say you have a notice you want to send customers:

```
  <letter>
  Dear <customer>John Doe</customer>,
  We are happy you chose to purchase <product>Happy Fun Ball</product> however,
  we are temporarily out of stock.

  <company>Widgets Inc.</company>
</letter>
```

As you can see, we have an element <letter> that contains both text and elements. So, how do we declare this? Let's take a look.

```
<xs:element name="letter">
  <xs:complexType mixed="true">
    <xs:sequence>
      <xs:element name="customer" type="xs:string"/>
      <xs:element name="product" type="xs:string"/>
      <xs:element name="company" type="xs:string"/>
    </xs:sequence>
  </xs:complexType>
</xs:element>
```

We start by declaring the element `<letter>`, which contains a `complexType`. That type has a `mixed` attribute, with a value of `true`, which is used to indicate that character data can occur between any of the child elements.

What follows next is a sequence of elements that are in the mixed content model. In this case, we have a `<customer>`, `<product>`, and `<company>` element within the content of the `<letter>` element.

Mixed content models can become very complex very quickly, so be careful when you are constructing elements with mixed content. The most common error made when working with mixed content in schemas is to forget that the ordering of elements in mixed content is important: Elements in the XML instance document must occur in the order and number in which they occur in the schema document.

Empty Elements

There are instances when you might want to declare an empty element—for example, an element that has only attributes. This is possible to do by exploiting the `complexContent` element:

```
<xs:element name="emptyElement">
  <xs:complexType>
    <xs:complexContent>
      <xs:restriction base="xs:anyType"/>
    </xs:complexContent>
  </xs:complexType>
</xs:element>
```

What has occurred here is that we have declared an element called *`emptyElement`* and have given it a complex type. Then, we've specified that the `complexType` has `complexContent`, which is a restriction of the `anyType` (a built-in type). But because we do not give any restrictions, the element is treated as an empty element.

Substitution Groups

One new powerful feature of XML Schemas is a Substitution group, which is simply a grouping of elements that can be substituted for one another. The element that serves as the basis for the group is called the *head* element. Let's look at an example:

```
<xs:element name="customer" type="xs:string" />
<xs:element name="myspace:phone" type="xs:string" />

<xs:element name="USphone" type="xs:string"
        substitutionGroup="myspace:phone"/>

<xs:element name="INTphone" type="xs:string"
        substitutionGroup="myspace:phone"/>

<xs:element name="contact">
  <xs:complexType>
    <xs:sequence>
      <xs:element ref="customer"/>
      <xs:element ref="myspace:phone"/>
```

```
    </xs:sequence>
  <xs:complexType>
</xs:element>
```

In this example, we start by declaring a <customer> element for the name of our customer, and then declare a <phone> element for our customer phone number. Notice that we also declare the <phone> element with a Namespace prefix. We do this because Substitution groups must take the form of qualified names.

Next, we declare the <USphone> and <INTphone> elements, but you will notice that we added an attribute to these declarations called *substitutionGroup*. That attribute accepts a value in the form of a Namespace-qualified name that represents the head element for which the newly declared element may be substituted.

Note

Elements in a Substitution group must all be of the same type. For example, you could not have an element called *<name>* that was a string and another called *<quantity>* that was an integer, and place them both in the same Substitution group.

Finally, we declare the <contact> element with an element content model that includes our <customer> and <phone> elements. The result is that all the following XML instances are valid against our schema declarations:

```
<contact>
<customer>John Doe</customer>
<myspace:phone>555-1212</myspace:phone>
</contact>

<contact>
<customer>John Doe</customer>
<myspace:USphone>312-555-1212</myspace:USphone>
</contact>

<contact>
<customer>John Doe</customer>
<myspace:INTphone>+1-312-555-1212</myspace:INTphone>
</contact>
```

In each case, the only aspect that changes is the phone USphone and INTphone elements, which may be substituted in the instance for each other because they are all members of the same Substitution group.

Substitution groups provide for a great deal of flexibility in the construction of XML instance documents.

<sequence>

Sometimes you may want to restrict the authors of your instance documents so that they don't have a choice over what is included in a complexType. In fact, you might want to be even more restrictive than you normally are.

For example, if you are creating an <address> element based on the standard address format in the United States, the address takes the form:

Name

Street Address

City, State Zip

If you were to write it:

City, Street Address

Zip, Name

State

it *might* get to the proper place, but you would be making enemies at the post office and relying on their good nature for your letter to be delivered. Because we can impose some rules in an XML document, why not state specifically that within an <address> element, there must be

```
<name>
<street>
<city>
<state>
<zip>
```

and that they must occur in that order? Well, with the sequence element, you can do just that. The sequence element lets you specify that the content must appear as it is outlined within the sequence element itself, in that order. Let's take a look:

```
<xs:element name="address">
 <xs:complexType>
  <xs:group>
   <xs:sequence>
    <xs:element name="name" type="xs:string"/>
    <xs:element name="street" type="xs:string"/>
    <xs:element name="city" type="xs:string"/>
    <xs:element name="state" type="xs:string"/>
    <xs:element name="zip" type="xs:string"/>
   </xs:sequence>
  </xs:group>
 </xs:complexType>
</xs:element>
```

Now, the sequence element requires that all the elements declared within it—<name>, <street>, <city>, <state>, and <zip>—must appear in that same order when they are used in an instance document. We could still provide some customization. For example, let's say we wanted to make <name> optional, or as a choice between <name> and <company> and then we also wanted to add an optional <street2> for a second street address line:

```
<xs:element name="address">
 <xs:complexType>
  <xs:group>
   <xs:sequence>
```

```
    <xs:group>
     <xs:choice>
      <xs:element name="name" type="xs:string"/>
      <xs:element name="company" type="xs:string"/>
     </xs:choice>
     </xs:group>
    <xs:element name="street" type="xs:string"/>
    <xs:element name="street2" type="xs:string" minOccurs="0"/>
    <xs:element name="city" type="xs:string"/>
    <xs:element name="state" type="xs:string"/>
    <xs:element name="zip" type="xs:string"/>
   </xs:sequence>
  </xs:group>
 </xs:complexType>
</xs:element>
```

Now, in this example, you'll notice that we have nested a `<choice>` within our `<sequence>`. The end result is we now have a choice between a `<name>` element for our address and a `<company>` element. Also, by adding the `<street2>` declaration, we can have a second street address line; however, because it may occur zero times, it is essentially optional. Therefore, in an instance document, we could have

```
<address>
 <name>John Doe</name>
 <street>2135 North Damen</street>
 <city>Chicago</city>
 <state>IL</state>
 <zip>60647</zip>
</address>
```

or we could have

```
<address>
 <company>Widgets, Inc.</company>
 <street>1608 North Milwaukee</street>
 <street2>Suite 800</street2>
 <city>Chicago</city>
 <state>IL</state>
 <zip>60622</zip>
</address>
```

Both would fit the content model described by our use of the `complexType` as shown in the preceding example.

<all>

Finally, there is another possible child element for the `complexType`: `<all>`. Just as the `<sequence>` element is used to define a sequence of elements, and `<choice>` is used to define a choice between multiple elements, the `<all>` element is used to denote *all* the elements that are declared or referenced in the `complexType`.

`<all>` is a little different from `<choice>` and `<sequence>`, however—there are some restrictions regarding the use of `<all>`.

- <all> must be the top-level element. This means that an <all> element *cannot* be the child of a <choice> or <sequence>.
- <all> may contain only elements. This means that an <all> element may not contain a <sequence> or a <choice>—it can contain only an actual element declaration or the reference to an element declaration.

Also, the <all> element does not place any restrictions on the ordering of the elements it contains—it merely means that they must be present. For example, let's say that we have a <contact> element, and we want to ensure that every contact has at least a name and a phone number:

```
<element name="contact">
 <complexType>
 <all>
  <element name="name" type="string"/>
  <element name="phone" type="string"/>
 </all>
 </complexType>
</element>
```

With this declaration, an instance document could be either

```
<contact>
<name>John Doe</name>
<phone>812-555-1212</phone>
</contact>
```

or

```
<contact>
<phone>812-555-1212</phone>
<name>John Doe</name>
</contact>
```

Because order is not important, the elements can appear in any order. However, you could ***not*** have

```
<contact>
<name>John Doe</name>
</contact>
```

This is not valid because the <all> element specified that <contact> had to contain both a <name> *and* a <phone>.

ATTRIBUTE DECLARATIONS IN XML SCHEMAS

Attributes are declared in an XML Schema using an <attribute> element, which has a number of attributes itself. Those attributes are used to place constraints on the properties of the attribute declaration.

The scope of an attribute declaration is determined by its placement within the XML Schema. To declare a global attribute, you would declare the attribute as a child of the <schema> element:

```
<xs:schema>
  <xs:attribute name="myAttribute"/>
  <xs:element name="someElement type="xs:string"/>
</xs:schema>
```

In this example, the `myAttribute` attribute would be declared globally, because it is the child of the `<schema>` element, and not an element declaration. This means that the attribute could be referenced by an element in the document, or by any attribute group as well.

If we wanted to locally declare an attribute so that it was available to only a specific element, we could do that by placing the attribute as a child of the element declaration itself:

```
<xs:schema>
  <xs:element name="someElement
  <xs:complexType>
    <xs:attribute name="myAttribute"/>
  </xs:complexType>
  </xs:element>
</xs:schema>
```

You'll notice that the element declaration has changed some—it now contains a `<complexType>` element, which in turn contains the `attribute` declaration. The `attribute` declaration itself hasn't changed at all—it is the same `attribute` declaration used before. However, because it is now a child of the `<complexType>` element *within* the `<element>` declaration, it is now scoped locally. We could not reference the attribute for another element.

This is how scope is defined for many components, including `<element>` declarations. So, you should be careful when planning your schemas to determine whether you will need to reuse an element or attribute with other components. If you do, it would be best to declare the attribute globally, and then reference it in the `element` declaration.

<attribute>

You've already seen an `attribute` declaration or two—they take the form of an `<attribute>` element, which can have a number of attributes used to define properties of the `attribute` declaration itself. So, let's take a look at the actual attributes that can be used with the `<attribute>` declaration.

name

The first attribute we use with the `<attribute>` declaration is the `name` attribute. This is used to specify the name of the attribute we are declaring. So, if you wanted to declare an attribute called `"sku"` for a sku number in a catalog, for example, you would use

```
<attribute name="sku"/>
```

The names of attributes must be valid XML names. Another aspect of naming to watch out for is naming conflicts. For example, you couldn't have two attributes declared using the same name:

```
<attribute name="sku" type="string"/>
<attribute name="sku" type="integer"/>
```

This would create a conflict because you would have two attributes with the same name, but different types. If they were declared globally, there would be no way to differentiate between the two attributes.

You can, however, have different components that have the same name. For example:

```
<element name="sku" type="xs:string" />
<attribute name="sku" type="xs:string" />
```

This is valid because one declaration is for an element, and the other is for an attribute.

`default`

The `default` attribute allows you to place a value constraint on the attribute being declared. By specifying a default value, you are defining what the value of the attribute will default to if the author of an XML instance document does not specify a value for the attribute. The default attribute takes a value in the form of a string.

For example, let's say that we have an attribute called *`size`* for items in a catalog. We want the author of an XML document to be able to specify a size, but we also don't ever want the size to be blank. We can use the `default` attribute to declare a default value for the attribute:

```
<attribute name="size" default="medium" type="xs:string" />
```

Now, with this declaration, if we had an item in an instance document:

```
<shirt/>
```

even without having the `size` attribute listed, the value of `size` as determined by the XML parser would be "`medium`."

`fixed`

There may be times when you want the value of an attribute to be `fixed`—for example, if there is an internal code that you want associated with an element, but do not want the author of an XML document to be able to change the value of an attribute. In that case, you can use the `fixed` attribute to declare a fixed value for the attribute declaration:

```
<attribute name="areacode" fixed="317" />
```

In this case, anytime the "`areacode`" attribute is used in a document, the value will always be "`317`."

`id`

The `id` attribute is analogous to the ID in XML 1.0. This allows you to provide a unique identifier for the attribute, so that it can be referenced by other schema components.

Note

In addition to reference by the ID, you can also reference attributes by name, and, in fact, that is the more common usage within an XML Schema.

5

`ref`

The `ref` attribute is used to provide a mechanism to reference another attribute declaration. There are some restrictions:

1. A globally declared attribute may not contain a reference—it must contain a `name`.
2. An attribute declaration that contains a `ref` may not also contain a `name`.

Here's an example. Let's say that we wanted to declare an attribute for a phone number, called `phone`, and that we wanted to be able to use it with multiple elements, such as `<business>` and `<personal>`.

```
<?xml version="1.0" encoding="utf-8"?>
<xs:schema xmlns:xs="http://www.w3.org/2001/XMLSchema">

<xs:element name="contact">
  <xs:complexType>
    <xs:sequence>
      <xs:element name="personal">
        <xs:complexType mixed="true">
          <xs:attribute ref="phone"/>
        </xs:complexType>
      </xs:element>
      <xs:element name="business">
        <xs:complexType mixed="true">
          <xs:attribute ref="phone"/>
        </xs:complexType>
      </xs:element>
    </xs:sequence>
  </xs:complexType>
</xs:element>

<xs:attribute name="phone" type="xs:string"/>

</xs:schema>
```

This example showcases a couple of aspects of schemas. First, notice that each of the element declarations contains an attribute declaration that is actually a reference. Here, they are referencing the `phone` attribute declaration, which will allow both `<personal>` and `<business>` to have `phone` attributes. The actual `<attribute>` declaration is declared globally; otherwise, it could not be referenced. You also will notice that the references occur in the schema **before** the actual attribute declaration. That kind of forward reference is actually allowed in XML Schemas.

In an XML instance document, we could use the elements and attributes like this:

```
<?xml version="1.0" ?>
<contact>
<personal phone="317-555-1212">John Doe</personal>
<business phone="812-555-1212">My Company, Inc.</business>
</contact>
```

Using the `ref` attribute for references is a great way to make the structure of your schemas easier to read and more versatile.

`type`

The `type` attribute is used to specify the datatype associated with the attribute value in the XML instance document. There are a number of types that can be used for attribute values, some of which include

- `boolean`
- `integer`
- `decimal`
- `float`
- `date`
- `time`
- `string`

There are more types available as well, but all the types have one thing in common: They are simple types. Unlike elements, attributes cannot be declared complex types. Therefore, all attribute declarations have to be based on the built-in simple types, or derived simple type, based on a restriction of another simple type.

`use`

The `use` attribute is used to limit the usage of an attribute within an XML instance document. The attribute accepts one of three values:

- `optional`
- `prohibited`
- `required`

5

The default value (if none is specified in the attribute declaration) is "`optional`."

If an attribute use is defined as optional, the attribute may or may not be used by the author of an instance document. If the use value is `"required"` then the attribute **must** be present in the XML instance document.

The final possible value for the `use` attribute is "`prohibited`." If the attribute use is declared as "`prohibited`" then the attribute may not be used at all.

attributeGroup

We discussed earlier how you can make use of the `ref` attribute to make a reference to an attribute declaration that is declared globally within your schema:

```
<?xml version="1.0" encoding="utf-8"?>
<xs:schema xmlns:xs="http://www.w3.org/2001/XMLSchema">
```

```
  <xs:attribute name="sku" type="xs:string"/>

  <xs:element name="catalog">
    <xs:complexType>
      <xs:sequence>
        <xs:element name="item">
          <xs:complexType>
            <xs:attribute ref="sku"/>
          </xs:complexType>
        </xs:element>
      </xs:sequence>
    </xs:complexType>
  </xs:element>
</xs:schema>
```

References are one way to organize your attributes and to reuse attributes—another way is the attribute group.

An <attributeGroup> allows you to declare attributes together within a common structure, and then reference that structure in place of individual attribute declarations.

For example, let's say you had a number of attributes:

```
<attribute name="sku" type="xs:string"/>
<attribute name="price" type="xs:string"/>
<attribute name="size" type="xs:string"/>
<attribute name="color" type="xs:string"/>
```

You could add these all to an element with four different references. However, there is an easier way—declare the attributes within an <attributeGroup>:

```
<attributeGroup name="itemInfoGroup">
  <attribute name="sku" type="xs:string"/>
  <attribute name="price" type="xs:string"/>
  <attribute name="size" type="xs:string"/>
  <attribute name="color" type="xs:string"/>
</attributeGroup>
```

Now, the entire set of attributes can be referred to in an element declaration using the name of the group:

```
<?xml version="1.0" encoding="utf-8"?>
<xs:schema xmlns:xs="http://www.w3.org/2001/XMLSchema">

  <xs:attributeGroup name="itemInfoGroup">
    <xs:attribute name="sku" type="xs:string"/>
    <xs:attribute name="price" type="xs:string"/>
    <xs:attribute name="size" type="xs:string"/>
    <xs:attribute name="color" type="xs:string"/>
  </xs:attributeGroup>

  <xs:element name="catalog">
    <xs:complexType>
      <xs:sequence>
        <xs:element name="item">
          <xs:complexType>
            <xs:attributeGroup ref="itemInfoGroup"/>
          </xs:complexType>
```

```
        </xs:element>
      </xs:sequence>
    </xs:complexType>
  </xs:element>

</xs:schema>
```

With the attributeGroup included with the element by referencing the group definition by name, we could have the following XML:

```
<?xml version="1.0"?>
<catalog xsi:noNamespaceSchemaLocation="catalog2.xsd" xmlns:
➥xsi="http://www.w3.org/2001/XMLSchema-instance">
  <item sku="012345" price="1.25" size="Medium" color="blue"/>
</catalog>
```

There are several advantages to using an attribute group in this way. First, it allows you to declare a group of attributes with a global scope. This allows you to reuse the attributes as much as you need to, with more than just one element, simply with a reference to the attribute group.

Second, this can make your element declarations easier to read, by allowing you to use multiple attributes in the element declaration with a single reference.

The <attributeGroup> element itself accepts three attributes:

- id
- name
- ref

The id attribute allows you to specify an ID for the attribute group. The name attribute specifies the name of the group, which is then used when referencing the attribute group. Finally, you can actually reference other attribute groups within an attribute group, which is why <attributeGroup> also accepts the ref attribute.

5

As for the content of the <attributeGroup> element itself, it may contain <attribute> declarations, as we saw in the previous example. It may also contain other attributeGroup elements, as references to create a group of groups.

Enumerations

Enumerations are simply lists. For example, if you had an address element, you might want it to include an attribute called state and you might want to force the user to choose from one of the 50 states in the United States.

With XML 1.0, enumerations can be used only with attributes, which is why we are going to discuss them here. However, it is important for you to keep in mind that enumerations with XML Schemas can actually be used with elements as well.

An enumeration is implemented by using a restriction of a `simpleType`. To define an enumeration, you would use the `<enumeration>` element as a child of the `<restriction>` element. Let's look at an example. Say you were defining an element called *<phone>* and you wanted the author to be able to specify an attribute called *location* from which they could choose one of "`work`, `home`, `fax`, `cell`, or `pager`" as the location of the phone number. That's a perfect use for an enumeration:

```
<xs:attribute name="location">
  <xs:simpleType>
    <xs:restriction base="xs:string">
      <xs:enumeration value="work"/>
      <xs:enumeration value="home"/>
      <xs:enumeration value="fax"/>
      <xs:enumeration value="cell"/>
      <xs:enumeration value="pager"/>
    </xs:restriction>
  </xs:simpleType>
</xs:attribute>

<xs:element name="phone">
  <xs:complexType>
  <xs:attribute ref="location"/>
  </xs:complexType>
</xs:element>
```

As you can see in the attribute declaration, the enumeration is formed by restricting a `simpleType`—in this case, "`string`."

Each choice for the enumeration is specified using an `<enumeration>` element that takes an attribute called *value*, which specifies the value for that enumeration choice.

Enumerations are found everywhere in computing applications, such as pulldown menus, so they are a very useful construct to be aware of when authoring your XML Schemas.

ASSOCIATING SCHEMAS WITH XML DOCUMENTS

There are a number of elements described by the XML Schemas: Structures Recommendation that are designed to link XML Schemas to the XML instance documents with which they are to be used in conjunction. Those elements have actually been given their own namespace:

```
http://www.w3.org/2001/XMLSchema-instance
```

The XML Instance namespace is a very important one, even though it does not contain many elements. It is how you associate an XML Schema with a document.

Let's look at a very simple schema and an XML document. This will simply be a document for storing a person's name and telephone number. Our schema might look something like this:

```
<?xml version="1.0" encoding="UTF-8" ?>
<xs:schema xmlns:xs="http://www.w3.org/2001/XMLSchema">
```

```
 <xs:element name="contact">
  <xs:complexType>
   <xs:sequence>
       <xs:element name="name" type="string"/>
       <xs:element name="phone" type="string"/>
   </xs:sequence>
  </xs:complexType>
  </xs:element>
</xs:schema>
```

This schema would define a document with a `contact` root element, which would contain the two elements `name` and `phone`, each of which may contain a string. A valid XML document for this schema might look something like this:

```
<?xml version="1.0" encoding="UTF-8" ?>
<contact>
<name>David Gulbransen</name>
<phone>812-555-1212</phone>
</contact>
```

But how do we **know** that this is a valid XML document? How does an application parsing this document know that we have even defined a schema for the document, let alone know where that schema is? Well, if we were using a DTD with the document, we would use the "DOCTYPE" declaration to point a parser to the DTD file that described this document. But because we are using an XML Schema, we will use an XML-Instance element.

Note

The XML-Instance namespace is commonly associated with the "`xsi`" prefix. Because it is a namespace, you could actually use any prefix you wanted, so long as you were consistent. However, because the XML Schema Recommendation uses the "`xsi`" convention, it probably is a good idea to stick to that unless you have a compelling reason not to.

There are four elements defined in the XML Schema: Structures Recommendation in the XML-Instance namespace that are particularly important to using Schemas with your XML documents:

- `xsi:type`
- `xsi:nil`
- `xsi:schemaLocation`
- `xsi:noNamespaceSchemaLocation`

To use any of these attribute types with your XML documents, you must first define the `xsi` namespace, using the following:

```
xmlns:xsi="http://www.w3.org/2001/XMLSchema-instance"
```

After that has been defined, you may use the XML-Instance attributes in the following manner:

- `xsi:type`

  The XML-Instance `type` attribute is a way for you to explicitly assert a type for the instance of a particular element. For example, let's say that your schema had an element called *phone* for storing a phone number. You might also have defined several derived datatypes for the phone element, such as `USPhone`, `UKPhone`, and so on, to allow for international phone number formats. If you then used the `<phone>` element in your document, you could use the `xsi:type` attribute to assert a specific type—for example, `<phone xsi:type="USPhone">`.

- `xsi:nil`

  The XML-Instance `nil` attribute is used to denote that an element may still be considered valid with empty content, even if the element is supposed to have content according to the schema. Valid values for the attribute are "true" and "false." If you have an element which is supposed to have content, but does not for some reason, such as an item that normally has a SKU number, but is temporarily out of stock, you can set the `xsi:nil` equal to "true" and then the element could be empty even though it is normally supposed to contain a value.

- `xsi:schemaLocation`

  The XML-Instance `schemaLocation` attribute is used to specify the location of an XML Schema associated with an XML document. The attribute value is a pair of URIs, the first of which is the `targetNamespace` for the XML Schema, and the second is the URI that points to the location of the schema.

- `xsi:noNamespaceSchemaLocation`

  The XML-Instance `noNamespaceSchemaLocation` attribute is very similar to the `schemaLocation` attribute, in that it allows you to specify the location of a schema for use with your document. However, because a schema is not required to have a `targetNamespace`, this attribute can be used for schemas that do not have a namespace.

That covers the XML Instance attributes that you will use with your XML Schemas. Let's take a look at using the XML Instance attributes to link an XML Schema to an XML document.

Say that we save the preceding XML Schema to a file called "*contact.xsd*" to our server, located at `www.mycompany.com`. If we then wanted to create a document based on that schema, it would look something like this:

```
<?xml version="1.0" encoding="UTF-8" ?>
<contact xmlns="http://www.mycompany.com/contact"
        xmlns:xsi="http://www.w3.org/2001/XMLSchema-instance"
    xsi:schemaLocation="http://www.mycompany.com/contact
                        http://www.mycompany.com/contact.xsd">
<name>David Gulbransen</name>
<phone>812-555-1212</phone>
</contact>
```

The key to using the schema lies in the attributes we have used with the <contact> element. The first attribute

```
xmlns="http://www.mycompany.com/contact"
```

is used to describe the default namespace for the document. That will usually be the same as the targetNamespace of the schema, but not always. Next, we have the xsi namespace

```
xmlns:xsi="http://www.w3.org/2001/XMLSchema-instance"
```

This defines the "xsi" prefix for use with the XMLSchema-instance namespace, which will allow us to use those attributes associated with the namespace. Finally, we have

```
xsi:schemaLocation="http://www.mycompany.com/contact
                    http://www.mycompany.com/contact.xsd">
```

The xsi:schemaLocation attribute here has two values. The first value is the default, or targetNamespace of the XML Schema to which we are pointing. The second value is the actual location of the .xsd file that defines the Schema. This will let any XML Parser processing the document know 1) the targetNamespace of the document and the Schema, and 2) the location of the schema on a server. The targetNamespace is the namespace for which our Schema contains the appropriate declarations. We'll take a closer look at targetNamespaces, and namespaces in general in Chapter 6.

Datatypes in XML Schemas

One of the most promising new features of XML Schemas is the ability to specify datatypes for your elements and attributes. Datatypes are commonly used in programming languages and in databases to enforce data integrity by requiring the data stored to be of a certain type—for example, by forcing number to be only integers, or to have only two decimal places. XML Schemas introduce datatypes into XML with the second part of the XML Schema Recommendation: Datatypes.

5

What Is a Datatype?

There are really two broad divisions among the users of XML. First, there is the document camp. Those users are using XML to create structured documents in a format, which we all think of as a "document"—that is, large blocks of text, such as a book or a letter. The document camp might have XML documents that look like this:

```
<title>Introducing Datatypes</title>
<intro>This chapter introduces XML Schema Datatypes</intro>
<text> There are really two broad divisions among the users of XML. First,
there is the document camp… etc. </text>
```

This type of document is a perfectly legitimate and very useful application of XML.

The second XML camp is the data camp. The data users of XML are using XML for data applications that previously might not have had any standard. For example, a manufacturer keeping track of items in a database:

```
  <item sku="3487112">
  <manufacture_Date>2001-07-27</manufacture_Date>
  <ship_Date>2001-07-27</ship_Date>
  <warehouse>21200</warehouse>
  <price>59.95<price>
</item>
```

These XML "documents" contain interrelated pieces of information, and the structure of the XML document is designed to reflect those relationships. This is also a perfectly legitimate use of XML.

XML documents provide a great way to exchange information that is primarily datasets. Because XML is a widely supported, W3C-based standard, any communication based on XML is also likely to be widely supported.

Another advantage comes from making use of common base standards and a set of related standards for accessing the information stored in XML documents. For example, previously, if two financial institutions used differing formats for storing data about their transactions, they would need to build complicated customized translators in order to exchange data. XML provides a way for them to work together to build a common format; and, even if translations are necessary because the documents in question are all based on an XML standard, the translation is much easier.

How Datatypes Are Useful

Interoperability is where datatypes really come in handy. A datatype is a way of defining a lexical meaning for the value of an element or an attribute.

For example, consider the following element:

```
<date>03-11-01</date>
```

What information is represented in this element? Well, as a human reader, we can surmise that it is a date from the element name. But to an application processing it, the word "`date`" is just another string of letters—it doesn't necessarily have any meaning at all.

Then there is the matter of what this element's value means. Take a look at the date. It could represent March 11, 2001, or it could represent November 3, 2001 or November 1, 2003 or January 11, 2003. If we don't agree on what the number represents, in terms of `YY-MM-DD` or `DD-MM-YY`, there is no way for us to make real use of the data without the possibility of introducing errors into our data.

That is what datatypes really provide: a mechanism for us to agree on the representation of the data in our dataset. The benefit we gain from that is that when we all agree, for example, that a data should always be Year-Month-Day, then we all know that "03-11-01" is November 1, 2003. That way, our customer gets the item they ordered on time. Or an item in stock that has an expiration date can be removed when it goes bad.

Datatypes are very useful in computing applications, and if you have done any programming with languages such as Java or C++ then you are probably already familiar with datatypes and their uses. Datatypes are also important for storing information in databases, for similar reasons that we outlined above: They are a way to ensure the integrity of your data.

However, with the original XML specifications, what you could accomplish in terms of datatypes was somewhat limited. Addressing those limitations was one of the major motivators for the XML Schemas recommendation.

Using XML and DTDs as specified in the XML 1.0 Recommendation, there was no way to define a datatype, such as a date. Therefore, people who needed to use a datatype to restrict element and attribute values were limited to creating their own mechanisms to do so during XML parsing. But with no standard, people might implement datatypes differently, which takes data applications with XML back to square one.

However, now with the XML Schemas: Datatypes Recommendation, there is not only a common set of datatypes that can be used by schema and XML instance authors, but also a grammar for deriving new customized datatypes. Therefore, authors can create virtually any datatype they need for their documents, but in a specific way so that anyone using their schemas or documents can also use those same datatypes.

NAMESPACES AND DATATYPES

As is the case with schemas in general, there are some namespace considerations when you are working with datatypes. There are two namespaces associated with XML Schema Datatypes:

```
http://www.w3.org/2001/XMLSchema
http://www.w3.org/2001/XMLSchema-Datatypes
```

The first namespace can be used with datatypes in the schema, and it is actually the namespace for the entire Schema Recommendation, both Part 1: Structures and Part 2: Datatypes. The second namespace is a namespace for just the Datatypes, and it is provided to be used in applications where you need to reference the datatypes in the Schema Recommendation, but don't necessarily care about the other schema components.

When you derive your own datatypes, they have their own namespace, which is the namespace of the schema in which you are defining the new datatypes themselves.

PRIMITIVE BUILT-IN DATATYPES

The Schemas provide for two different types of datatypes: primitive datatypes and derived datatypes.

Primitive datatypes are defined within the Schemas Part 2: Datatypes section of the Recommendation, and the only way that new primitive datatypes can be introduced is through the W3C adding them to the official Recommendation.

The primitive datatypes included in the Recommendation are there for a number of reasons. First, these datatypes are datatypes that are already in common usage in other applications, such as databases and programming languages. Because of the likelihood that these common datatypes would be used in XML in addition to other computing applications, they were included in the Recommendation so that you don't have to expend energy defining them yourself.

Another reason for including the primitive datatypes is that they serve as the basis for building other kinds of datatypes. For example, you could build a house out of wood, brick, or stone. Those basic building materials would be the primitive datatypes that are used to construct additional, more complicated datatypes, which brings us to derived datatypes.

Derived datatypes are datatypes that are constructed from other datatypes, either through extension or restriction—that is, extending the content model of the original datatype.

The schema Recommendation also provides a number of derived datatypes as well, which are also commonly used datatypes, provided for the convenience of XML Schema authors. However, schema authors may also create their own derived datatypes, which we will discuss later in this chapter and others as well.

There are a number of datatypes that are built into the XML Schema for the convenience of schema authors. The first set of built-in datatypes are the primitive datatypes.

The primitive datatypes are important for several reasons. First, there are many times when you will find that a primitive datatype does exactly what you need, and therefore you will not need to create your own datatype. Second, primitive datatypes can be used as the base for building new types. That is why it is important for you to have a good understanding of the primitive datatypes. To build your own datatypes using the primitives as your base, you will need to understand what each datatype represents and how its value set may be manipulated.

Now let's look at some of the most common primitive datatypes and the types of data they can be used to represent.

Note

The primitive datatypes and facets discussed in this chapter are by no means a comprehensive listing of all the available types and facets. To accomplish this task would necessitate far more than one chapter in an XML title, and could indeed consist of an entire book. What we have tried to cover here are some of the most common types, to get you started and familiar with the types you will see in Schemas most often.

string

The `string` datatype is a primitive datatype used to represent strings of characters. The character is considered the atomic unit of a string, and what constitutes a character is defined in the XML 1.0 Recommendation. The value set for a string will be dependent on the character set being used in the XML document, just as the characters in the English alphabet are different from the characters in the Russian alphabet.

The constraining attributes that can be used with the string datatype are

- `length`
- `minLength`
- `maxLength`

- pattern
- enumeration

Properties such as these that make up the characteristics of types are known as *facets*. Facets are expressed and manipulated with types as attributes, and changing the value of the attribute changes the limitations or values of the facet.

The `length`, `minLength`, and `maxLength` facets accept values of integers, which represent the number of characters in the string. The `pattern` facet accepts a value in the form of a regular expression that can be used for pattern matching against the value of the string.

The `enumeration` facet allows you to specify a list of choices for the value of a string, listing each choice for the value space as a separate enumeration facet.

Let's take a look at a couple of examples using the string type. Let's say that you wanted to create an element called `description`, which could contain a string describing something:

```
<xs:element name="description" type="xs:string"/>
```

That's all there is to declaring an element using the `string` type. However, you can also create new datatypes using the `string` type by restricting those constraining facets. For example, we could create a new simple datatype called `passwd` based on the `string` type, and limit the number of characters in the password to fit into a range of 6–8 characters:

```
<xs:simpleType name="passwd">
 <xs:restriction base="xs:string">
  <xs:minLength value="6"/>
  <xs:maxLength value="8"/>
 </xs:restriction>
</xs:simpleType>
```

By using the `string` type as a base, and then the `minLength` and `maxLength` constraining facets, we are left with a new datatype called *`password`*, which we could then use with an element declaration:

```
<xs:element name="password" type="passwd"/>
```

If you were to use `<password>` in an instance document, the value of the element would have to be a string of characters at least 6 characters long, and a maximum of 8 characters long.

As you can see from these examples, each of the primitive types can be used directly in an element declaration, or they can be used in a type definition to create a new type.

boolean

A `boolean` is a datatype that is used to represent the mathematical concept of binary-valued logic. Practically speaking, that translates to true and false.

The boolean type has a predefined value set of "true, false, 1, 0" where 1 is the same as true, and 0 is the same as false.

A boolean can be used when you need a datatype that represents a true condition or a false condition. For example, if you wanted to create an element called "`attendance`" for keeping track of meeting attendees:

```
<xs:element name="attendance" type="xs:boolean"/>
```

In the instance document, the element could be either

```
<attendance>true</attendance> or <attendance>false</attendance>
```

depending on whether the person in question had attended or not. Booleans are a very useful datatype, so don't forget that they are available to you as a primitive.

decimal

There are not many data-centric XML documents in which numbers won't play some role in the data, and that is where the `decimal` type comes in. The `decimal` type is used to represent decimal numbers with arbitrary precision.

The `decimal` type allows for a leading sign of "+" or "-" to specify a positive or negative number, although the "+" is the default, so it is not necessary to use it. The type supports any theoretical amount of digits to the right or left of the decimal point, although XML processors are required to support only at least 18 total digits.

Some valid values for decimals include `4`, `5.2`, `-6.3`, or `3.14159`.

There are a number of constraining attributes that can be used with the decimal type:

- `totalDigits`
- `fractionDigits`
- `minInclusive`
- `maxInclusive`
- `minExclusive`
- `maxExclusive`

The `totalDigits` attribute can be used to constrain the total number of digits that are allowed in the decimal type. This applies to the digits on both the right and the left of the decimal place.

To limit the number of digits to the right of the decimal, you can use the `fractionDigits` attribute, which allows you to limit the number of digits, or decimal places, to the right of the decimal point. This mechanism can effectively be used to determine precision.

The `minInclusive`, `maxInclusive`, `minExclusive`, and `maxExclusive` attributes can be used to express a range for the value of the decimal, but describing the bounds, either inclusively or exclusively.

Let's look at some ways in which decimals can be used in XML Schemas. One way is to create a datatype called *currency*, which could be used to keep track of monetary values. Because monetary values are expressed in decimal form, with two digits in the decimal place, such as $1.25, we can use a decimal type for currency, if we limit the "`fractionDigits`" to 2:

```
<xs:simpleType name="currency">
 <xs:restriction base="xs:decimal">
  <xs:fractionDigits value="2"/>
 </xs:restriction>
</xs:simpleType>
```

In addition to manipulating the fraction digits, we can manipulate the total digits as well. For example, say we wanted to create a type for a PIN number. We could accomplish that by limiting the `fractionDigits` to `"0"`, because `PIN`s cannot have decimals, and then limit the `totalDigits` to `"4"`:

```
<xs:simpleType name="PIN">
 <xs:restriction base="decimal">
  <xs:totalDigits value="4"/>
  <xs:fractionDigits value="0"/>
 </xs:restriction>
</xs:simpleType>
```

Of course, there are other types (such as `integer`) which might be easier to use; however, `integer` is based on `decimal`, with some of the limitations performed already. Another way to place limits is to make use of the min/max bounds. For example, if we wanted to set a `"price"` type, which could not be more than $9.99, we could first use `minInclusive` set to `"0"` to ensure that we don't have a negative price. Then, we can use the `maxExclusive` with a value set to `"10"` to limit the value set to anything under 10, but because the bound is exclusive, the value could not be 10. Here's how we would define the type:

```
<xs:simpleType name="price">
 <xs:restriction base="decimal">
  <xs:fractionDigits value="2"/>
  <xs:minInclusive value="0"/>
  <xs:maxExclusive value="10"/>
 </xs:restriction>
</xs:simpleType>
```

5

As you can see, `decimal` is a very flexible type, and although you might not make use of it directly in your schemas, many practical types can be derived from `decimal`.

date

The `date` type represents a date. The data refers to a date in Gregorian calendar, and takes the `YYYY-MM-DD` format. So, May 16th, 2005 would be

```
2005-05-16
```

The constraining attributes you can use with `date` also are similar to those of `decimal`:

- `minInclusive`
- `maxInclusive`

- `minExclusive`
- `maxExclusive`

`hexBinary`

One of the limitations of the XML 1.0 Recommendation is the lack of real mechanisms for dealing with binary data. Binary data can be referenced in XML documents using notations; however, under the 1.0 Recommendation, there is no way to include binary data within an XML document.

The ability to include binary data is one of the new features that comes with the XML Schema recommendation. The first way to include binary data in an XML document is to use the `hexBinary` datatype.

The `hexBinary` type is used to represent hex-encoded binary data. That is binary data that has been converted from binary form (111110110111) into a binary octet hexadecimal form (0FB7).

Many applications are capable of converting between hexadecimal and binary formats, and it is a commonly used format for exchanging files. The advantage to using `hexBinary` types is that the information is encoded using ASCII text characters, so it will not cause conflicts with applications that can handle only text.

`base64Binary`

Another datatype that can be used to represent binary data in an XML document is the `base64Binary` type. This type is similar to the `hexBinary` type in that it allows you to include binary data in an XML document. Also, the base64-encoded binary is "text safe" as the encoding method uses only ASCII and EBCDIC characters in the encoding.

The `base64Binary` is a good type to use for including binary information in your documents because it is also a very common format, used for exchanging MIME documents via applications.

DERIVING SIMPLE TYPES

Although there are a number of built-in simple types available for your usage, there are still times when you may want to derive your own new simple types. You can't derive a new simple type from extension, because if you extend a simple type, it becomes a complex type. So, now, let's take a look at deriving new simple types by restriction.

DERIVATION BY RESTRICTION

The most common way of deriving a new simple type is through a restriction. When deriving a new simple type by restriction, what you are doing is manipulating the constraining attributes of the type.

The constraining attributes you have available to change will vary from type to type, so it's always a good idea to check and make sure the attribute you want applies, and to see what it expresses. But restrictions all take the same basic form.

For example, let's say we wanted to create a new type called "Pen" which we could then use with various elements in a stationery store catalog. We want the simple type to be a choice between Ball Point pens, Roller Ball pens, and Gel pens. Our type definition might look something like this:

```
<xs:simpleType name="Pen">
 <xs:restriction base="string">
  <xs:enumeration value="BallPoint"/>
  <xs:enumeration value="RollerBall"/>
  <xs:enumeration value="Gel"/>
 </xs:restriction>
</xs:simpleType>
```

In this simple type definition, we name the new type "Pen" so that we can reference it in element or attribute declarations later in the schema. And then we use the <restriction> element to denote that the type is a restriction, based on the "string" type. We then use the "enumeration" facet for "string" to specify that the value set of our new "Pen" type must consist of "BallPoint", "RollerBall", or "Gel".

Restrictions can be used in any of the simple types. All restrictions will follow this basic form, and by using the appropriate base class in conjunction with its constraining attributes, you can create your own simple types that are more suited to your needs.

DERIVING COMPLEX TYPES

5

Simple datatypes do offer a lot of power within an XML Schema, in terms of managing your data. However, they do lack the flexibility to define new complex representations of data within the content model of an element.

For defining complex types, XML Schemas provide the <complexType> mechanism, which allows you to define your own complex types for element content models.

Complex types can also be defined independently of element declarations, so that they can be applied to multiple elements, or so that you may derive new complex types, based on previous types that you have defined in a schema. There are two mechanisms that you can use for deriving new complex types: restriction and extension.

COMPLEX TYPES BY RESTRICTION

Just as you can derive new simple types using a restriction, you can also use a restriction to define a new complex type. For example, let's start with the following complex type definition:

```
<xs:complexType name="beverages">
  <xs:sequence>
   <xs:element name="name" type="xs:string"/>
   <xs:element name="ingredients" type="xs:string"/>
   <xs:element name="type" type="xs:string"/>
```

```
  </xs:sequence>
 </xs:complexType>
```

This creates a complex type called `beverages` which has a number of elements, such as `name`, `ingredients`, and `type`. Now, in the complex type as we have defined it here, each one of these elements must occur once in this type.

Now, we could use this complex type as the base for a new type, called `juice`, which would be used for specific kinds of beverages. But suppose that with `juice` we want the `ingredients` element to be optional, and for the `type` we want to have an enumeration of values, such as `apple` and `orange`.

We can do this with a restriction, because we aren't really adding any new elements or attributes to the type; instead, we are placing constraining facets on the existing elements in the type. So, our new type, which is a restriction of the `beverages` type, would look like this:

```
 <xs:complexType name="juice">
  <xs:complexContent>
   <xs:restriction base="beverages">
    <xs:sequence>
     <xs:element name="name" type="xs:string"/>
     <xs:element name="ingredients" type="xs:string" xs:minOccurs="0"/>
     <xs:element name="type">
      <xs:simpleType>
       <xs:restriction base="xs:string">
        <xs:enumeration value="apple"/>
  <xs:enumeration value="orange"/>
       </xs:restriction>
      </xs:simpleType>
     </xs:element>
    </xs:sequence>
   </xs:restriction>
  </xs:complexContent>
 </xs:complexType>
```

The first thing you will notice is that in the `<complexContent>` element within the type definition, we use the `<restriction>` element, with a base of `beverages` which is the complex type we are restricting.

Next, we include the type definition for `<name>`, just as it appears in the `beverages` definition, because in a restriction, we have to include all the definitions from the original complex type, even if we are not changing them. Next, however, we include the new declaration for the `<ingredients>` element, with a new `minOccurs` attribute, set to `"0"` to denote that the element is optional.

Finally, we use a new declaration for the `<type>` element, which uses another simple type definition, along with another restriction to specify the enumeration values for the new type:

```
     <xs:element name="type">
      <xs:simpleType>
       <xs:restriction base="xs:string">
        <xs:enumeration value="apple"/>
  <exs:numeration value="orange"/>
       </xs:restriction>
```

```
    </xs:simpleType>
   </xs:element>
```

The result is that we now have a type called `juice`, which is derived from the `beverages` type. If we use this type with an element declaration, such as

```
<xs:element name="drink" type="juice"/>
```

then the XML instance could look like this:

```
<drink>
<name>Natural Stuff</name>
<type>Apple</type>
</drink>
```

The advantage of deriving a complex type by restriction is that although you do have to duplicate a number of items between the two definitions, you establish a type hierarchy that defines a relationship between the different types.

COMPLEX TYPES BY EXTENSION

In addition to derivation by restriction, complex types can also be derived by extension. Deriving types by extension allows you to add new functionality to a complex type, to *extend* the base type with a new definition. For example, let's revisit the `"beverages"` base class from before:

```
<xs:complexType name="beverages">
  <xs:sequence>
   <xs:element name="name" type="xs:string"/>
   <xs:element name="ingredients" type="xs:string"/>
   <xs:element name="type" type="xs:string"/>
  </xs:sequence>
 </xs:complexType>
```

Now, let's say that we want to use all the elements defined in the complex type definition for `beverages` with a new `juice` type, but rather than placing any restrictions on the new type, we want to extend the type by adding a new attribute called `temp` that we can use to indicate whether the beverage is hot or cold.

The extension of our `beverages` type would look like this:

```
<xs:complexType name="juice">
  <xs:complexContent>
   <xs:extension base="beverages">
   <xs:attribute name="temp">
    <xs:simpleType">
     <xs:restriction base="xs:string >
      <xs:enumeration value="Hot"/>
      <xs:enumeration value="Cold"/>
     </xs:restriction>
    </xs:simpleType>
   </xs:attribute>
   </xs:extension>
  </xs:complexContent>
 </xs:complexType>
```

The first, and most significant, difference between the extension and restriction is that with an extension, it is not necessary to duplicate the elements defined in the original base type. These elements are assumed to be a part of the extension type, so all that we need to do is add the new element or attribute we are adding to the new, extended type. In this case, that is our new `temp` attribute declaration. With that added to the `juice` type, our new complex type has all the elements from our original `beverages` type, but also includes our new attribute declaration.

So, if we declare a new element based on our new extended complex type:

```
<xs:element name="drink" type="juice"/>
```

the instance document might look like this:

```
<drink temp="Cold">
<name>Nature Made</name>
<ingredients>Apples, Water</ingredients>
<type>Apple</type>
</drink>
```

Creating a new extended type also helps establish a relationship between the new type and the base type, but unlike the restriction, it also provides a shorthand for including the declarations of the original base type, which saves you retyping the definitions.

SCHEMA DESIGNS

Now you have the fundamentals of element and attribute declarations in XML Schemas, as well as the basics of datatypes and how they can be used in XML Schemas. There are a number of different design philosophies that can be used when approaching schema authoring. So, now let's take a look at some schema examples that will put the schema authoring skills to use and showcase the various methods for constructing XML Schemas.

Note

There is an excellent discussion of Schema Design Issues, including information regarding these patterns and further discussions of Schema Best Practices, located at `http://www.xfront.com/BestPracticesHomepage.html`.

RUSSIAN DOLL DESIGN

The Russian Doll design for schemas involves nesting all the component definitions and declarations within the schema structure itself. Everything is declared locally with the exception of the parent element of the document.

The result is a schema that can be hard to read, but directly reflects the design of the XML instance document it describes. For example, let's examine a schema for a newspaper article:

```
<?xml version="1.0" encoding="UTF-8" ?>
<xs:schema xmlns:xs="http://www.w3.org/2001/XMLSchema"
       xmlns="http://www.w3.org/2001/XMLSchema">
```

```
<xs:element name="article">
 <xs:complexType>
  <xs:sequence>
   <xs:element name="headline">
    <xs:simpleType>
     <xs:restriction base="xs:string">
      <xs:maxLength value="50"/>
     </xs:restriction>
    </xs:simpleType>
   </xs:element>
   <xs:element name="dateline">
    <xs:complexType>
     <xs:sequence>
      <xs:element name="submission" type="xs:date"/>
      <xs:element name="publication" type="xs:date"/>
     </xs:sequence>
    </xs:complexType>
   </xs:element>
   <xs:element name="byline" minOccurs="0">
    <xs:simpleType>
     <xs:restriction base="xs:string">
      <xs:maxLength value="25"/>
     </xs:restriction>
    </xs:simpleType>
   </xs:element>
   <xs:element name="text" type="xs:string"/>
  </xs:sequence>
 </xs:complexType>
</xs:element>
</xs:schema>
```

With a schema written using the Russian Doll design, we have a schema that reflects the structure of an instance document:

```
<article>
 <headline>Mars Invades Earth</headline>
 <dateline>
  <submission>2001-04-01</submission>
  <publication>2001-04-01</publication>
 </dateline>
 <byline>Alan Smithee</byline>
 <text>Today the planet of Mars launched an invasion…</text>
</article>
```

In a Russian Doll design, all the components, except the parent element, are declared locally. The Russian Doll design does have some advantages.

First, we mentioned that it follows the structure of the instance document. Therefore, following a Russian Doll schema to build an instance document is often quite easy.

Because all the declarations are local in scope, and self-contained, there can't be references to a declared component in another section of the schema. As a result, what you see is what you get.

Another advantage is that namespaces are localized. If we declared a `targetNamespace` for our schema, and our schema was then imported into another schema, we would need to worry only about namespace qualification with the `<article>` element, as the other elements would be local to `<article>`. For example, had we declared a namespace for the preceding example, such as "`xmlns:article`" in an instance document, our code would look like this:

```
<?xml version="1.0">
<article:article xmlns:article="http://www.mysever.com/article/">
 <headline>Mars Invades Earth</headline>
 <dateline>
  <submission>2001-04-01</submission>
  <publication>2001-04-01</publication>
 </dateline>
 <byline>Alan Smithee</byline>
 <text>Today the planet of Mars launched an invasion…</text>
</article:article>
```

Note that only the parent `<article>` document has the namespace prefix, because the other elements are local to the `<article>` element by definition. This can help avoid namespace confusion and clutter in instance documents.

This also has the advantage of shielding instance documents somewhat, because if your schema is included in another schema, only the parent element is exposed. That means that the integrity of the element is harder to compromise. (Not impossible—it could still be redefined, for example; however, the child elements cannot be accessed out of the context of the parent element.)

For example, our `<article>` might be included into a schema describing a `<magazine>`. That magazine might include other types of content, such as a `<review>` or `<editorial>`. Now, because all of our elements are locally scoped, if we change the declaration for anything within an `<article>`, it only affects the article, not any of the other elements. But had we declared `<byline>` globally, and then our `<byline>` element was included as the byline for `<review>` or `<editorial>`, then, if we made a change to our article schema, the impact would be broader than just the `<article>` element. This can be seen as an advantage, or a disadvantage, almost entirely dependent on how much control you want to exert over the original schema, and how you want to allow others to reuse your design.

However, reuse of components is one of the great features of schemas, and the Russian Doll design lacks the flexibility to reuse components.

SALAMI SLICE DESIGN

The Salami Slice design approach to structuring your schemas involves splitting the component declarations into smaller segments, and then building the complete parent element by reference to the previous declarations.

The Salami Slice design still relies heavily on element declarations as opposed to type definitions, but most of the element declarations are declared globally, so they are potentially exposed to other schemas, and are free to be referenced in other locations within your own schema document.

Let's take a look at the same example we used for the Russian Doll design, only now the schema has been modified to reflect the Salami Slice design:

```
<?xml version="1.0" encoding="UTF-8" ?>
<xs:schema xmlns:xs="http://www.w3.org/2001/XMLSchema"
xmlns="http://www.w3.org/2001/XMLSchema">

<xs:element name="headline">
 <xs:simpleType>
  <xs:restriction base="xs:string">
   <xs:maxLength value="50"/>
  </xs:restriction>
 </xs:simpleType>
</xs:element>

<xs:element name="dateline">
 <xs:complexType>
  <xs:sequence>
   <xs:element name="submission" type="xs:date"/>
   <xs:element name="publication" type="xs:date"/>
  </xs:sequence>
 </xs:complexType>
</xs:element>

<xs:element name="byline">
 <xs:simpleType>
  <xs:restriction base="xs:string">
   <xs:maxLength value="25"/>
  </xs:restriction>
 </xs:simpleType>
</xs:element>

<xs:element name="text" type="xs:string"/>

<xs:element name="article">
 <xs:complexType>
  <xs:sequence>
   <xs:element ref="headline"/>
   <xs:element ref="dateline"/>
   <xs:element ref="byline" minOccurs="0"/>
   <xs:element ref="text"/>
  </xs:sequence>
 </xs:complexType>
</xs:element>

</xs:schema>
```

Now, with this example you can see that most of the elements are contained in their own, standalone declarations. The parent element for the `<article>`, then, is built by referencing the declarations.

The Salami Slice design is certainly more verbose than the Russian Doll design. The overall schema itself is not self-contained, and instead is broken up into much smaller parcels of information. However, an advantageous side effect is that each component declaration is clearly visible, and easy to read. It's easy for us to locate and look at the structure of any one particular component, as opposed to the overall document structure.

This design also provides us with a great deal more flexibility with our elements. For example, because the elements are declared globally, we could take advantage of Substitution groups if we wanted. And because the components are all declared globally, we could access them in other schemas as well.

For example, if we were building a `journal` schema, we could include our article schema:

```
<?xml version="1.0" encoding="UTF-8" ?>
<xs:schema xmlns:xs="http://www.w3.org/2001/XMLSchema"
xmlns="http://www.w3.org/2001/XMLSchema">

<xs:include schemaLocation="http://www.myserver.com/article.xsd"/>

<xs:element name="journal">
 <xs:complexType>
  <xs:sequence>
   <xs:element ref="article" maxOccurs="unbounded"/>
   <xs:element name="editorial" maxOccurs="unbounded">
    <xs:complexType>
     <xs:sequence>
      <xs:element ref="headline"/>
      <xs:element ref="byline"/>
      <xs:element ref="text"/>
     </xs:sequence>
    </xs:complexType>
   </xs:element>
  </xs:sequence>
 </xs:complexType>
</xs:element>

</xs:schema>
```

In this example, we can use the `<article>` element, from the imported schema, but we can also make use of the components that make up the `<article>` element, such as "`headline`" and "`byline`," in order to create a new element called `<editorial>`. This kind of flexibility in reuse is offered by the Salami Slice design.

There is one major caveat to this methodology, though, when it comes to namespace use. For example, if we had declared a `targetNamespace` for our `article.xsd` schema:

```
targetNamespace=http://www.myserver.com/article
```

and we wanted to use the namespace qualified version in our instance document:

```
xmlns:article="http://www.myserver.com/article"
```

the resulting instance would need to look like this:

```
<article:article>
 <article:headline>Mars Invades Earth</article:headline>
 <article:dateline>
  <article:submission>2001-04-01</article:submission>
  <article:publication>2001-04-01</article:publication>
 </article:dateline>
 <article:byline>Alan Smithee</article:byline>
 <article:text>Today the planet of Mars launched an invasion…</article:text>
</article:article>
```

It is important to consider the impact of the namespace usage when using this approach. Namespaces can be very advantageous in this situation, even though they add clutter to the schema itself. By using the namespaces explicitly, you can ensure avoiding possible namespace collisions. Namespaces are covered in greater detail in Chapter 6, "Avoiding XML Confusion with XML Namespaces."

Venetian Blind Design

The third style of XML Schema design addresses the issue of namespace localization similar to the Russian Doll design, while still allowing the global declarations of components similar to the Salami Slice design.

This design is called the Venetian Blind design (named because it is sliced like the Salami Design, but allows the toggling on/off of namespace qualification, like the Russian Doll design).

The Venetian Blind design is very similar to the Salami Slice design in that each component is declared globally for exposure and ease of reading and management. However, rather than being declared as elements, components are defined as types whenever possible, and then those types are used when declaring the elements within the content model of the parent component.

Let's look at an `article.xsd` schema, designed using the Venetian Blind method:

```
<?xml version="1.0" encoding="UTF-8" ?>
<xs:schema xmlns:xs="http://www.w3.org/2001/XMLSchema"
xmlns="http://www.w3.org/2001/XMLSchema">

<xs:simpleType name="headline">
 <xs:restriction base="xs:string">
  <xs:maxLength value="50"/>
 </xs:restriction>
</xs:simpleType>

<xs:complexType name="dateline">
 <xs:sequence>
  <xs:element name="submission" type="xs:date"/>
  <xs:element name="publication" type="xs:date"/>
 </xs:sequence>
</xs:complexType>

<xs:simpleType name="byline">
 <xs:restriction base="xs:string">
  <xs:maxLength value="25"/>
 </xs:restriction>
</xs:simpleType>

<xs:complexType name="article">
 <xs:sequence>
  <xs:element name="headline" type="headline"/>
  <xs:element name="dateline" type="dateline"/>
  <xs:element name="byline" type="byline" minOccurs="0"/>
  <xs:element name="text" type="xs:string"/>
 </xs:sequence>
```

5

```
</xs:complexType>

<xs:element name="article" type="article"/>

</xs:schema>
```

As you can see, we now have a number of global types, such as "`headline`" and "`byline`," which we could include in another document. For example, our journal would look like this:

```
<?xml version="1.0" encoding="UTF-8" ?>
<xs:schema xmlns:xs="http://www.w3.org/2001/XMLSchema"
xmlns="http://www.w3.org/2001/XMLSchema">

<xs:include schemaLocation="http://www.myserver.com/article.xsd"/>

<xs:element name="journal">
 <xs:complexType>
  <xs:sequence>
   <xs:element ref="article" maxOccurs="unbounded"/>
   <xs:element name="editorial" type="article" maxOccurs="unbounded"/>
  </xs:sequence>
 </xs:complexType>
</xs:element>

</xs:schema>
```

By including the article schema, we gain access to both the `<article>` element and the "`article`" type, which means we can use both, greatly simplifying our journal schema by reusing those components.

We also have a much finer degree of control over namespaces, allowing you to "toggle" off and on namespace qualification in documents using the "`elementFormDefault`" attribute, which by default will hide the namespaces in your documents.

In general, the Venetian Blind schema design offers the best of both the Russian Doll design and the Salami Slice design, so it should be the design choice you examine first when considering design approaches. Of course, if limiting exposure of the components of your schema is important, then the Russian Doll design is always an alternative.

There is no "right" or "wrong" approach to using any of these design models presented here; however, there are better choices than others, and by taking a look at how you intend to use your schema, one of these design models will likely present itself as the best choice for you to use when authoring.

SCHEMA ALTERNATIVES

Just as DTDs are not the only way to create a schema for use with XML, there are also alternatives to XML Schemas. The two most popular alternatives to XML Schemas include RELAX NG and Schematron.

RELAX NG

The most promising schema alternative currently being developed is the RELAX NG standard, which is being sponsored by the Organization for the Advancement of Structured Information Standards (OASIS). The RELAX NG standard is the result of a positive reception among developers to both TREX and RELAX, two older schema alternatives, and the desire to see features of each incorporated into the other, culminating in RELAX NG, a merger of TREX and RELAX.

OASIS has released a formal standard for RELAX NG, which can be found at

```
http://www.oasis-open.org/committees/relax-ng/spec-20011203.html
```

Because OASIS is a very powerful, vendor-neutral standards organization, RELAX NG is a very viable alternative to XML Schema.

RELAX NG combines the features of TREX and RELAX into one syntax, and it is also XML based. The goal of RELAX NG is to provide a simple, easy-to-learn syntax for describing grammars that are not necessarily hampered by backward compatibility and complexity, as is the case with XML Schemas.

SCHEMATRON

Schematron was developed by Rick Jelliffe, and is not so much an alternative to XML Schemas as it is a supplemental technology. Jelliffe has described Schematron as a feather duster that reaches into the corners that the XML Schemas vacuum cleaner can't reach. Schematron is supported via a Web site located at

```
http://www.ascc.net/xml/schematron
```

What makes Schematron different from the other schema alternatives is that Schematron is **not** grammar based. Instead, it is rules based, and therefore provides a level of validity checking simply not possible with XML Schemas.

For example, Schematron allows you to check the content of elements and attributes, and then check for dependencies based on those results. Schematron also provides you with a mechanism for returning "plain English" error messages that are easily understood.

For example, let's say you had the following XML instance:

```
<employee SSN="331001234">Jane Doe</employee>
```

Schematron would allow you to check to make sure that the `<employee>` element had the "`SSN`" attribute, and it would allow you to count the digits in the "`SSN`" attribute, as well as to check to make sure that a name was included for the element content. And if there was a problem, using Schematron, you could specify an error message such as

> "Social Security numbers should be exactly 9 digits"

Schematron is very flexible, and, in fact, it can be used not only with XML Schemas, but also with RELAX Modules and TREX Grammars!

As if that weren't enough, Schematron is also very simple. There are only six basic elements in Schematron, and the technology is built using XSLT and XPath. So, if you already know XPath and XSLT, Schematron can be learned **very** quickly.

Schematron works by using XPath to specify the location and conditions that are being checked, and it uses XSLT to perform the manipulation of the Schematron Schema and the application of the Schematron Schema to your instance documents.

Another advantage of Schematron is that because it is based on core XML technologies, Schematron Schemas can actually be nested directly within XML Schema–based schemas, using an `<annotation>` and the `<appinfo>` elements.

Schematron is an excellent choice for a supplementary technology to provide a finer level of validation than possible with XML Schemas.

ADDITIONAL RESOURCES

XML Schemas are a complicated technology, and can by no means be covered completely in one chapter. You should have a good handle on the basics of XML Schemas, and when it would be appropriate to use them. You should also be able to author some pretty advanced schemas. However, if you need more information about XML Schemas, here are some additional resources you can consult:

- XML Schemas Part 0: Primer (`http://www.w3.org/TR/xmlschema-0/`) This first part (numbered 0) of the XML Schema Recommendation is actually a tutorial addressing many issues of XML Schema authoring, and can be a very valuable resource for learning about the intricacies of schema authoring.
- XML Schemas Part 1: Structures (`http://www.w3.org/TR/xmlschema-1/`) The XML Schemas Recommendation: Strucutures, deals with the physical structures for authoring XML Schemas. Physical structures include element declarations, attribute declarations, and so on, and this is the Recommendation that should be consulted for any Schema issues that are not specific to datatypes.
- XML Schemas Part 2: Datatypes (`http://www.w3.org/TR/xmlschema-2/`) The second part of the Schema Recommendation deals with datatypes. This Recommendation defines how datatypes are used, and defines the primitive and built-in derived datatypes as well.
- Relax NG (`http://www.oasis-open.org/committees/relax-ng/spec-20011203.html`) The RELAX NG standard was developed and maintained by OASIS, and it can be found here at the OASIS site. If you are interested in learning more about XML Schema alternatives, this is an excellent resource to consult.
- Schematron (`http://www.ascc.net/xml/schematron`) Rick Jelliffe maintains this site as a resource center related to Schematron, another XML Schema alternative. The site includes the Schematron specification, as well as some tutorial information.

- *Special Edition: Using XML Schemas* (ISBN 0-7897-2607-6) This title also from Que by David Gulbransen covers XML Schema in greater detail, from structures to datatypes, and includes examples and information on best practices.

ROADMAP

XML Schemas fit nicely into the XML family of technologies, providing a way to create a set of rules to structure your XML documents and create valid XML. Schemas supplement or replace Document Type Definitions, and as such are an important XML technology.

It would be hard not to notice that XML Schemas make pretty extensive use of XML Namespaces to accomplish datatypes, and to link the XML Schemas to XML instance documents. In Chapter 6, we will take a much closer look at XML Namespaces, how they are used with XML documents and with XML Schemas as well. From there, we will be ready to move on to the technologies for displaying XML in print and on the Web: XSL.

CHAPTER 6

Avoiding XML Confusion with XML Namespaces

In this chapter

by David Gulbransen

INTRODUCTION TO NAMESPACES

The Namespaces in XML Recommendation from the W3C is an incredibly simple, incredibly short Recommendation that causes a lot of confusion and argument among XML developers.

The Recommendation itself is fewer than 10 pages long, and the syntax for Namespaces is simple, even though it might not look very pretty. So, why all the fuss over Namespaces?

Well, the first stumbling block with Namespaces is conceptual. Many people learning about XML for the first time are coming from Web design or document management backgrounds, and might not be familiar with the concept of Namespaces. For developers coming from an application programming background, Namespaces might be more natural because those developers may have encountered them in another form using a programming language.

Either way, Namespaces exist for one simple reason: to help keep track of components and to ensure that people don't create elements and attributes that conflict with each other.

For example, let's say that we have an XML document for a journal:

```
<?xml version="1.0"?>
<journal>
 <article>
  <headline>Introduction to Namespaces</headline>
  <byline>Jane Doe</byline>
  <body>Namespaces are simple…</body>
 </article>
</journal>
```

This is a pretty straightforward XML document with a few elements to store journal articles, with `headline`, `byline`, and `body` elements for the actual data.

Now, what would happen, though, if we wanted to include some HTML markup along with our XML data? For example:

```
<?xml version="1.0"?>
<journal>
 <html>
  <article>
   <head>
    <title>
    <headline>Introduction to Namespaces</headline>
    </title>
   </head>
   <body>
    <i><byline>Jane Doe</byline></i>
    <body>Namespaces are simple…</body>
   <body>
  </article>
 </html>
</journal>
```

First, the preceding example is confusing and hard to read, because we have both XML and HTML tags intermixed, with no real way to tell the two apart. But we also have a much bigger problem: two `<body>` tags. One of the `<body>` tags represents the HTML `<body>` whereas the other is the `<body>` element for our XML journal document. When we mix the two together, there is no way for an XML parser or a browser to tell the difference between the two. That is why we need Namespaces.

Namespaces allow you to create a way of uniquely identifying components as being members of a specific Namespace. That allows XML processors to differentiate between two elements that might have the same name, because one element would be the member of one Namespace, whereas the other element would be the member of a different Namespace. It would be like knowing two people with the name Jim Smith, one from New York and one from California. If you call one New York Jim and the other Cali Jim, you can easily keep them straight, even though they have the same name.

So, if we add Namespaces to our example, we have something that looks like this:

```
<?xml version="1.0"?>
<journal xmlns="http://www.myserver.com/journal"
        xmlns:html="http://www.w3.org/TR/REC-html40">
 <html:html>
  <article>
   <html:head>
    <html:title>
    <headline>Introduction to Namespaces</headline>
    </html:title>
   </html:head>
   <html:body>
    <html:i><byline>Jane Doe</byline></html:i>
    <body>Namespaces are simple…</body>
   <html:body>
  </article>
 </html:html>
</journal>
```

Now you will notice that all the tags in our document that are HTML tags have the "`html:`" prefix added to them. That is how Namespaces are identified in XML. If you recall from Chapter 3 in our discussion on naming elements, we mentioned that the colon "`:`" was reserved for use in Namespaces. Names that make use of a Namespace prefix with the colon are said to be Qualified or Namespace Qualified names. Now let's take a closer look at the Namespaces syntax.

6

SPECIFYING NAMESPACES

Specifying Namespaces is very simple—so simple, in fact, that many people assume something else must be involved, so they make it needlessly complicated. The really difficult issues surrounding Namespaces involve when to use them, which we will discuss later in this chapter.

Namespaces are specified using the `xmlns` attribute to declare the Namespace with an element. The attribute takes the general form

```
<element xmlns:prefix="Namespace URI">
```

in which the *element* is the element for which we are declaring the Namespace, the *prefix* is the prefix we will use with our element names, and the *Namespace URI* is the identifier of the Namespace itself. The prefix is actually optional—if it is left out, the Namespace declaration is considered the default Namespace, and all the elements in the document will be treated as members of that Namespace unless they are marked otherwise.

The *Namespace URI* often causes some confusion as well. Generally, this takes the form of a URL, which serves as a good unique identifier, because it includes the domain name, and is easily understood by Web-enabled software. The most common misconception resulting from the use of a URL here is that the URL necessarily points to something, when, in fact, it does not. The URL is simply used as a string to identify the Namespace—it does not necessarily point to any specific document (although it can if you want it to) and there is no syntax or standard for creating a Namespace document to live on your server.

Basically, the URL is just treated as a Substitution string by the XML processor. For example, when you create an XML document such as

```
<personal:document xmlns:personal="http://www.myserver.com/document">
</personal:document>
```

what the XML processor sees when it parses the document is

```
<http://www.myserver.com/document:document
xmlns:personal="http://www.myserver.com/document">
</http://www.myserver.com/document:document>
```

That's really all there is to declaring Namespaces. It's a very simple syntax, even though it is not necessarily easy to read with all the URLs and colons.

INTEGRATING NAMESPACES IN XML DOCUMENTS

There are a few ways in which we can incorporate Namespaces into our XML documents. All of these methods still use the same syntax we just covered for declaring the Namespace, with some variations on where the declaration is placed, and how the prefixes are used.

A SINGLE DEFAULT NAMESPACE

The simplest application of Namespaces is for documents that have only one Namespace, so that a default Namespace can be declared. This is a useful technique for declaring a Namespace for XML documents that you are going to share with other users, either within your organization or in the public, so that if they use the document with other documents, you can avoid Namespace collisions. It is good XML style to include a default Namespace, even if you do not intend to do much with the document and Namespaces.

To declare a default Namespace for your document, you simply use the `xmlns` attribute with your document's `root` element:

```
<?xml version="1.0"?>
<journal xmlns="http://www.myserver.com/journal">
 <article>
  <headline>Introduction to Namespaces</headline>
  <byline>Jane Doe</byline>
  <body>Namespaces are simple…</body>
 </article>
</journal>
```

The advantage of declaring a default Namespace in this manner is that we do not need to use any prefix on any of the elements within the document. This keeps the document clean and easy to read, but we still have a Namespace declared so that if later we integrate this document with other documents or share it, we can avoid possible collisions between elements or attributes of the same name.

Multiple Prefixed Namespaces

Declaring a default Namespace can make a document more readable; however, there are instances in which you may want to explicitly use a prefix with all the elements in your document. You might want to do this to ensure that if the file is imported or included in other documents, the users are aware of the Namespace issues, or even just to make sure anyone who reads the document will notice that the document uses multiple Namespaces.

To make all the Namespaces in the document require a prefix, we use the same basic structure as declaring a default Namespace, only we add the : *prefix* to the `xmlns` attribute:

```
<?xml version="1.0"?>
<journal:journal xmlns:journal="http://www.myserver.com/journal"
        xmlns:html="http://www.w3.org/TR/REC-html40">
 <html:html>
  <journal:article>
   <html:head>
    <html:title>
    <journal:headline>Introduction to Namespaces</journal:headline>
    </html:title>
   </html:head>
   <html:body>
    <html:i><journal:byline>Jane Doe</journal:byline></html:i>
    <journal:body>Namespaces are simple…</journal:body>
   <html:body>
  </journal:article>
 </html:html>
</journal:journal>
```

6

Note

In this example, you will notice that even the root element `journal` has the Namespace prefix, resulting in a `journal:journal` element. That is necessary because even though we are defining the Namespace in this element with the `xmlns` attribute, the `journal` root element is still part of the Namespace.

Because we have declared both Namespaces in this document with a prefix, there is no default Namespace, and we have to use a prefix with all the elements in the document. Although this does slightly impact the ease of readability, it is now explicitly clear which elements belong to which Namespace.

DEFAULT AND PREFIXED NAMESPACES

Most commonly, you will find that XML documents that utilize multiple Namespaces will use a mixture of a default Namespace and Namespaces that require the colon prefix. This can be accomplished by declaring both Namespaces—one as the default and one requiring a prefix—in the `xmlns` attribute with the `root` element:

```
<?xml version="1.0"?>
<journal xmlns="http://www.myserver.com/journal"
        xmlns:html="http://www.w3.org/TR/REC-html40">
 <html:html>
  <article>
   <html:head>
    <html:title>
    <headline>Introduction to Namespaces</headline>
    </html:title>
   </html:head>
   <html:body>
    <html:i><byline>Jane Doe</byline></html:i>
    <body>Namespaces are simple…</body>
   <html:body>
  </article>
 </html:html>
</journal>
```

The advantage of this method is that now both Namespaces are declared globally. That is because they are declared in the `root` element, and the default Namespace applies to any element without a prefix in the document. Because the second Namespace is also declared globally, any element in the document can be made part of that Namespace by appending the prefix.

We could also declare the default Namespace globally, but then have the second Namespace declared locally:

```
<?xml version="1.0"?>
<journal xmlns="http://www.myserver.com/journal">
 <article>
  <headline>Introduction to Namespaces</headline>
  <byline>Jane Doe</byline>
  <body>Namespaces are simple… an HTML Example
   <html:html xmlns:html="http://www.w3.org/TR/REC-html40">
   <html:b>This is HTML</html:b>
   </html:html>
  </body>
 </article>
</journal>
```

This allows us to restrict the usage of the second Namespace to the children of the `<html>` element, because the Namespace is not declared at the root level, but instead it is declared as an attribute of the <html> element. In fact, in the preceding example we used the html: prefix to underscore which elements were members of which Namespace, but that is not actually necessary. Because the second Namespace is being declared locally, we could eliminate the prefix altogether, and essentially declare a local default Namespace:

```
<?xml version="1.0"?>
<journal xmlns="http://www.myserver.com/journal">
 <article>
  <headline>Introduction to Namespaces</headline>
  <byline>Jane Doe</byline>
  <body>Namespaces are simple… an HTML Example
   <html xmlns="http://www.w3.org/TR/REC-html40">
    <b>This is HTML</b>
   </html>
  </body>
 </article>
</journal>
```

Using this technique, all the children of the <html> element will be considered part of the http://www.w3.org/TR/REC-html40 Namespace, because that is the declared default Namespace for the <html> element. However, because this is a locally scoped declaration, when we close the <html> element, all the elements from that point on will be members of the document default Namespace—only the children of the <html> element will be members of the local Namespace.

There are a number of ways in which you can use Namespaces in your documents, and how you choose to incorporate Namespaces will depend largely on the specifics of your XML implementation. You may just want to declare a simple default Namespace for all of your documents, or you may want to incorporate several different Namespaces in your documents.

Namespaces apply to many of the XML technologies we are describing in this title. So, let's take a look at how Namespaces apply specifically to some of those technologies.

NAMESPACES AND SCHEMAS

Quite possibly, the most confusing aspect of XML Schemas and XML Schema authoring is that of Namespaces. You may recall from Chapter 5 that Namespaces were used pretty heavily in the schema examples we provided. Although implementing Namespaces themselves is trivial, keeping track of how those Namespace declarations impact your schemas and instance documents can be confusing.

6

Caution

Although XML Schemas make extensive use of Namespaces, this is because XML Schemas are, in fact, XML documents. Because DTDs have their own unique syntax, Namespace issues do not apply to DTDs at all because DTDs cannot make use of Namespaces.

There are three major issues that will confront most authors when dealing with Namespaces and XML schemas:

- Expose or hide Namespaces. This applies to Namespaces in the instance documents the users of your schema will be creating. Do you limit the users' exposure to Namespaces? Or do you require full Namespace disclosure?
- Default Namespaces. What is the best approach for declaring default Namespaces in your schema, and what is the impact on using the schema with other schemas and instance documents?
- Multiple Schemas, Multiple Namespaces. What is the best Namespace approach when you are creating multiple document schemas? Should they all share one Namespace? No Namespaces? Should each schema have its own Namespace?

Let's examine each of these issues in greater detail and see what might constitute the best practices.

NAMESPACES AND INSTANCE DOCUMENTS

Many users of instance documents find the use of Namespaces unappealing. The prefixes often make it difficult for them to read the instance documents, and there is often much confusion over what Namespace applies where.

With designs such as the Russian Doll design and the Venetian Blind design, you have the ability to shield users by keeping Namespaces localized to the schema, or exposing them in the instance document. So, which is the better approach? Neither.

This area, like many in XML, is a gray area. There are advantages and disadvantages to both approaches. For example, let's say that you are building a specification for mobile phones, importing two schemas:

```
<?xml version="1.0" encoding="UTF-8" ?>
<xs:schema xmlns:xs="http://www.w3.org/2001/XMLSchema"
xmlns:nokia="http://www.nokia.com"
xmlns:motorola="http://www.motorola.com"
targetNamespace="http://www.mobilephone.com"
xmlns="http://www.mobilephone.com"
elementFormDefault="unqualified">

<import namespace="http://www.nokia.com" schemaLocation="nokia.xsd"/>
<import namespace="http://www.motorola.com" schemaLocation="motorola.xsd"/>

<xs:element name="phone">
 <xs:complexType>
  <xs:complexContent>
   <xs:element name="features" type="nokia:features"/>
   <xs:element name="description" type="motorola:description"/>
  </xs:complexContent>
 </xs:complexType>
</xs:element>

</xs:schema>
```

There is actually a lot going on with Namespaces in this simple document. First, we have the Namespace declaration for the Schema elements themselves:

```
<xs:schema xmlns:xs="http://www.w3.org/2001/XMLSchema"
```

Next, we have the Namespaces for the `nokia` and the `motorola` schemas. This way, we will be able to distinguish between the two imported Namespaces:

```
xmlns:nokia="http://www.nokia.com"
xmlns:motorola=http://www.motorola.com
```

Now we need to declare a target Namespace for our Schema. The target Namespace is the Namespace that we are defining with this schema—it is the Namespace to which our final XML Instance documents will belong. This is an important element in our document, as we are using Namespaces from other Schemas, so by declaring a `targetNamespace`, we are ensuring that our schema will define a new Namespace, separate from these:

```
targetNamespace=http://www.mobilephone.com
```

We then define the default Namespace for the document the same as the `targetNamespace`:

```
xmlns="http://www.mobilephone.com"
```

Finally, we are going to use an attribute called *`elementFormDefault`*, which allows us to specify how elements should appear in the final XML Instance document:

```
elementFormDefault="unqualified">
```

Because we have chosen `"unqualified"`, the elements in an XML document based on our schema will need to have only unqualified NCNames for the elements. This means that we do not have to use the Namespace prefix with the colon. As a result, we have an instance document that looks like this:

```
<?xml version="1.0" encoding="UTF-8" ?>
<phone xmlns="http://www.mobilephone.com"
   xmlns:xsi="http://www.3.org/2001/XMLSchema-Instance"
   xsi:schemaLocation="http://www.mobilephone.com
   http://www.mobilephone.com/phone.xsd">

<features>Silent Ringing</features>
<description>Sleek and small…</description>
</phone>
```

6

This is descriptive, and the user is unaware that the `<features>` element and the `<description>` element are both being imported from different Namespaces. In many cases, that might not be important. But it also means that users will be unaware that if one of those imported schemas changes, they will need to change their instance documents. If we alter the Schema to change the `elementFormDefault` to `qualified`, we toggle on the Namespaces, and the instance document looks like this:

```
<?xml version="1.0" encoding="UTF-8" ?>
<phone xmlns="http://www.mobilephone.com"
       xmlns:xsi="http://www.3.org/2001/XMLSchema-Instance"
       xsi:schemaLocation="http://www.mobilephone.com
       http://www.mobilephone.com/phone.xsd"
```

```
        xmlns:motorola="http://www.motorola.com"
        xmlns:nokia="http://www.nokia.com">

<nokia:features>Silent Ringing</nokia:features>
<motorola:description>Sleek and small…</motorola:description>
</phone>
```

Now it is clear to the user that these elements have been imported from another Namespace. There are advantages and disadvantages to both approaches. However, there is no clear-cut reason to use one over the other. How you choose to use Namespaces depends on your design goals for the final instance documents.

DEFAULT NAMESPACES

When you are declaring the Namespaces for your schema, you can declare a number of different Namespaces for the schema document. How the Namespaces are declared for your document impacts your ability to effectively import and include other schemas and their components.

Schemas that do not have a `targetNamespace` are called *Chameleon* schemas because when they are imported, they effectively become a part of your schema. So, what happens when we have a schema that does not have a default Namespace declaration

```
<?xml version="1.0" encoding="UTF-8" ?>
<xs:schema xmlns:xs="http://www.w3.org/2001/XMLSchema"
        xmlns:my="http://www.myserver.com"
        targetNamespace="http://www.myserver.com">
</xs:schema>
```

In this case, we have two Namespaces: the XML Schema Namespace and the "`http://www.myserver.com`" Namespace, both of which have prefixes assigned. The problem with this design is that if we now try to import a Chameleon schema, it will by nature become part of the default Namespace, which in this case doesn't exist. And that will break things.

Another approach would be to declare the default Namespace to be the `XMLSchema` Namespace:

```
<?xml version="1.0" encoding="UTF-8" ?>
<xs:schema xmlns:xs="http://www.w3.org/2001/XMLSchema"
        xmlns:my="http://www.myserver.com"
        targetNamespace="http://www.myserver.com"
        xmlns="http://www.w3.org/2001/XMLSchema">
</xs:schema>
```

Now we do have a default Namespace, so when we import our Chameleon schema, it will be treated as part of the default Namespace, which in this case, is the `XMLSchema` Namespace.

Of course, this would create errors as well, because now the imported components would be treated as part of the XML Schema Namespace, but, of course, none of the elements and attributes we need are declared within the XML Schema Namespace.

The correct approach to this issue, therefore, is to declare the `targetNamespace` as the default Namespace:

```
<?xml version="1.0" encoding="UTF-8" ?>
<xs:schema xmlns:xs="http://www.w3.org/2001/XMLSchema"
        targetNamespace="http://www.myserver.com"
        xmlns="http://www.myserver.com"
</xs:schema>
```

This is the best practice, because this allows for all of your schema declarations to be qualified (using the "xs" prefix) but imported Chameleon schemas are automatically considered a part of the `targetNamespace` you are in the process of defining. Therefore, each declaration will be part of the proper Namespace, and you will not run into errors because of Namespace conflicts or trying to reference components that are not defined.

MULTIPLE NAMESPACES

The Chameleon approach of not declaring a target Namespace for your schemas is one way to manage multiple-part schemas when building a single schema from multiple files. However, this is not the only approach to the problem. The issue basically involves three choices:

- Many Namespaces
- One Namespace
- Zero Namespaces

So, let's take a look at these approaches and their impacts.

MANY NAMESPACES

The first approach we might use would be to have a `targetNamespace` declared for each one of our multiple schemas:

```
<?xml version="1.0" encoding="UTF-8" ?>
<xs:schema xmlns:xs="http://www.w3.org/2001/XMLSchema"
        targetNamespace="http://www.myserver.com/Name"
        xmlns="http://www.myserver.com/Name">
<xs:element name="name" type="xs:string"/>
</xs:schema>

<?xml version="1.0" encoding="UTF-8" ?>
<xs:schema xmlns:xs="http://www.w3.org/2001/XMLSchema"
        targetNamespace="http://www.myserver.com/Address"
        xmlns="http://www.myserver.com/Address">
<xs:element name="address" type="xs:string"/>
</xs:schema>

<?xml version="1.0" encoding="UTF-8" ?>
<xs:schema xmlns:xs="http://www.w3.org/2001/XMLSchema"
        targetNamespace="http://www.myserver.com/Phone"
        xmlns="http://www.myserver.com/Phone">
<xs:element name="phone" type="xs:string"/>
</xs:schema>
```

Here, we have three schemas, each representing a different Namespace, and now we want to build a new schema by including each of these schemas. The result would look like this:

```
<?xml version="1.0" encoding="UTF-8" ?>
<xs:schema xmlns:xs="http://www.w3.org/2001/XMLSchema"
        xmlns:name="http://www.myserver.com/Name"
        xmlns:address="http://www.myserver.com/Address"
        xmlns:phone="http://www.myserver.com/Phone"
        targetNamespace="http://www.myserver.com/Contact"
        xmlns="http://www.myserver.com/Contact">

<xs:import namespace="http://www.myserver.com/Name" schemaLocation="Name.xsd"/>
<xs:import namespace="http://www.myserver.com/Address"
schemaLocation="Address.xsd"/>
<xs:import namespace="http://www.myserver.com/Phone" schemaLocation="Phone.xsd"/>

<xs:element name="contact">
 <xs:complexType>
  <xs:sequence>
   <xs:element ref="name:name"/>
   <xs:element ref="address:address"/>
   <xs:element ref="phone:phone"/>
  </xs: sequence>
 </xs:complexType>
</xs:element>

</xs:schema>
```

The biggest disadvantage of this approach is the clutter created in your schema (and instance documents). There is a great deal of Namespace information to keep track of even in our simple example, which uses only three declarations.

It does, however, have the advantage of strict control over the Namespace itself, which means that if you are publishing the Namespaces to a wide audience, this approach might be the best. In terms of avoiding potential Namespace conflicts, it is certainly the safest. By declaring Namespace information for each schema, you can ensure that users of your schemas will be bound to your Namespace, and therefore conflicts will be kept to a bare minimum.

ONE NAMESPACE

Another alternative is to use a single, umbrella Namespace, with each schema belonging to that Namespace:

```
<?xml version="1.0" encoding="UTF-8" ?>
<xs:schema xmlns:xs="http://www.w3.org/2001/XMLSchema"
        targetNamespace="http://www.myserver.com/Contact"
        xmlns="http://www.myserver.com/Contact">

<xs:element name="name" type="xs:string"/>
</xs:schema>


<?xml version="1.0" encoding="UTF-8" ?>
<xs:schema xmlns:xs="http://www.w3.org/2001/XMLSchema"
```

```
        targetNamespace="http://www.myserver.com/Contact"
        xmlns="http://www.myserver.com/Contact">

<xs:element name="address" type="xs:string"/>
</xs:schema>


<?xml version="1.0" encoding="UTF-8" ?>
<xs:schema xmlns:xs="http://www.w3.org/2001/XMLSchema"
        targetNamespace="http://www.myserver.com/Contact"
        xmlns="http://www.myserver.com/Contact">
<xs:element name="phone" type="xs:string"/>
</xs:schema>
```

The resulting "umbrella" schema will look like this:

```
<?xml version="1.0" encoding="UTF-8" ?>
<xs:schema xmlns:xs="http://www.w3.org/2001/XMLSchema"
        targetNamespace="http://www.myserver.com/Contact"
        xmlns="http://www.myserver.com/Contact">

<xs:include schemaLocation="Name.xsd"/>
<xs:include schemaLocation="Address.xsd"/>
<xs:include schemaLocation="Phone.xsd"/>

<xs:element name="contact">
 <xs:complexType>
  <xs:sequence>
   <xs:element ref="name"/>
   <xs:element ref="address"/>
   <xs:element ref="phone"/>
  </xs:sequence>
 </xs:complexType>
</xs:element>
```

Because all the schemas are part of the same Namespace, we can include the schemas, and we also can eliminate much of the clutter from the multiple-Namespace approach.

However, one distinct disadvantage is that although our Namespace is reflected in each of the documents, none of them is a complete definition of the components in the Namespace. This means, if we publish these schemas, someone could reference one of our multiple parts, and gain access to only a portion of the Namespace, but be under the impression they are accessing the whole Namespace.

ZERO NAMESPACES

The Chameleon approach has the benefits of using the umbrella approach, in that it allows importing, and it also eliminates clutter. The multiple parts of the schema do not have any Namespace declaration:

```
<?xml version="1.0" encoding="UTF-8" ?>
<xs:schema xmlns:xs="http://www.w3.org/2001/XMLSchema">
 <xs:element name="name" type="xs:string"/>
</xs:schema>
```

```
<?xml version="1.0" encoding="UTF-8" ?>
<xs:schema xmlns:xs="http://www.w3.org/2001/XMLSchema">
 <xs:element name="address" type="xs:string"/>
</xs:schema>

<?xml version="1.0" encoding="UTF-8" ?>
<xs:schema xmlns:xs="http://www.w3.org/2001/XMLSchema">
 <xs:element name="phone" type="xs:string"/>
</xs:schema>
```

But then we can create another "umbrella" schema as before:

```
<?xml version="1.0" encoding="UTF-8" ?>
<xs:schema xmlns:xs="http://www.w3.org/2001/XMLSchema"
        targetNamespace="http://www.myserver.com/Contact"
        xmlns="http://www.myserver.com/Contact">

<xs:include schemaLocation="Name.xsd"/>
<xs:include schemaLocation="Address.xsd"/>
<xs:include schemaLocation="Phone.xsd"/>

<xs:element name="contact">
 <xs:complexType>
  <xs:sequence>
   <xs:element ref="name"/>
   <xs:element ref="address"/>
   <xs:element ref="phone"/>
  </xs:sequence>
 </xs:complexType>
</xs:element>
```

Because Chameleon schemas take on the Namespace characteristics of the document in which they are included, this has a similar effect to the "one Namespace" approach outlined in the previous section. However, now we have a set of schemas that can be used easily not just with this schema, but with any others in our organization as well, without worry about Namespace restrictions. And we still have one single schema that accurately describes the complete Namespace we were describing.

The main drawback to this technique, however, is that it leaves the door wide open for potential Namespace collisions if you are not very mindful of the schemas that are being imported. Although on the surface it is the easiest approach in terms of implementing, and it's very readable, using this approach requires authors to be very attentive to the details of your schema content and declarations to avoid possible Namespace conflicts.

NAMESPACES WITH XML VOCABULARIES

One goal of XML is to further facilitate the exchange of information; therefore, it makes sense that most XML documents will be designed to be shared with other users, be they developers, designers, or so on. This is why there are so many XML vocabularies currently being developed, ranging from MathML to SVG. One feature all these vocabularies have in common is their own unique Namespaces associated with them.

Having a Namespace associated with a vocabulary is a good way to assist users in using your vocabularies. For example, it may be desirable to mix and match different vocabularies within a single XML document. For instance, if you are writing a paper for submission to a mathematics journal, you might have a generic XML format for the article; however, you might want to include some MathML markup for your formulas, or perhaps some SVG markup for diagrams or illustrations.

The ability to utilize multiple vocabularies within a single document because they are all well-formed XML is one of the great aspects of XML that makes it so "extensible." However, to avoid possible Namespace conflicts between different vocabularies and each other, or with your own document, you should always use Namespaces when working with XML documents based on a publicly published XML vocabulary.

Here's a list of the Namespaces for some of the technologies discussed in this book:

XML Schemas	`http://www.w3.org/2001/XMLSchema`
XML Schema Instance	`http://www.3.org/2001/XMLSchema-Instance`
XSL	`http://www.w3.org/1999/XSL`
XSLT	`http://www.w3.org/1999/XSL/Transform`
XSL-FO	`http://www.w3.org/1999/XSL/Format`
XLink	`http://www.w3.org/1999/xlink`
XInclude	`http://www.w3.org/2001/XInclude`
XHTML	`http://www.w3.org/1999/xhtml`
SVG	`http://www.w3.org/2000/svg`
SMIL	`http://www.w3.org/2001/SMIL20/`
RDF	`http://www.w3.org/1999/02/22-rdf-syntax-ns#`

Keep in mind that as Recommendations are updated, the Namespace associated with the Recommendation's current version may change as well. For example, when XML 2.0 is released, it will likely have a different Namespace from v1.0 to avoid confusion between the versions.

6

ADDITIONAL RESOURCES

Because the technical details of Namespaces are relatively simple, and the debate on when and why to use Namespaces rages on, there are not many resources available for learning more about XML Namespaces that will provide you with definitive answers. However, you can consult

- Namespaces in XML (`http://www.w3.org/TR/REC-xml-names/`)—This is the official W3C Namespaces Recommendation, and it should be the first source you consult if you have a question about Namespaces or using Namespaces in your documents.
- XML.com (`http://www.xml.com/pub/rg/74`)—XML.com has a number of articles and tutorials regarding XML Namespaces, and they can be found at the preceding link.

> This is simply an archive of articles, so pay attention to when the articles were written, as changes may have occurred in practices since an article was first published.

If you have concerns about the use and implementations of Namespaces in your projects, you might also consider posting to XML-DEV or comp.text.xml. You are likely to get a deluge of opinions—some useful, some not—but the feedback can be valuable and raise issues you may not have considered.

Roadmap

XML Namespaces might be simple, but they impact a wide variety of XML technologies, from well-formed XML documents, to XML Schemas, to various XML vocabularies. Namespaces are quite possibly the best example of a member of the XML family of Recommendations that touches nearly every other aspect of XML.

Namespaces are also the final tool in the set of "core" XML technologies that deal directly with the creation of well-formed and valid XML documents. You now have an understanding of well-formed XML, valid XML, Document Type Definitions, and XML Schemas. And you now know how XML Namespaces relates to those technologies as well. That completes the core set of XML technologies, so we can now branch out into related technologies that take the power of XML to the next level.

Specifically, in the next part we will address the technologies that can be used to take the plain text files of XML and display them in various formats such as the Web and print. In Chapter 7, "Using XML with Existing Stylesheet Technologies (CSS)," we will look at how you can use XML with Cascading Stylesheets. In Chapter 8, "The New Wave of Stylesheets: XSL," we will take a look at the Extensible Stylesheet Language. In Chapter 9, "Transforming XML Data into Other Formats with XSLT," we will discuss XSL Transformations, a powerful tool for manipulating XML documents. Finally, in Chapter 10, "The Nuts and Bolts of XSL: Formatting Objects," we will focus on XSL-Formatting Objects, the final step in taking your XML documents from text to the Web to print.

PART II

XML Presentation Technologies

CHAPTER 7

Using XML with Existing Stylesheet Technologies (CSS)

In this chapter

by David Gulbransen

XML DISPLAY IN THE BROWSERS

When XML first debuted, none of the Web browsers were capable of displaying XML documents, except as text documents. Although that is a valid way to view XML documents, it also represents a step backward from the display of HTML.

Eventually, the browsers began to add support for XML. Internet Explorer was the first, with the ability to display an XML document as a tree, which could be collapsed or expanded in the browser display.

XML was around approximately two years (as an official Recommendation) before XSL. During that time, browser manufacturers wanted a way to display XML in the browser, and CSS was already supported. And because HTML is a markup language and XML vocabularies are markup languages, it didn't take much to display XML using CSS.

In fact, the CSS Level 2 Recommendation from the W3C even includes a tutorial for using XML and CSS. However, keep in mind that the CSS2 Recommendation was written before XML became an official Recommendation, so that information might be somewhat dated.

WHEN TO USE CSS

Many users wonder which stylesheet language is the appropriate choice, and the answer really depends upon your goals. For example, if you want to use a stylesheet to convert your XML document into WML, you really have no choice but to use XSLT—CSS simply cannot handle transformations.

In fact, if you are manipulating the XML in any way other than for the purposes of display, the answer is to use XSL. However, if you are using XML for display in a Web browser, you have the option of using CSS.

In this situation, most users will find that it is much easier to use CSS. There is any number of WYSIWYG editors available for working with CSS. More browsers support CSS than XSL, and CSS is much easier to master than XSL. When you take all of these factors into consideration, it's clear that if you are simply applying formatting rules, and are doing pretty straightforward formatting, CSS is probably the choice for you.

CSS BASICS

So, now, let's take a look at some of the basics of CSS. First, Cascading Stylesheets are cascading. That means that you can actually build hierarchies of stylesheets, by importing one stylesheet into another. When you do this, the rules from the sheets are combined, and you can use this to build complex stylesheets from a series of simple stylesheets.

For our purposes of discussion, we will not do much with cascading. In this chapter, we will work with a one-stylesheet-to-one-XML-document model. If you're interested in learning more about cascading and multiple stylesheets, there are thousands of CSS tutorials and hundreds of CSS books available on the market.

Rules and Selectors

A CSS Stylesheet is simply a series of rules that describe how elements in an HTML document are to be displayed in a browser. A typical rule looks like this:

```
BODY {font-family: "Arial", sans-serif}
```

The first part of the rule, `BODY`, is called the *selector*. This is the portion of the rule that selects what element the rule applies to. In this case, the selector is `BODY`, which will select the HTML `<body>` element.

The second portion of the rule, `{font-family: "Arial", sans-serif}` is called the *declaration*. Each declaration consists of a set of properties and their associated values. In this case, the property is `font-family` and the values are `"Arial"` and `sans-serif`.

Inheritance

One of the nice features of CSS is that of property inheritance. That is, all the child elements of the element selected inherit the property of the selected element.

So, with our sample rule

```
BODY {font-family: "Arial", sans-serif}
```

because we have selected the `<body>` element, any child elements of the body will also have the same font properties. That means that `<h1>`, `<h2>`, and so on will all be either `"Arial"` or another sans-serif font if Arial is unavailable.

We can also override the inherited properties, simply by declaring another rule, which is more specific. For example, if we had

```
BODY {font-family: "Arial", sans-serif}
H3 {font-family: "Times New Roman", serif}
```

then all `body` elements would be rendered in Arial, sans-serif, with the exception of the `h3` elements, which would be in Times New Roman, serif.

You can also group selectors together to select multiple elements and apply the same properties to them:

```
BODY {font-family: "Arial", sans-serif}
H3, H2, H1 {font-family: "Times New Roman", serif}
```

This example groups the `<h3>`, `<h2>`, and `<h1>` elements together, so that they all share the same font properties described in the descriptor.

We can also use multiple properties within the descriptor

```
BODY {font-family: "Arial", sans-serif; font-size: 24pt; color: blue}
```

Here there are multiple properties specified in the descriptor, each separated from the other by a semicolon.

CSS PROPERTIES

The CSS properties represent the physical display properties, which can be manipulated in order to affect the appearance of an element when it is rendered in the browser. Each of the following categories of properties is grouped based on the type of display it alters. This is by no means a complete list of all the CSS properties, but this is a very good start to work with formatting XML documents.

Properties are listed as a keyword, followed by a colon, which separates the property from the property value

```
SELECTOR {property: value; property: value}
```

Now let's examine some of the more common properties and their acceptable values.

COLORS AND BACKGROUNDS

There are a number of properties that are related to changing the color of elements or the background of elements. These include

- `color`—The `color` property allows you to select a color for the selected element. Color values can be given as either keywords or as RGB color triplets.
- `background`—The `background` property allows you to select the background for the selected object.
- `background-color`—This property allows you to select a color for the background, either as a Web color keyword, or as an RGB triplet.
- `background-image`—This property allows you to specify a background image.

Color values can be specified using predefined color keywords, or as RGB values:

```
BODY {background-color: red}
BODY {background-color: rbg(255, 0, 0)}
```

The background properties can accept either color values or URLs as their content:

```
BODY {background: red}
BODY {background: url("http://www.myserver.com/bg.gif")}
```

FONTS

Because so much of the content on the Web is text based, the ability to manipulate the font properties of the text being displayed is critical to any stylesheet mechanism. CSS is no exception, and there are several properties that exist exclusively for dealing with fonts. Some of these include

- `font`—This is the generic `font` property, which can be used to establish any of the following properties.

- `font-family`—This property allows you to select the value of the font family for an element. The font family can be either the name of a specific font in quotation marks, or a generic family type, such as `serif` or `sans-serif`:

  ```
  BODY {font-family: "Arial", sans-serif}
  ```

- `font-style`—This property allows you to specify the font style. The default value is normal, but you can choose from values of `normal`, `italic`, or `oblique`.
- `font-variant`—This property allows you to specify a font-variant. The default value is `normal` or you can specify `small-caps` for a small-caps font.
- `font-weight`—The default font weight is `normal`, which corresponds to a value of **`400`**. Font weight can be specified with a keyword of `normal`, `bold`, `bolder`, or `lighter`, or it can be specified with a numeric range from 100 to 900, with 400 representing normally weighted type.
- `font-size`—The `font-size` expresses the size of the font, which can be defined in a value of point size (for example, 12pt) or percentages (for example, 150%).

This is by no means a complete list, but these are the most commonly used font-properties, and if you understand their usage, you should be able to understand the use of the other properties, which you can find in a CSS-specific reference.

TEXT

It might seem as though text and font should be the same thing; however, in the context of stylesheets they are different. The text properties relate to the way that text is formatted in terms of alignment, underlining, and letter and word spacing as well as whitespace issues. Text is closely related to fonts; however, these properties are their own, in a separate category.

- `text-indent`—This property sets the amount of space a text block is to be indented. The value takes the form of a length, either as an explicit measurement (for example, 14pt) or as a percentage (for example, 125%).
- `text-align`—This property is used to define how the text object is to be aligned. Keyword choices include `left`, `right`, `center`, or `justify`.
- `text-decoration`—The `text-decoration` property allows you to specify a text decoration for your text block, such as an `underline`. Other keyword values include `overline`, `line-through`, or the awful `blink`.
- `letter-spacing`—This property allows you to specify the letter spacing in the text block. The value is expressed as a measurement, using any of the following units: pt (points), em (em spaces), cm (centimeters), in (inches).
- `word-spacing`—This property allows you to specify the word spacing of the text block, and it accepts any of the same measurements as `letter-spacing`.
- `white-space`—The default value for the `white-space` property is `normal`, but you may also select `pre`, which collapses any whitespace or newlines in the text block, or `nowrap`, which also collapses whitespace, with the exception of newline characters such as `<br>`.

TABLES

Tables are a fantastic way to organize data into an easily readable format. That's why there is pretty robust support for table formatting built into CSS. The properties can be combined to create advanced formatting for HTML tables in CSS:

- `table`—This property represents the entire table, and can be used to change any of the following properties.
- `table-row`—This property represents the table-row, which can be used by setting the `display` property to "`display: table-row`."
- `table-column`—This property represents the table-column, which can be used by setting the `display` property to "`display: table-column`."
- `table-cell`—This property represents the table-cell, which can be used by setting the `display` property to "`display: table-cell`."
- `table-caption`—This property represents the table-caption, which can be used by setting the `display` property to "`display: table-caption`."

The table properties are most useful in conjunction with HTML table elements that correspond directly to these properties with a one-to-one name relationship. However, you can use table properties with the `display` property and your XML elements as well.

The `display` property is used to manipulate the manner in which objects are displayed, such as inline, or in a block. We will discuss the `display` property later in the chapter.

LISTS

Another method of organizing data is the list. Lists are everywhere, and these properties enable you to specify how the items contained in a list are displayed.

- `list-style`—This property enables you to change any of the following list properties.
- `list-style-type`—This refers to the style of bullet that is used to offset list items. Some choices include

  disc

  circle

  square

  lower-roman

  upper-roman

  decimal

  The `lower-roman` value would number the list using lowercase Roman numerals (i,ii,iii); `upper-roman` would be uppercase Roman numerals (I, II, III); and `decimal` would be numbered with integers (1,2,3).
- `list-style-image`—This property enables you to specify an image (in the form of a URL) to be used as the list item marker.

- `list-style-position`—The default value for this property is `outside`, which results in the list being numbered with the marker outside the list item text:

  ```
  - This is outside
    the list item text.
  ```

  A value of `inside` places the item inside the list item text:

  ```
  - This is inside
  the list item text.
  ```

Borders

The border properties enable you to specify how borders are drawn around elements such as `display` blocks or other elements that can have borders. `Display` blocks are an easy mechanism for developing graphic elements such as borders.

- `border-style`—This is the general border style property, which can be used to define any of the following properties.
- `border-top-width`—This property represents the width of the top border of an area. The width value can be established using any of the units of measure mentioned earlier (pt, px, cm, in, em).
- `border-bottom-width`—This property represents the width of the bottom border of an area. The width value can be established using any of the units of measure mentioned earlier (pt, px, cm, in, em).
- `border-right-width`—This property represents the width of the right border of an area. The width value can be established using any of the units of measure mentioned earlier (pt, px, cm, in, em).
- `border-left-width`—This property represents the width of the left border of an area. The width value can be established using any of the units of measure mentioned earlier (pt, px, cm, in, em).
- `border-top-color`—This property represents the color of the top border of an area. The color value can be established with a keyword or with an RGB value.
- `border-bottom-color`—This property represents the color of the bottom border of an area. The color value can be established with a keyword or with an RGB value.
- `border-right-color`—This property represents the color of the right border of an area. The color value can be established with a keyword or with an RGB value.
- `border-left-color`—This property represents the color of the left border of an area. The color value can be established with a keyword or with an RGB value.

Comments

Comments in CSS stylesheets do not share the same form as those of XML. Instead, they share the same comment style as C++ and other programming languages, with the start of the comment denoted by `/*` and the end of the comment with `*/`. This is an example of a CSS comment:

```
/* CSS Comments are not the same as XML comments. */
```

MARGINS AND PADDING

The `margin` and `padding` properties are used to establish areas of the page where text cannot be placed. You can establish the margins for pages, display blocks, and so on. Padding functions similarly to margins, in that it enables you to specify an area where no text is supposed to be flowed.

- `margin`—This is the margin property, which enables you to specify all the following margin-related properties.
- `margin-top`—This represents the top margin of an area or block. The margin size is specified using any of the units of measure mentioned before, such as pt, px, cm, in, and so on.
- `margin-bottom`—This represents the bottom margin of an area or block. The margin size is specified using any of the units of measure mentioned before, such as pt, px, cm, in, and so on.
- `margin-left`—This represents the left margin of an area or block. The margin size is specified using any of the units of measure mentioned before, such as pt, px, cm, in, and so on.
- `margin-right`—This represents the right margin of an area or block. The margin size is specified using any of the units of measure mentioned before, such as pt, px, cm, in, and so on.
- `padding`—This is the padding property, which enables you to specify all the following padding-related properties.
- `padding-top`—This represents the top padding of an area or block. The padding size is specified using any of the units of measure mentioned before, such as pt, px, cm, in, and so on.
- `padding-bottom`—This represents the bottom padding of an area or block. The padding size is specified using any of the units of measure mentioned before, such as pt, px, cm, in, and so on.
- `padding-left`—This represents the left padding of an area or block. The padding size is specified using any of the units of measure mentioned before, such as pt, px, cm, in, and so on.
- `padding-right`—This represents the right padding of an area or block. The padding size is specified using any of the units of measure mentioned before, such as pt, px, cm, in, and so on.
- `display`—This property is not really a margin or padding, but instead is used to establish how an element is to be displayed. For example, a value of `block` causes the element to be displayed in a block box, which has margin, padding, and border properties. Other options for display include

  `inline`

  `block`

```
list-item

table
```

These properties enable you to control the placement and relationships of items on the page by treating them as rectangular areas that can have margins, padding, and border properties applied to them. This is particularly useful when working with XML because it provides a mechanism for grouping together "blocks" of things, which can then be formatted as a single object.

PSEUDO ELEMENTS

Normally, all the elements that are selected are normal elements that are part of the document tree. Pseudo elements are special elements that are not part of the document tree. These elements are defined in the CSS Recommendation, and can be used by you to accomplish special formatting tricks, such as a dropped cap.

- `:first-letter`—This pseudo element represents the first letter in a block of text. This can be useful for designing elements such as an initial, or *drop*, cap.
- `:first-line`—This pseudo element represents the first line in a section of text, which could be used to create an initial line of small caps or a similar graphic element.

Pseudo elements are selected by appending the pseudo-element onto the element it is altering. For example, to select the pseudo element `first-letter` of an `<h2>` element, you would use the syntax

```
H2:first-letter {color: blue}
```

which would result in the first letter of all `<H2>` elements appearing blue.

PSEUDO CLASSES

Pseudo classes function similarly to pseudo elements; however, pseudo classes do not need to be linked to a specific physical element. For example, if you wanted to use the pseudo class to make all the links in your document bold and 14 point, you could use the following:

```
:link {font-style: bold; font-size: 14pt}
```

The pseudo classes function similarly to the pseudo elements; however, they do not need to be linked to real elements in order to be used in a style sheet.

- `:link`—The `:link` pseudo class refers to all hypertext links in the document.
- `:visited`—The `:visited` pseudo class refers to all hypertext links in the document which have already been visited by the user.
- `:active`—The `:active` pseudo class refers to the hypertext link in the document which is currently being selected by the user.

The pseudo classes enable you to establish styles for a broad category of elements within the document, such as links with one rule. However, most of the pseudo class related to links, and so on, will not have much meaning in the context of an XML document.

USING CSS FORMATTING WITH XML

Now that you have seen how CSS rules are formed and are familiar with some of the properties and values that you can manipulate to influence how your elements are displayed, we can look at an example of an XML document formatted with CSS.

Listing 7.1 shows a `newspaper.xml` document which we are going to format for display with CSS. This document is a regular, well-formed XML document, with only one special line, which is immediately following the XML Declaration. That line is

```
<?xml-stylesheet type="text/css" href="newspaper.css"?>
```

This line is a processing instruction, which is used to link our stylesheet to the XML document. It has two attributes, one of which is `type` that is used to specify the type of stylesheet being applied, which in this case is "`text/css`". The second attribute is `href`, which is a URL that points to the location of the stylesheet, which in this case is just the name of the stylesheet because both files are in the same directory.

LISTING 7.1 A NEWSPAPER.XML DOCUMENT WITH A NEWSPAPER.CSS CSS STYLESHEET ASSOCIATED WITH IT

```
<?xml version="1.0"?>
<?xml-stylesheet type="text/css" href="newspaper.css"?>

<newspaper>
 <masthead>The Web Times</masthead>
 <edition>Morning Edition</edition>
 <section>
  <header>Technology</header>
  <article>
   <headline>DTDs Made Easy</headline>
   <byline>Jane Doe</byline>
   <story>Let's look at a Document Type Definition...</story>
  </article>
  <article>
   <headline>CSS Formatting XML</headline>
   <byline>John Smith</byline>
   <story>Using CSS to format XML documents is easy...</story>
  </article>
    <article>
   <headline>Browser Security Hole</headline>
   <byline>Sally Jones</byline>
   <story>Security experts today announced another security risk...</story>
  </article>
 </section>
 <section>
  <header>Arts</header>
  <article>
```

Listing 7.1 continued

```
    <headline>La Boheme at Lyric</headline>
    <byline>Susan Doe</byline>
    <story>The Chicago Lyric Opera season...</story>
   </article>
   <article>
    <headline>New Underground Film</headline>
    <byline>Kenneth Smith</byline>
    <story>Radio Ridge Productions today announced a new...</story>
   </article>
   <article>
    <headline>Seventh Season for ARTS</headline>
    <byline>Fred Smythe</byline>
    <story>The ARTS community theatre is currently in the 7th...</story>
   </article>
 </section>
</newspaper>
```

With the XML document ready to go and linked to the stylesheet, we now have to create the `newspaper.css` file in order to display the file properly.

There are no special headers or declarations associated with a CSS stylesheet, so we can begin with our rules immediately. First, we will establish the rule for our root element, which all the children in the document will inherit. In this case, we are going to specify a general font family using `"Times New Roman"` and, if that is not available, a generic serif font. Next, we will create a solid border around the newspaper, 3 points wide, and with a 20-point padding area. Then, by setting the `display` property to `block`, we create the block in which this element will be displayed:

```
newspaper {
 font-family: "Times New Roman", serif;
 border-style: solid;
 border-width: 3pt;
 padding: 20pt;
 display:block
}
```

Next, we want to format the masthead of our newspaper, *The Web Times*. First, we select the `masthead` element with our selector, and then we apply the font properties. In this case, we're going to make the masthead `"Arial"`, a sans-serif font, 36 points, and in the color blue. Again, to apply the style settings, we will set the display to `block`:

```
masthead {
 font-family: "Arial", sans-serif;
 font-size: 36pt;
 color: blue;
 display: block
}
```

7

With the masthead formatted, we can now format the `edition`. This rule looks very similar to the masthead; however, with the `edition`, we will rely on inheriting the `font-family` from the `newspaper` parent. We'll also change the font style to `italic` and add a margin at the bottom of the element to introduce some whitespace to our design:

```
edition {
 font-size: 24pt;
 font-style: italic;
 color: blue;
 margin-bottom: 15pt;
 display: block
}
```

Next, we're ready for the section `header`. For the section headers, we will also be inheriting our `font-family`, but we will still be manipulating the `font-size` and `font-style`. We also want to create a special effect with the section headers: a blue line that separates them from the text below. To create the blue line, we will make use of the `border` properties to essentially create a bottom border that is solid, blue, and 1 point wide. We'll also use the `margin` properties to add a bit of padding around our blue line:

```
header {
 font-size: 18pt;
 font-style: bold;
 color: blue;
 border-color: blue;
 border-bottom-width: 1pt;
 border-bottom-style: solid;
 margin-top: 10pt;
 margin-bottom: 5pt;
 display: block
}
```

Now all the mastheads and section heads are formatted and we are ready to start formatting the section content. First, we will format the article `headline`, for which we will be selecting a new `font-family` and `style`. We will also add some margin padding to keep the headline separate from the byline:

```
headline {
 font-family: "Arial", sans-serif;
 font-size: 14pt;
 font-style: bold;
 margin-top: 10pt;
 display: block
}
```

The `byline` formatting follows the same basic outline as the headline, but with a slightly smaller font and italic text, rather than bold:

```
byline {
 font-family: "Arial", sans-serif;
 font-size: 12pt;
 font-style: italic;
 display: block
}
```

Finally, we are ready for the `story` text itself. The `story` will inherit the font properties of the `newspaper`, although we will set the size at 12 points. We will also add some margins at the top and bottom, to separate the story from the byline and from the next story headline on the page:

```
story {
 font-size: 12pt;
 margin-top: 5pt;
 margin-bottom: 5pt;
 display: block
}
```

The one remaining thing we're going to do is to make use of one of the pseudo classes to add a bit of flourish to the page. In this case, we're going to use the `:first-letter` pseudo class in order to create a drop-cap at the start of each article. We can do this by setting the `font-size` at 18 points, which is larger than our `story` font size. Next, we will set the letter to `float` on the left. Then we will vertically align the letter with the top of the story text with `vertical-align: text-top`. Finally, we set the right margin to 2 pixels, so that the letter doesn't stand too far off from the article text:

```
story:first-letter {
 font-size: 18pt;
 float: left;
 vertical-align: text-top;
 margin-right: 2px
 }
```

The result is a drop-cap letter at the start of every story.

When we bring all of these rules together into a stylesheet, the result is what you see in Listing 7.2.

LISTING 7.2 THE COMPLETE NEWSPAPER.CSS CSS STYLESHEET

```
/* A CSS Stylesheet for the newspaper.xml file */

newspaper {
 font-family: "Times New Roman", serif;
 border-style: solid;
 border-width: 3pt;
 padding: 20pt;
 display:block
}

masthead {
 font-family: "Arial", sans-serif;
 font-size: 36pt;
 color: blue;
 display: block
}

edition {
 font-size: 24pt;
 font-style: italic;
 color: blue;
 margin-bottom: 15pt;
 display: block
}
```

LISTING 7.2 CONTINUED

```
header {
 font-size: 18pt;
 font-style: bold;
 color: blue;
 border-color: blue;
 border-bottom-width: 1pt;
 border-bottom-style: solid;
 margin-top: 10pt;
 margin-bottom: 5pt;
 display: block
}

headline {
 font-family: "Arial", sans-serif;
 font-size: 14pt;
 font-style: bold;
 margin-top: 10pt;
 display: block
}

byline {
 font-family: "Arial", sans-serif;
 font-size: 12pt;
 font-style: italic;
 display: block
}

story {
 font-size: 12pt;
 margin-top: 5pt;
 margin-bottom: 5pt;
 display: block
}

story:first-letter {
 font-size: 18pt;
 float: left;
 vertical-align: text-top;
 margin-right: 2px
 }
```

When the original XML document is viewed in a browser that supports XML and CSS, the result is a document that is displayed in the browser in accordance with the rules in the XML document, as shown in Figure 7.1.

Of course, this stylesheet could be reused with other `newspaper.xml` documents as well, which is one of the benefits of stylesheets. As you can see, CSS is easy to work with, and does offer good flexibility and display potential.

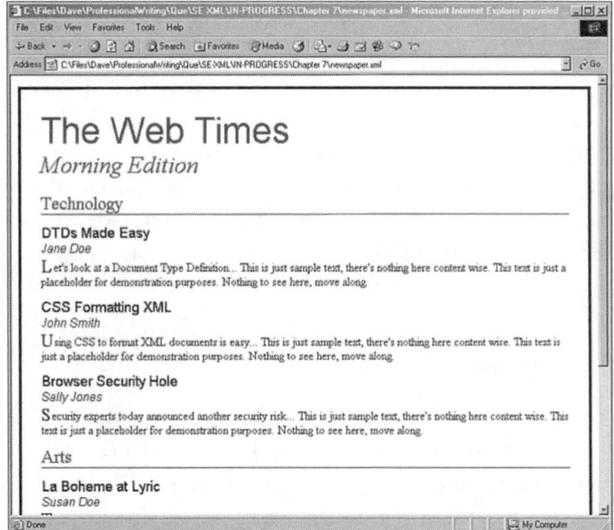

Figure 7.1
The `newspaper.xml` document as rendered in Internet Explorer with the `newspaper.css` stylesheet.

Additional Resources

There are a number of resources on the Web dedicated to learning CSS, and CSS is a well-established technology with respect to HTML. There are fewer resources available for using CSS with XML, although there are a few very good sites:

- W3C CSS Home Site (`http://www.w3.org/Style/CSS/`)—This is the main W3C site for Cascading Style Sheets. There are links here to tutorials and the CSS Recommendation.
- How to Add Style to XML (`http://www.w3.org/Style/styling-XML`)—This tutorial from the W3C details how you can use CSS in conjunction with your XML documents.
- Which Should I Use? (`http://www.w3.org/Style/CSS-vs-XSL`)—This article from the W3C addresses the issue of when to use CSS for formatting XML versus when to use XSL.
- Associating Stylesheets with XML (`http://www.w3.org/TR/xml-stylesheet/`)—This is the Recommendation that defines how stylesheets are associated with XML documents.

Any of the various sites dedicated to Web authoring, such as `builder.com` and `webmonkey.com`, will have a number of articles specifically dealing with CSS. If you have mastered CSS with HTML, applying CSS to XML is really a trivial matter of applying the stylesheet to XML elements rather than to HTML elements.

Roadmap

Cascading Stylesheets were designed to work with HTML, but they were never intended for use with XML. Although CSS is a very nice tool for working with layout and design, there are still a number of features that would be nice for working with XML documents that CSS does not afford.

Because of those shortcomings, the W3C developed the Extensible Stylesheet Language, which is designed specifically for working with XML documents. In fact, XSL is divided into two parts, one of which is called XSL Transformations, or XSLT, which deals with stylesheets designed for transforming XML. With XSLT, you can convert your XML documents from one XML vocabulary to another, such as from XML to WML. You can also convert XML documents into HTML. After you convert your XML document to HTML, you can even use CSS with the HTML as you normally do.

However, you could also take advantage of XSL Formatting Objects, or XSL-FO, to format the XML directly for display on the Web or in print.

From here, we'll go on to Chapter 8, "The New Wave of Stylesheets: XSL," where we will take a first look at XSL, discuss how XSL stylesheets are structured, and introduce XSLT and XSL-FO. From there, in Chapter 9, "Transforming XML Data into Other Formats with XSLT," we will look at XSLT in more detail. Finally in Chapter 10, "The Nuts and Bolts of XSL: Formatting Objects," we will look at XSL-FO and applying stylesheets for display and generating PDFs.

CHAPTER

THE NEW WAVE OF STYLESHEETS: XSL

In this chapter

by David Gulbransen

INTRODUCTION TO XSL

The idea of stylesheets is not a new concept; and, in fact, stylesheets have been around for a long time, both in the structured markup world and in the world of computing applications in general.

In many computing applications, data is not separated from display information. For example, in word processing documents, the text of the document is integrated with information about the typeface, font size, and special formatting information such as tabs, justification, and so on. The same is true for documents on the World Wide Web. HTML documents contain both the information that is to be displayed and the markup that details how the information is to be displayed.

However, there are many benefits of separation of data and display markup. Separation of the two tasks enables you to edit the data without the hindrance of visual markup information. And having separate display information also enables you to apply the same formatting information to multiple documents, which can be a real timesaving device when working with large amounts of data that is all similarly formatted. Separating the data from the display markup also makes it easier for developers to write applications that interact directly with the data, in essence making it easier for machines to read as well.

That is why Cascading Stylesheets have become popular on the Web—they make it easier to maintain complex Web sites. And as we saw in Chapter 7, "Using XML with Existing Stylesheet Technologies (CSS)," CSS can be used in conjunction with XML.

However, stylesheets for structured markup predate XML, going back to SGML. The mechanism for creating stylesheets with SGML is called *Document Style Semantics and Specification Language (DSSSL)*. DSSSL is a very powerful stylesheet language, which is very near to an actual procedural programming language.

Although CSS can be used to create stylesheets for XML, the W3C recognized the utility of a stylesheet system that was more flexible and specifically created to work with XML. As was the case with SGML, the W3C also recognized that the complexity and power of DSSSL would be a bar to entry for many Web users, and that a simpler, yet still powerful technology should be developed.

That gave rise to the Extensible Stylesheet Language (XSL) which is designed to facilitate the display of XML in a variety of applications, from display on the Web to print output.

XSL AS A DISPLAY TECHNOLOGY

The genesis of XSL is to provide a way for XML to be displayed properly in a variety of formats. Because XML files are simply text, they do not have the potential for the same range of dynamic display that is possible with HTML.

However, XSL enables XML authors to design stylesheets that are designed to work with XML, and to specify how the elements and attributes within their XML documents are to be displayed in the browser or on the printed page.

Producing PDFs

Although there are many ways to produce printed documents, from word processing applications to layout applications, one technology that has become popular in the past few years that can also be used on the Web is the Portable Document Format (PDF), which was developed by Adobe to provide a mechanism for producing graphically rich documents to be viewed on any platform and also printed out.

PDFs have become a very popular format for exchanging documents, and PDFs can be produced with a number of applications, from word processors to layout applications. And, of course, you can also use XSL to produce PDFs from your XML files.

There are a number of software tools that can generate PDF files from XML documents with an XSL stylesheet. The Formatting Objects defined in the XSL Recommendation allow you to control aspects such as color, size, and positioning of your XML data, and these XSL engines then can apply the stylesheet to the XML and generate a PDF which can then be published on the Web or printed.

Direct Browser Support

Although it is very useful to be able to print XML documents, XML is designed for use on the Web, so it is important to be able to display XML documents on the Web as well.

To achieve the display of XML on the Web, it's necessary to have direct browser support for XSL. Currently, Microsoft Internet Explorer and Netscape Navigator offer only rudimentary support for XSL processing. The W3C browser Amaya offers some XSL support, as does a browser called *X-Smile*.

XSL is becoming an established technology, and the major browser vendors are committed to increasing the support of XSL in their products. Soon you will be able to display XML documents with XSL directly in Internet Explorer and Netscape Navigator as they ship.

XSL As a Transformation Technology

In 1999, the authors of the XSL Working Group decided to split the Recommendation into two parts. The first part became the XSL 1.0 Recommendation, and the second part became the XSL Transformations Recommendation (XSLT).

In a sense, all stylesheets transform XML, given that you start with a plain-text document and you end up with the XML data, which can be displayed with a design and layout. This is one application of stylesheets. However, the editors of the XSL Recommendation realized the potential for the ability to transform XML from one format to another, which is the goal of XSLT.

XSLT allows you to take an XML document and transform the data in the document into another XML format, or even another language, such as HTML.

XML TO XML

XSLT enables authors to write a stylesheet that starts with a well-formed XML document, and then using a set of rules, or templates, convert that document from one set of XML tags to another. For example, using XSLT we could start with the following XML document:

```
<catalog>
 <item part="MS223">
  <name>Shirt</name>
  <description>Men's Shirt</description>
  <msrp>49.99</msrp>
 </item>
</catalog>
```

and create an XSLT stylesheet that would convert the data into the following document:

```
<inventory>
 <item>
  <name>Shirt</name>
  <description> Men's Shirt </description>
  <price>49.99</price>
  <sku>MS223</sku>
 </item>
</inventory>
```

Here's a preview of the stylesheet we used to accomplish this:

```
<xsl:stylesheet version="1.0"
   xmlns:xsl="http://www.w3.org/1999/XSL/Transform" >

<xsl:output method="xml"/>

<xsl:template match="catalog">
 <xsl:element name="inventory">
  <xsl:apply-templates select="item"/>
 </xsl:element>
</xsl:template>

<xsl:template match="item">
 <xsl:element name="item">
  <xsl:apply-templates select="name"/>
  <xsl:apply-templates select="description"/>
  <xsl:apply-templates select="msrp"/>
  <xsl:apply-templates select="@part"/>
 </xsl:element>
</xsl:template>

<xsl:template match="name">
 <xsl:copy>
  <xsl:apply-templates/>
 </xsl:copy>
</xsl:template>

<xsl:template match="description">
 <xsl:copy>
  <xsl:apply-templates/>
 </xsl:copy>
</xsl:template>
```

```
<xsl:template match="msrp">
 <xsl:element name="price">
  <xsl:apply-templates />
 </xsl:element>
</xsl:template>

<xsl:template match="@part">
 <xsl:element name="sku">
  <xsl:value-of select="."/>
  <xsl:apply-templates/>
 </xsl:element>
</xsl:template>

</xsl:stylesheet>
```

We'll take a closer look at the mechanics of how this is accomplished later in Chapter 9, "Transforming XML Data into Other Formats with XSLT."

This could be very useful in applications in which your organization has already implemented an internal format for your XML data, but you are receiving information from an outside source, such as a supplier or vendor, which you need to integrate into your own. XSLT enables you to accomplish this task with a stylesheet that can take one XML document and output another XML document, with elements and attributes rewritten.

Producing HTML

HTML is a markup language, so it make sense that if you are able to convert an XML document into another document using XML, you should also be able to take an XML document and create HTML with an XSLT stylesheet. In fact, XSLT is a very useful technology for outputting HTML, and other markup languages as well, such as WML, from an XML document.

Let's look at an example, starting with our `catalog.xml`:

```
<catalog>
 <item part="MS223">
  <name>Shirt</name>
  <description>Men's Shirt</description>
  <msrp>49.99</msrp>
 </item>
</catalog>
```

The goal is to convert the document into HTML so that the document can be displayed in any HTML-compatible browser. Here's the stylesheet that we can use to accomplish that task:

```
<xsl:stylesheet version="1.0"
   xmlns:xsl="http://www.w3.org/1999/XSL/Transform" >

<xsl:output method="html"/>

<xsl:template match="name">
 <title>Catalog</title>
 <h2><xsl:value-of select="."/></h2>
</xsl:template>
```

```
<xsl:template match="description">
 <i><xsl:value-of select="."/></i>
 <br/>
</xsl:template>

<xsl:template match="msrp">
 <b>$<xsl:value-of select="."/></b>
</xsl:template>

</xsl:stylesheet>
```

When this stylesheet is applied to the XML document, the result is the following HTML code:

```
<title>Catalog</title>
<h2>Shirt</h2>
<i>Men's Shirt</i>
<br>
<b>$49.99</b>
```

We'll take a closer look at using XSL to produce HTML in Chapter 9 when we examine XSLT in greater detail.

STYLESHEET PROCESSING

There is a lot that can be accomplished with XML and XSL, from converting between XML, to XML and outputting HTML. Now, let's take a look at the mechanism that is employed when processing stylesheets.

First, to process a stylesheet, you will need a piece of software capable of reading both the XML file and the stylesheet and then processing the templates contained in the stylesheet. This piece of software is commonly referred to as an XSL *processor*, or *engine*. There are a number of XSL processors available, but for the examples used in this and the following chapter, we have used Saxon. For the examples using XSL-FO in Chapter 10, "The Nuts and Bolts of XSL: Formatting Objects," we have used FOP. Both of these products are open-source, Java-based solutions, which are easy to use, free, and portable. More information about both can be found at the end of the chapter in the "Additional Resources" section.

When an XML processor is used to process an XSL stylesheet, the XML document is parsed, in what is termed *document order*. Document order means that the XSL processor reads the document from top to bottom, as it would be encountered if you were reading it. So, first, the root element is read, then the next element, then any children of that element, until there are no more, and then on to the next element in the document. Elements in an XML document are called *nodes*, and the document itself is called the *source tree*. After the source tree is built, the processor then applies, in order, the XSL stylesheet templates to the source tree to create a new version of the document, complete with changes, called the *result tree*.

The result tree is the finished product of the stylesheet transformation, or formatting, and it is in turn output by the processor.

TEMPLATES

If you look at the earlier stylesheet examples in this chapter, you will notice that the majority of the information contained in the stylesheets themselves is contained in elements called *templates*, which take the following form:

```
<xsl:template match="description">
 <i><xsl:value-of select="."/></i>
 <br/>
</xsl:template>
```

The "`xsl:`" is simply the Namespace prefix that identifies the element as part of the XSL Stylesheet Namespace.

The template itself consists of two major parts—the first is the `match` attribute, which makes use of an XPath pattern to specify the component being selected by the template for transformation. The second part is the content, or body, of the template, which is where the transformation information is specified.

For example, in the previous template, the `match` attribute contains `"description"`, which will match the element `<description>` in our XML document. The body of the template contains the HTML code which is to be output, and the `value-of` element enables us to select the value from the XML into which we want to insert the HTML code. In this case, the `select` attribute has a value of "`.`", which means that the current selected value, which is the value of the matched `description` element, should be inserted.

This is a very simple example of a template and an XPath expression that accompanies it. However, as you will see in the next chapter, these can both become more complex.

AREA MODELS

Templates are an essential part of stylesheets that are designed for transformation. However, there are also some mechanisms that are used primarily by stylesheets designed for formatting. Area models are conceptually important for using stylesheets as a formatting mechanism. When the XSL processor creates formatted output based on the transformations in your stylesheet, it is creating a specialized type of result tree called the *area tree*.

The area tree consists of formatted rectangular areas based on the information specified in your stylesheet.

Every area has three parts, which can be manipulated by the stylesheet mechanism:

- Content-rectangle—This is the rectangle that actually bounds the content of the node processed.
- Padding—As with a table cell, this represents the area between the content rectangle and the border.
- Border—This is the border area of the content-rectangle, similar to the border of a table cell.

There are four types of general areas that are used to describe the formatted page:

- Regions—Regions describe broad areas on a page—for example, a page in a word processor might have three regions, such as a header, body, and footer. However, in XSL, there are actually a number of regions: In addition to top, bottom, and left and right margins, there is a region-body that is the document body, and it is bounded by a region-before, region-after, region-start, and region-end. The relationship of these regions is shown in Figure 8.1.
- Block areas—Block areas are areas that represent block-level elements, such as a paragraph of text. Block elements are placed into regions for the sake of formatting.
- Line areas—Block areas are composed of line areas. For example, a line of text in a paragraph would be a line area. Line areas are composed of inline areas and inline spaces.
- Inline areas—Inline areas are the building blocks, such as characters, which together form line areas.

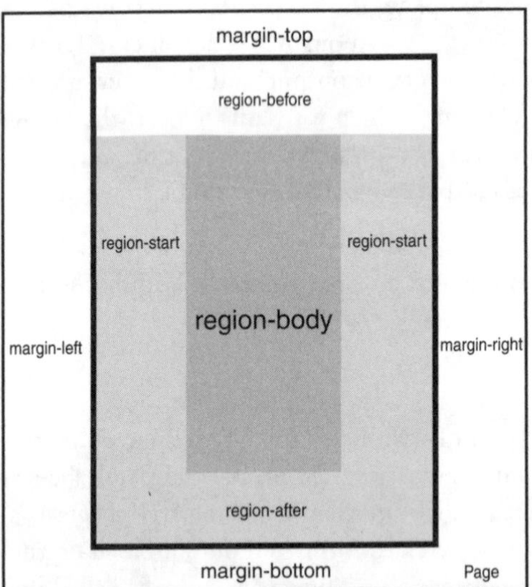

Figure 8.1
The relationship between the region area elements in XSL.

FORMATTING OBJECTS AND PROPERTIES

When the W3C first moved from a complex stylesheet language such as DSSSL to XSL, the standard quickly became very comprehensive and complex. That led to the XSL standard being split into XSL and XSL Transformations. Remaining as the bulk of the XSL Recommendation are Formatting Objects, which is a vocabulary that enables authors to express very high-level formatting in an XML-based syntax. Formatting Objects allow authors to control page layout, document pagination, and typesetting styles. When used in conjunction with XSL Transformations, the Formatting Objects allow very tight control over the formatting of XML documents for print applications, such as output to PDF files.

For the purposes of layout and visual formatting, there are a number of XSL Formatting Objects that can be manipulated to change the display properties that are applied to an XML document. Each one of these objects will also have a number of properties that can be manipulated to specify the details of the layout.

FORMATTING OBJECTS

There are more than 50 Formatting Objects specified for XSL. Each one of these objects describes some aspect of the layout of your document. Each object has a number of properties that can be changed to change the way that object is rendered in the final output. Just as XML elements act as nouns, and attributes as adjectives, Formatting Objects are more concrete, with additional information that can be used to modify the object itself.

For example, the `fo:table` object is used to describe how a table is to be formatted. Depending on the type of documents you are working with, some of these objects might be of little use; however, you should glance over what objects are available to become familiar with the resources you have at hand. Table 8.1 shows a summary of the Formatting Objects, which you might find useful.

TABLE 8.1 A SUMMARY OF THE MOST COMMONLY USED FORMATTING OBJECTS

Formatting Objects Summary	
Declarations and Pagination and Layout Formatting Objects	`fo:root`
	`fo:declarations`
	`fo:color-profile`
	`fo:page-sequence`
	`fo:layout-master-set`
	`fo:page-sequence-master`
	`fo:single-page-master-reference`
	`fo:repeatable-page-master-reference`
	`fo:repeatable-page-master-alternatives`
	`fo:conditional-page-master-reference`
	`fo:simple-page-master`
	`fo:region-body`
	`fo:region-before`
	`fo:region-after`
	`fo:region-start`
	`fo:region-end`
	`fo:flow`

TABLE 8.1 CONTINUED

Formatting Objects Summary	
	`fo:static-content`
	`fo:title`
Block-level Formatting Objects	`fo:block`
	`fo:block-container`
Inline-level Formatting Objects	`fo:bidi-override`
	`fo:character`
	`fo:initial-property-set`
	`fo:external-graphic`
	`fo:instream-foreign-object`
	`fo:inline`
	`fo:inline-container`
	`fo:leader`
	`fo:page-number`
	`fo:page-number-citation`
Formatting Objects for Tables	`fo:table-and-caption`
	`fo:table`
	`fo:table-column`
	`fo:table-caption`
	`fo:table-header`
	`fo:table-footer`
	`fo:table-body`
	`fo:table-row`
	`fo:table-cell`
Formatting Objects for Lists	`fo:list-block`
	`fo:list-item`
	`fo:list-item-body`
	`fo:list-item-label`

As you can see, there is a wide range of Formatting Objects: objects that allow you to create page masters for your documents, objects that allow you to change color and font properties within your documents, and even objects that are designed to allow you to format your data into lists or tables.

We will take a closer look at the Formatting Objects and their usage when we explore XSL-FO in more detail in Chapter 10.

PROPERTIES

Each of the XSL Formatting Objects has a number of properties associated with it. These are the properties of which you will change the values in order to change the appearance of elements in your XML file. For example, a block object might have various font properties, such as the font face and size, which you can change to modify the appearance of lines of text that appear within the block.

Table 8.2 contains a summary of some of the more common formatting object properties that you will encounter when working with XSL-FO.

TABLE 8.2 COMMONLY USED FORMATTING OBJECT PROPERTIES

Common Formatting Object Properties	
Common Absolute Position Properties	`absolute-position`
	`top`
	`right`
	`bottom`
	`left`
Common Border, Padding, and Background Properties	`background-attachment`
	`background-color`
	`background-image`
	`background-repeat`
	`background-position-horizontal`
	`background-position-vertical`
	`border-before-color`
	`border-before-style`
	`border-before-width`
	`border-after-color`
	`border-after-style`
	`border-after-width`
	`border-start-color`
	`border-start-style`
	`border-start-width`
	`border-end-color`
	`border-end-style`
	`border-end-width`
	`border-top-color`

TABLE 8.2 CONTINUED

Common Formatting Object Properties	
	border-top-style
	border-top-width
	border-bottom-color
	border-bottom-style
	border-bottom-width
	border-left-color
	border-left-style
	border-left-width
	border-right-color
	border-right-style
	border-right-width
	padding-before
	padding-after
	padding-start
	padding-end
	padding-top
	padding-bottom
	padding-left
	padding-right
Common Font Properties	font-family
	font-selection-strategy
	font-size
	font-stretch
	font-size-adjust
	font-style
	font-variant
	font-weight
Common Margin Properties-Block	margin-top
	margin-bottom
	margin-left
	margin-right
	space-before

Table 8.2 continued

Common Formatting Object Properties	
	space-after
	start-indent
	end-indent
Area Alignment Properties	alignment-adjust
	alignment-baseline
	baseline-shift
	display-align
	dominant-baseline
	relative-align
Area Dimension Properties	block-progression-dimension
	content-height
	content-width
	height
	inline-progression-dimension
	max-height
	max-width
	min-height
	min-width
	scaling
	scaling-method
	width
Block and Line-related Properties	hyphenation-keep
	hyphenation-ladder-count
	last-line-end-indent
	line-height
	line-height-shift-adjustment
	line-stacking-strategy
	linefeed-treatment
	white-space-treatment
	text-align
	text-align-last
	text-indent

TABLE 8.2 CONTINUED

Common Formatting Object Properties	
	white-space-collapse
	wrap-option
Character Properties	character
	letter-spacing
	suppress-at-line-break
	text-decoration
	text-shadow
	text-transform
	treat-as-word-space
	word-spacing
Color-related Properties	color
	color-profile-name
	rendering-intent
Layout-related Properties	clip
	overflow
	reference-orientation
	span
Leader and Rule Properties	leader-alignment
	leader-pattern
	leader-pattern-width
	leader-length
	rule-style
	rule-thickness
Pagination and Layout Properties	blank-or-not-blank
	column-count
	column-gap
	extent
	flow-name
	force-page-count
	initial-page-number
	master-name
	master-reference

TABLE 8.2 CONTINUED

Common Formatting Object Properties	
	maximum-repeats
	media-usage
	odd-or-even
	page-height
	page-position
	page-width
	precedence
	region-name
Table Properties	border-after-precedence
	border-before-precedence
	border-collapse
	border-end-precedence
	border-separation
	border-start-precedence
	caption-side
	column-number
	column-width
	empty-cells
	ends-row
	number-columns-repeated
	number-columns-spanned
	number-rows-spanned
	starts-row
	table-layout
	table-omit-footer-at-break
	table-omit-header-at-break

Again, as with the Formatting Objects themselves, this table is provided as some summary information for your use as we begin to work with stylesheets in more detail. We will look at the mechanism for working directly with object properties in Chapter 10.

INTRODUCING XPATH

To perform formatting or transformations on an XML document, you must have some mechanism for locating the elements and attributes you want to either transform or apply formatting data to. That is where XPath comes in. XPath is a Recommendation from the W3C that deals specifically with locating elements and attributes within an XML document. There is an entire syntax and structure associated with XPath that is quite flexible and powerful—so powerful, in fact, that we have given it a separate chapter, and we will be covering XPath in much greater detail in Chapter 11, "Locating Components in XML Documents with XPath."

However, to effectively talk about using XSLT and XSL-FO in the next few chapters, it is necessary to discuss a little bit about XPath here. For example, in the previous stylesheet examples shown, we've already used XPath in our `<xsl:template>` and `<xsl:value-of>` elements:

```
<xsl:template match="description">
```

```
<xsl:value-of select="."/>
```

So, now let's start with a simple XML document, which doesn't really have any meaning, but we've chosen colors for our element names for the purposes of demonstration:

```
<colors>
 <red tint="pink">
  <green>
   <blue/>
  </green>
 </red>
</colors>
```

Now, if we are working with this document and an XSL Stylesheet, we'll start processing at the root node. The root node is the parent of all the nodes in a document. There is only one root node per document. It includes all processing instructions, comments, and elements. In this case, the root contains all the elements beginning with `<color>`, which is the root element.

So, in that context, let's see what some of the XPath expressions would accomplish:

- `red`

  This expression would match any `red` elements within the current context.

- `red/green`

  This expression would match any `green` elements that are children of a `red` element.

- `/`

  Matches the root node of the document.

- `red//blue`

  Matches any `blue` element with `red` as an ancestor. Keep in mind that this matches all `blue` elements that are descendants of any `red` element.

- `//green`

  Matches any `green` element anywhere in the document.

- `.`

  This is used to represent the current node.

- `.//green`

  Matches any `green` elements that are descendants of the current node.

- `red[@tint]`

  Matches any `red` element that has a `tint` attribute present, regardless of the attribute value.

- `red[@tint="pink"]`

  Matches any `red` elements that have a `tint` attribute with the value of `"pink"`.

Now you should have enough of XPath to follow the discussion in the next couple of chapters. We might still use some XPath syntax you aren't familiar with, but this is a good starting point, and you can revisit any examples in Chapters 9 and 10 which are not clear after you've finished mastering XPath in Chapter 11.

For now, let's move on to take a closer look at XSLT in Chapter 9.

Additional Resources

There is certainly no shortage of XSL and XSLT resources on the Web, ranging from the official resources at the W3C to vendor sites describing XSL products and tutorials, to articles on XSL at various XML sites.

The extensive resources for would be too numerous to list here. However, there are some sites that are much better than others, offer some important software, or can serve as a good jumping point for other XSL resources. Here is a selection of those sites for you to find out more about XSL.

- W3C XSL Site (`http://www.w3.org/Style/XSL/`)—The W3C maintains this site, which contains links to the official XSL and XSLT Recommendation. In addition, there are links to a number of tutorials, articles, and other resources for working with XSL.
- W3C XSL Recommendation (`http://www.w3.org/TR/xsl/`)—This is the link to the official XSL 1.0 Recommendation. The XSL Recommendation includes information about XSL-FO.
- W3C XSLT Recommendation (`http://www.w3.org/TR/xslt`)—This is the link to the XSL Transformations Recommendation.
- XSL FAQ (`http://www.dpawson.co.uk/xsl/xslfaq.html`)—This is the Frequently Asked Questions site for all things related to XSL, including both XSL-FO and XSLT.
- FOP (`http://xml.apache.org/fop/`)—FOP is an open-source, Java-based XSL-FO formatting engine that is released by the Apache Project.

- Saxon (`http://saxon.sourceforge.net/`)—Saxon is an open-source, Java-based XSLT engine. There are two versions available, one complete with source code, and another called "Instant Saxon," which is a simple Java executable.
- XSL Cover Pages (`http://xml.coverpages.org/xsl.html`)—Robin Cover maintains a site dedicated to tracking information related to all areas of XML. This is a link to the area of the site that deals specifically with XSL.
- XML.com (`http://www.xml.com/style/`)—XML.com also is a general XML resource; however, this is a link to the section of the site that contains information, articles, and tutorials directly related to XSL.

ROADMAP

In Chapter 7 we saw how XML could be displayed in browsers with Cascading Stylesheets. Although that is certainly a viable method for display, CSS was not designed to work with XML, and it does have some limitations.

We have seen how to work with CSS, and have been introduced to the concepts of working with XSL. Now we can move on to look more closely at the practical aspects of working with XSL.

The next step is to take a look at XSL Transformations and see how we can use XSLT to take XML and convert it into other formats, such as HTML, or how we can take an XML document with one set of tags and convert it into another XML document. The power to transform XML is one of the most powerful applications of XSL.

Then, we will move on to working with XSL as a formatting technology, looking at Formatting Objects and how we can use XSL-FO to display XML in print and for XSL-enabled browsers.

It's easy to see how display technologies such as XSL work with XML, because without them, XML would just be a text format, and although that might still be useful for working with XML as a data format, it would represent a step backward in terms of sharing information on the Web.

CHAPTER 9

Transforming XML Data into Other Formats with XSLT

In this chapter

by David Gulbransen

XSL TRANSFORMATIONS

Although you can use existing markup languages to process XML, as we saw with CSS in Chapter 7, "Using XML with Existing Stylesheet Technologies (CSS)," there are better solutions for working with XML—specifically, the Extensible Stylesheet Language (XSL).

As we learned in Chapter 8, "The New Wave of Stylesheets: XSL," there are a number of things you can do with XSL, not just limited to formatting XML for display in print or on the Web. Although XSL Formatting Objects deal with formatting XML for display, there is another Recommendation closely tied to XSL, which is XSL Transformations, or XSLT.

XSLT was created in 1999 as a spinoff Recommendation from the XSL Recommendation. The editors of the XSL draft recognized the potential for the ability to transform XML dynamically, and therefore XSLT was born. XSLT is an evolving standard; and, in fact, the W3C has already released a working draft for XSLT2.0.

XSLT enables you to create a stylesheet which, when applied to an XML document by an XSL parser, can actually manipulate the contents of the document. The potential ranges from the ability to insert HTML elements into your documents, to turning XML elements into HTML elements, to changing an element from one type of XML element to another.

The result is that you can use XSLT to create HTML documents from your XML, or you can use it to process and change XML documents from one XML vocabulary to another. The power to work with your XML documents that this creates is nearly limitless. So, now let's take a closer look at the components of XSLT, how they function, and how we can apply them to some sample XML documents.

THE XML FILE

XSLT by itself doesn't necessarily mean much, because the goal of authoring stylesheets is to apply it to an XML document. Therefore, for the sake of discussion and illustration as we explore XSLT, Listing 9.1 shows a well-formed XML document which we will be using as the basis for our examples.

LISTING 9.1 A SAMPLE WELL-FORMED XML DOCUMENT THAT WILL BE USED TO CLARIFY EXAMPLES IN THIS CHAPTER

```
<?xml version="1.0" ?>
<address_book>
 <contact>
  <name>
   <first>Jane</first>
   <last>Doe</last>
  </name>
  <address location="office">
   <street>123 Fake Street</street>
   <city>Springfield</city>
   <state>IL</state>
   <zip>49201</zip>
  </address>
```

Listing 9.1 continued

```
    <number type="office">708-555-1212</number>
    <number type="mobile">708-855-4848</number>
    <number type="fax">800-555-1212</number>
   </phone>
   <email>jane@doe.com</email>
  </contact>
  <contact>
   <name>
    <first>John</first>
    <last>Smith</last>
   </name>
   <address location="home">
    <street>205 Peaceful Lane</street>
    <city>Bloomington</city>
    <state>IN</state>
    <zip>47401</zip>
   </address>
   <address location="office">
    <street>8192 Busy Street</street>
    <city>Bloomington</city>
    <state>IN</state>
    <zip>47408</zip>
   </address>
   <phone>
    <number type="office">812-555-1212</number>
    <number type="mobile">812-855-4848</number>
    <number type="fax">800-333-0999</number>
   </phone>
   <email>john@smith.com</email>
   <email>johns@feemail.com</email>
  </contact>
 </address_book>
```

The XSLT Namespace

XSLT stylesheets, like all XSL stylesheets, are simply well-formed XML documents. They are text files, and must conform to all the rules of XML. Because XSLT stylesheets are text files, it's necessary to let parsers know that the elements contained in the document are a part of the XSLT Namespace—that is, that they are not just any generic XML elements and attributes, but that they are specifically stylesheet elements and attributes.

XSLT has the following Namespace, as defined in the Recommendation:

```
http://www.w3.org/1999/XSL/Transform
```

In practice, it is a very good idea to use this Namespace with a prefix when you are authoring your stylesheets. That's because you will be mixing a number of different types of elements in your sheet, such as HTML, and using the XSLT Namespace ensures that your documents will be parsed correctly.

Every XSL stylesheet has a root element, which is called `stylesheet`, which is where you would define the Namespace:

```
<xsl:stylesheet version="1.0"
  xmlns:xsl="http://www.w3.org/1999/XSL/Transform" >
```

Now let's examine the elements that make up the stylesheet itself.

`xls:stylesheet` AND `xsl:transform`

We mentioned that every stylesheet will have a root element called `stylesheet`. In fact, there are two root elements to choose from, either `stylesheet` or `transform`. Both of these elements are synonymous and therefore can be used interchangeably (although your start/end tags must still match). Some authors use the `stylesheet` element with XSL-FO sheets, and the `transform` element with XSLT, to provide some differentiation; however, there are no hard and fast rules, and it is perfectly acceptable to always use `stylesheet`.

The `stylesheet` element also has a number of attributes, which you can use with it to provide additional information, such as extensions. The most common attributes you will use, however, are

- `id`
- `version`

`id` is an attribute that allows you to specify an ID for the stylesheet. This can be useful later if you are importing stylesheets or working with multiple stylesheets.

The second is the `version` attribute, which must be used to specify the version of XSLT, which the stylesheet uses for processing. This attribute is required so always be sure to specify the version to avoid errors.

The `stylesheet` element can also have a number of elements as children. The more common of these child elements include

- `import`
- `include`
- `output`
- `decimal-format`
- `namespace-alias`
- `attribute-set`
- `variable`
- `template`

In the following sections, we will take a look at each of these child elements and their attributes and see how they are used within the stylesheet.

`xsl:include` AND `xsl:import`

Cascading stylesheets are designed to "cascade," or be linked together. Although XSL stylesheets aren't specifically designed to be linked together, there are a couple of mechanisms that can be used to link different sheets together, either by including them or importing them.

Both `xsl:include` and `xsl:import` have the same attribute:

- `href`

This is simply the reference to the sheet that is being imported, in the form of a URI. It can be either a relative path (such as just the filename if the stylesheets are in the same directories) or a URL that points to the stylesheet on the server.

9

The only practical difference between `include` and `import` is how rules are processed. If a stylesheet is included then the rules of the included stylesheet are processed just as if they were part of the including stylesheet. If a stylesheet is imported then the stylesheet that is importing the new stylesheet takes precedence over the stylesheet being imported.

xsl:output

As we learned in Chapter 8, when an XSL stylesheet is processed, the XSL engine reads the document tree, or source tree, and applies the stylesheet rules to produce a result tree. But what happens to that result tree next is up to the processor. XSL processors are not required to output the result tree, although most do. To help you specify how that result tree is output, you can use the `xsl:output` element to define some characteristics of how the final document is written.

The way in which outputting is performed is defined by a number of attributes:

- `method`—This attribute allows you to select which type of document is to be output, either "`xml`," "`html`," or "`text`." XSLT will add "`xhtml`" as an option. The default is "`xml`," although some processors may automatically select "`html`" if they detect that the first element in your result tree is an `<html>` element.
- `version`—The `version` attribute allows you to specify the version of the output method. For example, you could use this attribute to choose between HTML 3.2 or 4.0.
- `encoding`—This attribute allows you to specify a character encoding type for the document.
- `omit-xml-declaration`—This attribute accepts a value of either "yes" or "no" and specifies whether or not the processor should output the XML declaration.
- `standalone`—This attribute also accepts a value of "yes" or "no" and is used to specify whether the processor should output a "standalone" attribute.
- `doctype-public`—This attribute is used to specify the value of the "PUBLIC" identifier if you are working with a DOCTYPE declaration.
- `doctype-system`—This attribute is used to specify the value of the "SYSTEM" identifier if you are working with a DOCTYPE declaration.
- `cdata-section-elements`—This attribute allows you to specify any elements in your document which should have their content output within a CDATA section. This is useful only with `xml` output.

- `indent`—This accepts a value of "yes" or "no" to specify whether or not the output should be indented.
- `media-type`—This attribute allows you to specify a MIME content type for the document.

As you can see, there is a great deal of flexibility for working with output from XSLT. We'll look at how to use output later on in the chapter when we present some stylesheet examples.

xsl:decimal-format

In the United States, it is customary to represent decimal places with a period (.) and to separate groups of numbers using a comma (,). For example, we would write one thousand dollars and 23 cents as "$1,000.23." However, if we were dealing with the same amounts in many European countries, we might write the number as "1.000,23." Both are examples of different decimal formats.

The `decimal-format` element allows you to set how you want decimal numbers to be formatted within an element or stylesheet. There are a number of attributes that you can use to define the `decimal-format`:

- `name`—This attribute allows you to give a name to the decimal format, such as "`USA`," so that you can reference the format by name.
- `decimal-separator`—The `decimal-separator` attribute accepts a character as its value. For instance, if we wanted to specify that the separator were to be a comma, as in Europe, we would use this attribute.
- `grouping-separator`—This attribute also accepts a character, which is used to represent the character used to separate hundreds from thousands, from millions, and so on. In the U.S. decimal format, this is a comma.
- `infinity`—This allows you to specify a string that is used to represent infinity. The default value is the string `"Infinity"`.
- `minus-sign`—This allows you to specify a character that is used to represent the minus sign. The default value is the hyphen-minus character (`-`).
- `NaN`—This allows you to specify a string that is used to represent something that is not a number. The default value is the string `"NaN"`.
- `percent`—This allows you to specify a character that is used to represent a percentage. The default value is the percent sign (`%`).
- `zero-digit`—This allows you to specify a character that is used to represent zero. The default value is the character (`0`).
- `digit`—This allows you to specify a character that is used to represent digits. The default value is the character number sign (`#`).
- `pattern-separator`—This allows you to specify a character that is used as a pattern separator. The default value is the semicolon (`;`).

So, if we were to use the following:

```
<xsl:decimal-format decimal-separator="," grouping separator="."/>
```

the result would be decimal numbers in the format "`1.000,00`".

TEMPLATES

At the heart of the XSLT stylesheet are `template` elements. All the information in your stylesheet that is output will pass through a `template`. In short, they are the most important element in a stylesheet, and they are where you will define all the information for how text, elements, and attributes are to be output by your stylesheet.

There are a few elements that are related to templates and their use, so let's take a closer look at templates and how they function in XSL.

xsl:template

The most important element in the stylesheet is `xsl:template`. This element has several attributes, including `priority`, `mode`, `name`, and `match`. The `priority` attribute allows you to specify a numeric priority level for the template. The `mode` attribute allows you to assign a mode name to the template, so that you can apply it only to elements with the same mode name. The two attributes with which you will become intimately familiar as you use XSL are `name` and `match`.

The `name` attribute allows you to specify a name for a template, so that the template can be called later by the `call-templates` element, which we will discuss later.

The `match` attribute is a very important attribute, because this is what will determine what component your template will be applied to in the XML document. The value of the `match` attribute takes the form of an XPath expression, as we discussed in Chapter 8. XPath will also be covered in greater detail in Chapter 11, "Locating Components in XML Documents with XPath."

Now, let's see how templates work. Take our sample XML document. Let's say that we wanted to write a template, which would output our `<email>` element as an HTML tag with italic:

```
<xsl:stylesheet version="1.0"
   xmlns:xsl="http://www.w3.org/1999/XSL/Transform" >

<xsl:template match="address_book">
 <html>
 <xsl:apply-templates select="contact/email"/>
 </html>
</xsl:template>

<xsl:template match="email">
  Email: <i><xsl:value-of select="."/></i>
</xsl:template>
</xsl:stylesheet>
```

The result of this template would be

```
<html>
 Email: <i>jane@doe.com</i>
 Email: <i>john@smith.com</i>
 Email: <i>johns@feemail.com</i>
</html>
<xsl:template-match="/">
  <xsl:apply-templates/>
</xsl:template-match>
```

```
Node type--Rule

Element - Call <xsl:apply-templates> to process the child nodes.
Attributes - Copy the attribute value as text to the result tree
Text - Copy the text to the result tree
Comments - Do nothing
PIs - Do nothing
Namespaces - Do nothing
```

```
<?xml version="1.0" encoding="utf-8"?>



    Jane
   Doe

    123 Fake Street
   Springfield
   IL
   49201

    708-555-1212
   708-855-4848
   800-555-1212

   <html>
  Email: <i>jane@doe.com</i></html>



    John
   Smith
    205 Peaceful Lane
   Bloomington
   IN
   47401
   8192 Busy Street
   Bloomington
   IN
   47408
   812-555-1212
   812-855-4848
   800-333-0999
  <html>
  Email: <i>john@smith.com</i></html>
```

```
  <html>
  Email: <i>johns@feemail.com</i></html>

<xsl:template match="address_book">
 <html>
 <xsl:apply-templates select="contact/email"/>
 </html>
</xsl:template>

<xsl:template match="email">
  Email: <i><xsl:value-of select="."/></i>
</xsl:template>
</xsl:stylesheet>
```


because this template would first match the `address_book` element, and then apply the `email` template to any children of `contact` elements. When the `email` template is applied, the resulting value of the `email` element is inserted into the HTML code in the second template. The first thing that you should notice about the template is that the contents of the template include plain text, HTML tags, and additional XSL tags. Whatever is in the body of the template will be output, so you can directly place text and HTML in the body of the template. The HTML and text are kept separate from the XSL because of the "`xsl:`" Namespace that is used with XSL elements.

The other piece of the puzzle in the template is the XSL element:

```
<xsl:value-of select="."/>
```

This element is used to specify the value of whichever element or attribute we want to insert into the template body. Because the value of our `<email>` elements is the actual e-mail address, that is what is inserted into the HTML code.

We could also take the entire contents of our sample file and dump them out as text with one simple template:

```
<xsl:template match="/">
 <xsl:apply-templates />
</xsl:template>
```

The `apply-templates` element is used to communicate to the processor that it should apply the template to the current selected node. In the previous example, the node is specified as "`/`," or the root element, so it contains the entire document. Therefore, the output would be the text content of the file, stripped of elements and attributes:

```
Jane
Doe
office
123 Fake Street
Springfield
Etc…
```

xsl:value-of

The `xsl:value-of` element is used to insert the value of a component into the template. The `value-of` element has a `select` attribute for specifying the element or attribute you want to select the value of, using an XPath expression. As you can see, XPath plays a considerable role in the use of XSLT. Let's look at some `value-of` elements we might use with our example. If we wanted to insert the value of the `name` element to display the first and last names, we could use

```
<xsl:stylesheet version="1.0" xmlns:xsl="http://www.w3.org/1999/XSL/Transform"
xml:space="preserve">
<xsl:template match="contact">
 <html>
  <xsl:value-of select="name/first" /> <xsl:value-of select="name/last" />
 </html>
</xsl:template>

</xsl:stylesheet>
```

We have placed the two `value-of` elements side-by-side, because that is how they will be replaced in the document. Because XSLT ignores whitespace, in order to preserve the space between the names, we need to set the `xml:space` attribute to `"preserve"` in order to preserve the space in the output document.

```
<xsl:stylesheet version="1.0" xmlns:xsl="http://www.w3.org/1999/XSL/Transform"
xml:space="preserve">
```

You should also note that the template selects the contact node, which then becomes our context for locating the `first` and `last` elements, which are children of the `name` element.

`xsl:apply-templates`

Apply templates instruct the XSL processor to cycle through child elements of the selected node, which allows you to actually apply templates to more than just the root node of your document. You can use either the `apply-templates` element with no selector, as we did previously, which will process the current node, or a `select` attribute to specify a node to apply the template to. For example:

```
<xsl:template match="/">
 <xsl:apply-templates select="//address"/>
</xsl:template>
```

will first match the root node, and then apply the template to any `address` children because of the `apply-templates` element. The result is the output of the content of any address node children, such as `street`, `city`, `state`, and `zip`:

```
123 Fake Street
Springfield
IL
49201
205 Peaceful Lane
Bloomington
IN
47401
8192 Busy Street
Bloomington
IN
47408
```

For example, if we wanted to process the `name` elements, which are children of the `contact` element in our example, we could use

```
<xsl:template match="contact">
    <xsl:apply-templates select=".//name"/>
</xsl:template>
```

The resulting output would be

```
Jane
Doe
John
Smith
```


NAMED TEMPLATES

You can also call `templates` in your documents by name—for example, if you have the following template:

```
<xsl:template name="get-names" match="contact">
    <xsl:apply-templates select=".//name"/>
</xsl:template>
```

you could actually invoke this template using `call-template`:

```
<xsl:call-template name="get-names"/>
```

This has basically the same result as using `apply-templates`; however the biggest difference is that `call-template` does not have a `select` attribute that allows you to change the context.

GENERATING XML

So far, we've seen how you can use templates to insert new information, such as HTML tags, into the content of your XML documents. There are also some ways in which we can actually use XSLT to write elements and attributes into the output, effectively changing the XSL from one vocabulary to another.

xsl:element

The `xsl:element` element enables you to use a `template` to create a new element in your output. The `element` element takes three attributes:

- `name`—The `name` attribute allows you to specify the name of the element. This either can be a straightforward name, or it can take the form of an expression. This provides you with the power to generate dynamic names for your elements based on the content of the XML document being processed.
- `namespace`—This attribute can be used to establish a Namespace for your element.
- `use-attribute-sets`—This attribute is used to specify an attribute-set to be appended to the element. An attribute-set is simply a grouping of attributes, which can then be used with element generation.

Let's take a look how we could use the xsl:element with our address document. Say we wanted to convert our generic phone element into a set of elements, based on the type of phone number specified in the attribute:

```
<xsl:template match="address_book">
  <xsl:apply-templates select="contact/phone"/>
</xsl:template>

<xsl:template match="number">
  <xsl:element name="{@type}">
    <xsl:value-of select="."/>
  </xsl:element>
</xsl:template>
```


```
<xsl:template match="address_book">
  <xsl:apply-templates select="contact/phone"/>
</xsl:template>

<xsl:template match="number">
  <xsl:element name="{@type}">
    <xsl:value-of select="."/>
  </xsl:element>
</xsl:template>
```


In the previous example, the name of the new element is actually generated by the expression "{@type}", which results in the content of the type attribute for the phone number being used as the name. The result is a new element for each separate number:

```
<office>708-555-1212</office>
<mobile>708-855-4848</mobile>
<fax>800-555-1212</fax>

<office>812-555-1212</office>
<mobile>812-855-4848</mobile>
<fax>800-333-0999</fax>
```

xsl:attribute

In addition to being able to generate elements, you can also use the xsl:attribute element to generate attributes in the output. There are two attributes you can use with the xsl:attribute element:

- name—Specifies the name of the attribute.
- namespace—Specifies the Namespace for the attribute.

The use of the xsl:attribute follows the form of the element pretty closely; however, the attribute element must be nested within an element, or a tag pair:

```
<xsl:template match="contact">
<xsl:element name="office">
 <xsl:attribute name="phone">
  <xsl:value-of select="phone/number"/>
```

```
 </xsl:attribute>
</xsl:element>
</xsl:template>
```

xsl:attribute-set

Attribute sets are a mechanism for grouping together commonly used attributes, which can then be assigned to use with an `xsl:element` element using the `use-attribute-set` attribute.

9

An attribute set has two attributes:

- `name`—This enables you to define a name for the attribute set.
- `use-attribute-sets`—You can include other attribute sets within an attribute set by referencing an existing attribute set in this attribute. Keep in mind that it is an error for an attribute set to reference itself.

The `attribute-set` itself will contain any number of `attribute` elements. For example:

```
<xsl:attribute-set name="specs">
 <xsl:attribute name="size">
  <xsl:value-of select="item/@size"/>
 </xsl:attribute>
 <xsl:attribute name="color">
  <xsl:value-of select="item/@color"/>
 </xsl:attribute>
</xsl:attribute-set>
```

This attribute set could then be used with `xsl:element`:

```
<xsl:element name="shirt" use-attribute-set ="specs">
</xsl:element>
```

which will result in the created element having attributes of `size` and `color`.

Attribute sets can be a great way to group together a large number of attributes that are going to be used with a single element, or to create a group for attributes that are going to be used repeatedly.

xsl:text

The `xsl:text` element allows you to insert text into the output. It has only one attribute:

- disable-output-escaping

which allows you to toggle on and off the escaping of symbols in the text stream. The use of `xsl:text` is straightforward:

```
<xsl:text>This will insert text into the output.</xsl:text>
```

xsl:comment

Commenting your code is not only good style, it's an easy way to pass along messages to people who might be using your documents. The `xsl:comment` element enables you to insert comments into the output. For example:

```
<xsl:comment>This file was generated automatically with XSLT</xsl:comment>
```

would result in the following comment being inserted into the final output document:

```
<!-- This file was generated automatically with XSLT -->
```

xsl:copy

There are times when you might simply want to copy the contents of an element from one document to another without any changes. To accomplish this, you can use the `xsl:copy` element, which simply copies the element from the document tree to the result tree.

You can use the `use-attribute-sets` attribute with the `xsl:copy` element if you want to add an attribute set to the element during the copy.

If we wanted to copy the name element without any intervention, we could use the following template:

```
<xsl:template match="name">
  <xsl:copy>
   <xsl:apply-templates/>
  </xsl:copy>
 </xsl:template>
```

REPETITION

Repetition is natural in the processing of XML documents. The nature of the tree involves stepping through the document node-by-node and applying the transformations laid out in the templates. There are many occasions when you will want to apply the same formatting to a number of the same type of elements. For example, if you had an XML document that described the employees in your company, and you were transforming it into an HTML document for the Web, you might want to create a table with each employee's name in it. For this operation, you would basically want to repeat the operation for the number of times an element occurred.

Fortunately, there is a mechanism built into XSLT, which makes this kind of repetitious processing very easy—the `xsl:for-each` element.

xsl:for-each

The `xsl:for-each` element can contain a template, or other structures, for creating elements, and has one attribute, `select`. The `select` attribute allows you to choose what condition the repetition will be based on.

For example, let's say that we wanted to create an element for our phone numbers in our address XML document. We could use the `for-each` structure to create a new element for each of the `number` children for each `phone`:

```
<xsl:template match="contact">
 <xsl:for-each select="phone/number">
 <xsl:element name="{@type}">
  <xsl:value-of select="."/>
```

```
    </xsl:element>
    </xsl:for-each>
   </xsl:template>
```

CONDITIONAL PROCESSING

One of the more powerful features of XSL is the ability to do conditional processing. If you are familiar with any programming or scripting languages, then you are probably already familiar with conditional processing.

9

The idea is that you establish a condition, a test, and if that test is met, you continue with the remainder of the processing. The most common structure for conditional processing is an "if…then" structure.

XSLT does have some structures for conditional processing: `if`, `choose`, `when`, and `otherwise`.

`xsl:if`

The `xsl:if` element allows you to perform a test, and if that test turns out to be true, you can then perform some transformation. The element accepts one attribute:

- `test`

The `test` attribute must be a boolean XPath expression. XPath will be covered in greater detail in Chapter 11. However, there are a number of functions that can be used to perform tests. For now, it's just important to know that the test either returns true, and the contents of the `if` element are executed, or it returns false and they are not.

For example, if we wanted to generate a list of the people in our address book, and insert a dashed line between entries; however, we did not want to have the line after the last entry, we could use:

```
<xsl:template match="address_book">
  <xsl:apply-templates select="contact"/>
</xsl:template>

<xsl:template match="contact">
  <xsl:value-of select="."/>
  <xsl:if test="position() != last()">--------</xsl:if>
</xsl:template>
```


```
<xsl:template match="address_book">
  <xsl:apply-templates select="contact"/>
</xsl:template>

<xsl:template match="contact">
  <xsl:value-of select="."/>
  <xsl:if test="position() != last()">--------</xsl:if>
</xsl:template>
```

xsl:choose, xsl:when, xsl:otherwise

If you are familiar with conditionals from other areas, you might also be familiar with a mechanism that allows you to choose between different cases, such as "case…switch." The idea here is that you have a few different tests you want to perform, with a different template or transformation to perform based on which test is true.

To perform this type of conditional processing, you need to make use of three structures:

- xsl:choose
- xsl:when
- xsl:otherwise

The first element, choose, is the parent element for both the when and the otherwise elements. The tests are specified in the when element using a test attribute. You can use any number of when elements as children of the choose.

The when element functions similarly to an if element, allowing you to perform a test, and if the test is true, then perform the transformation. If the test is false, then the processor moves on to evaluate the next when.

The final element in the structure is the otherwise element, which acts as a catchall. If none of the when tests turns out to be true, the transformation specified in the otherwise is performed instead. Here's what the structure looks like:

```
<xsl:choose>
 <xsl:when test="Some test">
  <!-- Transformation One -->
  </xsl:when>
  <xsl:when test="Another test">
  <!-- Transformation Two -->
  </xsl:when>
  <xsl:otherwise>
  <!-- Transformation Three -->
  </xsl:otherwise>
</xsl:choose>
```

Just as with the if element, the tests are expressed using XPath, which is covered in more detail in Chapter 11.

SORTING

Another feature of XSLT is the ability to sort elements based on a specific set of criteria.

xsl:sort

Attributes:

- select—This attribute uses an XPath expression to select the component, which is used as the key for the sort.

- `lang`—This attribute allows you to select the language for the sort, which will govern how alphabetical sorting will occur, based on the character set for the specified language.
- `data-type`—This attribute allows you to specify the datatype of the key values, which are used in sorting, and can accept values of `text` or `number`. If `text` is selected, then the sort is performed in accordance with the rules for sorting text, based on the language selected. If `number` is selected, then the sort is performed based on a numbered order.
- `order`—This allows you to specify if the sort should result in the sorted items being in `ascending` or `descending` order. Those are the only two acceptable values for this attribute.
- `case-order`—Case order accepts one of two values, `upper-first` or `lower-first`. This determines how two of the same character, but different case, should be sorted. For example, with `upper-first`, "a" would sort as "A a." With `lower-first`, it would sort "a A."

For example, if we wanted to sort the names of our contacts in descending order, we could use the following templates:

```
<xsl:template match="address_book">
    <xsl:apply-templates select="contact">
      <xsl:sort order="descending" select="name/last"/>
    </xsl:apply-templates>
</xsl:template>

<xsl:template match="contact">
    <xsl:value-of select="name/last"/>,<xsl:value-of select="name/first"/>
    <xsl:text>
    </xsl:text>
</xsl:template>
```

NUMBERING

In addition to sorting, you can also use XSLT to automate the numbering of items. For example, if you had a list of names that you wanted to number, you could use the `xsl:number` element to automatically process the names for numbering.

xsl:number

The `xsl:number` element allows you to number items automatically, based on criteria you select, and with a numbering system, which you specify. The element accepts a number of attributes, including

- `format`—The `format` attribute allows you to specify the number format to be used for numbering. The default value is "1"; however, you can also substitute characters, to number items with letters—for instance A, B, C.... Common values for `format` include "A," "a," "I," and "i."

- `value`—This attribute is an XPath expression that is used to match the item being numbered. For instance, "position()" will cause the item to be numbered by its document position.
- `level`—The level attribute lets you select how deep in the source tree items should be considered for numbering. The default value is `single`, which means that only one level will be recursed for numbering. You can also specify `multiple` or `any`.
- `count`—The `count` attribute enables you to specify a pattern for what nodes should be counted at a specific level. This allows you to narrow the number of items to be counted.
- `from`—The `from` attribute enables you to specify the node from where counting should begin (based on an XPath pattern).
- `lang`—This attribute enables you to select the language of the numbering system.
- `grouping-separator`—This attribute enables you to specify the character used to separate groupings in the number—for instance, the comma in the number 1,000.
- `grouping-size`—The `grouping-size` has a default value of three (3), which is the number of digits grouped and separated by the `grouping-separator`.

For example, let's say we wanted to number the phone numbers in our address XML document. To do this, we could first select the phone element and sort the numbers, and then we would apply the numbering based on position:

```
<xsl:stylesheet version="1.0"
  xmlns:xsl="http://www.w3.org/1999/XSL/Transform" >

<xsl:template match="contact">
  <xsl:value-of select="name"/>
  <xsl:for-each select="phone/number">
    <xsl:sort select="."/>
      <xsl:number value="position()" format="1. "/>
      <xsl:value-of select="."/>
      <xsl:text>
      </xsl:text>
  </xsl:for-each>
</xsl:template>

</xsl:stylesheet>
```

Applying this template to our document would result in the following output:

```
   Jane
   Doe
  1. 708-555-1212
  2. 708-855-4848
  3. 800-555-1212


   John
   Smith
  1. 800-333-0999
  2. 812-555-1212
  3. 812-855-4848
```

AN XML-TO-XML TRANSFORMATION EXAMPLE

With all of these basic elements of XSLT, it is actually possible to accomplish quite a bit. We have steered away from some of the more advanced XSLT topics, which require a more full understanding of stylesheets than is possible in one chapter in this book. But that doesn't mean that you can't actually get some practical things done using the processes outlined in this chapter.

So, now let's take a look at exactly what we can do, starting with the conversion of an XML document from one XML syntax to another.

In this example, we're going to start with an XML document that describes some travel information for airline ticket holders. The data here is contact information, and information related to the flight, such as seat assignments, gates, and so on.

This is all the type of information that the airline needs for ticketing, but which travel agents also provide to clients in the form of an itinerary.

In this example, we're going to take our `travel.xml` document and using XSLT, transform the document into an `itinerary.xml` document.

Let's start by looking at the first XML document, shown in Listing 9.2.

LISTING 9.2 THE TRAVEL.XML DOCUMENT THAT WILL BE TRANSFORMED USING VARIOUS STYLESHEETS

```
<?xml version="1.0" ?>
<travel>

 <passenger>
  <name>Sally Smith</name>
  <address>
   <street>555 W. 3rd</street>
   <city>Chicago</city>
   <state>IL</state>
   <zip>60647</zip>
  </address>
  <phone>312-555-1212</phone>
  <ticket>
   <departure date="10/10/02" time="10:00 AM" gate="A6">
    <flight number="839" seat="6F" meal="None"/>
    <airport code="ORD"/>
   </departure>
   <arrival date="10/10/02" time="10:45 AM" gate="B12">
    <flight number="839"/>
    <airport code="IND"/>
   </arrival>
  </ticket>
 </passenger>

<passenger>
  <name>John Dough</name>
  <address>
```

LISTING 9.2 CONTINUED

```
    <street>123 Fake Street</street>
    <city>Chicago</city>
    <state>IL</state>
    <zip>60622</zip>
   </address>
   <phone>773-888-1234</phone>
   <passport issued="3/15/00" expires="3/15/05" origin="US" number="00000092"/>
   <ticket>
    <departure date="8/13/02" time="2:00 PM" gate="C23">
     <flight number="082" seat="A2" meal="Vegetarian"/>
     <airport code="ORD"/>
    </departure>
    <connecting date="8/13/02" time="5:00 PM" gate="F15">
     <flight number="332" seat="B3" meal="Vegetarian"/>
     <airport code="JFK"/>
    </connecting>
    <arrival date="8/14/02" time="7:00 AM" gate="B10">
     <flight number="332"/>
     <airport code="LHR"/>
    </arrival>
    <notes>Super Mile Program #22233</notes>
   </ticket>
  </passenger>

</travel>
```

We want to convert this document into an itinerary format supplied by the travel agent, resulting in the document shown in Listing 9.4.

First, we need to start with the XSL Namespace and the `stylesheet` element:

```
<xsl:stylesheet version="1.0"
   xmlns:xsl="http://www.w3.org/1999/XSL/Transform" >
```

Next, we want to specify the output method as "xml" and we want to indent our output to help keep things readable. If this were an entirely automated process, we might not care much about the indentation, but here we certainly do:

```
<xsl:output method="xml" indent="yes"/>
```

The next step is to define our first template, which we will use to select the root element and get to the passenger information:

```
 <xsl:template match="travel">
  <xsl:element name="travel_information">
   <xsl:apply-templates select="//passenger"/>
  </xsl:element>
 </xsl:template>
```

Here, we are matching the `travel` element of our original document and then writing a new element called `travel_information`, which is the new root element for our new document. We are then using the `apply-templates` to call the template for the `passenger` elements in our document.

Next, we have the template, which will match our passenger element, that looks like a rather complex template. However, if you look closely, all we are really doing is starting with the passenger element and then writing out a new element called itinerary. The itinerary will then contain a contact element, which has children of the name and address elements that are called with the apply-templates:

```
<xsl:template match="//passenger">
 <xsl:element name="itinerary">
  <xsl:element name="contact">
   <xsl:apply-templates select="name"/>
   <xsl:apply-templates select="address"/>
  </xsl:element>
  <xsl:element name="departing">
   <xsl:apply-templates select="ticket/departure"/>
  </xsl:element>
  <xsl:element name="connecting">
   <xsl:apply-templates select="ticket/connecting"/>
  </xsl:element>
  <xsl:element name="arriving">
   <xsl:apply-templates select="ticket/arrival"/>
  </xsl:element>
 </xsl:element>
</xsl:template>
```

After defining the contact element, we actually write the remaining three elements in the itinerary, which are departing, connecting, and arriving.

If you look closely, though, we don't actually do anything with those elements, but we use apply-templates to match those elements. Let's now look at the other templates.

First, we have the name element, which is actually the same in both documents. Because the content is the same, we can actually use the xsl:copy element to copy the element from one document to the next:

```
<xsl:template match="name">
 <xsl:copy>
  <xsl:apply-templates/>
 </xsl:copy>
</xsl:template>
```

In the previous template, the match element selects the context of the name element, and then copy copies the element.

Moving on to the address, we have another situation where we are primarily copying elements. We start by matching the address element and then applying the templates for the individual address components:

```
<xsl:template match="address">
 <xsl:copy>
  <xsl:apply-templates select="street"/>
  <xsl:apply-templates select="city"/>
  <xsl:apply-templates select="state"/>
  <xsl:apply-templates select="zip"/>
 </xsl:copy>
</xsl:template>
```

The address elements themselves are just a series of `xsl:copy` elements because the address information isn't changing, and neither are the elements for the address information:

```
<xsl:template match="street">
 <xsl:copy>
  <xsl:apply-templates/>
 </xsl:copy>
</xsl:template>

<xsl:template match="city">
 <xsl:copy>
  <xsl:apply-templates/>
 </xsl:copy>
</xsl:template>

<xsl:template match="state">
 <xsl:copy>
  <xsl:apply-templates/>
 </xsl:copy>
</xsl:template>

<xsl:template match="zip">
 <xsl:copy>
  <xsl:apply-templates/>
 </xsl:copy>
</xsl:template>

<xsl:template match="phone">
 <xsl:copy>
  <xsl:apply-templates/>
 </xsl:copy>
</xsl:template>
```

Now we are ready to deal with the departing, connecting, and arriving information for each passenger. Here, we start with a template, which will match the `departure` element in our original document:

```
<xsl:template match="ticket/departure">
```

From there, we will create the first element in our `departing` element, which will be the airport information. We select the `airport` element, and then insert the value of the `code` attribute, using the `xsl:value-of` element:

```
  <xsl:element name="airport">
   <xsl:value-of select="airport/@code"/>
  </xsl:element>
```

This is the same basic process that we use for each of the remaining pieces of information. First, we select the appropriate element, and then we specify the attribute which we are using as the value of our new element, using `xsl:value-of`:

```
  <xsl:element name="date">
   <xsl:value-of select="@date"/>
  </xsl:element>
  <xsl:element name="time">
```

```
    <xsl:value-of select="@time"/>
   </xsl:element>
   <xsl:element name="flight">
    <xsl:value-of select="flight/@number"/>
   </xsl:element>
   <xsl:element name="seat">
    <xsl:value-of select="flight/@seat"/>
   </xsl:element>
   <xsl:element name="gate">
    <xsl:value-of select="@gate"/>
   </xsl:element>
 </xsl:template>
```

The process is essentially the same for the information relating to connecting and arrival information:

```
 <xsl:template match="ticket/connecting">
   <xsl:element name="airport">
    <xsl:value-of select="airport/@code"/>
   </xsl:element>
   <xsl:element name="date">
    <xsl:value-of select="@date"/>
   </xsl:element>
   <xsl:element name="time">
    <xsl:value-of select="@time"/>
   </xsl:element>
   <xsl:element name="flight">
    <xsl:value-of select="flight/@number"/>
   </xsl:element>
   <xsl:element name="gate">
    <xsl:value-of select="@gate"/>
   </xsl:element>
 </xsl:template>

<xsl:template match="ticket/arrival">
   <xsl:element name="airport">
    <xsl:value-of select="airport/@code"/>
   </xsl:element>
   <xsl:element name="date">
    <xsl:value-of select="@date"/>
   </xsl:element>
   <xsl:element name="time">
    <xsl:value-of select="@time"/>
   </xsl:element>
   <xsl:element name="flight">
    <xsl:value-of select="flight/@number"/>
   </xsl:element>
   <xsl:element name="gate">
    <xsl:value-of select="@gate"/>
   </xsl:element>
 </xsl:template>
</xsl:stylesheet>
```

When we bring all of these pieces together, the resulting stylesheet is shown in Listing 9.3.

LISTING 9.3 THE ITINERARY.XSL STYLESHEET THAT WILL BE APPLIED TO THE TRAVEL.XML DOCUMENT TO GENERATE THE NEW ITINERARY.XML DOCUMENT

```
<xsl:stylesheet version="1.0"
  xmlns:xsl="http://www.w3.org/1999/XSL/Transform" >

 <xsl:output method="xml" indent="yes"/>

 <xsl:template match="travel">
  <xsl:element name="travel_information">
   <xsl:apply-templates select="//passenger"/>
  </xsl:element>
 </xsl:template>

 <xsl:template match="//passenger">
  <xsl:element name="itinerary">
   <xsl:element name="contact">
    <xsl:apply-templates select="name"/>
    <xsl:apply-templates select="address"/>
   </xsl:element>
   <xsl:element name="departing">
    <xsl:apply-templates select="ticket/departure"/>
   </xsl:element>
   <xsl:element name="connecting">
    <xsl:apply-templates select="ticket/connecting"/>
   </xsl:element>
   <xsl:element name="arriving">
    <xsl:apply-templates select="ticket/arrival"/>
   </xsl:element>
  </xsl:element>
 </xsl:template>

 <xsl:template match="name">
  <xsl:copy>
   <xsl:apply-templates/>
  </xsl:copy>
 </xsl:template>

 <xsl:template match="address">
  <xsl:copy>
   <xsl:apply-templates select="street"/>
   <xsl:apply-templates select="city"/>
   <xsl:apply-templates select="state"/>
   <xsl:apply-templates select="zip"/>
  </xsl:copy>
 </xsl:template>

 <xsl:template match="street">
  <xsl:copy>
   <xsl:apply-templates/>
  </xsl:copy>
 </xsl:template>

 <xsl:template match="city">
  <xsl:copy>
   <xsl:apply-templates/>
```

LISTING 9.3 CONTINUED

```
  </xsl:copy>
 </xsl:template>

 <xsl:template match="state">
  <xsl:copy>
   <xsl:apply-templates/>
  </xsl:copy>
 </xsl:template>

 <xsl:template match="zip">
  <xsl:copy>
   <xsl:apply-templates/>
  </xsl:copy>
 </xsl:template>

 <xsl:template match="phone">
  <xsl:copy>
   <xsl:apply-templates/>
  </xsl:copy>
 </xsl:template>

 <xsl:template match="ticket/departure">
   <xsl:element name="airport">
    <xsl:value-of select="airport/@code"/>
   </xsl:element>
   <xsl:element name="date">
    <xsl:value-of select="@date"/>
   </xsl:element>
   <xsl:element name="time">
    <xsl:value-of select="@time"/>
   </xsl:element>
   <xsl:element name="flight">
    <xsl:value-of select="flight/@number"/>
   </xsl:element>
   <xsl:element name="seat">
    <xsl:value-of select="flight/@seat"/>
   </xsl:element>
   <xsl:element name="gate">
    <xsl:value-of select="@gate"/>
   </xsl:element>
 </xsl:template>

 <xsl:template match="ticket/connecting">
   <xsl:element name="airport">
    <xsl:value-of select="airport/@code"/>
   </xsl:element>
   <xsl:element name="date">
    <xsl:value-of select="@date"/>
   </xsl:element>
   <xsl:element name="time">
    <xsl:value-of select="@time"/>
   </xsl:element>
   <xsl:element name="flight">
    <xsl:value-of select="flight/@number"/>
   </xsl:element>
   <xsl:element name="gate">
```

9

LISTING 9.3 CONTINUED

```
      <xsl:value-of select="@gate"/>
    </xsl:element>
  </xsl:template>

  <xsl:template match="ticket/arrival">
    <xsl:element name="airport">
      <xsl:value-of select="airport/@code"/>
    </xsl:element>
    <xsl:element name="date">
      <xsl:value-of select="@date"/>
    </xsl:element>
    <xsl:element name="time">
      <xsl:value-of select="@time"/>
    </xsl:element>
    <xsl:element name="flight">
      <xsl:value-of select="flight/@number"/>
    </xsl:element>
    <xsl:element name="gate">
      <xsl:value-of select="@gate"/>
    </xsl:element>
  </xsl:template>
</xsl:stylesheet>
```

When we process this stylesheet using an XSLT engine such as Saxon (the Web site for Saxon can be found later in the resources section at the end of the chapter), we have the resulting new XML document that is shown in Listing 9.4.

LISTING 9.4 THE `itinerary.xml` FILE GENERATED BY APPLYING THE `itinerary.xsl` STYLESHEET TO THE `travel.xml` DOCUMENT

```
<?xml version="1.0" encoding="utf-8"?>
<travel_information>
   <itinerary>
      <contact>
         <name>Sally Smith</name>
         <address>
            <street>555 W. 3rd</street>
            <city>Chicago</city>
            <state>IL</state>
            <zip>60647</zip>
         </address>
      </contact>
      <departing>
         <airport>ORD</airport>
         <date>10/10/02</date>
         <time>10:00 AM</time>
         <flight>839</flight>
         <seat>6F</seat>
         <gate>A6</gate>
      </departing>
      <connecting/>
      <arriving>
         <airport>IND</airport>
```

LISTING 9.4 CONTINUED

```
         <date>10/10/02</date>
         <time>10:45 AM</time>
         <flight>839</flight>
         <gate>B12</gate>
      </arriving>
   </itinerary>
   <itinerary>
      <contact>
         <name>John Dough</name>
         <address>
            <street>123 Fake Street</street>
            <city>Chicago</city>
            <state>IL</state>
            <zip>60622</zip>
         </address>
      </contact>
      <departing>
         <airport>ORD</airport>
         <date>8/13/02</date>
         <time>2:00 PM</time>
         <flight>082</flight>
         <seat>A2</seat>
         <gate>C23</gate>
      </departing>
      <connecting>
         <airport>JFK</airport>
         <date>8/13/02</date>
         <time>5:00 PM</time>
         <flight>332</flight>
         <gate>F15</gate>
      </connecting>
      <arriving>
         <airport>LHR</airport>
         <date>8/14/02</date>
         <time>7:00 AM</time>
         <flight>332</flight>
         <gate>B10</gate>
      </arriving>
   </itinerary>
</travel_information>
```

AN XML-TO-HTML TRANSFORMATION EXAMPLE

Now let's look at an example of converting an XML document into an HTML document. We will start with the XML document in Listing 9.2, our `travel.xml` document, and work to produce an HTML-formatted itinerary.

As with any stylesheet, we start with the `stylesheet` element and Namespace:

```
<xsl:stylesheet version="1.0"
   xmlns:xsl="http://www.w3.org/1999/XSL/Transform" >
```

Next, we specify that the output method is HTML, and we will be indenting again for the sake of readability:

```
<xsl:output method="html" indent="yes"/>
```

The first template will match our root node, and will actually contain all the markup that we will have in the document:

```
<xsl:template match="/">
```

Now, because we are working with HTML, we can insert our markup directly into the template. We start with the `head` and `title` elements:

```
<head>
<title>Travel Itinerary</title>
</head>
```

Next, we want to step through the document and produce an itinerary for each passenger in the document. For this, we will use a `for-each` element, selected for the `travel/passenger`:

```
<xsl:for-each select="travel/passenger">
```

Then we add the markup, and where we want to include information from the source XML document, we do so with the `xsl:value-of`:

```
<h2>Travel Itinerary for <xsl:value-of select="name"/></h2>
<hr/>
<b><xsl:value-of select="name"/></b><br/>
<xsl:value-of select="address/street"/><br/>
<xsl:value-of select="address/city"/>, <xsl:value-of select="address/state"/>
<xsl:text> </xsl:text>
<xsl:value-of select="address/zip"/>
<br/>
<xsl:value-of select="phone"/><p/>
<b>Departing:</b>
<p/>
<ul>
```

Our `value-of` selects are pretty straightforward—usually just the element name or the element path to the child element we're using. When we want to use an attribute, we use the path to the attribute, and then the attribute is represented with the `@attribute`:

```
  Airport: <xsl:value-of select="ticket/departure/airport/@code"/><br/>
  Date: <xsl:value-of select="ticket/departure/@date"/><br/>
  Time: <xsl:value-of select="ticket/departure/@time"/><br/>
  Gate: <xsl:value-of select="ticket/departure/@gate"/><br/>
  Flight: <xsl:value-of select="ticket/departure/flight/@number"/><br/>
  Seat: <xsl:value-of select="ticket/departure/flight/@seat"/><br/>
 </ul>
 <p/>
...
<b>Arriving</b>
 <p/>
 <ul>
  Airport: <xsl:value-of select="ticket/arrival/airport/@code"/><br/>
  Date: <xsl:value-of select="ticket/arrival/@date"/><br/>
```

```
   Time: <xsl:value-of select="ticket/arrival/@time"/><br/>
   Flight: <xsl:value-of select="ticket/arrival/flight/@number"/><br/>
   Gate: <xsl:value-of select="ticket/arrival/@gate"/><br/>
  </ul>
  <p/>
</xsl:for-each>
  <p/>
  <hr/>
```

Although every passenger will have departing and arriving information, not every passenger will have connecting information. That's why we will use another `for-each` construct to make sure that the HMTL code is generated only for each `connecting` element:

```
<xsl:for-each select="ticket/connecting">
 <b>Connecting:</b>
 <p/>
 <ul>
  Airport: <xsl:value-of select="//connecting/airport/@code"/><br/>
  Date: <xsl:value-of select="//connecting/@date"/><br/>
  Time: <xsl:value-of select="//connecting/@time"/><br/>
  Gate: <xsl:value-of select="//connecting/@gate"/><br/>
  Flight: <xsl:value-of select="//connecting/flight/@number"/><br/>
  Seat: <xsl:value-of select="//connecting/flight/@seat"/><br/>
 </ul>
 <p/>
 </xsl:for-each>
```

This is a great deal simpler than our previous example, because we're not really changing anything from the source document—we're just inserting values into the HTML code. When we bring all of these elements together, the resulting code is shown in Listing 9.5.

LISTING 9.5 THE `html.xsl` STYLESHEET THAT WILL BE APPLIED TO THE `travel.xml` DOCUMENT TO GENERATE THE NEW `itinerary.html` DOCUMENT

```
<xsl:stylesheet version="1.0"
   xmlns:xsl="http://www.w3.org/1999/XSL/Transform" >

<xsl:output method="html" indent="yes"/>

<xsl:template match="/">
 <head>
 <title>Travel Itinerary</title>
 </head>
 <xsl:for-each select="travel/passenger">
 <h2>Travel Itinerary for <xsl:value-of select="name"/></h2>
 <hr/>
 <b><xsl:value-of select="name"/></b><br/>
 <xsl:value-of select="address/street"/><br/>
 <xsl:value-of select="address/city"/>, <xsl:value-of select="address/state"/>
 <xsl:text> </xsl:text>
 <xsl:value-of select="address/zip"/>
 <br/>
 <xsl:value-of select="phone"/><p/>
 <b>Departing:</b>
 <p/>
 <ul>
```

LISTING 9.5 CONTINUED

```
  Airport: <xsl:value-of select="ticket/departure/airport/@code"/><br/>
  Date: <xsl:value-of select="ticket/departure/@date"/><br/>
  Time: <xsl:value-of select="ticket/departure/@time"/><br/>
  Gate: <xsl:value-of select="ticket/departure/@gate"/><br/>
  Flight: <xsl:value-of select="ticket/departure/flight/@number"/><br/>
  Seat: <xsl:value-of select="ticket/departure/flight/@seat"/><br/>
 </ul>
 <p/>
 <xsl:for-each select="ticket/connecting">
 <b>Connecting:</b>
 <p/>
 <ul>
  Airport: <xsl:value-of select="//connecting/airport/@code"/><br/>
  Date: <xsl:value-of select="//connecting/@date"/><br/>
  Time: <xsl:value-of select="//connecting/@time"/><br/>
  Gate: <xsl:value-of select="//connecting/@gate"/><br/>
  Flight: <xsl:value-of select="//connecting/flight/@number"/><br/>
  Seat: <xsl:value-of select="//connecting/flight/@seat"/><br/>
 </ul>
 <p/>
 </xsl:for-each>
 <b>Arriving</b>
 <p/>
 <ul>
  Airport: <xsl:value-of select="ticket/arrival/airport/@code"/><br/>
  Date: <xsl:value-of select="ticket/arrival/@date"/><br/>
  Time: <xsl:value-of select="ticket/arrival/@time"/><br/>
  Flight: <xsl:value-of select="ticket/arrival/flight/@number"/><br/>
  Gate: <xsl:value-of select="ticket/arrival/@gate"/><br/>
 </ul>
 <p/>
 </xsl:for-each>
 <p/>
 <hr/>

</xsl:template>

</xsl:stylesheet>
```

This stylesheet can then be applied to the XML document using an engine such as Saxon, and the result is an HTML file that can be read by any browser, as shown in Listing 9.6.

LISTING 9.6 THE FINAL `itinerary.html` HTML DOCUMENT GENERATED BY PROCESSING THE `travel.xml` FILE WITH THE `html.xsl` STYLESHEET

```
<html>
<head>
<meta http-equiv="Content-Type" content="text/html; charset=utf-8">
<title>Travel Itinerary</title>
</head>
<h2>Travel Itinerary for Sally Smith</h2>
<hr><b>Sally Smith</b><br>555 W. 3rd<br>Chicago, IL 60647<br>312-555-1212
<p></p><b>Departing:</b><p></p>
```

Listing 9.6 continued

```
<ul>
   Airport: ORD<br>
   Date: 10/10/02<br>
   Time: 10:00 AM<br>
   Gate: A6<br>
   Flight: 839<br>
   Seat: 6F<br></ul>
<p></p><b>Arriving</b><p></p>
<ul>
   Airport: IND<br>
   Date: 10/10/02<br>
   Time: 10:45 AM<br>
   Flight: 839<br>
   Gate: B12<br></ul>
<p></p>
<h2>Travel Itinerary for John Dough</h2>
<hr><b>John Dough</b><br>123 Fake Street<br>Chicago, IL 60622<br>773-888-1234
<p></p><b>Departing:</b><p></p>
<ul>
   Airport: ORD<br>
   Date: 8/13/02<br>
   Time: 2:00 PM<br>
   Gate: C23<br>
   Flight: 082<br>
   Seat: A2<br></ul>
<p></p><b>Connecting:</b><p></p>
<ul>
   Airport: JFK<br>
   Date: 8/13/02<br>
   Time: 5:00 PM<br>
   Gate: F15<br>
   Flight: 332<br>
   Seat: B3<br></ul>
<p></p><b>Arriving</b><p></p>
<ul>
   Airport: LHR<br>
   Date: 8/14/02<br>
   Time: 7:00 AM<br>
   Flight: 332<br>
   Gate: B10<br></ul>
<p></p>
<p></p>
<hr>
</html>
```

As you can see, stylesheets need not be complicated—they often involve a number of repetitious steps, which, if you break them down piece-by-piece, are not beyond reach. The key is to know in advance what your beginning document looks like, and to have a prototype of how you want the result document to appear. Then, you can walk through the source document component-by-component until you reach the end goal.

With the components outlined in this chapter, you can design some stylesheets to format your XML in HTML or to convert between XML documents. The more complicated your documents, the more complicated your stylesheets, and as you become more advanced in your XSLT work, you may want to consult a title which is solely dedicated to the topic of XSLT.

ADDITIONAL RESOURCES

There are literally hundreds of articles available on the Web that are related to XSLT. It would be impossible to list them all here, but these are some good starting places to learn more about XSTL:

- W3C XSL Home (`http://www.w3.org/Style/XSL/`)—The W3C XSL home page contains links to the XSLT Recommendation, as well as links to tutorials and software related to both XSL and XSLT.
- XSLT Recommendation (`http://www.w3.org/TR/xslt`)—This is the official W3C XSL Transformations (XSLT) version 1.0.
- Saxon (`http://saxon.sourceforge.net`)—Saxon is a Java-based, open-source XSLT parser. It is the processor that was used to process all the examples in this chapter.
- XSLT.com (`http://www.xslt.com/`)—This is a portal Web site that is dedicated to tracking resources for XSLT, including tutorials, articles, and software.
- XSL Cover Pages (`http://www.oasis-open.org/cover/xsl.html`)—Robin Cover maintains this site, which functions as a general XML resource. This is a link to the area of the site that deals specifically with XSL resources, including XSLT.
- XML.com (`http://www.xml.com/style/`)—XML.com is a general XML resource; however, this is a link to the section of the site that covers stylesheet activity.

ROADMAP

Now you should have a better understanding of how stylesheets work and how to format XML documents using CSS. You also are now aware of how XSL Transformations can be used to create HTML documents from XML sources, or to change XML into other flavors of XML. This chapter is only the tip of the iceberg for working with XSLT, which is powerful enough that we could easily fill a book talking about the variations of what is possible and how to accomplish various transformations.

However, now you know what is possible, and you have the tools at your hands to begin manipulating XML with XSLT. From here, it's time to look at how you can actually format XML for display using Formatting Objects, or XSL-FO, to display them on the Web or in a browser or prepare them for printing.

That will round out the technologies for working directly with XML for display purposes, and you'll be ready to move on to the next part, which deals with location technologies, some of which, such as XPath, we have touched on here.

CHAPTER 10

The Nuts and Bolts of XSL: Formatting Objects

In this chapter

by David Gulbransen

THE NUTS AND BOLTS OF XSL: FORMATTING OBJECTS

Although XSLT is a very important part of XSL, it does not deal directly with the physical layout and formatting of XML documents. XML-FO exists to provide the mechanisms for applying presentation and style controls over structured XML documents. The functionality of XSL-FO is similar to that of Cascading Style Sheets; however, XSL-FO does go beyond the functionality provided by CSS, offering features such as page numbering, improved margins, footnotes, and a host of other features which have been added to XSL-FO to deal with laying out complex documents.

There are many similarities between XSL-FO and CSS; however, the biggest similarity is that CSS properties and XSL-FO properties represent the same type of information. That doesn't mean that the syntax is always the same, but it does mean that the properties represent the same functionality. This makes it much easier for someone familiar with CSS to transition to the use of XSL-FO without learning an extensive set of new properties.

For example, if we wanted to define a background image for the `<BODY>` of an HTML document, we would use the following CSS:

```
<STYLE type="text/css">
 BODY { background-image: url("http://www.myserver.com/texture.gif") }
</STYLE>
```

If we wanted to create a background image using XSL-FO, we would use

```
<fo:block background-image="http://www.myserver.com/texture.gif">
</fo:block>
```

The `background-image` property remains the same. The difference between the two applications is largely semantic, with XSL-FO following the structure of well-formed XML, with the property values defined as XML attributes.

Another key difference is that CSS is designed primarily to bring a stylesheet language to the Web; however, XSL-FO is not designed strictly for Web applications. In fact, those readers coming from a print background, who may be familiar with layout applications such as QuarkXPress or Adobe PageMaker, may already be familiar with some of the concepts associated with XSL-FO, such as page masters. Those readers coming from a Web background might not be familiar with these types of objects, but their usage and uses will become quickly apparent.

BASICS OF XSL-FO

XSL layout control is based on Formatting Objects, which are rectangular areas similar to boxes in CSS. These areas have a number of properties, and they can contain other areas, images, text, and so on.

An easy way to look at this is to look at some of the objects used to represent tables:

- `fo:table`
- `fo:table-column`

- fo:table-row
- fo:table-cell

Each of these XSL-FO elements represents a different object, some of which contain other objects, such as fo:table which can contain table-column, table-row, and table-cell objects. Those objects in turn contain objects (rows and columns contain cells) or they can contain content: table-cell objects will contain the text or images contained in the table.

Each of these objects will also have properties associated with it, either specific to the object, or generic properties that can be applied to multiple objects. For example, if we wanted to specify that the font to be used in a table cell:

```
<fo:table-cell>
 <fo:block font-family="Helvetica, Arial, sans" font-size="12pt">
Some Content
 </fo:block>
</fo:table-cell>
```

Here we have a table-cell object, which contains a block object. That block object contains some text, but it also makes use of the font-family property to specify the type of font that should be used in rendering the contents of that cell.

A Basic XSL-FO Document

Now, let's see how a typical XSL-FO document might be structured. For the sake of discussion and learning about Objects and Properties, we are going to work with content inserted directly into the XSL document. However, at the end of the chapter, we will explore some examples with XSL-FO integrated with XSL, to use stylesheets as they were intended, to dynamically format data from XML files.

For now, though, let's look at a very basic XSL-FO document, which will simply display the text "Hello World" in a 64pt sans-serif font:

```
<?xml version="1.0"?>
<fo:root xmlns:fo="http://www.w3.org/1999/XSL/Format">
 <fo:layout-master-set>
  <fo:simple-page-master master-name="title_page">
  <fo:region-body/>
 </fo:simple-page-master>
</fo:layout-master-set>

<fo:page-sequence master-name="title_page">
 <fo:flow flow-name="xsl-region-body">
  <fo:block font-size="64pt" font-family="sans-serif">
  Hello World
  </fo:block>
 </fo:flow>
</fo:page-sequence>

</fo:root>
```

When we render this document, the result is a single page, with the text displayed in a large, sans-serif font, as shown in Figure 10.1.

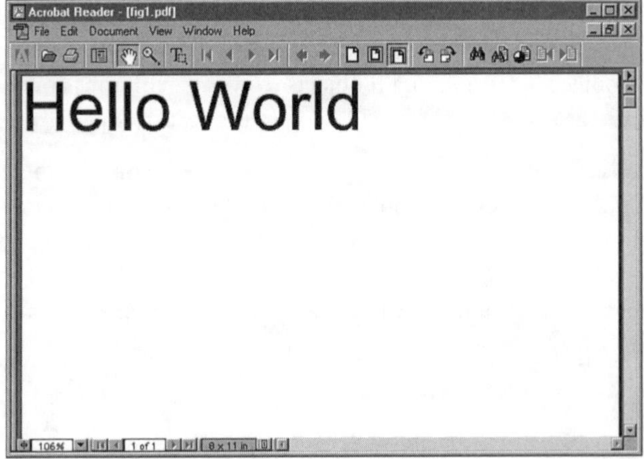

Figure 10.1
A simple XSL-FO document rendered using FOP and displayed as a PDF file.

Don't worry about the layout and page master objects for now—we will explore those objects a bit later, as we discuss the structure and layout of pages in XSL.

There are three things you should note about this first simple document.

First, the document is well-formed XML; the document begins with an XML declaration, specifying that this is an XML document, based on XML version 1.0.

Second, the entire document is contained within an `fo:root` element, which serves as a container for the rest of the XSL-FO object elements. This is also where we specify that the XSL-FO objects are members of the "`http://www.w3.org/1999/XSL/Format`" Namespace. The current convention is to use the "`fo`" prefix for formatting objects, which allows you to keep them straight from other XML elements, or XSLT elements within the document.

Finally, you should notice that the object elements have property attributes that are used to configure the appearance of information in the final rendered document. For example:

```
<fo:block font-size="64pt" font-family="serif"></fo:block>
```

Here we have a `block` object, with the `font-size` and `font-family` properties specified for that particular block object. Because properties are inherited, if we placed additional block objects within this block, they would inherit the font properties, unless we specifically overrode them.

Keep this relationship between objects and properties in mind as we take a closer look at the Formatting Objects and Properties outlined in the XSL Recommendation.

AREAS

Processing a stylesheet involves breaking down the whole document into increasingly smaller pieces, and then applying formatting information to each of those pieces. For example, if we wanted to format a book, we would have a number of different pieces that made up the book: a cover, a title page, and chapters. Each chapter, in turn, would consist of paragraphs, made up of sentences, composed of characters.

XSL stylesheets work in a similar fashion, only abstracted to allow for a variety of document types. The highest level in XSL are regions. Regions, in turn, are broken down into block areas, which consist of line areas and inline areas.

REGIONS

Regions are large rectangular areas at the top of the object hierarchy. For example, a page in XSL is a region, which in turn is divided into a number of smaller subregions. A page can be divided into five regions:

- `region-body`
- `region-start`
- `region-end`
- `region-before`
- `region-after`

These objects represent regions that will then contain the other areas in the document.

Most of the properties associated with these objects will relate to the size and margins of the pages that make up your document. We will take a closer look at how these region objects relate to one another and form pages when we look at the page objects a little later.

BLOCK AREAS

Block areas also represent rectangular areas, which may contain other block areas, or they may contain content. Block areas are "flowed" within regions—that is, their location is not given with coordinates, but instead in relation to the other block elements that make up a document.

Some examples of Formatting Objects that produce block areas include

- `block`
- `table`
- `table-and-caption`
- `list-body`
- `list-item`

Most documents will be composed of a large number of block areas, and we will look in depth at block areas, including tables and lists later in this chapter.

LINE AREAS

Line areas are a special type of area in XSL. The text content of a block area is laid out in line areas, which are used to determine how text should wrap within a block, for example. The principal difference between line areas and block areas is that line areas are not configured by the stylesheet author.

With block areas, the stylesheet author uses the applicable properties to configure how a block area should be rendered. When that block area contains text content, however, the XSL processor actually makes use of line areas within the block to perform tasks such as wrapping the text. The author does not create line areas, but they are stylesheet areas nonetheless.

INLINE AREAS

Although stylesheet authors don't have direct control over line areas, there are instances when you will want to have direct control over inline areas—for example:

- `character`
- `page-number`
- `leader`
- `external-graphic`

These types of objects allow you to manipulate inline areas to produce items such as footnote references, page numbers, and rule/leader lines, or to include external graphics, such as gifs or jpegs, within a block area.

PAGES

XSL-FO documents are composed of pages, which are in turn composed of several different regions. When a document is rendered using Formatting Objects, text is flowed from page to page as required until the entire document has been generated.

Each page is composed of five regions, which are generated by the following object elements:

- `fo:region-body`

  The `fo:region-body` object creates the body region of the page. This region actually contains all the page content, including the other `region-before`, `region-after`, `region-start`, and `region-end` areas. This can be quite confusing—the naming scheme would imply that one region comes before or after the other, but, in fact, the coordinates of the regions have to be set appropriately to ensure that they do not overlap.

- `fo:region-before`

  The `region-before` area is located at the top of the page, inside the `margin-top`. It can be used to place header information on a page, but keep in mind that unless formatted otherwise, it will naturally overlap with the body region.

- `fo:region-after`

  The `region-after` area is located at the bottom of the page, and is ended at the `margin-bottom`. It can be used as a footer area on the page; however, like the `region-before`, it may overlap with the body region.

- `fo:region-start`

  The `region-start` area is located on the left side of the page, when used with a Western-based language. It is bounded on the left by the `margin-left`. Similar to the other regions, it naturally overlaps the body region.

- `fo:region-end`

  The `region-end` area is located on the right side of the page, bounded by the `margin-right`. It also overlaps the body region.

Caution

Region placement is based on the assumption of top-to-bottom, left-to-right text. Therefore, in the standard model, the `region-start` object occurs on the left, and the `region-end` object occurs on the right, because Western text is written left-to-right. However, if you are working with a character set and language such as Arabic or Hebrew, which is written right-to-left, the placement of these areas will be reversed.

In addition to these body regions, pages also have margins that can be expressed with the following formatting object elements:

- `fo:margin-top`

  This object defines the top margin of the page.

- `fo:margin-bottom`

  This object defines the bottom margin of the page.

- `fo:margin-left`

  This object defines the margin on the left side of the page.

- `fo:margin-right`

  This object defines the margin on the right side of the page.

Unlike the body regions, the margins do not overlap with the other areas on the page. These objects also do not change with respect to the orientation of the text. The left margin is always the left margin.

PAGE MASTERS

Because the model for laying out documents in XSL-FO is based on pages, there exists a mechanism for defining master pages, which serve as templates for the pages generated by the XSL processor when the document is being rendered.

Page masters in XSL-FO function similarly to page masters in other graphic design/layout programs, such as QuarkXPress. After defining the properties associated with a master page, that master page can then be referenced within the stylesheet to construct a page, which, in turn, inherits the properties of the page master. Let's see how this works in XSL-FO.

First, page masters are contained in an object element called the *`layout-master-set`*. This is a container object, which can be used to group multiple page masters for complex documents. For example, you may want to have multiple masters for different pages in your document, such as a title page, or other specially formatted pages.

All page masters are defined using the `fo:simple-page-master` object, which is used to manipulate the actual properties of the physical page layout. You can create any number of `simple-page-master` pages, which can then be used in conjunction with the `page-sequence-master` to create more complex layout schemes.

For example, if we wanted to define a page master for a simple, 8.5×11-inch letter-size page, we would use

```
<fo:layout-master-set>
 <fo:simple-page-master master-name="Letter"
     page-width="8.5in"
     page-height="11.0in"
     margin-top="0.5in"
     margin-bottom="0.5in"
     margin-left="0.5in"
     margin-right="0.5in">
  <fo:region-body/>
 </fo:simple-page-master>
</fo:layout-master-set>
```

The `page-width` and `page-height` properties define the size of the page, and can be expressed using the following units of measure:

- `cm` Centimeters
- `mm` Millimeters
- `in` Inches
- `pt` Points
- `pc` Picas
- `px` Pixels

Each of the four margins can also be specified using these units of measure. In this case, because we are defining a simple, blank page, we need to use only a single region for the body; any content we place on the page will then be flowed into that region. Here's another example of a simple master, which defines a legal-size page:

```
<fo:layout-master-set>
 <fo:simple-page-master master-name="Legal"
     page-width="8.5in"
     page-height="14.0in"
     margin-top="0.5in"
     margin-bottom="0.5in"
     margin-left="0.5in"
     margin-right="0.5in">
  <fo:region-body/>
 </fo:simple-page-master>
</fo:layout-master-set>
```

Note

For those curious about international paper sizes, `http://www.cl.cam.ac.uk/~mgk25/iso-paper.html` has a good explanation of the various sizes available.

10

Now, if we wanted to make use of the region areas on the page, we could do so by defining the size and margins of the regions in the page master, and then utilizing those regions elsewhere in the document.

For example, let's say we wanted to create a letterhead, with a header and a footer that would appear on the page. We could do this by utilizing the `region-before` and `region-after` areas.

The length of the `region-before` and `region-after` areas is determined by using the `extent` property. For example, to define a header 1 inch, we would use

```
<fo:region-before extent="1.0in"/>
```

To define the footer, we would use

```
<fo:region-after extent="1.0in"/>
```

Next, in defining the `region-body`, we need to make use of the margin properties to make sure that the body region does not overlap our header and footer. Remember, the body naturally encompasses the `before`, `after`, `start`, and `end` areas, so by using the margin properties, we make sure that the body content is separated from the header/footer areas:

```
<fo:region-body margin-top="1.0in" margin-bottom="1.0in"/>
```

If we put those objects together into a page master, we have a page with a header and footer which we could use as a letterhead—for example:

```
<fo:layout-master-set>
 <fo:simple-page-master master-name="Letter"
     page-width="8.5in" page-height="11.0in"
     margin-top="0.5in" margin-bottom="0.5in"
     margin-left="0.5in" margin-right="0.5in">
  <fo:region-before extent="1.0in"/>
```

```
  <fo:region-body margin-top="1.0in" margin-bottom="1.0in"/>
  <fo:region-after  extent="1.0in"/>
 </fo:simple-page-master>
</fo:layout-master-set>
```

Listing 10.1 shows how these regions could then be used as a header and a footer, containing information such as might be included on a company letterhead. Don't worry about how the `block` elements are formatted for now—we will cover those shortly. However, note how the `simple-page-master` is formatted and then referenced by the `page-sequence`.

LISTING 10.1 AN EXAMPLE OF USING REGIONS TO ESTABLISH PAGE HEADER AND FOOTER AREAS

```
<?xml version="1.0"?>
<fo:root xmlns:fo="http://www.w3.org/1999/XSL/Format">
 <fo:layout-master-set>
  <fo:simple-page-master master-name="Letter"
      page-width="8.5in" page-height="11.0in"
      margin-top="0.5in" margin-bottom="0.5in"
      margin-left="0.5in" margin-right="0.5in">
   <fo:region-before extent="1.0in"/>
   <fo:region-body margin-top="1.0in" margin-bottom="1.0in"/>
   <fo:region-after  extent="1.0in"/>
  </fo:simple-page-master>
 </fo:layout-master-set>
 <fo:page-sequence master-name="Letter">
  <fo:static-content flow-name="xsl-region-before">
   <fo:block font-size="18pt" font-family="serif"
       font-weight="bold" text-align="center">
    Mythical Company, Inc.
    <fo:leader leader-pattern="rule" leader-length="7.0in" />
   </fo:block>
  </fo:static-content>

  <fo:static-content flow-name="xsl-region-after">
   <fo:block font-size="18pt" font-family="serif" text-align="center">
    <fo:leader leader-pattern="rule" leader-length="7.0in" />
    1-800-555-1212 or e-mail sales@mycompany.com
   </fo:block>
  </fo:static-content>

  <fo:flow flow-name="xsl-region-body">
   <fo:block font-size="12pt" font-family="serif">
    The contents of the letter...
   </fo:block>
  </fo:flow>
 </fo:page-sequence>
</fo:root>
```

The rendered results for the stylesheet in Listing 10.1 is shown in Figure 10.2.

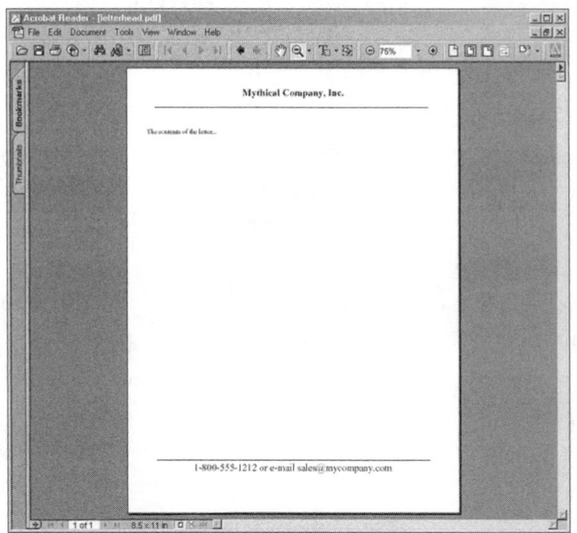

Figure 10.2 The rendered results of the `letterhead.fob` stylesheet—note the `region-begin` and `region-end` areas rendered at the top and bottom of the page.

Although so far we have looked at only the `simple-page-master` object, there are a number of other ways to use page masters. By using the `page-sequence-master` object, you can group a number of different types of references to `simple-page-masters` together. This is done by using a number of different `reference` objects, such as

- `fo:single-page-master-reference`

  The `single-page-master-reference` can be used to describe a page master that is limited to one page in length. Under normal circumstances, pages are flowed, one to the next, until the document has been rendered. Using a `single-page-master-reference` limits the display to one page. This could be used to create a master for a title page, for example.

- `fo:repeatable-page-master-reference`

  Even though the `simple-page-master` does flow, you might want to create a `repeatable-page-master-reference` to coincide with the single page master, which could be used for the rest of the document—say, the report that follows a title page.

The `conditional-page-master-reference` allows you to create references to a set of page masters, which can then be used depending on certain conditions, such as being the first or last page of the document. For example, if we wanted to create a set of page masters for a chapter, with a Title Page master, a master for the chapter text, and another master for an index on the last page, we would use a conditional master set:

```
<fo:layout-master-set>
 <fo:page-sequence-master master-name="chapter">
  <fo:repeatable-page-master-alternatives>
   <fo:conditional-page-master-reference page-position="first"
       master-name="title_page"/>
   <fo:conditional-page-master-reference page-position="rest"
       master-name="chapter_text"/>
```

```
    <fo:conditional-page-master-reference page-position="last"
        master-name="index"/>
  </fo:repeatable-page-master-alternatives>
 </fo:page-sequence-master>
</fo:layout-master-set>
```

Each of the conditional-page-master-reference objects in turn references a simple-page-master definition that constructs the page layout itself. The conditional-page-master-reference allows you to create page masters that are used depending on one of three criteria:

- page-position—The page-position can be first, last, rest, or any, which are used to denote the position of the page(s) relative to the other pages in the document.
- odd-or-even—The odd-or-even trait can be used to denote either all odd pages, all even pages, or any page.
- blank-or-not-blank—The blank-or-not-blank trait can denote blank pages, not-blank pages, or any page.

The use of masters can be very flexible, and provides the fine level of control that graphic designers are accustomed to, although as the control level increases, so does the complexity of the stylesheet.

PAGE SEQUENCES

Page sequences consist of multiple document pages as rendered by the XSL processor.

For simpler documents, the page-sequence object is used to create instances of pages, based on the page master:

```
<?xml version="1.0"?>
<fo:root xmlns:fo="http://www.w3.org/1999/XSL/Format">
<fo:layout-master-set>
<fo:simple-page-master master-name="the_page_master">
<fo:region-body/>
</fo:simple-page-master>
</fo:layout-master-set>

<fo:page-sequence master-name="the_page_master">
<fo:flow flow-name="xsl-region-body">
<fo:block/>
</fo:flow>
</fo:page-sequence>
</fo:root>
```

The page-sequence has a master-name property that is used to reference the appropriate page master. Unless you are using a page master that restricts the number of pages in the document, the page-sequence will be used to create as many pages as necessary to render the complete document.

CONTENT AREAS

Now that you have an idea of how pages are structured and instantiated by the XSL processor, let's examine how content is arranged on the page. There are three objects that are used to place content on the page: `flows`, `static-content`, and `blocks`. Flows and static-content objects are actually containers, in which blocks can be placed to render the actual content. Let's take a look at these objects and their syntax.

`flow` AND `static-content`

There are actually two kinds of "flow" objects: `flow` and `static-content`.

The `flow` object is used as a container for block elements that are designed to flow from one page to another, such as the text of a chapter. The control of the flow is determined by the XSL processor, based on the constraints placed on the page using object properties.

`static-content` is used as a container for content which is not flowed from page to page, but remains static in one region of a page, such as the information we placed in the header and footer of the letterhead example. Because that content is not flowed, it is considered static.

Each `flow` object can contain multiple block level objects, such as a `block`, `table`, `list-body`, and so on. Each `flow` object also has a `flow-name` property, that is used to define the region on the page which the content will be flowed into. The acceptable values for the `flow-name` include

- `xsl-region-begin`
- `xsl-region-end`
- `xsl-region-start`
- `xsl-region-end`
- `xsl-region-body`

Each region needs only one `flow` object, so there should never be more than five `flow` objects in a sequence.

`static-content` object elements work similarly to `flow` objects—there is only one `static-content` object per region on the page. The primary difference between the `static-content` object and a `flow` object is that the content of `flow` objects is flowed from page to page in the document. However, `static-content` appears in the same position on every page of the document that is created when the document is rendered. That is what makes `static-content` appropriate for elements such as headers or footers that are to appear on each page in a document.

BLOCKS

The content of `flow` objects and `static-content` objects includes Block-level objects. Blocks enclose content, such as text or images. `Block` objects also can be used with a variety of properties to format the text that appears in the block. Properties can be manipulated from `block` to `block`, and each block in a `flow` object is rendered with a line break between the blocks. This makes the `block` object appropriate for formatting headlines, paragraphs, or a number of text-content types within a document.

For example, in this XSL-FO document, we have three different `block` elements, each of which contains a small snippet of text. Each of the `block` objects in our example also makes use of several font properties, so you can see how each block is rendered differently in the final document:

```
<?xml version="1.0"?>
<fo:root xmlns:fo="http://www.w3.org/1999/XSL/Format">
 <fo:layout-master-set>
  <fo:simple-page-master master-name="title_page">
   <fo:region-body/>
  </fo:simple-page-master>
 </fo:layout-master-set>

 <fo:page-sequence master-name="title_page">
  <fo:flow flow-name="xsl-region-body">
   <fo:block font-size="24pt" font-family="sans-serif">Block One</fo:block>
   <fo:block font-size="48pt" font-family="serif">Block Two</fo:block>
   <fo:block font-size="24pt" font-family="sans-serif">Block Three</fo:block>
  </fo:flow>
 </fo:page-sequence>

</fo:root>
```

The final rendered output from this stylesheet appears in Figure 10.3.

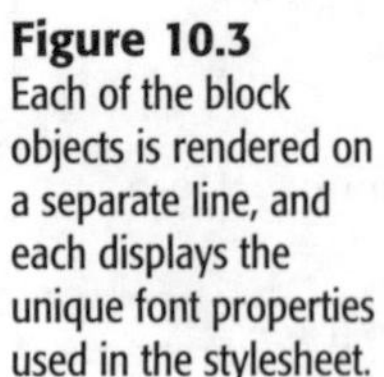

Figure 10.3
Each of the block objects is rendered on a separate line, and each displays the unique font properties used in the stylesheet.

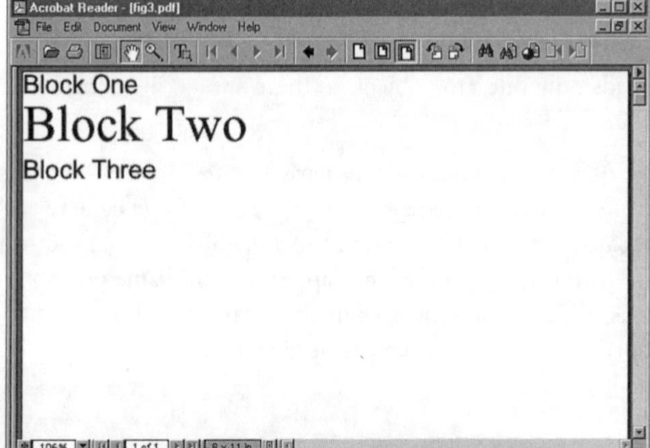

`block` objects can be grouped together, using the `block-container` object as well, to create a reference area of blocks which can then be manipulated as a unit.

Inline Objects

In addition to block formatting objects, there are a number of other objects that are inline objects.

These objects are designed to be integrated into lines within block objects, or within sections of text. These inline objects allow you to manipulate sentences, words, or characters.

The inline objects include

- `bidi-override`—This overrides the direction in which text is written. Normally, the default will be appropriate to the language. However, there are times when the algorithm might make the wrong choice, or where you want to write text in a different way. Although English is top-to-bottom, left-to-right, other languages or specific applications (such as engineering specifications) might be written differently.
- `character`—This object allows you to apply detailed formatting to a single letter (or glyph). Unlike most objects, you don't put the character inside the tags—you use the character object's `character` property.
- `inline`—This is used to format a section of text inside a block. It can be used to add a border, change fonts and/or background, keep text together, and so on. We will look at this more when we discuss working with text later in the chapter.
- `inline-container`—This is an inline object that serves as a reference area, such as a `block-container`.
- `leader`—The `leader` object is used to create both leaders and rules, which can be inserted into text lines in a block.
- `page-number`—The `page number` object is used to insert page numbers into your document, such as placing a page number in the page's footer.
- `basic-link`—This object is used to create a link to another document or position within the same document. Internal links use the `internal-destination` property and jump to a position base on the `id` property. External links use the `external-destination` property and use a URI.
- `external-graphic`—This is used to embed a graphic stored in an external file. The `src` property takes the form of a URI pointing to the file to be included, much like an HTML `<img>` tag. You can specify a height and width or let it be automatically determined.
- `instream-foreign-object`—This object is used to embed a graphic or other object described as XML, such as an SVG-based graphic.

The most commonly used of the inline objects will relate to including graphics in documents, both in the form of images and rule lines. Another very common use of inline objects is including page numbers. So, let's take a closer look at both of these applications.

WORKING WITH GRAPHICS

Many documents include graphics along with text, from charts and graphs to logos and photographs. Graphic images included in a stylesheet are treated as inline objects, and can take one of a few forms.

The `instream-foreign-object` object can be used to contain a section of XML-based code, which generates a graphic. That code might take the form of an SVG image, or a MathML-formatted equation, or some yet-to-be-developed format.

More common, though, will be the inclusion of familiar graphic formats such as .gif or .jpeg images, similarly to how images are included in HTML pages.

To include an external graphic in an XSL-FO document, the `external-graphic` object is used, which accepts a URI pointing to the image to be included:

```
<fo:external-graphic src="http://www.myserver.com/logo.jpg"/>
```

The URI can be either an absolute or relative URI. For example, if we wanted to include a photograph with a caption, we would use the following:

LISTING 10.2 INCLUDING GRAPHICS WITH XSL-FO AND THE `external-graphic` OBJECT

```
<?xml version="1.0"?>
<fo:root xmlns:fo="http://www.w3.org/1999/XSL/Format">
 <fo:layout-master-set>
  <fo:simple-page-master master-name="page">
   <fo:region-body/>
  </fo:simple-page-master>
</fo:layout-master-set>

 <fo:page-sequence master-name="page">
  <fo:flow flow-name="xsl-region-body">   <fo:block>
    <fo:external-graphic src="L.jpg"/>
   </fo:block>

   <fo:block font-size="14pt" font-family="serif">
    Trains in Chicago are called the "L" for eLevated.
   </fo:block>
  </fo:flow>
 </fo:page-sequence>

</fo:root>
```

This creates a document with an inline graphic, in the form of a JPEG image, and then places a caption underneath the image. The rendered results are shown in Figure 10.4.

In addition to graphics in the form of imported images, another common type of graphic element used in documents comes in the form of the rule line. So, now let's take a look at how rules are handled in XSL-FO.

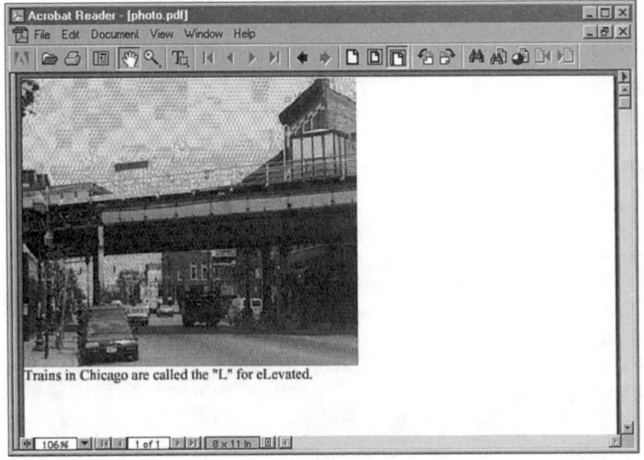

Figure 10.4
A photo and a caption generated using blocks and the inline `external-graphic` object.

LEADERS AND PAGE NUMBERS

XSL-FO treats leaders and rules as the same object. A leader is a series of glyphs linking two pieces of text. For example, in a table of contents:

```
Chapter 5.............................................................. 40
```

The series of "dots" linking the Chapter label and the page number is a leader. Leaders can be composed of any character, and the `leader` object allows you to set the character used with the `leader-pattern` property, which is also how XSL-FO handles rule lines.

A rule line is a horizontal graphic line, used to separate sections or as a decorative element. In HTML, rule lines are created using the <hr> tag. With XSL-FO, rules are created using the `leader` object, and setting the `leader-pattern` value to `rule`.

For example, to create a rule line 60 picas long (approximately 5 inches), we would use

```
<fo:leader leader-pattern="rule" leader-length="60pc" />
```

The `leader-pattern` could also be set to a color value, which would create a colored rule line.

One use for creating a rule line might be to set apart a page footer that contained a page number for the page. To include page numbers in a document, we would need to use the `page-number` object, and include it in a `static-content` object, located in the appropriate region on our page.

Let's say that we wanted to create a footer that included a rule line and a page number:

```
<fo:static-content flow-name="xsl-region-after">
 <fo:block font-size="12pt" font-family="serif" text-align="center">
  <fo:leader leader-pattern="rule" leader-length="7.0in" />
  Page # <fo:page-number/>
 </fo:block>
</fo:static-content>
```

We accomplish this by creating a `static-content` object in the `region-after` area of the page. Within that object, we have a `leader` object and a `page-number` object. The complete document looks like this:

Listing 10.3 Using the `leader` and `page-number` Objects to Create a Page Footer

```
<?xml version="1.0"?>
 <fo:root xmlns:fo="http://www.w3.org/1999/XSL/Format">
 <fo:layout-master-set>
  <fo:simple-page-master master-name="Letter"
      page-width="4in" page-height="4in"
      margin-top="0.5in" margin-bottom="0.5in"
      margin-left="0.5in" margin-right="0.5in">
   <fo:region-body margin-top="1.0in" margin-bottom="1.0in"/>
   <fo:region-after  extent="0.5in"/>
  </fo:simple-page-master>
 </fo:layout-master-set>
 <fo:page-sequence master-name="Letter">
  <fo:static-content flow-name="xsl-region-after">
   <fo:block font-size="12pt" font-family="serif" text-align="center">
    <fo:leader leader-pattern="rule" leader-length="7.0in" />
    Page # <fo:page-number/>
   </fo:block>
  </fo:static-content>  <fo:flow flow-name="xsl-region-body">
   <fo:block font-size="12pt" font-family="serif">
    The contents of the page...
   </fo:block>
  </fo:flow>
 </fo:page-sequence>
</fo:root>
```

When rendered, the complete page appears as shown in Figure 10.5, complete with our footer, separated by a rule line and containing a page number.

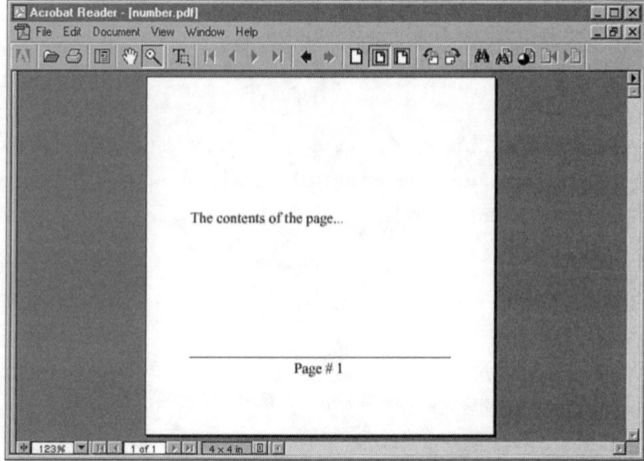

Figure 10.5
A page with a footer featuring a leader object and a page number.

Because the pages are generated dynamically by the XSL processor, the page numbers are also determined automatically by the XSL processor. By manipulating the various `page-number` properties (see Appendix B "Guide to Reading the XML Recommendation" for a full list), you can control how page numbers appear, such as only numbering even or odd pages, or skipping the first page, and start numbering the document with page 2.

TABLES

One of the most common formatting techniques is the creation of tables. A myriad of information can be stored in tables, and as any HTML author is aware, tables can function as more than simply storage units for data, they can contain virtually any kind of text and images, sometimes in ways that are not even represented as tables.

Because of the formatting power of XSL-FO, there is no longer really a need to use tables to hack together page layouts. However, tables are still a very useful formatting element. There are a number of XSL Formatting Objects that are explicitly used in the creation and formatting of tables. They are

- `table-and-caption`—This tag is only used to provide a container for a table and its caption. It should contain a table object and a caption object. You can use the table object without this if you do not need a caption.
- `table`—The `table` object is used to create a table. Although it can be used within a `table-and-caption` object, it can also be used on its own to create a table.
- `table-caption`—This object contains a block, which is the caption for a table.
- `table-column`—This describes the columns of the table and their formatting.
- `table-header`—This contains the first row (header), normally column titles for the table.
- `table-footer`—This contains last row (footer) of a table, which can be used for titling, totaling, and so on. It acts much the same way as a table-header.
- `table-body`—This contains the main body of the table. It holds the `table-row` objects.
- `table-row`—This contains a single row of table data. It holds a set of `table-cell` objects.
- `table-cell`—This describes a single cell (data contents of a particular column and row) and holds a `block` object. These are normally contained in a `table-row` object, but can be used on their own with the `starts-row` and `ends-row` properties.

Let's look at how these objects come together to create a table. We are going to create a table for some part numbers and information about the parts. We will have a table header and store the table data in individual cells. We start the table off using the `table` object, and we use some of its properties to establish a border style, color, and the width of the border—in this case, a 1-point line. (We will discuss border properties in greater detail later in the Borders and Padding section.)

```
<fo:table border-collapse="separate" border-style="solid" border-color="black"
➥border-width="1pt">
```

Next, we need to establish the columns for our table:

```
<fo:table-column column-width="8pc"/>
<fo:table-column column-width="12pc"/>
<fo:table-column column-width="8pc"/>
<fo:table-column column-width="4pc"/>
```

The column width can be specified using any of the units of measure we mentioned before (such as in, cm, mm, and so on). In this case, we have used picas.

Next, we establish the table header, and for the header we are using a `background-color` property and the `color` property to make the header a black band with red text:

```
<fo:table-header>
 <fo:table-row background-color="black" color="red">
  <fo:table-cell number-columns-spanned="4" padding="2pt">
   <fo:block>Part Catalog</fo:block>
  </fo:table-cell>
 </fo:table-row>
</fo:table-header>
```

With the table structure established, we are ready to create the body for the table. Within the `table-body`, we will be defining each of the table rows, and the table cells that contain the actual data for our table:

```
 <fo:table-body>
  <fo:table-row background-color="grey" color="white">
   <fo:table-cell padding="2pt"><fo:block>Part Number</fo:block></fo:table-cell>
   <fo:table-cell padding="2pt"><fo:block>Description</fo:block></fo:table-cell>
   <fo:table-cell padding="2pt"><fo:block>Unit Price</fo:block></fo:table-cell>
   <fo:table-cell padding="2pt"><fo:block>In Stock</fo:block></fo:table-cell>
  </fo:table-row>
 </fo:table-body>
</fo:table>
```

When we pull this all together and add the rest of our data, the result is the code shown in Listing 10.4.

Listing 10.4 A Complete Table Built Using XSL Formatting Objects

```
<?xml version="1.0"?>
<fo:root xmlns:fo="http://www.w3.org/1999/XSL/Format">
 <fo:layout-master-set>
  <fo:simple-page-master master-name="Catalog"
      page-width="6in" page-height="8.0in"
      margin-top="0.5in" margin-bottom="0.5in"
      margin-left="0.5in" margin-right="0.5in">
   <fo:region-before extent="1.0in"/>
   <fo:region-body margin-top="1.0in" margin-bottom="1.0in"/>
   <fo:region-after  extent="1.0in"/>
  </fo:simple-page-master>
 </fo:layout-master-set>
 <fo:page-sequence master-name="Catalog">
  <fo:static-content flow-name="xsl-region-before">
```

LISTING 10.4 CONTINUED

```
   <fo:block text-align="center" font-family="sans-serif"
       font-size="18pt" font-weight="bold">
    Widgets, Inc.
   </fo:block>
  </fo:static-content>
  <fo:static-content flow-name="xsl-region-after">
   <fo:block text-align="center" font-family="sans-serif"
       font-size="12pt" font-style="italic">
     Last updated January 1, 2002
   </fo:block>
  </fo:static-content>
  <fo:flow flow-name="xsl-region-body">
   <fo:block>
    Please consult your product manual for part numbers.
   </fo:block>
   <fo:table border-collapse="separate" border-style="solid"
       border-color="black" border-width="1pt">
    <fo:table-column column-width="8pc"/>
    <fo:table-column column-width="12pc"/>
    <fo:table-column column-width="8pc"/>
    <fo:table-column column-width="4pc"/>

    <fo:table-header>
     <fo:table-row background-color="black" color="red">
      <fo:table-cell number-columns-spanned="4" padding="2pt">
       <fo:block>Part Catalog</fo:block>
      </fo:table-cell>
     </fo:table-row>
    </fo:table-header>

    <fo:table-body>
     <fo:table-row background-color="grey" color="white">
      <fo:table-cell padding="2pt"><fo:block>Part Number</fo:block>
➥</fo:table-cell>
      <fo:table-cell padding="2pt"><fo:block>Description</fo:block>
➥</fo:table-cell>
      <fo:table-cell padding="2pt"><fo:block>Unit Price</fo:block></fo:table-cell>
      <fo:table-cell padding="2pt"><fo:block>In Stock</fo:block></fo:table-cell>
     </fo:table-row>
     <fo:table-row background-color="white" color="black">
      <fo:table-cell padding="4pt"><fo:block>AB2992</fo:block></fo:table-cell>
      <fo:table-cell padding="4pt"><fo:block>Casters</fo:block></fo:table-cell>
      <fo:table-cell padding="4pt"><fo:block>$19.99</fo:block></fo:table-cell>
      <fo:table-cell padding="4pt"><fo:block>Yes</fo:block></fo:table-cell>
     </fo:table-row>
     <fo:table-row background-color="white" color="black">
      <fo:table-cell padding="4pt"><fo:block>CY9932</fo:block></fo:table-cell>
      <fo:table-cell padding="4pt"><fo:block>Handle</fo:block></fo:table-cell>
      <fo:table-cell padding="4pt"><fo:block>$5.99</fo:block></fo:table-cell>
      <fo:table-cell padding="4pt"><fo:block>Yes</fo:block></fo:table-cell>
     </fo:table-row>
     <fo:table-row background-color="white" color="black">
      <fo:table-cell padding="4pt"><fo:block>DF9921</fo:block></fo:table-cell>
      <fo:table-cell padding="4pt"><fo:block>Drawer</fo:block></fo:table-cell>
      <fo:table-cell padding="4pt"><fo:block>$9.99</fo:block></fo:table-cell>
      <fo:table-cell padding="4pt"><fo:block>Yes</fo:block></fo:table-cell>
```

10

LISTING 10.4 CONTINUED

```
      </fo:table-row>
      <fo:table-row background-color="white" color="black">
       <fo:table-cell padding="4pt"><fo:block>XV2201</fo:block></fo:table-cell>
       <fo:table-cell padding="4pt"><fo:block>Storage Unit</fo:block>
➥</fo:table-cell>
       <fo:table-cell padding="4pt"><fo:block>$99.99</fo:block></fo:table-cell>
       <fo:table-cell padding="4pt"><fo:block>No</fo:block></fo:table-cell>
      </fo:table-row>
      <fo:table-row background-color="white" color="black">
       <fo:table-cell padding="4pt"><fo:block>FG2231</fo:block></fo:table-cell>
       <fo:table-cell padding="4pt"><fo:block>Print Manual</fo:block>
➥</fo:table-cell>
       <fo:table-cell padding="4pt"><fo:block>$2.99</fo:block></fo:table-cell>
       <fo:table-cell padding="4pt"><fo:block>Yes</fo:block></fo:table-cell>
      </fo:table-row>
     </fo:table-body>
    </fo:table>  </fo:flow>
  </fo:page-sequence>
</fo:root>
```

The results of the rendered file are shown in Figure 10.6.

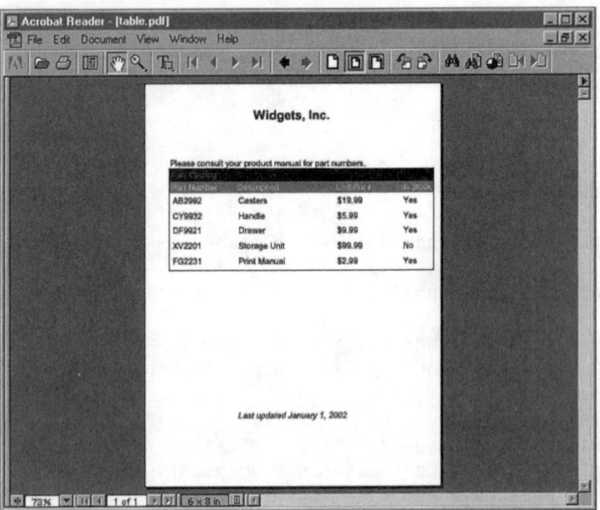

Figure 10.6
A fully formatted XSL-FO table, which makes use of colors and borders.

XSL-FO `table` objects are very powerful, especially when combined with XSLT, which allows for the automatic creation and population of tables using XSL. We will take a closer look at using XSLT and XSL-FO later in the "Integrating XSLT and XSL-FO" section.

LISTS

Another common formatting technique involves lists. There are a number of objects that are used explicitly for the creation and formatting of lists. These include

- `list-block`—This object contains the data and describes the formatting for a list of items.
- `list-item`—This contains an individual list item that consists of a `list-item-label` object and `list-item-body` object.
- `list-item-label`—This contains the label block (such as an individual character or graphics) for an individual list item.
- `list-item-body`—This contains the block of data for an individual list item.

Now let's see how these objects work together to create a list. This list will contain a list of customers for an imaginary company. We start with the `list-block` object, which contains a `list-item` object:

```
<fo:list-block>
<fo:list-item></fo:list-item>
</fo:list-block>
```


The `list-item` object will contain the `list-item-label`, which is the bullet that precedes items on the list. The `list-item-label` also has some properties, such as `start-indent` and `end-indent`. These properties determine the amount of space that will come between the item label and the list item itself:

```
<fo:list-item-label start-indent="2pt" end-indent="label-end()">
<fo:block>-</fo:block>
</fo:list-item-label>
```

Next, we have to define the list item itself, using the `list-item-body` object. This object also has a `start-indent` property, which is used to determine the offset from the `item-label` by determining where in its area the list starts:

```
<fo:list-item-body start-indent="body-start()">
<fo:block>American Manufacturing</fo:block>
</fo:list-item-body>
```

When we bring these objects together, along with the content of our list, the results are shown in Listing 10.5.

LISTING 10.5 A LIST CREATED USING THE XSL-FO LIST OBJECTS

```
<?xml version="1.0"?>
<fo:root xmlns:fo="http://www.w3.org/1999/XSL/Format">
 <fo:layout-master-set>
  <fo:simple-page-master master-name="Page"
      page-width="6in" page-height="8.0in"
      margin-top="0.5in" margin-bottom="0.5in"
      margin-left="0.5in" margin-right="0.5in">
  <fo:region-before extent="1.0in"/>
  <fo:region-body margin-top="1.0in" margin-bottom="1.0in"/>
  <fo:region-after  extent="1.0in"/>
  </fo:simple-page-master>
 </fo:layout-master-set>
 <fo:page-sequence master-name="Page">
  <fo:static-content flow-name="xsl-region-before">
```

LISTING 10.5 CONTINUED

```
    <fo:block font-size="18pt" font-family="serif"
        font-weight="bold" text-align="center">
     Widgets, Inc.
     <fo:leader leader-pattern="rule" leader-length="7.0in" />
    </fo:block>
   </fo:static-content>

   <fo:static-content flow-name="xsl-region-after">
    <fo:block font-size="12pt" font-family="serif" text-align="center">
     <fo:leader leader-pattern="rule" leader-length="7.0in" />
     Confidential, property of Widgets, Inc.
    </fo:block>
   </fo:static-content>

   <fo:flow flow-name="xsl-region-body">
    <fo:list-block>
     <fo:list-item>
      <fo:list-item-label start-indent="2pt" end-indent="label-end()">
       <fo:block>-</fo:block>
      </fo:list-item-label>
      <fo:list-item-body start-indent="body-start()">
       <fo:block>American Manufacturing</fo:block>
      </fo:list-item-body>
     </fo:list-item>
     <fo:list-item>
      <fo:list-item-label start-indent="2pt" end-indent="label-end()">
       <fo:block>-</fo:block>
      </fo:list-item-label>
      <fo:list-item-body start-indent="body-start()">
       <fo:block>Kyoto Manufacturing Concern</fo:block>
      </fo:list-item-body>
     </fo:list-item>
     <fo:list-item>
      <fo:list-item-label start-indent="2pt" end-indent="label-end()">
       <fo:block>-</fo:block>
      </fo:list-item-label>
      <fo:list-item-body start-indent="body-start()">
       <fo:block>Midwest Manufacturing</fo:block>
      </fo:list-item-body>
     </fo:list-item>
     <fo:list-item>
      <fo:list-item-label start-indent="2pt" end-indent="label-end()">
       <fo:block>-</fo:block>
      </fo:list-item-label>
      <fo:list-item-body start-indent="body-start()">
       <fo:block>Joe's Tools</fo:block>
      </fo:list-item-body>
     </fo:list-item>   </fo:list-block>
   </fo:flow>
  </fo:page-sequence>
</fo:root>
```

When this stylesheet is rendered, the resulting list is shown in Figure 10.7.

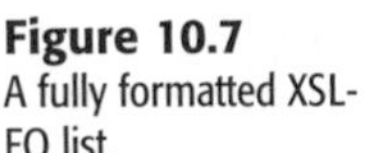

Figure 10.7
A fully formatted XSL-FO list.

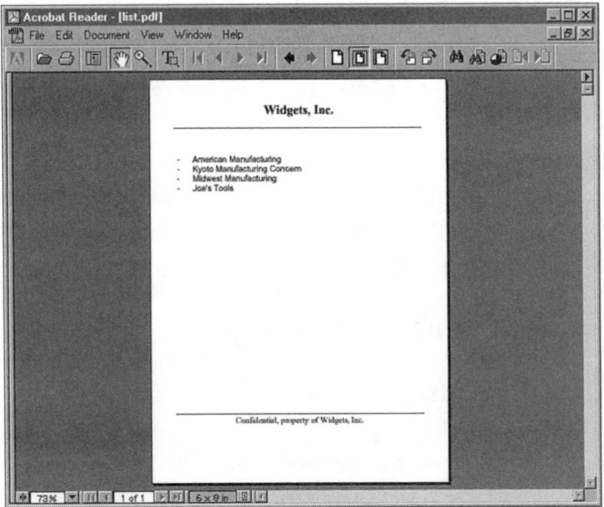

Both table and list objects can be very powerful, yet easy-to-use mechanisms for formatting documents with XSL. However, the power of these objects really comes from the manipulation of the properties that define the object's characteristics. Although we've already used a number of these properties, because it is really impossible to work with stylesheets without using them, now let's take a closer look at some of the more common properties and how they function with the XSL-FO objects.

PROPERTIES

The XSL-FO objects themselves would not be nearly as useful were it not for the properties that can be manipulated to affect how an object is rendered. In the XSL-FO examples we have used so far, you have already seen properties such as `font-size`, which is a property used to specify the size (in points) of the font being used to display a line of text.

Properties are used to express a variety of qualities with objects, from the size and color of borders, to padding inside block areas, to background images and font sizes and colors. The XSL-FO properties are expressed as attributes, which are used with XML elements that represent objects. For example, with the `block` object element, we can use the `font-family` property attribute to specify the font family to be used to render the text of the block.

BACKGROUND AND COLOR PROPERTIES

The background and color properties allow you to manipulate the quality of the background in areas and regions, and the color of an area. These properties include

- `background-color`—The `background-color` property is used to specify a color to be used as the background for an area. The area could be a region, or a `block` object, or any number of `table` objects.

- `background-image`—This property can be used to specify an image to be used as an object background. It accepts a URI (absolute or relative) as the value for the attribute.
- `background-repeat`—This property can be used to repeat a graphic image as a background, to achieve texture effects.
- `color`—The `color` property can be applied to a variety of objects and is used to set the value of the color of the object. The `color` property sets the value of the foreground color, so most commonly it can be used with the `block` object to manipulate the color of the font.

Let's take a look at an example. Say we wanted to change the color of the background of a text area to yellow. We could accomplish this by using the `background-color` property with the `block` object:

```
<?xml version="1.0"?>
<fo:root xmlns:fo="http://www.w3.org/1999/XSL/Format">
 <fo:layout-master-set>
  <fo:simple-page-master master-name="title_page">
  <fo:region-body/>
 </fo:simple-page-master>
 </fo:layout-master-set>

 <fo:page-sequence master-name="title_page">
  <fo:flow flow-name="xsl-region-body">
   <fo:block background-color="yellow" font-size="64pt" font-family="serif">
   A Yellow Background
   </fo:block>
  </fo:flow>
 </fo:page-sequence>

</fo:root>
```

The results of this are shown rendered in Figure 10.8. The result is that the area of the `block` object, which contains our text, is rendered with a bright yellow background.

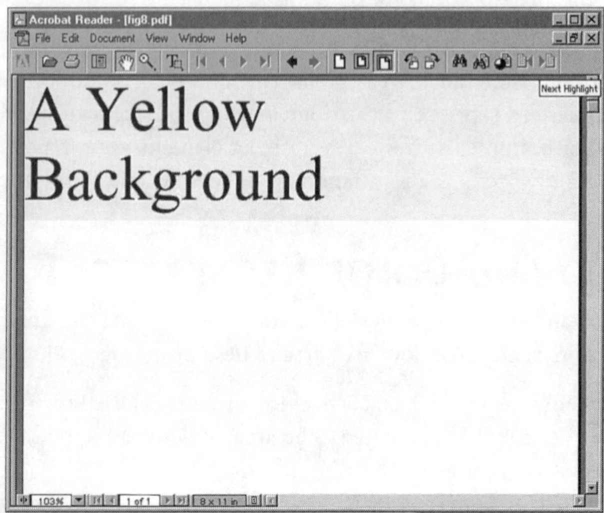

Figure 10.8 Manipulating a document's background using the `background-color` property.

BORDERS AND PADDING

Although border and padding properties can be used with many objects, including `block` objects, they are most commonly used with tables. These properties include

- `border-style`—This property allows you to select the style of the border for an object. Values for the `border-style` include `solid`, `dotted`, `dashed`, `groove`, and so on.
- `border-width`—This property defines the width of the border and accepts unit values, such as pt, px, and so on.
- `border-color`—The `border-color` property defines the color of the border of an area. It accepts color keyword values or hex color values.
- `padding`—The `padding` property specifies the amount of padding (in units) from the edge of an area rectangle. One of the most common uses for padding is to establish a buffer between a table border and the table content.

For example, if we wanted to create a table with a 4pt red border, and some padding for the cells, we would use the following:

```
<?xml version="1.0"?>
<fo:root xmlns:fo="http://www.w3.org/1999/XSL/Format">
 <fo:layout-master-set>
  <fo:simple-page-master master-name="title_page">
   <fo:region-body margin-left="1.0in"/>
  </fo:simple-page-master>
 </fo:layout-master-set>

 <fo:page-sequence master-name="title_page">
  <fo:flow flow-name="xsl-region-body">
   <fo:block>A simple table:</fo:block>

   <fo:table  border-style="solid" border-color="red" border-width="5pt">
    <fo:table-column column-width="12pc"/>
    <fo:table-column column-width="12pc"/>
    <fo:table-body>
     <fo:table-row>
      <fo:table-cell padding="5pt"><fo:block>5 point padding</fo:block>
➥</fo:table-cell>
      <fo:table-cell padding="10pt"><fo:block>10 point
➥padding</fo:block></fo:table-cell>
     </fo:table-row>
    </fo:table-body>
   </fo:table>
  </fo:flow>
 </fo:page-sequence>
</fo:root>
```

The results of this stylesheet are shown in Figure 10.9.

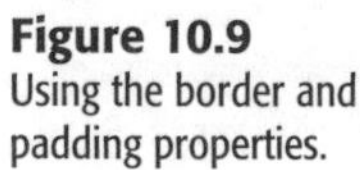

Figure 10.9
Using the border and padding properties.

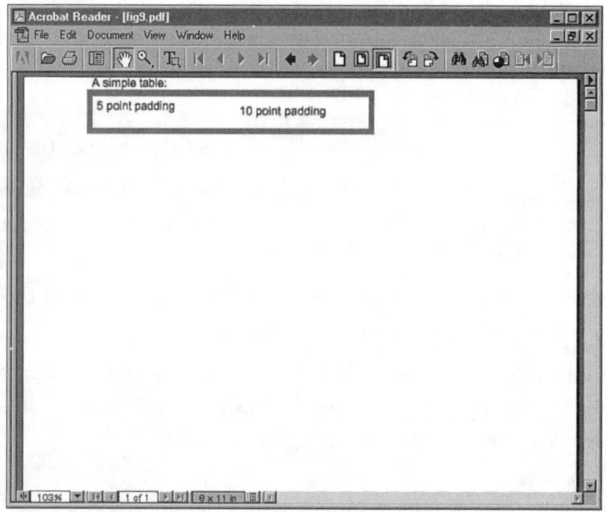

You can see the difference between the first and second table cells, based on the `padding` property, which creates a buffer zone between the border and the content of the table cells.

FONT PROPERTIES

One of the properties that will have the most visible impact on the appearance of your documents is the font face used to display the text. Manipulating the font style, size, and other aspects will bring dramatically different results to the final rendered document.

Here are some of the more common font properties you can use with XSL-FO:

- `font-family`—The `font-family` property allows you to choose the generic family of font to be used, such as `serif` or `sans-serif` fonts. Although you can specify specific typefaces, specifying a family ensures that the general appearance of your font will be acceptable, as not all font faces will be available to all XSL processors.
- `font-size`—This property allows you to set the size of the font the text should be rendered in. Typically, font sizes are specified using points (pt).
- font-style—The font style property accepts values such as `italic`, `oblique`, or `backslant`. These are common styles that can be applied to a variety of typefaces.
- `font-weight`—The font weight allows you to control the weight of the font, such as `bold`, or specify a numeric value, such as 100, 200, 300, and so on. The value of 700 is equivalent to `bold`.

Let's take a look at a stylesheet that shows off some of the changes the font properties can have on the text within a `block` object:

```
<?xml version="1.0"?>
<fo:root xmlns:fo="http://www.w3.org/1999/XSL/Format">
 <fo:layout-master-set>
```

```
  <fo:simple-page-master master-name="title_page">
   <fo:region-body/>
  </fo:simple-page-master>
 </fo:layout-master-set>

 <fo:page-sequence master-name="title_page">
  <fo:flow flow-name="xsl-region-body">
   <fo:block font-size="10pt" font-family="serif">10 point type</fo:block>
   <fo:block font-size="24pt" font-family="serif">24 point type</fo:block>
   <fo:block font-size="36pt" font-family="serif">36 point type</fo:block>
   <fo:block font-size="48pt" font-family="serif">A Serif Family Type</fo:block>
   <fo:block font-size="48pt" font-family="sans-serif">A Sans-Serif
➥Family</fo:block>
   <fo:block font-size="48pt" font-family="sans-serif" font-
➥style="italic">Italics</fo:block>
   <fo:block font-size="48pt" font-family="sans-serif" color="red">RED
➥type</fo:block>
  </fo:flow>
 </fo:page-sequence>

</fo:root>
```

The rendered results of the file can be seen in Figure 10.10.

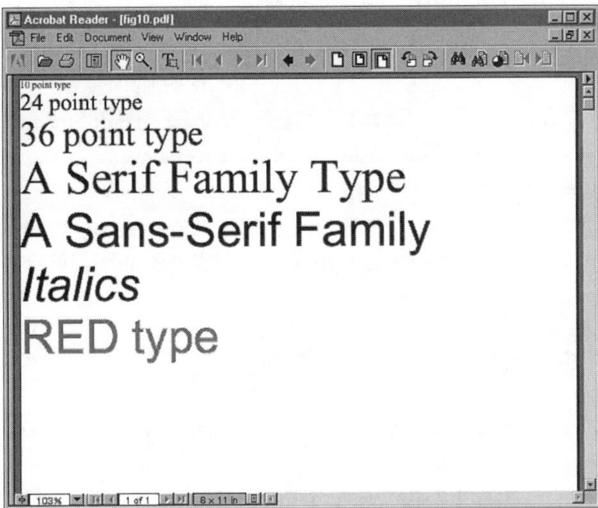

Figure 10.10
Manipulating type appearance with the font properties.

As you can see, manipulating the font properties of an object can have profound changes. Font manipulation is a very common way to alter the appearance of your documents.

TEXT

Finally, there are a number of properties that relate to the appearance and functionality of text in your documents. Not all of these properties will always be useful; however, these properties can be of vital importance if you are working with a non-Western language, or for gaining finer control over the flow of text within your documents.

Some of these text-related properties include

- `country`—This property allows you to specify the country code for the document being defined. The value of the country should be the recognized two-character country code.
- `language`—The `language` property allows you to control the language being used to render the document. This property will not directly affect the character encoding; however, it may affect how text is flowed within your document. For example, using a non-Western language such as Japanese or Arabic will cause text to be flowed in the appropriate direction for the language, rather than the top-to-bottom, left-to-right layout of English.
- `hyphenate`—This property allows you to turn hyphenation on or off.
- `wrap-option`—This property allows you to turn word wrapping on or off.
- `text-align`—This property determines how text is aligned within an object, such as a `block`. For example, text can be aligned `left`, `right`, or `center`.
- `letter-spacing`—This property allows you to specify the letter spacing used with a section of text.
- `word-spacing`—This property allows you to specify the word spacing used with a section of text.
- `break-before` and `break-after`—These two properties can be used to help keep areas of text (such as a `block`) together. You can choose to have the formatter insert page breaks before or after an object.
- `orphans` and `widows`—Orphans and widows are characters or lines of text that are separated significantly from the rest of their text—for example, the last sentence in a chapter that flows over onto a new page. These properties allow you to specify how much text is allowed to be orphaned or widowed before the processor will go back, and insert a page break and reflow the text in order to eliminate these stragglers.

Manipulation of these properties can allow you to produce vibrant, complete documents using a variety of character sets and languages, and to ensure that the text in your document appears exactly as you would like it to appear.

INTEGRATING XSLT AND XSL-FO

Of course, XSL-FO is a part of the XSL Recommendation, and as such, you shouldn't think of it as being entirely separate from other extremely useful aspects of XSL and XSLT. In fact, one of the most powerful applications of XSL-FO involves building the XSL-FO sheets dynamically using XSL Transformations.

In the examples we have used so far in this chapter, we have inserted the data our stylesheets are formatting directly into the stylesheet itself. However, separating content from display is one of the points of a structured markup language such as XML. One way in which we can use an XSL-FO stylesheet while still having our data separate in an XML file is through XSLT.

For example, let's say we had a very simple table, which was simply a list of first and last names:

First	Last
John	Doe
Jane	Doe
Billy	Doe

Now, the names from this table should be stored in an instance document that looks something like this:

```
<people>
 <name>
  <first>John</first>
  <last>Doe</last>
 </name>
 <name>
  <first>Jane</first>
  <last>Doe</last>
 </name>
 <name>
  <first>Billy</first>
  <last>Doe</last>
 </name>
</people>
```

Now, we could insert this information directly into an XSL-FO sheet:

```
<fo:table-body>
 <fo:table-row>
  <fo:table-cell><fo:block>John</fo:block></fo:table-cell>
  <fo:table-cell><fo:block>Doe</fo:block></fo:table-cell>
 </fo:table-row>
 <fo:table-row>
  <fo:table-cell><fo:block>Jane</fo:block></fo:table-cell>
  <fo:table-cell><fo:block>Doe</fo:block></fo:table-cell>
 </fo:table-row>
 <fo:table-row>
  <fo:table-cell><fo:block>Billy</fo:block></fo:table-cell>
  <fo:table-cell><fo:block>Doe</fo:block></fo:table-cell>
 </fo:table-row>
<fo:table-body>
```

However, then what happens if we add another name to the XML file? We could cut and paste the new name into the stylesheet, but this can introduce errors, creates more work, and isn't how XML should be used.

Instead, we can build the stylesheet dynamically with XSLT, along the lines of

```
<xsl:for-each select="name">
  <fo:table-body>
```

```
  <fo:table-row>
  <fo:table-cell><fo:block>
  <xsl:value-of select="first"/>
  </fo:block></fo:table-cell>
  <fo:table-cell><fo:block>
  <xsl:value-of select="last"/>
  </fo:block></fo:table-cell>
  </fo:table-row>
  </fo:table-body>
</xsl:for-each>
```

By using XSLT to extract the information for our final document directly from the XML file, we can be confident that anytime the XML file is updated, we can simply create a new document, and the update will be reflected. Let's look at another example.

Let's say the information regarding some customer and product data is stored in an XML document, such as shown in Listing 10.6.

LISTING 10.6 THE XML INSTANCE DOCUMENT CONTAINING COMPANY DATA

```
<?xml version="1.0"?>
<widgets-inc>
 <logo>logo.gif</logo>

 <catalog>
  <part number="AB2992">
   <item>Casters</item>
   <price>$19.99</price>
   <stock>Yes</stock>
  </part>

  <part number="CY9932">
   <item>Handle</item>
   <price>$5.99</price>
   <stock>Yes</stock>
  </part>

  <part number="DF9921">
   <item>Drawer</item>
   <price>$9.99</price>
   <stock>Yes</stock>
  </part>

  <part number="XV2201">
   <item>Storage Unit</item>
   <price>$99.99</price>
   <stock>No</stock>
  </part>

  <part number="FG2231">
   <item>Print Manual</item>
   <price>$2.99</price>
   <stock>Yes</stock>
  </part>
```

LISTING 10.6 CONTINUED

```
 </catalog>

 <customers>
  <company>American Manufacturing</company>
  <company>Kyoto Manufacturing Concern</company>
  <company>Midwest Manufacturing</company>
  <company>Joe's Tools</company>
 </customers>
</widgets-inc>
```

The data contained in our .xml shown in Listing 10.6 is a simple XML file. However, it is important to note that the file does not contain any formatting information. The information contained in the .xml file is all data. We can use XSL to apply formatting information to the file, to create a final rendered document. We start with an XSLT stylesheet, which combines the data from the .xml file with the XSL-FO code necessary to render the final document.

For example, to build the list of customers this memo is intended for, we can use the following template:

```
<xsl:template match="customers">
 <xsl:for-each select="company">
  <fo:list-item>
   <fo:list-item-label start-indent="2pt" end-indent="label-end()">
    <fo:block>-</fo:block>
   </fo:list-item-label>
   <fo:list-item-body start-indent="body-start()">
    <fo:block>
     <xsl:value-of select="."/>
    </fo:block>
   </fo:list-item-body>
  </fo:list-item>
 </xsl:for-each>
</xsl:template>
```

This will cause a separate list item to be created with each `<company>` instance that is encountered when we process the XSLT sheet. We can do something similar to build the table that contains our part listing:

```
<xsl:template match="catalog">
 <xsl:for-each select="part">
  <fo:table-row background-color="white" color="black">
   <fo:table-cell padding="2pt">
    <fo:block>
     <xsl:value-of select="@number"/>
    </fo:block>
   </fo:table-cell>
   <fo:table-cell padding="2pt">
    <fo:block>
     <xsl:value-of select="item"/>
    </fo:block>
   </fo:table-cell>
   <fo:table-cell padding="2pt">
```

```
      <fo:block>
       <xsl:value-of select="price"/>
      </fo:block>
     </fo:table-cell>
     <fo:table-cell padding="2pt">
      <fo:block>
       <xsl:value-of select="stock"/>
      </fo:block>
     </fo:table-cell>
    </fo:table-row>
   </xsl:for-each>
  </xsl:template>
```

This will populate our table with the part, and its associated information, for each part that is encountered in our XML document. This way, our table always reflects the content of the XML document. When we pull this information together into a complete XSLT stylesheet, we have the code shown in Listing 10.7.

LISTING 10.7 THE XSLT STYLESHEET USED TO GENERATE THE FINAL XSL-FO DOCUMENT

```
<?xml version="1.0"?>
<xsl:stylesheet version="1.0"
     xmlns:xsl="http://www.w3.org/1999/XSL/Transform"
     xmlns:fo="http://www.w3.org/1999/XSL/Format">
 <xsl:output indent="yes"/>
 <xsl:template match="/">

 <fo:root xmlns:fo="http://www.w3.org/1999/XSL/Format">
  <fo:layout-master-set>
   <fo:simple-page-master master-name="Catalog"
       page-width="8.5in" page-height="11.0in"
       margin-top="0.5in" margin-bottom="0.5in"
       margin-left="0.5in" margin-right="0.5in">
    <fo:region-before extent="2.0in"/>
    <fo:region-body margin-top="2.0in" margin-bottom="1.0in"/>
    <fo:region-after  extent="1.0in"/>
   </fo:simple-page-master>
  </fo:layout-master-set>

  <fo:page-sequence master-name="Catalog">
   <fo:static-content flow-name="xsl-region-before">
    <fo:block text-align="center">
     <fo:external-graphic src="logo.gif"/>
    </fo:block>
    <fo:block text-align="center" font-family="sans-serif"
        font-size="18pt" font-weight="bold">
     Widgets, Inc.
    </fo:block>
   </fo:static-content>

   <fo:static-content flow-name="xsl-region-after">
    <fo:block text-align="center" font-family="sans-serif"
        font-size="12pt" font-style="italic">
     Last updated January 1, 2002
    </fo:block>
   </fo:static-content>
```

LISTING 10.7 CONTINUED

```
   <fo:flow flow-name="xsl-region-body">
    <fo:block font-family="sans-serif" font-size="12pt" padding="1pc">
     Catalog Update Issued to the Following Customers:
    </fo:block>
    <fo:list-block>
     <xsl:apply-templates select="//customers"/>
    </fo:list-block>
    <fo:block padding="1pc">
     Please consult your product manual for part numbers.
    </fo:block>
    <fo:table border-collapse="separate" border-style="solid"
        border-color="black" border-width="1pt">
     <fo:table-column column-width="8pc"/>
     <fo:table-column column-width="12pc"/>
     <fo:table-column column-width="8pc"/>
     <fo:table-column column-width="4pc"/>

     <fo:table-header>
      <fo:table-row background-color="black" color="red">
       <fo:table-cell number-columns-spanned="4" padding="2pt">
         <fo:block>Part Catalog</fo:block>
       </fo:table-cell>
      </fo:table-row>
     </fo:table-header>

     <fo:table-body>
      <fo:table-row background-color="gray" color="white">
       <fo:table-cell padding="2pt"><fo:block>Part Number</fo:block>
➥</fo:table-cell>
       <fo:table-cell padding="2pt"><fo:block>Description</fo:block>
➥</fo:table-cell>
       <fo:table-cell padding="2pt"><fo:block>Unit Price</fo:block>
➥</fo:table-cell>
       <fo:table-cell padding="2pt"><fo:block>In Stock</fo:block></fo:table-cell>
      </fo:table-row>
      <xsl:apply-templates select="//catalog"/>
     </fo:table-body>
    </fo:table>
   </fo:flow>
  </fo:page-sequence>
 </fo:root>
</xsl:template>

  <xsl:template match="customers">
   <xsl:for-each select="company">
    <fo:list-item>
     <fo:list-item-label start-indent="2pt" end-indent="label-end()">
      <fo:block>-</fo:block>
     </fo:list-item-label>
     <fo:list-item-body start-indent="body-start()">
      <fo:block>
       <xsl:value-of select="."/>
      </fo:block>
     </fo:list-item-body>
    </fo:list-item>
```

LISTING 10.7 CONTINUED

```
    </xsl:for-each>
   </xsl:template>

   <xsl:template match="catalog">
    <xsl:for-each select="part">
    <fo:table-row background-color="white" color="black">
     <fo:table-cell padding="2pt"><fo:block>
       <xsl:value-of select="@number"/>
     </fo:block></fo:table-cell>
     <fo:table-cell padding="2pt"><fo:block>
      <xsl:value-of select="item"/>
     </fo:block></fo:table-cell>
     <fo:table-cell padding="2pt"><fo:block>
      <xsl:value-of select="price"/>
     </fo:block></fo:table-cell>
     <fo:table-cell padding="2pt"><fo:block>
      <xsl:value-of select="stock"/>
     </fo:block></fo:table-cell>
    </fo:table-row>
   </xsl:for-each>
  </xsl:template>
</xsl:stylesheet>
```

Listing 10.8 shows the result of building the stylesheet automatically, which is similar to what we might have coded by hand; however, this is guaranteed to be in sync with the XML document, although the cut-and-paste method could easily introduce errors.

LISTING 10.8 THE `xsl-fo` DOCUMENT THAT CAN BE USED TO RENDER THE FINAL DOCUMENT

```
<?xml version="1.0"?>
<fo:root xmlns:fo="http://www.w3.org/1999/XSL/Format">
 <fo:layout-master-set>
  <fo:simple-page-master master-name="Catalog"
      page-width="8.5in" page-height="11.0in"
      margin-top="0.5in" margin-bottom="0.5in"
      margin-left="0.5in" margin-right="0.5in">
   <fo:region-before extent="2.0in"/>
   <fo:region-body margin-top="2.0in" margin-bottom="1.0in"/>
   <fo:region-after  extent="1.0in"/>
  </fo:simple-page-master>
 </fo:layout-master-set>

 <fo:page-sequence master-name="Catalog">
  <fo:static-content flow-name="xsl-region-before">
   <fo:block text-align="center">
    <fo:external-graphic src="logo.gif"/>
   </fo:block>
   <fo:block text-align="center" font-family="sans-serif"
       font-size="18pt" font-weight="bold">
    Widgets, Inc.
   </fo:block>
  </fo:static-content>
```

LISTING 10.8 CONTINUED

```
<fo:static-content flow-name="xsl-region-after">
 <fo:block text-align="center" font-family="sans-serif"
     font-size="12pt" font-style="italic">
  Last updated January 1, 2002
 </fo:block>
</fo:static-content>

<fo:flow flow-name="xsl-region-body">
 <fo:block font-family="sans-serif" font-size="12pt" padding="1pc">
  Catalog Update Issued to the Following Customers:
 </fo:block>
 <fo:list-block>
  <fo:list-item>
   <fo:list-item-label start-indent="2pt" end-indent="label-end()">
    <fo:block>-</fo:block>
   </fo:list-item-label>
   <fo:list-item-body start-indent="body-start()">
    <fo:block>American Manufacturing</fo:block>
   </fo:list-item-body>
  </fo:list-item>

  <fo:list-item>
   <fo:list-item-label start-indent="2pt" end-indent="label-end()">
    <fo:block>-</fo:block>
   </fo:list-item-label>
   <fo:list-item-body start-indent="body-start()">
    <fo:block>Kyoto Manufacturing Concern</fo:block>
   </fo:list-item-body>
  </fo:list-item>

  <fo:list-item>
   <fo:list-item-label start-indent="2pt" end-indent="label-end()">
    <fo:block>-</fo:block>
   </fo:list-item-label>
   <fo:list-item-body start-indent="body-start()">
    <fo:block>Midwest Manufacturing</fo:block>
   </fo:list-item-body>
  </fo:list-item>

  <fo:list-item>
   <fo:list-item-label start-indent="2pt" end-indent="label-end()">
    <fo:block>-</fo:block>
   </fo:list-item-label>
   <fo:list-item-body start-indent="body-start()">
     <fo:block>Joe's Tools</fo:block>
   </fo:list-item-body>
  </fo:list-item>
 </fo:list-block>

 <fo:block padding="1pc">
  Please consult your product manual for part numbers.
 </fo:block>
 <fo:table border-collapse="separate" border-style="solid"
     border-color="black" border-width="1pt">
  <fo:table-column column-width="8pc"/>
  <fo:table-column column-width="12pc"/>
```

10

LISTING 10.8 CONTINUED

```
    <fo:table-column column-width="8pc"/>
    <fo:table-column column-width="4pc"/>

    <fo:table-header>
     <fo:table-row background-color="black" color="red">
      <fo:table-cell number-columns-spanned="4" padding="2pt">
       <fo:block>Part Catalog</fo:block>
      </fo:table-cell>
     </fo:table-row>
    </fo:table-header>

    <fo:table-body>
     <fo:table-row background-color="grey" color="white">
      <fo:table-cell padding="2pt"><fo:block>Part Number</fo:block>
➥</fo:table-cell>
      <fo:table-cell padding="2pt"><fo:block>Description</fo:block>
➥</fo:table-cell>
      <fo:table-cell padding="2pt"><fo:block>Unit Price</fo:block></fo:table-cell>
      <fo:table-cell padding="2pt"><fo:block>In Stock</fo:block></fo:table-cell>
     </fo:table-row>
     <fo:table-row background-color="white" color="black">
      <fo:table-cell padding="4pt"><fo:block>AB2992</fo:block></fo:table-cell>
      <fo:table-cell padding="4pt"><fo:block>Casters</fo:block></fo:table-cell>
      <fo:table-cell padding="4pt"><fo:block>$19.99</fo:block></fo:table-cell>
      <fo:table-cell padding="4pt"><fo:block>Yes</fo:block></fo:table-cell>
     </fo:table-row>
     <fo:table-row background-color="white" color="black">
      <fo:table-cell padding="4pt"><fo:block>CY9932</fo:block></fo:table-cell>
      <fo:table-cell padding="4pt"><fo:block>Handle</fo:block></fo:table-cell>
      <fo:table-cell padding="4pt"><fo:block>$5.99</fo:block></fo:table-cell>
      <fo:table-cell padding="4pt"><fo:block>Yes</fo:block></fo:table-cell>
     </fo:table-row>
     <fo:table-row background-color="white" color="black">
      <fo:table-cell padding="4pt"><fo:block>DF9921</fo:block></fo:table-cell>
      <fo:table-cell padding="4pt"><fo:block>Drawer</fo:block></fo:table-cell>
      <fo:table-cell padding="4pt"><fo:block>$9.99</fo:block></fo:table-cell>
      <fo:table-cell padding="4pt"><fo:block>Yes</fo:block></fo:table-cell>
     </fo:table-row>
     <fo:table-row background-color="white" color="black">
      <fo:table-cell padding="4pt"><fo:block>XV2201</fo:block></fo:table-cell>
      <fo:table-cell padding="4pt"><fo:block>Storage Unit</fo:block>
➥</fo:table-cell>
      <fo:table-cell padding="4pt"><fo:block>$99.99</fo:block></fo:table-cell>
      <fo:table-cell padding="4pt"><fo:block>No</fo:block></fo:table-cell>
     </fo:table-row>
     <fo:table-row background-color="white" color="black">
      <fo:table-cell padding="4pt"><fo:block>FG2231</fo:block></fo:table-cell>
      <fo:table-cell padding="4pt"><fo:block>Print Manual</fo:block>
➥</fo:table-cell>
      <fo:table-cell padding="4pt"><fo:block>$2.99</fo:block></fo:table-cell>
      <fo:table-cell padding="4pt"><fo:block>Yes</fo:block></fo:table-cell>
     </fo:table-row>
    </fo:table-body>
   </fo:table>
```

LISTING 10.8 CONTINUED

```
  </fo:flow>
 </fo:page-sequence>

</fo:root>
```

When the .xsl stylesheet is applied to the .xml document, the result is an XSL-FO stylesheet, which can be rendered to produce the final document, as shown in Figure 10.11.

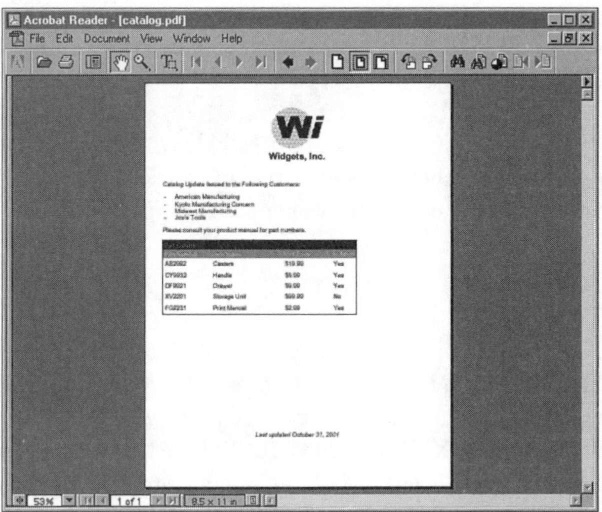

Figure 10.11
The final rendered output based on the .xml and .xsl files.

Depending on the structure of your XML files, and the desired output, you could even further customize the stylesheet—for example, pulling table headers from element or attribute names. The stylesheet can really be built as flexibly as you need.

The ability to utilize other areas of XSL, such as XSLT in conjunction with XSL-FO, is where you really begin to see the benefits of stylesheets. Using XML to create structured documents is the ideal way to separate content from presentation, and with XSLT you can then take that content and automatically generate the presentation files using all the features of XSL.

ADDITIONAL RESOURCES

Because XSL-FO is a relatively new technology, the support for XSL-FO is not as robust as the support for HTML or CSS. However, there are a number of resources that can help with your XSL-FO development:

- XSL-FO (`http://groups.yahoo.com/group/xsl-fo/`)—The XSL-FO discussion group/mailing list is a good resource for discussing XSL-FO solutions with other developers, and can be a source for news and information regarding the latest in XSL-FO.

- XSL Formatter (`http://www.antennahouse.com/axf20/AXF20topEN.htm`)—XML Formatter is an application that can be used with both XSL-T and XSL-FO stylesheets. More information on XML Formatter can be found at the manufacturer's site at the previous link.
- X-Smiles (`http://www.xsmiles.org/`)—X-Smiles is an XML-compliant browser that supports the rendering of XSL-FO stylesheets. Currently, X-Smile is the only browser that supports XML natively, and allows the display of XML in conjunction with XSL stylesheets.
- FOP (`http://xml.apache.org/fop/`)—FOP is an open-source XSL-FO formatter from the Apache Project. FOP is the rendering engine used in X-Smiles, and also was used to generate all the examples in this chapter.

With time, XSL, XSLT, and XSL-FO support will likely find its way into all the major browser vendors, as well as other types of layout applications. Until then, you might have to use some creative solutions; however, tools like FOP are progressing at a rapid pace.

ROADMAP

XSL-FO is the last piece of the XSL puzzle, bringing the stylesheet technology full circle from using XML on the Web to using XML in print (as PDFs). You've now seen how XSL Stylesheets are put together, and how you can use technologies like XSLT to transform your XML documents from plain XML into HTML, XHTML, and finally into an XSL-FO sheet. These XSL-FO sheets can then be used to generate PDF files which could be printed or downloaded by your organization's clients and customers.

XSL-FO really rounds out the last of the presentation technologies that are associated with XML. However, we've already touched on some of the technologies that will be covered now. For example, XSLT makes use of XPath to locate various elements and attributes within your XML documents. In Part III, "XML Location Technologies," we will take a closer look at the tools you can use with XML to locate XML components within larger documents, or to assemble document fragments into a single document. As we've already seen, location technologies go hand-in-hand with presentation technologies, and they will fit together with other pieces of the XML jigsaw puzzle as well.

PART III

XML Location Technologies

CHAPTER 11

Locating Components in XML Documents with XPath

In this chapter

by Andrew Watt

One of the fundamental things that you need to do when retrieving or manipulating any XML content is to locate the part of the XML document that you want to work on. If you want to extract selected XML information, you need a syntax to unambiguously express the parts of the XML document you want to extract. XPath provides that syntax.

WHAT IS XPATH?

XPath is a language intended to be used with XML documents in order to allow addressing of selected parts of an XML document. This allows some desired process to be carried out on that selected data—perhaps some form of data retrieval or manipulation.

One of the major advantages of XPath is that we simply declare the part of the document that we want to select. We don't have to spell out step-by-step in lengthy code how a processor does the work of locating and navigating to the desired node. The XPath processor does that work for us.

XPath is not written in XML. It more resembles the kind of path information that your operating system might show you or that you frequently see within URLs. One reason XPath is not written in XML is that it is frequently expressed as the value of an attribute on an XML element. If the XPath expression had to be written in XML syntax, it would be necessary to escape characters such as < (the less-than sign) and replace them with entities: in this case, `<`.

XPath can also be looked at as a data model for XML documents. XPath models an XML document as a tree of nodes. Just as a directory path structure can be seen as a hierarchy of directories, an XML document can be viewed as a hierarchy of nodes.

XPath provides a data model only for well-formed XML documents. Each well-formed XML document has a node, called the `root node`, which is at the base of the hierarchy. Just as a well-formed XML document might have only one document element, the `root node` is allowed to have only one child element node.

Listing 11.1 shows a skeleton XHTML 1.0 listing. In a moment, we will discuss how different parts of the document are represented in XPath.

LISTING 11.1 A SKELETON XHTML DOCUMENT (XHTML1.HTML)

```
<?xml version="1.0"?>
<!-- This is an XHTML comment. -->
<!DOCTYPE html
PUBLIC "-//W3C//DTD XHTML 1.0 Transitional//EN"
"DTD/xhtml1-transitional.dtd">
<html>
<head>
<title>XHTML 1.0 Transitional Template</title>
</head>
<body>
<!-- Some content would go here. -->
</body>
</html>
```

The following describes how the XPath model represents the parts of the XML document as a hierarchy of nodes.

XPath represents the document itself as a `root node`. The XML declaration and the `DOCTYPE` declaration that we can see in the code listing are, perhaps surprisingly, *not* represented at all in the XPath 1.0 data model. The root node has two child nodes—a `comment` node and a `html` element node. The `html` element node is the representation of the document `html` element in the listing. The root node can only have exactly one child element node.

The `html` element node has a `head` element node as its first child. The `head` element node has, in turn, a `title` element node as its child. The text content of the `title` element is represented as a `text node`, which is a child of the `title` element node.

The other child element node of the `html` element node is the `body` element node. The `body` element node has a single child comment node.

In addition to the node types just mentioned, XPath provides `namespace nodes`, `attribute nodes`, and `processing instruction nodes`. These will be discussed later in the chapter.

WHAT DOES XPATH DO?

XPath allows us to write declarative code that describes which parts of the tree model of any XML document we want to locate. Typically, XPath is used in conjunction with another XML-related technology. At the time of writing, XPath's most common usage is with the *Extensible Stylesheet Transformation Language (XSLT)*. XSLT is described in Chapter 9, "Transforming XML Data into Other Formats with XSLT."

11

For example, if we wanted to display the content of information elements that were not secret, we could use XPath, in conjunction with XSLT, to construct a simple HTML/XHTML Web page. Listing 11.2 shows the data we will work with.

LISTING 11.2 A DATA STORE CONTAINING PUBLICLY ACCESSIBLE AND SECRET INFORMATION (DATASTORE.XML)

```
<?xml version='1.0'?>
<DataStore>
 <Information type="public">
  George Bush is President.
 </Information>
 <Information type="secret">
  One and one is two.
 </Information>
 <Information type="public">
  Tony Blair is Prime Minister.
 </Information>
 <Information type="secret">
  XPath, just occasionally, is fun!
 </Information>
</DataStore>
```

In the simple data store, we have information we want to be publicly accessible and information we deem *secret*. We could use a simple XSLT stylesheet, such as the one shown in Listing 11.3, to create an HTML file that shows only the information intended for public consumption. After all, we wouldn't want anyone to know that XPath can be fun.

Listing 11.3 An XSLT Stylesheet to Create an XHTML Web Page Containing Only Non-Confidential Information (PublicViewing.xsl)

```
<?xml version='1.0'?>
<xsl:stylesheet
       xmlns:xsl="http://www.w3.org/1999/XSL/Transform"
       version="1.0">
<xsl:output
 indent="yes"
 doctype-public="-//W3C//DTD XHTML 1.0 Transitional//EN"
 doctype-system="DTD/xhtml1-transitional.dtd"
/>

<xsl:template match="/">
<html>
<head>
<title>Publicly available information from the data store</title>
</head>
<body>
<xsl:apply-templates select="//Information[@type='public']"/>
</body>
</html>
</xsl:template>

<xsl:template match="Information">
<p><xsl:value-of select="."/></p>
</xsl:template>

</xsl:stylesheet>
```

You were introduced to XSLT in Chapter 9, so hopefully the syntax of a short style sheet such as that in Listing 11.3 is familiar.

The XHTML file output when the XSLT style sheet is applied to the data store produces an appearance similar to that shown in Figure 11.1.

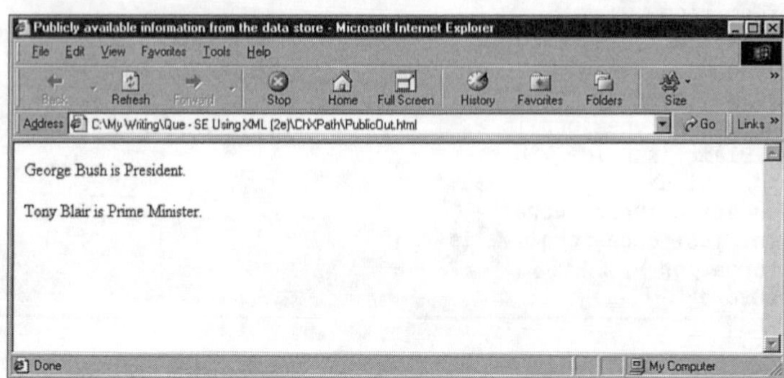

Figure 11.1 Only information suitable for public viewing is shown, as determined by the XPath predicate `[@type="public"]`.

The key to the working of the XSLT style sheet is the XPath path expression that is the value of the `select` attribute of the `xsl:apply-templates` element—`//Information[@type="public"]`. Briefly, the `//Information` part of the path expression indicates that the template should be applied to all `Information` element nodes within the source XML document. The `[@type="public"]` indicates that of those nodes, only those that have a `type` attribute which has a value of `public` are to be processed.

The XSLT Template that matches the XPath path expression `Information` (see the second `xsl:template` element in the listing) causes the output of an XHTML `p` element whose content is defined by another XPath path expression, `.`, a single period—which refers to the content of the `Information` element node being processed.

How Is XPath Used?

As you saw in the example from the previous section, XPath can be used with XSLT to process selected nodes. In addition, XPath can be used in XPointer, the XML Pointer Language.

Furthermore, XPath is also used in the emerging XForms specification and the XML Security standards such as Canonical XML and XML Signatures. The use of XPath in XForms is described in Chapter 25, "Using XML to Create Forms: XForms." Further information on Canonical XML Recommendation is located at `http://www.w3.org/TR/xml-c14n`. The XML Signatures Recommendation is located at `http://www.w3.org/TR/xmldsig-core/`.

11

XSLT

XSLT became a W3C Recommendation as far back as November 1999 and is currently the dominant use of XPath. Many XSLT tools are available for the transformation of XML documents, and all the recent tools implement XPath pretty much as described in the W3C XPath Recommendation.

XSLT is used to transform a source XML document and produce an output document or an output stream of bytes. The output document is, in most situations, often displayed onscreen or stored in an XML-based data store.

Listing 11.3 shows typical ways in which XPath is used. The `select` attribute of an `xsl:apply-templates` element has a value that is an XPath path expression. The following is another example of a simple path expression:

```
/html/head/title
```

If we applied it to the XHTML document in Listing 11.1, the `title` element node would be selected.

At the other end of the spectrum, XSLT can make use of very precise, lengthy XPath location paths such as the following:

```
/Book/Chapter[@number="3"]/Section[@title="Introduction"]/Paragraph[number="1"]
```

The preceding would select the first `Paragraph` element node in the `Introduction` section of the third chapter of a book.

XPOINTER

XPointer is a way to address fragments of an XML document. Using XPointer, it is possible to address nodes, just as in XPath, but XPointer extends XPath by adding addressing of two further types of fragments—`point` and `range`.

In XPath, we either select whole nodes or omit a node in its entirety. XPointer lets us select parts of a node and lets us make selections that cross the boundaries of a node. The kind of selection we can make onscreen illustrates what we can do with XPointer. Figure 11.2 shows a selection made by dragging onscreen. Listing 11.4 shows the source code.

LISTING 11.4 A SIMPLE XML DOCUMENT SUITABLE FOR SELECTIONS TO BE MADE (SELECTIONS.XML)

```
<?xml version='1.0'?>
<Selections>
<Selection>This is uninteresting</Selection>
<Selection>This is boring. This is fascinating.</Selection>
<Selection>This too is fascinating. This is dull</Selection>
</Selections>
```

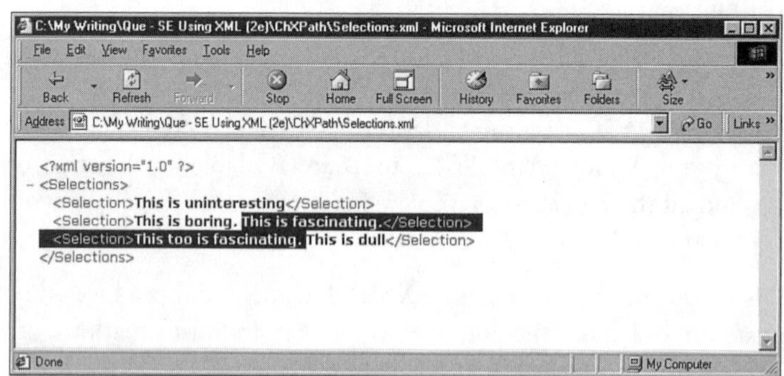

Figure 11.2
Selecting text across nodes. This is possible with XPointer, but not with XPath.

Think of the starting edge of the highlighted area as a `point` in XPointer. The selected text from the start point to the end point can be thought of as similar to an XPointer `range`. XPointer will be described more fully in Chapter 12, "Extending the Power of XPath with XPointer."

XQUERY

XQuery, or the XML Query Language, is designed to provide a query language for XML documents that is similar to those for relational database management systems.

As you've seen with XSLT, XPath already provides some useful means to query an XML document. However, XPath version 1.0 is inadequate to support a sophisticated query.

XQuery extends XPath to provide more functionality, such as the ability to compute join results.

XQuery is introduced in Chapter 20, “Query Documents Using XQuery.”

XPATH CONCEPTS

In this section, we will review the way in which an XPath processor views an XML document.

XML DOCUMENTS AS TREES

An XML document simply consists of a series of characters. The use of characters to create the logical structure for that document is constrained by the rules of XML 1.0. In XML 1.0 syntax, we might have elements nested within each other, as shown in the following code snippet:

```
<AnElement>
 <AnotherElement>
  <!-- Some more content -->
 </AnotherElement>
</AnElement>
```

The outermost element can also be viewed in the XPath data model as a node from which branches can spread out. The `AnElement` element is, in the XPath data model, represented by an element node—the `AnElement` element node. The `AnotherElement` element node is a child element node of the `AnElement` element node.

Whatever the complexity of the tree created from an XML document, it has one root node as the top of the hierarchy.

NODES

XPath represents all parts of an XML document, except the XML declaration (if present) and the `DOCTYPE` declaration, which have no representation, as nodes.

There are seven node types in XPath 1.0—root node, element node, text node, comment node, attribute node, namespace node, and processing instruction node. Each of these nodes will be described in more detail later in the chapter.

AXES

XPath Axes can be viewed as the directions you use to navigate around the XPath hierarchy of nodes. In total, XPath has 13 axes that will be described later in this chapter. The most commonly used axes are the child axis and the attribute axis.

EXPRESSIONS

XPath expressions can be evaluated to any of the four data types recognized by XPath—that is, to Boolean, node-set, string, or number values.

The subset of XPath expressions that return a node-set are termed a *location path*.

LOCATION PATHS

A location path returns a node-set. A location path is made up of one or more location steps. Each location step consists of an axis, a node test, and an optional predicate.

Let's look at an example that uses a single location step.

```
/child::Chapter[@number="1"]
```

In the preceding example, we start with the root node as context node. The `/` character indicates this. The axis is the `child` axis. The node test is `Chapter`, which indicates that of all possible child nodes, it is child element nodes with the name `Chapter` that are to be chosen. Finally, the predicate `[@number="1"]` indicates that of those `Chapter` element nodes selected by the axis and node test, only those whose `number` attribute has a value of `"1"` are to be selected.

An abbreviated XPath syntax allows us to write the following with the same meaning:

```
/Chapter[@number="1"]
```

Essentially, the child axis is the default axis and therefore doesn't need to be specified.

The following code allows us to look at a three-step location path:

```
<Invoice>
 <Purchaser id="12345">
  <Name>George Bush</Name>
  <Address1>1600 Pennsylvania Avenue</Address1>
  <City>Washington</City>
 </Purchaser>
</Invoice>
```

The following location path would select the element node corresponding to the `Address1` element:

```
/Invoice/Purchaser[@id="12345"]/Address1
```

Again, we start with the context node as the root node. The first location step has the implicit child axis, a node test of `Invoice` element nodes, and no predicate. The next `/` character is a separator between location steps. In the second location step, the implicit child axis is again used, the node test selects `Purchaser` element nodes, and the predicate `[@id="12345"]` selects `Purchaser` element nodes that possess an `id` attribute whose value is `"12345"`. The third location step has an implicit child axis and a node test that selects `Address1` element nodes. As you can see, except for the first forward slash, location steps are separated by forward slashes. The first forward slash signifies that location path is an absolute location path and selects the root node of the document containing the context node.

FUNCTIONS

XPath provides a library of core functions that can be used within XPath expressions. These will be described later in the chapter.

CONTEXT

Context in XPath refers to the location relative to which an XPath expression is evaluated. This is similar to a set of street directions. You need to know your starting point before being able to correctly interpret instructions such as, "Go along three streets, and the house is the first on the right with a green door."

You can explicitly set the context to be the root node by beginning a location path with the / character.

CONTEXT SIZE

The context size is one component of an XPath context.

```
<Chapter>
 <Paragraph>Some text.</Paragraph>
 <Paragraph>Some more text.</Paragraph>
 <Paragraph>Some additional text.</Paragraph>
 <Paragraph>Yet more text.</Paragraph>
</Chapter>
```

If the preceding snippet was an entire XML document and we had an XPath location path `/Chapter/Paragraph`, the context size would be four because four `Paragraph` element nodes in the document satisfy the requirements of the location path.

CONTEXT POSITION

The context position describes the position of a node in the current node list. The first position has a value of `"1"`—that is, counting starts from one, not zero. The maximum value for context position is equal to the context size.

In the example in the preceding section, we could select the `Paragraph` element whose content is `"Some additional text."` using the path expression `/Chapter/Paragraph[3]`.

VARIABLES

The final part of the context is a set of zero or more variable bindings. A variable binding maps a variable name to the value of that variable. When used with XSLT, the value of a global variable, for example, would be set using the XSLT `xsl:variable` element.

DATA TYPES

XPath provides four data types—node-sets, strings, numbers, and Booleans.

NODE-SETS

A node-set is the XPath term for an unordered collection of nodes returned by a location path. In practice, processing of a node-set often takes place either in forward document order or reverse document order. So although the node-set is technically or theoretically unordered, in practical usage it is often treated as an ordered list.

STRINGS

A `string` data type in XPath is a sequence of Unicode characters.

NUMBERS

A `number` data type in XPath is a floating point number.

BOOLEANS

In XPath, a Boolean value can take one of two values—`true` or `false`.

ABBREVIATED SYNTAX

XPath can appear very complex because it has four syntaxes—absolute unabbreviated, absolute abbreviated, relative unabbreviated, and relative abbreviated. In practice, most XPath location paths that you will see use the abbreviated syntax because the abbreviated syntax can express the selection of element nodes and attribute nodes, the two XPath node types most frequently included in XPath expressions.

Absolute unabbreviated syntax and absolute abbreviated syntax are used when the `root node` is the context node. For example, the code

```
/child::Book
```

is the absolute unabbreviated syntax to indicate with the root node as context node that we select any `Book` element nodes that are in the child axis. If the document looked like the following code, a node-set containing a single `Book` element node would be selected:

```
<Book>
<Chapter number="1">Some text</Chapter>
<Chapter number="2">Some further text.</Chapter>
</Book>
```

The code

```
/Book
```

is the absolute abbreviated syntax to select the same node.

The unabbreviated path expression `child::Author` is expressed in abbreviated syntax as `Author` because the child axis is effectively the default axis.

The unabbreviated path expression `attribute::type` can be replaced by the abbreviated form `@type`.

Some of the less commonly used XPath axes can only be expressed using unabbreviated syntax.

UNABBREVIATED SYNTAX

The `following` axis (to be described later), for example, as well as some other axes, can be expressed only using unabbreviated syntax.

If the context node was the first `Paragraph` element node in the following code, all other `Paragraph` nodes in the document would be chosen by the path expression `following::Paragraph` because all other `Paragraph` nodes follow the context node in document order.

```
<Book>
 <Chapter number="1">
  <Paragraph number="1">
   Some text.
  </Paragraph>
  <Paragraph number="2">
   Some more text.
  </Paragraph>
 </Chapter>
 <Chapter number="2">
  <Paragraph number="1">
   Some text.
  </Paragraph>
  <Paragraph number="2">
   Some more text.
  </Paragraph>
 </Chapter>
</Book>
```

Other axes that can be expressed only in unabbreviated syntax include the `preceding` axis, the `following-sibling` axis, and the `preceding-sibling` axis.

XPATH NODE TYPES

XPath 1.0 provides seven node types that are described in this section. Each node type corresponds to a part of the source XML document. Remember that two parts of the source XML document—the XML declaration, if present, and the DOCTYPE declaration—cannot be represented in XPath.

XPath is also unable to express an external parsed entity. If you want to address parts of such an entity, it is necessary to use XPointer.

ROOT NODE

All XML documents that are well-formed have a single root node. The root node corresponds broadly to the document entity in XML 1.0 and is not visible within the code of the XML document.

A root node has no parent node or ancestor node. The root node has no name.

ELEMENT NODES

Element nodes are the XPath representation of elements within the source XML document.

An element node can have a parent node. The parent node of an element node is either another element node or a root node. An element node has a name that corresponds to the element type name of the corresponding element in the source document.

ATTRIBUTE NODES

An attribute node corresponds to an attribute on an element in the source XML document. An attribute node can be selected only by using the `attribute` axis.

An attribute node has a name that corresponds to the relevant attribute name in the source document.

NAMESPACE NODES

A namespace node exists for each namespace in scope on an element node. A namespace node can be selected only by using the `namespace` axis.

A default XML namespace node is present in association with each element node, as well as namespace nodes for any namespaces declared in namespace declarations in the source document.

PROCESSING INSTRUCTION NODES

A processing instruction node is present for each processing instruction in the source document, except any processing instruction contained in the `DOCTYPE` declaration.

COMMENT NODES

Each comment in the source document is represented by a comment node in the XPath data model, except comments contained in the DOCTYPE declaration.

TEXT NODES

XPath creates a text node for text content of an element in the source document. Similarly, any `CDATA` section in the source document results in a text node being created. There is no way in XPath to distinguish a text node created from text content of an element from text contained in a `CDATA` section.

XPATH AXES

Axes in XPath (which we will describe shortly) provide an indication of the direction we, or an XPath processor, are to travel around the tree representation of an XML document.

DIRECTIONS OF AXES

Axes can be viewed as being `forward`—that is, in document order—or `reverse`—that is, in the opposite direction of document order.

PROXIMITY POSITION

The direction of an axis that forms part of a location step influences how any position in a predicate in that same location step is interpreted.

In a `forward` axis, a predicate `[2]` means that the second node in document order is selected.

```
<SEUsingXML>
<Chapter>The XML Jigsaw Puzzle</Chapter>
<Chapter>The Basics of XML</Chapter>
<Chapter>XML Building Blocks</Chapter>
<Chapter>Structuring XML Documents with DTDs</Chapter>
<Chapter>XML Schemas</Chapter>
<Chapter>XML Namespaces</Chapter>
</SEUsingXML>
```

For example, if the context node were the `Chapter` element node with the text content `XML Building Blocks`, the code

```
following::Chapter[2]
```

would select the `Chapter` element node that has a text node containing `XML Schemas`. The `following` axis is a forward axis, so we are moving toward the end of the document. As we go forward into the document, we meet a `Chapter` element node with text content `Structuring XML Documents with DTDs`, and the second node has the text content `XML Schemas`.

If the axis in the location step is a `reverse` axis, the predicate `[2]` would mean that the second node in reverse document order is selected by the predicate. If we again start at the third `Chapter` element node, the code

```
preceding::Chapter[2]
```

is as if we turned around to face the beginning of the document. The first `Chapter` element we meet has the text context of `The Basics of XML`. We carry on going toward the beginning of the document, and the second `Chapter` element node has the text content of `The XML Jigsaw Puzzle`.

PREDICATES

The direction of an axis also affects the way in which XPath predicates are interpreted as just described for proximity position.

AXES IN XPATH

In XPath 1.0, there are thirteen axes. These will now be described individually.

THE `child` AXIS

The `child` axis contains the children of the context node. The `child` axis represents an element nested immediately within another element. The `child` axis is a forward axis.

```
<Book>
 <Chapter>
  <Paragraph>
   Some text.
  </Paragraph>
 </Chapter>
</Book>
```

If the `Book` element node is the context node, the `Chapter` element node is in the child axis. The `Paragraph` element node is not in the child axis because it isn't a direct child of the `Book` element node.

Nodes that can occur in the child axis are element nodes, processing instruction nodes, comment nodes, and text nodes. Attribute nodes and namespace nodes cannot occur in the child axis.

THE descendant AXIS

The `descendant` axis includes all nodes that are descendants of the context node. A descendant is a child node of the context node, that child node's child nodes, and so on. The `descendant` axis is a forward axis.

THE parent AXIS

The `parent` axis selects the parent node of the context node. The `parent` axis is a reverse axis.

If, for example, the context node was an element node corresponding to the `paragraph` element in the following code, the parent node is the element node corresponding to the `chapter` element.

```
<chapter>
 <paragraph>
  Some paragraph text about XML
 </paragraph>
</chapter>
```

Only two types of nodes are found in the `parent` axis of any node—a root node or an element node—because only those types of nodes can be parent nodes.

THE ancestor AXIS

The `ancestor` axis includes all the ancestor nodes of the context node. An ancestor node is the parent of the context node, that node's parent node, and so on. The `ancestor` axis always stops at the root node because the root node has no parent node and therefore no ancestor nodes. The `ancestor` axis is a reverse axis.

THE following AXIS

The `following` axis selects nodes that follow the context node in document order. Descendants of the context node are not included in the results. It also excludes attribute nodes or namespace nodes. The `following` axis is a forward axis.

If the context node is an attribute node or a namespace node, the `following` axis is empty.

The code that follows will allow us to explore the use of the `following` axis.

```
<Book>
<Chapter number="1">
<Paragraph number="1">
```

```
Some text.
</Paragraph>
<Paragraph number="2">
Some extra text.
</Paragraph>
</Chapter>
<Chapter number="2">
<Paragraph number="1">
Some additional text.
</Paragraph>
<Paragraph number="2">
Some more text.
</Paragraph>
</Chapter>
</Book>
```

If the first `Paragraph` element node was the context node and the path expression was `following::Paragraph`, three nodes would be returned in the resultant node-set. The second `Paragraph` element node associated with Chapter 1 and both `Paragraph` element nodes associated with Chapter 2 would be included in the node-set because they are not in the descendant axis of the context node and occur later than the context node in document order.

THE `following-sibling` AXIS

The `following-sibling` axis selects nodes that are not present in the `descendant` axis of the context node and also share a parent with the context node. It also excludes attribute nodes and namespace nodes. The `following-sibling` axis is a forward axis.

11

If the context node is an attribute node or a namespace node, the `following-sibling` axis is empty.

Thus if we applied the path expression `following-sibling::Paragraph` to the document shown in the preceding section, the resulting node-set would only contain a single `Paragraph` element node—the second `Paragraph` element node associated with Chapter 1. The two `Paragraph` element nodes associated with Chapter 2 would not be included because those nodes do not share a common parent node with the context node.

THE `preceding` AXIS

The `preceding` axis selects nodes that are not in the ancestor axis of the context node and appear before it in document order. It also excludes attribute nodes or namespace nodes. The `preceding` axis is a reverse axis.

If the context node is an attribute node or a namespace node, the `preceding` axis is empty.

Let's use the example in the "`following` Axis" section again. If the second `Paragraph` element node relating to Chapter 2 was the context node and the path expression was `preceding::Paragraph`, three nodes would be returned in the resultant node-set. The first `Paragraph` element node associated with Chapter 2 and both `Paragraph` element nodes associated with Chapter 1 would be included in the node-set because they are not present in the ancestor axis for the context node and occur earlier than the context node in document order.

THE `preceding-sibling` AXIS

The `preceding-sibling` axis selects nodes that are not present in either the ancestor axis of the context node, which occur earlier in document order and also share a parent with the context node. It also excludes attribute nodes or namespace nodes. The `preceding-sibling` axis is a reverse axis.

If the context node is an attribute node or a namespace node, the `preceding-sibling` axis is empty.

Thus if we applied the path expression `preceding-sibling::Paragraph` to the same document we have been working with in the previous examples, the resulting node-set would only contain a single `Paragraph` element node—the first `Paragraph` element node associated with Chapter 2. The two `Paragraph` element nodes associated with Chapter 1 would not be included because those nodes do not share a common parent node with the context node.

THE `attribute` AXIS

The `attribute` axis selects attribute nodes associated with the context node. If the context node is not an element node, the `attribute` axis is empty.

THE `namespace` AXIS

The `namespace` axis selects namespace nodes associated with the context node. If the context node is not an element node, the `namespace` axis is empty.

THE `self` AXIS

The `self` axis refers to only the context node itself.

THE `descendant-or-self` AXIS

The `descendant-or-self` axis is the union of the `descendant` axis and the `self` axis. The `descendant-or-self` axis is a forward axis.

THE `ancestor-or-self` AXIS

The `ancestor-or-self` axis is the union of the `ancestor` axis and the `self` axis. The `ancestor-or-self` axis is a reverse axis.

XPATH FUNCTIONS

Version 1 of the XPath Recommendation provides a Core Function Library. The various functions provided in that library are described in this section.

XPath functions can return a data type that is one of the four XPath data types—`node-set`, `boolean`, `string`, or `number`.

CONTEXT FUNCTIONS

Context functions say something specifically about the current context or in relation to the current context as a starting point.

THE last() FUNCTION

The last() function is typically used in a predicate within a location path. It selects the last node in the current node list.

```
<Result>
<First>John Doe</First>
<Second>Jane Doe</Second>
<Third>Robert Kennedy</Third>
</Result>
```

If the result element node was the context node and the path expression was child::*[last()], the Third element node would be selected because it is the last child element node in position in document order.

THE position() FUNCTION

The position() function is typically used in a predicate within a path expression.

With the example XML source document shown in the preceding section, the XPath path expression child::*[position()=2] would choose the element child node second in position that is the Second element node. The same meaning can be expressed by the abbreviated path expression *[2].

11

THE lang() FUNCTION

The lang() function takes a single argument. If the argument of the lang() function is equal to the value of the xml:lang attribute (or is a subset of that language) for the selected node, a value of true is returned. Otherwise, a value of false is returned.

```
<Chapter xml:lang="en">
<Paragraph xml:lang="fr">
Bonjour.
</Paragraph>
</Chapter>
```

If the context node was the Chapter element node, the path expression lang(fr) would return false because the value of the xml:lang attribute is en meaning English. However, if the context node was the Paragraph element node, the path expression lang(fr) would return true.

NODE-SET FUNCTIONS

In addition to the position() and last() functions mentioned earlier, XPath provides a number of other functions that return a node-set or operate on a node-set.

THE count() FUNCTION

The count() function takes a single argument, which is a node-set, and returns a number that represents the number of nodes in the node-set.

```
<PurchaseOrder>
<Items>
<Item>Some item</Item>
<Item>A second item</Item>
<Item>A third type of thing</Item>
</Items>
</PurchaseOrder>
```

If the context node was the Items element node, the path expression count(Item) would return the number 3 because three Item element nodes are in the XPath representation of the document.

THE local-name() FUNCTION

The local-name() function takes an optional argument, which is a node-set. The local-name() function returns the local part of the expanded name of the first node in document order in the argument node-set if an argument is present. If the local-name() function has no argument, the function returns the local part of the expanded name of the context node.

Caution

Be careful not to confuse the term local-name() function with the local part of the expanded name. The naming of the XPath function and the component of the expanded name seem unnecessarily confusing. The potential for confusion means that you need to take a little extra care. For example, attempting to apply a (nonexistent) local-part() function will cause an error.

THE namespace-uri() FUNCTION

The namespace-uri() function takes an optional argument, which is a node-set. The namespace-uri() function returns the namespace URI of the first node in document order in the argument node-set if an argument is provided to the function. If the function has no argument, it returns the namespace URI of the context node.

THE name() FUNCTION

The name() function returns a string that is the name of the first node in document order present in the node-set argument, if one exists. If there is no argument, the name() function returns a string that is the name of the context node.

If the argument has no expanded name, the name() function and the local-name() functions will return the same string.

EVALUATION AND CONVERSION FUNCTIONS

XPath provides a number of functions that can be viewed as evaluation or conversion functions.

THE id() FUNCTION

The id() function takes a single argument that is an object and returns a node-set.

The path expression id("someID") returns the node that has a unique ID of value "someID". In the following document, it would be the third Paragraph node:

```
<Chapter>
<Paragraph id="abc123">
Some text
</Paragraph>
<Paragraph id="xyz123">
Some other text
</Paragraph>
<Paragraph id="someID">
Yet different text.
</Paragraph>
</Chapter>
```

THE boolean() FUNCTION

The boolean() function takes a single argument that is an object and returns a boolean value.

If the argument is a string of non-zero length, true is returned. If the string is of zero length, false is returned.

11

If the argument is a number and if that number is not equal to positive or negative zero or NaN (not a number), true is returned.

If the argument is a node-set and the node-set is empty, false is returned. Otherwise, true is returned.

THE string() FUNCTION

The string() function takes an optional single argument that is an object and returns a string.

If the argument is a node-set, the string returned by the string() function is equal to the string-value of the node in the argument node-set that is first in document order. If there is no argument, the context node is the node-set, and its string-value is returned.

If the argument is a number, typically the number is converted to a string. If the number is NaN, the string "NaN" is returned. If the number is Infinity, the string "Infinity" is returned. If the number is -Infinity, the string "-Infinity" is returned. If the argument is positive zero or negative zero, the string "0" is returned.

THE number() FUNCTION

The number() function takes a single argument that is an object and returns a number value.

If the argument is a number, the same number value is returned.

If the argument is a string that represents a numerical value, a number is returned corresponding to the string. However, if the string contains a non-numeric value, the value `NaN` is returned.

If the argument is a node-set, it is as if the `string()` function has been applied with the node-set as argument and the string returned by the `string()` function is converted to a number or `NaN` as just described.

STRING FUNCTIONS

XPath provides several functions that allow us to manipulate strings.

THE concat() FUNCTION

The `concat()` function takes two or more string arguments. It returns a string that is the concatenation of the string arguments.

For example, if the code was `concat("George", "Bush")`, the string returned by the `concat()` function would be `"George Bush"`.

THE starts-with() FUNCTION

The `starts-with()`function takes two string arguments. The function returns `true` if the first string argument starts with the second string argument. It returns `false` otherwise.

The code `starts-with("The sky is blue", "The")` would return `true`.

THE contains() FUNCTION

The `contains()` function takes two string arguments and returns a boolean value. If the first string value contains the second string value, the `contains()` function returns `true`. Otherwise, it returns `false`.

For example the code `contains("Jack and Jill went up the hill", "hill")` would return `true`.

THE substring-before() FUNCTION

The `substring-before()` function takes two string arguments and returns a string. The string returned is the substring of the first string argument that occurs before the occurrence of the second string argument.

The code `substring-before("The cat sat on the mat", "sat")` would return the string `"The cat "`. Notice the trailing space at the end of the returned substring.

THE substring-after() FUNCTION

The `substring-after()` function takes two string arguments and returns a string. The string returned is the substring of the first string argument that occurs after the occurrence of the second string argument.

The code `substring-after("The cat sat on the mat", "sat")` would return the string `" on the mat"`. Notice the leading space at the beginning of the returned substring.

THE `substring()` FUNCTION

The `substring()` function can take two or three arguments.

If there are two arguments, the first argument is a string and the second is a number. The number specifies the character of the first argument at which to start the returned string. The code `substring("This is a string", 9)` would return the string `"a string"`.

If there are three arguments, the third argument is a number that defines the length of the returned string. The code `substring("This is a string", 9, 1)` would return the string `"a"`.

THE `string-length()` FUNCTION

The `string-length()`function takes an optional string argument and returns a number.

If an argument is present, the `string-length()` function returns the number of characters in the string argument.

If there is no argument, the length of the string-value of the context node is returned.

THE `normalize-space()` FUNCTION

The `normalize-space()`function takes an optional string argument.

If a string argument is specified, the string returned is the string argument with any leading or trailing spaces stripped off and any sequences of more than one whitespace character replaced by a single space character.

If the `normalize-space()` function has no argument, the string-value of the context node is returned after any leading and trailing whitespace characters have been stripped and any sequences of whitespace characters have been replaced by a single space character.

THE `translate()` FUNCTION

The `translate()` function takes three string arguments and returns a string value.

Occurrences of characters in the second string argument are replaced in the first string argument by the corresponding characters in the third string argument.

For example, the code `translate("Martha", "Mary", "1ary")` returns `"1artha"`. The character `1` in the third string replaces any occurrence of `"M"` in the second string. Because that character occurs as the first character of `"Martha"`, the `"M"` is replaced by the `"1"` character.

BOOLEAN FUNCTIONS

XPath provides a number of functions to manipulate boolean values.

THE `not()` FUNCTION

The `not()` function negates the value of its argument. The argument for the `not()` function can be a simple value or can be a nested construct involving one or more XPath functions. If the argument evaluates to `true`, a value of `false` will be returned after the `not()` function has been applied. If the argument evaluates to `false`, a value of `true` will be returned after the `not()` function has been applied.

THE `true()` FUNCTION

The `true()` function takes no arguments and returns a boolean value of `true`.

THE `false()` FUNCTION

The `false()` function takes no arguments and returns a boolean value of `false`.

NUMBER FUNCTIONS

The number functions in XPath are rather limited. Those functions are described here.

THE `sum()` FUNCTION

The `sum()` function takes a node-set argument and returns a number. The string values of each node in the node-set are summed after those string values are converted to numbers.

THE `floor()` FUNCTION

The `floor()` function takes a single number argument and returns a number value. The number value returned is the largest integer value that is not greater than the argument. For example, the code `floor(3.5)` would return `3`.

THE `ceiling()` FUNCTION

The `ceiling()` function takes a single number argument and returns a number value. The number value returned is the smallest integer value that is greater than the argument. For example, the code `floor(3.5)` would return `4`.

THE `round()` FUNCTION

The `round()` function takes a single number argument and returns a number value. The number returned is the integer value closest to the argument. If the argument is exactly half way between two adjacent integer values, the integer value closest to positive infinity is returned.

EXTRA: XPATH 2.0

The future of XPath within the W3C family of XML technologies seems secure. The use of XSLT is already well established and seems likely to grow progressively for the foreseeable future.

The future of XPath is importantly interlinked with the emerging XML Query Language, XQuery. The first Working Draft for XPath 2.0 was issued shortly before this writing. The XPath 2.0 data model and the XPath 2.0 functions and operators drafts have been issued as a joint document for XPath 2.0 and XQuery 1.0.

XQuery is described in more detail in Chapter 21.

ADDITIONAL RESOURCES

The definitive resource available on the Web for learning about XPath is the W3C Recommendation. This is located at `http://www.w3.org/tr/xpath`.

ROADMAP

XPath is most commonly used in XSLT, which was described in Chapter 9. The XPath notion of a node is too restrictive for some purposes, and in Chapter 12 we will examine the XML Pointer Language, XPointer, which extends the XPath concept of a node to include the notions of *point* and *range*. XPointer therefore allows more flexibility in how we address fragments of an XML document.

CHAPTER 12

Extending the Power of XPath with XPointer

In this chapter

by Andrew Watt

In this chapter, we will look at the XML Pointer language, XPointer, which allows us to address parts of an XML document or an XML external parsed entity in ways in which the XML Path Language, XPath, version 1 does not support. You can, if you like, think of XPath 1.0 as a module in XPointer.

It might be helpful to understand parts of XPointer by comparing it to familiar hyperlinks on a Web page. A simple HTML hyperlink typically takes you to the beginning of the page to which it is linked. XHTML anchors can cause a Web browser to scroll to a selected part of the page. Being able to directly address parts of an HTML/XHTML document is very useful, particularly if the document is a lengthy one—the Web browser can take you directly to the part of the document that is of interest. XPointer is intended for use with XML documents and the XML Linking Language, XLink. XPointer aims to provide similar functionality to that provided by HTML/XHTML anchors for XML applications and to provide functionality that goes beyond that.

Caution

At the time of writing, XPointer is a W3C Candidate Recommendation. However, there is still a vigorous public debate about the scope of XPointer. Some interested parties want to see significant parts of XPointer, as described in this chapter, removed from the specification to create a slimmed down XPointer specification that is easier to implement. Be sure to check the W3C Web site for current information.

At the time of writing, there are few XPointer implementations, so much of the potential of XPointer has to be described in terms of what XPointer processors will be able to do in the future, once the XPointer specification is finalized.

WHAT IS XPOINTER?

XPointer is a language to be used with XML but, like XPath, is not written in XML. XPointer allows us to address fragments of an XML document. You might already be familiar with fragment identifiers in HTML/XHTML. Let's briefly look at a simple use of HTML/XHTML fragment identifiers to remind you how they work and also to examine their limitations.

To look at that, we need to create two simple XHTML files. The first, Listing 12.1, will contain a truncated table of contents for this book, and the second page, Listing 12.2, will contain a highly abbreviated version of some text representing the content of the book.

LISTING 12.1 A SIMPLIFIED TABLE OF CONTENTS FOR THIS BOOK IN XHTML (TOC.HTML)

```
<!DOCTYPE html
PUBLIC "-//W3C//DTD XHTML 1.0 Transitional//EN"
"DTD/xhtml1-transitional.dtd">
<html>
<head>
<title>SE Using XML (2nd Edition) - Table of Contents</title>
```

Listing 12.1 Continued

```
</head>
<body>
<h2>SE Using XML (2nd Edition)</h2>
<p>Welcome to SE Using XML, 2nd Edition. From this page
you can link directly to individual chapters in the book.</p>
<a href="BookText.html#Chapter1"><p>Chapter 1 - The XML Jigsaw Puzzle</p></a>
<a href="BookText.html#Chapter2"><p>Chapter 2 - The Basics of XML</p></a>
<a href="BookText.html#Chapter3"><p>Chapter 3 - Elements and Attributes</p></a>
<a href="BookText.html#Chapter4"><p>Chapter 4 -
Document Type Definitions</p></a>
<a href="BookText.html#Chapter5"><p>Chapter 5 - XML Schema</p></a>
</body>
</html>
```

Listing 12.1 provides the links, contained in XHTML a elements, to anchors in Listing 12.2. In XHTML, a # character in a hyperlink precedes the fragment identifier such as the fragment identifier `Chapter3` in `BookText.html#Chapter3`. The named anchors within Listing 12.2 provide the target for the fragment identifiers specified in Listing 12.1.

Listing 12.2 An Abbreviated Pseudo-text for This Book Demonstrating Linking to XHTML Anchors (BookText.html)

```
<!DOCTYPE html
PUBLIC "-//W3C//DTD XHTML 1.0 Transitional//EN"
"DTD/xhtml1-transitional.dtd">
<html>
<head>
<title>Highly Abbreviated Pseudo-Text of SE Using XML, 2nd Edition</title>
</head>
<body>
<h2>SE Using XML, 2nd Edition</h2>
<a name="Chapter1"><h3>Chapter 1</h3></a>
<p>Chapter 1 text would go here and describe the XML
Jigsaw Puzzle. Lots of &lt;br&gt; tags space the "chapters"
out so you can see anchors working in a Web browser.<p>
<br/><br/><br/><br/><br/><br/><br/><br/><br/><br/><br/><br/>
<a name="Chapter2"><h3>Chapter 2</h3></a>
<p>Chapter 2 text would go here and describe The Basics of XML.<p>
<br/><br/><br/><br/><br/><br/><br/><br/><br/><br/><br/><br/>
<a name="Chapter3"><h3>Chapter 3</h3></a>
<p>Chapter 3 text would go here and describe Elements and Attributes.<p>
<br/><br/><br/><br/><br/><br/><br/><br/><br/><br/><br/><br/>
<a name="Chapter4"><h3>Chapter 4</h3></a>
<p>Chapter 4 text would go here and describe Document Type Definitions.<p>
<br/><br/><br/><br/><br/><br/><br/><br/><br/><br/><br/><br/>
<a name="Chapter5"><h3>Chapter 5</h3></a>
<p>Chapter 5 text would go here and describe W3C XML Schema.<p>
<br/><br/><br/><br/><br/><br/><br/><br/><br/><br/><br/><br/>
<br/><br/><br/><br/><br/><br/><br/><br/><br/><br/><br/><br/>
</body>
</html>
```

If you click, for example, on the link to Chapter 4 in the Table of Contents, you will be taken to a page similar in appearance to that shown in Figure 12.1.

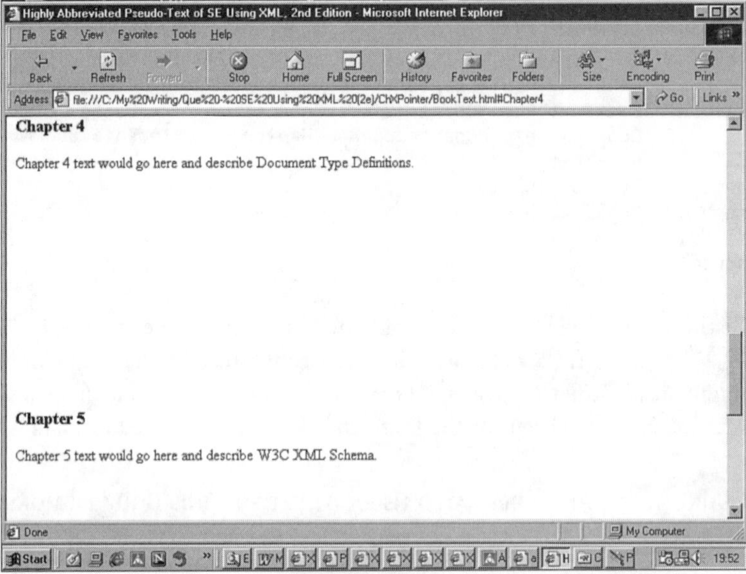

Figure 12.1
The anchor in the code of the book text page causes the browser to scroll to the selected chapter on the page.

The XHTML anchors in the target Web page representing the book allow us to link directly to the desired part of the Web page. But that functionality is available to us only if there are anchors to the part of the page that interests us. If there are no anchors, we can link to the beginning of the Web page and nowhere else.

So, we see that if we want to link to a part of the page not selected by the page author, we can't do it using XHTML fragment identifiers. This is a significant limitation and one that becomes increasingly important as the Web grows in size. It simply becomes impractical to contact page authors to ask for anchors to be added.

If we want to select, for example, several lines in some arbitrary way in a technical document, we find that XHTML fragment identifiers have no way of doing that unless the text of interest is itself written within an anchor. Clearly, there would be advantages in having a fragment identifier syntax that would allow us to link into an XML document at any point in which we, as document users, might choose to view. This might be useful, for example, to someone creating online courses who wants to point students to a particular segment of text and highlight the text, not just to scroll to the nearest anchor. XPointer processors will be able to provide functionality that scrolls to a selected fragment of the document and highlights it.

Beside targeting ranges of text or data, an XPointer processor will be able to target a specific point in an XML document without having a predefined anchor to that point in the document. If the application was similar to a word processor, for example, the cursor could be placed by means of an XPointer to exactly the desired point in the document.

The namespace URI for XPointer, at least at the Candidate Recommendation stage, is `http://www.w3.org/2001/05/XPointer`.

Let's move on to examine what XPointer has been created to do and how it can improve on the useful but limited functionality provided by anchors in HTML/XHTML.

WHAT DOES XPOINTER DO?

XPointer is designed to let us link to parts of an XML document that we want to pay particular attention to. Listing 12.3 illustrates the kind of things XPointer will be able to do.

LISTING 12.3 A HIGHLY SIMPLIFIED "BOOK" (BOOK.XML)

```
<?xml version='1.0'?>
<book>
<chapter number="1">
<paragraph number="1">
George Walker Bush is President of the United States of America.
</paragraph>
<paragraph number="2">
Anthony Charles Linton Blair is Prime Minister of the United Kingdom.
</paragraph>
<paragraph number="3">
Kofi Annan is General Secretary of the United Nations.
</paragraph>
</chapter>
<!-- More would go here. -->
</book>
```

In the last chapter, we learned that XPath provides a way to select nodes from a document. For example, XPath would allow us to select individual text nodes that were child nodes of `paragraph` element nodes. But what if we wanted to select, in code, part of the document similar to that illustrated in Figure 12.2? XPath is unable to do that, but XPointer can help us.

The advantage is that XPointer will be able to describe any arbitrary part of an XML document—similar to the arbitrary way we can highlight text in a word processor.

XPointer allows us to target a particular point in a document or a particular segment of a document. For example, if we were interested in a particular pair of sentences in a long document, an appropriately written XPointer could allow us to open the document with the document scrolled to the desired place and with the relevant sentences already highlighted.

Because XPointer is designed to be a general-purpose fragment identifier, the scrolling and highlighting just mentioned are functions of the containing application, perhaps a text editor or Web browser, rather than the XPointer syntax itself. The XPointer enables application-dependent processing of document fragments, such as selecting part of the text in a way similar to highlighting a piece of text in a word processor.

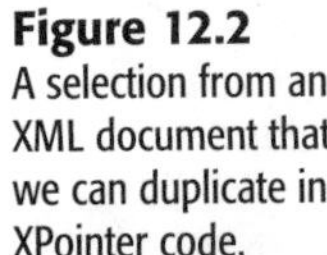

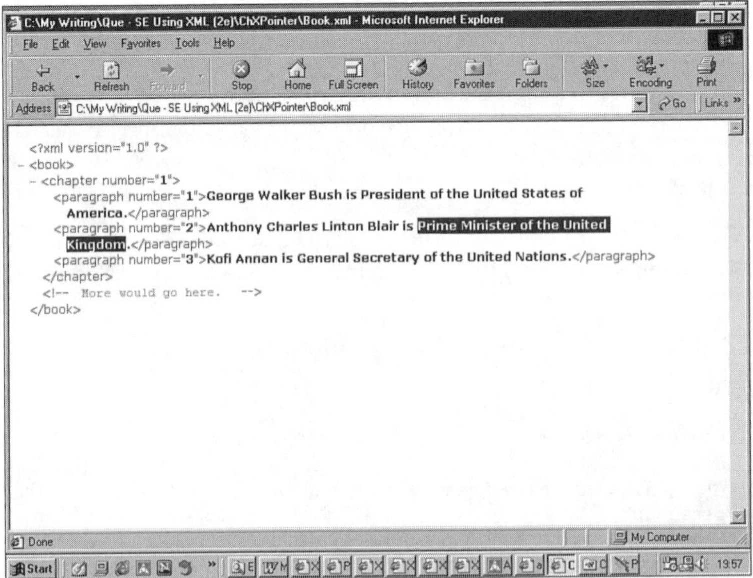

Figure 12.2
A selection from an XML document that we can duplicate in XPointer code.

In other uses of XPointer, perhaps in an XML-based search engine, the XPointer might be able to select and display the relevant part of a document that matches your search criteria. As XML-aware search engines begin to function, we could have more meaningful and intelligent search facilities combined with improved location functionality for any matching pages in the search. I would be misleading you if I suggested that this type of function would be routinely available immediately. But its potential usefulness should be obvious.

It's also possible that the selected part of a target XML document might not be displayed to a human user at all. It might simply be added to a relevant part of an XML data store. How a particular application makes use of a fragment identified by an XPointer is entirely up to the application.

XPointer is intended to be used with documents whose Internet media types are `text/xml`, `application/xml`, `text/xml-external-parsed-entity`, and `application/xml-external-parsed-entity`. Less formally, XPointer is intended for use with well-formed XML documents and external parsed entities. It is likely that in the future, documents of more specialized media types will also make use of XPointer as a fragment identifier language. Already the *Scalable Vector Graphics (SVG)* specification uses some XPointer syntax to reference selected parts of code to enable reuse of that code in other parts of an SVG image. Thus application-specific uses for XPointer might grow to include more than those described earlier. SVG is described more fully in Chapter 23, "Scalable Vector Graphics."

How Are XPointer and XPath Related?

The XPath specification was created by W3C because it recognized that some of the functionality needed by the *Extensible Stylesheet Language (XSL)* and the XML Pointer language was similar. XSLT, which became a W3C Recommendation late in 1999, and XPointer both needed to be able to address parts of XML documents. The W3C decided to consolidate the common functionality into XPath and allow XSLT and XPointer to provide additional functionality that built on the XPath foundation. You were introduced to XPath in Chapter 11, "Locating Components in XML Documents with XPath," and looked at how XSLT uses XPath in Chapter 9, "Transforming XML Data into Other Formats with XSLT."

Like XPath, XPointer works by using axes, location tests (which are similar to XPath node tests), predicates, and functions. In principle, all thirteen of the XPath axes are available to XPointer processors. A location test is similar to a node test in XPath, except that the location test is applied to XPointer points and ranges, as well as nodes. An XPointer predicate is very similar to an XPath predicate and, like XPath predicates, frequently makes use of functions—in this case, the functions can be from XPath or XPointer—to refine a location-set selected by earlier parts of the XPointer expression.

XPointer extends the notion of a tree of nodes, which was described in Chapter 11, for XPath. XPath is applicable only to well-formed XML documents. Therefore, the tree of nodes has a single root node that has a single child element node. XPointer, as already mentioned, can be used not only in connection with well-formed XML documents, but also with external general parsed entities. An external general parsed entity need not be well-formed: Therefore, the XPointer data model allows for that. In practice, this means that the root node of an XPointer tree can have any node as a child that an element node can have. Thus, the root node of an external parsed entity can have element nodes and text node children.

Similarly, the XPath notion of a node-set is extended in XPointer to the idea of a location-set. A node-set includes nodes only. A location-set can include nodes plus the XPointer ranges and points.

Among the functions that XPointer adds to the XPath Core Function Library are the `range-to()` function and the `string-range()` function. Each of these returns a location-set. The XPointer functions `here()` and `origin()` allow XPointers to be defined relative to the location of the XPointer that uses those functions. The functions `start-point()` and `end-point()` return the locations that delimit another location such as a range. The functions `range()` and `range-inside()` address what is termed a `covering range`. All the XPointer functions will be further described later in the chapter.

USES FOR XPOINTER

The most obvious way to use XPointers is in conjunction with XLink hyperlinks. If an XLink link relates to a whole XML resource, XPointer allows us to select part of that XML resource—in XPointer terminology, a `sub-resource`—for any appropriate use.

Additional experimental uses of XPointer are using it to replace XPath in use with XSLT. A couple of projects, called XSLT++ and XT++, are exploring how that might be implemented.

Let's move on to examine more closely the concepts that XPointer adds to what we already can do with XPath.

XPOINTER CONCEPTS

In this section, we will look at the concepts that XPointer adds to those provided in XPath.

LOCATIONS

A `location` generalizes the idea of a node, which you saw in Chapter 11 when we looked at XPath. A `location` can be a `node` (as in XPath), a `point`, or a `range`. In a moment, we will examine precisely what a `point` and a `range` are.

POINT LOCATIONS

Consider the following snippet of code:

```
<paragraph number="1">
This is the text in the first paragraph. This paragraph has two sentences.
</paragraph>
<paragraph number="2">
This is also a paragraph. It too has two sentences.
</paragraph>
```

In the XPath data model, the preceding code would have two `paragraph` element nodes and two text nodes—each text node being a child node of its parent element node. XPath offers the choice of addressing any of these as a whole node. There is no option to address part of a node.

For simplicity, we will talk in terms of cursor because that might help you visualize how an XPointer works. Suppose that we wanted to place the cursor exactly between the first and second sentences of the first paragraph—that is, to select a `point`, in XPointer terminology. Using XPath, we can't do it—but in XPointer, placing the cursor at that `point` is fairly straightforward.

Note

When we consider an XPointer `point`, we hit a place where different XML specifications clash, as far as XML terminology is concerned. What XPointer calls a `point`, the DOM Level 2 specification calls a `position`. (But it also uses the term point in that context too.) Of course, XPath too has the term `position`, but–as you will hopefully recall from Chapter 11–this refers to the position in document order in a selected node set and is accessed using the XPath `position()` function.

A location that is a `point` is described by a `container node` and a non-negative index enclosed in square brackets. A point can represent any position in an XML document corresponding to immediately before or after a character or immediately before or after a node.

When the `container node` is a root node or an element node, the index represents an index into the child nodes of the container node. In these circumstances, the point is termed a `node-point`.

```
<Chapter>
 <Paragraph number="1">
  Some text.
 </Paragraph>
 <Paragraph number="2">
  A second piece of text.
 </Paragraph>
 <Paragraph number="3">
  Yet more text.
 </Paragraph>
</Chapter>
```

If the context node was the root node and we wanted to create a node-point that was placed immediately before the second `Paragraph` element node, we could express that as `xpointer(/Chapter[1])`. The `xpointer()` syntax is one of two `schemes` specified in XPointer. As you see it contains a location. The `Chapter` element node is the container node and the index is `1`.

Caution

> The index of a node-point starts at zero, not one. An index of zero is immediately before the first child node. An index of one is immediately after the first child node or immediately before the second child node. This zero-based counting contrasts with, for example, the one-based approach of the XPointer `string-range()` function and the XPath `position()` function.

When the `container node` is of a node type that cannot have child nodes, the point location defined by an XPointer is a `character-point`. This applies to text nodes, processing instruction nodes, comment nodes, attribute nodes, and namespace nodes. The index in this case must be greater than or equal to zero and no greater than the string length of the text value of the node concerned.

12

If we wanted to address a `character-point` immediately before the word "piece" in the second `Paragraph` element, we could do so using the following XPointer:

```
xpointer(/Chapter/Paragraph[2]/text()[9])
```

The leading whitespace shown on the page for the source XML is for display purposes only. If there were whitespace characters in the actual code, an appropriate adjustment to the `index` would be required in order to locate the desired `character-point`.

Note

> Be sure to clearly distinguish the meaning of the numbers within square brackets in the preceding code. In `Paragraph[2]`, `2` refers to the value returned by the XPath `position()` function and could also be written as `Paragraph[position()=2]`. In `text()[9]`, `9` refers to the XPointer index of the character-point within the text node.

A point location does not have an expanded name. A point location has a string-value, which is empty.

The `self` axis of a point contains the point itself. The `parent` axis contains the point's container node. The `ancestor` axis contains the container node and any ancestor nodes it might have. The `ancestor-or-self` axis contains the point itself, its container node, and any ancestor nodes the container node has. The `descendant-or-self` axis contains only the point itself. All other axes are empty.

RANGE LOCATIONS

Another term and concept that XPointer adds is a `range`. It is helpful to split consideration of the topic into ranges that span multiple nodes and ranges that occur within a node.

Let's look at how to define a range that spans more than one node.

```
<Invoice>
<Name>John Doe</Name>
<Address1>1 Any Street</Address1>
<Address2>Some locality</Address2>
<City>AnyCity</City>
<ZipCode>12345</ZipCode>
<Country>USA</Country>
<Invoice>
```

Suppose we wanted to select the range that starts immediately before the `Name` element node and ends immediately after the `City` element node. An XPointer to select that range is shown here:

```
xpointer(/Invoice/Name to /Invoice/City)
```

Essentially, what we have as the content of the XPointer is a pair of location paths separated by the keyword `to`. The first location path selects the `Name` element node, and, in this context, indicates that the start of a range is immediately before the `Name` element node. The second location path selects the `City` element node. Because it is contained within an XPointer and follows the keyword `to`, it indicates that the range stops immediately after the node specified in the location path.

Let's move on to examine how we would select a range within a node.

If we wanted to select the first two words, `"A second"` of the second sentence in the first `Paragraph` element in the code we looked at in the previous section, XPath can't do it. In XPointer, choosing these two words within a text node would be choosing a `range within a node`.

Choosing a range such as the one we just mentioned is similar to choosing two character-points. The first character-point represents the *start-point* of the chosen string and the second character-point represents the *end-point* of the chosen string.

So let's work out how we would create a range containing the string `"A second"`. The start point is immediately before the `"A"` and is at an index of `0`. So, we could write the XPointer for the start point as `xpointer(/Chapter/Paragraph[2]/text()[0])`. Similarly, the end point is immediately after the `"d"` character of `"second"` and is therefore at an index of `8`. So we could locate the end point, as a character-point, using the XPointer `xpointer(/Chapter/Paragraph[2]/text()[8])`.

We can put the two XPointers together to create the XPointer for the desired range:

```
xpointer(/Chapter/Paragraph[2]/text()[0] to
/Chapter/Paragraph[2]/text()[8])
```

LOCATION SETS

A `location-set` is an unordered list of `locations` produced by an XPointer expression. A `location-set` generalizes the notion of a `node-set`, which is present in XPath.

COVERING RANGES

XPointer adds the notion of a covering range. A *covering range* defines the range that wholly contains a location. For a range, the covering range is equal to the range itself. Similarly, for a point, the covering range is equal to the point itself. For a root location, the covering range is equal to the location.

SUB-RESOURCES IN XML DOCUMENTS

XPointer uses the term `sub-resource` to refer to the portion of an XML document that is selected by an XPointer expression.

SCHEMES

XPointer, as drafted at the time of writing, has two *schemes* named `xpointer` and `xmlns`. The `xpointer` scheme is the one you have seen in examples earlier in this chapter and can be used where there are no namespace issues. The xpointer scheme is written, for example, as follows:

```
xpointer(someLocation)
```

or

```
xpointer(someLocation to someOtherLocation)
```

12

> **Note**
>
> Code such as `xpointer(//Chapter)` is termed an *XPointer part*. An XPointer part will have one scheme, either `xpointer` or `xmlns`, plus a location contained in parentheses.

THE `xpointer` SCHEME

The xpointer scheme can be used, as you have already seen, to select points—whether node-points or character-points—and ranges.

THE `xmlns` SCHEME

You might wonder why XPointer has an `xmlns` scheme at all. Can't the `xpointer` scheme cover all possible scenarios? In fact, you would be in good company to ask that because the W3C XLink Working Group was working on the same assumption until the issue that I will illustrate in a moment was raised. Although XPointer had been at the Candidate Recommendation stage, the issue was sufficiently serious that XPointer was demoted to a Working Draft again.

Consider what would happen if we had an XPointer such as the following one:

```
myDocument.xml#xpointer(//my:element)
```

At first, you might think that there is no problem. The XPointer returns a location set (which might or might not be a single location) that consists of all `my:element` node descendants of the document root. But suppose that the XML document to which it was applied resembled this:

```
<my:Document xmlns:my="http://www.edititwrite.com">
<my:element >Some content</my:element>
<my:element xmlns:my="http://www.svgspider.com">
Some other content
</my:element>
<my:Document>
```

This is perfectly legal XML. An XML processor would recognize that the first `my:element` is associated with the namespace `http://www.edititwrite.com`. The second `my:element` is associated with the namespace `http://www.svgspider.com`. This is no problem for a generic XML processor—it uses the namespace URI, not the namespace prefix, when it considers which element belongs to which namespace.

But there is a big problem for the XPointer that we just looked at. Does the XPointer `myDocument.xml#xpointer(//my:element)` refer to the `my:element` from the namespace `http://www.edititwrite.com`, to the `my:element` from the namespace `http://www.svgspider.com`, or to both?

It was to remove the possibility of such ambiguous code that the `xmlns` scheme was added to XPointer.

If we wanted to select the `my:element` element node from the namespace URI of `http://www.edititwrite.com`, we can do so unambiguously using the `xmlns` scheme, as shown in the following XPointer:

```
xmlns(my=http://www.edititwrite.com) xpointer(//my:element)
```

Caution

Be careful not to use quotes within an XPointer part from the `xmlns` scheme. Quotes are used in namespace declarations, but not with the `xmlns` XPointer scheme.

The use of the `xmlns` scheme within the XPointer disambiguates which `my` namespace prefix is being referred to, so there is no problem in interpreting the part of the XPointer from the `xpointer` scheme.

NAMESPACES IN XPOINTER

It is often forgotten that all XML documents are implicitly associated with the namespace URI `http://www.w3.org/1998/XML/namespace`. You can confirm that if you use XPath to display all the namespace nodes associated with an element node, for example. In addition to the XML namespace, an XPointer must also be initialized with respect to any namespace defined by the `xmlns` scheme.

XPOINTER FUNCTION EXTENSIONS TO XPATH

The function library defined in the XPath specification is available to XPointer processors. Several additional XPointer functions are also available.

LOCATION SET FUNCTIONS

XPointer adds `point` and `range` to the `node` of XPath, as explained earlier in the chapter. Because XPath lacks functions to operate on `locations` other than nodes, additional functions are required in XPointer to allow manipulation of non-node locations.

THE `range-to()` FUNCTION

The `range-to()` function takes a single `location-set` argument and returns a range for each member of the location-set argument.

Suppose we had a document that included the fragment shown here:

```
<paragraph id="para1" number="1">
<!-- Some content goes here -->
</paragraph>
<paragraph id="para2" number="2">
<!-- Some more content goes here -->
</paragraph>
```

12

To address this fragment, we could use the following XPointer, which makes use of the `range-to()` function:

```
xpointer(id("para1")/range-to(id("para2")))
```

The `range-to()` function is used here to express the range with the `paragraph` element whose `id` attribute has the value of `para1` as its start point and is used to identify a second point as end point, which also happens to be a `paragraph` element node that has an `id` attribute with value of `para2`.

The `range-to()` function adds to the permitted syntax of a location step as defined in XPath 1.0. The `range-to()` function is the only XPointer function that can be used in that way.

THE `string-range()` FUNCTION

The `string-range()` function takes two required arguments and two optional arguments. It returns a set of ranges. The first required argument is a `location-set`, and the second is a string.

Thus, we could write `string-range(//Paragraph, "XPointer")` to search all `Paragraph` element nodes for the string `"XPointer"`.

The third (optional) argument is a `number` that defines the position of the first character to be included in the returned range. The default is `1` if the third argument is omitted. If we had code such as

```
string-range(//Paragraph, "misunderstanding", 4)
```

it would result in ranges that contain the "understanding" part of "misunderstanding" because the third argument to the `string-range()` function indicates that we start at the fourth character.

The fourth (optional) argument is a `number` that defines the number of characters in the range that is returned.

If we had code such as

```
string-range(//Paragraph, "misunderstanding", 4, 5)
```

it would result in ranges that contain the "under" part of "misunderstanding" because the third argument to the `string-range()` function indicates that we start at the fourth character and the fourth argument indicates that the range is five characters long.

The default, when the fourth argument is omitted, is that the length of the content of the range returned equals the length of the second `string` argument to the function.

The `string-range()` function can also be used to return specific occurrences of a string. The following XPointer `string-range(//Paragraph, "XPointer")[5]` would return the fifth occurrence of the string `"XPointer"` in the location-sets specified in the first argument to the function.

THE `range()` FUNCTION

The `range()` function takes a single `location-set` argument and returns a set of ranges. For each location in the argument `location-set`, a range location representing the covering location is added to the returned location-set.

THE `range-inside()` FUNCTION

The `range-inside()` function takes a single `location-set` argument and returns a location-set which consists of ranges. The returned location-set contains a range for each location in the argument `location-set`.

If a location in the argument `location-set` is a range or a point, that location is added to the returned location-set.

Otherwise, the location in the argument `location-set` is used as the container node of the start-point and end-point of the range to be added to the returned location-set. The index of the start point of the returned location is zero. If the end point is a character-point, its index is the length of the string-value of the location in the argument. Otherwise, its index is the number of child locations of the location in the argument location.

THE start-point() FUNCTION

The `start-point()`function takes a single `location-set` argument and returns a location-set of start-points.

For each location in the argument `location-set`, the `start-point()` function adds a point to the returned location-set. The point returned represents the start point of the argument location.

THE end-point() FUNCTION

The `end-point()` function takes a single `location-set` argument and returns a location-set of end points.

For each location in the argument `location-set`, the `end-point()` function adds a point to the returned location-set. The point returned represents the end point of the argument location.

CONTEXT FUNCTIONS

The `here()` and `origin()`functions that XPointer adds can be viewed as context functions: They give information about the location of the context of the XPointer.

THE here() FUNCTION

The `here()` function returns a location-set and takes no arguments. The `here()` function can be used in a meaningful way only when the XPointer is contained in a well-formed XML document or an external parsed entity—in other words, when the `here()` function is used within an XML context. Otherwise, the `here()` function is uninterpretable. Because `"here"` cannot be in two places at one time, the location-set returned by the `here()` function contains only one member.

A special case occurs when the XPointer is situated within a text node that is the child of an element node. In that case, the `here()` function returns the parent element node in the location-set. In all other circumstances, the `here()` function returns the node within which the `here()` function is contained.

The `here()` function might be used to navigate through a set of slides. The following code could be used to move to the next slide:

```
<button
 xlink:type="simple"
 xlink:href="#xpointer(here()/ancestor::slide[1]/following::slide[1])">
  Next
</button>
```

The location step `ancestor::slide[1]` selects the first ancestor element node which is a `slide` element node, and the location step `following::slide[1]` selects the next `slide` element node in document order. Assuming typical ordering of elements in the desired display order, this will cause the next slide in the slide show to be displayed. Similarly, by using the XPath `preceding` axis, the code `preceding::slide[1]` could be used to display the previous slide.

THE `origin()` FUNCTION

The `origin()` function takes no argument and returns a location-set. To be meaningful, the `origin()` function must be processed in relation to an XPointer as part of a link traversal from an XML document. If the document from which the link is being traversed is anything other than XML, the `origin()` function cannot return a meaningful location-set.

WRITING XPOINTERS

When we start to write XPointers, we need to remember that an XPointer typically includes a URI. So, we might have code such as the following:

```
xlink:href="someDocument.xml#xpointer(id('someID'))"
```

Tip

To avoid syntax errors, remember to use one form of quote marks (either paired single quotes or paired double quotes) to mark out the limits of an attribute value. Use the other kind of quote marks to delimit within an XPointer, as when using single quotes within the `id()` function in the preceding code.

Because the XPointer can also be the value of an XML attribute, we also need to consider that aspect. Thus, we need to ensure that an XPointer satisfies any syntactic considerations for *Uniform Resource Identifiers (URIs)* and for XML. Therefore, certain characters need to be escaped.

In addition, we have the further consideration that XPointer uses certain characters in specific ways, which necessitates escaping the characters if we want to use them literally within an XPointer.

ESCAPING CHARACTERS

A full consideration of escaping is beyond the scope of this chapter, but the following description will give you an introduction to the types of issues involved.

XPOINTER ESCAPING

Parentheses are significant to the XPointer processor. Therefore, if you want to use unbalanced parentheses in an XPointer (which would otherwise likely cause an error) you can escape the unbalanced parenthesis character by preceding it with a circumflex. Thus, we would write Â(or Â) in order to escape the opening or closing unbalanced parenthesis character.

Note

All closing parentheses not being used as part of XPointer to balance an opening parenthesis, must be escaped using the circumflex even when the unbalanced parenthesis occurs within a literal.

Because the circumflex has the special function of escaping other characters in an XPointer, any literal use of the circumflex must be written as ÂÂ.

INTERNATIONALIZED URI ESCAPING

In Internationalized URIs, IURIs, the percent sign, `%`, is used to escape other characters. You have likely seen sequences such as `%20` (which represents a space character) in URIs, which illustrates how the `%` character can be used in this way. Therefore, when including a literal `%` character as part of an XPointer in an IURI, the `%` character must be written as `%25`. You cannot escape the `%` character in an IURI by writing `%%`.

A further issue arises because XPointer uses the same Unicode set of characters as XML does. The difficulty arises because some Unicode characters are disallowed in URIs. All non-ASCII characters are disallowed. To complicate matters further, the `#`, `%`, `[`, and `]` characters were disallowed in URIs at one time but were later re-instated.

Each disallowed character is converted to UTF-8 as one or more bytes. Those bytes corresponding to disallowed characters are escaped and expressed as `%XX`, where `XX` is the hexadecimal notation for the value of the character.

XML ESCAPING

Any characters in an XPointer expression that might be significant to an XML processor must be written—either as an entity reference or as a character reference. For example, if the `<` character were used in an XPointer expression, it would be written as `<`.

URI ESCAPING

For backward compatibility with applications that have not implemented the *Format for Literal IPv6 Addresses in URL's* (IETF RFC 2732), it is wise to escape square brackets. The opening square bracket character, `[`, should be replaced by `%5B`, and the closing square bracket character, `]`, should be replaced by `%5D`.

So, let's look at an example, modified from one in the XPointer specification. The example uses the full XPointer syntax. The XPointer we want to create might resemble this:

```
myDocument.xml#xpointer(string-range(//p, "a little circumflex ^"))
```

To satisfy the demands of XPointer syntax, we need to escape the circumflex so that it resembles the following code:

```
myDocument.xml#xpointer(string-range(//p, "a little circumflex ^^"))
```

So far, so good. There is no percent sign in the code, so we don't need to change anything further to comply with the syntax requirements for an IURI.

When it's time to place this within an XML document, we find that we need to escape the quotation marks. Therefore our code resembles this:

```
myDocument.xml#xpointer(string-range(//p, &quot;a little circumflex ^^&quot;))
```

Finally, we need to escape the quotation marks (replace with `%22`), spaces (replace with `%20`), and circumflexes (replace with %5E) to correspond to legal URI syntax:

```
myDocument.xml#xpointer(string-range(//p,
 %22a%20little%20circumflex%20%5E%5E%22))
```

As you can probably imagine, this can become a bit complex and tedious to get right at times.

FORMS OF XPOINTERS

The XPointer specification describes one full form of XPointer syntax and two shorthand ways of expressing XPointers. Let's look at the full syntax for XPointers in a little more detail.

FULL XPOINTERS

Most of the code snippets that you have seen earlier in the chapter are full XPointers. They use the `xpointer` scheme explicitly with or without the `xmlns` scheme.

BARE NAMES XPOINTERS

If you have used HTML/XHTML links to anchors, you are familiar with the syntax used in XPointer bare names. The *bare name* is simply the name used within the `id()` function of a full XPointer.

If you want to access the element with an `id` attribute of `someID` in the document `myDocument.xml`, we can write a bare names XPointer that resembles this:

```
myDocument.xml#someID
```

The corresponding full XPointer would be

```
myDocument.xml#xpointer(id('someID'))
```

The idea behind having the bare names syntax is to provide a succinct syntax that makes use of the value of `id` attributes. As you will see in a moment when we examine the use of child sequence XPointers, elements with an `id` attribute can be addressed irrespective of any changes in document structure. As long as the element has an `id` attribute that doesn't change, we can always address it using the bare names syntax.

CHILD SEQUENCE XPOINTERS

Child sequences operate by addressing parts of an XML document or external parsed entity by using the relative position of nodes within the tree representation of the source XML.

If we had a simple XML document such as that shown in Listing 12.4, we could use it to examine how child sequence XPointers operate.

LISTING 12.4 A BRIEF LISTING OF SOME XML TECHNOLOGIES (XMLTECHNOLOGIES.XML)

```
<?xml version='1.0'?>
<XMLTechnologies id="DocElement">
 <XMLTechnology>
 XML
 </XMLTechnology>
 <XMLTechnology>
 XML Schema
 </XMLTechnology>
 <XMLTechnology>
 XSLT
 </XMLTechnology>
</XMLTechnologies>
```

A child sequence is expressed as a sequence of integers separated by / characters. We could refer to the XMLTechnology element that contains the text "XSLT" using the following child sequence:

```
/1/3
```

The first / character represents the root node as in XPath. The 1 that follows selects the first child node of the root node; the second / character is a separator, and finally the 3 selects the third child node of the previously located element. Thus, the child sequence selects the third XMLTechnology element node of the first child node of the root node.

An alternative syntax, again using the child sequence syntax, would be

```
DocElement/3
```

On this occasion, DocElement refers to the value of the id attribute of the XMLTechnologies element. The 3 refers to the third child node (location) relative to that context. So again, the XMLTechnology element node (location) whose content is "XSLT" is chosen.

12

However, let's suppose we (or someone else) update our XML file when it is realized that no mention has been made of XPath and XPointer. Our new XML data store is shown in Listing 12.5.

LISTING 12.5 AN UPDATED XML DOCUMENT ENUMERATING XML TECHNOLOGIES (XMLTECHNOLOGIES2.XML)

```
<?xml version='1.0'?>
<XMLTechnologies id="DocElement">
 <XMLTechnology>
 XML
 </XMLTechnology>
 <XMLTechnology>
 XML Schema
 </XMLTechnology>
 <XMLTechnology>
 XPath
 </XMLTechnology>
 <XMLTechnology>
 XPointer
```

LISTING 12.5 CONTINUED

```
 <XMLTechnology>
 XSLT
 </XMLTechnology>
</XMLTechnologies>
```

With these minor changes, we find that neither of our previous pieces of code—`/1/3` or `DocElement/3`—select the desired element node (location).

You should see that child sequences are tightly coupled to the structure of an XML document.

Contrast that with what would happen if we had `id` attributes on each element, as shown in Listing 12.6, and used the bare names syntax that we considered in the previous section.

LISTING 12.6 THE ORIGINAL XML TECHNOLOGIES DOCUMENT WITH `id` ATTRIBUTES (XMLTECHNOLOGIESID1.XML)

```
<?xml version='1.0'?>
<XMLTechnologies id="DocElement">
 <XMLTechnology id="XML">
 XML
 </XMLTechnology>
 <XMLTechnology id="XMLSchema">
 XML Schema
 </XMLTechnology>
 <XMLTechnology id="XSLT">
 XSLT
 </XMLTechnology>
</XMLTechnologies>
```

Using bare names syntax, we would access the `XMLTechnology` element node directly using the following syntax:

```
XMLTechnologiesID1.xml#XSLT
```

If we add elements that refer to XPath and XPointer, as in Listing 12.7, the bare names XPointer still works.

LISTING 12.7 THE UPDATED XML TECHNOLOGIES DOCUMENT INCLUDING `id` ATTRIBUTES (XMLTECHNOLOGIESID2.XML)

```
<?xml version='1.0'?>
<XMLTechnologies id="DocElement">
 <XMLTechnology id="XML">
 XML
 </XMLTechnology>
 <XMLTechnology id="XMLSchema">
 XML Schema
 </XMLTechnology>
 <XMLTechnology id="XPath">
 XPath
```

LISTING 12.7 CONTINUED

```
 </XMLTechnology>
 <XMLTechnology id="XPointer">
 XPointer
 </XMLTechnology>
 <XMLTechnology id="XSLT">
 XSLT
 </XMLTechnology>
</XMLTechnologies>
```

We could still address the XMLTechnology element node as before (modifying only the filename for the purposes of this chapter):

```
XMLTechnologiesID2.xml#XSLT
```

Similarly, the full XPointer syntax could provide a stable way of addressing the desired element node whether or not the document was modified:

```
XMLTechnologiesID2.xml#xpointer(id('XSLT'))
```

We can add (or remove) as many elements as we want (other than the one of interest) and still find the element node we want. Thus, by using `id` attributes, we have a means of addressing into an XML document that is more stable than using child sequences to refer to a document that might be subject to amendment.

ADDITIONAL RESOURCES

At the time of writing, XPointer resources are few. Here are some relevant resources:

- XPointer specification (`http://www.w3.org/tr/xptr`). The URL given will take you to the latest version of the specification.
- Fujitsu (`http://www.labs.fujitsu.com/free/xlip/en/index.html`) has available as a free download an XLink processor, called XLiP, which in the February 2002 release, provides a useful XPointer processor.

ROADMAP

From here, we will look at the XML Linking Language, XLink. When it is used to address parts of resources, XLink will make use of the XPointer syntax that you have been introduced to in this chapter.

CHAPTER 13

LINKING INFORMATION: XLINK, XBASE, AND XINCLUDE

In this chapter

by Kynn Bartlett

EXPRESSING DOCUMENT RELATIONSHIPS IN XML

The basic XML syntax allows for creation of markup languages to convey structure and include content, but doesn't describe relationships between documents or portions of documents. That role is served in core XML by a series of technologies described in W3C Recommendations: *XML Base*, *XML Inclusion* (XInclude), and *XML Linking Language* (XLink). These related technologies establish relationships among resources, resource identifiers, documents, and sections of documents, building on XPath and XPointer.

XML BASE

WHAT IS XML BASE?

XML Base is a standard way to declare a "base" Uniform Resource Identifier (URI) in XML documents. This base URI is then used to resolve relative references. The functionality is the same as the `<base>` element in HTML, although XML Base is much broader. XML Base is an official W3C Recommendation that was issued on June 27, 2001, which can be found at

`http://www.w3.org/TR/xmlbase/`

When writing an HTML document, you can use the `<base href="...">` element to specify a base URI against which targets to relative documents are calculated. This applies to the entire document, as `<base>` is valid only within the <head> section and thus is applicable to the whole page. For example, in HTML:

```
<html>
  <head>
    <title>Kim's Page</title>
    <base href="http://www.khyri.com/">
  </head>
  <body>
    <h1>Kim's page!</h1>
    <p>
      Here is a picture of Kim:
      <br>
      <img src="kim/kim1m.jpg" alt="[Photo of Kim]">
      <br>
      Kim also has <a href="kan.htm">two sisters</a>.
    </p>
  </body>
</html>
```

In this example, the relative URI in the `<img>` element would resolve to "`http://www.khyri.com/kim/kim1m.jpg`" and the link to sisters would resolve to `http://www.khyri.com/kan.htm`, even if this HTML page were located on any Web site anywhere in the world, or even on someone's local machine.

XML Base goes beyond this, allowing for base URIs to be associated with smaller portions of a document by allowing any element to take an `xml:base` attribute. This provides even greater portability of XML documents, and has implications for XML Inclusion and XLink.

XML Base Support and XLink

To use XML Base, the application you're using must specifically recognize and use the `xml:base` attribute, and must define the context in which it uses that attribute. An application will use XML Base only if it's been designed to do so.

The only reason that the `href`, `src`, and `longdesc` attributes of HTML are recognized as URI references is that the browsers are programmed to treat them as such, because that's what the specification says to do. Thus, the base URI is applied to those attribute values but not to an attribute such as `height`, `alt`, or `border`. Unlike HTML, XML does not inherently attach meaning to any attributes, which means it is up to specific applications to define how `xml:base` applies.

XML Base support can reasonably be expected only for those XML applications and specifications which explicitly say that they support XML Base, and state how it's applied. Fortunately, the functionality of XML Base is both simple and effective, and so support for it is being written into many new W3C recommendations and other specifications.

One such specification is the XLink recommendation. The XLink specification explicitly states that XLink implementations must use XML Base when resolving relative URIs in `xlink:href` attribute values. The XLink specification does not state `xml:base` values apply to anything else; so, XML Base can't be used with the `xlink:role` attribute, for example. (The `xlink:href` and `xlink:role` attributes are explained later in this chapter.)

The `xml:base` Attribute

The XML Base specification defines a single global attribute `xml:base`, which can be applied to any XML element. The "`xml:`" prefix is a special Namespace; it does not need to be declared with an `xmlns:` prefix, and it should be honored even if the application does not normally support Namespaces. The `xml:lang` attribute is another case of a global attribute like `xml:base`. The official Namespace URI for `xml:base` is

```
http://www.w3.org/XML/1998/namespace
```

The acceptable values for XML Base are any valid URIs.

URIs must be escaped, which means using standard UTF-8 conversion to hexadecimal codes, such as `%20` for spaces.

Here's an example of the `xml:base` attribute:

```
<document xml:base="http://www.khyri.com">
...<!-- rest of the document here -->...
</document>
```

This would set the base URI for the `<document>` element, which happens to contain the entire document. However, it's also possible to set `xml:base` attributes on other elements, and these are interpreted relative to the base URIs of their parents, if any. For example:

```
<document xml:base="http://www.khyri.com">
  ...
  <content xml:base="/kim/">
```

13

```
      ...
    </content>
  </document>
```

The base URI of the document is "`http://www.khyri.com/`", but the base URI for the `<content>` element (and its children) is "`http://www.khyri.com/kim/`".

AN XML BASE EXAMPLE

In Listing 13.1, you can see a simple XML document which describes a collection of Web pages. Links to those Web pages are listed as "simple" XLinks, which are functionally similar in this instance to the `<a href="...">` construction in HTML. You'll learn more about XLinks later in this chapter.

We use XLink in our example because XLink is specifically stated to be compliant with the XML Base specification. This means that `xlink:href` attributes will be understood in the context of applicable xml:base values by an XLink processor.

LISTING 13.1 XML BASE IN ACTION

```
<sitemap xmlns:xlink="http://wwww.w3.org/1999/xlink"
         xml:base="http://kynn.com/">
  <pgroup title="Kynn's Web Site">
    <page xlink:type="simple" xlink:href="index.html">
      Kynn's Home Page
    </page>
    <pgroup type="Navigation Links"
            xml:base="/nav/">
      <page xlink:type="simple" xlink:href="people.html">
        Kynn's Friends
      </page>
      <page xlink:type="simple" xlink:href="causes.html">
        Kynn's Causes
      </page>
    </pgroup>
    <pgroup type="Journal Links"
            xml:base="http://www.livejournal.com/users/nextofkynn">
      <page xlink:type="simple" xlink:href="/">
        Kynn's Journal
      </page>
      <page xlink:type="simple" xlink:href="/friends/">
        Friends' Journals
      </page>
      <page xlink:type="simple" xlink:href="http://www.livejournal.com/">
        LiveJournal Site
      </page>
    </pgroup>
  </pgroup>
</sitemap>
```

How do the preceding `xlink:href` values get interpreted, by following XML Base? Table 13.1 lists each link (by the link text) and provides the URI for that link's destination.

Table 13.1 Interpreting XML Base Values

Link Text	Destination URI
Kynn's Home Page	`http://kynn.com/index.html`
Kynn's Friends	`http://kynn.com/nav/people.html`
Kynn's Causes	`http://kynn.com/nav/causes.html`
Kynn's Journal	`http://www.livejournal.com/users/nextofkynn/`
Friends' Journals	`http://www.livejournal.com/users/nextofkynn/friends/`
LiveJournal Site	`http://www.livejournal.com/`

XML Inclusion

What Is XInclude?

XML Inclusion, known as XInclude for short, is a method for including the content of one XML document or a portion of it (specified by an XPointer) inside another XML document. The ability to directly incorporate external sources of information is very useful in programming, and XInclude extends that functionality to XML-based markup applications.

The XInclude specification is (at time of writing) a W3C working draft, which means it has not yet been approved as an official W3C Recommendation. This section covers the most recent available draft, dated May 16, 2001. To review the current document, you can visit

`http://www.w3.org/TR/xinclude`

XML processors that support XInclude will resolve `xi:include` elements by including the appropriate external content into the source document. (Naturally, those XML processors that do not support XInclude will not do inclusion.)

XInclude Versus External Entity References

13

External entities, defined within an XML DTD, also allow for the inclusion of content into an XML document from an external source. However, XInclude and external entities are complementary technologies, not competing ones, because they do different things.

A reference to an external entity is processed when the XML document is being parsed, and is dependent upon the DTD and DOCTYPE statements. XML Inclusion, on the other hand, describes a process that occurs after the parsing of the document, when the data is stored abstractly as an XML infoset.

Note

The XML Information Set (XML Infoset) defines abstractions for the various parts of XML documents. The information set includes information on the context as well as the content of the document.

XML information sets are defined by the XML Infoset specification published at

`http://www.w3.org/TR/xml-infoset/`

By operating at this higher level, XInclude is able to preserve information such as the appropriate base URIs and Namespaces for included content.

THE `xi:include` ELEMENT

The `XInclude` specification defines a single element, `include`, which is part of the `XInclude` Namespace. The URI identifier associated with the `XInclude` Namespace is

`http://www.w3.org/2001/xinclude/`

By convention, the prefix "`xi:`" is associated with that when using `XInclude`, and thus the `include` element can be written as `xi:include` and we will follow that convention in this chapter. The syntax of the `xi:include` element and its attributes is

```
<xi:include
  xmlns:xi="http://www.w3.org/2001/xinclude"
  href="URI "
  parse="xml |text"
  encoding="encoding_type"/>
```

An `xi:include` element could conceivably have other attributes or contain content of some kind; the meaning of these is left undefined by the `XInclude` specification.

THE `href` ATTRIBUTE

The XML content to be included is designated by the `href` attribute. This attribute can take any escaped URI value, and it can be an XPointer expression to cover a range of elements, or a range of text, within an external document.

The `href` attribute is a required attribute, and cannot be omitted; without a reference to which resource to include, no XML Inclusion can occur. Inclusion can be nested—a document (or partial document) can be included if it contains an `xi:include` element itself, although inclusion loops are not allowed. A document cannot include itself or anything else that's already been parsed as part of the inclusion process.

THE `parse` ATTRIBUTE

The `parse` attribute can take one of two values: "`xml`" or "`text`." This specifies the mechanics by which the content is to be included.

- Parsing as "xml" means that the external resource is parsed as an XML document and the resulting infoset is incorporated into the original's infoset. If necessary, extra xmlns: or xml:base attributes may be added, so that information isn't lost when the infosets are merged.
- Parsing as "text" means that the external resource is converted to a text node, which means, among other things, that all <> brackets are converted to <> character entities. If you parse something as "text," this means that further inclusions will be converted to normal text so you don't have to worry about inclusion loops.

The parse attribute is optional; if it is not included then the value "xml" is assumed.

The encoding Attribute

The character encoding of included text can be specified with the encoding attribute, as it may not be obvious. This optional attribute is significant only if the parse attribute is "text"—it's ignored if the parse attribute's value is "xml." If an encoding attribute isn't provided, and the encoding can't be determined otherwise (from HTTP headers or media type, for example), an encoding of "UTF-8" is assumed.

XInclude Examples

Including Parsed XML

In Listing 13.2, we present a simple XML file that defines a message for display to the user. Using XInclude, we will include a standard disclaimer that might be included on other pages as well.

The disclaimer is listed in Listing 13.3, and is meant to be included as XML, so the parse attribute has the value "xml." (XLink attributes are explained later in this chapter.)

Listing 13.2 An Example of XInclude Syntax

```
<message xml:base="http://xml.kynn.com/lampshades">
  <para>
    Thank you for shopping at Amal's House of Lampshades.
  </para>
  <xi:include     xml:base="web/legal"

    href="standard-disclaimer.xml"
    parse="xml"
    xmlns:xi=http://www.w3.org/2001/Xinclude/>
</message>
```


Listing 13.3 A Standard Disclaimer to Be Included

```
<disclaimer
  xmlns:xlink="http://www.w3.org/1999/xlink">
  <para>
    <image
```

LISTING 13.3 CONTINUED

```
      xlink:type="simple"
      xlink:href="corplogo.png"
      xlink:show="embed"
      xlink:actuate="onLoad" />
    This material is copyright 2002 by Amal's House of Lampshades.
  </para>
  <para>
    Please see our
    <link
      xlink:type="simple"
      xlink:href="full-disclaimer.xml"
      xlink:show="new"
      xlink:actuate="onRequest">
      full disclaimer
    </link> for more details.
  </para>
</disclaimer>
```

The result of processing the inclusion is shown in Listing 13.4.

LISTING 13.4 THE RESULT OF INCLUDING THE DISCLAIMER

```
<message xml:base="http://xml.kynn.com/lampshades">
  <para>
    Thank you for shopping at Amal's House of Lampshades.
  </para>
  <disclaimer
    xmlns:xlink="http://www.w3.org/1999/xlink"
    xml:base="web/legal">
    <para>
      <image
        xlink:type="simple"
        xlink:href="corplogo.png"
        xlink:show="embed"
        xlink:actuate="onLoad" />
      This material is copyright 2002 by Amal's House of Lampshades.
    </para>
    <para>
      Please see our
      <link
        xlink:type"simple"
        xlink:href="full-disclaimer.xml"
        xlink:show="new"
        xlink:actuate="onRequest">
        full disclaimer
      </link> for more details.
    </para>
  </disclaimer>
</message>
```

INCLUDING TEXTUAL CONTENT

Listing 13.5 is both the source and the included file, as it references itself. As the content is not being parsed as XML but included as text (thanks to the `parse="text"` attribute value), this does not create a loop and thus is allowed in XInclude. The content to be included is listed in XPointer syntax.

LISTING 13.5 INCLUDING TEXT WITH XINCLUDE

```
<webLesson
  xmlns:xi="http://www.w3.org/2001/XInclude">
  <titleText>Lesson 14: XML Include</titleText>
  <lessonBody>
    <introBlurb>
      In this lesson we'll examine the XML source
      used to create this very lesson.
    </introBlurb>
    <sampleCode>
      <headlineText>Sample Code:</headlineText>
      <xi:include href="#xpointer(//lessonBody)"
                  parse="text"
                  encoding="UTF-8" />
    </sampleCode>
  </lessonBody>
</webLesson>
```

The result of the inclusion is shown in Listing 13.6; as you can see, the content has been escaped appropriate for listing markup in an XML document.

LISTING 13.6 THE RESULTS OF INCLUDING TEXT

```
<webLesson
  xmlns:xi="http://www.w3.org/2001/XInclude">
  <titleText>Lesson 14: XML Include</titleText>
  <lessonBody>
    <introBlurb>
      In this lesson we'll examine the XML source
      used to create this very lesson.
    </introBlurb>
    <sampleCode>
      <headlineText>Sample Code:</headlineText>
  &lt;lessonBody&gt;
    &lt;introBlurb&gt;
      In this lesson we'll examine the XML source
      used to create this very lesson.
    &lt;/introBlurb&gt;
    &lt;sampleCode&gt;
      &lt;headlineText&gt;Sample Code:&lt;/headlineText&gt;
      &lt;xi:include href="#xpointer(//lessonBody)"
                  parse="text" /&gt;
    &lt;/sampleCode&gt;
  &lt;lessonBody&gt;
    </sampleCode>
  </lessonBody>
</webLesson>
```

XLINK

WHAT IS XLINK?

To take full use of XML as a markup format, a generic method for providing links was created: XLink, the XML Linking Language. XLink is a W3C Recommendation that was released on 27 June 2001; this means that the W3C has declared this a stable, proven specification for use on the Web and elsewhere. The XLink specification is published at

`http://www.w3.org/TR/xlink/`

A link, in XLink terminology, is a relationship between one or more resources (or portions thereof) which are said to participate in the link. A resource is simply anything that can be addressed by a Uniform Resource Identifier (URI), such as a document on a Web site or an XML data repository. The use of XPointer allows for a portion of a resource to be identified as participating in a link.

There are two primary types of links which can be expressed with XLink—simple links, which are one way from a single local resource to a single remote resource, and extended links, which can have more complex relationships including links between multiple resources, bidirectional links, and third-party links (annotation links, left in a document by another reader).

There are no predefined XLink elements—any element can be made an XLink element by setting an XLink attribute, xlink:type, on the element. Additional XLink attributes can be set to further define the properties of the XLink element. The XLink Namespace is used to identify these global attributes.

SIMPLE, UNIDIRECTIONAL LINKS

In its simplest form, XLink is similar to the various elements in HTML that create an explicit relationship between the current document (or a portion of it) and some other content. The most obvious example is the anchor element, `<a>`, which specifies a hypertext link such as

```
<a href="http://www.webaim.org/">
  Web Accessibility In Mind
</a>
```

This creates a relationship between the local resource—that is, the fragment of the source document that includes the text "Web Accessibility in Mind"—and the remote resource identified by the URI "`http://www.webaim.org`." The exact behavior of that relationship is that the link text is presented in some way to indicate that it's a link (most commonly blue underlined text) and if that text is clicked, you're taken to the external resource.

Less obvious is the HTML `<img>` tag, which at first glance doesn't seem to be a link, but in terms of XLink, it's a link as well. It establishes a link between the location of the `<img>` tag and a remote resource (the image file), and the behavior is to replace the `<img>` tag with the graphical representation of the image when displaying it. A typical `<img>` tag would look like this:

```
<img src="mypic.jpg" alt="My Picture">
```

Other linking elements in HTML include `<link>`, `<object>`, and the elements for creating framesets.

In XLink terms, all of these are simple links: They go from one local resource to one remote resource. XLink simple links are expressed in simple markup, which is designed to be familiar to HTML authors. The XLink equivalents of the previously mentioned `<a>` and `<img>` tags are

```
<hyperlink xmlns:xlink="http://www.w3.org/1999/xlink"
           xlink:type="simple"
           xlink:href="http://www.webaim.org/">
   Web Accessibility In Mind
</hyperlink>

<image xmlns:xlink="http://www.w3.org/1999/xlink"
       xlink:type="simple"
       xlink:href="mypic.jpg"
       xlink:title="My Picture"/>
```

These are considered XLink elements because they have attributes from the XLink Namespace.

Complex Linking Structures

Beyond simple links, there may be uses for more complex links between elements; these are known as extended links in XLink terminology. Extended links can be used for a number of purposes including

- Bidirectional linking that goes two ways (even if you don't control one or both of the linked resources)
- Establishing multiple links that relate more than one starting resource to more than one ending resource
- Creating relationships with specific roles defined for each resource
- Defining third-party links that describe relationships between remote resources
- Referencing a linkbase (an XML collection of related links) of third-party links, such as annotations or indexes

13

An extended link consists of an XLink extended-type element, with several child elements that define the types of resources involved and the relationships among those resources.

Extended links can reference both local resources—those that are part of the content of the extended link element—and remote resources—those that are not contained within the markup of the XLink. Local resources are identified by an XLink resource-type element, and remote resources by a locator-type element. (Simple links identify the local resource by the content of the link element, and the remote resource by the `xlink:href` attribute. `xlink:href` attributes are also known as locator attributes.)

With those resources (local or remote) identified, relationships can be established between them by defining arcs. An arc is description of the starting and ending resources of a link, the direction of the relationship between them, and possibly more information on the behavior produced by activating that link. Activation of a relationship in a link is known as traversing the link.

The result of traversing the link is dependent upon the application used to process the link, but the author of the XLink can specify suggested roles and behavior. The `xlink:role` and `xlink:arcrole` attributes are used to define the meaning and purpose of the relationship. The `xlink:actuate` and `xlink:show` attributes specify when a link should be traversed, and how that traversal should be displayed to the end user.

XLINK SYNTAX

Although you might already be familiar with some of the attributes used with XLink in some applications, such as the `href` attribute with simple links, XLink actually has its own syntax for defining some of the more complex linking structures that are possible. All of these elements and attributes for defining XLinks are a part of its own namespace as well. So, now let's take a look at the specific syntax for defining links in XML.

XLINK NAMESPACE

XLink attributes belong to the XLink Namespace, which is

```
http://www.w3.org/1999/xlink
```

It is traditional to use a prefix of `xlink:` on XLink attributes (although because of the way Namespaces work, this could really be anything). For purposes of this book, however, we'll stick with tradition. Like all other uses of XML Namespaces, the XLink Namespace and prefix must be declared on the element that contains the XLink attributes, or on a parent of that element.

→ To review XML Namespaces, **see** "Avoiding XML Confusion with XML Namespaces," Chapter 6.

CREATING XLINK ELEMENTS

An XLink element is any element that has appropriate XLink attributes set. There are no native XLink elements—any XML element can become an XLink element if XLink attributes are placed on it. This is different from languages such as HTML, where only certain elements (such as `<link>`, `<a>`, `<object>`, and `<img>`) can contain links. XLink attributes are *global*, meaning they theoretically could be applied to any element and don't need to be attached to specific element names.

For example, the following XML contains an XLink element, `<xref>`, by virtue of the `xlink:type`, `xlink:href`, and `xlink:role` attributes set on that element:

```
...
<para>
  You can learn more about accessible web design from the
  <xref abbrev="Web Accessibility Initiative"
        xmlns:xlink="http://www.w3.org/1999/xlink/"
        xlink:type="simple"
        xlink:role="http://xml.kynn.com/linkprops/crossref"
        xlink:href="http://www.w3.org/WAI/">
    WAI
```

```
    </xref>
  </para>
  ...
```

The meaning of each attribute will be described in the rest of this chapter, along with other XLink attributes that could also be set. In short, this element (`<xref>`) creates a simple, one-way cross-reference link between the term "WAI" and the site of the W3C's Web Accessibility Initiative. It also uses the `abbrev` attribute to indicate the acronym expansion of the referenced term. This isn't part of XLink—this is simply one of the attributes defined by our XML language apart from XLink functionality. An XLink element can contain non-XLink attributes that support its role within the XML language but which don't relate directly to its function as a link.

Attribute Defaulting via DTD

Because XML DTDs allow default values to be specified when declaring attributes, certain values in XLink can be preset in the DTD and thus don't need to be written out for each XLink element—they will automatically be included by the XML parser when it processes the DTD.

A partial DTD for the previous example could define the `<xref>` element as follows:

```
...
<!ELEMENT xref
<!ATTLIST xref
  abbrev          CDATA          #IMPLIED
  xmlns:xlink     CDATA          #FIXED "http://www.w3.org/1999/xlink"
  xlink:type      (simple)       #FIXED "simple"
  xlink:role      CDATA          #FIXED "http://xml.kynn.com/linkprops/crossref">
  xlink:href      CDATA          #IMPLIED
>
...
```

This would reduce the number of attributes that need to be written, because fixed attributes do not need to be rewritten in the instance document; instead, the values are provided by the DTD:

```
  ...
  <para>
    You can learn more about accessible web design from the
    <xref abbrev="Web Accessibility Initiative"
          xlink:href="http://www.w3.org/WAI/">
      WAI
    </xref>
  </para>
  ...
```

13

Caution

Of course, this will work only if you're actually using a DTD with the appropriate attributes defined, and if your XLink processor properly parses the DTD. If it doesn't, you can't use attribute default values.

THE `xlink:type` ATTRIBUTE

The `xlink:type` attribute is the key attribute for creating an XLink, as it determines what function the element serves within the XLink structure. There are six possible values for `xlink:type`, as listed in Table 13.2.

TABLE 13.2 VALUES FOR THE `xlink:type` ATTRIBUTE

Value	XLink Type
`simple`	A simple link (one-way)
`extended`	An extended link (complex relationships)
`locator`	A locator in an extended link (a remote resource)
`resource`	A (local) resource in an extended link
`arc`	A relationship between resources in an extended link
`title`	A human-readable title for an extended link (or portion thereof)

An arc in XLink is simply a transversal path for the link. There can be several different types of arcs: inbound, outbound, or third party. An inbound arc is one in which the link goes from the local resource to an outside resource. An outbound arc, in which the link goes from a remote resource to a local resource, is the opposite of inbound. Third-party arcs refer to a link between two remote resources.

An element with an `xlink:type` attribute can be referred to as an "*-type element," such as "simple-type element" if the value is `simple`, or "arc-type element" if the value is `arc`.

With extended links, an XLink element's children may or may not be significant within the context of an XLink. Nothing prevents the XLink element, its children, or content from having non-XLink significance; for example, in the preceding `<xref>` example, the `abbrev` attribute served a purpose apart from the XLink functionality.

The significance of the children or content of an XLink element is shown in Table 13.3. As you can see, only direct children are significant; other descendant elements are not significant within an XLink context.

TABLE 13.3 SIGNIFICANCE OF XLINK ELEMENT CONTENT OR CHILDREN

XLink Element Type	Significance
`simple`	The simple-type element itself, combined with the content of the simple link, is the local resource of the link, and other XLink elements within the `simple` element are not considered part of the `simple` link.
`extended`	The children of the `extended-type` link are only significant within an XLink context if they are of type `locator`, `arc`, resource, or title.
`locator`	Only `title-type` elements are significant as direct children of the `locator` element; other XLink elements within a locator have no meaning within the context of the `extended` link. Non-XLink content is allowed but has no specific meaning in the XLink context.

TABLE 13.3 SIGNIFICANCE OF XLINK ELEMENT CONTENT OR CHILDREN

XLink Element Type	Significance
`resource`	A `title-type` element is the only child element within a `resource-type` element that has any meaning in the XLink context. Any non-XLink content of the resource is a local resource that may participate in a relationship defined by an `arc-type` element.
`arc`	Only `title-type` elements are significant as direct children of the `arc-type` element; other XLink elements within an arc have no meaning within the context of the extended link. Non-XLink content is allowed but has no specific meaning in the XLink context.
`title`	An XLink element within a `title-type` element has no meaning relative to the extended link, `locator`, or `arc` which contains the `title-type` element. The content of the `title-type` element is a human-readable description for its parent element.

THE `xlink:href` ATTRIBUTE

The job of the `xlink:href` attribute is quite similar to the `href` attribute from HTML, but that's not the full story. It's incorrect to think of `xlink:href` as only establishing HTML-style hypertext links (blue underlined text). In XLink, the `xlink:href` serves to provide a reference to an external resource of any kind: This can include images, script files, multimedia presentations, and more. (The `xlink:show` attribute, described as follows, is used to define how the result of activating the XLink should be displayed. For example, activating the link may display the content of an image in place.) Thus, the `xlink:href` attribute also serves the same function as the `src` attribute on the `<img>` element in HTML.

Values for `xlink:href` should be valid URIs, escaped as for inclusion in XML files, and may be XPointers when referring to XML documents or portions thereof. Relative and absolute values for URIs are both acceptable, and XML Base references can be used to resolve the relative URIs.

The `xlink:href` attribute is valid only for XLink element types, which identify remote resources. These are the simple-type and locator-type elements. A locator-type element must have an `xlink:href` attribute; it's optional for simple-type elements, although a simple-type element that doesn't identify an ending resource cannot be traversed.

13

THE `xlink:role` ATTRIBUTE

The `xlink:role` attribute is metadata information, used to indicate the semantic role of the XLink element. An `xlink:role` value is an URI, and must be absolute (not relative). This value has two uses; as a unique identifier it conveys information in a way similar to Namespace URI, and as a URI it can reference a document which explains what the value means.

It's not actually necessary that the document on the other end of the `xlink:role` URI be in any specific format; what's more common is for an XLink-aware application to understand the specific unique identifiers rather than access and parse whatever the URI points to. For this reason, the XLink specification doesn't define what format that referenced document must take.

Only links (simple and extended) and resources (local and remote) can have roles, so the `xlink:role` attribute is restricted to those types. The `xlink:role` attribute is optional; if not included, that simply means that the role of the relationship is undefined by XLink.

THE XLINK:ARCROLE ATTRIBUTE

The `xlink:arcrole` attribute is a metadata attribute very similar to the `xlink:role` attribute, but the purpose is to define the properties of the relationship between two (or more) resources in the XLink. Although `xlink:role` describes the resource, `xlink:arcrole` defines how they relate.

For example, consider a simple link between two books. Each of the books could be identified with a role URI, which is agreed to mean "a book," whereas the arcrole between them both means "a sequel" (in the direction from the first book to the second):

```
<bookdata>
  <booktitle>A Game of Thrones</booktitle>
  <author>George R.R. Martin</booktitle>
  <related xmlns:xlink="http://www.w3.org/1999/xlink"
           xlink:type="simple"
           xlink:href="http://xml.kynn.com/book.php?isbn=0553579908"
           xlink:role="http://xml.kynn.com/linkprops/book"
           xlink:arcrole="http://xml.kynn.com/linkprops/sequel">
    A Clash of Kings
  </related>
  ...
</bookdata>
```

Notice that in this example you could change the role of the related resource by giving a different URI identifier such as "`http://xml.kynn.com/linkprops/videotape`" (presumably to designate a videotape), or change the role of the link to something like "`http://xml.kynn.com/linkprops/prequel`" for a prequel story—assuming that whatever application you're using will understand what those URIs mean.

The `xlink:arcrole` attribute is appropriate only for XLink elements that define relationships between resources, which means only the `simple` and `arc` element types can have an `xlink:arcrole`. The `xlink:arcrole` element describes the role of the remote resource, and is optional. However, if omitted, it means that the specific relationship is not defined within the context of the XLink.

THE xlink:show ATTRIBUTE

The `xlink:show` and `xlink:actuate` attributes allow you to define the behavior of an XLink relationship. The `xlink:show` attribute answers the question "What do I do with this?" whereas the `xlink:actuate` attribute answers "And when do I do it?"

XLink 1.0 defines five types of values that can be assigned to an `xlink:show` attribute. Those values are "`new`," "`replace`," "`embed`," "`other`," and "`none`," and their meanings are listed in Table 13.4.

TABLE 13.4 POSSIBLE VALUES FOR xlink:show

Value	Behavior
new	Display the target content in a new context; for example, in a new window or frame. (In HTML, this is accomplished by a link with a target="_blank" attribute.)
replace	Display the target content in the same context as the starting resource, replacing it. (In HTML, this is default link behavior: You follow a link, and the new page loads in the same window as the page you were on before.)
embed	Display the target content within the same context as the starting resource; in effect, replacing the link with the rendered version. (In HTML, this is how the <object> and <img> elements work, by embedding the presentation of the referenced object or image where the <object> or <img> element itself is located within the HTML page.)
other	This is a catchall in XLink; the meaning is that XLink doesn't define the show behavior, but the application should use other attributes to determine what should be done. (One analogous situation in HTML is the <link> element, which uses the "rel" attribute to determine the meaning of a link. For example, a value of "stylesheet" means that the linked document is a stylesheet.)
none	This is a second catchall, but this one means XLink doesn't define the meaning, and neither does any other attribute. This doesn't mean the link should be ignored, just that there is no explicitly defined "show" behavior.

Only those XLink elements that define relationships can take an xlink:show attribute, so this attribute can be set only on simple and arc element types. If the xlink:show attribute is omitted, the display behavior is undefined by XLink.

THE xlink:actuate ATTRIBUTE

As xlink:show is used to indicate how a link should be handled, the xlink:actuate attribute is used to define when that happens. The valid values for xlink:actuate are "onLoad," "onRequest," "other," and "none", as shown in Table 13.5.

TABLE 13.5 POSSIBLE VALUES FOR xlink:actuate

Value	Behavior
onLoad	When the source document is loaded, the link should be actuated. (In HTML, this is the way <img> elements work—i.e., the referenced image is loaded when the page is loaded.)
onRequest	The link doesn't take effect until a request is given, such as clicking on link text. (This is the way most hypertext links work.)
other	Like the other value for xlink:show, this is a catchall that means look for additional information in the markup to determine when to actuate the link.
none	This means, like xlink:show="none", that the details on how to actuate the link are specifically not defined in XLink or the markup, and are left for the application to infer.

Like `xlink:show`, `xlink:actuate` can be used only on XLink elements that describe a relationship link: simple-type and arc-type elements. The `xlink:actuate` attribute is optional; if no value is given then the actuation behavior of the link is undefined.

THE `xlink:label` ATTRIBUTE

The `xlink:label` element is used on XLink locator-type and resource-type elements within extended links to identify them as participating in XLink arcs. These labels are used in `xlink:to` and `xlink:from` attributes to describe the starting and ending resources for relationships.

Values for `xlink:label` must be of XML type `NMTOKEN`, which means they must start with an alphabetic letter and can only contain letters or numbers—that is, no spaces and no punctuation. A value for `xlink:label` is not an XML ID, however, meaning that it does not have a requirement to be unique. Multiple XLink resources or locators can share the same value; arcs defined by such labels will be defined to or from all of those elements.

Only XLink resource or locator element types can have an `xlink:label` attribute. The `xlink:label` attribute is optional; if an `xlink:label` is not set on an XLink resource-type or locator-type element, that element cannot be part of an arc in an extended link—except for arcs which do not specify an `xlink:to` or `xlink:from` attribute. (Such arcs define relationships that start or end with all resources or locators in the extended XLink.)

THE `xlink:from` ATTRIBUTE

The `xlink:from` attribute of an XLink arc-type element defines the starting resource that originates the relationship described by the link. This is only necessary when using extended links; simple links fully define the starting resource as the content of the simple link itself.

The possible values for an `xlink:from` attribute are any labels, which have been given to XLink locator-type or resource-type elements using the `xlink:label` attribute. If more than one locator-type or resource-type element has the same `xlink:label`, then the `xlink:from` element identifies relationships, which originate with all of those resources.

The `xlink:from` attribute can only be set on XLink arc-type elements. If no `xlink:from` value is supplied, the relationship is defined as going from all resources or locators within the extended XLink.

THE `xlink:to` ATTRIBUTE

The `xlink:to` attribute is the partner of the `xlink:from` attribute; together they define the starting and ending resources for an arc in an extended XLink. As with `xlink:from`, the value must be the same as a previously defined `xlink:label` on a resource-type or locator-type element. If the `xlink:to` value is a label for more than one resource-type or locator-type element, all that are labeled with that value are the ending resources defined by the link. It's possible to have an arc with the same `xlink:from` and `xlink:to` values; such a resource simply links back to itself.

Only XLink arc-type elements can have xlink:to attributes; in simple links, the ending destination is given via the `xlink:href` attribute. If the `xlink:to` value is not specified then all available XLink resources or locators in the extended link are the ending resources. An `arc` element lacking both an `xlink:from` attribute and an xlink:to attribute defines a relationship from all resources and locators to all resources and locators in the extended link.

THE `xlink:title` ATTRIBUTE

The `xlink:title` attribute is used to provide a human-readable title for an XLink element. Human-readable titles can be multiple words and are meant to be presented to the user (in some manner) rather than used only by the XLink processor.

All XLink elements can take `xlink:title` attributes, except for the title elements—which themselves function as human-readable text for their XLink parent object. The `xlink:title` element is optional.

AN XLINK EXAMPLE

Let's look an example of using XLink to establish relationships among documents. We'll use the Virtual Dog Show (`www.dogshow.com`) in our example. The Virtual Dog Show is an online dog competition, whereby owners can enter their pooches via the Web for judging by qualified judges around the world. Dogs are judged on five pictures—a headshot, a side view, and up to three other pictures of the owner's choice.

In Listing 13.7, we've encoded the information in a simple XML format—the `<dogshow>` element contains at least one instance (and in this case, exactly one) of the <dog> element. The `<dog>` element has an `id` attribute that identifies the entry number of the dog, and child elements representing the dog's name(s), gender, date of birth, breed, judge, owner, and pictures.

LISTING 13.7 VIRTUAL DOG SHOW DATA WITHOUT XLINKS

```
<dogshow>
  <!-- Expressed without XLink, in XML -->
  <dog id="0002">
    <name kind="formal">Drokkytshang Nying Chhem-Po</name>
    <name kind="pet">Kim</name>
    <gender>Dog</gender>
    <dob>25-December-1989</dob>
    <breed code="tibm">
      Tibetan Mastiff
    </breed>
    <judge page="http://xml.dogshow.com/judges.html#bobhayes">
      Bob Hayes
    </judge>
    <owner>
      <ownername>Liz Bartlett</ownername>
      <address withheld="withheld"/>
      <email>khyri@idyllmtn.com</email>
    </owner>
    <pic src="http://xml.dogshow.com/images/0002-01.jpg"
         alt="Headshot" />
```

13

LISTING 13.7 CONTINUED

```
    <pic src="http://xml.dogshow.com/images/0002-02.jpg"
         alt="Side View" />
    <pic src="http://xml.dogshow.com/images/0002-03.jpg"
         alt="Other View" />
  </dog>
</dogshow>
```

It's a simple but reasonably effective document, but it's got some shortcomings, too, which can be remedied through the use of XLink. These include

- The attributes of `page` and `src` have no inherent meaning as links; they simply contain CDATA that may or may not equate to URIs, which may or may not be links between information.
- The behavior and role of these implied links is not explicitly stated. Do we display them inline, in new windows, or what?
- We have to repeat the owner's information for each dog instance. If someone enters more than one dog, it seems more effective to refer to the owner than to repeat the information, doesn't it?
- The "breed code" is used by an application to create a link to the breed page in the show catalog. We can probably include this explicitly in the data structure rather than requiring a lookup table.

One major benefit of using XLink is that we can make those relationships explicit, in a standardized manner, which means we can used generalized applications to deal with these relationships, rather than having to hard-wire or special-case each relationship with nongeneric code. XLink provides a way to explicate these links that's very similar to the philosophy of XML.

ADDING SIMPLE XLINKS

In Listing 13.8, we've rewritten the document to use simple XLinks. Notice that we're now able to add information on the behavior and activation of each link—via `xlink:show` and `xlink:actuate` attributes—as well as defining what each link means by use of the `xlink:role` attribute. We've also changed the breed reference so it's no longer a raw attribute that needs to be specially processed, but directly links to the breed display page.

LISTING 13.8 EXAMPLE WITH SIMPLE LINKS ADDED

```
<dogshow
  xmlns:xlink="http://www.w3.org/1999/xlink">
  <!-- with simple xlinks -->
  <dog id="0002">
    <name kind="formal">Drokkytshang Nying Chhem-Po</name>
    <name kind="pet">Kim</name>
```

LISTING 13.8 CONTINUED

```
    <gender>Dog</gender>
    <dob>25-December-1989</dob>
    <breed xlink:type="simple"
           xlink:href="http://xml.dogshow.com/breed.php?code=tibm"
           xlink:role="http://xml.dogshow.com/linkprops/breed"
           xlink:title="Tibetan Mastiff"
           xlink:show="replace"
           xlink:actuate="onRequest" />
    <judge xlink:type="simple"
           xlink:href="http://xml.dogshow.com/judges.html#bobhayes"
           xlink:role="http://xml.dogshow.com/linkprops/judge"
           xlink:title="Judge Bob Hayes"
           xlink:show="replace"
           xlink:actuate="onRequest" />
    <owner xlink:type="simple"
           xlink:href="http://xml.dogshow.com/show.php?owner=khyri@idyllmtn.com"
           xlink:role="http://xml.dogshow.com/linkprops/owner"
           xlink:title="Owner Liz Bartlett"
           xlink:show="replace"
           xlink:actuate="onRequest" />
    <pic xlink:type="simple"
         xlink:href="http://xml.dogshow.com/images/0002-01.jpg"
         xlink:role="http://xml.dogshow.com/linkprops/picture"
         xlink:title="Headshot"
         xlink:show="embed"
         xlink:actuate="onLoad" />
    <pic xlink:type="simple"
         xlink:href="http://xml.dogshow.com/images/0002-02.jpg"
         xlink:role="http://xml.dogshow.com/linkprops/picture"
         xlink:title="Side View"
         xlink:show="embed"
         xlink:actuate="onLoad" />
    <pic xlink:type="simple"
         xlink:href="http://xml.dogshow.com/images/0002-03.jpg"
         xlink:role="http://xml.dogshow.com/linkprops/picture"
         xlink:title="Other View"
         xlink:show="embed"
         xlink:actuate="onLoad" />
  </dog>
</dogshow>
```

13

As we create these links, we're assigning roles to each one with the `xlink:role` attributes. Each role value is a URI within the `http://xml.dogshow.com/linkprops` directory—but what do they refer to? According to the XLink specification, a role value URI "identifies some resource that describes the intended property." In this particular case, each reference is to a text file that describes the specific meaning of that role—but, more importantly, this unique URI can be used to uniquely identify the type of relationship. It doesn't matter what the relationship is as long as we can refer it to in some unique, consistent manner.

These relationships we've defined, and their meanings, are listed in Table 13.6. As we develop this example further, we'll want to keep a list of what these roles mean.

TABLE 13.6 ROLE DEFINITIONS FOR DOG SHOW MARKUP

Role URI	Link Meaning ("A link to...")
`http://xml.dogshow.com/linkprops/breed`	The catalog page for the dog's breed
`http://xml.dogshow.com/linkprops/judge`	The page about the judge evaluating this dog
`http://xml.dogshow.com/linkprops/owner`	The owner's profile page
`http://xml.dogshow.com/linkprops/picture`	A picture of the dog

SETTING ATTRIBUTE DEFAULTS

You may have noticed that Listing 13.8 is much longer than Listing 13.7. Although we've made our relationships explicit, we've also greatly increased the size of our file over the earlier version. We can reduce the size by writing a DTD that provides default, fixed values for specific attributes of our elements. When our document is processed, these default values will be included on the attributes even if they're not written out in our document.

Listing 13.9 is the rewritten document with simple links, according to the DTD in Listing 13.10.

LISTING 13.9 SIMPLE LINKS WITH ATTRIBUTE DEFAULT VALUES IN THE DTD

```
<dogshow>
  <!-- with simple xlinks and attribute defaults in the DTD -->
  <dog id="0002">
    <name kind="formal">Drokkytshang Nying Chhem-Po</name>
    <name kind="pet">Kim</name>
    <gender>Dog</gender>
    <dob>25-December-1989</dob>
    <breed xlink:href="http://xml.dogshow.com/breed.php?code=tibm"
           xlink:title="Tibetan Mastiff" />
    <judge xlink:href="http://xml.dogshow.com/judges.html#bobhayes"
           xlink:title="Judge Bob Hayes" />
    <owner xlink:href="http://xml.dogshow.com/show.php?owner=khyri@idyllmtn.com"
           xlink:title="Owner Liz Bartlett" />
    <pic xlink:href="http://xml.dogshow.com/images/0002-01.jpg"
         xlink:title="Headshot" />
    <pic xlink:href="http://xml.dogshow.com/images/0002-02.jpg"
         xlink:title="Side View" />
    <pic xlink:href="http://xml.dogshow.com/images/0002-03.jpg"
         xlink:title="Other View" />
  </dog>
</dogshow>
```

LISTING 13.10 DTD FOR LISTING 13.9

```
<!ELEMENT dogshow (dog+)>
<!ATTLIST dogshow
  xmlns         CDATA         #IMPLIED
  xmlns:xlink   CDATA         #FIXED "http://www.w3.org/1999/xlink">
```

LISTING 13.10 CONTINUED

```
<!ELEMENT dog (name+,gender,dob,breed,judge+,owner,pic*))>
<!ATTLIST dog
  id              ID               #IMPLIED
>

<!ELEMENT name #PCDATA>
<!ATTLIST name
  kind            (formal|pet)     #IMPLIED
>

<!ELEMENT gender #PCDATA>

<!ELEMENT dob #PCDATA>

<!ELEMENT breed EMPTY>
<!ATTLIST breed
  xlink:type      (simple)         #FIXED "simple"
  xlink:href      CDATA            #REQUIRED
  xlink:role      CDATA            #FIXED
"http://xml.dogshow.com/linkprops/breedcode"
  xlink:title     CDATA            #IMPLIED
  xlink:show      (replace)        #FIXED "replace"
  xlink:actuate   (onRequest)      #FIXED "onRequest"
>

<!ELEMENT judge EMPTY>
<!ATTLIST judge
  xlink:type      (simple)         #FIXED "simple"
  xlink:href      CDATA            #REQUIRED
  xlink:role      CDATA            #FIXED "http://xml.dogshow.com/linkprops/judge"
  xlink:title     CDATA            #IMPLIED
  xlink:show      (replace)        #FIXED "replace"
  xlink:actuate   (onRequest)      #FIXED "onRequest"
>

<!ELEMENT owner EMPTY>
<!ATTLIST owner
  xlink:type      (simple)         #FIXED "simple"
  xlink:href      CDATA            #REQUIRED
  xlink:role      CDATA            #FIXED "http://xml.dogshow.com/linkprops/owner"
  xlink:title     CDATA            #IMPLIED
  xlink:show      (replace)        #FIXED "replace"
  xlink:actuate   (onRequest)      #FIXED "onRequest"
>

<!ELEMENT pic EMPTY>
<!ATTLIST pic
  xlink:type      (simple)         #FIXED "simple"
  xlink:href      CDATA            #REQUIRED
  xlink:role      CDATA            #FIXED
"http://xml.dogshow.com/linkprops/picture"
  xlink:title     CDATA            #REQUIRED
  xlink:show      (embed)          #FIXED "embed"
  xlink:actuate   (onLoad)         #FIXED "onLoad"
>
```

Note

You'll notice that I made the `xlink:title` attribute `#REQUIRED` for the `<pic>` element. Why? Because this is the equivalent of an `alt` attribute in an HTML `<img>` element: Textual equivalents for graphical content are necessary to enable access by nonvisual users, such as users with visual disabilities or blindness. When designing XML DTDs or Schemas, it's important to consider the needs of your audience who may not be able to access all information.

CREATING AN EXTENDED LINK

So far, this example has used only simple links. However, what we really have here is a larger set of links that could be represented by extended links in XLink. Listing 13.11 rewrites the dog show data as an extended link.

LISTING 13.11 AN EXTENDED LINK REPLACES SEVERAL SIMPLE LINKS

```
<dogshow
  xmlns:xlink="http://www.w3.org/1999/xlink">
  <!-- with extended xlinks -->
  <dog xlink:type="extended">
    <doginfo id="0002"
            xlink:type="resource"
            xlink:role="http://xml.dogshow.com/linkprops/doginfo"
            xlink:label="doginfo">
      <name kind="formal">Drokkytshang Nying Chhem-Po</name>
      <name kind="pet">Kim</name>
      <gender>Dog</gender>
      <dob>25-December-1989</dob>
    </doginfo>
    <breed xlink:type="locator"
          xlink:href="http://xml.dogshow.com/breed.php?code=tibm"
          xlink:role="http://xml.dogshow.com/linkprops/breed"
          xlink:title="Tibetan Mastiff"
          xlink:label="breed" />
    <human xlink:type="locator"
          xlink:href="http://xml.dogshow.com/judges.html#bobhayes"
          xlink:title="Bob Hayes"
          xlink:label="bobhayes" />
    <human xlink:type="locator"
          xlink:href="http://xml.dogshow.com/show.php?owner=khyri@idyllmtn.com"
          xlink:title="Liz Bartlett"
          xlink:label="lizbartlett" />
    <pic xlink:type="locator"
        xlink:href="http://xml.dogshow.com/images/0002-01.jpg"
        xlink:role="http://xml.dogshow.com/linkprops/picture"
        xlink:label="pic1" />
    <pic xlink:type="locator"
        xlink:href="http://xml.dogshow.com/images/0002-02.jpg"
        xlink:role="http://xml.dogshow.com/linkprops/picture"
        xlink:label="pic2" />
    <pic xlink:type="locator"
        xlink:href="http://xml.dogshow.com/images/0002-03.jpg"
        xlink:role="http://xml.dogshow.com/linkprops/picture"
        xlink:label="pic3" />
```

Listing 13.11 Continued

```
    <doglink xlink:type="arc"
             xlink:arcrole="http://xml.dogshow.com/linkprops/isbreed"
             xlink:from="doginfo"
             xlink:to="breed"
             xlink:title="Breed"
             xlink:show="replace"
             xlink:actuate="onRequest" />
    <doglink xlink:type="arc"
             xlink:arcrole="http://xml.dogshow.com/linkprops/judgedby"
             xlink:from="doginfo"
             xlink:to="bobhayes"
             xlink:title="Judge"
             xlink:show="replace"
             xlink:actuate="onRequest" />
    <doglink xlink:type="arc"
             xlink:arcrole="http://xml.dogshow.com/linkprops/ownedby"
             xlink:from="doginfo"
             xlink:to="lizbartlett"
             xlink:title="Owner"
             xlink:show="replace"
             xlink:actuate="onRequest" />
    <piclink xlink:type="arc"
             xlink:arcrole="http://xml.dogshow.com/linkprops/picturedin"
             xlink:from="doginfo"
             xlink:to="pic1"
             xlink:title="Headshot"
             xlink:show="embed"
             xlink:actuate="onLoad" />
    <piclink xlink:type="arc"
             xlink:arcrole="http://xml.dogshow.com/linkprops/picturedin"
             xlink:from="doginfo"
             xlink:to="pic2"
             xlink:title="Side View"
             xlink:show="embed"
             xlink:actuate="onLoad" />
    <piclink xlink:type="arc"
             xlink:arcrole="http://xml.dogshow.com/linkprops/picturedin"
             xlink:from="doginfo"
             xlink:to="pic3"
             xlink:title="Other View"
             xlink:show="embed"
             xlink:actuate="onLoad" />
  </dog>
</dogshow>
```


In Listing 13.11, we created a new child element of `<dog>`, `<doginfo>`, which contains specific information on this specific dog which functions as a local resource for XLink purposes. Also, we've eliminated the difference between `<judge>` and `<owner>`, and rewritten them as a single `<human>` element—the exact relationship of that human to the dog will be defined by the `arc type defined, which is described by the` xlink:arcrole `attribute.` Each `xlink:arcrole` attribute serves as a label for the relationship established by the `arc` type. The advantage of using extended links here, over the simple links, is that we now have a set of arcs that more accurately describe the relationships among our various links. Rather than just a set of links, we have a pattern of relationships established among the dog, the owner, and the judge; and, those relationships are better documented through the `arcrole` attribute.

These are identified by their labels, via the `xlink:to` and `xlink:from` attributes on the XLink arc-type elements and the `xlink:label` on the resource-type or locator-type elements. The specific meanings we've given to these arcrole values are listed in Table 13.7.

TABLE 13.7 ARCROLE DEFINITIONS FOR DOG SHOW MARKUP

Arcrole URI	Link Meaning
`http://xml.dogshow.com/linkprops/isbreed`	...is of the breed shown on page...
`http://xml.dogshow.com/linkprops/judgedby`	...will be judged by...
`http://xml.dogshow.com/linkprops/ownedby`	...is owned by...
`http://xml.dogshow.com/linkprops/picturedin`	...is pictured in...

Notice that instead of describing what the resource or locator is, as the roles in Table 13.6 do, the arcroles instead describe how the resources or locators relate to one another.

SETTING ATTRIBUTE DEFAULTS FOR EXTENDED LINKS

Listing 13.12 is a rewrite to put default attribute values into the DTD, which is shown in Listing 13.13.

LISTING 13.12 EXTENDED LINK PLUS ATTRIBUTE DEFAULTS IN THE DTD

```
<dogshow
  xmlns="http://xml.dogshow.com/dogML-5.dtd">
  <!-- with extended xlinks and attribute defaults -->
  <dog xlink:type="extended">
    <doginfo id="0002">
      <name kind="formal">Drokkytshang Nying Chhem-Po</name>
      <name kind="pet">Kim</name>
      <gender>Dog</gender>
      <dob>25-December-1989</dob>
    </doginfo>
    <breed xlink:href="http://xml.dogshow.com/breed.php?code=tibm"
           xlink:title="Tibetan Mastiff" />
    <human xlink:href="http://xml.dogshow.com/judges.html#bobhayes"
           xlink:title="Bob Hayes"
           xlink:label="bobhayes" />
    <human
      xlink:href="http://xml.dogshow.com/show.php?owner=khyri@idyllmtn.com"
           xlink:title="Liz Bartlett"
           xlink:label="lizbartlett" />
    <pic xlink:href="http://xml.dogshow.com/images/0002-01.jpg"
         xlink:label="pic1" />
    <pic xlink:href="http://xml.dogshow.com/images/0002-02.jpg"
         xlink:label="pic2" />
    <pic xlink:href="http://xml.dogshow.com/images/0002-03.jpg"
         xlink:label="pic3" />
    <doglink xlink:arcrole="http://xml.dogshow.com/linkprops/isbreed"
             xlink:from="doginfo"
             xlink:to="breed"
```

LISTING 13.12 CONTINUED

```
              xlink:title="Breed" />
    <doglink xlink:arcrole="http://xml.dogshow.com/linkprops/judgedby"
             xlink:from="doginfo"
             xlink:to="bobhayes"
             xlink:title="Judge" />
    <doglink xlink:arcrole="http://xml.dogshow.com/linkprops/ownedby"
             xlink:from="doginfo"
             xlink:to="lizbartlett"
             xlink:title="Owner" />
    <piclink xlink:from="doginfo"
             xlink:to="pic1"
             xlink:title="Headshot" />
    <piclink xlink:from="doginfo"
             xlink:to="pic2"
             xlink:title="Side View" />
    <piclink xlink:from="doginfo"
             xlink:to="pic3"
             xlink:title="Other View" />
  </dog>
</dogshow>
```

LISTING 13.13 DTD FOR LISTING 13.12

```
<!ELEMENT dogshow (dog+)>
<!ATTLIST dogshow
  xmlns           CDATA           #IMPLIED
  xmlns:xlink     CDATA           #FIXED "http://www.w3.org/1999/xlink"
>

<!ELEMENT dog (doginfo,breed,human+,pic*,doglink*,piclink*)>
<!ATTLIST dog
  xlink:type      (extended)      #FIXED "extended"
>

<!ELEMENT doginfo (name|gender|dob)>
<!ATTLIST doginfo
  id              ID              #REQUIRED
  xlink:type      (resource)      #FIXED "resource"
  xlink:role      CDATA           #FIXED
"http://xml.dogshow.com/linkprops/doginfo"
  xlink:label     (doginfo)       #FIXED "doginfo"
>

<!ELEMENT name #PCDATA>
<!ATTLIST name
  kind            (formal|pet)    #IMPLIED
>

<!ELEMENT gender #PCDATA>

<!ELEMENT dob #PCDATA>

<!ELEMENT breed EMPTY>
<!ATTLIST breed
  xlink:type      (locator)       #FIXED "locator"
  xlink:href      CDATA           #REQUIRED
```

13

LISTING 13.13 CONTINUED

```
  xlink:role      CDATA           #FIXED
"http://xml.dogshow.com/linkprops/breedcode"
  xlink:title     CDATA           #IMPLIED
  xlink:label     (breed)         #FIXED "breed"
>

<!ELEMENT human EMPTY>
<!ATTLIST human
  xlink:type      (locator)       #FIXED "locator"
  xlink:href      CDATA           #REQUIRED
  xlink:title     CDATA           #IMPLIED
  xlink:label     NMTOKEN         #IMPLIED
>

<!ELEMENT pic EMPTY>
<!ATTLIST pic
  xlink:type      (locator)       #FIXED "locator"
  xlink:href      CDATA           #REQUIRED
  xlink:role      CDATA           #FIXED
"http://xml.dogshow.com/linkprops/picture"
  xlink:title     CDATA           #REQUIRED
  xlink:label     NMTOKEN         #FIXED "pic"
>

<!ELEMENT doglink EMPTY>
<!ATTLIST doglink
  xlink:type      (arc)           #FIXED "arc"
  xlink:arcrole   CDATA           #IMPLIED
  xlink:from      NMTOKEN         #IMPLIED
  xlink:to        NMTOKEN         #IMPLIED
  xlink:title     CDATA           #IMPLIED
  xlink:show      (replace)       #FIXED "replace"
  xlink:actuate   (onRequest)     #FIXED "onRequest"
>

<!ELEMENT piclink EMPTY>
<!ATTLIST piclink
  xlink:type      (arc)           #FIXED "arc"
  xlink:arcrole   CDATA           #FIXED
"http://xml.dogshow.com/linkprops/picturedin"
  xlink:from      NMTOKEN         #IMPLIED
  xlink:to        NMTOKEN         #IMPLIED
  xlink:title     CDATA           #IMPLIED
  xlink:show      (embed)         #FIXED "embed"
  xlink:actuate   (onLoad)        #FIXED "onLoad"
>
```

USING XML BASE, BACKLINKS, AND THIRD-PARTY LINKS

In Listing 13.14, we shorten our URI paths by adding `xml:base` statements to the DTD (additions to the DTD are shown in Listing 13.15), as well as adding additional arcs. Backlinks from remote resources (identified by `<human>` locators) to the local resource (`<doginfo>`) identify these links as going in both directions. Third-party links established by the `<nextpic>` and `<prevpic>` arcs determine a browsing order between the pictures, which could be used to create a slideshow of the dog show pictures.

Listing 13.14 Extended Link with Attribute Defaults, `XML:Base`, Backlinks, and Third-Party Links

```
<dogshow
  xmlns="http://xml.dogshow.com/dogML-7.dtd">
  <!-- with extended xlinks, attribute defaults, xml:base,
       xml:base defaults, and backlinks -->
  <dog>
    <doginfo id="0002">
      <name kind="formal">Drokkytshang Nying Chhem-Po</name>
      <name kind="pet">Kim</name>
      <gender>Dog</gender>
      <dob>25-December-1989</dob>
    </doginfo>
    <breed xlink:href="breed.php?code=tibm"
           xlink:title="Tibetan Mastiff" />
    <human xlink:href="judges.html#bobhayes"
           xlink:title="Bob Hayes"
           xlink:label="bobhayes" />
    <human xlink:href="show.php?owner=khyri@idyllmtn.com"
           xlink:title="Liz Bartlett"
           xlink:label="lizbartlett" />
    <pic xlink:href="0002-01.jpg"
         xlink:title="Headshot" />
    <pic xlink:href="0002-02.jpg"
         xlink:title="Side View" />
    <pic xlink:href="0002-03.jpg"
         xlink:title="Other View" />
    <doglink xlink:arcrole="http://xml.dogshow.com/linkprops/isbreed"
             xlink:from="doginfo"
             xlink:to="breed"
             xlink:title="Breed" />
    <doglink xlink:arcrole="http://xml.dogshow.com/linkprops/judgedby"
             xlink:from="doginfo"
             xlink:to="bobhayes"
             xlink:title="Judge" />
    <doglink xlink:arcrole="http://xml.dogshow.com/linkprops/judgefor"
             xlink:from="bobhayes"
             xlink:to="doginfo" />
    <!-- New links describing the relationship between the breed and
         the judge -->
    <doglink xlink:arcrole="http://xml.dogshow.com/linkprops/judgedby"
             xlink:from="breed"
             xlink:to="bobhayes"
             xlink:title="Breed Judge" />
    <doglink xlink:arcrole="http://xml.dogshow.com/linkprops/judgefor"
             xlink:from="bobhayes"
             xlink:to="breed" />
    <doglink xlink:arcrole="http://xml.dogshow.com/linkprops/ownedby"
             xlink:from="doginfo"
             xlink:to="lizbartlett"
             xlink:title="Owner" />
    <doglink xlink:arcrole="http://xml.dogshow.com/linkprops/ownerof"
             xlink:from="lizbartlett"
             xlink:to="doginfo" />
    <piclink xlink:from="doginfo"
             xlink:to="pic1"
```

LISTING 13.14 CONTINUED

```
              xlink:title="Headshot" />
    <piclink xlink:from="doginfo"
             xlink:to="pic2"
             xlink:title="Side View" />
    <piclink xlink:from="doginfo"
             xlink:to="pic3"
             xlink:title="Other View" />
    <nextpic xlink:from="pic1"
             xlink:to="pic2" />
    <prevpic xlink:from="pic2"
             xlink:to="pic1" />
    <nextpic xlink:from="pic2"
             xlink:to="pic3" />
    <prevpic xlink:from="pic3"
             xlink:to="pic2" />
  </dog>
</dogshow>
```

LISTING 13.15 PARTIAL DTD FOR LISTING 13.14

```
...
<!ELEMENT dogshow (dog+)>
<!ATTLIST dogshow
  xmlns          CDATA            #IMPLIED
  xmlns:xlink    CDATA            #FIXED "http://www.w3.org/1999/xlink"
  xml:base       CDATA            #FIXED "http://xml.dogshow.com/"

...

<!ELEMENT pic EMPTY>
<!ATTLIST pic
  xlink:type     (locator)        #FIXED "locator"
  xlink:href     CDATA            #REQUIRED
  xlink:role     CDATA            #FIXED
"http://xml.dogshow.com/linkprops/picture"
  xlink:title    CDATA            #REQUIRED
  xlink:label    NMTOKEN          #FIXED "pic"
  xml:base       CDATA            #FIXED "/images/"
>

...

<!ELEMENT nextpic EMPTY>
<!ATTLIST nextpic
  xlink:type     (arc)            #FIXED "arc"
  xlink:arcrole  CDATA            #FIXED
"http://xml.dogshow.com/linkprops/preceeds-pic"
  xlink:from     NMTOKEN          #IMPLIED
  xlink:to       NMTOKEN          #IMPLIED
  xlink:title    CDATA            #IMPLIED
  xlink:show     (replace)        #FIXED "replace"
  xlink:actuate  (onRequest)      #FIXED "onRequest"
>
```

LISTING 13.15 CONTINUED

```
<!ELEMENT prevpic EMPTY>
<!ATTLIST prevpic
  xlink:type      (arc)           #FIXED "arc"
  xlink:arcrole   CDATA           #FIXED
"http://xml.dogshow.com/linkprops/follows-pic"
  xlink:from      NMTOKEN         #IMPLIED
  xlink:to        NMTOKEN         #IMPLIED
  xlink:title     CDATA           #IMPLIED
  xlink:show      (replace)       #FIXED "replace"
  xlink:actuate   (onRequest)     #FIXED "onRequest"
>
```

The new arcroles in Listing 13.14 are shown in Table 13.8, which extends the listing in Table 13.7.

TABLE 13.8 ADDITIONAL ARCROLES FOR DOG SHOW EXAMPLE

Arcrole URI	Link Meaning
`http://xml.dogshow.com/linkprops/judgefor`	...will be the judge for...
`http://xml.dogshow.com/linkprops/ownerof`	...is the owner of...
`http://xml.dogshow.com/linkprops/preceeds-pic`	...comes before (in slideshow order)...
`http://xml.dogshow.com/linkprops/follows-pic`	...comes after (in slideshow order)...

Notice that we can even use the arcrole `http://xml.dogshow.com/linkprops/judgefor` to establish links between the judge's `<human>` element and the `<breed>` element, indicating that this judge is not only judging the dog in question, but also the specific breed.

RESOURCES

There are a limited number of resources surrounding XBase, XInclude, and XLink, primarily because although they are capable of helping you build some pretty complex relationships, the technologies themselves are inherently simple. However, here are a few good resources to get you started working with XLink and its related technologies:

- W3C XBase Recommendation (`http://www.w3.org/TR/xmlbase/`). As always, the first stop for information regarding XBase should be here, the official Recommendation.
- W3C XInclude Candidate Recommendation (`http://www.w3.org/TR/xinclude/`). XInclude is currently in the form of a candidate recommendation, which is only one small step away from being an official Recommendation. You should feel free to use this as a resource—just be aware that there might be some small changes when the official Recommendation is released.
- XInclude Engine (`http://www.ibiblio.org/xml/XInclude/`). This is a Java-based XInclude processor that is designed to work with both SAX and DOM parser implementations.

- XInclude Transformer (`http://xml.apache.org/cocoon/userdocs/transformers/xinclude-transformer.html`). This is another XInclude processor—this one from the Apache Project.
- W3C XLink Recommendation (`http://www.w3.org/TR/xlink/`). This is the W3C official Recommendation for XLink.
- XML.com XLink Introduction (`http://www.xml.com/pub/a/2000/09/xlink/part1.html`). XML.com features this introductory article on XLink, which provides a basic view of the technology and some examples.
- XML.com XLink Reference (`http://www.xml.com/pub/a/2000/09/xlink/part2.html`). Also from XML.com, and a continuation of the XLink Introduction, this section offers more advanced XLink advice.
- XGuru (`http://www.xguru.com/tutorial/news.asp?id=19`). The XGuru site contains information about a number of XML technologies, including this XLink Tutorial.

ROADMAP

The XBase, XInclude, and XLink technologies are all important, as they help establish the relationships among the dates in various XML documents. And, because the entire point of XML is to help develop documents in which the content is separated from the markup, this is a very important aspect of developing robust XML solutions that accurately convey the meaning of your information.

This chapter rounds out the location technologies currently used with XML. We've seen how to use XPath and XPointer to navigate the data within XML documents. And now we've seen how XBase, XInclude, and XLink can help you link together data in different documents, and navigate through data in document sets, rather than in a single document.

In the next section, we will be taking a look at the technologies you can use to automate the processing of XML documents. We will look at how XML can be used with technologies such as Microsoft's .NET and Sun's Java. And, then, we will move on to real-world XML applications.

PART IV

XML Programming and Scripting

CHAPTER 14

XML and the Document Object Model

In this chapter

by Alexander Kachur

Platform-Independent Interface for XML Documents

One of the reasons for today's widespread usage of the XML technologies is that they provide the developers with a standard way of structuring documents and dealing with those documents the same way, regardless of technologies used in conjunction with XML documents.

XML Documents and DOM

To make it even easier to access XML documents from different platforms through different sets of technologies, the World Wide Web Consortium developed a specification of the Application Programming Interface (API) which allows accessing XML and HTML documents through an object model.

This API specification—the Document Object Model (DOM)—is an *implementation*-independent (that is, *platform*- and *language*-neutral) specification of interfaces for accessing the tree structure of the XML documents.

Note

Note that W3C does not provide any implementation of the API as their goal was just to develop a common implementation independent standard.

DOM Specification Overview

The genesis of DOM is based on different APIs provided with the browsers such as Microsoft Internet Explorer or Netscape Navigator for accessing HTML documents in the sense that the DOM utilizes the idea of representing documents with an object model, which is accessible to applications through a standard API.

The DOM treats documents as hierarchical tree structures containing objects that represent the components of a document.

Note

A tree is a specially organized collection of objects usually referred to as *Nodes*. The structure of a tree is organized based on the following rules:

- Every node must have one parent node and zero or more child nodes.
- The very first node in the tree does not have a parent.

Later in this chapter, we will discuss the organization of XML documents in more detail.

Because most of today's Web documents are HTML based, the DOM API specification has been designed with non-XML tree-structured documents, such as HTML, in mind.

DESIGN LEVELS

The W3C decided to split the DOM specification into three different levels of implementation, allowing the implementers to choose how much functionality they need to support.

These design levels are

- Level 1
- Level 2
- Level 3

DOM LEVEL 1

The main part of the DOM API Level 1 is a set of *core interfaces*, which is a must for any DOM API implementation. The core interfaces contain methods useful for any type of tree-structured document as well as some XML-specific extensions.

In addition to core interfaces, the specification defines an API for accessing HTML document trees.

DOM LEVEL 1 CORE

The DOM Level 1 Core Interfaces Specification defines two types of interfaces:

- *Fundamental*—Ones that should be realized in any DOM Level 1–compliant implementation.
- *Extended*—Interfaces that are not required in some implementations—for example, in HTML-only implementations of DOM Level 1.

The W3C specification of DOM gives Interface Definition Language (IDL) definitions of interfaces that provide implementation-neutral and language-independent means to define them. All the interfaces could be easily defined and implemented in any language that supports interface definitions, such as Java.

The interfaces are defined in such a way that they are easy to use in any object-oriented language, such as Java, C++, and so on, or platform, such as DCOM.

However, for performance-critical applications as well as for easy access from non–Object-Oriented languages, such as C, there is one interface defined (see the following Node interface definition) that has a lot of functionality available in it. For the price of code readability through this interface, XML documents can be performance-efficiently accessed without querying other interfaces.

Let's look more closely at the DOM Level 1 Fundamental Core Interfaces.

FUNDAMENTAL CORE INTERFACES

The Document Object Model defines a document as a tree hierarchy of *Nodes*. A node can have other nodes as children or it can be a *leaf*, so it cannot have children. A Node represents any element of the XML document tree hierarchy. An element, such as `<author>`, is a node. An element with an attribute, such as `<author ID="1234567">`, is a node as well.

The DOM operates with the following types of nodes:

- Document
- Document Type
- DocumentFragment
- Notation
- Element
- Attribute
- Text
- CDATA Section
- Entity
- Entity Reference
- Processing Instruction
- Comment

Each of them has its own interface derived from the base interface Node.

There are also two interfaces defined in the specification that do not belong to the `html` or `xml` document model but are used to provide the developers with some helper functionality. These interfaces are the `DOMImplementation` and `DOMException`.

`DOMImplementation` The `DOMImplementation` interface defines only one method, `hasFeature`, which is a helper function provided for the purpose of testing whether the requested feature and its version are supported by the implementation of DOM Level 1 used by a developer.

The method takes two `DOMStrings`: the XML name of a feature to test and the version of the feature.

> **Note**
>
> The `DOMString` is a sequence of characters encoded using UTF-16 encoding. In Java, it corresponds to the `String` class.

As we mentioned before, the DOM level 1 consists of two modules: XML and HTML; hence, the two feature names defined in the specification are *"XML"* and *"HTML."*

`DOMException` There is only one exception interface defined in DOM. Any exceptions or errors related to the operation of the DOM implementation should be encapsulated into the implementation of this class. At the time this book was being written, there were 10 exception codes defined and the W3C reserves the right to use other codes in the future. Table 14.1 lists the exception codes.

Table 14.1 Exception Codes Defined in the `DOMException` Interface

Exception Code	Description
`DOMSTRING_SIZE_ERR`	The exception is raised if the text string size does not fit into a `DOMString`.
`HIERARCHY_REQUEST_ERR`	This condition happens when the operation on the node (insert, replace, and so on) cannot be done because of the hierarchy restrictions: an attempt to insert a child into a node that cannot have children, or an attempt to insert into a nonexisting parent note.
`INDEX_SIZE_ERR`	The code means that the operation failed because the index or size was outside the range of acceptable values.
`INUSE_ATTRIBUTE_ERR`	The exception is raised when there is an attempt made to add or replace an attribute that is already in use.
`INVALID_CHARACTER_ERR`	An operation failed because of an illegal character in a name or other property.
`NOT_FOUND_ERR`	An operation on the node failed because the node does not exist.
`NOT_SUPPORTED_ERR`	This exception is raised when the implementation of the DOM does not support the requested operation or object.
`NO_DATA_ALLOWED_ERR`	This code means that the node type does not support the data specified.
`NO_MODIFICATION_ALLOWED_ERR`	An operation failed because of an attempt to modify something that is not allowed to be changed.
`WRONG_DOCUMENT_ERR`	This code is raised when an attempt is made to use a node within a document it doesn't belong to.

Node The XML or HTML document can be built from different types of nodes, such as *Element*, *CDATA Section*, *Comment*, and so on. All of them have their own interfaces and specific methods defined in DOM Level 1. These interfaces are inherited from Node, which defines basic properties and methods independent from the node type.

The Node interface defines a set of basic methods that provide access to node elements and their children. Together with the Node properties, which will be discussed later, these methods are the minimum you need to work with XML or HTML documents. The methods are described in Table 14.2.

TABLE 14.2 METHODS OF THE NODE INTERFACE

Name	Parameters	Description, Returns, Throws

`insertBefore`	`newChild`—Node. A node to insert.
	`refChild`—Node. The child node before which the new one should be inserted.
		Description
		Inserts the `newChild` node before the existing `refChild`. If `refChild` already exists, it is replaced by the new instance.
		Return value
		Node—The inserted node.
		Exception
		Throws `DOMException`:
		`HIERARCHY_REQUEST_ERR`
		`WRONG_DOCUMENT_ERR`
		`NO_MODIFICATION_ALLOWED_ERR`
		`NOT_FOUND_ERR`

`replaceChild`	`newChild`—Node. A node to replace with.
	`oldChild`—Node. An old child node, which should be replaced.
		Replaces one node with another. If the `newChild` node already exists, it is replaced.
		Returns:
		Node—The `oldChild` node.
		Throws `DOMException`:
		`HIERARCHY_REQUEST_ERR`
		`WRONG_DOCUMENT_ERR`
		`NO_MODIFICATION_ALLOWED_ERR`
		`NOT_FOUND_ERR`

`removeChild`	*`oldChild`—Node. A child node to remove.*	Removes a child node from the tree.
		Returns:
		Node—The `oldChild` node.
		Throws `DOMException`:
		`NO_MODIFICATION_ALLOWED_ERR`
		`NOT_FOUND_ERR`

`appendChild`	*`newChild`—Node. A node to append.*	Appends a new node to the end of the list of children of this node. The methods removes `newChild` from the tree if it already exists.
		Returns:
		Node—The inserted node.
		Throws `DOMException`:
		`HIERARCHY_REQUEST_ERR`
		`WRONG_DOCUMENT_ERR`
		`NO_MODIFICATION_ALLOWED_ERR`

`HasChildNodes-Boolean`	*None*	Returns a value that indicates whether the node has children. Returns: boolean—True if there are child nodes, false otherwise. Throws: No exceptions.

TABLE 14.2 CONTINUED

Name	Parameters	Description, Returns, Throws
cloneNode	*deep—boolean. Whether to recursively clone the subtree.*	Creates a clone of the node. The created clone will have no parent. If the deep is true, this method will create a clone that includes all of the subnodes, also. Returns: Node—The newly created clone. Throws DOMException: NOT_SUPPORTED_ERR

Among its properties, the Node interface has four that give enough information to describe the node without obtaining specialized interfaces. Table 14.3 describes these properties.

TABLE 14.3 FOUR PROPERTIES DESCRIBING THE TYPE AND CONTENTS OF THE NODE

Name, Type	Description	Comment
nodeType, readonly unsigned short	This property describes the node type, which can be used to make a decision regarding further processing of the node.	One of the following constants: ELEMENT_NODE—The node object represents an *Element*. ATTRIBUTE_NODE—The node is an *Attribute*. TEXT_NODE—This node is a *Text*. CDATA_SECTION_NODE—The node object represents a *CDATASection*. ENTITY_REFERENCE_NODE—This is an *EntityReference*. ENTITY_NODE—The object is an *Entity*. PROCESSING_ INSTRUCTION_NODE—This is a *ProcessingInstruction*. COMMENT_NODE—The node represents a *Comment*. DOCUMENT_NODE—This node is a *Document*. DOCUMENT_TYPE_NODE—This node is a *DocumentType*. DOCUMENT_FRAGMENT_NODE —This is a *DocumentFragment*. NOTATION_NODE—The node object represents a *Notation*.

TABLE 14.3 CONTINUED

Name, Type	Description	Comment
nodeName, `readonly DOMString`	The name of the node.	The value of this property depends on the `nodeType`. Refer to Table 14.2 for details.
nodeValue, `read-write DOMString`	The value of the node.	The value of this property depends on the `nodeType`. Refer to Table 14.2 for details.
attributes, `readonly NamedNodeMap`	Attributes of the node.	This property contains all the attributes of the node of type *`Element`* or *`null`* for all the other node types.

Depending on the value of the *`nodeType`* property, three of the properties described have different meanings as shown in Table 14.4.

TABLE 14.4 VALUES OF THE `nodeName`, `nodeValue`, AND `attributes` PROPERTIES DEPENDING ON THE `nodeType`

Node Type	`nodeName`	`nodeValue`	Attributes
`ELEMENT_NODE`	The name of the element tag.	null	All the element attributes.
`ATTRIBUTE_NODE`	The name of the attribute.	The value of the attribute.	null
`TEXT_NODE`	The string literal "`#text`".	The content of the node.	null
`CDATA_SECTION_NODE`	The string literal "`#cdata-section`".	The content of the CDATA section node.	null
`ENTITY_REFERENCE_NODE`	The name of the entity referenced.	null	null
`ENTITY_NODE`	The name of the entity.	null	null
`PROCESSING_INSTRUCTION_NODE`	The target of the processing instruction.	The remaining content of the processing instruction excluding the target.	null
`COMMENT_NODE`	The string literal "`#comment`".	The contents of the comment.	null
`DOCUMENT_NODE`	The string literal "`#document`".	null	null
`DOCUMENT_TYPE_NODE`	The document type name.	null	null

TABLE 14.4 CONTINUED

Node Type	nodeName	nodeValue	Attributes
DOCUMENT_FRAGMENT_NODE	The string literal "#document fragment".	null	null
NOTATION_NODE	The notation name.	null	null

These are not the only properties defined in the Node interface. Table 14.5 describes the remainder.

TABLE 14.5 OTHER PROPERTIES DEFINED IN THE NODE INTERFACE

Name, Type	Description	Comment
parentNode, readonly Node	The parent of the node.	Null if: The node has not been added to a tree yet (just created) or, The node has been removed from the tree or, The node represents Attr, Document, DocumentFragment, Entity, and Notation.
childNodes, readonly NodeList	All the children of the node.	Empty NodeList if there are no children (not null!).
firstChild, readonly Node	The first child of the node.	Null if there are no children in the node.
lastChild, readonly Node	The last child of the node.	Null if there are no children in the node.
previousSibling, readonly Node	The node preceding this one under the same parent node in the document.	Null if there are no preceding node or if the node is the root of the document.
nextSibling, readonly Node	The node that follows this one under the same parent node in the document.	Null if there is no following node or if the node is the root of the document.
ownerDocument, readonly Document	The Document object which owns the node.	Null if the node is a Document.

`NodeList` In many cases, a developer needs to get a collection of the children that belong to a node and iterate through them using an index. Such a collection is accessible in DOM Level 1 from the `NodeList` interface, which has one method and one property in it as shown in Tables 14.6 and 14.7 respectively.

TABLE 14.6 METHOD OF THE NodeList INTERFACE

Name	Parameters	Description, Returns, Throws
item	index—unsigned long.	Returns a node by its index in the collection. The first node has an index of 0. Throws: No exceptions.

TABLE 14.7 PROPERTY OF THE NodeList INTERFACE

Name, Type	Description	Comment
length, *readonly* unsigned long	The number of nodes in the collection.	

NamedNodeMap The NamedNodeMap interface is another way of accessing a node's children. Unlike NodeList, this interface allows us to access nodes by their names.

In addition to *item* method and *length* property, which are the same as in NodeList, there are three more methods defined in the NamedNodeMap.

TABLE 14.8 METHODS OF THE NamedNodeMap INTERFACE

Name	Parameters	Description, Returns, Throws
GetNamedItem	nodeName—DOMString. The name of the node to retrieve.	The method searches for a node by its name—specified as a parameter. Returns: Node—The node found or null. Throws: No exceptions.
SetNamedItem	newNode—Node. The node to add to the collection.	Adds a new node to the collection. The node's nodeName property is then used as the node's name in the map. Returns: null or the previous node if the operation results in replacement of a node with the same name. Throws DOMException: INUSE_ATTRIBUTE_ERR WRONG_DOCUMENT_ERR NO_MODIFICATION_ALLOWED_ERR
removeNamedItem	nodeName—Node. The name of the node to remove.	The method searches for a node by its name, specified as a parameter, and removes the node. Returns: Node—The node removed or null if the node cannot be found. Throws DOMException: NOT_FOUND_ERRNO_MODIFICATION_ ALLOWED_ERR

TABLE 14.8 CONTINUED

Name	Parameters	Description, Returns, Throws
item	index—unsigned long.	Returns a node by its index in the collection. The first node has an index of 0. If the index is out of range, the method returns null. Throws: No exceptions.

TABLE 14.9 PROPERTY OF THE NamedNodeMap INTERFACE

Name, Type	Description	Comment
length, readonly unsigned long	The number of nodes in the collection.	

DOCUMENT The Document object is the root node of an XML document tree and any node object, other than the root, created using a DOM API implementation, should have an owner document. The Document interface inherits the Node interface. In addition to the methods and properties defined in the Node, it provides a set of factory methods to create any other types of Node objects, such as Elements, Processing Instructions, and so on.

TABLE 14.10 METHODS OF THE DOCUMENT INTERFACE

Name	Parameters	Description, Returns, Throws
CreateElement	tagName—DOMString. The name of the element to create.	Creates a new node of type Element with a tag name specified in the parameter. The newly created element should then be attached to some node in a document tree with a call to a method such as appendChild(). Returns: Element—The new Element object created. Throws DOMException: INVALID_CHARACTER_ERR NOT_SUPPORTED_ERR
CreateDocument-Fragment	None	Creates a new empty DocumentFragment. Returns: DocumentFragment—The new *DocumentFragment* object created. Throws: No exceptions.

14

TABLE 14.10 CONTINUED

Name	Parameters	Description, Returns, Throws
createTextNode	data—DOMString. The node's text string.	Creates a new Text node and inserts the specified string as its content. Returns: Text—The new *Text* object created. Throws: No exceptions.
CreateComment	data—DOMString. The node's comment string.	The node's comment string. Creates a new node of type Comment node and inserts the specified string as its textual content. Returns: CommentNode—The new *Comment* object created. Throws: No exceptions.
createCDATASection	data—DOMString. The node's text.	Creates a new CDATASection node and inserts the specified string as its content. Returns: Node—The new *CDATASection* object created. Throws DOMException: NOT_SUPPORTED_ERR
createProcessing-Instruction	target—DOMString. data—DOMString.	Creates a new ProcessingInstruction node with the name and content specified as parameters. Returns: Node—The new ProcessingInstruction object created. Throws DOMException: NOT_SUPPORTED_ERR INVALID_CHARACTER_ERR
createAttribute	name—DOMString. The name of the attribute.	Creates a new Attr node using the name specified as a parameter. Returns: Attr—The new Attr objectcreated. Throws DOMException: INVALID_CHARACTER_ERR
createEntityReference	name—DOMString. The name of the Entity to reference.	Creates a new EntityReference node using the name of the referenced Entity object as a parameter. Returns:

Table 14.10 Continued

Name	Parameters	Description, Returns, Throws

		`Entityreference`—The new `EntityReference` object created.
		Throws `DOMException`:
		`INVALID_CHARACTER_ERR`
		`NOT_SUPPORTED_ERR`

`getElementsByTagName`	`tagName`—`DOMString`. The name of a tag to get elements of.	Return a `NodeList` containing all the Element node objects with the tag name specified—or a list of all of the Elements that belong to a Document if an asterisk is specified as a tag name. Returns: `NodeList`—A list of Elements. Throws: No exceptions.

Table 14.11 Properties of the Document Interface

Name, Type	Description	Comment
`docType`, `readonly DocumentType`	This property contains a DTD specification of the Document.	This property returns `null` if the document does not have a Document Type Definition associated with it.
`implementation`, `readonly DOMImplementation`	The `DOMImplementation` object that can be used to find out about the capabilities of the DOM implementation being used.	
`documentElement`, `readonly` Element	An instance of the root Element of the document tree.	

`DocumentFragment` The `DocumentFragment` interface represents a section of the XML or HTML document tree. It is derived from the Node interface and it is a node containing a fragment of a bigger document. It is a very useful lightweight version of the Document interface especially dedicated to perform temporary operations such as holding a portion of a tree that is being moved from one location to another, and so on. For example, you can create a `DocumentFragment` using the factory method `createDocumentFragment()` on the Document interface, assemble a subtree attaching child nodes with calls to the `appendChild()` method on the `DocumentFragment` interface, and then place the fragment in another location in the document.

The `DocumentFragment` interface does not have any methods or properties other than those defined within the Node interface.

ELEMENT The Element interface represents an XML or HTML document Element.

It inherits all the methods of the Node interface and introduces a bit more flexibility in accessing elements' attributes.

TABLE 14.12 METHODS OF THE ELEMENT INTERFACE

Name	Parameters	Description, Returns, Throws
getAttribute	`name`—`DOMString`. The name of the element attribute to get.	The method returns the value of the requested attribute. Returns: `DOMString`—A value of the attribute or null if there is no specified or default value. Throws: No exceptions.

setAttribute	`name`—`DOMString`. The name of the element attribute to set.
	`value`—`DOMString`. The value of the attribute.
		Adds a new attribute with the name and value specified to the element node.
		Changes the value of the attribute with the same name if it already exists.
		Returns:
		No return value.
		Throws `DOMException`:
		`INVALID_CHARACTER_ERR`
		`NO_MODIFICATION_ALLOWED_ERR`

removeAttribute	`name`—`DOMString`. The name of the element attribute to remove.	Removes the attribute specified from the element node or changes the value of the attribute to default if a default value exists for this attribute. Returns: No return value. Throws `DOMException`: `NO_MODIFICATION_ALLOWED_ERR`
getAttributeNode	`name`—`DOMString`. The name of the element attribute to set.	Unlike the `getAttribute` this method returns the Node object associated with the requested attribute rather than the attribute string value. Returns: `Attr`—An object of type `Attr` or null if the attribute does not exist. Throws: No exceptions.

TABLE 14.12 CONTINUED

Name	Parameters	Description, Returns, Throws
setAttributeNode	newAttr—Attr. An Attr to add to an element.	Adds a new attribute to the element node. Replaces the attribute with the same name if it already exists. Returns: Attr—The old attribute object if the method replaced it or null otherwise. Throws DOMException: WRONG_DOCUMENT_ERR NO_MODIFICATION_ALLOWED_ERR INUSE_ATTRIBUTE_ERR
removeAttributeNode	oldAttr—Attr. The attribute to remove.	Removes the attribute specified from the element node or changes the value of the attribute to the default if the default value exists for this attribute. Returns: Attr—The attribute object removed. Throws DOMException: NO_MODIFICATION_ALLOWED_ERR NOT_FOUND_ERR
getElementsByTagName	name—DOMString. The name used to match descendant element names.	Returns a NodeList collection of all the descendant elements whose name matches the one given in the parameter. If the special character * is used, all element descendants will be returned. Returns: NodeList—A collection of Element nodes. Throws: No exceptions.
normalize	None	The method parses a subtree below the Element node and concatenates all the Text nodes that do not have any markup between each other. This is useful when you need to make sure the DOM tree structure is the same after the document has been saved to a file and loaded again. Returns: No return value. Throws: No exceptions.

14

TABLE 14.13 PROPERTIES OF THE ELEMENT INTERFACE

Name, Type	Description	Comment
tagName, readonly DOMString	The name of an XML or HTML tag—that is, the element name.	Note that for XML documents the cproperty is in the same case as it is in the document. For HTML documents the property contains a canonical uppercase tag name.

Attr The Attr object is a very special kind of node object. It is a property of an element node and is not treated by the DOM as a child of the element or as a part of the document tree.

TABLE 14.14 PROPERTIES OF THE Attr INTERFACE

Name, Type	Description	Comment
name, readonly DOMString	The name of the attribute.	
value, readonly DOMString	The value of the attribute.	
specified, readonly boolean	This property indicates whether the attribute has been explicitly set by a user or taken by the DOM from the DTD.	True if the attribute has been assigned a value by a user through DOM or false if the default attribute value has been used based on the document's DTD, which is accessible through the DocumentType interface.

CharacterData The *CharacterData* interface is derived from Node, also. In addition to the basic methods and properties provided by its parent, it has a set of methods and properties that can be used to access or manipulate character data within the XML document.

In DOM Level 1, the CharacterData is a base interface for the following interfaces:

- Text
- Comment

TABLE 14.15 METHODS OF THE CharacterData INTERFACE

Name	Parameters	Description, Returns, Throws
substringData	offset—unsigned long. The starting position within the node's character data of the substring to retrieve. count—unsigned long. The size of the substring to retrieve.	Retrieves a range of data from the node's character data. Returns: DOMString—The substring retrieved. Throws DOMException: NO_MODIFICATION_ALLOWED_ERR INDEX_SIZE_ERR

Table 14.15 Continued

Name	Parameters	Description, Returns, Throws
appendData	arg—DOMString. The string to append to the end of the node's character data.	Appends a string to the node's character data. Returns: No return value. Throws DOMException: NO_MODIFICATION_ALLOWED_ERR
insertData	offset—unsigned long. The starting position within the node's character data, where the data will be inserted. arg—DOMString. The substring to insert.	Inserts data into the node's chara ter data at the specified offset. Returns: No return value. Throws DOMException: NO_MODIFICATION_ALLOWED_ERR INDEX_SIZE_ERR
deleteData	offset—unsigned long. The offset within the node's character data of the substring to delete. count—unsigned long. The number of characters to delete.	Deletes a substring from the node's character data at the specified offset. Returns: No return value. Throws DOMException: NO_MODIFICATION_ALLOWED_ERR INDEX_SIZE_ERR
replaceData	offset—unsigned long. The offset of the substring to replace. count—unsigned long. The number of characters to replace. arg—DOMString. The substring to replace with.	Replaces a substring in the node's character data at the specified offset Returns: No return value. Throws DOMException: NO_MODIFICATION_ALLOWED_ERR INDEX_SIZE_ERR

Table 14.16 Properties of the CharacterData Interface

Name, Type	Description	Comment
data, DOMString.	The character data of the node.	Reading the value may throw DOMException: DOMSTRING_SIZE_ERR Setting the value may throw DOMException: NO_MODIFICATION_ALLOWED_ERR
length, readonly unsigned long.	Length of the character data of the node.	

14

Text The Text interface is derived from CharacterData and should implement all the methods defined in its parent. In addition to the base methods, there is one more defined in the Text (see Table 14.17).

Nodes of type Text represent the text data of an `Element` or `Attr` node. Note that the DOM specification allows an element to have multiple adjacent Text nodes as its children (for example, as a result of calling the `splitText()` method on a Text node). However, XML does not have any means of storing adjacent Text nodes persistently and adjacent Text nodes will become a single node after the document has been saved and reloaded.

TABLE 14.17 METHODS OF THE TEXT INTERFACE

Name	Parameters	Description, Returns, Throws

splitText	`offset`—unsigned long. Offset in the Text node where node will be split.	Splits a `Text` node into two separate nodes. After a successful call, the text in this node contains the first part of the text before a split point.
		Returns:
		`Text`—The new Text node containing the second part of the text.
		Throws `DOMException`:
		`INDEX_SIZE_ERR`
		`NO_MODIFICATION_ALLOWED_ERR`

COMMENT The comment interface inherits the `CharacterData` interface and does not implement any additional methods.

Comment nodes represent comment sections of XML and HTML documents enclosed in `<!--` and `-->` tags.

EXTENDED INTERFACES

The interfaces discussed in the previous section are required for any implementation of the DOM Level 1 API. However, the specification also defines a set of extended interfaces that are only mandatory for implementations supporting XML. If an implementation is to be used only with HTML documents, there is no need to support any of the extended interfaces.

> **Note**
>
> To find out whether an implementation supports extended interfaces, you can use the `hasFeature()` method passing it two `DOMStrings`: `"XML"` and `"1.0"` as parameters. If the return value is true then the extended interfaces are present.

`DocumentType` The document type interface provides a set of methods to access a list of entities and notations from the document, such as entities declared in the DTD for an XML document.

In future versions of DOM when the W3C standardization efforts produce some final specifications for XML Schemas and DTDs, this interface may be extended to give DOM implementations more flexibility to provide validation of documents, strong type checking, and so on.

At the date of this writing, there are only three properties defined in the interface:

TABLE 14.18 PROPERTIES OF THE `DocumentType` INTERFACE

Name, Type	Description	Comment
name, readonly `DOMString`	The name of the XML Schema or DTD associated with the document.	
entities, *readonly* `NamedNodeMap`	A `NamedNodeMap` of Entity objects declared in the DTD.	
notations, *readonly* `NamedNodeMap`	A `NamedNodeMap` of Notation objects declared in the DTD.	

NOTATION The Notation interface, derived from the Node interface, describes the notation declared in the DTD.

TABLE 14.19 PROPERTIES OF THE NOTATION INTERFACE

Name, Type	Description	Comment
publicId, readonly `DOMString`	The notation's public identifier.	The value is null if the id is missing.
systemId, readonly `DOMString`	The notation's system identifier.	The value is null if the id is missing.

ENTITY Like many others, the Entity interface is derived from the Node interface. It describes an entity defined in a document. However, it's a special kind of node, which does not belong to any parent—it's rather a property of the document than a part of the document tree.

The specification leaves it up to the XML processor implementer to decide whether it should perform the validation of documents. Consequently, any entities may be expanded by the processor before the document structure is exposed as a DOM tree.

TABLE 14.20 PROPERTIES OF THE ENTITY INTERFACE

Name, Type	Description	Comment
publicId, readonly `DOMString`	The entity's public identifier.	The value is null if the id is missing.
systemId, readonly `DOMString`	The entity's system identifier.	The value is null if the id is missing.
notationName, readonly `DOMString`	The name of the notation used for entity.	The value is null if the entity is a parsed entity.

`EntityReference` When an XML processor parses a document, it can use objects of type *`EntityReference`* to hold references to any entities found in that document. However, the specification allows parsers to resolve any entities and perform all necessary substitutions in the document tree instead of building up `EntityReference` objects.

The `EntityReference` interface is declared as an empty interface derived from the Node; therefore, it implements only the methods and properties defined in its parent interface.

`ProcessingInstruction` When a DOM parser encounters a processing instruction in the document being parsed, it creates and populates an object which implements the *`ProcessingInstruction`* interface derived from the Node interface. A processing instruction consists of the specification of its target and data associated with it.

TABLE 14.21 PROPERTIES OF THE `ProcessingInstruction` INTERFACE

Name, Type	Description	Comment
`target`, `readonly DOMString`	The target of the instruction.	
`data`, `DOMString`	The data associated with the instruction.	This property is writable; however, if the node is not allowed to be modified, updating the property may throw `DOMException`: `NO_MODIFICATION_ALLOWED_ERR`

`CDATASection` The last, but not least, of the XML-specific interfaces of the DOM Level 1 is the `CDATASection`. Objects implementing this interface correspond to CDATA sections in the XML documents—special placeholders for text that may confuse parsers and therefore should not be parsed.

`CDATASection` interface inherits the Text interface. Objects of type `CDATASection` are usually treated in exactly the same way as Text objects so that there is no need to have any additional methods or properties implemented in the `CDATASection` interface.

DOM LEVEL 2

We've gone through all the interfaces of the DOM Level 1. Now we are going to take a quick look at the other levels of the DOM specification.

We will not be able to explore them thoroughly, but when we are finished, you will be oriented in most of the specifications and will know where to get the additional information you may need.

Level 2 of the DOM was approved by the W3C as a W3C Recommendation in November 2000. The full specification can be found at the official Web site of the consortium at `http://www.w3.org/TR/DOM-Level-2-Core`. Since the release of the specification, software vendors have started incorporating support for DOM 2 into browsers (IE 5.5 and later, Netscape 6), DOM parsers, and APIs. The Java 2 Standard Edition, Version 1.4, includes support for Level 2. Later in this chapter, we will discuss the tools and levels of the DOM they support.

The DOM Level 2 is an extension to Level 1 specification and it defines all the interfaces found in it, but also extends them with some extra features. These features are

- Events
- Views
- Styles
- Traversal and Ranges

The Level 2 specification has also introduced some changes to the core interfaces defined in Level 1.

Modifications to the Core Interfaces

The specification of the DOM Level 2 Core builds on the DOM Level 1, meaning that almost all the interfaces and methods that are present in Level 1 can also be found in Level 2. However, as the specification introduces new functionality, some changes have been made to the core interfaces. The specification discusses the differences between Level 1 and Level 2 in detail, which we will examine briefly.

The following changeshave been made to the Core Interfaces in Level 2:

- *`Attr`*—The `Attr` node has an additional property that references to its owner Element.
- *`Document`*—The `Document` interface has five extra methods, which are useful to work with Namespaces and move nodes from one document to another.
- *`NamedNodeMap`*—Three more methods have been added to make it easier to use Namespaces.
- *`Node`*—The `Node` interface now has three more properties and two extra methods. It is now possible to determine whether a particular node supports a feature and whether it has attributes.
- *`DocumentType`*—This interface has been extended with three more properties.
- *`DOMImplementation`*—This interface now allows creating new documents with association to a specific Namespace and document type. A factory for empty `DocumentType` nodes has also been added.
- *`Element`*—This is the most affected interface as it has eight new methods mostly for operating with Namespaces.
- *`DOMException`*—New exception codes have been added.

Note

The feature string corresponding to the set of core interfaces in a call to `DOMImplementation.hasFeature()` method is "Core" and the version for any Level 2 feature is "2.0."

14

SUPPLEMENTAL SPECIFICATIONS

The DOM Level 2 specification is separated into 14 modules that support particular groups of features. Unlike the DOM Level 1, the Level 2 allows implementers to implement only the modules they need (the core module still has to be implemented).

EVENTS

The first of the modules is an *Events* module, which describes the event model for the DOM. There are several types of events (UI events, mouse events, and so on) and an implementation can support some or all of them.

The source of any event in the DOM is always a document processor. The Events module provides developers with interfaces and methods to register their event targets and listeners and handle them according to their needs.

Note

The feature string corresponding to the event model in a call to `DOMImplementation.hasFeature()` method is "Events" and the version is "2.0." For particular types of events, it is also possible to call this method with the following strings:

- `"UIEvents"`
- `"MouseEvents"`
- `"MutationEvents"`
- `"HTMLEvents"`

VIEWS

The same XML document can be presented to a user in multiple ways. The presentation of a document can change in response to any changes to the document. To make it easier to associate views with an XML document, there is a "Views" module in the Level 2 specification.

The implementation of actual views is beyond the scope of the specification, so it is really just a foundation for implementing custom views, which gives a standard way of associating them with documents.

Note

The feature string corresponding to the event model in a call to `DOMImplementation.hasFeature()` method is "Views," and the version is "2.0."

`Styles`

The `styles` section of the Level 2 specification defines a standard way of associating documents with style sheets of any kind. The Styles module contains just a few base interfaces that can be extended by a developer.

Note

The feature string corresponding to the event model in a call to `DOMImplementation.hasFeature()`method is "Styles" and the version is "2.0." For particular features, it is also possible to call this method with the following strings:

- `"StyleSheets"`
- `"CSS"`
- `"CSS2"`

TRAVERSAL

The traversal module defines a few handy interfaces for traversal of XML documents, such as `NodeIterator`, `TreeWalker`, and `NodeFilter`.

Note

The feature string corresponding to the event model in a call to `DOMImplementation.hasFeature()`method is "Traversal," and the version is "2.0."

RANGE

Finally, the Range section of the DOM Level 2 specification defines could be handy for implementing applications that operate with ranges of data in an XML document.

Interfaces implemented in the Range module are useful, for example, for selecting, copy-pasting, deleting, and so on, of ranges of Elements in a document.

Note

The feature string corresponding to the event model in a call to `DOMImplementation.hasFeature()` method is "Range," and the version is "2.0."

DOM LEVEL 3

The third level of the DOM specification is just additional development of Level 2. It has all the features of its predecessors—some of them modified—plus further enhancement. At the time of this writing, the specification had an official status of the Working Draft. Further changes are still possible.

Level 3 adds the following features to the DOM API:

- Abstract Schemas and Load and Save—These modules provide object models for accessing the XML abstract schemas, such as DTDs and XML Namespaces and loading/saving DOM representations from/to XML files. The Abstract Schemas module comprises two sets of interfaces: a set for editing documents and a set for editing abstract schemas. To determine which of the sets is supported by an implementation, you can call the `hasFeature()` method with a parameter `"AS-DOC"` for the first set and `"AS-EDIT"` for the latter one. The `"LS"` feature name stands for the Load and Save module.
- Events (enhancement of Level 2)—The Events module (the feature name is "Events") builds on the same module of Level 2 providing additional features and some changes to the Level 2 interfaces. The specification focuses on providing a flexible event model for working with DOM documents—keeping in mind the need for a high degree of backward compatibility with old HTML event models provided with IE 3.0 and Netscape 3.0 browsers. The following features can be optionally included into implementations: `UIEvents`, `MouseEvents`, `TextEvents`, `MutationEvents`, and `HTMLEvents`.
- XPath—This module (`XPath` is the feature name) enables DOM applications to locate nodes using the `XPath` expressions. An important point is that the specification focuses on different compatibility issues between the XPath and DOM and defines interfaces that are free from compatability problems.

Note

Earlier versions of the DOM Level 3 included one more feature, Views, which was supposed to extend the Level 2 Views module. Later, it was removed from the specification.

IMPLEMENTATIONS OF THE DOM

There are several implementations of the DOM API available. Most of them are available free of charge; some are distributed under the terms of open-source license. Let's look at a few of them.

CRIMSON/XERCES

Crimson is a subproject of the Apache XML project derived from the Sun Project X parser. It is implemented in Java and is shipped as a part of Sun's products. Currently, it is one of the most common XML parsers in the Java world; however, Sun plans to make it part of another Apache project, Xerces Java 2, which we will discuss in the next section.

Crimson supports the following APIs:

- JAXP—Java API for XML Parsing—an XML processor-independent API, which will be discussed later in Chapter 16 "Working with XML and Java."
- SAX—The Simple API for XML. For details on this event-based API, refer to Chapter 15 "Parsing XML Based on Events."

- SAX 2.0—Version 2 of the SAX, which will be also discussed in Chapter 15.
- DOM Level 2 Core.

Xerces is another baby of the Apache XML project, which is a new-generation XML processor. In addition to the features and APIs supported by Crimson, it also includes

- Implementation of DOM Level 2 Core and Events
- Partial implementation of the DOM Level 3 Core, Abstract Schemas, and Load and Save

Currently, implementations of Xerces are available in Java, C++, and Perl.

Note

Crimson, Xerces, GNUJAXP, and other JAXP-compliant XML processors will be discussed in detail in Chapter 16.

MSXML

The Microsoft's XML parser MSXML incorporates not only fully supported DOM Level 1 API (partial support for level 2), but also an alternative approach to parsing XML documents—event-based parsing (SAX parser), which we will discuss in Chapter 15.

The product can be downloaded from the Microsoft Web site.

→ http://www.microsoft.com/xml

DOM PARSING: PROS AND CONS

The DOM API is quite simple and straightforward to use and this is the strongest advantage of it. The tree structure of the XML document corresponds directly to the DOM tree structure and the API gives a lot of freedom in accessing tree elements.

The price for that is the performance. Try loading a five-meg document with a DOM parser and you'll run out of patience—try a bigger document and you'll run out of memory.

Unfortunately, the DOM requires the whole document to be loaded into memory *before* the DOM tree is made available to a developer. That is why the DOM is ideal for applications operating with small XML documents and its benefits quickly fade after the size of documents reaches hundreds or thousands of megabytes.

In the next chapter, we will discuss alternative approaches to XML parsing, which are free of such problems—event-based parsing and the SAX parser. But, before that, we'll give you some useful links to DOM-related resources.

ADDITIONAL RESOURCES

Most of the specifications used when this chapter was written had an official status of W3C Recommendation; some of them were W3C Working Drafts. Everything is changing rapidly in the XML world and it is possible that some DOM specifications will change. This section will be your guide through some of the most useful resources where you can find up-to-date information regarding the DOM.

- XML 1.0 Recommendation (`http://www.w3.org/TR/REC-xml`). The XML 1.0 Recommendation (Second Edition) from the W3C is the final word on XML. If you have a question about a technical aspect of XML, this should be the first source you consult.
- W3C Home site (`http://www.w3c.org`). This is a home site of the World Wide Web Consortium. If you are up to the latest news, links, and specifications, try this first.
- DOM Level 1 Specification (`http://www.w3.org/TR/REC-DOM-Level-1`). The latest version of the DOM Level 1 specification can be found at this URL.
- The DOM Level 2 Core Specification is located here: `http://www.w3.org/TR/DOM-Level-2-Core`.
- The DOM Level 2 Events Specification is located here: `http://www.w3.org/TR/DOM-Level-2-Events`.
- The DOM Level 2 Views Specification is located here: `http://www.w3.org/TR/DOM-Level-2-Views`.
- The DOM Level 2 Style Specification is located here: `http://www.w3.org/TR/DOM-Level-2-Style`.
- The DOM Level 2 Traversal and Ranges Specification is located here: `http://www.w3.org/TR/DOM-Level-2-Traversal-Range`.
- The DOM Level 2 HTML Specification is located here: `http://www.w3.org/TR/DOM-Level-2-HTML`.
- The DOM Level 3 Core Specification is located here: `http://www.w3.org/TR/DOM-Level-3-Core`.
- The DOM Level 3 Abstract Schemas and Load and Save Specification is located here: `http://www.w3.org/TR/DOM-Level-3-ASLS`.
- The DOM Level 3 Events Specification is located here: `http://www.w3.org/TR/DOM-Level-3-Events`.
- The DOM Level 3 XPath Specification is located here: `http://www.w3.org/TR/DOM-Level-3-XPath`.
- Microsoft MSDN home site (`http://msdn.microsoft.com`). For the latest information regarding the MSXML, refer to this site.
- Apache XML Project home site (`http://xml.apache.org`). Here you can download the latest versions of Crimson and Xerces, as well as relevant documentation.

ROADMAP

If you don't feel confident after reading this chapter and there is something you can't grasp, it may be a good idea to refer to some of the other chapters of this book. Here is a roadmap, which will assist you.

Chapter 1, "The XML Jigsaw Puzzle," and Chapter 2, "The Basics of XML," will remind you about the structure of an XML document, its relation to schemas, and DTDs.

Chapter 3, "XML Building Blocks: Elements and Attributes," focuses more on elements and attributes, which are the most commonly used nodes in document trees.

Chapter 4, "Structuring XML Documents with DTDs," and Chapter 5, "Defining XML Document Structures with XML Schemas," will be useful to understand the `DocumentType` node and interface as well as entities and notations.

The next chapter, Chapter 15, "Parsing XML Based on Events," will help you understand another approach to XML parsing and teach you how to choose between DOM and SAX parsing.

You will find Chapter 16, "Working with XML and Java," useful if you are interested in more details on parsing XML documents in Java.

Chapter 17, "Working with XML and .NET," will be useful for developers using Microsoft's products fans—we will discuss MSXML and other XML-related technologies there.

CHAPTER 15

Parsing XML Based on Events

In this chapter

by Alexander Kachur

EVENT-BASED PARSING OF XML

The XML API discussed in the previous chapter was based on a tree representation of an XML document, which is a logical approach because XML document content forms a tree structure. However, for many types of applications, this way of handling documents is extremely inefficient—like reading a thousand Yellow Pages entries to find a phone number of a restaurant.

This chapter will discuss another way of dealing with XML documents. This API—the Simple API for XML—is not a Recommendation of the W3C, but it is a de facto standard for XML parsing and is absolutely free for both commercial and noncommercial use.

SAX: A SIMPLE API FOR XML

The SAX is a result of a successful attempt to bring together ideas implemented in different products available in 1997 to provide a common interface for Java programmers.

Unlike the DOM, the SAX started as a purely Java-based project and evolutionized in open discussions among the members of the XML-DEV mailing list under the leadership of David Megginson.

At the time of this writing, the current version of the API is SAX 2.0, originally released in May 2000. The SAX 2.0 r2 (release 2) is in prerelease stage. Although the SAX API was initially implemented in Java, it later evolved into a standard supported by other languages including C++, Visual Basic, COM, Perl, and Pascal.

DOM VERSUS SAX

There is a huge difference between the approaches used by the developers of DOM and SAX. It is so large that it's impossible to say that one is better than another—they are just to be used in different types of applications.

The DOM parser reads the entire document into memory and then builds a DOM tree of the parsed XML structure, making the tree available to a developer only after the entire tree is built.

The SAX parser reads an XML document and generates notifications on different types of events depending on the content being read. The developer then filters and handles these events using easy-to-implement event handlers.

TREES VERSUS EVENTS

The main problem with the tree-based parsing such as the DOM is that a parser has to load an entire document into memory before preparing its tree image, even if all you need to do is to read just one element out of thousands. In fact, the DOM API is unusable on large documents.

Note

On a Pentium 4–based PC with Sun JDK 1.4, it takes several minutes to load a 5MB XML file and get a DOM tree.

Larger documents require increasing the memory allocation beyond the default for the JVM instance–otherwise, you will get an out-of-memory exception.

If you are interested in concrete benchmark results, you can get some figures at `http://www.sosnoski.com/opensrc/xmlbench/index.html`.

On the other hand, after the DOM tree is ready, it provides developers with full random access to any node of the document it represents.

It is also easy to edit documents using the DOM API—as SAX events are one way and there is no way to apply changes to existing documents through an event-based API of this sort.

CHOOSING BETWEEN DOM AND SAX

Whenever you have to choose between DOM and SAX, try answering a few questions, as follows:

- Do you need to handle large documents? If yes, choose SAX; if no, then consider another question:
- Is the performance an issue in your application? If yes, SAX will be better; if no, ask yourself the next question:
- Do you need to search for or retrieve content of any specific node of the document? If yes, choose SAX; if no, go on to the next question:
- Does your application heavily rely on random access to nodes across the document? If yes, your solution is DOM; if no, the last question is
- Do you need to update documents? If yes, your choice will be the DOM API.

If this is not enough to make up your mind, it is probably wise to think more about the requirements of your application.

SAX OVERVIEW

Unlike the DOM, SAX is not an object model. A SAX parser represents a document using events initiated sequentially while parsing the document tags. For example, the portion of the XML document demonstrated in Listing 15.1 will translate into the following sequence of events:

- `startElement`
- characters
- `endElement`

LISTING 15.1 SAMPLE XML DOCUMENT

```
...
<my-element>
    this is sample text
</my-element>
...
```

SAX PARSERS

SAX is designed in such a way that it is very easy to use the API with different implementations of parsers. The only requirement is that parsers should implement a set of standard interfaces—otherwise, there is considerable freedom in implementing SAX-compliant parsers.

Currently, there are several implementations of SAX parsers available in Java and other languages. Some of the most well known include

- Crimson
- Xerces
- Oracle XML Parser for Java 2
- Microsoft MSXML

Let's have a quick look at each of them.

CRIMSON Crimson is a part of Apache XML Project. It supports XML 1.0 through multiple APIs, such as

- SAX 2.0
- SAX 2 Extensions 1.0
- DOM Level 2 Core
- JAXP 1.1

Crimson ships with Sun products. It is available in binaries and source code. At the date of this writing, there are plans to move the Crimson codebase into the Xerces Java 2 project. Crimson can be found at `http://xml.apache.org/crimson`.

Note

In Chapter 16, we will discuss the Java API for XML Processing, JAXP, in detail. Crimson is one of the JAXP-compliant parsers.

XERCES Xerces is also a child of the Apache XML Project. When this book reaches its readers, Xerces Java Parser 2 will probably be available, which will include the codebase from Crimson and many new features. Version 1.4.4, the latest at the date of writing this book, includes the following:

- SAX 1.0
- SAX 2.0
- SAX 2 Extensions 1.0
- DOM Level 1
- DOM Level 2 (Core + Events + Traversal and Ranges)
- JAXP 1.1
- XML Schema Recommendation Version 1.0

> **Note**
> Xerces is also one of the JAXP-compliant parsers, which we will discuss in Chapter 16, "Working with XML and Java."

Xerces can be found at `http://xml.apache.org/xerces-j/`. Xerces2 may be found at `http://xml.apache.org/xerces2-j/`.

Xerces is available for several programming languages.

ORACLE XML PARSER FOR JAVA 2 XML Parser for Java 2 is a part of Oracle XDK—a family of XML libraries that can be used by developers to stick together XML and Oracle 8i databases. The support is provided for

- SAX 2.0
- DOM Level 2 (Core + Mutation Event + Traversal)
- XML Namespaces Recommendation
- JAXP 1.1 (was available only in XDK Beta Release at the date of writing)
- SAX 2 Extensions 1.0 (was available only in XDK Beta Release at the date of writing)

Oracle's XML Developer kit can be obtained by visiting `http://www.oracle.com/xml/` and registering to become a member of the Oracle Technology Network. Registration is free.

Oracle also provides several implementations for different programming languages.

MICROSOFT MSXML Microsoft MSXML is a COM-based implementation of various APIs for accessing XML 1.0. The APIs are provided through an object model and are best used from non-Java platforms, such as C++, VisualBasic, and so on. The features supported are

- SAX
- DOM
- SAX-DOM integration
- XML Schema Recommendation Version 1.0

For additional information about MSXML, visit its Web site at `http://www.microsoft.com/xml`.

Now that we know when to choose SAX and which parsers can be used with it, it's time to talk about implementing SAX-driven applications.

JAVA INTERFACES AND CLASSES

Basically, any SAX-based XML processing application consists of two parts—a SAX parser and a set of handlers that should be implemented by a developer. Some helper classes also make life easier.

The core of SAX2 API contains two packages:

- `org.xml.sax`
- `org.xml.sax.helpers`

Some additional nonstandard features can be implemented in a standard way in the third package, `org.xml.sax.ext`, which is not a part of the SAX core.

CORE INTERFACES

We won't repeat the SAX 2 documentation, which is available for download on the official Web site of the project (see references at the end of the chapter).

Instead, we will discuss the steps that have to be taken and the classes that have to be implemented by developers of SAX-driven applications and by developers of SAX-compliant parsers.

INSTANTIATING A PARSER

First, an instance of a SAX parser must be instantiated before an application can use the SAX API to access XML documents. It is up to the developer to decide which parser to use with the application. All SAX-compliant parsers realize standard interfaces so that it's very easy to stick in any of the parsers available.

For the purpose of this discussion, we will not focus on any particular implementation of a SAX parser. The examples given will work with any SAX implementation that supports the SAX API in Java. For more details about using specific parsers, you can refer to Chapter 16.

The developer has two choices in instantiating an instance of a parser:

- Using an implementation of the interface XMLReader supplied by a parser.
- Instantiating a parser with a factory provided by the SAX API.

A few lines of code that follow demonstrate the first approach. Again, the example is implemented in Java and works with any parser that provides support for SAX API in Java.

```
import org.xml.sax.XMLReader;
import javax.xml.parsers.SAXParser;

...

XMLReader myReader = new javax.xml.parsers.SAXParser();
```

The second approach is demonstrated here

```
import org.xml.sax.XMLReader;
import org.xml.sax.XMLReaderFactory;
import org.xml.sax.SAXException

...

try
{
    XMLReader myReader =
➥XMLReaderFactory.createXMLReader("javax.xml.parsers.SAXParser");
}
catch(SAXException se)
{
    // Report a problem
}
```

The second example instantiates a parser passing its class name to a factory method as a string, which can be loaded from a config file, or taken as a startup parameter. This approach is usually more flexible as it allows changing compliant parsers on-the-fly without recompiling any source code.

USING THE `XMLReader` INTERFACE

The `XMLReader` interface used in this example has a lot of interesting methods, which provides developers with the control over event handlers associated with the document being parsed, features of the parser in effect, and so on. Table 15.1 lists the methods of the interface.

TABLE 15.1 METHODS OF THE `XMLReader` INTERFACE

Name	Parameters	Description, Returns, Throws
`getContentHandler`	None.	Retrieves a content handler registered with a call to the `setContentHandler` method. Returns: `ContentHandler`—an implementation of a `ContentHandler` interface or `null`—if `ContentHandler` has not been registered. Throws: No exceptions.

TABLE 15.1 CONTINUED

Name	Parameters	Description, Returns, Throws
setContentHandler	*handler*, ContentHandler—an implementation of a content handler to register with the parser.	Registers a content handler with the parser. The parser starts sending events to this handler immediately. Returns: No return value. Throws: java.lang.NullPointerException
getDTDHandler	None.	Retrieves a DTD handler registered with a call to the setDTDHandler method. Returns: DTDHandler—an implementation of a DTDHandler interface or null—if DTDHandler has not been registered. Throws: No exceptions.
setDTDHandler	*handler*, DTDHandler—an implementation of a DTD handler to register with the parser.	Registers a DTD handler with the parser. The parser starts sending events to this handler immediately. Returns: No return value. Throws: java.lang.NullPointerException
getErrorHandler	None.	Retrieves an error handler registered with a call to the setErrorHandler method. Returns: ErrorHandler—an implementation of an ErrorHandler interface or null—if ErrorHandler has not been registered. Throws: No exceptions.
setErrorHandler	*handler*, ErrorHandler—an implementation of an error handler to register with the parser.	Registers an Error handler with the parser. The parser starts sending events to this handler immediately. Returns: No return value. Throws: java.lang.NullPointerException
getEntityResolver	None.	Retrieves an EntityResolver registered with a call to the setEntityResolver method. Returns: EntityResolver—an implementation of the EntityResolver interface or null—if EntityResolver has not been registered. Throws: No exceptions.

15

TABLE 15.1 CONTINUED

Name	Parameters	Description, Returns, Throws
setEntityResolver	*handler*, EntityResolver—an implementation of an entity resolver to register with the parser.	Registers an entity resolver with the parser. The parser starts sending events to the resolver immediately. Returns: No return value. Throws: java.lang.NullPointerException
parse	*source*, InputSource—the source to read the document from.	A call to this method starts parsing a document. Any events encountered will be sent to registered handlers or ignored if there is no appropriate handler registered. The method will not return unless the parsing is complete or an exception has occurred. Returns: No return value. Throws: java.io.Exception or org.xml.sax.SAXException
parse	*systemId*, String—the URI of the source to read the document from.	The same as the previous one with the only exception that the parser itself creates an InputSource object from the document located at the given URI.
getFeature	*name*, String—the name of the feature represented as a fully qualified URI.	Checks whether a feature is supported by the implementation of SAX parser. Some feature values may be available only in specific contexts, such as before, during, or after a parse. Returns a boolean: *true* if the requested feature is supported or *false* if it is not. Throws: SAXNotRecognizedException or SAXNotSupportedException
setFeature	*name*, String—the name of the feature represented as a fully qualified URI. *value*, Boolean—the status of the feature.	Sets the status of the requested feature of the parser being used with the SAX. Some feature values may be immutable or mutable only in specific contexts, such as before, during, or after a parse. Returns: No return value. Throws: SAXNotRecognizedException or SAXNotSupportedException
getProperty	*name*, String—the name of the property represented as a fully qualified URI.	Checks the value of the requested property. Some property values may be available only in specific contexts, such as before, during, or after a parse.

TABLE 15.1 CONTINUED

Name	Parameters	Description, Returns, Throws
		Returns: The property value as a `java.lang.Object`. Throws: `SAXNotRecognizedException` or `SAXNotSupportedException`
`setProperty`	`name`, `String`—the name of the property represented as a fully qualified URI. `value`, `java.lang.Object`—the value of the property.	Sets the value of the requested property for the parser being used with the SAX. Some property values may be immutable or mutable only in specific contexts, such as before, during, or after a parse. Returns: No return value. Throws: `SAXNotRecognizedException` or `SAXNotSupportedException`

The `XMLReader` interface is a replacement for the `Parser` interface from version 1.0 and is a required interface for any SAX 2 driver (parser).

As you can see from Table 15.1, the `XMLReader` interface provides us with methods that can be used to register event handlers. This is what interests us in the next step.

REGISTERING EVENT HANDLERS

After we have an instance of an `XMLReader`, we can register event handlers for the events we are interested in.

To do so, we have a choice of methods on the `XMLReader` interface, but before setting a handler we have to implement it.

IMPLEMENTING THE `ContentHandler` INTERFACE

To start with, we need to implement a `ContentHandler` interface—the methods of which will be invoked by the parser, or *called back*, every time it encounters something interesting in the document being parsed.

Note

Callback methods are often utilized to handle events programmatically. For example, callbacks are used in the Windows operating system to report mouse events (and many other kinds of events), such as a mouse movement, to applications. The use of callbacks usually involves two steps–registration and handling.

Registration is needed to advise the source of events about the parties that are interested in receiving event notifications. Methods or functions are bound to an event type through registration.

Handling is what callback methods are written for. When an event occurs, the source of events (a parser in our case) invokes (or calls back) the methods registered to handle this particular type of event.

For every event, there can be multiple handlers registered. They are usually invoked in the order of registration.

Table 15.2 lists the methods of the `ContentHandler` interface, which have to be implemented by an application developer.

TABLE 15.2 METHODS OF THE `ContentHandler` INTERFACE

Name	Parameters	Description, Returns, Throws
`characters`	*`ch`*, `char[]`—an array of characters from the XML document. *`start`*, `int`—the starting position of the chunk of data in the array. *`length`*, `int`—the length of the chunk.	This callback method is called by the parser to report character data encountered in the parsed XML document. No assumptions should be made regarding the way this method is used by parser. A parser can return all the characters in a single chunk or it may be necessary to call the method more than once to retrieve all the characters. Also, the developers should keep in mind that reading beyond the range specified by the start and length parameters could bring unpredictable results. Returns: No return value. Throws: SAXException
`ignorableWhitespace`	*`ch`*, `char[]`—an array of characters from the XML document. *`start`*, `int`—the starting position of the chunk of data in the array. *`length`*, `int`—the length of the chunk.	This callback method is called by the parser to report ignorable whitespace in element content. Validating parsers should always use this method; non-validating ones can also use it. Returns: No return value. Throws: SAXException
`startDocument`	None.	Parser calls this method only once when it starts parsing a document and before invoking any other handler events. Returns: No return value. Throws: SAXException

TABLE 15.2 CONTINUED

Name	Parameters	Description, Returns, Throws
`endDocument`	None.	Parser calls this method only once when it reaches the end of a document. No other events can be initiated after invoking this method. Returns: No return value. Throws: SAXException
`startElement`	`namespaceURI`, `String`—the namespace used with the element name. `localName`, `String`—the name of the element. `qName`, `String`—the qualified name of the element. `atts`, Attributes—the collection of attributes found within the element tag.	This method is called by the parser when it encounters an opening tag of an element. Returns: No return value. Throws: `SAXException`
`endElement`	`namespaceURI`, `String`—the namespace used with the element name. `localName`, `String`—the name of the element. `qName`, `String`—the qualified name of the element.	This method is called by the parser when it encounters a closing tag of an element. Returns: No return value. Throws: SAXException
`setDocumentLocator`	`locator`, `Locator`—the locator object that can return an origin of events associated with the document being parsed.	The `Locator` object supplied in a call to this method can be used by an application to find a place in the document where an event came from.Parsers are not required to supply this object. Returns: No return value. Throws: SAXException
`startPrefixMapping`	`prefix`, `String`—the namespace prefix. `uri`, `String`—the namespace URI.	The event is initiated by parser when it enters a namespace prefix to URI mapping. Returns: No return value. Throws: SAXException
`endPrefixMapping`	`prefix`, `String`—the namespace prefix.	The event is initiated by parser when it leaves a namespace prefix to URI mapping. Returns: No return value. Throws: `SAXException`

15

TABLE 15.2 CONTINUED

Name	Parameters	Description, Returns, Throws
processing-Instruction	*target*, String—the target of the processing instruction. *data*, String—data supplied with the instruction.	The event is initiated by parser when it encounters a processing instruction in the document being parsed. Returns: No return value. Throws: SAXException
skippedEntity	*name*, String—the nameof the entity skipped.	Depending on the parser's feature set, the parser can decide to skip an entity. If this is the case, it has to initiate this event. Returns: No return value. Throws: SAXException

SAX provides a default implementation of this interface that can be used as a base class for any custom implementation. This default class is the *DefaultHandler* and it implements do-nothing versions of the callbacks defined in the interface *ContentHandler* (and three other handler interfaces). Application developers can inherit their implementations from it and override the methods they need.

IMPLEMENTING THE ErrorHandler INTERFACE

After the content handler has been implemented, we need to make sure our software is able to respond to any problems that may occur during the parsing.

Three kinds of errors can occur during the parsing:

- Fatal Error—This error occurs when something prevents the parser from further processing the document. A fatal error in SAX is defined by the W3C XML 1.0 Recommendation, Section 1.2.
- Error—This error is reported by the parser when it encounters a problem with the document but is able to recover and continue processing. An error in SAX is defined by the W3C XML 1.0 Recommendation, Section 1.2.
- Warning—This event is reported to an application when a SAX parser wants to report something that is neither an error nor a fatal error according to Section 1.2 of the W3C XML 1.0 Recommendation.

Using these categories of errors, the ErrorHandler interface defines three callback methods that any parser expects to be implemented by application developers. These methods are described in Table 15.3:

TABLE 15.3 METHODS OF THE `ErrorHandler` INTERFACE

Name	Parameters	Description, Returns, Throws
fatalError	*exception*, SAXParseException	Called when the application is requested to process a fatal error that occurred during the parsing process. Returns: No return value. Throws: SAXException
error	*exception*, SAXParseException	Called when the application is requested to process an error that occurred during the parsing process. Returns: No return value. Throws: SAXException
warning	*exception*, SAXParseException	Called when the application is requested to process a warning that occurred during the parsing process. Returns: No return value. Throws: SAXException

And, again, the developers of SAX have taken care of implementing the default error handler for us. The class *DefaultHandler* discussed earlier also implements methods of the `ErrorHandler` interface as empty methods.

IMPLEMENTING THE INTERFACE `DTDHandler`

The next interface to implement is `DTDHandler`. It fires events upon encountering notation and unparsed entity declarations that can be used by application developers.

Note

Note that this interface does not have anything to do with validation of DTDs. To perform the validation, an application should call the setFeature method on the implementation of the XMLReader interface with a parameter `http://xml.org/sax/features/validation` and set this parameter to true.

Because the future of DTDs is rather unclear and it looks as though XML Schemas will preempt the concept of DTDs, it is unlikely that many of the readers will have to implement this handler. However, if needed, Table 15.4 shows the methods to implement.

TABLE 15.4 METHODS OF THE DTDHandler INTERFACE

Name	Parameters	Description, Returns, Throws
notationDecl	*name*, String—notation name. *publicId*, String—public identifier of the notation. *systemId*, String—system identifier of the notation.	Process the declaration of a notation. Returns: No return value. Throws: SAXException
unparsedEntityDecl	*name*, String—entity name. *publicId*, String—public identifier of the entity. *systemId*, String—system identifier of the entity.	Process the declaration of an unparsed entity. Returns: No return value. Throws: SAXException

The DefaultHandler class implements empty methods for this handler.

IMPLEMENTING THE EntityResolver INTERFACE

The EntityResolver interface is normally not needed to be implemented by application developers. The only use of this interface is to handle external entities before the parser tries to open them.

It may be useful to implement the interface in such cases when an application uses nonstandard system identifiers or nonstandard ways of resolving the system identifiers.

The only method of the interface is described in Table 15.5. The DefaultHandler class contains a default implementation of the interface.

TABLE 15.5 METHODS OF THE EntityResolver INTERFACE

Name	Parameters	Description, Returns, Throws
ResolveEntity	*publicId*, String—public identifier of the entity. *systemId*, String—system identifier of the entity.	Called when an external entity is encountered and before the parser opens the entity. Returns: InputSource—an object which can be used by the parser to read an entity resolved by the application or null when the application requests the parser to try resolving it itself. Throws: SAXException or java.io.IOException

Having instantiated a parser to read through XML documents and implemented the handlers to process events, your application is now ready to work with XML documents. However, there are other useful features of SAX, such as the ability to change or eliminate events that can make your life much easier when it comes to processing XML input.

FILTERING EVENTS

One of the advantages of event-based processing is that it allows developers to build data processing solutions from chains or sequences of filters and handlers, which process and possibly modify data while events "flow" through them.

For that purpose, there are a special interface *`XMLFilter`* and its default implementation class *`XMLFilterImple`* available in SAX 2.0. The `XMLFilter` is a simple extension to the `XMLReader`, which adds methods to enable filtering of events initiated during the processing of documents.

`XMLFilter` INTERFACE There are only two methods in the `XMLFilter interface` as described in Table 15.6.

TABLE 15.6 METHODS OF THE `XMLFilter` INTERFACE

Name	Parameters	Description, Returns, Throws
`setParent`	*`parent`*, `XMLReader`—the reader object to use with the filter.	Sets the source of events for the filter, i.e. links the filter with the `XMLReader` which will supply the filter with events. It is possible to build a chain of filters using this method—just pass another `XMLFilter` object to a call to the method. Returns: No return value. Throws: No exceptions.
`getParent`	None.	Retrieves the parent reader or filter, which is the source of events for this filter. Returns: `XMLReader`—an object implementing the `XMLReader` or `XMLFilter` interface. Throws: No exceptions.

`XMLFilterImpl` CLASS The `XMLFilterImpl` class provides application developers with a convenient default implementation of the `XMLFilter` interface together with all four handler interfaces previously discussed.

All you need to do to implement your filter handlers is to derive your handler class from this default implementation and provide your implementations of the handlers you want to use.

Following is a simple Java example of a Y2K-aware filter, which replaces all the letters Y with K (that's why it's Y2K-aware) in element names:

LISTING 15.2 A SIMPLE Y2K FILTER—REPLACES "Y" WITH "K" AND "Y" WITH "K"

```
public class y2kFilter extends XMLFilterImpl
{
    public y2kFilter(XMLReader rdr)
    {
        super(rdr);
    }


    public void startElement(
                String uri,
                String localName,
                String qName,
                Attributes atts) throws SAXException
    {
        localName = localName.replace("Y", "K");
        localName = localName.replace("y", "k");
        super.startElement(uri, localName, qName, atts);
    }

    public void endElement(
                String uri,
                String localName,
                String qName) throws SAXException
    {
        localName = localName.replace("Y", "K");
        localName = localName.replace("y", "k");
        super.endElement(uri, localName, qName);
    }

}
```

As a result of this processing, see the following portion of an XML file:

```
<january>
    <new-year-day date = "1">
        <celebrate drink = "champagne" />
    </new-year-day>
</january>
<february>

</february>
```

The handler following our y2kFilter will receive `startElement` and `endElement` events with the following element names.

TABLE 15.7 ELEMENT NAMES AS A RESULT OF Y2K FILTER `startElement` AND `endElement` EVENTS

Event Callback	Element Name
`startElement`	januark
`startElement`	new-kear-dak

TABLE 15.7 CONTINUED

Event Callback	Element Name
`startElement`	Celebrate
`endElement`	Celebrate
`endElement`	new-kear-dak
`endElement`	Januark
`startElement`	Februark
`endElement`	Februark

IMPLEMENTING SAX PARSERS

Now that you have been introduced to several of the interfaces in SAX, you may want the details on the implementation of SAX parsers. Although we cannot delve into the details of implementing SAX parsers in this book, we can give you a list of the interfaces that you must implement to write your own.

SAX provides implementations of most of the interfaces needed for both application and parser writers. The minimum set of parser interfaces that have to be implemented is as follows:

- *`XMLReader`* (*`Parser`* for SAX 1–compliant parsers)—This interface in used to set features of the parser and start the parsing process. The implementation of this class will be the source of events for applications.
- *`Locator`*—Is used by an application whenever it needs to associate an event received from the parser with the location of a node in the document being parsed.
- *`Attributes`* (`AttributeList` for SAX 1–compliant parsers)—Applications use this interface for obtaining lists of elements' attributes.

SAX EXTENSIONS

In addition to the set of core interfaces discussed before, the SAX 2 specification defines some features that are optional for parsers but are standardized to make all the SAX-compliant parsers compatible and transparent to applications.

The standard SAX Extension 1.0 provides the following additional interfaces:

- *`DeclHandler`*—Provides application developers with the ability to do more complex handling of DTD declarations than through the standard handlers.
- *`LexicalHandler`*—An additional handler interface to deal with lexical events. Operates with CDATA sections, comments, entities, and DTD declarations.
- *`Attributes2`*—A bit more advanced version of the `Attributes` interface.

- *EntityResolver2*—A more complicated extension to the `EntityResolver` interface.
- *Locator2*—In addition to the services provided in the `Locator` interface, this one defines methods to retrieve the information regarding the encoding of the XML document and the version of XML.

ADDITIONAL RESOURCES

To make it easier for readers searching for further information, following is a collection of useful links to SAX-related sites.

- The SAX project (`http://sax.sourceforge.net`) is being developed within the SourceForge Open Source Development Network.
- David Megginson's original SAX project (`http://www.megginson.com/SAX`). This site is no longer updated; the only official source of the latest information is the SourceForge site. However, there is interesting historical material related to SAX, and David has other useful work there.
- Java XML Representations Benchmark (`http://www.sosnoski.com/opensrc/xmlbench/index.html`). Dennis Sosnoski has developed benchmarks to test software that manipulates XML documents. He has also benchmarked several popular suites.
- Apache Crimson (`http://xml.apache.org/crimson`). Information about the Crimson project.
- Apache Xerces for Java (`http://xml.apache.org/xerces-`). The Apache XML Project site also hosts information on the Xerces project.
- JAXP (`http://java.sun.com/xml/jaxp`). More information on the JAXP API can be found here. You may also want to look at Sun's other XML initiatives. Sun has been a leading contributor for quite a while.
- MSXML (`http://msdn.microsoft.com`). Microsoft MSDN is the best place to find resources related to MSXML and other Microsoft XML–based technologies.
- Oracle XML Developer Kits (`http://otn.oracle.com/tech/xml/content.html`). Oracle's useful site has information about its XDK and XML in general.

ROADMAP

If some of the concepts we've explained seem unclear, it may be useful to review some of the earlier chapters.

A discussion of some basics, such as an XML document structure, schemas, and DTDs can be found in Chapter 1, "The XML Jigsaw Puzzle," and Chapter 2, "The Basics of XML."

Chapter 3, "XML Building Blocks: Elements and Attributes," focuses more on elements and attributes, which are the most commonly used nodes in document trees.

Chapter 4, "Structuring XML Documents with DTDs," and Chapter 5, "Defining XML Document Structures with XML Schemas," will be useful to understand entities and notations.

Event-based parsing is only one possible way of dealing with XML documents. Chapter 14, "XML and the Document Object Model," will help you understand the DOM, a Recommendation of the W3C—and another approach to XML parsing.

In Chapter 16, "Working with XML and Java," you will learn how to use Java to work with XML in much more detail.

Chapter 17, "Working with XML and .NET," will be useful for developers using Microsoft's XML products—we will discuss MSXML and other related XML technologies there.

CHAPTER 16

WORKING WITH XML AND JAVA

In this chapter

by Kenrick Rawlings

INTRODUCTION

In this chapter, we will cover various techniques of working with XML via Sun's Java programming language. Java has been a driving force in the acceptance and utilization of XML. Therefore, it has quite a variety of interfaces and tools for working with XML.

The previous two chapters covered the standard Application Programming Interfaces (APIs) DOM and SAX for working with XML. This chapter starts putting those APIs into practice with the popular programming language Java from Sun Microsystems. After an introduction and some preparation, the specific methods for accessing XML via Java with SAX and DOM are covered. Next, navigating and transforming XML in Java via XPath and XSLT are introduced. Finally, the last two sections provide an introduction to other Java XML standards and tools you might find useful.

PREPARATION

Before we get started with the nuts and bolts of XML and Java, you should be familiar with the technical prerequisites and software that need to be installed on your computer.

REQUIREMENTS

We assume that you have a working knowledge of programming with Sun's Java Programming Language and are familiar with the installation of Java software development kits and Java libraries. If you aren't, check out an introductory Java Book, such as *Special Edition Using Java 2 Standard Edition*, also available from Que Publishing.

SOFTWARE

Make sure that the following software is installed on your machine:

The Java 2 Platform Software Development Kit (SDK), Standard Edition v1.3.1 or higher, available from Sun Microsystems at `http://java.sun.com/j2se/`.

The Java XML Pack, available from Sun Microsystems at `http://java.sun.com/xml/downloads/javaxmlpack.html`.

Note

Installing the Java 2 SDK is straightforward, but getting the Java XML Pack working correctly can be tricky. Make sure that you carefully read the documentation provided by Sun. As of the time of this writing, two class libraries are essential to running the examples provided in this chapter: "xalan.jar" and "xerces.jar". Both are contained in the Java API For XML Processing (JAXP) subdirectory of the Java XML Pack. Make sure that you add these to the classpath of the IDE or compilation tool that you are using.

We will be using the following sample XML Document throughout this chapter:

```
<?xml version="1.0"?>
<java_xml>
```

```
  <standards>
    <standard href="http://java.sun.com/xml/jaxp">
      Java API for XML Processing(JAXP)
    </standard>
    <standard href="http://www.w3.org/DOM/">
      Document Object Model(DOM)
    </standard>
    <standard href="http://www.saxproject.org/">
      Simple API for XML(SAX)
    </standard>
  </standards>
  <parsers>
    <parser href="http://xml.apache.org/xerces-j/">Xerces</parser>
    <parser href="http://xml.apache.org/crimson/index.html">Crimson</parser>
    <parser href="http://www.gnu.org/software/classpathx/jaxp/">GNUJAXP</parser>
  </parsers>
</java_xml>
```

16

JAVA XML CONCEPTS

When working with XML, there are varied technologies programmers need to work with, depending on the focus of the desired business results. These technologies fall broadly into categories that we will cover over the course of this chapter.

First, programmers need basic methods that allow the data contained within XML Documents to be parsed and accessed programmatically. There are two common approaches to this issue. Event based parsing is the lowest level method, which does not retain any document structure. The standard method in Java for event based parsing is the *Simple API for XML (SAX)*. Document based parsing is the other method. Document based parsing is a higher-level method that keeps information about the parsed document stored in memory. The standard method in Java for document based parsing is the *Document Object Model (DOM)*.

Second, methods are required to allow parsed XML to be navigated and transformed. Navigation is accomplished with technologies such as XPath, XQuery, and more recently with technologies that actually bind the structure of XML directly to Java code like JDOM and JAXB. Transformation is accomplished with implementations of XSLT and XSL:FO, which allow the transformation of XML into various other formats such as HTML, PDF, or SVG.

Finally, new more advanced technologies have recently become available that build on this foundation and enable higher level and more complex XML activities to be accomplished. For instance, XML is now being commonly used as a standard protocol for communications between businesses, using specifications such as SOAP and XML-RPC.

The Java XML landscape has changed quite a bit over the last few years. As is often the case, the early technologies available consisted of many different *APIs (Application Programming Interfaces)* that competed for mind-share. Although some of the various XML APIs have become standardized by organizations such as the W3C, the methods for accessing these interfaces from Java were often different from implementation to implementation until recently. This made working with XML difficult and sometimes confusing.

JAVA API FOR XML

As mentioned previously, there are many competing software implementations of the common XML standards (DOM, SAX, XPath, XSLT, and so on). Naturally, they are programmatically accessed by various methods. For example, the method for creating an instance of an XML parser with the original Microsoft XML Parser for Java was completely different from the method used for the IBM XML for Java parser. This has often caused confusion and difficulty when moving a developed XML application from one implementation to another.

Fortunately, however, Sun has decided to standardize and integrate the APIs for working with XML with the official "Java API for XML." These interfaces are rapidly gaining industry acceptance, and will form the foundation that we will be working with in this chapter.

The Java API for XML consists of five technologies (see Figure 16.1):

- Java API for XML Processing (JAXP), which encompasses basic XML Processing tasks such as parsing XML, accessing it via event based and document based interfaces and transforming it.
- Java API for XML Messaging (JAXM), which allows applications to communicate with each other through structured XML documents
- Java API for XML Registries (JAXR), which provides a method for Java applications to connect to XML Web Service Registries.
- Java API for XML-based RPC (JAX-RPC), which allows Java applications to communicate with other applications over the Internet via the standard Simple Object Access Protocol (SOAP).
- Java Architecture for XML Binding (JAXB), which allows programmers to generate XML documents and work with existing XML documents directly through Java classes.

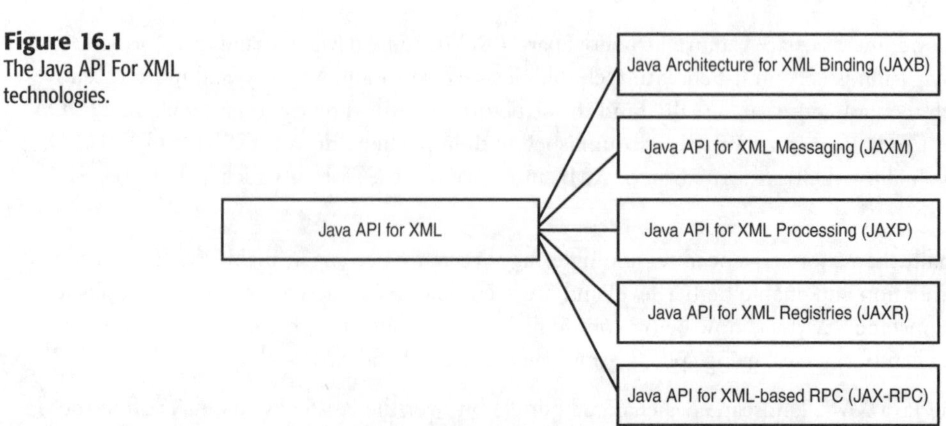

Figure 16.1
The Java API For XML technologies.

JAVA API FOR XML PROCESSING

The goal of the Java API for XML Processing (`http://java.sun.com/xml/jaxp/index.html`) is to allow programmers to develop applications that parse and work with XML without having to use tool and parser specific code. Implementations that conform to the Java API for XML Processing will allow programmers to switch to a different implementation without changing how that implementation is accessed in their code. JAXP supports the following interfaces:

- DOM
- SAX
- XSLT

Why is JAXP necessary if DOM, SAX, and XSLT are standard XML interfaces? A different standardized Java interface is needed because although these interfaces specify how to interact with already parsed XML data, they do not standardize how to actually start up the various parsers and tools. They also do not provide standard interfaces for specifying exactly what XML data you want to work with. JAXP provides these higher-level interfaces. In this way, it can be seen as a "wrapper" around the other XML standards.

It is important here to distinguish between interfaces and implementations. The JAXP programming interfaces merely specify the interfaces and methods that programmers use to work with XML. They do not specifically mandate (or provide) an implementation. The Java XML Pack does provide a default implementation, but you are free to choose from any JAXP compliant implementation. Several of the dominant Java XML parsers will be covered later in this chapter.

The JAXP API is a relatively recent development in the Java XML community, and a great deal of legacy code uses parser-specific interfaces, especially for creating, starting, and stopping the parsing process. Because only a few dominant parsers exist on the Java platform, it might be tempting to continue to use these proprietary interfaces. However, by limiting code to the use of the standard interfaces, a new parser can be seamlessly plugged into your application. This can be useful because different parsers might make various trade-offs: One might be faster but consume much more memory, another parser might be especially good at handling international characters, and so on.

JAXP is by far the most important of the Java API for XML interfaces, and the technologies it standardizes are the focus of this chapter. However, there are several other JAVA XML API's for XML that you might want to investigate. These will be discussed in the following sections.

JAVA API FOR XML REGISTRIES

The JAVA API for XML Registries (JAXR) is the standard Java API for accessing XML Registries. An XML registry is defined as "an enabling infrastructure for building, deploying, and discovering Web services." These Web services are language and operating system independent, and can be accessed via a variety of different methods. The JAXR specification is available at `http://java.sun.com/xml/jaxr/index.html`.

In order to understand what JAXR is and why it is needed, it is helpful to first understand what a Web service is. In the most straightforward sense, a Web service is a server that communicates over the Internet via standard Web protocols, such as the *Hypertext Transfer Protocol (HTTP)* and the *Simple Object Access Protocol (SOAP)*, and provides some sort of service. However, a Web service is not a Web server in a traditional sense. Unlike a Web server, you do not usually connect with Web services via a Web browser. Instead, a custom client program communicates with the Web service, and then provides the results of the communication with that service. This client might then pass that information on to a Web browser, or it might use a completely different interface, such as a Java Swing Graphical User Interface.

These Web services are seen as becoming increasingly important to the expansion of the Internet into new areas, particularly with *business-to-business (B2B)* communications. As part of the standardization of this infrastructure, it is necessary to be able to store information about Web services into registries, and the higher-level document format that has been chosen for these registries is XML. These XML registries are a recent development, but are already garnering quite a bit of attention.

As of this writing, there are two important XML Registries:

- ebXML—Whose purpose is to "enable enterprises of any size, in any location to meet and conduct business through the exchange of XML-based messages." The ebXML specification is available at `http://www.ebxml.org/`.
- UDDI—Whose purpose is to become "the building block that will enable businesses to quickly, easily, and dynamically find and transact business with one another using their preferred applications." The UDDI specification is available at `http://www.uddi.org`.

The Java API for XML Registries provides an abstract method for accessing various XML registries, such as ebXML and UDDI. Although the various registries might have different methods for describing their content and metadata, the Java API for XML Registries provides a standardized information model to allow this data to be accessed in a consistent manner.

JAVA API FOR XML-BASED RPC

Although the Java API for XML Processing provides extensive tools for the handling of XML documents on a single machine, the rise of the Internet has made applications that are able to communicate with one another over the network extremely important. In previous years, this communication was usually through Internet sockets (TCP, UDP, and so on), or in more advanced cases via standards like Java RMI (Remote Method Invocation) that actually allowed client software to access other software running on a machine somewhere else on the network. These procedures were useful, but involved a great deal of coding effort in the case of sockets, or were difficult to use between different programming languages as in the case of any Java RMI.

By using a higher-level abstraction called the *Remote Procedure Call (RPC)*, a local client can talk to a remote server and information can be communicated back and forth in a language and operating system independent manner. The server defines a group of procedures that can be accessed by remote clients, and then the clients communicate with the server via the RPC. Various types of RPC protocols have been used within different operating systems, but interoperability has been difficult to achieve.

With the advent of XML, a standard has been developed to allow RPC services to be made available in a high-level manner, using a communications protocol based on XML. This high-level abstraction allows any language and platform to create clients and servers that can communicate with one another. This specification is called the *Simple Object Access Protocol (SOAP)*, which is in the process of being standardized by the W3C and is available at `http://www.w3.org/TR/SOAP/`.

In order to facilitate the growth of XML Remote Procedure Calling services, Sun has created an API for Java programmers to access XML-based remote procedures in a high-level manner. This API is called the *Java API for XML-based RPC (JAXR)* and is available at `http://java.sun.com/xml/jaxrpc/`.

In addition, the Java API for XML-based RPC provides interfaces for describing the services that are being made available via the *Web Service Description Language (WSDL)*.

Java API for XML Messaging

The Java API for XML Messaging allows Java applications to send and receive messages to and from one another in a structured document form. Java API for XML Messaging uses SOAP to transmit these messages back and forth. This relieves the programmer from having to worry about such low-level issues as how the connection is made and how the XML is generated and decomposed. Therefore, complex document-oriented communications can be accomplished with minimal programming effort on the part of the implementer. The Java API for XML Messaging specification is available at `http://java.sun.com/xml/jaxm/index.html`.

Recently, the JAXM specification added the concept of Messaging Profiles. This allows for a higher-level definition of the protocol of the document-based messaging that is to be done. For instance, a Messaging profile for ebXML (`http://www.ebxml.org/`) facilitates XML-based electronic communications for businesses to meet and conduct business through the exchange of XML-based messages.

This additional level of specification allows for more advanced communication features than the basic SOAP specification allows. For instance, constraints on the communication that enhance security, scalability, and robustness are often added in this layer.

Java Architecture for XML Binding

The *Java Architecture for XML Binding (JAXB)*, available on the Web at `http://java.sun.com/xml/jaxb/index.html`, provides a very high-level method of working with XML documents. Although SAX specifies a low-level interface for working with XML and DOM specifies a document-based interface for working with XML, JAXB takes this process one step further and actually generates Java code to directly access XML data.

How does JAXB accomplish this? The Java XML Binding architecture requires that an XML Schema be provided for the XML documents that are to be worked with. (More information about XML Schemas is available in Chapter 5, "Defining XML Document Structures with XML Schemas.") JAXB provides a tool that then will turn this XML Schema into Java classes.

These generated Java classes then handle all parsing and handling of the XML documents through the generated code. This frees up the programmer to concentrate on higher-level issues in his programs without worrying about low-level parser issues. Validation of the document and enforcements of the constraints specified by the XML schema are handled automatically by the generated classes.

In addition, according to Sun, JAXB applications often use less memory and are faster than Applications that use SAX or DOM interfaces. However, as is often the case, there is a tradeoff for using JAXB. As mentioned previously, all the lower-level handling of the parsing of the XML documents and working with the document data is managed by JAXB. This means that you lose quite a bit of flexibility in the process of how your access to the XML data is structured. In addition, JAXB requires XML Schemas. So, if you are working with well-formed XML or use a method of constraint different from XML Schema, JAXB is not an option.

CHOOSING A PARSER

Although the JAVA API for XML Processing defines standard interfaces to connect to XML parser implementations, various parsers are available to choose from. In this section, the three major parsers currently available in XML will be presented: the Apache Xerces Parser, the Apache Crimson Parser, and the GNU GNUJAXP parser (see Table 16.1).

TABLE 16.1 MAJOR JAVA PARSERS

Name	License	Features	Location
Xerces	Apache License	JAXP 1.1 (with Xalan XSLT)	`http://xml.apache.org/xerces-j/`
Crimson	Apache License	JAXP 1.1 minus the javax.xml.transform package	`http://xml.apache.org/crimson/index.html`
GNUJAXP	GNU Public License	JAXP v1.1	`http://www.gnu.org/software/classpathx/jaxp/`

Note

In addition to the open source standalone Java parsers that implement the Java API for XML processing, third-party vendors have also begun to announce JAXP support in their customized parsers. One example is Oracle's XML Developer's Kit for Java, available on the Web at `http://technet.oracle.com/tech/xml/xdk_java/content.html`.

CRIMSON

The Apache Crimson XML parser was originally written by Sun Microsystems and initially served as the reference implementation of the Java API for XML Processing. It has since been donated to the Apache Project (`http://www.apache.org`) and has become a completely open source project. The source code has been made available under the Apache License, which is a generous source code license that allows commercial and noncommercial use of the product.

The Crimson Parser is available at `http://xml.apache.org/crimson/index.html` and implements the following specifications:

- Java API for XML Processing (JAXP) 1.1, minus the javax.xml.transform package
- SAX 2.0
- SAX2 Extensions version 1.0
- DOM Level 2 Core Recommendation

As previously listed, the Crimson Parser implements the entire Java API for XML Processing specification, minus the XSLT transformation package. However, because of the pluggable architecture of the Java API for XML Processing, external implementations of the transformation package can be coupled with the Crimson parser.

XERCES

Early on in the development of XML, *International Business Machines (IBM)* became actively involved in the development of tools to process and work with XML. IBM has also been a very active supporter of Sun Microsystems' Java initiatives. Therefore, it was a good fit for IBM to devote resources to providing a robust Java Parser for XML. The result of that initiative was the IBM XML For Java (XML4J) parser, which has been used for several years in many products, both commercial and noncommercial.

Recently, IBM decided to contribute its parser to the Apache project, much as Sun did with the Crimson parser. The parser has been renamed the Apache Xerces XML Parser and is undergoing active development. It is widely regarded as the most robust XML Parser for Java, and Sun has even begun including Xerces as the reference implementation parser for the Java API for XML Processing. The Apache Xerces source code is also made available under the Apache License, and can be used for both commercial and noncommercial products.

As of the publication of this book, the Xerces parser is the reference implementation for the Java XML APIs that is provided by default in the Java XML Pack. Therefore, all the examples in this chapter will use the Apache parser

The Apache Xerces Parser is available at `http://xml.apache.org/xerces-j/`, and Xerces implements the following specifications:

- XML 1.0
- XML Namespaces
- Document Object Model (DOM) Level 2 Core, Events, and Traversal and Range Recommendations
- Simple API for XML (SAX) 2.0 Core and Extension
- Java APIs for XML Processing (JAXP) 1.1
- XML Schema 1.0 Structures and Datatypes Recommendations

The reasons for Apache having two Java parsers are historical rather than technological: Crimson was developed by Sun, and Xerces had been developed by IBM. The Apache project is solving this by combining the best technology of both Crimson and the original Xerces parser into a new parser called Xerces 2, which is currently in beta and is available on the Web at `http://xml.apache.org/xalan-j/index.html`.

GNUJAXP

The GNU Project (`http://www.gnu.org`) has a long history of advocating free software and providing free implementations of various technology standards. One of its premier projects is the GNU Classpath Extensions project, which provides a wide variety of Java technologies. GNUJAXP is the part of that implementation that provides a free implementation of the standard Java API for XML Processing. The GNUJAXP parser is made available under the GNU General Public License with the "library exception." Normally, the GNU General Public License only allows the use of GNU software in non-commercial projects; however, GNUJAXP has an exception that allows it to be used for non-free software. There are still some restrictions, though, and it would be worthwhile to read the license carefully before considering use of GNUJAXP in a commercial product.

GNU GNUJAXP is available at `http://www.gnu.org/software/classpathx/jaxp/` and implements the following standards:

- SAX Parser API
- DOM Level 2 generic XML data structures
- JAXP v1.1 interfaces, with no XSLT support

EVENT BASED PARSING WITH SAX UNDER JAVA

The most straightforward method of parsing XML under Java is with the *Simple API for XML (SAX)*. This section provides examples of the use of SAX with the Java API for XML Processing and focuses on Java-specific issues. Refer to Chapter 15, "Parsing XML Based on Events," for a more detailed introduction to SAX.

CREATING A SAX PARSER INSTANCE

In order to parse XML documents with SAX, we first need a method to generate a parser that supports the SAX API. In JAXP, parsing with SAX is made available through the creation of an instance of the JAXP `SaxParser` class. Because of the extremely general nature of the Java APIs for XML Processing, this is a multistep process.

First, a `SAXParserFactory` needs to be generated. A SAXParserFactory is not the parser itself. Instead, it is a wrapper class that, when called, generates a `SAXParser`. This could be any parser currently available on the system (Apache Crimson, Apache Xerces, and so on) that supports SAX. If none is specified, a default parser will be chosen. A specific parser can be chosen by setting the `"org.xml.sax.driver"` Java system property. In this case, however, we will use the default parser implementation:

```
parserFactory = SAXParserFactory.newInstance();
```

In addition, the `parserFactory` allows users to specify whether they want to have a namespace aware parser. Because namespaces are becoming more common, we will enable this feature of the SAXParserFactory:

```
parserFactory.setNamespaceAware(true);
```

It is also possible to tell the Parser Factory whether you want to have a validating XML Parser. Because our example document (see the beginning of the chapter) doesn't use a DTD, for this example a non-validating parser will be chosen.

```
parserFactory.setValidating(false);
```

Now that a Parser Factory has been created, an actual parser can be generated. The methods available to the `SAXParser` are listed in Table 16.2.

```
SAXParser saxParser = parserFactory.newSAXParser();
```

TABLE 16.2 `SAXParser` METHODS

getParser	The current SAX `Parser` that this class encapsulates
getProperty	Gets a SAX `XMLReader` property
getXMLReader	The underlying `XMLReader` associated with this parser
isNamespaceAware	A `boolean` value that specifies whether this parser understands namespaces
isValidating	A `boolean` value that specifies whether this parser validates against DTDs and Schemas

TABLE 16.2 CONTINUED	
`parse`	Parses the specified XML document
`setProperty`	Sets a SAX `XMLReader` property

Note

JAXP 1.1 and higher are based on SAX2, and therefore include methods to work with the SAX2 XMLReader interfaces. If you are using a tool based on the older JAXP 1.0 standard (which was based on SAX1), these methods will not be available.

HANDLING EVENTS

The Simple API for XML is an event-based parser interface. Whenever a node in the XML document is parsed, a matching callback function in the SAX implementation is called. In the case of Java, this is done via the `DefaultHandler` interface of the Java SAX specification. For our example, the various methods will print out information about the document that is available at each step of the parsing.

For the Java SAX example, the first handlers to be provided are for the `startDocument` and the `endDocument`. These notify the application when the parser has begun and when it has finished parsing the document. This can be especially helpful when processing long documents:

```
public void startDocument ()
{
  System.out.println("[Start Of Document]");
}
  public void endDocument ()
{
  System.out.println("[End Of Document]");
}
```

Similar methods are registered to be called when an element is started (`startElement`) and when an element is ended (`endElement`). It is important to note that the `endElement` method might be called long after the `startElement` is called because an element might include many elements beneath it. Keeping track of this sort of information is one of the subtle complexities of using the SAX API, and it is one reason some applications are better suited to a higher level API such as the *Document Object Model (DOM)*.

```
public void startElement (String uri, String name, String qName, Attributes atts)
{
  System.out.println("[Start element: " + qName + "]");
}
public void endElement (String uri, String name, String qName)
{
  System.out.println("[End element: " + qName + "]");
}
```

Finally, the event handler for character data must be provided. In the case of XML parsers, whitespace such as new lines in documents is preserved. In order to make the printing of the character data more pleasant to read, all the characters except the new lines will be printed.

```
public void characters (char ch[], int start, int length)
{
  for (int i = start; i < start + length; i++)
  {
    if (ch[i] != '\n')
    {
      System.out.print(ch[i]);
    }
  }
  System.out.println();
}
```


PARSING THE DOCUMENT

A SAX Parser has now been generated. However, this parser can be used over and over again. In order to use it specifically for our document, an object called an `XMLReader` must be created from the SAX Parser. An `XMLReader` is the object that actually implements the SAX interfaces for the event based parsing that is to be done.

```
XMLReader xmlReader = saxParser.getXMLReader();
```

Similarly, the SAX Event Handlers have been programmed, but the SAX Parser does not yet know that those handlers are the ones to use for this document. Therefore, those handlers must be placed in a custom class. In this case, our class is called `SimpleSax`. Then, an instance of that class must be generated, and the SAX Event Handlers set to use that class.

```
SimpleSAX saxHandler = new SimpleSAX();
xmlReader.setContentHandler(saxHandler);
xmlReader.setErrorHandler(saxHandler);
```

At this point, all that still needs to be done is to actually parse the document. This is accomplished through the parse method of the `XMLReader` object. That parse method requires a Java `InputSource` to parse, so first a Java `FileReader` is created for the example, `"example.xml"`, and then that `FileReader` is used to create an `InputSource`:

```
FileReader fileReader = new FileReader("example.xml");
InputSource inputSource = new InputSource(fileReader);
```

Finally, the parse method of the `XMLReader` is called, and the document is parsed:

```
xmlReader.parse(inputSource);
```

The full source code to this example is shown in Listing 16.1, and the output from the example is shown in Listing 16.2.

LISTING 16.1 SAX EXAMPLE IN JAVA

```
import java.io.FileReader;

import javax.xml.parsers.SAXParserFactory;
import javax.xml.parsers.SAXParser;
import org.xml.sax.XMLReader;
```

LISTING 16.1 CONTINUED

```
import org.xml.sax.Attributes;
import org.xml.sax.InputSource;
import org.xml.sax.helpers.XMLReaderFactory;
import org.xml.sax.helpers.DefaultHandler;

public class SimpleSAX extends DefaultHandler
{

  // Could also specify org.xml.sax.driver
  public static void main (String args[])    throws Exception
  {
    // Generate a parser factory that will provide a parser implementation
    SAXParserFactory parserFactory = SAXParserFactory.newInstance();

    // Tell the parser factory to generate a parser
    // that is aware of namespaces
    parserFactory.setNamespaceAware(true);

    // Tell the parser factory to generate a parser that does not validate
    parserFactory.setValidating(false);

    // Using the parser factory, generate a new SAX Parser
    SAXParser saxParser = parserFactory.newSAXParser();

    // Generate a specific XML Reader from the SAX Parser
    XMLReader xmlReader = saxParser.getXMLReader();

    // Create an instance of the SimpleSAX class that implements the
    // SAX DefaultHandler interface
    SimpleSAX saxHandler = new SimpleSAX();

    // Tell the XML Reader that we wish to use the generated SimpleSAX
    // Class for parsing event callbacks
    xmlReader.setContentHandler(saxHandler);

    // Tell the XML Reader to use the generated SimpleSAX class for errors as well
    xmlReader.setErrorHandler(saxHandler);

    // Open a Java fileReader for the example file
    FileReader fileReader = new FileReader("example.xml");

    // Create an InputSource based on the File Reader
    InputSource inputSource = new InputSource(fileReader);

    // Parse the document with the Input Source created from the example file.
    xmlReader.parse(inputSource);
  }

  // SAX Event Handlers

  public void startDocument ()
  {
    System.out.println("[Start Of Document]");
  }
```

Listing 16.1 continued

```
  public void endDocument ()
  {
    System.out.println("[End Of Document]");
  }


  public void startElement (String uri, String name, String qName, Attributes
➥atts)
  {
  System.out.println("[Start element: " + qName + "]");
  }


  public void endElement (String uri, String name, String qName)
  {
  System.out.println("[End element: " + qName + "]");
  }


  public void characters (char ch[], int start, int length)
  {

    // Print out all of the characters provided by the parser, ignoring newlines.
    for (int i = start; i < start + length; i++)
    {
      if (ch[i] != '\n')
      {
      System.out.print(ch[i]);
      }
    }
    // Since newlines are suppressed, generate a newline at the end of the
    // characters
    System.out.println();
  }

}
```


Listing 16.2 Sample Java SAX Application Output

```
[Start Of Document]
[Start element: java_xml]
[Start element: standards]
[Start element: standard]
Java API for XML Processing(JAXP)
[End element: standard]
[Start element: standard]
Document Object Model(DOM)
[End element: standard]
[Start element: standard]
Simple API for XML(SAX)
[End element: standard]
[End element: standards]
[Start element: parsers]
[Start element: parser]
Xerces
```

LISTING 16.2 CONTINUED

```
[End element: parser]
[Start element: parser]
Crimson
[End element: parser]
[Start element: parser]
GNUJAXP
[End element: parser]
[End element: parsers]
[End element: java_xml]
[End Of Document]
```

DOCUMENT BASED PARSING WITH DOM UNDER JAVA

Although event based parsing with the Simple API for XML is fast and memory efficient, it does not provide any context for where the current element is in the hierarchy of the document. This is due to the fact that parsing via SAX is effectively a one-shot operation: The parser only knows about the current element at the moment when it notifies the event handler and then promptly forgets about it.

For applications in which it is useful to have the parser remember more of this contextual information, using a parser that implements DOM is appropriate. DOM has the advantage of storing a complete copy of the XML document in memory at all times, allowing programmers to traverse through the hierarchy of elements without worrying about keeping track of the state of the document. This has the advantage of providing a much higher-level interface to XML documents than a SAX interface, but at a serious efficiency and memory cost, because all the information from the document must be stored in memory at all times.

This section provides an example of working with DOM in Java. For more specific information on the Document Object Model and its interfaces, see Chapter 14, "XML and the Document Object Model."

CREATING THE DOM PARSER INSTANCE

In order to parse XML documents with DOM, we first need a method to generate a DOM Parser. Under the Java API for XML Processing, this is done in a very similar way to how SAX Parsers are built: with a factory object that creates parsers on request. Under the JAXP interfaces, a DOM parser is referred to as a Document Parser, and the parser factory responsible for generating a Document Parser is the `DocumentBuilderFactory`. Therefore, our example starts with the creation of the `DocumentBuilderFactory`. (The methods available to the resulting `DocumentBuilder` are shown in Table 16.3.)

```
DocumentBuilder documentBuilder = documentBuilderFactory.newDocumentBuilder();
```

Table 16.3 DocumentBuilder Methods

Method	Description
getDOMImplementation	The DOMImplementation associated with this document builder
isNamespaceAware	A boolean value that specifies whether this parser understands namespaces
isValidating	A boolean value that specifies whether this parser validates against DTDs and Schemas
newDocument	Creates a new W3C DOM Document object that can be manipulated
parse	Parses the specified XML document
setEntityResolver	Sets the event callback that will be used to resolve entity references in the document
setErrorHandler	Sets the event callback that will be called when an error is encountered during the parsing of the document

Parsing the Document

At this point, there is a marked difference in how documents are parsed between the DOM and SAX parsers. Under SAX, a SAXParser must be created and then an XMLReader is created from the parser to actually parse the document. When using the DOM interface, the process is much more streamlined: The filename to be parsed is passed directly to the parse method of the DocumentBuilder. This method returns a Document object. The next step in the example is to use this method to parse our sample "example.xml" XML file.

```
Document document = documentBuilder.parse("example.xml");
```

This Document object represents an in-memory representation of the entire XML document. There are various methods for querying the Document object for details about the XML document that has been parsed. (See Chapter 14 if you are interested in more detailed information about these interfaces.) For our example, we start by retrieving the root node of the document. This is referred to by the Document Object Model specification (somewhat confusingly) as the Document Element, and is retrieved by the method getDocumentElement().

```
Element elem = document.getDocumentElement();
```

Now that the root element of the document has been retrieved, it's time to harness the power of the Document Object model in Java to find out some specific information from our example XML file. If you refer back to the example file at the beginning of the chapter, you will notice that an XML element called <standards> contains several children <standard> elements that each name a standard in the text of the element and provide the Web address for each of them in the href attribute of the element. Let's add the ability to our example to print out the information for each of those standards.

First, a list of all the elements with the name "standards" needs to be retrieved. This is done with the DOM method getElementsByTagName, which returns a NodeList that contains all of the elements.

```
NodeList standards_list = root_element.getElementsByTagName("standards");
```

For this example, there is only one `<standards>` element in the document, so the item method of the `NodeList` can be called to retrieve the first element in the `NodeList`. Although the Document Object Model specifies that a `NodeList` contains DOM nodes, in this case we know ahead of time that the `Node` is actually a DOM `Element`. Therefore, a Java typecast is used to convert the returned `Node` into a DOM `Element`:

```
Element standards_element = (Element) standards_list.item(0);
```

Now we have a handle on the `<standards>` element, which can be then used to navigate to all of its children. In this case, the children are all a group of individual elements with the name `<standard>`. Therefore, we use the `getElementsByTagName()` method again, but in this case we find all `<standard>` elements:

```
NodeList children = standards_element.getElementsByTagName("standard");
```

Unlike the previous use of `getElementsByTagName`, where there was only one element to be retrieved, in this case several different elements need to be visited because the `<standards>` element contains several `<standard>` elements. Therefore, the `getLength` method of the children `NodeList` object is called, which returns the number of elements contained in the `NodeList`. This value is then used to cycle through returned children via a Java `for` loop:

```
for (int n=0; n<children.getLength(); n++) {
```

Upon each pass through the `for` loop, the `NodeList` item method is used to select the current element in the list:

```
Element standard = (Element)children.item(n);
```

Next we want to print out the names of each of the standards. We start by notifying the user that the standard's name will be printed:

```
System.out.println("The standard named: \n\t");
```

At this point, the process becomes slightly more complicated. The name of each standard is represented as text contained within each `<standard>` element. Unfortunately, something like a `getText` method that retrieves all that text is not available, because the Document Object Model specifies that any text contained within an element is represented as child text nodes of that element. Therefore, we need to iterate over the child nodes of each `<standard>` element, looking for text nodes and then appending them to the result string:

```
String value = "";
// Collect the text beneath each node
NodeList child = standard.getChildNodes();
for(int i = 0; i < child.getLength(); i++ ) {
        Node current_child = child.item(i);
        // If a node is a Text Node then it is part of the standard name
        if( current_child.getNodeType() == Node.TEXT_NODE ) {
                value = value + current_child.getNodeValue();
        }
}
System.out.println(value);
```

This process is very similar to the one used previously to navigate into the children of the `<standard>` and `<standards>` elements. However, one important difference to note is the use of the `getNoteType` method of the DOM `Node`, which in this case is used to discover whether the current node is a text node. If it is, the value of the text `Node` (obtained via the `getNodeValue` method) is used to add that text to the current string. If it is not a text node, it is ignored.

Finally, for each `<standard>` element, the Web address for each standard is printed. Retrieving attributes from the DOM in Java is much easier than retrieving text. Each `Element` object has a `getAttribute` method that, when given the name of an attribute, returns the text value of that attribute. This method is used here to find the `"href"` attribute for each element and print it to the console.


```
System.out.println("Can be accessed on the web at: \n\t");
String href = standard.getAttribute("href");
System.out.println(href);
System.out.println();
```

The full source code for this example is shown in Listing 16.3, and the output from the example is shown in Listing 16.4.

Listing 16.3 DOM Example in Java

```
//SimpleDOM.java

import javax.xml.parsers.DocumentBuilderFactory;
import javax.xml.parsers.DocumentBuilder;
import javax.xml.parsers.ParserConfigurationException;
import org.xml.sax.SAXException;
import org.w3c.dom.Document;
import org.w3c.dom.Element;
import org.w3c.dom.NodeList;
import org.w3c.dom.Node;
import java.io.IOException;

public class SimpleDOM {

  public static void main(String[] args)
  {

    try
    {
      // Generate a Document Builder Factory that will allow
      // DOM Parsers to be generated
      DocumentBuilderFactory documentBuilderFactory =
➥ DocumentBuilderFactory.newInstance();
      // Using the Document Builder Factory, generate a DOM Parser
      DocumentBuilder documentBuilder =
➥ documentBuilderFactory.newDocumentBuilder();

      System.out.println("Start Processing: example.xml");

      // Using the generated DOM parser, parse the example file
      Document document = documentBuilder.parse("example.xml");

      // Get the Root Element of the Document
      Element root_element = document.getDocumentElement();
```

LISTING 16.3 CONTINUED

```
      // Get a list of all elements with the name "standard"
      NodeList standards_list = root_element.getElementsByTagName("standards");
      Element standards_element = (Element) standards_list.item(0);

      // Take the first element with the name "standard" and get all of its
      // children named "standards"
      NodeList children = standards_element.getElementsByTagName("standard");

      // Cycle through the NodeList containing elements named standards
      for (int n=0; n<children.getLength(); n++)
      {
        // Get each individual standard element one at a time
        Element standard = (Element)children.item(n);

        System.out.println("The standard named: \n\t");
        String value = "";
        // Collect the text beneath each node
        NodeList child = standard.getChildNodes();
        for(int i = 0; i < child.getLength(); i++ ) {
          Node current_child = child.item(i);
          // If a node is a Text Node then it is part of the standard name
          if( current_child.getNodeType() == Node.TEXT_NODE ) {
            value = value + current_child.getNodeValue();
        }
      }
      System.out.println(value);
      // Print out the standard location, which is contained as an attribute
      System.out.println("Can be accessed on the web at: \n\t");
      String href = standard.getAttribute("href");
      System.out.println(href);
      System.out.println();
    }
    System.out.println("End Processing: example.xml");
  } catch (ParserConfigurationException e)
    {
      System.out.println("Parser Configuration Exception :" + e);
    } catch (SAXException e)
    {
    System.out.println("SAX Exception :" + e);
    } catch (IOException e)
    {
      System.out.println("Input Output Exception :" + e);
    }
  }
}
```

LISTING 16.4 OUTPUT FROM DOM EXAMPLE

```
Start Processing: example.xml
The standard named:
Java API for XML Processing(JAXP)
Can be accessed on the web at:
http://java.sun.com/xml/jaxp
The standard named:
Document Object Model(DOM)
```

LISTING 16.4 CONTINUED

```
Can be accessed on the web at:
http://www.w3.org/DOM/
The standard named:
Simple API for XML(SAX)
Can be accessed on the web at:
http://www.saxproject.org/
End Processing: example.xml
```


XML TRANSFORMATIONS IN JAVA

The final crucial component of the *Java API For XML Processing (JAXP)* is the ability to programmatically transform XML documents via XSLT. Details of XSLT transformations are covered in detail in Chapter 9, "Transforming XML Data into Other Formats with XSLT." This section focuses on methods for using Java to produce these XSLT transformations.

The reference implementation for the JAXP transformation engine is the Apache Xerces Xalan XSLT engine, and it is the transformation engine that will be used for the example in this section. The Apache Xalan XSLT engine source code is made available under the open source Apache License and is contained in the Java XML Pack that is available for downloading at `http://xml.apache.org/xalan-j/index.html`.

The JAXP specification provides an extremely straightforward method for doing XSLT transformations in Java. As an example, we will build a small application that transforms the XML file example from the beginning of this chapter into HTML. The XSLT file that will be used for this example is shown in Listing 16.7. This XSLT transformer takes our example XML file and turns it into an HTML file that prints out all the standards listed in the document.

As with all the other Java API for XML interfaces, the XSLT transformation engine isn't instantiated directly, but is instead generated via a factory—in this case a `TransformerFactory` that queries the system for the available transformers and generates one on demand:

```
TransformerFactory transformerFactory =  TransformerFactory.newInstance();
```

Now that a `TransformerFactory` has been created, it is necessary to prepare the data sources that will be transformed. Because files will be used in this example, Java IO File Objects are created for the XML and XSLT file examples:

```
File xmlFile = new File("example.xml");
File xsltFile = new File("example.xslt");
```

The Java Transformation API cannot use raw Java File objects for transformation. Instead, it defines a custom interface called `Source` to which all XML data sources must conform. Luckily, a wrapper object called `StreamSource` is provided that will convert Java IO file objects into `StreamSource` objects that implement the `Source` interface.

```
Source xmlSource =  new StreamSource(xmlFile);
Source xsltSource =   new StreamSource(xsltFile);
```

Now that the source objects have been created, we need to specify a location for the transformed XML data to be placed into. This can be another file, a network communications pipe, or—as is the case here—a standard `PrintStream` like the System Console. A `StreamResult` object is created from the desired output stream similar to how `StreamSource` objects were created for the input stream:

```
StreamResult streamResult = new StreamResult(System.out);
```

Now the Transformation engine object must be created. The Transformation engine object is created from the `TransformerFactory` object created earlier, and it is created via the `newTransformer` method. When the `Transformer` object is created, the XSLT `Source` object is passed in as part of the call to the `newTransformer`. This creates a `Transformer` tied to that specific XSLT Stylesheet and can be used over and over again to transform multiple documents with the style sheet. (The methods available to the `Transformer` object are shown in Table 16.4.)

```
Transformer transformer = transformerFactory.newTransformer(xsltSource);
```

TABLE 16.4 TRANSFORMER METHODS

clearParameters	Clears all the XSLT parameters that have been set.
getErrorListener	Returns the error handler for this transformation.
getOutputProperties	Returns the output properties for this transformation.
getOutputProperty	Returns a single output property for this transformation.
getParameter	Returns an XSLT parameter that has been set.
getURIResolver	Returns the handler used to resolve URIs.
setErrorListener	Sets the error handler for the transformation.
setOutputProperties	Sets the output properties for this transformation.
setOutputProperty	Sets a single output property for this transformation.
setParameter	Sets an XSLT parameter for this transformation.
setURIResolver	Sets the handler used to resolve URIs.
transform	Transforms the specified XML document using the specified XSLT and outputs the results.

We're now ready to run the XSLT transformation. The `Transformer` object contains a method called `transform` that actually runs the transformation. This method takes two arguments. The first is the `StreamSource` to be used to fetch the XML document to be transformed, which in our case is the `xmlSource` object corresponding to the sample XML file. The second is the `StreamResult` object to send the transformed document to, which in this case is the `streamResult` object corresponding to the System Console.

```
transformer.transform(xmlSource, streamResult);
```

That's it. The full implementation of code for this example is contained in Listing 16.6. The HTML output generated by the transformation example is shown in Listing 16.5, and finally the output displayed in a Web browser is contained in Figure 16.2.

LISTING 16.5 HTML OUTPUT FROM THE TRANSFORMER EXAMPLE

```
<html>
<head>
<META http-equiv="Content-Type" content="text/html; charset=UTF-8">
<title>Example Transformation</title>
</head>
<body>
<center>
<h1>Example Transformation</h1>
</center>
<h1>Standard</h1>
<h2>Java API for XML Processing(JAXP)</h2>
<h1>Standard</h1>
<h2>Document Object Model(DOM)</h2>
<h1>Standard</h1>
<h2>Simple API for XML(SAX)</h2>
<h1>Parser</h1>
<h2>Xerces</h2>
<h1>Parser</h1>
<h2>Crimson</h2>
<h1>Parser</h1>
<h2>GNUJAXP</h2>
</body>
</html>
```


LISTING 16.6 JAVA XSLT TRANSFORMER CODE EXAMPLE

```
import java.io.File;
import javax.xml.transform.Result;
import javax.xml.transform.Source;
import javax.xml.transform.Transformer;
import javax.xml.transform.TransformerException;
import javax.xml.transform.TransformerFactory;
import javax.xml.transform.stream.StreamSource;
import javax.xml.transform.stream.StreamResult;
public class SimpleTransform
{
  public static void main(String[] args) throws TransformerException
  {
    // Generate a Transformer Factory that will allow Transformers to be
    // generated
    TransformerFactory transformerFactory =  TransformerFactory.newInstance();
    // Create Java File object to load the example xml file from
    File xmlFile = new File("example.xml");
    // Create Java File object to load the example xslt file from
    File xsltFile = new File("example.xslt");
    // Create StreamSource object for the example xml file
    Source xmlSource =  new StreamSource(xmlFile);
    // Create StreamSource object for the example xslt file
    Source xsltSource =   new StreamSource(xsltFile);
```

LISTING 16.6 CONTINUED

```
    // Create the StreamResult object to inform the transformer where to send
    // the transformed document
    StreamResult streamResult = new StreamResult(System.out);
    // Create the transformer for this XSLT document from the generated
    // TransformerFactory object,
    Transformer transformer = transformerFactory.newTransformer(xsltSource);
    // Finally, run the XSLT transformation against the StreamSource generated
    // from sample XML file passing the results to the specified StreamResult,
    // which in this case is the Console
    transformer.transform(xmlSource, streamResult);
  }
}
```

LISTING 16.7 SAMPLE XSLT FILE

```
<?xml version="1.0"?>
<xsl:stylesheet xmlns:xsl="http://www.w3.org/1999/XSL/Transform" version="1.0">
<xsl:template match="/">
<html>
  <head>
    <title>Example Transformation</title>
  </head>
  <body>
    <center>
      <h1>Example Transformation</h1>
    </center>
<xsl:apply-templates/>
    </body>
</html>
</xsl:template>

<xsl:template match="standard">
  <h1>Standard</h1>
  <h2><xsl:value-of select="."/></h2>
</xsl:template>

<xsl:template match="parser">
  <h1>Parser</h1>
  <h2><xsl:value-of select="."/></h2>
</xsl:template>

</xsl:stylesheet>
```

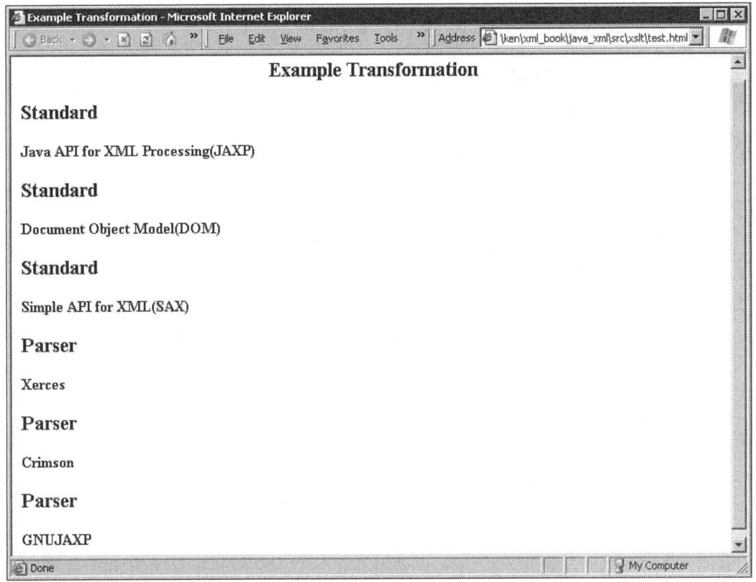

Figure 16.2
Browser displaying the output from the Transformer example.

NAVIGATING THE DOCUMENT VIA XPATH IN JAVA

Another important method for navigating XML documents is via XPath. XPath is a non-XML based specification for addressing arbitrary locations in XML Documents. The XPath syntax is described in detail in Chapter 11, "Locating Components in XML Documents with XPath." A basic usage of XPath with Java is provided in this section.

Unfortunately, a standard interface for XPath is not yet part of the standard Java API for XML provided by Sun. However, a robust implementation available for XPath works seamlessly with implementations of the Java API for XML like Xerces and Xalan. That XPath implementation is called Jaxen (available at `http://jaxen.org`).

Jaxen is a native Java implementation of the full XPath Specification and is capable of working with multiple Java XML access methods. For this section, we will use the familiar DOM interface with Jaxen.

Note

Jaxen isn't part of the standard Java XML Pack; therefore, to use this example you will need to download the Jaxen implementation from `http://jaxen.org` and install it. The only installation that is currently required is to add the "jaxen-full.jar" and saxpath.jar file from the Jaxen installation to the classpath for your IDE project (along with the standard xerces.jar and xalan.jar from the Java XML pack). However, be sure to read the installation documentation carefully to ensure correct functionality.

Using XPath via Jaxen is a straightforward process. First, because we will be using a DOM interface to work with the Jaxen engine, a DOM document is needed that represents the example XML document. Because Jaxen works seamlessly with the Java API For XML Processing, the process used to build this `Document` object is exactly the same as in the earlier section on DOM.

```
DocumentBuilderFactory factory = DocumentBuilderFactory.newInstance();
factory.setNamespaceAware(true);
DocumentBuilder builder = factory.newDocumentBuilder();
Document document = builder.parse( "example.xml" );
```

Now that the DOM document has been created, we're ready to execute the desired XPath expression. The API for this call is extremely simple. First, an `XPath` object is created with the XPath expression that we want to execute on the document. In this case, we will use the following XPath expression: `"//standards/standard"`. This XPath expression will return all the XML elements named `"standard"` that are children of the `"standards"` element.

```
XPath xpath = new XPath( "//standards/standard" );
```

In order to run the `XPath` object against our document, the `selectNodes` method of the `XPath` object is called with the DOM document as the parameter. This allows the same `XPath` object to be executed with many different XML documents, which greatly increases efficiency.

```
List xpathResults = xpath.selectNodes(document);
```

Now that the results have been generated, we need to access them. The process of accessing the results is a little different than in the Java API for XML, which uses the DOM object model to return lists of results. Here, the standard Java collection classes `List` and `Iterator` are used instead. The `selectNodes` method returns a Java List, which we can then iterate over with its Java `Iterator`:

```
Iterator resultsIterator = xpathResults.iterator();
while ( resultsIterator.hasNext() )
{
        Element resultElement = (Element) resultsIterator.next();
        System.out.println(resultElement.getTagName());
        System.out.println(resultElement.getAttribute("href"));
}
```

Each of the results contained in the Java List is a DOM `Node`. In this case, because our XPath expression queries for XML `Elements`, we know ahead of time that `Elements` will be returned. So each returned result is converted to a DOM `Element` and then the name of the `<standard>` element and the URL `href` attribute that it contains is printed out to the system console.

The full implementation of code for this example is contained in Listing 16.8, and the console output generated by the Jaxen XPath example is provided in Listing 16.9.

16

LISTING 16.8 JAVA XPATH EXAMPLE

```
import javax.xml.parsers.DocumentBuilder;
import javax.xml.parsers.DocumentBuilderFactory;
import java.io.IOException;
import org.w3c.dom.Document;
import org.w3c.dom.Element;
import org.xml.sax.SAXException;
import org.jaxen.dom.XPath;
import org.saxpath.SAXPathException;
import org.saxpath.XPathSyntaxException;
import javax.xml.parsers.ParserConfigurationException;
import java.util.List;
import java.util.Iterator;

public class SimpleXpath
{
  public static void main(String[] args)
 {
    try
   {
     // Generate a Document Builder Factory that will allow
     // DOM Parsers to be generated
     DocumentBuilderFactory factory = DocumentBuilderFactory.newInstance();
     // Set the factory to respect XML Namespaces
     factory.setNamespaceAware(true);
     // Using the Document Builder Factory, generate a DOM Parser
     DocumentBuilder builder = factory.newDocumentBuilder();

     // Using the generated DOM parser, parse the example file
     Document document = builder.parse( "example.xml" );

     // Build an XPath object with the desired expression
     XPath xpath = new XPath( "//standards/standard" );

     // Run the XPath expression against the current document, returning a
     // list of matched elements
     List xpathResults = xpath.selectNodes(document);

     // Generate a Java iteratory that will allow the returned elements
     // to be traversed
     Iterator resultsIterator = xpathResults.iterator();

     System.out.println("Results:" );

     // Loop over each element, while there are elements remaining ,
     // printing out the values of each.
      while ( resultsIterator.hasNext() )
      {
        Element resultElement = (Element) resultsIterator.next();
        System.out.println(resultElement.getTagName());
        System.out.println(resultElement.getAttribute("href"));
      }
    }
    catch (XPathSyntaxException e)
    {
```

LISTING 16.8 CONTINUED

```
      System.err.println(e);
    }

    catch (ParserConfigurationException e)
    {
      System.err.println(e);
    }
    catch (SAXException e)
    {
      System.err.println(e);
    }
    catch (IOException e)
    {
      System.err.println(e);
     }
  }
}
```

Note

This example depends on several Java libraries. If you have any problems compiling and running it, make sure that your classpath contains references to the standard Java XML Pack libraries (currently xerces.jar and xalan.jar), as well as references to the Jaxen libraries (currently jaxen-full.jar and saxpath.jar). In addition, make sure that you read the installation documentation to ensure correct installation.

LISTING 16.9 JAVA XPATH EXAMPLE OUTPUT

```
Results:
standard
http://java.sun.com/xml/jaxp
standard
http://www.w3.org/DOM/
standard
http://www.saxproject.org/
```

OTHER JAVA XML STANDARDS

The common tools and technologies for working with XML in Java have now been covered. However, occasionally there are cases in which a more specialized Java XML technology can be helpful. Several of these technologies are discussed in this section.

JDOM

JDOM is a standard for directly accessing, manipulating, and outputting XML documents from Java code. In this sense, it is very similar to the *Java API for XML Binding (JAXB)*. However, although JDOM is not an official Sun Java standard, it has been available for a much longer time and has a more mature implementation. The reference JDOM implementation is available at `http://www.jdom.org/`.

XSL:FO

Although XSLT is a great technology for transforming XML documents into other XML-like formats, there is occasionally a need for those documents to be transformed into a radically different format. *XSL Formatting Objects (XSL:FO)*, discussed in detail in Chapter 10, "The Nuts and Bolts of XSL: Formatting Objects," is a standard for these types of transformations.

The Apache project has developed a robust implementation of XSL:FO available as a Java library. This implementation is called FOP and is available at (`http://xml.apache.org/fop/index.html`).

FOP was the first XSL:FO print formatter developed and is quite mature. In addition to supporting the XSL:FO specification, the formatter is also output independent and can render pages to multiple output formats. The primary output format for FOP is PDF, but the following formats are also supported by the current FOP implementation:

- Portable Document Format (PDF)
- Printer Control Language (PCL)
- Postscript (PS)
- Structure Vector Graphics (SVG)
- XML area tree representation
- Java Abstract Windowing Toolkit (AWT)
- Framemaker Interchange Format (MIF)
- Text Format (TXT)

XQuery

Until recently, the default method for querying XML documents was XPath. Although XPath is a useful technology, it is limited to simple types of XML queries. The W3C is in the process of proposing a more advanced specification for queries against XML documents called XQuery. XQuery is discussed in more detail in Chapter 20, "Querying Documents Using XQuery," and the current working draft of this specification is available at `http://web3.w3.org/TR/xquery/`.

Although XQuery is not yet a formal specification, the development of an advanced query technology for XML is widely regarded as an important advancement. In response to this demand, three XQuery implementations are already available, although as of the time of this writing all are in the early stages of development.

Quip has been developed by Software AG and is available at `http://www.softwareag.com/developer/quip/`.

Quip is currently a Windows only application, but it provides a standard API that allows it to be accessed from Java.

Galax is an XQuery implementation being developed by Bell Labs. Information of Galax is available at `http://www-db.research.bell-labs.com/galax/`.

IPSI-XQ is an XQuery implementation being developed in collaboration with Technical University of Darmstadt, and information on IPSI-XQ is available at `http://xml.darmstadt.gmd.de/xquerydemo/`.

XML-RPC

Although the Java API for XML-RPC provides a high-level API for Java communications via the SOAP protocol, there is also another standard for remote procedure calls done via XML over HTTP called (confusingly enough) XML-RPC. XML-RPC is a much simpler protocol than the official SOAP protocol, and although it has more limited functionality, it also has been available longer, and many existing Web services are available using the XML-RPC format. The XML-RPC specification is available at `http://www.xmlrpc.com/`.

Like SOAP, XML-RPC can be used from many different languages. The Apache project has made a Java implementation of XML-RPC available called Apache XML-RPC (`http://xml.apache.org/xmlrpc/`). It is made available under the Apache license and can be used for commercial and non-commercial applications.

TOOLS

In addition to the various implementations of standards to work with XML available in Java, there are also high-level tools that leverage those standard implementations to enable advanced applications. In this section, several of those tools are examined.

COCOON

Apache Cocoon is a high-level framework for the publishing of XML documents on the Web. It allows for the complete separation of document content, application logic, and style transformation while still maintaining a central repository and high performance implementation that seamlessly serves the document content in a variety of formats.

The Apache Cocoon server is built on top of the Apache Xerces XML parsing suite and the Apache XSLT transformation engine. Apache Cocoon is available at `http://xml.apache.org/cocoon/index.html`.

BATIK SCALABLE VECTOR GRAPHICS TOOLKIT

Although many technologies are available for XML text processing, the Batik Scalable Vector Graphics toolkit breaks the mold and has been built to produce graphics content from XML documents. The *Scalable Vector Graphics (SVG)* format is a standard format for Web graphics that has been proposed by the W3C (the specification is available at `http://www.w3.org/TR/SVG/`) and is rapidly gaining acceptance on the Internet.

The Batik SVG toolkit is a set of modules that allows Scalable Vector Graphics documents to be parsed, generated, and accessed via the Document Object Model. In addition, Batik also provides a reference implementation of an SVG viewer that can be used to view SVG documents in browsers that do not yet support SVG but do support Java. Finally, Batik includes a useful tool that can turn SVG graphics documents into various raster image file formats such as JPEG and PNG.

The Batik Scalable Vector Graphics toolkit is made available at `http://xml.apache.org/batik/` under the liberal Apache License and can be used for commercial development.

Additional Resources

A number of additional resources are available on the Web to help you with learning about working with XML in Java. Here are a few of the best ones to consult:

- Sun Java and XML Technologies (`http://java.sun.com/xml/`)—This page, provided by Sun Microsystems, is the home for information on all the official Java XML standards.
- The Apache XML Project (`http://xml.apache.org/`)—This site is at the forefront of Java XML development, providing many tools and standards implementations.
- IBM developerWorks XML zone (`http://www-106.ibm.com/developerworks/xml/`)—IBM has been active in Java XML development since the beginning of XML standardization and provides a great deal of Java XML documentation and software at this site.

Roadmap

Now that working with XML in Java has been presented, we will move on in Chapter 17, "Working with XML and .NET," to discuss working with XML in a similar but competing technology. The Microsoft .NET framework provides similar functionality to Java, and includes built-in libraries for many of the common XML technologies we've worked with in this chapter, such as DOM, XSLT, and XPath. These libraries, and examples to demonstrate them, are covered in the next chapter. Then, in Chapter 18, "XML and Databases," we'll move on to working with XML in the popular web programming language Perl.

CHAPTER 17

Working with XML and .NET

In this chapter

by Kenrick Rawlings

PREPARATION

We assume that you have a basic knowledge of programming with Microsoft's C# Programming Language and are familiar with the installation of the .NET software development kit. If you are not, check out an introductory C# .NET Book or visit the Microsoft .NET site at `http://www.microsoft.com/net/`.

In this chapter, various methods for working with XML in Microsoft's .NET framework are presented. Microsoft .NET is a new and exciting framework for application development. Because .NET is new, we will start with the preparation and prerequisites for .NET development, followed by an introduction to the .NET XML Framework concepts. Next, various methods of parsing XML are presented, including both a SAX-like and a DOM method. Support for XML in .NET is extensive. The .NET framework also includes built-in support for XPath navigation and XSLT Transformation, which are covered in the final sections of the chapter.

Make sure that the following software is installed on your machine:

- The Microsoft .NET Platform SDK is available at `http://msdn.microsoft.com/downloads/default.asp`. All the libraries that will be used in this chapter are contained within the Microsoft .NET Platform SDK.
- An Integrated Development Environment (IDE) is optional, but highly recommended. The premier IDE is Microsoft's Visual Studio .NET, which is a commercial product. More information is available at `http://msdn.microsoft.com/vstudio/`.
- One great alternative is SharpDevelop, which is a free .NET Integrated Development Environment, made available under an open source license at `http://www.icsharpcode.net/`.

We will be using the following sample XML Document throughout this chapter:

```
<?xml version="1.0" ?>
<!DOCTYPE net_xml [
  <!ELEMENT net_xml        (standards, parsers)>
  <!ELEMENT standards (standard)+>
  <!ELEMENT parsers (parser)+>
  <!ELEMENT parser (#PCDATA)>
  <!ELEMENT standard (#PCDATA)>
  <!ATTLIST parser
     href      CDATA    #REQUIRED
  >
  <!ATTLIST standard
     href      CDATA    #REQUIRED
  >
]>
<net_xml>
  <standards>
    <standard href="http://www.dotnetexperts.com/ecma/index.html">
      .NET Standards Documents
    </standard>
    <standard href="http://www.w3.org/DOM/">
      Document Object Model(DOM)
```

```
    </standard>
    <standard href="http://www.saxproject.org/">
      Simple API for XML(SAX)
    </standard>
  </standards>
  <parsers>
    <parser href="">
      XmlTextReader
    </parser>
    <parser href="">
      XmlNodeReader
    </parser>
    <parser href="">
      XmlValidatingReader
    </parser>
  </parsers>
</net_xml>
```


INTRODUCTION

The Microsoft .NET platform is a new initiative designed by Microsoft to provide a broad framework for the creation of next generation applications. In many ways, .NET is Microsoft's answer to Sun's Java initiative. In this chapter, we will be focusing on the XML capabilities of .NET.

Because Java and .NET are such similar technologies, we will attempt to track the concepts and examples in a manner as similar as possible to Chapter 16, "Working with XML and Java." Although many of the interfaces are slightly different, as you will see they are similar enough that you should be able to convert code fairly easily between the two.

The .NET platform has several compelling features:

- Processor/Operating System Independence—Much like Java, .NET applications are not tied to one specific processor or operating system. Although the only currently available .NET implementation is from Microsoft for Windows, Microsoft is also developing an implementation for FreeBSD, and there are two initiatives for producing a .NET infrastructure under Linux: The Mono Project, available at `http://www.go-mono.com/`, and the DotGnu project, available at `http://www.gnu.org/projects/dotgnu/`.
- Language Independence—Although Sun's Java initiative is processor and operating system independent, the downside is that programmers are forced to use a single language (Java) to write their applications. Thankfully, Java is a great language, but different programmers prefer various types of languages. The Microsoft .NET runtime is designed to be completely language independent. So, if you prefer to write in the standard .NET language C#, that's great, but you can also write applications in Visual Basic, C++, Eiffel, Python, Perl, or even Fortran.
- Extensive Class Libraries—Probably the most compelling feature of the .NET platform is the thousands of libraries that are contained by default within the runtime system, called the *Common Language Runtime (CLR)*. This chapter focuses on the XML features

of the Common Language Runtime, but the CLR also contains classes for many common programming tasks like Windowing User Interfaces, Networking, Regular Expressions, Web Services, Cryptography, Multithreading, and the generation of Web User Interfaces.

- Native Support for Web Services—One of the largest and most controversial aspects of the .NET platform is the .NET My Services initiative (formerly named Hailstorm), which is Microsoft's vision for the next generation of application deployment. Under the .NET My Services infrastructure, applications would not be delivered to users directly via installers, but instead would be hosted on a centralized Microsoft server. Although this solution has many advantages, it is also a fundamentally different method of delivering software than programmers are used to, and there is some question as to how successful it will be. Luckily, whereas the My Services/Hailstorm component generated the most adverse reaction, the rest of the .NET platform can be used completely independently and provides a great environment for programmers to write next-generation applications.

.NET XML Framework Concepts

Although .NET is a new platform, Microsoft realizes that XML is a fundamentally important technology. So, .NET has been designed to contain extensive XML support right from the beginning. This chapter covers various techniques of working with XML via Microsoft's .NET Interfaces that programmers will need to help them achieve their desired results.

First, programmers need basic methods that allow the data contained within XML Documents to be parsed and accessed programmatically. There are two common approaches to this issue. The lower-level method cycles through the document reporting whenever a node is parsed. There are several standards for this method of parsing, such as the *Simple API for XML (SAX)*. Microsoft has chosen a custom mechanism for this type of parsing and implemented it with its `XmlReader` interface. With this parsing interface, the parser moves through the document on demand, informing the calling application what has most recently been parsed.

Document based parsing is the other common method for accessing data in an XML Document. The W3C has standardized an interface for this type of access in the *Document Object Model (DOM)*. DOM is discussed in detail in Chapter 14, "XML and the Document Object Model." Microsoft implements a variant of DOM with its `XmlDocument` interface.

Second, more advanced methods are required to allow parsed XML to be navigated and transformed. Navigation is accomplished with technologies such as XPath. Transformation is accomplished with implementations of XSLT, which allow the transformation of XML into various other formats such as HTML, PDF, or SVG. Both XPath and XSLT interfaces are included in .NET.

Finally, new more advanced technologies have recently become available that build on this foundation and enable higher level and more complex XML activities to be accomplished.

For instance, XML is now being commonly used as a standard protocol for communications between businesses, using specifications such as SOAP and XML-RPC.

CHOOSING A LANGUAGE FOR .NET

Because the Microsoft .NET platform supports a large variety of languages, programmers can access the .NET interfaces through whatever language they prefer. However, for the purposes of this chapter, one language has been chosen to focus on. That language is the Microsoft C# programming language, which is rapidly becoming the dominant language for .NET programming. Although the code examples will be discussed in C# format, all examples will also be provided in Visual Basic .NET format. The syntax of C# and Visual Basic .NET are relatively close, and those with Visual Basic experience should have no problems following the examples.

PARSING WITH THE .NET XmlReader CLASSES

Microsoft supplies three parsers that implement the `XmlReader` interface (see Figure 17.1):

- `XmlTextReader`—The simplest and most straightforward XML parser in .NET `XmlTextReader` is a one-pass, forward-only parser. `XmlTextReader` doesn't support validation, cannot expand general entities, and default attributes aren't made available. However, although it has several downsides, the `XmlTextReader` is an extremely fast and efficient parser.
- `XmlValidatingReader`—The `XmlValidatingReader` uses a parser like the `XmlTextReader` to add several extended features. First, the `XmlValidatingReader` validates the document against a Document Type Definition or XML Schema while the document is being parsed. In addition, it adds support for the expansion of general entities and attaches the default attributes specified in the Document Type Definition or Schema.
- `XmlNodeReader`—The `XmlNodeReader` parser is a fundamentally different parser in target usage than the standard `XmlTextReader` parser. The `XmlNodeReader` does not parse text documents into their equivalent XML form. Instead, it is used to read from XML documents that have already been parsed into a W3C Document Object Model (DOM) tree.

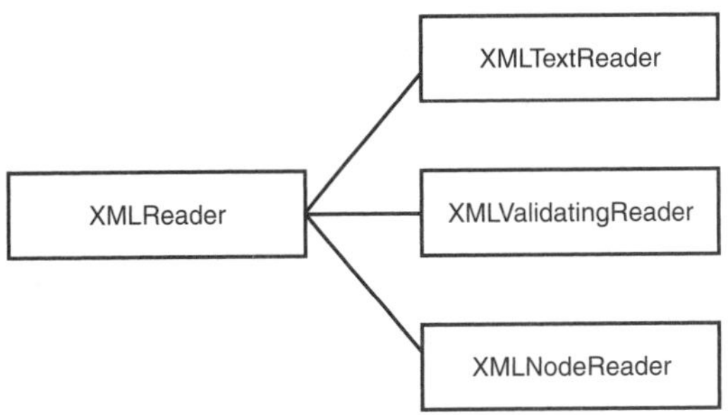

Figure 17.1
The Microsoft .NET `XmlReader` parsers.

PARSING WITH XmlTextReader

The simplest method of parsing XML with .NET is using the XmlTextReader class. This section provides an example of the use of XmlTextReader to accomplish basic parsing tasks. XmlTextReader is similar in functionality, though not in interface, to SAX, which is discussed in Chapter 15, "Parsing XML Based on Events." In this section, we will develop a simple application that reads all the nodes in the document, informing the user of all the elements in the documents and printing any text contained within them.

In order to parse XML documents with the .NET XmlTextReader class, we will first need to generate an instance of the XmlTextReader. This is done simply by passing the name of the document to be parsed—in this case passing "example.xml" to the XmlTextReader constructor:

```
XmlTextReader xmlTextReader = new XmlTextReader("example.xml");
```

Here, we are parsing a local file, but the XmlTextReader is extremely flexible. It can be passed in almost any type of W3C Universal Resource Identifier (URI). For example, if you wanted to parse a document on the Web located at "http://www.mylocalcompany.com/payroll.xml", you could instead use the following declaration:

```
XmlTextReader xmlTextReader =
➥new XmlTextReader("http://www.mylocalcompany.com/payroll.xml");
```

The XmlTextReader is a one-pass parser that moves forward through the supplied XML document node by node. Unlike SAX, which is event based, the XmlTextReader waits until the program asks for the next node to provide it. This has the advantage of letting the programmer decide when to parse the next section of the document because the programmer controls the flow of processing rather than responding to it.

The method called to inform the XmlTextReader to read the next node in the XML Document is the Read method of the XmlTextReader object.

```
xmlTextReader.Read()
```

For our example program, we'll want to read every node in the document, so the Read method call is placed in a while loop:

```
while ( xmlTextReader.Read() )
```

It's important to note that the Read method of the XmlTextReader object does not actually return any data. It's easiest to think of the XML parser in this case as an assembly line: The Read method merely moves the assembly line forward one step.

However, the XmlTextReader does make it extremely easy to get access to the currently parsed XML data. Whenever the Read method is called, the currently parsed XML data is placed into the XmlTextReader object that is in use, and that data is made available via the various properties of the XmlTextReader object (see Table 17.1).

TABLE 17.1 XmlTextReader PROPERTIES

AttributeCount	The number of attributes the current node contains
BaseURI	The base URI of the current node
CanResolveEntity	A boolean value indicating whether this reader can parse and resolve entities
Depth	The depth of the current node in the XML document
Encoding	The encoding attribute for this document
EOF	A value indicating whether XmlReader is positioned at the end of the stream
HasAttributes	A Boolean indicating whether the current node has any attributes
HasValue	A Boolean indicating whether the node can have a Value
IsDefault	A Boolean indicating if the current value was generated automatically by the DTD or schema
IsEmptyElement	A Boolean indicating whether the current element is an empty element (for example, <element/>)
Item	The value of the element's attribute with the specified index
LineNumber	The line number where the reader is currently
LinePosition	The line position where the reader is currently
LocalName	The current node's local name
Name	The current node's qualified name
Namespaces	A boolean value indicating whether namespaces are supported
NamespaceURI	The namespace URI (as defined by the W3C Namespace Specification) of the current node
NameTable	The XmlNameTable associated with this XmlTextReader
NodeType	The node type of the current node
Normalization	A boolean value indicating whether whitespace is normalized
Prefix	The current node's namespace prefix
QuoteChar	The type of quotation mark used to enclose the attribute node (if the current node is an attribute node)
ReadState	The current reader state
Value	The value of the current node as text
WhitespaceHandling	A property that specifies the manner in which whitespace is handled
XmlLang	The current scope according to the xml:lang specification
XmlResolver	A property that allows the XmlResolver used for DTD references to be modified
XmlSpace	The current scope according to the xml:space specification

17

For this example, it will be necessary to keep track of when an element is started, when an element is ended, and when a text node is available. In each of these cases, a process for determining the current type of the node is needed. The type of node that has just been parsed is stored in the `NodeType` property of the `XmlTextReader`. The `NodeType` property contains a value that matches the possible values of the `XmlNodeType` enumeration, which can have the values listed in Table 17.2.

TABLE 17.2 POSSIBLE `XmlNodeType` VALUES

Attribute	An XML attribute
CDATA	A CDATA section
Comment	A comment
Document	A Document object, which serves as the root of the entire XML Document
DocumentFragment	An association to a node or a subtree of another document
DocumentType	A Document Type Declaration
Element	An XML element. Specifically, the start of an XML element
EndElement	The end of an XML element
Entity	An Entity Declaration
EntityReference	An Entity Reference
None	The value of the `NodeType` property of `XmlReader` before the `Read()` method has been called to parse a document
Notation	A Document Type Declaration notation
ProcessingInstruction	An XML processing instruction
SignificantWhiteSpace	Whitespace that is placed between nodes if there is a mixed content model
Text	The text contained within an element
Whitespace	Insignificant whitespace placed between nodes
XMLDeclaration	An XML declaration node

Now that we're able to parse the documents into XML nodes and determine the type of each node, we're ready to print out the information desired for each node. The first type of node is the `Element`. Keep in mind that an element node doesn't contain the entire element; it is informing the program that the start of an element has been encountered (much like the SAX `StartElement` event handler). Specifically, the children of the current element have not yet been parsed and they will be encountered after further parsing. The name of the XML element that has been parsed is placed in the `Name` property of the `XmlTextReader`.

```
if (xmlTextReader.NodeType == XmlNodeType.Element)
{
  // Signal the start of the element
```

```
    Console.WriteLine("Start Element: " +  xmlTextReader.Name);
  }
```

The next type of node that the program needs to be watching for is the `Text` node. Whenever a text node is encountered, its contents are placed in the `Value` property of the `XmlTextReader`. As part of the example application, the text of a node needs to be printed, so the value of the `Text` node is printed out.

```
else if (xmlTextReader.NodeType == XmlNodeType.Text)
{
  Console.WriteLine(xmlTextReader.Value);
}
```

Finally, whenever the end of an element is reached, an `EndElement` node is placed in the `XmlTextReader`. The name of the XML element that is ending is placed in the `Name` property of the `XmlTextReader`.

```
else if (xmlTextReader.NodeType == XmlNodeType.EndElement)
{
  // Signal the end of the element
  Console.WriteLine("End Element: " + xmlTextReader.Name);
}
```

17

As it turns out, using the `XmlTextReader` interface is actually quite similar to using SAX. The main difference is that instead of the parser determining when the next node is to be parsed and then notifying the application, the application has direct control over the parsing of the next node. The full source code to this example is shown in Listing 17.1 (with the Visual Basic .NET version in Listing 17.2), and the output from the example is shown in Listing 17.3.

LISTING 17.1 C# XmlTextReader EXAMPLE

```
using System;
using System.Xml;
using System.Text;
class SimpleXmlTextReader
{
  static void Main(string[] args)
  {
    try
    {
      //Create an instance of the XMLTextReader.
      XmlTextReader xmlTextReader = new XmlTextReader("example.xml");
      // This method reads the XML file and generates the output
      Console.WriteLine("Start of Document");
      while ( xmlTextReader.Read() )
      {
        // Process a start of element node.
        if (xmlTextReader.NodeType == XmlNodeType.Element)
        {
          // Signal the start of the element
          Console.WriteLine("Start Element: " +  xmlTextReader.Name);
        }
        // Process a text node.
        else if (xmlTextReader.NodeType == XmlNodeType.Text)
```

LISTING 17.1 CONTINUED

```
        {
          //Add the text data to the output.
          Console.WriteLine(xmlTextReader.Value);
        }
        //Process an end of element node.
        else if (xmlTextReader.NodeType == XmlNodeType.EndElement)
        {
          // Signal the end of the element
          Console.WriteLine("End Element: " + xmlTextReader.Name);
        }
      } // End while loop
      xmlTextReader.Close();
    }
    catch (XmlException ex)
    {
      Console.WriteLine("An XML exception occurred: " + ex.ToString());
    }
    catch (Exception ex)
    {
      Console.WriteLine("A general exception occurred: " + ex.ToString());
    }

    Console.WriteLine("End of Document");
  }
} //End SimpleXmlTextReader
```

LISTING 17.2 VISUAL BASIC .NET `XmlTextReader` EXAMPLE

```
Imports System
Imports System.Xml
Imports System.Text
Module SimpleXmlTextReaderVB
  Sub Main()
    Try
      'Create an instance of the XMLTextReader.
      Dim xmlTextReader As XmlTextReader
      xmlTextReader = New XmlTextReader("example.xml")
      Console.WriteLine("Start of Document")
      ' Continually read the next element that is available in the parsed
      ' document until there are no more.
      Do While xmlTextReader.Read()
        ' Process a start of element node.
        If xmlTextReader.NodeType = XmlNodeType.Element Then
          ' Signal the start of the element
          Console.WriteLine("Start Element: " + xmlTextReader.Name)
          ' Process a text node.
        ElseIf xmlTextReader.NodeType = XmlNodeType.Text Then
          'Add the text data to the output.
          Console.WriteLine(xmlTextReader.Value)
          'Process an end of element node.
        ElseIf xmlTextReader.NodeType = XmlNodeType.EndElement Then
          ' Signal the end of the element
          Console.WriteLine("End Element: " + xmlTextReader.Name)
        End If
```

LISTING 17.2 CONTINUED

```
      Loop
      xmlTextReader.Close()
      Catch ex As XmlException
        Console.WriteLine("An XML exception occurred: " + ex.ToString())
      Catch ex As Exception
        Console.WriteLine("A general exception occurred: " + ex.ToString())
    End Try
    Console.WriteLine("Endt of Document")
  End Sub
End Module
```

LISTING 17.3 SAMPLE JAVA SAX APPLICATION OUTPUT

```
Start of Document
Start Element: net_xml
Start Element: standards
Start Element: standard
.NET Standards Documents
End Element: standard
Start Element: standard
Document Object Model(DOM)
End Element: standard
Start Element: standard
Simple API for XML(SAX)
End Element: standard
End Element: standards
Start Element: parsers
Start Element: parser
XmlTextReader
End Element: parser
Start Element: parser
XmlNodeReader
End Element: parser
Start Element: parser
XmlValidatingReader
End Element: parser
End Element: parsers
End Element: net_xml
End of Document
```


.NET PARSING WITH VALIDATION IN .NET WITH XmlValidatingReader

The `XmlTextReader` covered in the previous section is an extremely fast and efficient parser, but it does have the downside of not doing any validation of the XML document. The .NET XML architecture provides a higher-level parser called `XmlValidatingReader` that provides this functionality. We will investigate the `XmlValidatingReader` in this section and use it to create an example that checks the validity of a document using a DTD.

The `XmlValidatingReader` doesn't parse text directly. Instead, it relies on another `XmlReader` like `XmlTextReader` for that lower-level functionality. Because we've just covered the `XmlTextReader` in the last section, that is the parser we'll use for our example. Therefore, first a standard `XmlTextReader` is constructed.

```
XmlTextReader xmlTextReader = new XmlTextReader("example.xml");
```

Next, we create an `XmlValidatingReader`. Instead of passing the name of the file to be parsed into the `XmlValidatingReader` constructor, the `XmlTextReader` that will actually do the text parsing is passed into the constructor.

```
xmlValidatingReader xmlValidatingReader = new XmlValidatingReader(xmlTextReader);
```

Now we're ready to tell the `XmlValidatingReader` what type of validation we want to have done to the document. This is done by setting the `ValidationType` property of the `XmlValidatingReader` to the desired validation type. The `XmlValidatingReader` supports five types of validation:

- DTD—Validate the Document according to DTD.
- None—Do Not Validate the Document.
- Schema—Use an XSD schema to validate the document.
- XDR—Validate against an XML-Data Reduced Schema.
- Auto—Attempt to determine from the document what type of validation to use.

Note

In addition to supporting the W3C XSD schema standard, the Microsoft *XML Data Reduced (XDR)* schema standard is supported. The XDR schema standard is based on early W3C work on schemas. Although it is similar to XSD schemas, it is not compatible.

For our example, we will validate our document against a DTD.

```
xmlValidatingReader.ValidationType = ValidationType.DTD;
```

Handling Validation Errors

Validation handling is done with an event-based architecture, similar to SAX. The document is still parsed on demand as it was with the `XmlTextReader`. However, in order to receive notification that a validation error has occurred, a callback must be registered with the `XmlValidatingReader`. This is done by first generating a helper class that will be used to construct the callback. Because events are used to signal validation, a `Boolean` variable called `success` will be added to the class to keep track of whether a validation error has occurred:

```
class ValidationHelper
{
  public bool success = true;
}
```

Now we're ready to add the event handler. Under .NET, an event callback is called a *delegate* and is constructed from a reference to a method in a class. Therefore, a method to be called whenever a validation event needs to be added. This method takes two arguments.

- First, an `object` is passed to the handler containing the `object` that sent the event.
- Second, a `ValidationEventArgs` object is passed with information on the validation event that triggered the call. The `ValidationEventArgs` object contains a string property called `message` that includes the relevant validation error.

For this example, the event handler will signal that an error has occurred by writing the error message to the console. Finally, the event handler sets the success variable to false so that it can be checked later.

```
public void ValidationCallBack (object sender, ValidationEventArgs args)
{
  Console.WriteLine("Validation error:");
  Console.WriteLine(args.Message);
  Console.WriteLine();
  success = false;
}
```

17

Now that the validation handler has been constructed, it needs to be registered in the main program. This is done in .NET by constructing a `ValidationEventHandler` object that refers to the method that is to be called. First, an instance of the `ValidationHelper` class is created. Then a reference to the `ValidationCallBack` method is added to the list of handlers to be called by the `XmlValidatingReader` whenever a validation error occurs:

```
ValidationHelper validationHelper = new ValidationHelper();
xmlValidatingReader.ValidationEventHandler += new ValidationEventHandler
 (validationHelper.ValidationCallBack);
```

Validating the Document

Now that the mechanism for reporting errors has been put in place, we can go ahead and start parsing the document. This is done using the same method as the `XmlTextReader`: calling the `Read` method of the `XmlValidatingReader` object until there are no remaining nodes. In this case, we are only interested in validation, so a `while` loop is used to cycle over every node without acting on any of the nodes. This will work because validation errors are signaled as events to the `ValidationEventHandler`.

```
while ( xmlValidatingReader.Read() )  {    }
```

Now that the entire document has been parsed, we want to report back to the user whether validation was successful. Because we have a reference to the `ValidationHelper` object, all that needs to be done is to check the Boolean success variable inside that object and use it to report whether validation was successful or unsuccessful.

```
if (validationHelper.success == true)
  Console.WriteLine("Validation was successful");
else
  Console.WriteLine("Validation was unsuccessful");
```

The full C# code to this example is shown in Listing 17.4, and the equivalent Visual Basic .NET code is shown in Listing 17.5. If the sample document at the beginning of the chapter is used with this example, `"Validation was successful"` is reported. However, if we modify the example slightly to be invalid, as shown in Listing 17.6, the following validation errors are reported:

```
Validation error:
The required attribute 'href' is missing. An error occurred at file:
file://src/XmlValidatingReader/bin/Debug/example2.xml(18, 4).

Validation error:
Element 'parsers' has invalid content. Expected 'parser'. An error occurred at
file:file://src/XmlValidatingReader/bin/Debug/example2.xml(25, 4).

Validation error:
The 'extra' element is not declared. An error occurred at
file://src/XmlValidatingReader/bin/Debug/example2.xml(25, 4).

Validation was unsuccessful
```

LISTING 17.4 VALIDATING EXAMPLE IN C#

```
using System;
using System.Xml;
using System.Text;
using System.Xml.Schema;

namespace SimpleXmlValidatingReader
{
  class ValidationHelper
  {
    public bool success = true;
    public void ValidationCallBack (object sender, ValidationEventArgs args)
    {
      Console.WriteLine("Validation error:");
      Console.WriteLine(args.Message);
      Console.WriteLine();
      success = false;
    }
  }

  class SimpleXmlValidatingReader
  {
    static void Main(string[] args)
    {
      try
      {
        //Create an instance of the xmlValidatingReader.
        XmlTextReader xmlTextReader = new XmlTextReader("example2.xml");
        XmlValidatingReader xmlValidatingReader =
                      new XmlValidatingReader(xmlTextReader);
        xmlValidatingReader.ValidationType = ValidationType.DTD;

        // Add a validation handler to the Document
        ValidationHelper validationHelper = new ValidationHelper();
        xmlValidatingReader.ValidationEventHandler +=
```

LISTING 17.4 CONTINUED

```
                        new ValidationEventHandler
➥(validationHelper.ValidationCallBack);
        // Read through the entire document
        while ( xmlValidatingReader.Read() )  {    }
        xmlValidatingReader.Close();

        // Report whether validation was successful
        if (validationHelper.success == true)
          Console.WriteLine("Validation was successful");
        else
          Console.WriteLine("Validation was unsuccessful");
      }
      catch (XmlException ex)
      {
        Console.WriteLine("An XML exception occurred: " + ex.ToString());
      }
      catch (Exception ex)
      {
        Console.WriteLine("A general exception occurred: " + ex.ToString());
      }
    }
  }
}
```


LISTING 17.5 VALIDATING EXAMPLE IN VISUAL BASIC .NET

```
Imports System
Imports System.Xml
Imports System.Text
Imports System.Xml.Schema

Module XmlValidatingReaderVB

  Public Class ValidationHelper
    Public success As Boolean = True
    Public Sub ValidationCallBack(ByVal sender As Object,
➥ByVal args As ValidationEventArgs)
      Console.WriteLine("Validation error:")
      Console.WriteLine(args.Message)
      Console.WriteLine()
      success = False
    End Sub
  End Class

  Public Class SimpleXmlValidatingReader
    Public Shared Sub Main()
      Try
        'Create an instance of the xmlValidatingReader.
        Dim xmlTextReader As XmlTextReader
        xmlTextReader = New XmlTextReader("example2.xml")

        Dim xmlValidatingReader As XmlValidatingReader
        xmlValidatingReader = New XmlValidatingReader(xmlTextReader)
        xmlValidatingReader.ValidationType = ValidationType.DTD
```

LISTING 17.5 CONTINUED

```
        ' Add a validation handler to the Document
        Dim validationHelper As ValidationHelper
        validationHelper = New ValidationHelper()
        AddHandler xmlValidatingReader.ValidationEventHandler, AddressOf
➥validationHelper.ValidationCallBack

        ' Read through the entire document
        While xmlValidatingReader.Read()
        End While
        xmlValidatingReader.Close()

        ' Report whether validation was successful
        If validationHelper.success = True Then
          Console.WriteLine("Validation was successful")
        Else
          Console.WriteLine("Validation was unsuccessful")
        End If
        Catch ex As XmlException
          Console.WriteLine("An XML exception occurred: " + ex.ToString())
        Catch ex As Exception
          Console.WriteLine("A general exception occurred: " + ex.ToString())
      End Try
    End Sub
  End Class
End Module
```

LISTING 17.6 SAMPLE INVALID DOCUMENT

```
<?xml version="1.0" ?>
<!DOCTYPE net_xml [
  <!ELEMENT net_xml        (standards, parsers)>
  <!ELEMENT standards (standard)+>
  <!ELEMENT parsers (parser)+>
  <!ELEMENT parser (#PCDATA)>
  <!ELEMENT standard (#PCDATA)>
  <!ATTLIST parser
      href     CDATA    #REQUIRED
  >
  <!ATTLIST standard
      href     CDATA    #REQUIRED
  >
]>
<net_xml>
  <standards>
    <standard>.NET Standards Documents</standard>
    <standard href="http://www.w3.org/DOM/">Document Object Model(DOM)</standard>
    <standard href="http://www.saxproject.org/">Simple API for XML(SAX)</standard>
  </standards>
  <parsers>
    <parser href="">XmlTextReader</parser>
    <parser href="">XmlNodeReader</parser>
    <extra>bogus element</extra>
  </parsers>
</net_xml>
```

DOCUMENT-BASED PARSING WITH DOM UNDER .NET

Although event-based parsing is fast and memory efficient, as you saw in the previous sections, it doesn't provide any context for where the current element is in the hierarchy of the document. This is due to the fact that parsing via a parser like `XmlTextReader` is effectively a one-shot operation: The parser only knows about the current element after each call is made to the `XmlTextReader.Read()` method and then promptly forgets about it.

For applications in which it is useful to have the parser remember more contextual information, using a parser that implements DOM is appropriate. DOM has the advantage of storing a complete copy of the XML document in memory at all times, allowing programmers to traverse through the hierarchy of elements without worrying about keeping track of the state of the document. This has the advantage of providing a much higher-level interface to XML documents than a SAX interface, but at a serious efficiency and memory cost, because all the information from the document must be stored in memory.

This section provides an example of working with DOM in .NET. For more specific information on the Document Object Model and its interfaces, see Chapter 14.

CREATING A DOM IMPLEMENTATION

In order to parse XML documents with DOM, we first need a method to generate a DOM implementation. With .NET the DOM implementation is called `XmlDocument`, which represents an entire parsed DOM document. The DOM implementation, however, is not its own parser. In fact, much like the `XMLValidatingReader`, it relies on a lower-level parser like the `XmlTextReader` to actually generate the parsed data for it. That's exactly what will be done in this example. First, an `XmlTextReader` is created for the example document.

```
XmlTextReader xmlReader = new XmlTextReader("example.xml");
```

Note

Although `XmlDocument` does provide an implementation of the Document Object Model, many of the methods and properties have been changed to better fit into the .NET framework. For instance, many of the DOM data types begin with the prefix "Xml," all of them begin with uppercase letters, and many methods that are used to get and set values are changed into .NET properties–as is the case here in which the DOM `getDocumentElement` method has been changed to the `DocumentElement` property. See the .NET Framework SDK Documentation for more details.

Next, the `XmlTextReader` is used to generate a DOM-based `XmlDocument`. The `XmlDocument` is created.

```
XmlDocument xmlDocument = new XmlDocument();
```

Then the `XmlDocument` uses the `XmlTextReader` to load the sample document:

```
xmlDocument.Load(xmlReader);
```

The `Load` method of the `XmlDocument` actually signals the DOM implementation to go through the entire XML document and place it into an in-memory representation of the DOM tree, where the nodes of the DOM document can be accessed via the properties of the `XmlDocument`. The properties available to `XmlDocument` are shown in Table 17.3. Only the properties declared by the `XmlDocument` class are shown. `XmlDocument` is inherited from `XmlNode`, and therefore includes the properties from that class as well. See the .NET Framework SDK documentation for more information.

TABLE 17.3 `XmlDocument` MEMBERS

`BaseURI`	The current node's base Universal Resource Identifier (URI)
`DocumentElement`	The root element (of type `XmlElement`) of the current document
`DocumentType`	The node containing the document's `DOCTYPE` declaration
`Implementation`	The current document's `XmlImplementation` object
`InnerXml`	The contained text that represents all the children of the current node
`IsReadOnly`	A Boolean indicating whether the current node is read-only
`LocalName`	The current node's local name
`Name`	The current node's qualified name
`NameTable`	The `XmlNameTable` associated with this `XmlDocument`
`NodeType`	The node type of the current node
`OwnerDocument`	The parent `XmlDocument` that contains the current node
`PreserveWhitespace`	A Boolean indicating whether whitespace is preserved
`XmlResolver`	A property that allows the `XmlResolver` used for DTD references to be modified

This `XMLDocument` object represents an in-memory representation of the entire XML document. There are various methods for querying the `XMLDocument` object for metadata about the XML document that has been parsed. See Chapter 14 if you are interested in more detailed information about these interfaces. For our example, we start by retrieving the root node of the document. This is referred to by the DOM specification (somewhat confusingly) as the Document Element, and is retrieved by the `DocumentElement` property:

```
XmlElement root_element = xmlDocument.DocumentElement;
```

Now that the root element of the document has been retrieved, we can use DOM to find out some specific information from our sample XML file. If you refer to the sample file at the beginning of the chapter, you will notice that an XML element called `<standards>` contains several children `<standard>` elements which each name a standard in the text of the element and provide the Web address for each of them in the `href` attribute of the element. Let's add to our example the ability to print out the information for each of those standards.

First, a list of all the elements with the name `"standards"` needs to be retrieved. This is done with the DOM method `GetElementsByTagName`, which returns an `XmlNodeList` that contains all the elements.

```
XmlNodeList standards_list = root_element.GetElementsByTagName("standards");
```

For this example, there is only one `<standards>` element in the document, so the `item` method of the `XmlNodeList` can be called to retrieve the first element in the node list. Note that DOM specifies that a `node list` contains DOM nodes. However, in this case we know ahead of time that the node is actually a element. Therefore, a C# typecast is used to convert the returned `XmlNode` into an `XmlElement`:

```
XmlElement standards_element = (XmlElement) standards_list.Item(0);
```

Now we have a handle on the `<standards>` element, which can then be used to navigate to all of its children. In this case, they are all a group of individual elements with the name `<standard>`. Therefore, we use the `GetElementsByTagName` method again, but in this case we find all `<standard>` elements:

17

```
XmlNodeList children = standards_element.GetElementsByTagName("standard");
```

Unlike the previous use of `GetElementsByTagName`, where there was only one element to be retrieved, in this case several different elements need to be visited because the `<standards>` element contains several `<standard>` elements. Therefore, the `Count` property of the `XmlNodeList` object is accessed, which returns the number of elements that are contained in the `node list`. This value is then used to cycle through returned children via a C# "`for`" loop:

```
for (int n=0; n<children.Count; n++) {
```

Upon each pass through the `for` loop, the `XmlNodeList Item()` method is used to select the current element in the list:

```
XmlElement standard = (XmlElement)children.Item(n);
```

Next we want to print out the names of each of the standards. We start by notifying the user that the standards' names will be printed.

```
Console.Write("The standard named: \n\t");
```

At this point, the process becomes slightly more complicated. The name of each standard is represented as text contained within each `<standard>` element. We need to iterate over the child nodes of each `<standard>` element, looking for text nodes and then appending them to the result string:

```
String value = "";
XmlNodeList child = standard.ChildNodes;
for(int i = 0; i < child.Count; i++ )
{
  XmlNode current_child = child.Item(i);
  if( current_child.NodeType ==  XmlNodeType.Text )
  {
```

```
      value = value + current_child.Value;
    }
  }
  Console.WriteLine(value);
```

This process is very similar to the one that was previously used to navigate into the children of the `<standard>` and `<standards>` elements. However, one important difference to note is the use of the `NodeType` property of the DOM `Node`, which in this case is used to discover whether the current node is a text node. (For a list of `Node` types, see Table 17.2 in the previous section.) If it is, the value of the `Node` (obtained via the `Value` property) is used to add that text to the current `String`. If it is not a text node, it is ignored.

Finally, for each `<standard>` element, the Web address for each standard is printed. Retrieving attributes from the DOM in C# is much easier than retrieving text. Each `Element` object has a `getAttribute` method that, when given the name of an attribute, returns the text value of that attribute. This method is used here to find the value of the `"href"` attribute for each element and print it to the console.

```
Console.Write("Can be accessed on the web at: \n\t");
String href = standard.Attributes.GetNamedItem("href").Value;
Console.WriteLine(href);
```

The full source code to this example is shown in Listing 17.7, the Visual Basic .NET version is shown in Listing 17.8, and the output from the example is shown in Listing 17.9.

LISTING 17.7 DOM EXAMPLE IN C#

```
using System;
using System.Xml;
namespace SimpleDom
{
  class SimpleDom
  {
    static void Main(string[] args)
    {
      try
      {
        // Create an instance of the XMLTextReader for use with the XmlDocument
        XmlTextReader xmlReader = new XmlTextReader("example.xml");
        // Generate the XmlDocument object
        XmlDocument xmlDocument = new XmlDocument();
        // Load (and parse) the Document via the XmlTextReader object
        xmlDocument.Load(xmlReader);
        // All DOM objects have an "Xml" prefix added to them
        // All uppercase as well, and many are properties instead of methods
        // Get the Root Element of the Document
        XmlElement root_element = xmlDocument.DocumentElement;
        // Get a list of all elements with the name "standard"
        XmlNodeList standards_list =
                   root_element.GetElementsByTagName("standards");
        // Take the first element with the name "standard" and get all
        // of its children named "standards"
        XmlElement standards_element = (XmlElement) standards_list.Item(0);
        XmlNodeList children =
```

LISTING 17.7 CONTINUED

```
                    standards_element.GetElementsByTagName("standard");
        // Cycle through the NodeList containing elements named standards
        for (int n=0; n<children.Count; n++)
        {
          // Get each individual standard element one at a time
          XmlElement standard = (XmlElement)children.Item(n);
          Console.Write("The standard named: \n\t");
          String value = "";
          // Collect the text beneath each node
          XmlNodeList child = standard.ChildNodes;
          for(int i = 0; i < child.Count; i++ )
          {
            XmlNode current_child = child.Item(i);
            // If a node is a Text Node then it is part of the standard name
            if( current_child.NodeType ==  XmlNodeType.Text )
            {
              value = value + current_child.Value;
            }
          }
          Console.WriteLine(value);
          Console.Write("Can be accessed on the web at: \n\t");
          // Print out the standard location, which is contained as an attribute
          String href = standard.Attributes.GetNamedItem("href").Value; ""
          Console.WriteLine(href);
          Console.WriteLine();
        }
        xmlReader.Close();
      }
      catch (XmlException e)
      {
        Console.WriteLine("An XML exception occurred: " + e.ToString());
      }
      catch (Exception e)
      {
        Console.WriteLine("A general exception occurred: " + e.ToString());
      }
    }
  }
}
```

LISTING 17.8 DOM EXAMPLE IN VISUAL BASIC .NET

```
Imports System.Xml
Module SimpleDomVB
  Sub Main()
    Try
      ' Create an instance of the XMLTextReader for use with the XmlDocument
    Dim xmlReader As XmlTextReader
    xmlReader = New XmlTextReader("example.xml")
    ' Generate the XmlDocument object
    Dim xmlDocument As XmlDocument
    xmlDocument = New XmlDocument()
    ' Load (and parse) the Document via the XmlTextReader object
    xmlDocument.Load(xmlReader)
```

17

LISTING 17.8 CONTINUED

```
    ' Get the Root Element of the Document
    Dim root_element As XmlElement
    root_element = xmlDocument.DocumentElement
    ' Get a list of all elements with the name "standard"
    Dim standards_list As XmlNodeList
    standards_list = root_element.GetElementsByTagName("standards")
    ' Take the first element with the name "standard" and get all of its
➥children named "standards"
    Dim standards_element As XmlElement
    standards_element = standards_list.Item(0)
    Dim children As XmlNodeList
    children = standards_element.GetElementsByTagName("standard")
    ' Cycle through the NodeList containing elements named standards
    Dim n As Int16
      For n = 0 To children.Count - 1
        ' Get each individual standard element one at a time
        Dim standard As XmlElement
        standard = children.Item(n)
        Console.WriteLine("The standard named: ")
        Dim value As String
        value = ""
        ' Collect the text beneath each node
        Dim child As XmlNodeList
        child = standard.ChildNodes
        Dim i As Int16
        For i = 0 To child.Count - 1
          Dim current_child As XmlNode
          current_child = child.Item(i)
          ' If a node is a Text Node then it is part of the standard name
          If current_child.NodeType = XmlNodeType.Text Then
            value = value + current_child.Value
          End If
        Next
        Console.WriteLine(value)
        Console.WriteLine("Can be accessed on the web at: ")
        ' Print out the standard location, which is contained as an attribute
        Dim href As String
        href = standard.Attributes.GetNamedItem("href").Value '""
        Console.WriteLine(href)
        Console.WriteLine()
      Next
      xmlReader.Close()
    Catch e As XmlException
      Console.WriteLine("An XML exception occurred: " + e.ToString())
    Catch e As Exception
      Console.WriteLine("A general exception occurred: " + e.ToString())
    End Try
  End Sub
End Module
```

LISTING 17.9 DOM EXAMPLE OUTPUT

```
The standard named:
  .NET Standards Documents
Can be accessed on the web at:
  http://www.dotnetexperts.com/ecma/index.html
The standard named:
  Document Object Model(DOM)
Can be accessed on the web at:
  http://www.w3.org/DOM/
The standard named:
  Simple API for XML(SAX)
Can be accessed on the web at:
  http://www.saxproject.org/
```


XML TRANSFORMATIONS IN .NET

A crucial component of the .NET XML framework is the ability to programmatically transform XML documents via XSLT. XSLT transformations are covered in detail in Chapter 9, "Transforming XML Data Into Other Formats with XSLT." This section focuses on methods for using .NET to produce these XSLT transformations.

The .NET XML Framework provides an easy to use and efficient method for doing XSLT transformations in .NET. As an example, we will build a small application that transforms the sample XML file from the beginning of this chapter into HTML. The XSLT file that will be used for this example is shown in Listing 17.10. This XSLT transformer takes our sample XML file and turns it into an HTML file that prints out all the standards listed in the document.

LISTING 17.10 SAMPLE XSLT STYLE SHEET

```
<?xml version="1.0"?>
<xsl:stylesheet xmlns:xsl="http://www.w3.org/1999/XSL/Transform" version="1.0">
<xsl:template match="/">
  <html>
  <head>
  <title>Example Transformation</title>
  </head>
  <body>
  <center>
  <h1>Example Transformation</h1>
  </center>
  <xsl:apply-templates/>
  </body>
  </html>
</xsl:template>
```

LISTING 17.10 CONTINUED

```
<xsl:template match="standard">
  <h1>Standard</h1>
  <h2><xsl:value-of select="."/></h2>
</xsl:template>

<xsl:template match="parser">
  <h1>Parser</h1>
  <h2><xsl:value-of select="."/></h2>
</xsl:template>
</xsl:stylesheet>
```

The first step to doing a transformation is to generate an `XmlReader`, much as we did when generating a DOM `XmlDocument`. This is a common theme in the .NET XML interfaces. By allowing the programmer to specify which parser they want to use to generate the output for the various operations to perform on them, greater flexibility is obtained.

```
XmlReader xmlReader = new XmlTextReader("example.xml");
```

The `XslTransform` object, whose members are listed in Table 17.4, does the work of XSLT transformation in .NET. The `XslTransform` does not know natively how to traverse a parsed XML document; instead it needs a programmatic method to navigate that document's XML hierarchy. This functionality is provided by the `XPathDocument`, which is discussed in more detail in the next section. However, for an XSLT transformation, all that is necessary is to generate an `XPathDocument` based on the just-created `XmlReader`.

```
XPathDocument xpathDocument = new XPathDocument(xmlReader);
```

TABLE 17.4 `XslTransform` MEMBERS

XmlResolver	A property that allows the `XmlResolver` used for DTD references to be modified
Load	Method that loads the desired XSLT style sheet
Transform	Method that actually performs the specified XSLT transformation

Now we are ready to start working with the `XslTransform` transformation engine. The first step is to create an `XslTransform` object to be used:

```
XslTransform xslTransform = new XslTransform();
```

Now the example document is loaded into the `XslTransform` object. In this case, the sample file is used, but any valid system URL is acceptable.

```
xslTransform.Load("example.xslt");
```

Finally, we're ready to actually run the transformation. This is done with a call to the `Transform` method of the `XslTransform` object. The first argument passed to the method is the `XPathDocument` object to navigate the loaded document; the second is a list of arguments to be passed from your program into the XSLT transformer (such as default variables, and so on). In this case there are none, so the value is set to `null`. Finally, a stream is passed into the method to inform the transformer where to send the output. Here, the System Console is used.

```
xslTransform.Transform(xpathDocument, null, Console.Out);
```

That's all the code necessary to implement an XSLT transformation in .NET. The full implementation of C# code for this example is contained in Listing 17.11, and the equivalent Visual Basic .NET code is contained in Listing 17.12. The HTML output generated by the transformation example is provided in Listing 17.13, and finally the output displayed in a Web browser is contained in Figure 17.2.

17

Listing 17.11 C# XSLT Example

```
using System;
using System.Xml;
using System.Xml.XPath;
using System.Xml.Xsl;
public class TransformationUtility
{
  public static void Main(String[] args)
  {
    try
    {
      // Create an instance of the XMLTextReader for use with the XpathDocument
      XmlReader xmlReader = new XmlTextReader("example.xml");
      // Generate an XPathDocumentObject to run the Transformation against
      XPathDocument xpathDocument = new XPathDocument(xmlReader);
      // Create the XslTransform Object
      XslTransform xslTransform = new XslTransform();
      // Load the Exaple XSLT Stylesheet into the transformation Engine
      xslTransform.Load("example.xslt");
      // Call the Transform method of the transformation engine with the output
      // sent to the console
      xslTransform.Transform(xpathDocument, null,
➥new XmlTextWriter(Console.Out));
    }
    catch(XmlException e)
    {
      Console.WriteLine("Transformation error: " + e.ToString());
    }
  }
}
```

Listing 17.12 XSLT Visual Basic .NET Example

```
Imports System
Imports System.Xml
Imports System.Xml.XPath
Imports System.Xml.Xsl
Module SimpleTransformVB
  Sub Main()
    Try
      ' Create an instance of the XMLTextReader for use with the XpathDocument
```

LISTING 17.12 CONTINUED

```
      Dim xmlReader As XmlReader
      xmlReader = New XmlTextReader("example.xml")
      ' Generate an XPathDocumentObject to run the Transformation against
      Dim xPathDocument As XPathDocument
      xPathDocument = New XPathDocument(xmlReader)
      ' Create the XslTransform Object
      Dim xslTransform As XslTransform
      xslTransform = New XslTransform()
      ' Load the Example XSLT Stylesheet into the transformation Engine
      xslTransform.Load("example.xslt")
      ' Call the Transform method of the transformation engine with the
      '  output sent to the console
      xslTransform.Transform(xPathDocument, Nothing, Console.Out)
    Catch e As XmlException
      Console.WriteLine("Transformation error: " + e.ToString())
    End Try
  End Sub
End Module
```

LISTING 17.13 HTML OUTPUT FROM XSLT EXAMPLE

```
<html>
 <head>
   <META http-equiv="Content-Type" content="text/html">
   <title>Example Transformation</title>
 </head>
 <body>
   <center>
     <h1>Example Transformation</h1>
   </center>
   <h1>Standard</h1>
   <h2>.NET Standards Documents</h2>
   <h1>Standard</h1>
   <h2>Document Object Model(DOM)</h2>
   <h1>Standard</h1>
   <h2>Simple API for XML(SAX)</h2>
   <h1>Parser</h1>
   <h2>XmlTextReader</h2>
   <h1>Parser</h1>
   <h2>XmlNodeReader</h2>
   <h1>Parser</h1>
   <h2>XmlValidatingReader</h2>
 </body>
```

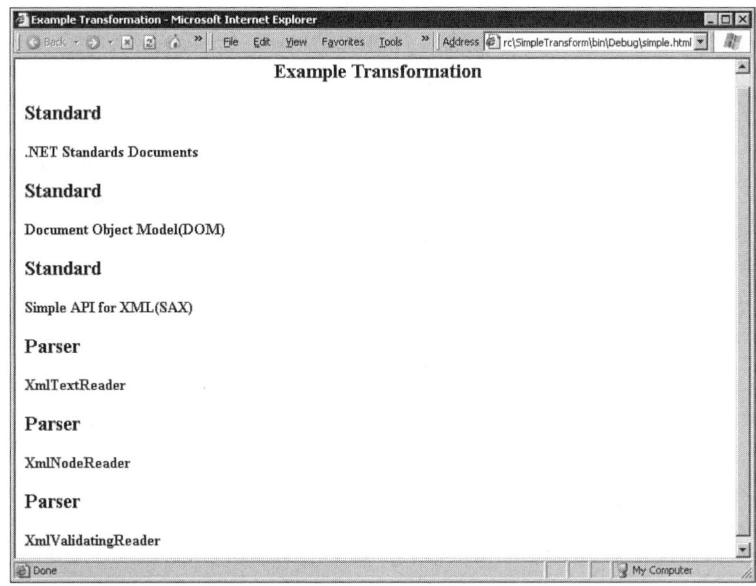

Figure 17.2
The XSLT example displayed in Internet Explorer.

NAVIGATING THE DOCUMENT VIA XPATH IN .NET

An important method for navigating XML documents is via XPath. XPath is a non-XML based specification for addressing arbitrary locations in XML documents. The XPath syntax is described in detail in Chapter 11, "Locating Components in XML Documents with XPath." A basic usage of XPath with .NET is provided in this section.

Using XPath via the .NET XML interfaces is a straightforward process. The XPath interfaces require an XML parser that has been instantiated against the desired document in order to do their work. The first step to doing an XPath addressing is to generate an `XmlReader`, much as we did when generating an `XmlDocument`.

```
XmlReader xmlReader = new XmlTextReader("example.xml");
```

Next, an `XPathDocument` object is created. This `XPathDocument` object creates the foundation for the execution of XPath expressions. Then, this `XPathDocument` object is used to create an `XPathNavigator` object.

```
XPathDocument xpathDocument = new XPathDocument(xmlReader);
XPathNavigator xpathNavigator = xpathDocument.CreateNavigator();
```

This `XPathNavigator` object is actually used to execute the desired XPath expression. In this case, we will use the following XPath expression: `"//standards/standard"`. This XPath expression will return all the XML elements named `"standard"` that are children of the "standards" element. The method used to run the XPath expression is the Select method of the XPathNavigator:

```
XPathNodeIterator xpathNodeIterator =
➥xpathNavigator.Select("//standards/standard");
```

Now that the results have been generated, we need to access them. The process of accessing the results is straightforward, and very similar to the process that we used earlier for the XmlTextReader. The XPathNodeIterator contains a MoveNext method that can be used to move sequentially through the results. We will use this inside a while loop to loop over all the matched nodes:

```
while (xpathNodeIterator.MoveNext()) {
```

Similarly to the XmlTextReader, each of the matched elements is available inside the XPathNodeIterator after each call to MoveNext. Because our XPath expression queries for <standard> elements, we know ahead of time that elements will be returned and will have an "href" attribute. So, the name of each returned standard is printed as well as its href.

```
Console.WriteLine(xpathNodeIterator.Current.Name);
Console.WriteLine(xpathNodeIterator.Current.GetAttribute("href", ""));
```

The full C# implementation of code for this example is contained in Listing 17.14, and the equivalent Visual Basic .NET code is provided in Listing 17.15. The console output generated by this example is provided in Listing 17.16.

LISTING 17.14 C# XPATH EXAMPLE

```
using System;
using System.Xml;
using System.Xml.XPath;
namespace SimpleXpath
{
  class SimpleXpath
  {
    static void Main(string[] args)
    {
      // Create an instance of the XMLTextReader for use with the XpathDocument
      XmlReader xmlReader = new XmlTextReader("example.xml");
      // Generate an XPathDocumentObject to run the XPath expression against
      XPathDocument xpathDocument = new XPathDocument(xmlReader);
      // Create an XPathNavigator to actually execute the XPath expression
      XPathNavigator xpathNavigator = xpathDocument.CreateNavigator();
      XPathNodeIterator xpathNodeIterator =
➥xpathNavigator.Select("//standards/standard");
      // Iterate through the results that show the element name and
      // the href attribute for each standard element
      while (xpathNodeIterator.MoveNext())
      {
        Console.WriteLine(xpathNodeIterator.Current.Name);
        Console.WriteLine(xpathNodeIterator.Current.GetAttribute("href", ""));
      }
    }
  }
}
```

LISTING 17.15 XPATH VISUAL BASIC .NET EXAMPLE

```
Imports System
Imports System.Xml
Imports System.Xml.XPath
Module SimpleXpathVB
  Sub Main()
    ' Create an instance of the XMLTextReader for use with the XpathDocument
    Dim xmlReader As XmlReader
    xmlReader = New XmlTextReader("example.xml")
    ' Generate an XPathDocumentObject to run the XPath expression against
    Dim xPathDocument As XPathDocument
    xPathDocument = New XPathDocument(xmlReader)
    ' Create an XPathNavigator to actually execute the XPath expression
    Dim xPathNavigator As XPathNavigator
    xPathNavigator = xPathDocument.CreateNavigator()
    Dim xPathNodeIterator As XPathNodeIterator
    xPathNodeIterator = xPathNavigator.Select("//standards/standard")
    ' Iterate through the results that show the element name and the href
    ' attribute for each standard element
    Do While xPathNodeIterator.MoveNext()
      Console.WriteLine(xPathNodeIterator.Current.Name)
      Console.WriteLine(xPathNodeIterator.Current.GetAttribute("href", ""))
    Loop
  End Sub
End Module
```


LISTING 17.16 XPATH SAMPLE OUTPUT

```
standard
http://www.dotnetexperts.com/ecma/index.html
standard
http://www.w3.org/DOM/
standard
http://www.saxproject.org/
```

ADDITIONAL RESOURCES

Because .NET is such a new technology, it's a great idea to use Web resources to stay up-to-date. A number of excellent resources are available on the Web for learning about .NET and XML:

- The Microsoft .NET Framework Home Page (`http://msdn.microsoft.com/netframework/`) is the definitive .NET resource. It contains many .NET resources, including tools and many technical articles to facilitate development.
- GotDotNet (`http://www.gotdotnet.com/`) is a .NET advocacy page with many technical articles and links to third-party tools and technologies.
- Microsoft Developer Network (MSDN) .NET Development (`http://msdn.microsoft.com/net/`) contains many high-level articles about developing for .NET.

- The Visual Studio .NET Home Page (`http://msdn.microsoft.com/vstudio/`) is a great resource for articles about, and add-ons to, Visual Studio, Microsoft's premier .NET Development tool.

ROADMAP

Now that we've covered working with XML from Microsoft's new .NET technologies, we will take a look at how to work with XML from the popular Web scripting language Perl in Chapter 18, "XML and Databases." Perl has a great variety of different modules and parsers to work with XML, which are discussed in the next chapter.

Chapter 18 concludes the introduction to XML Programming and Scripting, and we will then move on to Part V, "Real World XML."

PART V

Real World XML

CHAPTER 18

XML AND DATABASES

In this chapter

by Earl Bingham

XML and databases have an interesting relationship because XML documents organize data and style, and databases have been designed to store data and semantics.

Often relational databases that work with XML are referred to as XML-Enabled Databases because they have extensions that allow them to seamlessly transfer data between themselves and XML documents. Database vendors have been around for a long time and have developed mature repositories that can store your XML content. Each of the major database vendors have developed comprehensive XML solutions to work with XML-related content in their databases. In addition to the normal operations you can do with the data using the databases or with the DOM and SAX APIs, easy-to-use components are also provided by the major software vendors.

XML and Databases—Introduction to the History of Their Relationship

After the initial XML 1.0 specification in January 1998, a number of companies started offering various mechanisms to input or process XML data into their corresponding databases. These have taken a long time to mature to stable products that can be used for real-world applications. Implementations that are doing a lot of real-world problem solving have only been available for the past year or so.

XML and databases are often needed for complex messaging that takes place between enterprise applications. XML can assist in abstracting the complexities of the communication. XML's hierarchical structure allows for an infinite number of permutations of the XML message to be constructed. If a new set of data needs to be added to the communication between two systems, an element can be inserted into the schema associated with the communication.

Using XML documents can also be beneficial in debugging complex messaging problems that take place because you can easily debug the message.

Now you see large deployments of XML and database usage through the technology marketplace. By accessing the Internet, you can see these XML databases available for evaluation download. At the end of the chapter, you will find a list of related links and references.

In this chapter, we will go into how XML and databases can be used together by providing examples with some of the leading databases available. All the products discussed can be freely downloaded for evaluation.

By reviewing each of the XML API offerings these vendors have developed, you will have an understanding of what is available and which is the better solution to use.

Working with XML as Data

When working with XML, you often want to have a system that can handle a large number of XML documents. XML documents can be classified into two areas: document-centric

XML documents and data-centric XML documents. Both have a different design philosophy associated with them. *Document-centric* XML documents are for presentation and human-readable format. *Data-centric* XML documents are for messaging and transaction management. They can have attributes of each other, but the design is fundamentally different in various aspects.

Document-Centric XML Documents

XML files that have presentation information associated with them are normally considered document-centric XML documents. Normally, these XML documents will be viewed or edited by humans. The entire structure and syntax is stored in your database repository. Document-centric design involves a liberal use of free-form text that is "marked up" with elements.

Examples of document-centric XML documents include XHTML, WML, cHTML, and voiceXML documents.

Data-Centric XML Documents

XML documents used for transmitting information are considered data-centric XML documents. These documents are not designed to be human readable, but for machine-to-machine communication. The messages sent and received from other subsystems in an enterprise would be qualified as data-centric XML documents. These documents usually just have data needed to process a specific event.

Examples of data-centric documents include SOAP, WSDL, ebXML, and Rosettanet documents.

Are document-centric better than data-centric documents? Sometimes there's no obvious answer. Most XML documents should typically be data-centric.

XML and Relational Databases

When constructing the logical data design of the actual data you're using, there is a number of items to consider. SQL databases and XML documents have a set of similarities that can be used to associate specific data with the XML representation of that data.

As you construct your logical data model, the first step is to identify the entities that are going to be modeled. *Entities* can be any person, place, thing, or concept. These entities are analogous to structural elements in an XML database.

The next step would be to identify individual data points that are used to describe the entities we defined earlier. These are normally referred to as *attributes*, in which they are associated "adjectives" that describe elements.

Relationships in XML can be expressed in various ways. One mechanism is called structural containment, which could be a one-to-one relationship or a one-to-many relationship. The following XML represents a one-to-more relationship:

```
<PressReleases>
    <Article> Company Goes Public </Article>
    <Article> Company's Stock Soars! </Article>
    <Article> Company's Releases 3rd Quarter Earnings </Article>
    <Article> Company's Shares Double After Earnings Statement </Article>
</PressReleases>
```

This same XML document can be enhanced to have associated attributes. Each article element has an associated ID attribute. There is a one-to-one relationship with the ID attribute and the article element:

```
<PressReleases>
    <Article ID="0012"> Company Goes Public </Article>
    <Article ID="0023"> Company's Stock Soars! </Article>
    <Article ID="0156"> Company's Releases 3rd Quarter Earnings </Article>
    <Article ID="0345"> Company's Shares Double After Earnings Statement
    </Article>
</PressReleases>
```

This attribute can be used for indexing content so that specific content can be retrieved quickly, providing an infrastructure for versioning and time critical information.

MAPPING XML DATA TO RELATIONAL DATABASES

To map XML data to relational databases, you must define the associated data that is going to be represented in both formats. For database designers, this represents table structures of the data. Here is an example:

```
CREATE TABLE PressRelease (
    PressReleaseKey integer IDENTITY PRIMARY KEY,
    PressReleaseTitle varchar(30),
    PressReleaseDate datetime)
CREATE TABLE Article (
    ArticleKey integer IDENTITY PRIMARY KEY,
    Paragraphs varchar(10000))
CREATE TABLE TechnicalDocument (
    TechDocKey integer IDENTITY PRIMARY KEY,
    Paragraphs varchar(10000),
    CONSTRAINT FK_PressRelease FOREIGN KEY (PressReleaseKey)
        REFERENCES PressRelease (PressReleaseKey))
CREATE TABLE BusinessDocument (
    BusDocKey integer IDENTITY PRIMARY KEY,
    Paragraphs varchar(10000),
    CONSTRAINT FK_PressRelease FOREIGN KEY (PressReleaseKey)
        REFERENCES PressRelease (PressReleaseKey))
```

This example shows how you can use the normal foreign key to primary key relationship to be mapped to an XML document. The corresponding XML document would look like

```
<PressRelease ID="0011">
  <PressReleaseTitle>Company Goes Public</PressRelease>
  <PressReleaseDate>2001-11-23</PressReleaseDate>
  <Article ID="0012">
    <Paragraph>This could be a lot of text about the Company.</Paragraph>
    <Paragraph>This could be another paragraph about the Company.</Paragraph>
  </Article>
```

```
  <TechnicalDocument ID="0013">
    <Paragraph>This is text for technical information on Company.</Paragraph>
    <FK_PressRelease>0011</FK_PressRelease>
  </TechnicalDocument>
</PressRelease>
```

XML AND ORACLE

Oracle has a number of products that utilize the strengths of XML with its database. Oracle has been putting a lot of effort in the area of developing a suite of development tools and associated components to assist others in implementing enterprise applications with their database.

Oracle9*i*'s XML-enabled database technology is well documented. Oracle's documentation describes how XML data can be stored, managed, and queried in the database using Oracle XML-enabled technology and the appropriate Oracle development tools. You can obtain copies of the documentation from the Web at `http://otn.oracle.com/docs/`. We won't repeat what you can learn from that documentation here—instead, we will provide a brief overview of this technology and a couple of relevant examples.

In general, XML documents for the Oracle database are processed in one of two ways: as *composed* XML documents, stored as a "*Large Object*" *(LOB)* or as *decomposed* XML document fragments, stored in relational tables, with the XML tags mapped to their respective columns in the database tables. The decomposed or fragmented XML documents can then be regenerated into composed XML documents.

Note

Oracle8*i* supports the following two types of LOBs: those stored in the database either in-line in the table or in a separate tablespace–such as a *binary large object (BLOB)*, a *character large object (CLOB)*, or a *national character large object (NCLOB)*–and those stored as operating system files (such as BFILEs). BFILEs are large binary data objects stored in operating system files outside database tablespaces.

An example of loading LOB data from delimited fields of a document into Oracle would be

Control file

```
LOAD DATA
INFILE 'sample.xml'
INTO TABLE person_table
FIELDS TERMINATED BY ','
   (name        CHAR(25) ENCLOSED BY '<resumeName>' AND '</resumeName>',
1   "RESUME"    CHAR(507) ENCLOSED BY '<startlob>' AND '</startlob>')
```

Data file (sample.xml)

```
<resumeName>John Smith</resumeName>
<startlob>        John Smith
                          500 Oracle Parkway
                          jsmith@us.oracle.com ...   </startlob>
 <resumeName>Jack Sample</resumeName> .......
```

Oracle's SQL*Loader utility is a very powerful text parser. You can do a lot of neat tricks for loading XML when the document is very big, but consistent in its tags. Listings 18.1 and 18.2 show an example that uses the Oracle SQL*Loader utility to put into a database specific values from an XML document:

LISTING 18.1 EXAMPLE.XML

```
<resultset>
    <contact>
        <first>...</first>
        <last>...</last>
        <middle>...</middle>
    </contact>
    <friend>
        <first>...</first>
        <last>...</last>
        <middle>...</middle>
    </friend>
</resultset>
```

LISTING 18.2 EXAMPLE.CTL—FIELD DEFINITION PART OF THE SQL LOADER CONTROL FILE

```
field list ....
(
    contact COLUMN OBJECT ....
    (
            first    char(40) enclosed by "<first>" and "</first>",
            last    char(40) enclosed by "<last>" and "</last>",
            middle    char(40) enclosed by "<middle>" and </middle>"
      )
        friend COLUMN OBJECT ....
      (
            first    char(40) enclosed by "<first>" and "</first>",
            last    char(40) enclosed by "<last>" and "</last>",
            middle    char(40) enclosed by "<middle>" and </middle>"
      )
)
```

As you can see, Oracle has made it very easy to bring XML content into their databases. Oracle's commitment to XML extends well beyond this. Oracle has developed the Oracle XML Developer's kit (XDK) that can be used with most programs that developers are writing. They have API's for Java and C++. The developer kits include the following:

- XML Parsers—Supporting Java, C, C++, and PL/SQL, they create and parse XML using industry standard DOM and SAX interfaces.
- XSLT Processor—Transforms or renders XML into other text-based formats such as HTML.
- XML Schema Processor—Supporting Java, C, and C++, it allows the use of simple and complex XML data types.

- XML Class Generator—Automatically generates Java and C++ classes from DTDs and Schemas to send XML data from Web forms or applications.
- XML Transviewer Java Beans—Java Beans that allow a programmer to view and transform XML documents and data via Java components.
- XML SQL Utility—Supporting Java, it generates XML documents, DTDs and Schemas from SQL queries.
- XSQL Servlet—Combines XML, SQL, and XSLT in the server to deliver dynamic Web content.

Another item of note: With the Oracle 9*i* release, a suite of development tools is provided that are really good for developing XML applications that connect into the database. One of these, Oracle Jdeveloper, is a Java IDE that features support for editing and validating XML documents, as well as for producing Web Services via useful wizards. To learn more about Oracle's XML strategy, visit `http://otn.oracle.com/tech/xml/content.html`.

XML AND SQL SERVER 2000

As the need to present dynamic data to various sources has grown, the need for this information to be in a format for the Web has grown as well. More and more Web sites are now "data-driven" and interface directly to databases to provide a view of their data.

To ensure that you do not have to write a lot of complex ASP code to display data in ASP pages, SQL Server 2000 has functionality to make data available in an XML format. This set of new functionality allows us to literally view the entire relational database as XML, thereby providing the ability to write entire end-to-end XML applications.

These features allow you to treat your SQL Server 2000 data as a series of XML documents while leaving the data itself untouched, so none of your current applications are affected. This means that you can expose the data you already have as XML documents for building the next generation of XML-based applications. These XML technologies can be broken up into two categories: middle tier and server side features. In this section, we will briefly go over each tier.

After installing the latest version of SQL Server 2000, there are a number of components that come with the product. These include

- Support for *XDR (XML-Data Reduced)* schemas and the ability to specify XPath queries against XML data that is described by these schemas
- The ability to retrieve and write XML data with the following three mechanisms:

  Retrieve XML data using the `SELECT` statement and the `FOR` XML clause

  Write XML data using the OPENXML rowset provider

  Retrieve XML data using the XPath query language

On the server side, there are a few features we need to discuss. The first is the `For XML` query extension. Adding "for XML" to the end of a standard rowset producing query causes the SQL Server query processor to send the results of the query through a post-processing step that changes the rowset to a stream of XML. This is part of Microsoft's Transact-SQL, an extension of standard SQL. However, if the client making the request is SQLOLEDB, the XML is returned as a tokenized stream of SQL data type objects, which is converted to normal XML in the SQLOLEDB driver. This means that the more processor-intensive part of XML generation is done on the client, where processor cycles aren't as precious as on the database server.

"`For XML`" queries can be made in three modes: `Raw`, `Auto`, and `Explicit`. The mode is selected by appending the mode name to the end of the query. `Raw` would be similar to comma-separated text files. Each row in the query result becomes a single element in the returned XML. This is probably an efficient way to do your query if your application requires moving a lot of XML quickly. But not many XML applications can use XML in this format.

"`For XML Auto`" returns XML in a more usable format, with each table in the `from` clause becoming an element and each column becoming either an attribute or subelement.

Nesting of the XML is determined by scanning across the row in the resultset. Each time a column comes from a table different from the previous one, a subelement is created. This creates a nice XML hierarchy without a lot of processing overhead. However, if your application requires XML in a predefined format, you might find that "`For XML Auto`" won't create XML in the format you need.

`Explicit` mode requires a more complex query syntax, yet it provides the greatest control over the result. These queries define XML fragments in terms of a universal table (the rowset produced by executing a query), which consists of a column for each piece of data you require and two additional columns that are used to define the metadata for the XML fragment. Universal tables use the names of their data columns to dictate how the data will be defined in an XML document. The first two columns of the universal table are named "Tag" and "Parent." The remainder of the column names in a universal table consist of up to four arguments, as shown here:

```
ElementName!TagNumber!AttributeName!Directive
```

These arguments are used to express the name of the element, the nesting of the element, and other XML features such as the number and values of attributes. Each row of data in the universal table represents an element in the resulting XML document.

The Tag column uniquely identifies the XML tag that will be used to represent each row in the results, and the Parent column is used to store the tag number of the parent element. An example of a universal table is shown in Table 18.1.

TABLE 18.1 UNIVERSAL TABLE

TAG	Parent	AddressID	ZipCode
1	NULL	11	10048
1	NULL	42	10048
1	NULL	72	10048

The Transact-SQL code required to produce this table from the data in the Address table is shown here:

```
SELECT 1 AS Tag,
NULL AS Parent,
AddressID AS [Address!1],
ZipCode AS [Address!1!ZipCode]
FROM [Address]
WHERE ZipCode = 10048
```

The `Tag` and `Parent` values are explicitly assigned in the `SELECT` statement. This ensures that every row in the rowset returned by this query will have a Tag column with a value of `1` and a Parent column with a value of `NULL`. To generate the required XML document, add the `FOR XML Explicit` clause to the query. Here are the results:

```
<Address ZipCode="10048">11</Address>
<Address ZipCode="10048">42</Address>
<Address ZipCode="10048">72</Address>
```

18

Another API that SQL Server 2000 supports is the ability to use XPath expressions to retrieve specific data. XPath queries can be thought of as an easy way to write "`For XML Explicit`" queries. The XPath query processor parses the XPath you pass in and uses your query criteria and the information supplied in the mapping schema to build a "`For XML Explicit`" statement that will return an XML document that satisfies your query. The major difference between this and writing your own explicit queries is that with XPath, you have only limited control over the format of the `Explicit` query generated.

Here is an example mapping schema that you would then use with an XPath expression for querying information from the database:

```
<?xml version="1.0" ?><Schema
xmlns="urn:schemas-microsoft-com:xml-data"
xmlns:sql="urn:schemas-microsoft-com:xml-sql"
xmlns:dt="urn:schemas-microsoft-com:datatypes" >

  <ElementType name="Address" sql:relation="Addresses">
    <AttributeType name="ID"/>
    <AttributeType name="name"/>
    <AttributeType name="Address"/>
    <AttributeType name="City"/>
    <AttributeType name="State"/>

    <attribute type="ID"/>
    <attribute type="name"/>
```

```
    <attribute type="Address"/>
    <attribute type="City"/>
    <attribute type="State" sql:field="Region"/>

    <element type="AddressBook">
      <sql:relationship key-relation="Addresses" key="AddressID"
      foreign-relation="AddressBooks" foreign-key="AddressID"/>
    </element>

  </ElementType>

  <ElementType name="AddressBook" sql:relation="AddressBooks">
    <AttributeType name="AddressBookID"/>
    <attribute type="AddressBookID" sql:field="AddressBookID"/>
  </ElementType>
</Schema>
```

With this Schema Mapping, you could develop XPath queries such as `"Address[@ID='0013']"`. The same query for an SQL statement would be very long. So, the power of using XPath is that you can develop queries to the information in the repository that are much simpler. However, they would also be somewhat limited in capabilities.

Another interesting part of SQL Server 2000 is the virtual directory that is provided with Microsoft's Internet Information Server (IIS). This allows you to develop mechanisms to access data through your Web site in an efficient manner with XML. These include the ability to build URLs that provide the following:

- Accessing database objects directly
- Executing template files
- Executing XPath queries

These concepts are discussed next.

ACCESSING DATABASE OBJECTS DIRECTLY

In this case, the URL would include a virtual name of `dbobject` type. The database objects, such as tables and views, can be specified as part of the URL, and an XPath can be specified against the database object, as follows:

```
http://IISServer/nwind/dbobjectVirtualName/XpathQuery
```

In the URL, `dbobjectVirtualName` is the virtual name of the `dbobject` type that is created using the IIS Virtual Directory Management for SQL Server utility.

Note

When an operation that requires resources such as memory (for creating temporary tables and temporary stored procedures, declaring cursors, executing `sp_xml_preparedocument`, and so on) is executed at the URL, the resources must be freed by executing appropriate corresponding commands (such as, DROP TABLE, DROP PROCEDURE, DEALLOCATE the cursor, or EXECUTE *sp_xml_removedocument*).

EXECUTING TEMPLATE FILES

A template is a valid XML document consisting of one or more SQL statements. When a template file is specified at the URL, the SQL commands stored in the template file are executed. SQL queries can be directly specified at the URL, but this is not recommended for security reasons.

EXECUTING XPATH QUERIES

The XPath queries are executed against an annotated mapping schema file specified as part of the URL. Here is an example Schema:

```
<?xml version="1.0" ?>
<Schema xmlns="urn:schemas-microsoft-com:xml-data"
        xmlns:dt="urn:schemas-microsoft-com:datatypes"
        xmlns:sql="urn:schemas-microsoft-com:xml-sql">

  <ElementType name="Address" sql:relation="AddressBook" >
    <AttributeType name="AddressID" />
    <AttributeType name="ContactName" />
    <AttributeType name="Phone" />

    <attribute type="AddressID" />
    <attribute type="ContactName" />
    <attribute type="Phone" />
  </ElementType>
</Schema>
```

18

If the query returns more than one customer, you must specify the `root` keyword to return a well-formed XML document. The following XPath query returns all the customers. In the URL, the `root` keyword is specified:

```
http://IISServer/testdb/schema/Schema2.xml/Address?root=root
```

This is the partial result:

```
<?xml version="1.0" encoding="utf-8" ?>
<root>
   <Address AddressID="ALFKI" ContactName="John Smith"
            Phone="030-0074321" />
   <Address AddressID="ANATR" ContactName="Jane Doe"
            Phone="(5) 555-4729" />
     ...
</root>
```

XML AND DB2

IBM has done a lot of work in the XML area, and its XML initiatives for DB2 are well formulated as well. In this section, we will briefly go over the current work that has been done with DB2 and XML.

One project is an XML Registry/Repository package that uses DB2 for persisting the content of the XML documents. This package is available at

```
http://www.alphaworks.ibm.com/tech/xrr
```

The IBM XML Registry/Repository (XRR) is a data management system that manages and provides services for XML artifacts including schemas (DTD, XSD), style sheets (XSL), and instance documents (WSDL, WSFL, and XML). Users can implement XRR to obtain an XML artifact automatically, search or browse for an XML artifact, deposit an XML artifact with or without related data, and register an XML artifact without deposit.

XRR is a system that provides five services. The first service is a registry in which organizations submit and register DTDs, schemas, style sheets, and other types of XML documents. Once approved, these documents are referred to as registered objects. The registry provides a search of registered objects based on their metadata.

The second service is termed "*registration*," which is when an organization must first register itself with the registry as a *submitting organization (SO)* before it can make submissions. SO makes submissions through one of its contacts whose role is referred to as a *submitter*. The "submitter" must always be authenticated. Only an SO can make submissions.

The third service is the ability to search and retrieve a registered object. Anyone can search the registry for registered objects based on their metadata. No authentication is required.

The fourth service is administration— a registry administrator can change user status and get the registry content.

Finally, the fifth service provides access to registered objects. Through the repository, a user can download a registered object using standard identifiers (URLs) .

XML and Open Source Databases

A number of open source databases are available on the Internet today. MySQL is an open source database that is free to download and use. MySQL is available free under the GNU General Public License (GPL). Commercial licenses are available as well.

The MySQL developers "don't believe that one should have native XML support in the database, but will instead add the XML support our users request from us on the client side. We think it's better to keep the main server code as 'lean and clean' as possible and instead develop libraries to deal with the complexity on the client side. This is part of the strategy mentioned above of not sacrificing speed or reliability in the server."

Another open source initiative of note can be found at the xmldb.org Web site. Xmldb.org was formed to facilitate the development of technology specifications for managing the data in XML Databases, contribute to reference implementations of those specifications under an Open Source License, formulate a community in which XML database vendors and users can ask questions and exchange information to learn more about XML database technology and applications, and evangelize XML database products and technologies to raise the visibility of XML databases in the marketplace. For additional information on MySQL, visit `http://www.mysql.com`.

NATIVE XML DATABASES

The term "native" with Native XML Databases refers to the notion of a data storage application that keeps the XML document intact. The application, by its very nature, keeps the structure of the XML pure and does not transform the XML into another data structure for relational or object-oriented database applications. The data model in this context is often referred to as similar structures that XPath, XML infoset, DOM, and SAX implement.

Native XML databases can often be broken into two groups for the functionality they address. Some are document-centric, meaning that they work well with large documents that require features for the document structure. This is applicable to systems that have XML representations of specific forms or documents that are used for reference or business systems.

Another group is message-centric native XML databases. These systems work well with storage and retrieval in information that is message oriented. For example, say that you have an enterprise system that is sending and receiving a number of Web service messages that need to be persisted for future transactions, or the capability to rollback a number of transactions that have taken place. The applications are often referred to as transactional supporting deployments that support the ability to store information on transactions that are taking place with the system. XML is used as an integration or B2B data-exchange mechanism between two applications, each of which sit atop a relational database.

Native XML databases can also be broken up into two technology segments that include text-based or model-based storage. The major difference in this area is that with text-based storage, the syntax of the document stays intact. Single or double quotes used in the creation of the document would stay intact and not be modified. With a model-based approach, the XML document is stored into a DOM data structure and then stored into the database as a binary format.

The benefits of a native XML database include the ability to store XML content easily and index that information effectively, providing a simple mechanism for storage and retrieval.

CONCEPTS BEHIND XML DATABASES

Native XML databases differ from XML-Enabled databases in three main ways:

- Native XML databases can preserve physical structure (entity usage, CDATA sections, and so on), as well as comments, PIs, DTDs, and so on. XML-enabled databases can do this in theory, but it is generally not done in practice.
- Native XML databases can store XML documents without knowing their schema (DTD), assuming one even exists. Although XML-enabled databases could generate schemas on-the-fly, this is impractical in practice, especially when dealing with schemaless documents.

- The only interface to the data in native XML databases is XML and related technologies, such as XPath, the DOM, or an XML-based API. XML-enabled databases, on the other hand, are likely to offer direct access to the data. XML-enabled databases, as discussed previously, provide a number of APIs to the associated content.

FUTURE DIRECTIONS

With the growth of the Internet and content-rich applications, it has become imperative that databases support a data type that fulfills the ability to store unstructured data. Unstructured data in this context is any information that does not include metadata about the data. These databases need to be optimized for large amounts of unstructured data and provide a uniform way of accessing large amounts of unstructured data within the database or outside.

Vendors such as IBM, Microsoft, and Oracle will have to add additional functionality to their XML offerings to compete with each other. The APIs and tools they have developed will mature to become easier to implement and extend. As standards emerge and mature from the W3C and other consortiums, these will be integrated into their offerings as well.

ADDITIONAL RESOURCES

A number of very good additional resources are available on the Web for learning about XML. Here is one of the best to consult:

- XML 1.0 Recommendation (`http://www.w3.org/TR/REC-xml`) The XML 1.0 Recommendation (Second Edition) from the W3C is the final word on XML. If you have a question about a technical aspect of XML, this should be the first source you consult.

ROADMAP

The next chapter goes into further detail on how XML relates to being persisted and stored on computer systems. Various repositories store information differently based on the needs of the application being developed. Because XML has become such a standard mechanism of organizing content, it is important to understand the various ways XML can be stored and used.

CHAPTER 19

XML and Document Repositories

In this chapter

by Earl Bingham

Document Repositories include a number of various software products on the market today. This chapter only covers XML related document repositories.

XML AND REPOSITORIES—INTRODUCTION TO XML REPOSITORIES

In previous chapters, you learned how XML documents are used for a number of various purposes. This chapter focuses on how XML structures can be stored and the facilities that make this storage useful. This chapter further discusses the strengths of XML as a data source for information storage.

XML is used for structuring messages that are exchanged between machines or for producing content that is read or used by humans in some way. XML also describes and organizes information. Naturally, that information has to come from somewhere. The XML content is stored or produced dynamically from a repository.

The mechanisms for storing XML documents have been broken up into a few categories. These include native XML databases, file management systems, document management systems, and content management systems. The differences between the categories of document repositories are difficult to define—they are roughly based on the number of features provided, the target market and customers the products are geared toward, and the history of those software application groups.

You will learn how each of these categories is fundamentally used and how it addresses customer needs in their businesses.

The most common persistent storage is by file. File management systems help us to deal with files. They allow us to create, delete, retrieve, and organize files. The organization of the data at a file system level is atomic at the file level. We usually only have a small amount of information that we can use to help us—a name, a type, a creation date, an owner, and so on. Filesystems do not usually inspect the content of a file to help organize the information.

Microsoft's Windows operating systems come with Explorer, which in many respects is a simple file management system. Explorer provides a user interface for creating, deleting, and opening files on your computer. More complex management systems will allow for managing files between systems that are networked together.

XML-enabled file management systems can also be associated with the HTML editing software products that are available. When you use these products, they illustrate the concept of a sitemap for a Web project. This allows you to develop the relationship between documents—and you could potentially use these applications to manage XML documents instead of HTML documents.

When we move to the document level, we have collected information (which might be in several files) and produced a higher level abstraction. The kind of information about the document can be much more comprehensive than the information about files. Microsoft Word, for example, allows us to store information about the author, the version, the title, the category, keywords, and so on.

Document management systems provide access to this information to provide more sophisticated management. We can now organize documents by authors or version or collect files to produce larger documents such as books.

Moving to the next level, we explore information in even more depth. The content itself is described and organized. For example, information can be partitioned into paragraphs, which might use metadata to identify the subject. Content management systems allow us to manage information at a very granular level. We can get to fragments of information, or "*content components*." and produce relationships between them or aggregate them to produce larger entities, such as documents. Content Management Systems can notify us when data is updated or changed to desired values. *Workflow management systems (WMS)* often build on these capabilities. Content Management Systems often provide the flexibility to display content to various output devices in various formats. These include printer formats, wireless devices, large screens, and others.

Potentially underlying any of these systems, native XML databases have XML documents as their core component for persistence of information. They manage a set of XML documents that include basic database functionality for querying, updating, deleting, and searching through the information in the databases.

The most common persistent storage is by file. File management systems help us to deal with files. File systems allow us to create, delete, retrieve and organize files. The organization of the data at a file system level is atomic at the file level. We usually only have a small amount of information that we can use to help us—a name, a type, a creation date, an owner, etc. When we move to the document level, we have collected information (which may be in several files) and produced a higher level of abstraction. The kind of information about the document (the meta-data) can be much more comprehensive than the information about files. Word, for example allows us to store information about the author, the version, the title, the category, keywords, and so on. Document management systems provide access to this information to provide more sophisticated management. Moving to the next level, we explore information in even more depth. The content itself is described and organized, and content management systems allow us to manage at that level. We can get to fragments of information or "content components," and produce relationships between them. We can build documents.

THE INTERNET AS GLOBAL STORAGE FOR INFORMATION

The Internet is a collection of computer systems that communicate with each other in various protocols. Each of these computer systems contain documents that, in the form of HTML pages, can be easily distributed to other computers. These documents are also indexed by many modern search engines and by earlier systems such as the *Wide Area Information Servers (WAIS)*. A number of initiatives exist to classify data to make the information more meaningful. The Internet can be thought of as the largest document repository in the world: a repository that users can leverage for themselves.

PROBLEMS OF INDEXING AND SEARCHING THE GLOBAL NETWORK

A number of problems exist with searching and indexing the content that is available on the Internet.

The content currently available on the Internet is in a format suitable for viewing only. So the actual content has no association to the categorization of the information. This limits the capability of search mechanisms to be as comprehensive as they potentially could be. It is the *meaning* of the content that indexing algorithms have difficulty assembling to provide users with information relevant to what they are looking for.

The sheer size of the Internet is another problem for indexing. The number of Web pages on the Internet is growing rapidly, and the existing pages are changing constantly. Google, the most comprehensive search engine for the Web, has more than 3 billion Web pages indexed. Some sources estimate that more than 186 million Internet hosts have content available on the Internet. Trying to index all this information is a large and difficult task.

Even though there are a number of difficulties with managing the content of the Internet, there are a number of initiatives that help in this regard. A major one is the Open Directory Project, which is the largest, most comprehensive human-edited directory of the Web. It is constructed and maintained by a vast, global community of volunteer editors.

The goal of the open directory project is to be the definitive catalog of the Web. To achieve this goal, the database of Web content classified by humans is freely given away. It is currently powering the core directory services for the Web's largest and most popular search engines and portals. This includes AOL Search, Google, Lycos, HotBot, DirectHit, and hundreds of others.

Note

If you want to contribute to the Open Directory Project effort, you can go to the Web site at `http://dmoz.org/` and fill out the application for a specific area.

Search engine technology is also becoming better. In addition to providing a very competent search engine, Google also hosts a newsgroup repository. Google has fully integrated the past 20 years of Usenet archives into Google Groups, which now offers access to more than 700 million messages dating back to 1981. This is, by far, the most complete collection of Usenet articles ever assembled and a fascinating first-hand historical account.

Note

Google has compiled, and is compiling, some of the most especially memorable articles and threads in the creation of the Internet. For example, you can read Tim Berners-Lee's announcement of what became the World Wide Web or Linus Torvalds' post about his "pet project."

What Are Document Repositories?

A document repository is often thought of as an application that manages documents in some manner. Based on which category of document repository you're discussing, there is a number of *value adds* that a document repository adds: namely, storing libraries of related documents, discovery and retrieval, versioning, security, and collaboration and sharing, to name a few. Documents can be stored in their entirety with sections of the documents available for use.

An application that can manage HTML pages or MS Word documents would be a document repository.

Another definition for a document repository is an apparatus that supports the current state of information in a task. This definition is in relation to enterprise applications that need to store and recall transaction data for persistence and performance reasons. For example, when a company receives a purchase order, the document repository needs to store and recall the purchase order information.

Many companies have built software products that provide a number of features for creating and managing documents. Currently, a number of companies are providing peer-to-peer document sharing functionality to users. Also, a number of Web sites support online document repositories and file sharing.

XML Repositories Versus Existing Solutions

Existing content repositories use proprietary formats for indexing and managing the content placed in these applications. Non-XML repositories have complex and incongruous mechanisms for indexing and managing their content.

Often, the format of meta information on the content cannot be migrated to other solutions. With XML, the content is structured in a universal format that may allow a multitude of other applications to index and manage XML content.

Non-XML Document Storage Solutions

Many document storage solutions normally entail relational or object-oriented databases, file management systems, and other systems that are unaware of the structure of information formatted with XML. These applications were available for a number of years before SGML and XML started to become popular. Because XML is a relatively new standard and technology, there are still a number of benefits of using one of these solutions. Often, they are less expensive and have features that have been developed over many years.

For example, Microsoft's Content Management Server (`http://www.microsoft.com/cmserver/`) provides a framework for businesses to quickly empower their employees to create, manage, and publish their own content with a Web-based user interface. The Oracle9*i* database also includes a framework for content management (`http://www.oracle.com/ip/index.html?cm_consideration.html`).

STRUCTURED HIERARCHY OF XML DOCUMENTS

The structured format of XML provides many benefits over other data representations. One benefit is the ability to manage elements within elements, which can be difficult to manage in traditional relational databases.

The hierarchical structure of XML allows for complex relationships between data that is more difficult to express using relational structures. For example, in HTML, tables are often embedded within tables, which allows for complex display logic to be described in a hierarchical structure without too much complexity in the structure of the document.

```
<body>
<table>
 <tr>
  <td>
   <table>
    <tr>
   </table>
  </td>
 </tr>
</table>
</body>
```

The nesting of tags creates a tree-like structure that greatly simplifies the handling of these documents. You have already learned how XML documents are easily manipulated with DOM and SAX. In the next chapter, you will learn about XQuery and will see how XML documents can be queried by searching for a particular value or by identifying relationships.

To create a nested hierarchy of parent/child data that is similar to XML in a relational database, you will have to add other tables to the schema and define special SQL queries. This can be significantly more complex.

XML REPOSITORIES AND NON-XML DOCUMENTS

XML Repositories are used as the infrastructure that underlies many electronic business applications and integration efforts. Therefore, other kinds of content and documents will also need to be placed into these XML Repositories—not only for persistence of workflow transactions, but also for Meta or other business information.

With many XML Repositories, data structures of any kind can normally be expressed in XML format and can thus be stored and treated as XML objects. This also applies to information types that usually aren't stored in databases, for example, multimedia files such as video and sound. The relationship between these and other data can be expressed as links within the XML document.

Many XML repositories promote the notion of being able to simply drop content into them without needing a structured schema to define the mechanisms of the state in which the information will reside. This mechanism provides a framework for accommodating information diversity and change. As business models, standards, and components change, a repository needs to be able to facilitate this change in some way.

Documents that are semi-structured can also be adapted for use in XML Repositories. *Tidy* is a product that can parse poorly structured HTML or other markup documents and map them to well-formed XML. Tidy allows normal HTML documents that do not adhere to XML standards to be placed into an XML repository. Tidy has been included in many products to ensure that marked-up documents can be mapped to a more structured format so that they can be indexed within the repository. Tidy can be found at `http://www.w3.org/People/Raggett/tidy/`.

REPOSITORIES AND DATABASES

The difference between a repository and a database is defined by the form and function of their business uses. A *repository* is often thought of as a collection of organized files, whereas a *database* is a collection of organized data in company-specific data format. However, there's quite a bit of flexibility in the definitions. In this section, we'll think of repositories as places where documents or document fragments are kept and maintained. Databases will provide storage and management for the underlying pieces.

BUILDING XML REPOSITORIES ON RELATIONAL DATABASES

A number of benefits to using a relational database for storing XML information now exist. Each of the major vendors has built XML APIs into their databases that can be taken advantage of in many ways. This was discussed in Chapter 18, "XML and Databases." As you saw in that chapter, the vendors have tried to make it easy to import data into their databases and to make data available externally as XML.

A number of applications of large databases are being implemented that use these features and benefits.

These systems also have a number of features that newer native XML databases do not have yet. For instance, transaction management—the ability to roll back transactions that have taken place that need to be removed from the system—is a feature that almost all relational databases offer. Other features of relational databases include enhanced failover clustering, distributed partitioned views to deliver more scalability, and full-text searching.

A number of other components are available for connecting systems together that use XML and relational databases. The flexibility of XML and other standards for transforming XML, such as XSL, make XML a simple mechanism to use for integrating information systems.

Examples of software used to connect to databases can be found at `http://www.xmlsoftware.com`. Several products are available to developers that enable you to easily build connections between databases and other applications, such as Web servers and other data repositories. Castor, available at `http://castor.exolab.org`, is a framework for transforming XML into objects or persisting it into a relational database. Data Junction (`http://www.datajunction.com/default.asp`) provides commercial implementations of software that facilitates flexible application integration.

XML REPOSITORIES AND OBJECT-ORIENTED DATABASES

Object-oriented databases are thought of as the integration of database capabilities with object-oriented programming language capabilities. An object-oriented database management system provides a framework for constructing objects that are persisted in a database and can be used with an object-oriented programming language.

An interesting example of object-oriented programming and XML documents is a product named Castor XML. This product is open source and allows developers to build mechanisms to work with XML documents. An XML document can be used to construct Java objects or persist Java object information into an XML document. To do this, a developer will marshal or unmarshal a stream of data (in XML) to or from an object. Go to `http://www.castor.org` for additional information and a download of the software.

There are many benefits of linking XML repositories to OO databases. For example, if you have complex data, you can use the persistence of XML Repositories with some of the interesting mechanisms provided with object-oriented databases. Complex data can be defined as

- Data that does not have naturally unique identification—Unlike data that is organized into a structure suitable for a relational database, a unique ID isn't necessary for each entry. The hierarchical structure of the data can serve to distinguish one instance of data from another. For instance, if a document was a collection of words, we could easily find the fifth instance of the word *and*. It isn't necessary for each word (or the element that describes a word) to be unique in a document.
- A large number of many-to-many relationships—Many-to-many relationships are somewhat difficult to model with relational databases. They require an additional table to keep track of the relationships. Object-oriented databases often make many-to-many relationships easier to work with than the relational database equivalent.
- With complex data, fragments of an OO database can be thought of as representations of an XML data structure that is stored as objects.
- To understand the strengths of OODBMs and XML is to descript some examples of these two technologies. A many-to-many relationship exists when there are bidirectional relationships between objects. For example, a family might have more than one phone that they share. Perhaps each family member owns a cell phone and the family has a home phone also. Trying to map phone numbers to family members and family members to phone numbers would result in a many-to-many relationship. A daughter or son could use any of the phones. Similarly, calling one of the phone numbers could potentially result in a call to any member of the family.
- An example of a type code would be an AddressType field that could be in a normal relational database table. This field would be used to differentiate processing for various types of addresses, based on country or current political standard. Different type codes could identify the address format in an addressbook database. With an object-oriented database, you can have a clean representation of address information based on the country on which you are inserting information compared to a pure relational model that would have empty fields or fields that are used for different purposes based on country information.

Here we have described how OODB and complex data can be used for addressing complex issues of persistence of data. Yet to finalize the information concerning XML and OODB, we need to discuss some of the real-world implementations that have been successful these past few years as XML has grown in popularity.

One company that has a very efficient database is Object Design's Objectstore product. With Objectstore, the persistence of XML is stored as a data structure, without any mapping of code. The XML content is cached for performance, and Objectstore also offers the ability to have dynamic data modeling take place as information is stored or updated. For more information about ObjectDesign's Objectstore product, visit `http://www.objectdesign.com/htm/object_prod_oview.asp`.

Another exciting company that has developed a mature XML component to its object-oriented database is Versant. For its enJin product, it has an XML Interchange that allows for object graphs to be converted to XML or XML documents converted into object graphs. For additional information on the enJin product, go to `http://www.versant.com/products/enjin/index.html`.

By nature, object-oriented databases support user-defined types.

USING NATIVE XML DATABASES FOR BUILDING THE REPOSITORIES

As stated previously, native XML databases store XML documents in their pure entire form. This is different from other systems because they will normally transform the XML document into another format for storage.

The benefits of using an NXDB include

- Reduced "footprints" of the content compared to analogous database or flat-file structures.
- Dynamic linking and cross-collection aggregation of content is used so that any representation of the information can be queried quickly.
- Inherent multi-language support within the XML and Unicode standards.
- Support for XML standards for querying.

XPath is the primary query language used to access XML documents in an NXDB. XPath can be used to query multiple XML document collections, but it has limitations of sorting, grouping, data types, and cross-document joins. XQuery is also supported by a number of NXDBs. A true query language, XQuery is more suitable than XPath, but it still isn't a fully developed standard.

Now that major database vendors are shipping XML APIs to their back-end systems, a *native XML database (NXDB)* can be very useful as an intermediate cache, sitting between the back-end database and middle-tier application components. System architects can use this feature to achieve their goal of creating a framework that will allow for quick and easy expansion to the persistence of new data content or workflow design.

INDEXING DOCUMENTS IN XML REPOSITORIES

Indexes are used to efficiently search for specific content within documents of an XML repository. Many XML Repositories have mechanisms for indexing the content in their repositories. Indexes normally refer to a dictionary of indexed terms and a list of occurrences that store the position of each term in every document.

Indexes can be broken up into specific types: Word indexes are associated with specific words in a document. Date and time indexes help search for specific times or dates or a range of times or dates within a document. More complex searching would be associated with full text or string indexes that include all the content of an XML element. Finally, a numeric index is used to allow searching for integers, decimal numbers, or intervals in documents.

It is important to note that searching XML Repositories is the number one reason that Fortune 500 companies are currently using XML. Converting data into XML allows their employees to access data they couldn't reach before. Employees can now search across the structured data in a database and the unstructured data that was formerly in large collections of files. By using the metadata of the XML documents, employees can perform more precise searches and obtain more relevant information.

SEARCHING THE DOCUMENTS THROUGH A STRUCTURED HIERARCHY

This power of a structured hierarchy can be used in various ways for creating an index of data. This index can then be used for searching for specific content. For example, a numeric search can be applied, even when values contain mixed unit designations. For example, searching for the number `128` could return a collection of entries associated with various elements such as "`128 feet`," "`128MB`," and so on.

You can also search using name/value parameters, in which you can construct a search to find information in any of the tags of an XML document. Another search could be to restrict the search to a portion of the hierarchy of an XML document.

Because of the special nature of hierarchical XML data, many applications support searching that can limit the results to precise combinations of fields and subfields. For example, in a Shakespeare XML database, you could search for

- All the words spoken by a specific actor
- All the scenes that contain specific props or actors
- All the scenes that contain a specific word or phrase

XML REPOSITORIES IN REAL-WORLD APPLICATIONS

The current usage of XML repositories in the industry today provides a number of insightful implementations of the potential of what can be done for customers and the Internet. What follows is a few implementations of XML repositories that provide a number of business enablers that are unique and have benefited their customer base with these features.

SOFTWARE AG'S TAMINO XML SERVER

Software AG has a product line named Tamino, which is an XML database that provides support for Web Services, WebDav, XQuery, XPath, and application plug-ins. They are built on a set of core service components that Software AG has designed for flexibility. The XML engine and Data Map allow for the integrated native XML data store to be managed effectively with a suite of software that allows you to update and retrieve XML content. The Tamino X-tension service is an API that can be used to build various software applications that can then work with the content in their data store. The Tamino Manager and Security Manager are Web-based management tools for administering products to create a database, start/stop server, back up, restore, load, and so on. Tamino supports schema configuration for mapping of XML objects to internal Tamino structures. Additional flexibility can be created by installing the Tamino X-Tension component.

Associated with these core components and services is a set of services for development using EJBs, JSPs, HTTP, Clients, and access via WebDAV. To further compliment Software AG's product offering, it has another product called X-Node that allows the system to act as a virtual XML Repository to other disparate systems. For additional information on the product, visit Software AG's Web site at `http://www.softwareag.com/tamino/`.

NEOCORE XMS

NeoCore is a fairly new /company to introduce an offering for the XML Repository market. Its technology and product suite is founded on its patented technology called *Digital Pattern Processing (DPP)*. DPP describes infinite-width fields of the component content and indices of XML documents that are introduced to the NeoCore XMS. This mechanism effectively indexes every tag, element, and combination so that all queries are index based.

DPP generates numerical icons that symbolically represent the original data. The NeoCore XMS matches the icons with known patterns at up to 10 million matches per second.

NeoCore also claims that XMS will normally store XML documents 2 1/2 times smaller than their original size. This is important for the performance and scalability of the system. XMS offers security by providing access control to data and the various components of the repository. To find more information about NeoCore's products, visit `http://www.neocore.com/products/products.htm`.

B-BOP XFINITY SERVER

Another native XML server of note is B-Bop's Xfinity Server. This XML data management system includes the ability to access data that is located in legacy applications, filesystems, RDBMs, and text files, providing high performance XML data transaction and storage in a natural XML format.

B-Bop's Xfinity Server is unique in its capability to provide a schema-independent, native XML storage and retrieval using any standard RDBMS. Xfinity eliminates the need for any schema design or development of XML-to-RDB mapping programs. Leveraging existing relational databases, it delivers several benefits including proven scalability, reliability, and transaction support. Xfinity provides a flexible repository in which persistent XML data can be used by multiple applications. The system is optimized to handle complex XML Queries that can be generated with large data sets efficiently. Xfinity's capability to store and query XML documents at a granular level allows users to create new documents from sections of other documents or data sources.

The XML query engine supports W3C standards such as XPath. It utilizes B-Bop's own XQuery language, called TQL. TQL provides mechanisms similar to the XQuery W3C draft, which is a combination of XPATH and SQL. For example, if you have a document structure that looks like

```
<addresses>
<address>
 <firstname>John</firstname>
 <lastname>Smith</lastname>
 <addressField>123 Main Street</addressField>
 ...
```

and, if you want to search for the `addressField`'s of people with the last name of `Smith`, the TQL XML document would look like this:

```
<query>
 <select>
  <returnNodes>
   <nodePath>//addresses</nodePath>
</returnNodes>
  <where>
   <nodeTest>
    <nodePath>//addresses/address/lastname/text()</nodePath>
    <operator>eq</operator>
    <nodeValue>Smith</nodeValue>
   </nodeTest>
</where>
<returnNodes>
   <nodePath>//addresses/address/addressField</nodePath>
</returnNodes>
</select>
</query>
```

Another major component of the Xfinity server is the built-in transformation engine. With it, you can construct a chain of XSL transformations that become a pipeline which provides the desired output. This framework for transformations is cached on the server to improve performance and reliability.

Xfinity's XML/XSL publishing framework provides mechanisms for clearly separating logic, content, and style. Multiple client types, such as Web browsers and WAP-enabled devices, can be easily supported with this framework. They also support user profiling for customized Web pages and presentation.

Xfinity also has the features you would expect from a capable NXDB for remote administration, role-based security, and multi-platform support. Xfinity works with any J2EE-compliant application server. It includes a set of lightweight application services that facilitates session management, database connection pooling, and access control. The server supports most major open standards, including XSLT, SAX, DOM, XPath, SSL, HTTPS, and many components of the J2EE architecture. To get additional information about B-Bop's product line, visit `http://www.b-bop.com`.

XML and Other Document Repositories

In addition to the commercial products, a number of open source XML repositories are available for download. Each of these software packages can help the developer learn more about the benefits and actual real-world usefulness of these products.

The first XML repository of note is Xindice, which is a native XML database. Xindice is a Java-based application that is lightweight and modular in design. This database server can handle a large number of small, message-oriented XML documents. It provides a number of mechanisms for accessing the information in XPath expressions. Please visit `http://www.dbxml.org` for more information.

Another interesting open source XML database is Exist, located at `http://exist.sourceforge.net/`. This product allows for a full-text search for specific content in which an index is created using MySQL as the relational database backend. The performance for specific access of data is interesting to note. XPath support is still preliminary.

Conclusion

When contemplating XML Repositories, you need to consider their support for transaction management. A transaction is made up of a sequence of activities that must be completed together. Transaction management ensures that the transaction completes successfully or not at all. If any step of the transaction fails, the transaction manager will undo all the actions performed to that point. Many of the XML Repositories available today do not have this capability. If a bad update takes place, you have to manually go back and try to remove the transaction, which could be potentially impossible. So when making a decision about the platform to use for your application, be sure to make a complete list of the features you need to handle normal system failures.

Additional Resources

A number of very good additional resources are available on the Web for learning about XML. Here are a few of the best ones to consult:

- XML 1.0 Recommendation—(`http://www.w3.org/TR/REC-xml`). The XML 1.0 Recommendation (Second Edition) from the W3C is the final word on XML. If you have a question about a technical aspect of XML, this should be the first source you consult.
- The Open Directory Project—(`http://dmoz.org/about.html`)
- The Google newsgroup archive—(`http://www.google.com/grphp?hl=en`)

- Yahoo! Groups provides the ability to make groups and share files. Go to `http://groups.yahoo.com` for more information.
- "Introduction to Native XML Databases" by Kimbro Staken—(`http://www.xml.com/pub/a/2001/10/31/nativexmldb.html`)
- XMLDB.org—List of XML database resources—(`http://www.xmldb.org/resources.html`)
- List of XML databases—(`http://www.xmlsoftware.com/database/`)

ROADMAP

From here we will look at how specific standards are being used for bridging the gap between databases and XML. XQuery is a fairly new standard that a number of technology companies are using to provide easy to use mechanisms to extract content from collections of XML files like a database.

CHAPTER 20

Querying Documents Using XQuery

In this chapter

by Andrew Watt

Increasing quantities of data are stored in XML or in situations where XML can be used as an intermediate format. Thus, a query language to efficiently and declaratively access such data forms is an important part of the XML technologies jigsaw. There is no point in having a lot of data if you can't effectively query it!

XQuery, the XML Query Language, is an important, large, and potentially complex specification currently under development at the W3C. It is intended to allow the querying of "real and virtual" XML documents. In other words, although XQuery can be used to query static XML files, the XML being queried need not exist as files and can be simply streams of bytes.

The functionality of XQuery 1.0 builds on certain capabilities of XPath 1.0 and XSLT 2.0 (both in development at W3C) but differs sufficiently from them in that neither fully meets the needs of XQuery.

Because XQuery 1.0 is closely related to the development of XPath 2.0 and XSLT 2.0, XQuery is being developed jointly by the XSL Working and XQuery Working Groups at the W3C.

At the time of writing, several W3C documents exist that define XQuery 1.0 and its related specifications. All these documents are at the Working Draft stage of development. XSLT 2.0 and XPath 2.0, which are being developed in conjunction with XQuery 1.0, are only at the first public Working Draft stage of development. Thus, it is likely that further changes could occur before these interrelated specifications proceed to W3C Recommendation status. Be sure to check the latest version of the documents.

INTRODUCING XQUERY

XQuery is intended to work with single XML documents or collections of XML documents. In addition, XQuery will be able to query XML document fragments or collections of fragments. It borrows syntax from XSLT 1.0 and XPath 1.0.

For example, to query the `chapter` elements in a document named book.xml, we could use an XQuery expression—a path expression—such as the following:

```
document("book.xml")//chapter
```

As you can see, an XQuery expression is not written in XML. You might recognize the use of the `document()` function from XSLT 1.0 and a path expression, `//chapter`, from XPath 1.0. Less basic XQuery expressions add XQuery-specific syntax.

XQuery is not the first attempt at an XML query language. Other such query languages include Quilt and XQL.

In fact, XSLT can be seen as the W3C's first XML query language because it has many aspects of the functionality proposed for XQuery. Some perceptive commentators observed that the power they saw in XSLT derived from similarities to the RDBMS query language, SQL. However, the current expectation is that XQuery and XSLT will follow distinct but closely related development paths at the W3C. The possibility that XSLT will be the XML-based version of XQuery syntax now seems very unlikely with the advent of a first draft of XQueryX.

WHAT CAN XQUERY QUERY?

One of the most basic questions about the capabilities of a query language relates to what type of data model it is capable of querying.

At its simplest, the answer is that XQuery can query XML. But what functionality is available? What is XQuery likely to be useful for? Let's split our brief look at this topic into consideration of two broad uses of XML—document-centric and data-centric queries.

DOCUMENT-CENTRIC QUERIES

Suppose you had a large technical document—what kind of things are you likely to want to do with it? You might want to create a table of contents by identifying parts of the document that are, for example, chapter headers, section headers, and so on and use the query result to create a table of contents automatically. Equally, you might want to identify keywords within a document and use those to automatically create an index for the document. XQuery can help do either.

Listing 20.1 contains a highly simplified full text of a fictional book on XQuery.

LISTING 20.1 A FICTIONAL BOOK ON XQUERY (XQUERYBOOK.XML)

```
<?xml version='1.0'?>
<Book>
 <Title>
  XQuery Answers
 </Title>
 <Chapter number="1" title="The First Chapter">
  <Section number="1">First Section</Section>
  <Section number="2">Second Section of Chapter 1</Section>
  <!-- And so on ..... -->
 </Chapter>
 <Chapter number="2" title="The Second Chapter">
  <Section number="1">First Section</Section>
  <Section number="2">Second Section of Chapter 1</Section>
  <!-- And so on ..... -->
 </Chapter>
<!-- And so on with many more chapters ... -->
</Book>
```

A first attempt at creating a query to produce a table of contents might simply include the number and title of each chapter. We could create a first attempt at a simple table of contents using the XQuery query shown in Listing 20.2.

LISTING 20.2 CREATING A SIMPLE TABLE OF CONTENTS CONSISTING OF BOOK TITLE AND CHAPTER NUMBERS AND TITLES (XQUERYTOC.TXT)

```
<TOC>
{
  FOR $Chapter IN document("XQueryBook.xml")//Chapter
  RETURN
   <ChapterHead>
   {string($Chapter/number)}..{string($Chapter/title)}
   </ChapterHead>
}
</TOC>
```

Note

Element constructors allow new XML elements to be created in the output. They are used similarly to literal result elements in XSLT 1.0–the start tag is written, any content is created using XQuery expressions, and the literal end tag is written.

Let's break the XQuery query down line by line. The first line creates a literal output start tag for the element `TOC`. The XQuery expression

```
FOR $Chapter IN document("XQueryBook.xml")//Chapter
```

creates a variable `$Chapter` and assigns to that variable a `sequence` of nodes that can consist of one or more (in this case two) nodes. The `IN` keyword precedes the location or document that provides the sequence of nodes. You might recognize the `document()` function from XSLT. We are applying the query to the document XQueryBook.xml, which must be situated in the same directory as the query. The final part of the `FOR` statement, `//Chapter`, selects any `Chapter` element nodes in the document XQueryBook.xml.

The `RETURN` statement defines what is output for each node that appears in the `sequence` defined by the variable `$Chapter`. For each `Chapter` element node in the source XML document, a literal `ChapterHead` start tag is output first. Then the expression `{string($Chapter/@number)}` causes the value of the `number` attribute of the current `Chapter` element to be output literally. Once again, you will recognize the use of the abbreviated XPath syntax to describe the `attribute` axis—the `@` character, followed by the attribute name. That is followed by two literal periods and the result of evaluating the expression `{string($Chapter/@title)}`, which selects the value of the `title` attribute of the current node and adds it to the content of the `ChapterHead` element. Finally, an end tag for the `ChapterHead` element is output.

Because two `Chapter` elements are in the source XML document, the query produces two `ChapterHead` elements with content made up of the values of the `number` and `title` attributes from each `Chapter` element in the source document.

Finally, a literal end tag for the `TOC` element is output.

The document output by the preceding XQuery query is shown in Listing 20.3.

LISTING 20.3 THE FIRST CUT AT A TOC, PRODUCED BY APPLYING XQUERY (XQUERYBOOKTOC.XML)

```
<TOC>
 <ChapterHead>
  1..The First Chapter
 </ChapterHead>
 <ChapterHead>
  2..The Second Chapter
 </ChapterHead>
</TOC>
```

It is straightforward to modify this simple query to output an XHTML document that could be displayed in a Web browser. Listing 20.4 shows an XQuery to create a simple XHTML page.

LISTING 20.4 AN XQUERY TO PRODUCE A SIMPLE TABLE OF CONTENTS IN AN XHTML PAGE (XQUERYBOOKTOC.TXT)

```
<html>
 <head>
  <title>XQuery Answers Table of Contents</title>
 </head>
 <body>
  {
    FOR $Chapter IN document("XQueryBook.xml")//Chapter
    RETURN
      <p>
      {string($Chapter/@number)}..{string($Chapter/@title)}
      </p>
  }
 </body>
</html>
```

We simply provide whatever literal output we want around the XQuery statements. You might recognize similarities to the use of literal result elements in XSLT or to ASP or JSP Web pages.

You might want to query an XML document in another way. For example, you might want to find every occurrence of a selected word or phrase in a document.

XQuery will provide at least some support for regular expressions in string functions. For example, the `match()` function as currently drafted will accept a regular expression as one of its arguments and return a set of integers, indicating the position of the specified regular expression within a string argument to the `match()` function. This gives the basis for useful text search functionality.

XQuery intends to provide these and other useful types of document-centric query functionality.

20

DATA-CENTRIC QUERIES

Because XML can be used directly as a data store or can be produced from conventional relational database management systems by middleware, the querying of XML-related data stores is of great importance.

The most frequently used type of SQL query from a database is to retrieve data that is already in the database. Data is entered once, but it can be retrieved many times. Not surprisingly, retrieval type queries are well supported in XQuery. We will look at various examples of using XQuery in this way later in the chapter.

One important type of query currently missing from the XQuery 1.0 documents is a mechanism to update data by means of an update query syntax. This has major implications for the usefulness of XQuery because adding new data to a data store, changing a value in a data store, or deleting an item in a data store all require the ability to update the content of that data store.

At the time of writing, there is a lively ongoing debate about whether update queries should be included in XQuery 1.0. Nobody seems to be making a case that update queries are unnecessary. All seem to agree that they are very important. The discussion centers on the delay that would result from adding update queries to the current drafts for XQuery. If the facility to update XML data stores is important to you, consult the latest XQuery documents to see what the outcome of the discussions proves to be.

THE XQUERY SPECIFICATION DOCUMENTS

XQuery has several specification documents that are listed next. The URL given for each document will take you to the latest version of each document rather than to the version that is current at the time of writing. In earlier drafts, the XQuery Working Group has amalgamated documents or changed document titles, so the documents listed might not all be taken through to Recommendation status.

- XML Query Requirements—`http://www.w3.org/TR/xmlquery-req`
- XQuery 1.0, An XML Query Language—`http://www.w3.org/TR/xquery`
- XML Query Use Cases—`http://www.w3.org/TR/xmlquery-use-cases`
- XML Syntax for XQuery 1.0 (XQueryX)—`http://www.w3.org/TR/xqueryx`
- XQuery 1.0 and XPath 2.0 Data Model—`http://www.w3.org/TR/query-datamodel/`
- XQuery 1.0 and XPath 2.0 Functions and Operators—`http://www.w3.org/TR/xquery-operators/`
- XQuery 1.0 Formal Semantics—`http://www.w3.org/TR/query-semantics/`

As you will likely gather by the sheer number of specification documents, XQuery is a sizeable and complex technology. This chapter can only give you a hint of the capabilities that the final specification might provide.

XQuery 1.0 is also interrelated to the following specification documents that are also under development by the W3C:

- XPath 2.0—`http://www.w3.org/TR/xpath20`
- XSLT 2.0—`http://www.w3.org/TR/xslt20`

XQuery syntax has some similarities to the syntax of the *Structured Query Language (SQL)*. That is not surprising because both SQL and XQuery are intended to provide a declarative means to query data stores. XQuery also shares much functionality with XSLT, which was envisaged by some as the SQL of the XML world. The arrival of XQuery has displaced XSLT from that potential role.

One important aspect of XQuery (shared by XSLT and SQL) is that XQuery queries are *closed*. This means that the result of any XQuery query is also a suitable input to a following XQuery query.

How XQuery Relates to XPath

The first thing to say here is that XQuery relates primarily to version 2.0 of XPath, which is being developed in parallel with XQuery version 1.0 and XSLT version 2.0. The functionality provided by XPath 1.0 is inadequate to support the needs of XQuery 1.0. However, many XPath 1.0 concepts are applicable to your understanding of XQuery 1.0.

Both XPath 1.0 and XQuery 1.0 are able to query XML documents using element type names as well as attribute names and values.

XQuery will probably have fewer axes than XPath 1.0. The axes likely to be available in XQuery 1.0 are the `self` axis as well as the `child`, `descendant`, `descendant-or-self`, `parent`, and `attribute` axes.

Terminology in XQuery 1.0 changes from that in XPath 1.0. For example, the term *axis step* replaces *location step*. An axis step selects a *sequence* of nodes rather than a *node-set* as in XPath 1.0.

XQuery, XPath, and Data Types

At the time that XPath 1.0 was created, the only XML schema available was the *Document Type Definition (DTD)*, which is described in the XML 1.0 Recommendation. The DTD was carried over from the *Standard Generalized Markup Language (SGML)* whose main use was in document-centric applications. With the realization that XML could be readily used for data-centric purposes, the inadequacies of the DTD to define data types moved from being a vague theoretical concern to a real practical problem. XPath 1.0 does implement four data types—node-set, string, number, and Boolean—but XPath's datatyping is feeble in comparison to the sophisticated and extensible datatyping facilities provided by XSD Schema (W3C XML Schema), which was finalized in mid-2001.

Note

In this chapter when a reference is being made to specific XSD Schema data types, the indicative namespace prefix `xsd` will be used without necessarily including a namespace declaration that would be required in a full listing. For example, the XSD Schema `duration` data type will be shown as `xsd:duration`.

XQuery will make use of data types derived from W3C XML Schema (also called XSD Schema). This provides a substantially greater functionality to define and customize data types compared to the fairly limited range of node-sets, Booleans, strings, and numbers in XPath 1.0. The availability of XSD Schema datatyping will remove the necessity for significant amounts of custom coding to check that correct data types are present.

MULTI-DOCUMENT FUNCTIONALITY

XPath 1.0 is essentially designed to address parts of a single XML document. All XPath location paths are directly (as in absolute location paths) or indirectly (in relative location paths) interpreted relative to a root node in a particular document. The facility to extend an XPath 1.0 query to one or more external documents is added by the XSLT `document()` function.

An XQuery 1.0 query is capable of following inter-document and intra-document links. This more fully integrates multi-document queries than is possible with XPath 1.0.

THE XQUERY DATA MODEL

The XQuery Data Model is based on the XML Information Set, often called the Infoset. The XML Information Set Recommendation is described at `http://www.w3.org/TR/xml-infoset/`.

The Infoset is intended to provide an abstract representation of XML documents (or the most important parts of them) and is intended for use by other XML specifications. The XQuery 1.0 and XPath 2.0 Data Model will be built on the infoset.

THE XQUERY FUNCTIONS AND OPERATORS

The XQuery 1.0 and XPath 2.0 Functions and Operators document lists, in abstract terms, are an extensive range of functions and operators that will be available for use in XQuery 1.0 and XPath 2.0 (and also XSLT 2.0). Not every function needs to be used in any particular language.

The range of functions provided substantially extends what was available in XPath 1.0, even with the addition of the functions provided by XSLT 1.0. Because XQuery is strongly datatyped, it becomes both possible and necessary to augment the range of functions that can handle specific data types, particularly those data types allowed by XSD Schema but not recognized among the four XPath 1.0 data types.

For example, XQuery will provide an extensive range of functions and operators that will operate on date-related data types. The current working draft lists more than twenty functions that operate specifically on date/time values. These are divided into three groups—duration and datetime constructors, comparisons of duration and datetime values, and, finally, component extraction functions on datetime values.

XSD Schema provides nine datetime data types—`xsd:duration`, `xsd:dateTime`, `xsd:date`, `xsd:time`, `xsd:gYear`, `xsd:gYearMonth`, `xsd:gMonthDay`, `xsd:Month`, and `xsd:Day`.

The functions and operators are currently presented in an abstract syntax such as `xf:date` and `op:numeric-add`. The implemented syntax within XQuery, XQueryX, XPath 2.0, and XSLT 2.0 might vary.

Note

> The indicative namespace prefix for XQuery functions is `xf`. This indicative namespace prefix refers, for the working draft current at the time of writing, to the URI `http://www.w3.org/2001/12/xquery-functions`. XQuery operators have an indicative namespace prefix of `op` that relates to the namespace URI `http://www.w3.org/2001/12/xquery-operators`.

One example of a duration and datetime constructor function is the `xf:duration` function, which takes a string argument and creates a result that is of `xsd:duration` data type. If the string argument does not correspond to the `xsd:duration` type, an error is raised. Similarly, the `xf:date` function takes a string argument and returns a result that is of `xsd:date` data type.

The functions that perform comparisons on `xsd:dateTime` and `xsd:duration` values have a number of limitations but are, nonetheless, very useful additions to what was available in XPath 1.0. These functions are, because of limitations in XSD Schema 1.0, able to return only an `xsd:boolean` value after performing a comparison. Additionally, only certain datetime constructs can be taken by these functions as arguments. The argument to these functions must be either of the form that contains only years and months or of the form that contains days, hours, minutes, and seconds.

For example, the `op:duration-less-than()` operator takes two arguments and returns an `xsd:boolean` value.

The component extraction functions treat a datetime value as if it were constructed of distinct components. Intuitively this makes sense. A date value of `2003-01-15`—corresponding to January 15, 2003—has three *components*, a year, a month, and a day.

For example, the `xf:get-Century-from-dateTime()` function can take an argument of `xsd:dateTime` data type and return an integer value corresponding to the century part of the `xsd:dateTime` data type. If we use the `xf:get-Century-from-dateTime()` function as in this code,

```
xf:get-Century-from-dateTime(xf:dateTime('2003-01-15T15:35:00'))
```

it will return the integer value `20`. The `xf:dateTime()` function converts the string argument to an `xsd:dateTime` data type, which is the legal argument data type for the `xf:get-Century-from-dateTime()` function.

Caution

Be careful to distinguish the *century* returned by `xf:get-Century-from-dateTime()` from the common English means of the expression of century. When we would talk of the twenty-first century, the function will return the integer value of `20`.

If, however, the string we want to use corresponds to the `xsd:date` data type, `2003-01-15` for example, we must use a separate function `xf:get-Century-from-date()` function as shown here:

```
xf:get-Century-from-date(xf:date('2003-01-15'))
```

As you have hopefully seen from these brief examples, XQuery 1.0 provides new functions not present in XPath 1.0 or XSLT 2.0. There will likely be dozens of new functions. Those quoted give you an indication of the functions likely to be available. Datatyping provides useful new functionality, but the strict datatyping means that you will need to have a good working understanding of the differences between the relevant XSD Schema data types and which are legal arguments for which XQuery function(s).

THE XQUERY QUERY LANGUAGES

It might seem odd, but the XML Query Language will have more than one syntax. One syntax will be expressed in non-XML syntax and the other, XQueryX, will be expressed in a syntax that is compliant with the requirements of XML version 1.0. The non-XML syntax, XQuery, will be more easily human readable, and will be similar to XPath syntax.

XQUERY

XQuery is the non-XML syntax for the XML Query Language.

One form of XQuery query uses a path expression syntax, so called because of its close similarities to XPath 1.0 syntax.

For example, if you had a document called book.xml that contained several `chapter` elements—each of which had a `title` element nested within it—you could retrieve the title of all the chapters in the book by issuing a query similar to the following:

```
document("book.xml")//chapter/title
```

Similarly, you could retrieve the titles of all appendixes in the book with a query such as

```
document("book.xml")//appendices/title
```

XQuery expressions make extensive use of the so-called "flower" expressions. The name arises from the initials of the keywords `FOR`, `LET`, `WHERE`, and `RETURN`.

A FLWR expression uses at least two of the four keywords just mentioned. Because we will invariably want something to be returned (at least in non-update queries), the RETURN keyword will always be used.

Listing 20.5 shows a highly simplified inventory of items to which we can apply an XQuery query.

LISTING 20.5 AN INVENTORY OF ITEMS WITH PRICES (INVENTORY.XML)

```
<?xml version='1.0'?>
<Inventory>
<Article>
 <Name>Article 1</Name>
 <Price>21.50</Price>
</Article>
<Article>
 <Name>Article 2</Name>
 <Price>41.00</Price>
</Article>
<Article>
 <Name>Article 3</Name>
 <Price>25.00</Price>
</Article>
<Article>
 <Name>Article 4</Name>
 <Price>55.00</Price>
</Article>
<Article>
 <Name>Article 5</Name>
 <Price>19.99</Price>
</Article>
<Article>
 <Name>Article 6</Name>
 <Price>21.50</Price>
</Article>
</Inventory>
```

A query to select all articles in which there was a unique value for the Price element that was less than 30.00 is shown in Listing 20.6.

LISTING 20.6 TESTING FOR UNIQUE VALUES OF THE Price ELEMENT THAT ARE LESS THAN 30.00 (ITEMQUERY.TXT)

```
<Results>
  {
    FOR $Price in distinct-values(document("Inventory.xml")//Article/Price)
    LET $Name := $Price/../Name
    WHERE $Price < 30.00
    RETURN
      <Article price={ $Price/text() }>
        <Name>{ $Name/text() }</Name>
      </Article>
  }
</Results>
```

Let's walk through the query line by line. The first line indicates that a literal start tag for a `Results` element is to be output. The `{` character indicates the start of an XQuery expression.

The `FOR` statement applies the `distinct-values()` function to the result of applying the `document()` function to the file Inventory.xml and the path expression `//Article/Price`. If we review Listing 20.5, we see that the value of the `Price` element for the first and sixth `Article` elements is the same—`21.50`. Strictly, the choice of which of two nodes is discarded in this situation is up to an individual application. We will assume that the first is retained and the later duplicate is discarded.

Thus, we have five `Price` element nodes that satisfy line 3 of the code in Listing 20.6.

The `LET` statement simply assigns to the variable `$Name` the value of the `Name` element node, which is a sibling of the `Price` element used in the `SPrice` variable.

The `WHERE` statement applies a test to the value of the `$Price` variable. If its value is less than `30.00`, the `RETURN` statement is applied. If its value is `30.00` or greater, the `RETURN` statement is bypassed.

The value contained in the `Price` element for the second and fourth articles exceeds `30.00`. Therefore, the `RETURN` statement is bypassed for those articles.

For the first, third, and fifth articles, the `RETURN` statement causes a literal `Article` element to be output with a `price` attribute whose value is obtained from the XQuery expression `$Price/text()`. The content of each `Article` element also includes a `Name` element whose content is defined by the XQuery expression `$Name/text()`.

Listing 20.7 shows the document output.

LISTING 20.7 RESULTS FROM APPLYING THE LISTING 20.6 QUERY TO THE LISTING 20.5'S INPUT DOCUMENT (INVENTORYOUT.XML)

```
<Inventory>
 <Article price="21.50">
  <Name>Article 1</Name>
 </Article>
 <Article price="25.00">
  <Name>Article 3</Name>
 </Article>
 <Article price="19.99">
  <Name>Article 5</Name>
 </Article>
</Inventory>
```

The `FOR`, `LET`, `WHERE`, and `RETURN` statements can be combined in potentially very complex nested constructs to allow multiple criteria to be applied in a single search.

XQUERYX

One of the requirements contained in the XQuery Requirements document is that the functionality of XQuery should be expressed in an XML-based query syntax. XQueryX is the XML syntax currently under development at W3C.

At the time of writing, the XQueryX working draft has not been updated to take account of subsequent syntax changes in XQuery. Listing 20.8 is an example from the June 2001 Working Draft that shows equivalent XQuery and XQueryX syntax for a query.

LISTING 20.8 A QUERY EXPRESSED IN XQUERY (AQUERY.TXT)

```
FOR $b IN document("bib.xml")//book
WHERE $b/publisher = "Morgan Kaufmann" AND $b/year = "1998"
RETURN $b/title
```

Contrast that with Listing 20.9, which is expressed in XQueryX.

LISTING 20.9 THE QUERY OF LISTING 20.8 EXPRESSED IN XQUERYX (AQUERY.XML)

```
<?xml version='1.0'?>
<q:query xmlns:q="http://www.w3.org/2001/06/xqueryx">
  <q:flwr>
    <q:forAssignment variable="$b">
      <q:step axis="SLASHSLASH">
        <q:function name="document">
          <q:constant datatype="CHARSTRING">bib.xml</q:constant>
        </q:function>
        <q:identifier>book</q:identifier>
      </q:step>
    </q:forAssignment>
    <q:where>
      <q:function name="AND">
        <q:function name="EQUALS">
          <q:step axis="CHILD">
            <q:variable>$b</q:variable>
            <q:identifier>publisher</q:identifier>
          </q:step>
          <q:constant datatype="CHARSTRING">Morgan Kaufmann</q:constant>
        </q:function>
        <q:function name="EQUALS">
          <q:step axis="CHILD">
            <q:variable>$b</q:variable>
            <q:identifier>year</q:identifier>
          </q:step>
          <q:constant datatype="CHARSTRING">1998</q:constant>
        </q:function>
      </q:function>
    </q:where>
    <q:return>
      <q:step axis="CHILD">
        <q:variable>$b</q:variable>
        <q:identifier>title</q:identifier>
      </q:step>
```

LISTING 20.9 CONTINUED

```
    </q:return>
  </q:flwr>
</q:query>
```

The XQueryX version is obviously much more verbose than the XQuery version of the query. The XQuery version is also more readable. Apart from situations in which XQueryX is generated by, for example, XSLT, it is difficult to envisage XQueryX often being hand coded because of the sheer length of even simple queries.

SOME ILLUSTRATIVE XQUERY USE CASES

In this section, we will look at how XQuery code for some typical XQuery use cases might be written. In the space available, the examples only serve to illustrate the type of queries that XQuery will be able to execute. The absence of a particular type of query in this section shouldn't lead you to think that XQuery lacks any particular functionality. Check the latest XQuery specification documents to establish the latest position.

One XQuery early implementation from X-Hive.com is available for use online and makes use of examples contained in the W3C XQuery Use Cases draft. To view the XQuery demo, visit `http://www.x-hive.com/xquery`.

Thus, you can work through the examples shown in this section online at X-Hive.com. Naturally, you can also create your own queries to learn more about XQuery.

The XML document we will use for our data is found in the XML Query Use Cases Working Draft, `http://www.w3.org/TR/2001/WD-xmlquery-use-cases-20011220`, and is shown in Listing 20.10. This document is extremely useful as you work to get up to speed with XQuery.

LISTING 20.10 THE W3C XML USE CASES SOURCE XML CODE (BIB.XML)

```
<bib>
 <book year="1994">
  <title>
   TCP/IP Illustrated
  </title>
  <author>
   <last>Stevens</last>
   <first>W.</first>
  </author>
  <publisher>Addison-Wesley</publisher>
  <price> 65.95</price>
 </book>
 <book year="1992">
  <title>
   Advanced Programming in the Unix environment
  </title>
```

Listing 20.10 Continued

```
  <author>
   <last>Stevens</last>
   <first>W.</first>
  </author>
  <publisher>Addison-Wesley</publisher>
  <price>65.95</price>
 </book>
 <book year="2000">
  <title>
   Data on the Web
  </title>
  <author>
   <last>Abiteboul</last>
   <first>Serge</first>
  </author>
  <author>
   <last>Buneman</last>
   <first>Peter</first>
  </author>
  <author>
   <last>Suciu</last>
   <first>Dan</first>
  </author>
  <publisher>Morgan Kaufmann Publishers</publisher>
  <price> 39.95</price>
 </book>
 <book year="1999">
  <title>
   The Economics of Technology and Content for Digital TV
  </title>
  <editor>
   <last>Gerbarg</last>
   <first>Darcy</first>
   <affiliation>CITI</affiliation>
  </editor>
  <publisher>Kluwer Academic Publishers</publisher>
  <price>129.95</price>
 </book>
</bib>
```

20

Listing 20.10 describes a number of books. The document element is a `bib` element. The structure of most `book` elements is the same, but notice that the final book has an `editor` element rather than one or more `author` elements.

A Simple Book Listing

Let's create a simple query that will retrieve the content of all the `publisher` and `title` elements. The `bib` and `book` elements are created literally, not retrieved from the document being queried.

Note

All queries in this section are based on the example XML document from the XQuery Use Cases document. These have been modified to be able to run on the X-Hive.com online demo. If you want to run these with other XQuery implementations of the Use Cases, you will likely have to alter paths to files, for example.

Note that in the third line of the query, the path to the bib.xml file is shown as the argument to the `document()` function. The path used is the path to allow you to use the data on the live X-Hive demo. To run the queries in another setting, you would have to appropriately modify the path to bib.xml.

LISTING 20.11 AN XQUERY QUERY TO RETRIEVE THE CONTENT OF PUBLISHER AND TITLE ELEMENTS (QUERY01.TXT)

```
<bib>
 {
  for $b in document("/XQuery/docs/XMP/bib.xml")/bib/book
  return
    <book>
     { $b/title }
     { $b/publisher }
    </book>
 }
</bib>
```

This is a form of the `FLWR` expression that contains `FOR` and `RETURN` statements.

The `FOR` statement sets the variable `$b` to correspond to a `book` element node in bib.xml. The `RETURN` statement creates a new literal `book` element for each node in `$b` and outputs a `title` element node and a `publisher` element node that are child nodes of the nodes represented by `$b`. Finally, an end tag for the `book` element is output.

Note

Notice that the keywords `FOR`, `LET`, `WHERE`, and `RETURN` are not case sensitive. In this respect, XQuery resembles SQL where keywords are not case sensitive.

The result from the query is shown in Listing 20.12.

LISTING 20.12 THE RESULT FROM THE QUERY SHOWN IN LISTING 20.11 (QUERY01OUT.XML)

```
<bib>
 <book>
  <title>
   TCP/IP Illustrated
  </title>
  <publisher>Addison-Wesley</publisher>
```

Listing 20.12 Continued

```
</book>
<book>
 <title>
  Advanced Programming in the Unix environment
 </title>
 <publisher>Addison-Wesley</publisher>
</book>
<book>
<title>
 Data on the Web
</title>
<publisher>Morgan Kaufmann Publishers</publisher>
</book>
<book>
 <title>
  The Economics of Technology and Content for Digital TV
 </title>
 <publisher>Kluwer Academic Publishers</publisher>
</book>
</bib>
```

A Listing of Recent Books

Suppose that you want to find books published after the year 1995 and create a new XML document whose document element is a name of your choosing, such as a RecentBooks element.

Listing 20.13 shows a query to create a literal RecentBooks element as the document element and to select books that have a year attribute whose value is greater than 1995. We use a WHERE statement to compare the year of publication with 1995.

Listing 20.13 An XQuery Query to Retrieve Books Published Since 1995 (Query02.txt)

```
<RecentBooks>
 {
  for $b in document("/XQuery/docs/XMP/bib.xml")/bib/book
  where $b/@year > 1995
  return
    <book year={ $b/@year }>
     { $b/title }
     { $b/publisher }
    </book>
 }
</RecentBooks>
```

The XML document created by the query in Listing 20.13 is shown in Listing 20.14.

20

Listing 20.14 Result of the XQuery Query to Select Books Published After 1995 (Query02Out.xml)

```
<RecentBooks>
 <book year="2000">
  <title>
   Data on the Web
  </title>
  <publisher>Morgan Kaufmann Publishers</publisher>
 </book>
 <book year="1999">
  <title>
   The Economics of Technology and Content for Digital TV
  </title>
  <publisher>Kluwer Academic Publishers</publisher>
 </book>
</RecentBooks>
```

Sorting the Query Results by Publisher

We can modify Listing 20.13 to sort the output by the value of the `publisher` element in the input document. Listing 20.15 shows how this can be done.

Listing 20.15 Query Selecting Books Published After 1995, Sorted Alphabetically by Publisher (Query03.txt)

```
<RecentBooks>
 {
  for $b in document("/XQuery/docs/XMP/bib.xml")/bib/book
  where $b/@year > 1995
  return
    <book year={ $b/@year }>
     { $b/title }
     { $b/publisher }
    </book>
   sortby(publisher/text() ascending)
 }
</RecentBooks>
```

The `sortby()` function sorts the output by the text value of the `publisher` element node.

The output, sorted alphabetically by publisher, is shown in Listing 20.16.

Listing 20.16 Books Published After 1995 Alphabetically Sorted by Publisher (Query03Out.xml)

```
<RecentBooks>
  <book year=" year="1999"">
    <title>The Economics of Technology and Content for Digital TV</title>
    <publisher>Kluwer Academic Publishers</publisher>
  </book>
  <book year=" year="2000"">
```

LISTING 20.16 CONTINUED

```
    <title>Data on the Web</title>
    <publisher>Morgan Kaufmann Publishers</publisher>
  </book>
</RecentBooks>
```

There is much, much more to XQuery than has been introduced in this chapter. It will, after the specification has been finalized, be a key area of knowledge for many who work with XML. If this is a topic that interests you, be sure to follow the development of the XQuery specification in all its facets as defined in the various W3C working drafts.

ADDITIONAL RESOURCES

The URLs for each of the XQuery and related W3C documents were given earlier in the chapter.

XQuery is at an early stage of development so there are only a limited number of good additional resources available on the Web at present.

- An important resource is the XML Query home page at W3C (`http://www.w3.org/XML/Query`).
- The official archives of the W3C discussion list for XQuery (`http://lists.w3.org/Archives/Public/www-ql/`).
- The XQuery Mailing List on YahooGroups.com (`http://www.yahoogroups.com/group/xquery`).

Some of the most useful resources are associated with XQuery demo implementations. Here are a few of the best sites to visit:

- The X-Hive XQuery demo (`http://www.x-hive.com/xquery/`). It's one of the best XQuery demos at the time of writing.
- Software AG's Quip implementation of XQuery (`http://www.softwareag.com/developer/quip/default.htm`).
- OpenLink Software's XQuery Demo (`http://demo.openlinksw.com:8891/xquery/demo.vsp`).
- Fatdog's XML Query Engine (`http://www.fatdog.com/`).

ROADMAP

The XML Query Language will be a very important XML specification because it is intended to provide a comprehensive query language for XML data stores. Because it is at an early stage of development, it isn't covered elsewhere in this book. Keep an eye on the W3C site for new developments.

PART VI

XML Related Technologies

CHAPTER 21

THE FUTURE OF THE WEB: XHTML

In this chapter

by Kynn Bartlett

WHAT IS XHTML?

The simplest definition of XHTML is nothing more than the following:

> *XHTML is HTML written according to XML rules.*

Because you've gotten this far in the book, you have a good idea as to what XML is and how you can use it. In this chapter, we'll look at what impact XML has had on the existing HTML language and what the peculiarities are about using them both together, including how to use XHTML modules in constructing new languages.

A SHORT HISTORY OF XHTML

As you know, *Hypertext Markup Language (HTML)* is the primary language used on the Web for the construction of Web pages and sites. Originally created by Tim Berners-Lee in 1990, HTML was designed to be a simple application of *Standard Generalized Markup Language (SGML)* for easy creation of collaborative content.

The first Web site was at the European Center for Nuclear Research (CERN), a physics research institute. For this reason, I like to say that early HTML was a great language for marking up physics papers, and little else. The first version of HTML was unnumbered and primarily represented Tim's ideas of what he needed at CERN.

A more formal version of HTML was published in November 1995 by the Internet Engineering Task Force's HTML Working Group, as RFC 1866. This was *HTML 2.0*, and it consists of a fairly stable baseline of elements and attributes that are generally supported by every HTML application or browser out there. Unfortunately, HTML 2.0 turned out to be one of the least exciting languages in the world if you were trying to create attractive, functional designs in a commercial context: That's the purpose to which the Web was quickly put.

Browser innovation and competition between early front-runner Mozilla and newcomer Netscape led to the introduction of new elements and attributes to make up for the presentational shortcomings of early HTML. New browser releases meant new tags to use, and Web developers furiously debated the value of these "Netscapisms." The loose nature of the HTML language meant that browser authors were free to interpret the source code however they liked, so you could never be sure that what worked for one browser would work for the other. With the arrival of Microsoft's Internet Explorer onto the scene and the start of so-called Browser Wars, it became obvious that something needed to be done, and soon.

To address the problems associated with fast and loose standards, the newly formed *World Wide Web Consortium (W3C)* gathered together a group of very intelligent people and sat down to work on HTML 3.0. As often happens when you have a group of very intelligent people, it was hard to reach an agreement on what the new HTML 3.0 specification should be. Should it describe an evolutionary change in HTML? A revolutionary change? Or should it simply standardize the existing tags to bring them into some sort of agreement?

After many fine ideas were proposed (some of which made it into later versions of HTML or other Web standards), it became obvious that there was still no clear consensus on new directions for HTML 3.0. Rather than issuing a new version of HTML with completely new features, the decision of the World Wide Web Consortium was to release, in January 1997 as *HTML 3.2*, a snapshot of the state of Web markup as of early 1996. Thus, HTML 3.2 represents the most reasonable and useful set of HTML tags supported by browsers available at that point in time.

Of course, this meant that HTML 3.2 did little in the way of extending the functionality of HTML. For this reason, work began on HTML 4.0. Also, a need was recognized for a way to extend HTML-like documents without necessarily using the full complexity of SGML: This effort to create an extensible markup language, of course, led to the creation of XML.

Back on the HTML front, *HTML 4.0* was issued as a W3C recommendation on December 18, 1997. Many existing elements and attributes were standardized (such as frames, which are not allowed in HTML 3.2) and new functionality was added as well. Most of the new functionality lacked support in then current browsers. (Only recently are major browsers beginning to fully support nearly all the HTML 4.0 specifications.)

One of the guiding principles of HTML 4.0 was to separate presentation markup from structural and semantic markup through the use of Cascading Style Sheets. The *Cascading Style Sheets Level One* recommendation was issued by the W3C in December 1996, but browser support has been even slower in coming than the support for HTML 4.0. This meant that if you were to use HTML 4.0 without presentational markup, most browsers out there would display it as if you were still using HTML 2.0 (for example, gray backgrounds, no color or font control, and so on).

The authors of the HTML 4.0 recommendation addressed this by creating so-called *flavors* of HTML. Strict HTML 4.0 removes nearly all presentational attributes and elements (such as `align`, `<font>`, and so on) and relies on CSS. Transitional HTML 4.0 retains those elements for legacy reasons, and was intended as a temporary measure until full support for HTML Strict and CSS was forthcoming from the browsers. A third flavor of HTML, Frameset HTML 4.0, is identical to Transitional HTML 4.0 except for the inclusion of frames. Each of the different flavors of HTML 4.0 is based on a separate DTD because HTML is actually an application of SGML, defined with DTDs.

With the issuance of XML as a W3C Recommendation in February 1998, the question arose as to how to integrate these technologies together, which shared the same genesis as an outgrowth of early HTML and of SGML. The W3C's HTML Working Group released two documents closely together in December 1990 and January 2000—*HTML 4.01*, which updated the HTML 4.0 specification in relatively minor ways, and *XHTML 1.0*, which was HTML 4.01 written according to the rules for XML. Methods of writing backward-compatible XHTML ensure that XHTML documents can be understood by older browsers which only understand HTML.

To meet the need for a more extensible version of XHTML, the HTML Working Group then worked on breaking down XHTML into discrete modules. This was published as "Modularization of XHTML" in April 2001, and "XHTML 1.1." XHTML 1.0 Strict expressed in modules followed in May 2001. Further work on HTML, such as the simpler subset of "XHTML Basic" or the forthcoming "XHTML 2.0," will be based on this concept of abstract modules codified in DTDs or Schemas.

ADVANTAGES OF HTML WRITTEN AS XML

The primary benefit of XHTML derives from its nature as XML. You can work with XHTML in any environment in which you can work with XML.

Some of those benefits include

- Using XML editors and tools to create XHTML
- Checking your work against an XML DTD or Schema
- Transforming from other languages to XHTML with XSLT
- Changing XHTML into SVG, XSL-FO, or other XML languages
- Dynamically altering the markup to meet the end user's needs
- Using XPointer or XInclude to reference fragments of your XHTML page
- Combining with other XML languages (such as MathML) to extend XHTML
- Embedding XML or RDF metadata within your XHTML
- Managing a site as an XML repository

As XML applications continue to be created and evolve in sophistication, it will become critical to have content and user interface models written up in an XML-based format. XHTML is the important first step toward that goal.

TYPES OF XHTML

All the varieties of XHTML share a basic similarity: They adhere to the syntax and grammar of XML languages, and they are designed primarily for use on the Web to display and navigate through information and interactive applications. On the surface level, they are not very different from each other nor from earlier non-XML versions of HTML. The semantics and display characteristics of XHTML are inherited from HTML, so the meaning of any XHTML document should be familiar to authors of HTML.

XHTML 1.0 is the version of XHTML that is closest to HTML 4.01. In fact, XHTML 1.0 is defined primarily by reference to the HTML 4.01 specification. It's a direct translation from the looser SGML-based HTML into XML terms. No new language features were added (although a few fixes were made in the change from HTML 4.0 to 4.01), and apart from learning the rules for XML conversion and browser compatibility, it should present little problem to anyone who has written HTML.

Like HTML 4.01 (and 4.0 before it), *XHTML 1.0* comes in three flavors: Strict, Transitional, and Frameset. *Strict XHTML 1.0* relies upon Cascading Style Sheets to control the presentation; *Transitional XHTML 1.0* has the presentational elements that were removed from Strict; and *Frameset XHTML 1.0* allows frames.

With the modularization of XTHML, things start getting a little more tricky. In *modularized XHTML*, the language is defined according to modules from the Modularization of XHTML specification. The XHTML 1.0 specification was broken apart into pieces, with each *abstract module* representing one type of functionality. Languages built using these documents are considered to be part of the *XHTML family*.

XHTML 1.1 is the newest version of HTML, and is built upon the modularized XHTML framework. XHTML 1.1 eliminates a number of deprecated and legacy elements and attributes, enforcing a uniform "strict" approach: There is no transitional version of XHTML 1.1. XHTML also adds Ruby tags for text annotation. Ruby tags are used to allow easier use of East Asian languages in documents, which we will discuss later in the chapter.

XHTML Basic is also an XHTML family language, and it defines a limited set of functionality for use on small devices. This is intended to complement or even replace the use of *Wireless Markup Language (WML)* in cellular phones.

XHTML 1.0

The 1.0 version of XHTML was written as a direct translation of HTML 4.01 (released simultaneously on January 26, 2000) into XML. The W3C recommendation defining "XHTML 1.0: The Extensible Hypertext Markup Language" can be found at

`http://www.w3.org/TR/xhtml1`

At time of writing, an updated version of XHTML 1.0 (XHTML 1.0 Second Edition) was a W3C working draft. XHTML 1.0 Second Edition does not extend or change XHTML 1.0 semantics or functionality. It merely incorporates errata and clarifications for the original recommendation. Check the preceding URL for the latest official version of XHTML 1.0.

The XHTML 1.0 specification does not actually describe the meaning and semantics of the tags it defines. Instead, it refers to the HTML 4.01 recommendation. The address for the HTML 4.01 specification is

`http://www.w3.org/TR/html401`

Differences Between HTML and XHTML

Because XML is generally more demanding when it comes to syntax, the key differences between HTML and XHTML derive from the requirements of XML.

Well-formedness Required

HTML browsers have always been rather forgiving of sloppy markup practices: perhaps too forgiving because many Web developers (or their software tools) never got in the habit of properly nesting elements. The well-formed requirement of XML forces XHTML to be well-formed.

HTML Example:

```
<h1>
<strong>Note: This is not valid HTML
</h1>
</strong>
```

21

XHTML Equivalent:

```
<h1>
  <strong>Note: This is well-formed XML
  </strong>
</h1>
```

ELEMENTS AND ATTRIBUTES IN LOWERCASE

HTML is not case sensitive in element and attribute names, allowing mixed or irregular use of case, whereas XML requires standardization. Therefore, in XHTML, all elements and attributes must be named in lowercase. Why lowercase and not upper? It's essentially an arbitrary decision that needed to be made, and the HTML Working Group chose lowercase letters. It could have been uppercase almost as easily: But keep in mind that lowercase saves wear and tear on the Shift or Caps Lock key.

HTML Example:

```
<DIV class="notice" onMouseOver="rollover()">
  <Strong>
    HTML element and attribute names are
    case-insensitive.
  </Strong>
</div>
```

XML Equivalent:

```
<div class="notice" onmouseover="rollover()">
  <strong>
    XHTML element and attribute names are
    case-sensitive.
  </strong>
</div>
```

END TAGS ARE REQUIRED

Certain elements in HTML had optional ending tags, and some (`<html>`, `<head>`, `<body>`) even had optional starting tags. XHTML requires ending tags on all elements, even those that were optional under HTML.

HTML Example:

```
<p>Opening and closing elements:
<ol>
  <li>First, put the opening tag.
  <li>Then, put the element's content.
  <li>For some elements, the closing tag is optional.
</ol>
```

XHTML Equivalent:

```
<p>Opening and closing elements:</p>
<ol>
  <li>First, put the opening tag.</li>
  <li>Then, put the element's content.</li>
  <li>Finally, always put the closing tag.</li>
</ol>
```

Empty Elements Must Be Ended

Similarly, XHTML requires that all empty elements be properly closed by using either `<tag/>` or `<tag></tag>`.

HTML Example:

```
<p>
  I like
  <br>
  blank lines.
</p>
<hr>
```

XHTML Equivalent:

```
<p>
  I like
  <br />
  blank lines.
</p>
<hr></hr>
```

Attribute Values Must Be Quoted

Attribute values in HTML did not have to be quoted unless they contained characters besides letters, numbers, a plus, a dash, or an underline. In XHTML, quotes are required on all attribute values.

HTML Example:

```
<table border=3 align=right>
  <tr>
    <td width=50>...</td>
    <td width=50>...</td>
  </tr>
</table>
```

XHTML Equivalent:

```
<table border="3" align="right">
  <tr>
    <td width="50">...</td>
    <td width="50">...</td>
  </tr>
</table>
```

Attributes Cannot Be Minimized

SGML (and thus HTML) allows attributes to be *minimized*—which means that names and values can be written as simply the attribute name, and the value is equal to the attribute name. XML does not allow this shorthand, and neither does XHTML.

21

HTML Example:

```
<select name="version" multiple>
  <option selected>HTML 4.01</option>
  <option>XHTML 1.0</option>
```

```
    <option disabled>XHTML 2.0</option>
  </select>
```

XHTML Equivalent:

```
<select name="version" multiple="multiple">
    <option selected="selected">HTML 4.01</option>
    <option>XHTML 1.0</option>
    <option disabled="disabled">XHTML 2.0</option>
  </select>
```

WHITESPACE STRIPPED FROM ATTRIBUTE VALUES

In XHTML, whitespace at the beginning or end of attribute values is stripped, and multiple whitespace characters within an attribute value are condensed to a single space character.

HTML Example:

```
<abbr title="This Abbreviation          Has A Lot
              of          Whitespace          ">
  TAHALOW
</abbr>
```

XHTML Equivalent:

```
<abbr title="Whitespace      Will Be Condensed
             in this Abbreviation            ">
  WWBCITA
</abbr>
```

INLINE SCRIPTS AND STYLES IN CDATA

In HTML, the usual way to include a script or embedded style sheet was to hide it with HTML comments, so it wouldn't be seen by older browsers. XML parsers strip out comments, making this ineffective. Scripts and styles within an XHTML document must be character data, which means that characters which might be interpreted as XML (such as `<`, `&`, `]]>`, or `--`) need to be escaped, or included in external script and style files.

HTML Example:

```
<style type="text/css">
  <!--
    body { font-family: Arial, sans-serif; }
    .new { color: red; }
  -->
</style>
```

XHTML Equivalent:

```
<style type="text/css">
  <![CDATA[
    body { font-family: Arial, sans-serif; }
    .new { color: red; }
  ]]>
</style>
```

name ATTRIBUTE DEPRECATED IN FAVOR OF id

One role of the name attribute in HTML is to identify specific locations or fragments (anchors) within the page, which can then be targeted by links, used by scripts, or invoked as image maps. In XML, this same function is served by the id attribute, so XHTML favors id over name.

HTML Example:

```
<div>
  <a href="#about">About Me</a>
  |
  <a href="#contact">Contact Me</a>
</div>
<h1>
  <a name="about">
    About Me
  </a>
</h1>
```

XHTML Equivalent:

```
<div>
  <a href="#about">About Me</a>
  |
  <a href="#contact">Contact Me</a>
</div>
<h1 id="about">
  About Me
</h1>
```

ENUMERATED ATTRIBUTE TYPES

In HTML and XHTML, some attributes can take any values, whereas others are restricted to only certain attribute values. For example, the <bdo> element (for bi-directional text) can only take values of ltr (left-to-right) and rtl (right-to-left). In HTML, these values can be in any case: But in XHTML 1.0, they must be in lowercase because that's how they're defined in the DTD.

HTML Example:

```
<table>
  <tr>
    <td align="LEFT" valign="Top">
      ...
    </td>
  </tr>
</table>
```

XHTML Equivalent:

```
<table>
  <tr>
    <td align="left" valign="top">
    ...
    </td>
  </tr>
</table>
```

SGML EXCLUSIONS NOT ENFORCED BY THE DTD

HTML, as an application of SGML, can define certain elements as unable to contain other elements as children or descendants at any level. Unfortunately, that limitation can't be expressed within an XML DTD, so errors of that type can't be checked by validation against the XHTML DTD.

Instead, the specification defines certain element prohibitions that cannot occur at any level. For example, the `<label>` element cannot contain another `<label>` element, nor is it valid to contain a `<strong>` element that contains a `<label>` element. The latter use is valid against the DTD, so the restriction is spelled out in words.

Elements that are not allowed within other elements in XHTML are listed in Table 21.1.

TABLE 21.1 ELEMENT PROHIBITIONS

Element	**Cannot Contain**
`a`	Other a elements
`button`	`iframe`, and other `form` elements: `button`,`fieldset`, `form`, `input`, `isindex`, `label`, `select`, `textarea`
`form`	Other `form` elements
`label`	Other `label` elements
`pre`	`img`, `object`, `big`, `small`, `sub`, or `sup` elements

FLAVORS OF XHTML 1.0

Like HTML 4.01 (and HTML 4.0), XHTML 1.0 actually defines three languages: Strict, Transitional, and Frameset. Within a document, the specific variety of XHTML used is defined by the `DOCTYPE` statement.

XHTML STRICT

XHTML 1.0 Strict is almost entirely clear of presentational markup: for example, attributes or elements that specify alignment, color, font properties, and so on. These presentational effects should instead be specified using Cascading Style Sheets.

To identify a document as XHTML 1.0 Strict, use the following `DOCTYPE` statement:

```
<!DOCTYPE html
  PUBLIC "-//W3C//DTD XHTML 1.0 Strict//EN"
  "DTD/xhtml1-strict.dtd">
```

You will want to use XHTML 1.0 Strict if you are going to rely on CSS for presentation, or if you don't mind users of older browsers receiving an unstyled rendering of your content.

XHTML Transitional

XHTML 1.0 Transitional is meant as a compromise between the ideals of Strict XHTML (firm separation of presentation from content) and the reality of today's browsers, which have offered irregular support for CSS. (Fortunately, CSS support in browsers is improving and many CSS-based designs are now much more reliable than they were in the past.)

To declare your XHTML page as XHTML 1.0 Transitional, use this DOCTYPE:

```
<!DOCTYPE html
  PUBLIC "-//W3C//DTD XHTML 1.0 Transitional//EN"
  "DTD/xhtml1-transitional.dtd">
```

As the name indicates, Transitional XHTML is meant to be a temporary measure. You'll want to use XHTML 1.0 Transitional whenever you need to support older (non-CSS or limited CSS) browsers.

XHTML Frameset

The XHTML 1.0 Frameset variety is based on XHTML 1.0 Transitional, but it includes support for framesets within the <html> element, after the <head> element. Otherwise, it's the same as XHTML 1.0 Transitional.

The DOCTYPE statement for XHTML 1.0 Frameset is

```
<!DOCTYPE
  PUBLIC "-//W3C/DTD XHTML 1.0 Frameset//EN"
  "DTD/xhtml1-frameset.dtd">
```

You only need to declare a document as XHTML 1.0 Frameset if you're using frames, and then only on the documents that contain the <frameset> element instead of the <body> element (as the second child of <html>). The pages that are referenced by your <frame> elements should be XHTML 1.0 Transitional, not XHTML 1.0 Frameset. (Just the pages that build the framesets need XHTML 1.0 Frameset.)

XHTML 1.0 and Browsers

The primary use of XHTML 1.0 (like HTML) is on the Web, which means that most user agents which process XHTML are likely to be Web browsers. Indexing spiders, XML parsers, intelligent agents, and proxy servers are among the nonbrowsers that might be accessing XHTML pages, but these will continue to be in the minority for some time.

Most existing browsers in general use at this time don't directly support XML or XHTML, but they clearly understand HTML. For the next few years, most XHTML should be written with the expectation that it's very likely an HTML browser, with no knowledge of XML, will be handling the document.

Rules for Browser Compatibility

When creating XHTML, it's very easy to write perfectly legitimate XHTML that will send HTML browsers into fits. For example,

```
<p>
  This is a test.
  <br></br>
  Did it pass or fail?
  <br/>
  I may never know.
</p>
```

According to the HTML standard, there's no such closing tag as `</br`. The `<br>` element is `EMPTY` and can never have a closing element. So that's one possible point of confusion, but it's generally harmless because the HTML browser will just ignore the confusing closing tag.

Another possible point of confusion is that the construct `<br/>`, which we know from XML means "a self-closing empty tag," is not valid HTML either. The browser is very likely to read it not as "the familiar `br` element that I know how to display" but as "some strange element called `br/` that isn't on my list of elements." Upon encountering such an element, of course, the browser ignores it, which means that there's no blank line inserted.

Fortunately, XML is somewhat flexible in how you write your tags. So it's valid XHTML to do the following:

```
<p>
  This is a test.
  <br />
  Did it pass or fail?
  <br />
  I may never know.
</p>
```

The space before the slash means that the HTML browser will correctly read the name of the tag as `br`. When it reaches the slash, it'll just assume that it's some poorly written attribute and ignore it, which is what we want it to do.

This is just one example of how valid XHTML can be confused by HTML browsers. Therefore, the following guidelines for writing XHTML so that it can be read by current browsers were issued by the HTML Working Group:

- Be careful about processing instructions, including the XML declaration (`<?xml version="1.0"?>`): These are sometimes rendered. It's valid to leave out the XML declaration, but remember that means you can only use UTF-8 or UTF-16 encoding in that document because those are the default encoding types.
- If you do change the character encoding, use both the `<?xml version="1.0" encoding="UTF-16"?>` declaration, and a `<meta>` element as well: `<meta http-equiv="Content-type" content='text/html;charset="UTF-16"' />`.
- For `EMPTY` elements, include a space before the slash, as shown previously for `<br />`.

- For non-EMPTY elements that happen to be empty (meaning that they don't have to be empty all the time, according to the DTD, but this current instance is empty), don't use the minimized form. For example, use `<textarea></textarea>`, not `<textarea />`, even though both are valid XHTML.
- Don't use comments to hide style sheets or scripts; instead, put them in an external file if they contain `<`, `&`, `]]>`, or `--`.
- Because you can't rely on XHTML's whitespace compression in attribute values, don't split your attribute values over multiple lines and don't include extra spaces with the assumption they'll be translated into a single space.
- Don't put more than one `<isindex>` element in the document head—even though this is allowable by the DTD. In fact, you probably shouldn't use `<isindex>` at all because it's deprecated, and the `<form>` and `<input>` elements provide a better version of the same functionality.
- Use both the `xml:lang` and `lang` attributes. The `lang` attribute is deprecated and thus on the way out because `xml:lang` is the new, standardized XML way of expressing languages. But most browsers and assistive technologies don't know this yet, and are looking for `lang` attributes.
- The `id` attribute is preferred over the `name` attribute in XHTML 1.0, so this could lead to confusion. Consider, for example, the following: `<a href="#skip">Skip Links</a>`. From an XHTML (and XML) viewpoint, that is a link to an element with an `id` attribute whose value is `"skip"`. From the older, HTML perspective, that is a link to an `<a>` element whose `name` attribute has the value `"skip"`. For compatibility's sake, it's best to set both attributes to the same value, such as `<a id="skip" name="skip">...</em>`.
- Some HTML browsers don't properly understand the shorthand that lets you write `<option selected>` when you mean `<option selected="selected">`, and they won't select the option if you use the latter case. In XHTML, you can't minimize the attribute, so the second version is the only valid one, which means that these browsers might have a problem. There's not an easy solution to this if you want to keep to valid XHTML. (If you did `<option selected selected="selected">`, it would probably work in HTML and XHTML browsers, but it wouldn't be valid.)
- The HTML DOM and the XML DOM specify different behavior for names of attributes and elements, as well as a few other differences. JavaScript authors should be aware of these differences when writing for XHTML; for example, HTML attribute names are capitalized and XHTML are lowercase.
- Attribute values that contain the ampersand character (`&`) should be encoded with character entity `&`—such as URIs that specify parameters in the string. For example, `<a href="http://xml.kynn.com/parse.php?user=kynn&host=imra">` should be written as `<a href="http://xml.kynn.com/parse.php?user=kynn&host=imra">`.
- Cascading Style Sheets rules should be written with lowercase letters and should not assume the presence of elements that can be implied in HTML but must be explicit in XHTML—such as the `<tbody>` element.

Remember that the goal of these guidelines is to produce valid XHTML that can be understood by HTML browsers: It isn't to produce code that is both XHTML and HTML at the same time. In fact, except for very simple code, it's generally impossible to have XHTML 1.0 that is also valid HTML. The goal of these guidelines is to support backward compatibility without breaking any browsers that directly support XHTML.

BROWSER SUPPORT FOR XHTML 1.0

So far, there has been limited browser support for XHTML 1.0 interpreted as XHTML (and not as HTML)—mostly because XHTML is relatively new. Recent versions of Netscape (6.0 and higher), Mozilla, and Opera (5.0 and higher) claim support for native interpretation of XHTML.

INTERNET MEDIA TYPES FOR XHTML

When serving XHTML 1.0, the document (MIME) type should be set to `text/html` when written for compatibility with HTML browsers as described previously. The MIME types `text/xml` or `application/xml` can also be used, although this might affect the parsing of data. For example, DOM and CSS parsing might be different for HTML than for XML.

The media type `application/xhtml+xml` has been submitted to the Internet Engineering Task Force (IETF) as a draft. At the time of this writing, it is still a work in progress. The draft can be found at

`http://www.ietf.org/internet-drafts/draft-baker-xhtml-media-reg-02.txt`

MODULARIZING XHTML

In April 2001, the W3C's HTML Working Group released the "Modularization of XHTML" document as a W3C recommendation. It can be found at

`http://www.w3.org/TR/xhtml-modularization`

The recommendation breaks down the XHTML 1.0 specification into *abstract modules*, each module containing related elements and attributes. This modular approach forms the basis for all further development in XHTML because future versions need simply declare new or updated modules. This is the approach taken in XHTML 1.1 and XHTML Basic.

BENEFITS OF MODULARIZATION

Specifying an HTML-based markup language in modules has a number of benefits, including

- Modularization provides a consistent framework for defining HTML-based XML languages.
- Modularization means not duplicating effort. You don't have to reinvent the `<img>` element if you want to use it.
- Modularization makes it easy to replace discrete portions of the specification while keeping the framework intact.

- Modularization reduces the difficulty of adding new elements by simply including them in compliant modules.
- Modularization allows for portions of the XHTML language to be included directly in specifications of other languages.

Who Uses XHTML Modules?

The purpose of modularizing XHTML is to allow people who are developing systems (for example, browsers, applications, Web editors, proxy services, and databases) to easily construct XHTML-based languages. It's not expected that the average Web developer will need to create an XHTML variant, and the DTD-based nature of building an XHTML module means that it will remain a task for people who build XML languages.

However, as XHTML 1.1 (and future versions) will be defined in terms of modules, it's important for Web developers to understand what a module is and what effect it has on markup. Web developers might not be creating XHTML modules, but they certainly will be using them.

For a tutorial on creating XHTML languages using XHTML modularization, see

`http://www.w3.org/MarkUp/Guide/xhtml-m12n-tutorial`

How Modularization Works

XHTML modules are defined in two ways. On the specification level, they're described by listing the following information:

- Elements (and their allowable attributes) in the module
- Additional attributes added to existing elements (those defined in other modules)
- Other elements (or groups of elements) that have their content models extended by the module
- Notes on how the module is used

On a technical level, modules are currently defined using XML DTDs. Each module consists of one or more DTD files that are assembled by a *driver* which draws in appropriate sub-declarations to build the complete language. A schema-based system for declaring XHTML modules is being worked on, but is still a W3C draft at the time of writing. The most current version of "Modularization of XHTML in XML Schema" can be found at

`http://www.w3.org/TR/xhtml-m12n-schema`

Attribute Collections

For ease of reference, groups of attributes have been arranged in *attribute collections*. These collections are then referenced in the element definitions, and thus they don't have to be repeated multiple times. It becomes easier to extend the language by designating, for example, that a new global attribute be added to the Core or Events attribute collections.

The main attribute collections, and the attributes they contain, are listed in Table 21.2.

TABLE 21.2 XHTML ATTRIBUTE COLLECTIONS

Collection Name	Attributes

Core attributes	`class`
	`id`
	`title`

I18N attributes	`xml:lang` `dir` (only if Bi-Directional Textmodule is selected)
Common attributes	Core attribute collection I18N attribute collection Events attribute collection (only if Intrinsic Events module is selected) Style attribute collection (only if Style Attribute module is selected)

The elements composing the Events attribute collection are listed with the Intrinsic Events module; the Style attribute collection is shown with the Style Attribute module.

CONTENT SETS

Modularized XHTML defines certain groups of elements as content sets used to group together elements that function in roughly the same manner and can be used in minimal content models. A content sent can also contain other content sets.

Each content set is defined in a specific module, and can be extended by subsequent modules. Therefore, the exact composition of a content set will depend on the net effect of all modules, which might define or extend that content set. Within the DTDs for XHTML modules, content sets are expressed as entities.

For example, the Text module defines the Block content set as consisting of the `address`, `blockquote`, `div`, `p`, and `pre` elements. The Presentation module extends the Block content set by adding the `hr` element. If the Presentation module is used, the Block content set consists of `address`, `blockquote`, `div`, `p`, `pre`, and `hr`.

The content sets used in modularized XHTML, and the modules that define or extend each, are listed in Table 21.3.

TABLE 21.3 CONTENT SETS IN MODULARIZED XHTML

Content Set	Definition Module (Extending Modules)
Block	Text (Presentation, Basic Forms, Forms, Basic Tables, Tables, Scripting, Legacy)
Flow	Text (List)
Form	Basic Forms or Forms

TABLE 21.3 CONTENT SETS IN MODULARIZED XHTML

Content Set	Definition Module (Extending Modules)
Formctrl	Basic Forms or Forms
Heading	Text
Inline	Text (Hypertext, Presentation, Inline, Bi-Directional Text, Basic Forms, Forms, Image, Client-Side Image Map, Object, Iframe, Scripting, Applet, Legacy)
List	List (Legacy)

MINIMAL CONTENT MODELS

Each element in an XHTML module is listed with a *minimal content model*, expressed in typical XML DTD style. For example, `((foo,bar+)|baz*)` means "either a `<foo>` element followed by at least one and possibly more `<bar>` elements, or zero or more `<baz>` elements."

Content models are often defined in terms of content sets within XHTML modules, which means that subsequent module inclusions might extend the minimal content modules.

XHTML FAMILY LANGUAGES

Any language that is built according to the rules for XHTML modularization can be considered an XHTML family language. The two basic types of XHTML family languages are host languages and integration sets.

XHTML HOST LANGUAGES

An *XHTML host language* is a language in the XHTML family that follows the same basic structure as XHTML—`<html>` elements with `<head>` and `<body>` children, and so on. An XHTML host language is basically a variant of XHTML built with modules.

To qualify as a valid XHTML host language, the following rules apply:

- The language must be defined using one of the implementation methods for XHTML family language definitions—that is to say, by using DTDs. (In the future, it will be possible to use schemas.)
- The PUBLIC name of the `DOCTYPE` defining the DTD must start with "XHTML." For example, `"XHTML Plus CORAL Extensions."`
- The language must include the Structure, Hypertext, Text, and List modules.
- If any other modules are included, they have to be fully included (elements, attributes, minimal content models).
- New elements and attributes must be in a new XML namespace.

21

XHTML INTEGRATION SETS

A language that is based on XHTML, but doesn't follow the structure of XHTML, is called an *XHTML integration set*. To qualify as an integration set, an XHTML-based language must meet these requirements:

- The language must be defined using one of the implementation methods for XHTML family language definitions—that is to say, by using DTDs. (In the future, it will be possible to use schemas.)
- The PUBLIC name of the `DOCTYPE` defining the DTD must contain the word "XHTML" but cannot start with it. For example, "`Semantically Enhanced XHTML`."
- The language must include the Hypertext, Text, and List modules. (Unlike an XHTML host language, the Structure module is not required.)
- If any other modules are included, they have to be fully included (elements, attributes, minimal content models).
- New elements and attributes must be in a new XML namespace.

CORE MODULES

The core modules listed next are essential for building any XHTML family language because they define not only the basic structures and elements for an XHTML language, but also the basic content sets as well.

STRUCTURE MODULE

The Structure module is the basic building block of an XHTML host language: It defines the `<html>`, `<head>` and `<body>` elements, as well as the `<title>`. This is a required module for all XHTML host languages, although it is optional for XHTML integration set languages. The elements and attributes of the XHTML Structure module are shown in Table 21.4.

TABLE 21.4 XHTML STRUCTURE MODULE

Element	Attributes	Content Set	Minimal Content Model
`body`	*Common*	—	(*Heading* | *Block* | *List*)*
`head`	*I18N*, `profile`	—	title
`html`	*I18N*, `version`, `xmlns`	—	`head, body`
`title`	*I18N*	—	PCDATA

TEXT MODULE

The Text module defines a number of elements that define the meaning of textual content. These all declare text (or other content, such as images) to have specific meanings—whether it's paragraph text, a definition, or an abbreviation.

This module is required for all XHTML host languages and XHTML integration sets. Table 21.5 shows the elements and attributes of the Text module.

TABLE 21.5 XHTML TEXT MODULE

Element	Attributes	Content Set	Minimal Content Model
`abbr`	*Common*	Inline	(PCDATA | *Inline*)*
`acronym`	*Common*	Inline	(PCDATA | *Inline*)*
`address`	*Common*	Block	(PCDATA | *Inline*)*
`blockquote`	*Common*, `cite`	Block	(PCDATA | *Heading* | *Block* | *List*)*
`br`	*Core*	Inline	EMPTY
`cite`	*Common*	Inline	(PCDATA | *Inline*)*
`code`	*Common*	Inline	(PCDATA | *Inline*)*
`dfn`	*Common*	Inline	(PCDATA | *Inline*)*
`div`	*Common*	Block	(PCDATA | *Flow*)*
`em`	*Common*	Inline	(PCDATA | *Inline*)*
`h1`	*Common*	Heading	(PCDATA | *Inline*)*
`h2`	*Common*	Heading	(PCDATA | *Inline*)*
`h3`	*Common*	Heading	(PCDATA | *Inline*)*
`h4`	*Common*	Heading	(PCDATA | *Inline*)*
`h5`	*Common*	Heading	(PCDATA | *Inline*)*
`h6`	*Common*	Heading	(PCDATA | *Inline*)*
`kbd`	*Common*	Inline	(PCDATA | *Inline*)*
`p`	*Common*	Block	(PCDATA | *Inline*)*
`pre`	*Common*, `xml:space`	Block	(PCDATA | *Inline*)*
`q`	*Common*, `cite`	Inline	(PCDATA | *Inline*)*
`samp`	*Common*	Inline	(PCDATA | *Inline*)*
`span`	*Common*	Inline	(PCDATA | *Inline*)*
`strong`	*Common*	Inline	(PCDATA | *Inline*)*
`var`	*Common*	Inline	(PCDATA | *Inline*)*

The Text module defines four content set groups, which are used and extended by a number of other modules. These content set groups are

- Heading—The `h1` through `h6` elements, used to create headline-style titles for content sections.
- Block—Elements that generate their own visual formatting box.

- Inline—Elements that are displayed inline within an existing visual formatting box. Inline elements almost always do not contain block elements.
- Flow—A very broad content set that consists of the Heading, Block, and Inline content sets.

These content groups and the elements they contain are summarized in Table 21.6.

TABLE 21.6 XHTML TEXT MODULE CONTENT SETS

Content Set	Defining Module	Elements
Heading	Flow	`h1|h2|h3|h4|h5|h6`
Block	Flow	`address|blockquote|div|p|pre`
Inline	Flow	`abbr|acronym|br|cite|code|em|kbd|q|samp|span|strong|var`
Flow	—	*Heading* | *Block* | *Inline*

HYPERTEXT MODULE

The Hypertext module defines the <a> (anchor) element that is used for creating simple one-way hypertext links. This is a required module for XHTML host languages and XHTML integration sets. The elements and attributes of the Hypertext module are shown in Table 21.7.

TABLE 21.7 XHTML HYPERTEXT MODULE

Element	Attributes	Content Set	Minimal Content Model
`a`	*Common*, `accesskey`, `charset`, `href`, `hreflang`, `rel`, `rev`, `tabindex`, `type`	Inline	(PCDATA | *Inline* - a)*

The Hypertext module extends the Inline content set by adding <a>, as shown in the following:

Content Set	Defining Module	Elements
Inline	Text	`+a`

LIST MODULE

The List module defines the basic list types in XHTML, which are

- Definition lists are associate pairs of values.
- Ordered lists are automatically numbered and imply a sequential relationship between the list items.
- Unordered lists are collections of items usually represented as bullet lists, and they are not in any specific sequence.

The List module is required for any XHTML host language or XHTML integration set. The elements and attributes for the List module are shown in Table 21.8.

TABLE 21.8 XHTML LIST MODULE

Element	Attributes	Content Set	Minimal Content Model
`dl`	*Common*	List	(`dt`|`dd`)+
`dt`	*Common*	—	(PCDATA|*Inline*)*
`dd`	*Common*	—	(PCDATA|*Flow*)*
`ol`	*Common*	List	`li+`
`ul`	*Common*	List	`li+`
`li`	*Common*	—	(PCDATA|*Flow*)*

The List module defines the List content set, which is added to the Flow content set as shown in Table 21.9.

TABLE 21.9 XHTML LIST MODULE CONTENT SETS

Content Set	Defining Module	Elements
List	List	`(dl|ol|ul)+`
Flow	Text	+*List*

TEXT EXTENSION MODULES

The Text Extension modules offer formatting choices beyond those in the Text or List modules.

PRESENTATION MODULE

The elements in the Presentation module describe generic text effects as well as horizontal rules. These overlap with the functionality provided by Cascading Style Sheets (see the Style Sheet, Style Attribute, and Link modules) as well as the default presentation of certain Text module elements. Care should be taken to use the correct element. For example, if your intent is to strongly emphasize something, employ the `<em>` element and not the `<i>` element even though most browsers will render them identically as italic text.

You should include the Presentation module in an XHTML family language if you need to support generic text formatting elements. The elements and attributes of the XHTML Presentation module are shown in Table 21.10.

TABLE 21.10 XHTML PRESENTATION MODULE

Element	Attributes	Content Set	Minimal Content Model
`b`	*Common*	Inline	(PCDATA | *Inline*)*
`big`	*Common*	Inline	(PCDATA | *Inline*)*
`hr`	*Common*	Block	EMPTY
`i`	*Common*	Inline	(PCDATA | *Inline*)*
`small`	*Common*	Inline	(PCDATA | *Inline*)*
`sub`	*Common*	Inline	(PCDATA | *Inline*)*
`sup`	*Common*	Inline	(PCDATA | *Inline*)*
`tt`	*Common*	Inline	(PCDATA | *Inline*)*

The Presentation module extends the Block and Inline content sets as shown by Table 21.11.

TABLE 21.11 XHTML PRESENTATION MODULE CONTENT SETS

Content Set	Defining Module	Elements
Block	Text	`+hr`
Inline	Text	`+(b|big|i|small|sub|sup|tt)`

EDIT MODULE

The Edit module defines `<del>` and `<ins>` elements that can indicate edits in a document, such as revisions or deletions. You should include this module in an XHTML family language if you require the ability to mark changes. The elements and attributes of the Edit module are shown in Table 21.12.

TABLE 21.12 XHTML EDIT MODULE

Element	Attributes	Content Set	Minimal Content Model
`del`	*Common*, `cite`, `datetime`	Inline	(PCDATA | *Flow*)*
`ins`	*Common* `cite` `datetime`	Inline	(PCDATA | *Flow*)*

The <ins> and <del> elements are both added to the Inline content set by this module as shown here:

Content Set	Defining Module	Elements
Inline	Text	+(del|ins)

Bi-Directional Text Module

The Bi-Directional Text module is important for internationalization (I18N) because not all natural languages flow in the same direction. The <bdo> element defines changes in the direction of the text relative to the default direction of the element—for example, if Hebrew (which is right to left, *rtl*) is embedded within an English document. The language being used can be indicated by the `xml:lang` attribute, which is part of the Core attribute collection.

You should use this module as part of an XHTML family language whenever you might be dealing with more than one natural language within a document.

Element	Attributes	Content Set	Minimal Content Model
`bdo`	*Core*, `dir`	Inline	(PCDATA|*Inline*)*

In addition to the <bdo> element, the Bi-Directional Text module also adds the `dir` attribute to the I18N attribute collection, as shown next. The `dir` attribute can be set on any element that allows the Common or I18N attribute collections, and it can take a value of either `ltr` or `rtl`.

Element	Attributes	Defining Module or Collection
I18N	`dir`	Style Attribute Collection

The Bi-Directional Text module also extends the Inline content set by adding the <bdo> element.

Content Set	Defining Module	Elements
Inline	Text	+bdo

Forms Modules

Modularized XHTML offers two options for interactive forms—the Basic Forms module, which provides minimum input form functionality, and the Forms module itself, which supports the full range of XHTML 1.0 form controls.

These modules are mutually exclusive and not additive; you can declare either one or the other as part of an XHTML family module, but not both. The Forms module is a Defining Module of the Basic Forms module, so to get full functionality you only need the Forms module itself.

Neither Forms module allows for form-based actions outside of submitting information to a Web server (via `POST` or `GET`). To use forms with event handlers or client-side scripting, use either Forms module with the Intrinsic Events or Script modules.

BASIC FORMS MODULE

This module defines simple support for the most basic of XHTML forms, and it includes the element `label` and the attributes `accesskey` and `tabindex`, which enable access by people with disabilities and others who rely on keyboard input. The Basic Forms module only supports `<input>` form controls of type `text`, `password`, `radio`, `submit`, `reset`, and `hidden`.

Use the Basic Forms module when creating an XHTML family language that needs minimal support for input forms. If you need advanced form features (such as the `file` or `image` types of `<input>`) use the full Forms module; the elements and attributes of which are shown in Table 21.13.

TABLE 21.13 XHTML BASIC FORMS MODULE

Element	Attributes	Content Set	Minimal Content Model
`form`	*Common*, `action`, `method`, `enctype`	Form	(*Heading* | *List* | *Block* - `form`)+
`input`	*Common*, `accesskey`, `checked`, `maxlength`, `name`, `size`, `src`, `tabindex`, `type`, `value`	Formctrl	EMPTY
`label`	*Common*, `accesskey`, `for`	Formctrl	(PCDATA | *Inline* - `label`)*
`select`	*Common*, `multiple`, `name`, `size`, `tabindex`	Formctrl	`option+`
`option`	*Common*, `selected`, `value`	PCDATA	
`textarea`	*Common*, `accesskey`, `cols`, `name`, `rows`, `tabindex`	Formctrl	PCDATA

The Basic Forms module defines two content sets: Form, which only contains the `form` element, and Formctrl for form controls. Note that you can't nest `<form>`s. The content sets for the Basic Forms module are shown in Table 21.14.

TABLE 21.14 XHTML BASIC FORMS MODULE CONTENT SETS

Content Set	Defining Module	Elements
Form	Basic Forms	`form`
Formctrl	Basic Forms	`input|label|select|textarea`
Block	Text	+*Form*
Inline	Text	+*Formctrl*

FORMS MODULE

The Forms module is a more complete version of the Basic Forms module, containing full definitions of all form elements and attributes in XHTML 1.0. Forms built with the Forms module can be more accessible and complex than those created in accordance with the Basic Forms module.

Table 21.15 references the definitions of the Basic Forms module, as shown in Table 21.13, but it's important to remember that the Forms module is not a second module containing only those additional definitions. The Forms module allows for all elements in Basic, and using both modules at once is unnecessary and incorrect.

You should use the Forms module whenever you need full XHTML forms features in your XHTML family language. Those features include `button` elements, `accept` and `accept-charset` attributes, `disabled` or `readonly` values for form controls, input fields of type `file` or `image`, and `fieldset`, `legend`, and `optgroup` elements for grouping complex controls.

TABLE 21.15 XHTML FORMS MODULE

Element	Attributes	Content Set	Minimal Content Model
`form`	*as Basic*, `accept`, `accept-charset`	Form	(*Heading* | *List* | *Block* - `form` | `fieldset`)+
`input`	*as Basic*, `accept`, `alt`, `disabled`, `readonly`	Formctrl	EMPTY
`label`	*as Basic*	Formctrl	(PCDATA | *Inline* - `label`)*
`select`	*as Basic*, `disabled`	Formctrl	(optgroup | option)+

21

TABLE 21.15 CONTINUED

Element	Attributes	Content Set	Minimal Content Model
`option`	*as Basic*, `disabled`, `label`	Formctrl	PCDATA
`textarea`	*as Basic*, `disabled`, `readonly`	Formctrl	PCDATA
`button`	*Common*, `accesskey`, `disabled`, `name`, `tabindex`, `type`, `value`	Formctrl	(PCDATA | *Heading* | *List* | *Block - Form* | *Inline - Formctrl*)*
`fieldset`	*Common*	Form	(PCDATA | `legend` | *Flow*)*
`legend`	*Common*, `accesskey`	—	(PCDATA | *Inline*)+
`optgroup`	*Common*, `disabled`, `label`	—	`option+`

The Forms module defines the Form and Formctrl content sets and adds them to the Block and Inline field sets, respectively, as shown in Table 21.16.

TABLE 21.16 XHTML FORMS MODULE CONTENT SETS

Content Set	Defining Module	Elements
Form	Forms	`form|fieldset`
Formctrl	Forms	`input|select|textarea|label|button`
Block	Text	*+Form*
Inline	Text	*+Formctrl*

TABLES MODULES

As with Basic Forms and Forms modules, tables in modularized XHTML are defined in two different modules. The Basic Tables module defines a simple markup for tabular data, whereas the Tables module offers an expanded model for complex table relationships. You should only use one or the other in your XHTML family language, not both.

BASIC TABLES MODULE

The Basic Tables module defines the `<table>`, `<tr>`, `<td>`, `<th>`, and `<caption>` elements from XHTML, along with attributes such as `axis`, `headers`, and `scope`, which can associate cells with headings for screenreaders and other programs used by people with disabilities. Using tables for page layout is not recommended. But if you do, make sure that your tables make sense when read in the order they appear in the source code to ensure access by non-graphical browsers.

You should use the Basic Tables module when your XHTML family language needs simple tables. If you're going to require support for complex tables, use the Tables module instead. The elements and attributes for the Basic Tables module are shown in Table 21.17.

TABLE 21.17 XHTML BASIC TABLES MODULE

Element	Attributes	Content Set	Minimal Content Model
`caption`	*Common*	—	(PCDATA | *Inline*)*
`table`	*Common*, `summary`, `width`	Block	`caption?`, `tr+`
`td`, `th`	*Common*, `abbr`, `align`, `axis`, `colspan`, `headers`, `rowspan`, `scope`, `valign`	—	(PCDATA | *Flow* - `table`)*
`tr`	*Common*, `align`, `valign`	—	(`td` | `th`)+

The Basic Tables module extends the Block content set, defined in the Text module, by adding the `<table>` element:

Content Set	Defining Module	Elements
Block	Text	`+table`

TABLES MODULE

The Tables module includes definitions for all the table elements and attributes in XHTML 1.0. Table 21.18 lists those elements and attributes that are not part of Basic Tables (see Table 21.17). The Tables module fully defines the elements and attributes in the Basic Tables module, so it's not necessary to use both.

21

Include the Tables module in your XHTML family language if you are going to be dealing with complex tabular data that will be grouped into collections of columns or rows, if you need to align data by a particular character (such as a period for numeric data), or if you need to adjust the border, cellpadding, cellspacing, and other display characteristics of the table. (You can also use Cascading Style Sheets for the latter effect, by including the Style Sheet, Style Attribute, or Link modules.)

TABLE 21.18 XHTML TABLES MODULE

Element	Attributes	Content Set	Minimal Content Model
caption	*as Basic*	—	(PCDATA | *Inline*)*
table	*as Basic*, border, cellpadding, cellspacing, datapagesize, frame, rules	Block	caption?, (col* | colgroup*), ((thead?, tfoot?, tbody+) | (tr+))
td, th	*as Basic*, char, charoff	—	(PCDATA | *Flow*)*
tr	*as Basic*, char, charoff	—	(td | th)*
col	*Common*, align, char, charoff, span, valign, width	—	EMPTY
colgroup	*Common*, align, char, charoff, span, valign, width	—	col*
tbody, thead, tfoot	*Common*, align, char, charoff, valign	—	tr+

The Tables module extends the Block content set (from the Text module) by adding the `<table>` element:

Content Set	Defining Module	Elements
Block	Text	`+table`

IMAGE AND OBJECT MODULES

The Image module, the Object module, and the two Image Map modules all deal with embedding external content (usually graphical, but sometimes audio or multimedia) within an XHTML document.

IMAGE MODULE

The Image module is simple and straightforward; it defines the `<img>` element and adds it to the Inline content set. You should use the Image module when creating your XHTML family language if you require the ability to display images, of course. The use of images as image maps requires the use of one (or both) of the image map modules. The elements and attributes of the Image module are shown in Table 21.19.

TABLE 21.19 XHTML IMAGE MODULE

Element	Attributes	Content Set	Minimal Content Model
`img`	*Common*, `alt`, `height`, `longdesc`, `src`, `width`	Inline	EMPTY

XHTML Image Module Content Sets

Content Set	Defining Module	Elements
Inline	Text	`+img`

CLIENT-SIDE IMAGE MAP MODULE

The Client-Side Image Map module provides definitions for the `<map>` and `<area>` elements, which define mappings between "hotspots" on images and hypertext links. The module also extends the attributes for the `<a>`, `<img>`, `<input>`, and `<object>` elements.

Your XHTML family language requires this module if you're going to be using client-side image maps. You will need to include the Image module or Object module if you want to use either the `<img>` or `<object>` elements as image maps, and if you require support for `<input>` form controls of type `image` used as images, you'll need to use the Forms module. You can use the Server-Side Image Map module with this one as well; they are compatible and not exclusive. The elements and attributes of the Client-Site Image Map module are shown in Table 21.20.

TABLE 21.20 XHTML CLIENT-SIDE IMAGE MAP MODULE

Element	Attributes	Content Set	Minimal Content Model
`area`	*Common*, `accesskey`, `alt`, `coords`, `href`, `nohref`, `shape`, `tabindex`	—	EMPTY
`map`	*I18N*, *Events*, `class`, `id`, `title`	Inline	((*Heading* | *Block*) | `area`)+

The additional attributes defined for elements from other modules are listed in Table 21.21. When you include this module in your XHTML family language, those elements are extended as shown.

TABLE 21.21 XHTML CLIENT-SIDE IMAGE MAP MODULE ATTRIBUTES

Element	Attributes	Defining Module or Collection
`a`	`coords`, `shape`	Hypertext
`img`	`usemap`	Image
`input`	`usemap`	Forms
`object`	`usemap`	Object

The Client-Side Image Map module extends the Inline content set by adding the `<map>` element, as shown here:

Content Set	Defining Module	Elements
Inline	Text	`+map`

SERVER-SIDE IMAGE MAP MODULE

The Server-Side Image Map module doesn't define any new elements, but it does extend the `<img>` and `<input>` elements. Thus, it should be used with the Image and Forms modules, respectively.

Server-side image maps tend to be less accessible to people with disabilities and users of non-graphical browsers than client-side image maps because the links are not communicated to the browser and require a connection to the server to resolve the link. In cases in which your type of content might make it impossible to use a client-side map (such as a geographic map that refocuses on whatever point is clicked), you will want to use the Server-Side Image Map module to define your XHTML family language. The elements and the attributes of the Server-Site Image Map module are shown in Table 21.22.

TABLE 21.22 XHTML SERVER-SIDE IMAGE MAP MODULE ATTRIBUTES

Element	Attributes	Defining Module or Collection
img	ismap	Image module
input	ismap	Forms module

OBJECT MODULE

The Object module is used for generic inline inclusion of external media objects and applications. It defines the `<object>` and `<param>` elements.

The Object module should be incorporated into your XHTML language family whenever you need to embed Java applications, multimedia presentations, or other external content. The Object module is favored over the Embed module, which is deprecated. Objects can be used as image maps by inclusion of the Client-Side Image Map module. The elements and attributes of the Object module are shown in Table 21.23.

TABLE 21.23 XHTML OBJECT MODULE

Element	Attributes	Content Set	Minimal Content Model
object	*Common*, archive, classid, codebase, codetype, data, declare, height, name, standby, tabindex, type, width	Inline	(PCDATA|*Flow*|param)*
param	id, name, type, value, valuetype	—	EMPTY

The Object module extends the Inline content set as shown here:

Content Set	Defining Module	Elements
Inline	Text	+object

21

FRAMES MODULES

Definitions for the frame-related elements and attributes of XHTML 1.0 are found in three different modules: the Frames module, the Target module, and the Iframe module.

FRAMES MODULE

The elements of the Frames module are used to create frames and describe their layout. When using frames, each `<frame>` should be given a `title` attribute that describes its function, and `<noframes>` elements should be provided for non-visual browsers.

To use the full functionality of XHTML 1.0 frames, you will need to include both the Frames module and the Target module in your XHTML family language. In addition to the `<frameset>`, `<frame>`, and `<noframes>` elements, the Frames module redefines the `<html>` element's minimal content set, as shown in Table 21.24.

TABLE 21.24 XHTML FRAMES MODULE

Element	Attributes	Content Set	Minimal Content Model
frameset	*Core*, cols, rows	—	(frameset|frame)+, noframes?
frame	*Core*, frameborder, longdesc, marginheight, marginwidth, noresize, scrolling, src	—	EMPTY
noframes	*Common*		body
html	—	—	(head, frameset)

TARGET MODULE

The Target module adds a single attribute, `target`, to a number of elements defined in other modules, as shown in Table 21.25. You'll want to include the Target module in your XHTML family language if you're using the Frames or Iframe module, or if you want to add the ability to open hypertext links in new windows. To support HTML-style frame targets, you will need to include the Name Identification module as well to use the `name` attribute in addition to `id`.

TABLE 21.25 XHTML TARGET MODULE ATTRIBUTES

Element	Attributes	Defining Module or Collection
a	target	Hypertext
area	target	Client-Side Image Maps
base	target	Base
link	target	Link
form	target	Basic Forms or Forms

IFRAME MODULE

The Iframe module defines the inline frame module, `<iframe>`, and adds it to the Inline content set. The `<iframe>` can be targeted by links if the Target module is also included in the definition of your XHTML family language. The Iframe module elements and attributes are shown in Table 21.26.

TABLE 21.26 XHTML IFRAME MODULE

Element	Attributes	Content Set	Minimal Content Model
iframe	*Core*, frameborder, height, longdesc, marginheight, marginwidth, scrolling, src, width	Inline	(PCDATA | *Flow*)*

XHTML Iframe Module Content Sets:

Content Set	Defining Module	Elements
Inline	Text	+iframe

COMMON ATTRIBUTE MODULES

The following modules extend the Common attribute collection by adding the Events or Styles attributes collections. These then apply to all elements that use the Common attribute collection. If the appropriate modules are not selected for inclusion in an XHTML family language, the attribute collections are empty.

21

INTRINSIC EVENTS MODULE

The Intrinsic Events module adds the Events attribute collection to the Common attribute collection, and defines additional event attributes to elements defined in other modules, as shown in Table 21.27. Earlier versions of non-XML HTML usually wrote these attributes in mixed case for ease of reading, such onMouseOver. In XHTML, this is not allowed, and they must be written in lowercase.

The Intrinsic Events module can be used without the Scripting module. However, to get the full XHTML 1.0 scripting support in your XHTML family language, you'll probably want to include both.

TABLE 21.27 XHTML INTRINSIC EVENTS MODULE ATTRIBUTES

Element	Attributes	Defining Module or Collection
Common	onclick, ondbclick, onmousedown, onmouseup, onmouseover, onmousemove, onmouseout, onkeypress, onkeydown, onkeyup	Events Attribute Collection
a	onblur, onfocus	Hypertext
area	onblur, onfocus	Client-Side Image Maps
body	onload, onunload	Structure
frameset	onload, onunload	Frames
form	onreset, onsubmit	Basic Forms or Forms
label	onblur, onfocus	Basic Forms or Forms
input, *textarea*	onblur, onchange, onfocus, onselect	Basic Forms or Forms
select	onblur, onchange, onfocus	Basic Forms or Forms
button	onblur, onfocus	Forms

STYLE ATTRIBUTE MODULE

The Style Attribute module adds the Style attribute collection to the Common attribute collection—and this consists of only one attribute, `style`, for inline styles in Cascading Style Sheets. Include the Style Attribute module if your XHTML family language needs support for inline styles. For embedded style sheets, see the Style Sheet module, and for linked style sheets, see the Link module.

Element	Attributes	Defining Module or Collection
Common	`style`	Style Attribute Collection

HEAD MODULES

The modules in this section define elements that can be set within the `<head>` element of the Structure module. Each module extends the minimal content model of the `<head>` element.

METAINFORMATION MODULE

The Metainformation module defines the `<meta>` element and adds it to the minimal content model for `<head>`, as shown in Table 21.28. Include the Metainformation module in your XHTML family language to provide metadata on your document.

TABLE 21.28 XHTML METAINFORMATION MODULE

Element	Attributes	Content Set	Minimal Content Model
`meta`	*I18N*, `content`, `http-equiv`, `name`, `scheme`	—	EMPTY
head	—	—	`+meta`

SCRIPTING MODULE

The Scripting module allows for embedded client-side scripting languages, such as JavaScript, to be included in documents. The `<script>` element can appear in Block or Inline content, or in the `<head>` element. Note that in XHTML, scripts should probably be written as CDATA blocks, and comments should not be used to "hide" scripts because the contents of comments are ignored by XML parsers.

If your XHTML family language requires the Scripting module, you might also need the Intrinsic Events module to define events off which to trigger scripts. The elements and attributes of the Scripting module are shown in Table 21.29.

TABLE 21.29 XHTML SCRIPTING MODULE

Element	Attributes	Content Set	Minimal Content Model
noscript	*Common*	*Block*, *Inline*	(*Heading* | *List* | *Block*)+
script	charset, defer, src, type, xml:space	*Block*, *Inline*	PCDATA
head	—	—	+script

The Scripting module adds the <script> and <noscript> elements to both the Block and Inline content sets, as shown in Table 21.30.

TABLE 21.30 XHTML SCRIPTING MODULE CONTENT SETS

Content Set	Defining Module	Elements
Block	Text	+(noscript | script)
Inline	Text	+(noscript | script)

STYLE SHEET MODULE

The Style Sheet module allows for embedded CSS style sheets (or other style languages), by defining the <style> element and adding it to the content model for <head>.

You'll want to include the Style module in your XHTML family language if you need to embed a style sheet. For external style sheets, use the Link module, and for inline styles, use the Style Attribute module. The elements and attributes of the Style Sheet module are shown in Table 21.31.

TABLE 21.31 XHTML STYLE SHEET MODULE

Element	Attributes	Content Set	Minimal Content Model
style	*I18N*, media, title, type, xml:space	—	PCDATA
head	—	—	+style

LINK MODULE

Links between documents, including the link to an external style sheet, can be described with <link> elements, which are defined by the Link module.

If users of your XHTML family language will need to link to an external style sheet or describe other relationships between documents, include the Link module. The elements and attributes of the Link module are shown in Table 21.32.

TABLE 21.32 XHTML LINK MODULE

Element	Attributes	Content Set	Minimal Content Model
`link`	*Common*, `charset`, `href`, `hreflang`, `media`, `rel`, `rev`, `type`	—	EMPTY
head	—	—	`+link`

BASE MODULE

The Base module defines the `<base>` element, which defines a base URI for the entire page. Use this module if you are going to need the ability to specify a base URI within your XHTML family language. The elements and attributes of the Base module are shown in Table 21.33.

TABLE 21.33 XHTML BASE MODULE

Element	Attributes	Content Set	Minimal Content Model
`base`	`href`	—	EMPTY
head	—	—	`+base`

DEPRECATED AND LEGACY MODULES

The following modules exist only to define elements allowed in previous versions of HTML or XHTML, but that are now deprecated. The use of these modules is not recommended by the W3C, but they are included here in case you need them—for example, if you are going to construct a language that will be generated by an XHTML-compliant application but will display on an older HTML browser without Cascading Style Sheets support.

APPLET MODULE

The Applet module defines the `<applet>` and `<param>` elements, which allow embedded scripts. Instead of the Applet module, you should consider using the Object module, which provides the same functionality within your XHTML language family. The elements and attributes of the Applet module are shown in Table 21.34.

TABLE 21.34 XHTML APPLET MODULE

Element	Attributes	Content Set	Minimal Content Model
applet	*Core*, alt, archive, code, codebase, height, object, width	Inline	(PCDATA | *Flow* | param)*
param	id, name, type, value, valuetype	—	EMPTY

XHTML Applet Module Content Set:

Content Set	Defining Module	Elements
Inline	Text	+applet

NAME IDENTIFICATION MODULE

In HTML, a number of elements could be identified by `name` attributes and referenced as anchors for links or used by scripting languages. XHTML instead uses the XML standard of the `id` attribute, so the `name` attribute is avoided in the preceding modules. This module adds the name attribute to the `<a>`, `<applet>`, `<form>`, `<frame>`, `<iframe>`, `<img>`, and `<map>` elements.

Use this module to define your XHTML family language if backward compatibility with older HTML browsers is important. The elements and attributes of the Name Identification module are shown in Table 21.35.

TABLE 21.35 XHTML NAME IDENTIFICATION MODULE ATTRIBUTES

Element	Attributes	Defining Module or Collection
a	name	Hypertext
applet	name	Applet
form	name	Basic Form or Forms
frame	name	Frames
iframe	name	Iframe
img	name	Image
map	name	Client-Side Image Maps

LEGACY MODULE

The Legacy module is a catchall for the presentation elements and attributes that are not present in XHTML 1.0 Strict, as well as for those deprecated elements and attributes that were not yet removed from the specification.

All elements and attributes in the Legacy module have their functionality duplicated by other XHTML elements, attributes, or by Cascading Style Sheets, so this module should not be included within your XHTML family language. The exception is if you know with certainty that legacy support is necessary. The Modularization of XHTML specification specifically states that markup language creators should not use these elements and attributes in their XHTML family language. The elements of the Legacy module are shown in Table 21.36, and the attributes are shown in Table 21.37.

TABLE 21.36 XHTML LEGACY MODULE ELEMENTS

Element	Attributes	Content Set	Minimal Content Model
`basefont`	`color`, `face`, `id`, `size`	Inline	EMPTY
`center`	*Common*	Block	(PCDATA | *Flow*)*
`dir`	*Common*, `compact`	List	(*li*)+
`font`	*Core*, *I18N*, `color`, `face`, `size`	Inline	(PCDATA | *Inline*)*
`isindex`	*Core*, *I18N*, `prompt`	Block	EMPTY
`menu`	*Common*, `compact`	List	(`li`)+
`s`	*Common*	Inline	(PCDATA | *Inline*)*
`strike`	*Common*	Inline	(PCDATA | *Inline*)*
`u`	*Common*	Inline	(PCDATA | *Inline*)*

TABLE 21.37 XHTML LEGACY MODULE ATTRIBUTES

Element	Attributes	Defining Module or Collection
body	alink, background, bgcolor, link, text, vlink	Structure
br	clear	Text
caption	align	Basic Table or Tables
div	align	Text
dl	compact, type	Lists
h1, h2, h3 h4, h5, h6	align	Text
hr	align, noshade, size, width	Presentation
img	align, border, hspace, vspace	Image
input	align	Basic Form or Forms
legend	align	Forms
li	type, value	Lists
ol	compact, start, type	Lists
p	align	Text
pre	width	Text
script	language	Scripting
table	align, bgcolor	Basic Table or Tables
tr	bgcolor	Basic Table or Tables
th, td	bgcolor, height, nowrap, width	Basic Table or Tables
ul	compact, type	Lists

The content sets extended by the Legacy module are shown in Table 21.38.

TABLE 21.38 XHTML LEGACY MODULE CONTENT SETS

Content Set	Defining Module	Elements
Inline	Text	+(basefont|font|s|strike|u)
Block	Text	+(center|isindex)
List	List	+(dir|menu)

XHTML 1.1

WHAT IS XHTML 1.1?

XHTML 1.1 is the latest official (W3C-approved) version of HTML, and it was issued as a W3C Recommendation on May 31, 2001. The specification can be found at

`http://www.w3.org/TR/xhtml11`

XHTML 1.1 documents must have the following `DOCTYPE` declaration:

```
<!DOCTYPE
  html PUBLIC "-//W3C/DTD XHTML 1.1//EN"
  "http://www.w3.org/TR/xhtml11/DTD/xhtml11.dtd">
```

The namespace for XHTML 1.1 is the XHTML namespace, which can be found here:

`http://www.w3.org/1999/xhtml`

MODULES COMPRISING XHTML 1.1

XHTML 1.1 is a reformulation of XHTML 1.0 Strict in modularized XHTML. Deprecated modules were dropped entirely, and frames are not available either because they're not included in XHTML 1.0 Strict.

The modules used to create XHTML 1.1 are shown in Table 21.39.

TABLE 21.39 XHTML 1.1 MODULES

Module Name	Elements or Attributes Defined
Structure	body, head, html, title
Text	abbr, acronym, address, blockquote, br, cite, code, dfn, div, em, h1, h2, h3, h4, h5, h6, kbd, p, pre, q, samp, span, strong, var
Hypertext	a
List	dl, dt, dd, ol, ul, li
Object	object, param

Table 21.39 Continued

Module Name	Elements or Attributes Defined
Presentation	b, big, hr, i, small, sub, sup, tt
Edit	del, ins
Bi-Directional Text	bdo
Forms	button, fieldset, form, input, label, legend, select, optgroup, option, textarea
Table	caption, col, colgroup, table, tbody, td, tfoot, th, thead, tr
Image	img
Client-side Image Map	area, map
Server-side Image Map	Attribute ismap on img
Intrinsic Events	Events attributes
Metainformation	meta
Scripting	noscript, script
Style Sheet	style
Style Attribute	style attribute
Link	link
Base	base
Ruby Annotation	ruby, rbc, rtc, rb, rt, rp

Differences Between XHTML 1.0 and XHTML 1.1

For the most part, XHTML 1.1 is a faithful translation of XHTML 1.0 Strict, but there are three important differences:

- The `lang` element has been removed; `xml:lang` should be used instead.
- The `name` attribute has been removed from the `a` and `map` elements, and `id` is used instead.
- The Ruby Annotation module has been added.

The Ruby Annotation Module

The Ruby Annotation module was created to meet a specific need common to East Asian languages. In those languages, `ruby` text is small characters that run alongside larger text to provide pronunciation or context clues as to the meaning of the larger ideographs. Use of `ruby` in XHTML 1.1 is not restricted to Asian languages. It can be useful to use `ruby` in English text in some cases.

Ruby was defined in a W3C Recommendation issued on May 31, 2001. It can be found at `http://www.w3.org/TR/ruby/`

The elements and attributes defined by the Ruby Annotation module are listed in Table 21.40.

TABLE 21.40 RUBY ANNOTATION MODULE ELEMENTS

Element	Attributes	Content Set	Minimal Content Model
`ruby`	*Common*	Inline	(rb,(rt | (rp,rt,rp)))
`rbc`	*Common*	—	`rb+`
`rtc`	*Common*	—	`rt+`
`rb`	*Common*	—	(PCDATA | *Inline* - `ruby`)*
`rt`	*Common*, `rbspan`	—	(PCDATA | *Inline* - `ruby`)*
`rp`	*Common*	—	PCDATA*

The Ruby Annotation module extends the Inline content set, as shown here, by adding the `<ruby>` element. The other elements are contained within the `<ruby>` container.

Content Set	Defining Module	Elements
Inline	Text	`+ruby`

THE `ruby` ELEMENT

The `ruby` element is a wrapper that contains the other elements used to define a `ruby`. It is a signal that a `ruby` exists within, although it doesn't mean that only `ruby` text is found inside. There are two possible content models for the `ruby` element: simple and complex.

A simple `ruby` contains a single `ruby` base element, `<rb>`, with a single `ruby` text element, `<rt>`. A pair of `ruby` parenthesis elements, `<rp>`, are optional.

```
<ruby>
  <rb>Ruby Base</rb>
  <rp>(</rp>
  <rt>Ruby Text</rt>
  <rp>)</rp>
</ruby>
```

A complex `ruby` contains a `ruby` base container element, `<rbc>`, and one or two `ruby` text containers, `<rtc>`. Complex `ruby` markup is used to associate `ruby` characters with specific words or ideographs.

```
<ruby>
  <rbc>
    <rb>Base 1</rb>
    <rb>Base 2</rb>
    <rb>Base 3</rb>
  </rbc>
  <rtc>
```

```
    <rt>Ruby Text One</rb>
    <rt>Ruby Text Two</rt>
    <rt>Ruby Text Three</rt>
  </rtc>
  <rtc>
    <rt rbspan="3">
      All Your Base
    </rt>
  </rtc>
</ruby>
```

THE rb ELEMENT

The ruby base element, <rb>, is used to identify the base text for a ruby. This is the larger text (or any inline markup) that will be annotated by the ruby. The <rb> element can appear as the first child of a <ruby> element, or as one of several children of the <rbc> element.

THE rt ELEMENT

The ruby text element, <rt>, contains the text displayed in smaller letters as the ruby annotates the ruby base, <rb>.

An <rt> element can appear as the second child of the <ruby> element, or as the third child if ruby parenthesis elements, <rp>, are used. In a complex ruby, multiple <rt> elements can be used in the <rtc> container, and the <rt> element can take the rtspan attribute to indicate that it applies to multiple ruby bases.

THE rp ELEMENT

Ruby parenthesis elements are used to indicate a fallback for browsers that don't yet understand ruby markup. The contents of the <rp> element are ignored by browsers that understand ruby, but those that don't will display the content inline. The <rp> element is optional. But, if it's used, it needs to be the second and fourth child of the <ruby> element—it can only be used in pairs.

THE rbc ELEMENT

The <rbc> element is a container for holding ruby base elements, <rb>. Each <rb> within an <rbc> maps to one of the <rt> elements within the associated <rtc> elements. There can only be one <rbc> element within any given <ruby>.

THE rtc ELEMENT

The ruby text container, <rtc>, holds <rt> elements within a complex ruby. There can be either one or two of these elements, but not more or less than that.

XHTML BASIC

The proliferation of new wireless technologies, PDAs, and other portable computing devices have led to people accessing the Web from just about anywhere. However, anyone who has used these technologies will notice a difference between surfing the Web on a top-of-the-line desktop versus a cellular phone.

In order to accommodate some of the devices that might want to display a subset of HTML, the basic essential elements, there is an appropriate language: XHTML Basic.

What Is XHTML Basic?

XHTML Basic is a simplified form of XHTML that represents basic HTML-style functionality. XHTML Basic is intended for use on small devices, such as PDAs or cell phones, with limited displays, processing power, and interaction ability.

XHTML Basic was issued as a W3C recommendation in December 2000, and can be found at

`http://www.w3.org/TR/xhtml-basic`

Modules Composing XHTML Basic

Like XHTML 1.1, XHTML Basic is an XHTML host language, and is defined by the modules shown in Table 21.41. Note that the basic versions of the Forms and Tables modules are used, and a large number of elements are not included. XHTML Basic is a very simple markup language, but it is still sufficient for many purposes, including mobile use.

Table 21.41 XHTML Basic Modules

Module Name	Elements or Attributes Defined
Structure	`body`, `head`, `html`, `title`
Text	`abbr`, `acronym`, `address`, `blockquote`, `br`, `cite`, `code`, `dfn`, `div`, `em`, `h1`, `h2`, `h3`, `h4`, `h5`, `h6`, `kbd`, `p`, `pre`, `q`, `samp`, `span`, `strong`, `var`
Hypertext	`a`
List	`dl`, `dt`, `dd`, `ol`, `ul. li`
Basic Forms	`form`, `input`, `label`, `select`, `option`, `textarea`
Basic Tables	`caption`, `table`, `td`, `th`, `tr`
Image	`img`
Object	`object`, `param`
Metainformation	`meta`
Link	`link`
Base	`base`

XHTML Basic provides the bare essentials for HTML style markup, and it is possible by combining various subsets from the XHTML modules—one of the ways in which modularization helps to easily create *new* markup languages with relative ease.

THE ONGOING EVOLUTION OF XHTML

With the solid base of modularized XHTML, all that's necessary to build new versions of XHTML is to define new or updated modules and build a language. That's exactly what was done with XHTML 1.1 and XHTML Basic, and that's what's planned for the future of XHTML. Forthcoming developments in XHTML include extended input forms, standardized event models, and XHTML 2.0.

XFORMS

The XForms specification is an ongoing work in progress by the XForms Working Group to create the next generation of interactive forms for use with XML-based languages, including XHTML.

→ See Chapter 25, "Using XML to Create Forms: XForms."

XML EVENTS

The XML Events specification is a W3C working draft at the time of writing. The goal is to develop a generic XML syntax for event listeners and handlers beyond the simple attributes available in XHTML. This syntax could then be used for XML-based markup languages, including XHTML, to associate behaviors with actions.

The draft of XML Events can be found at

`http://www.w3.org/TR/xml-events`

XHTML 2.0

Progress is underway to craft a new version, XHTML 2.0. Unlike XHTML 1.0 and XHTML 1.1, version 2.0 is designed to include new features and not simply limit itself primarily to those capabilities included in HTML 4. Because it is still a work in progress, the details of what will be included in the XHTML 2.0 specification aren't fully known yet. But, a working draft dated January 2000 was available at the time of writing.

Some of the changes from XHTML 1.1 might include

- Support for XLink instead of relying on `href` and `src` attributes
- A new Image module that provides more support for `<alt>` text
- Improved syntax for the `<object>` element
- Support for XPointer links
- Sections and dynamically numbered headers
- Support for XForms
- Replacement of Intrinsic Events with XML Events
- Support for XML:Base
- Schema Modularization in addition to DTD

Some of these are stated in the draft, and some of these are educated guesses—no one yet knows what XHTML 2.0 will look like when it is released. What is known is that it will be based on modularized XHTML, so the principles learned from XHTML 1.1 will help you put XHTML 2.0 into context.

ADDITIONAL RESOURCES

As with most XML technologies, the first place to turn when you have questions about the technology should be to the W3C. There you can find the recommendations themselves, which are invaluable resources. Here's a rundown of some of the best XHTML resources available:

- W3C Markup Language home page (`http://www.w3.org/MarkUp/`)—This is the W3C's home site for all things related to HTML. In addition to HTML and XHTML, this site has links to other Recommendations, Notes, Working Drafts, and other topics of interest to designers, markup authors, and developers alike.
- XHTML 1.0 Recommendation (`http://www.w3.org/TR/xhtml1/`)—This is the home of the official XHTML 1.0 Recommendation from the W3C. When in doubt, this document should serve as the authoritative answer.
- XHTML Basic (`http://www.w3.org/TR/xhtml-basic/`)—This is the official W3C Recommendation for the XHTML Basic subset of XHTML.
- Modularization of XHTML (`http://www.w3.org/TR/xhtml-modularization/`)—This is the official W3C Recommendation for the modularization of XHTML. This document outlines how the various XHTML modules are defined and work together to create custom sets of markup features.
- Modularization of XHTML in XML Schemas (`http://www.w3.org/TR/xhtml-m12n-schema/`)—This Working Draft describes the modularization of XHTML, with respect to XML Schemas.
- HTML Tidy (`http://www.w3.org/People/Raggett/tidy/`)—This open source application is a very useful utility for checking the well-formedness of your HTML documents, but it can also be used to help you in the transition between HTML and XHTML.
- HTML Validation Service (`http://validator.w3.org/`)—This is another utility, provided by the W3C, for checking the validity of your HTML and XHTML documents.
- XHTML.org (`http://www.xhtml.org/`)—This is a portal site dedicated to XHTML technologies. Here you can find links to scores of other resources from W3C Recommendations to tutorials.
- W3schools XHTML Tutorial (`http://www.w3schools.com/xhtml/`)—This is an online tutorial for XHTML from the W3Schools Web site.
- Yahoo! Groups XHTML-L (`http://groups.yahoo.com/group/XHTML-L/`)—This is the Yahoo! Groups mailing list for XHTML authors and developers. Anyone using XHTML is welcome to participate, and this can be a great resource for exchanging development tips, questions, and ideas.

ROADMAP

XHTML is just one of a number of specific applications of the Extensible Markup Language that is shaping the way the World Wide Web will look in the future. XHTML updates HTML, adds new features in a more flexible way through modularization, and helps erase some of the sloppy habits created in the past with browsers that did not enforce well-formedness rules properly.

From here, we will take a look at some other XML related applications, such as Wireless Markup Language, the Scalable Vector Graphics language, and the Resource Descriptor Framework. These and other XML-based technologies are helping Web professionals develop new Web services that are expanding the functionality of the Web daily. So read on and see how other XML applications are contributing to the growth of the Web, just like XHTML.

CHAPTER 22

XML and Wireless Technologies: WML

In this chapter

by Alexander Kachur

XML and Wireless Technologies

It took just a few years for XML to penetrate just about everywhere in the Internet. But the triumph of XML has continued even after that—to wireless technologies.

Need for Wireless Web

Users have long been able to receive messages on mobile devices. It makes sense that devices made for communicating would someday be extended to interact with the World Wide Web. Mobile solutions needed a lightweight markup language that can be used within a small device with limited computational resources, such as a mobile phone to access resources made available through the *Wireless Application Protocol (WAP)*.

It is very tempting to be able to do almost everything you can do with the Internet using your cell phone. Cell phones are now part of our everyday life. At the same time, the need for constant access to the information and services of the Internet has become so strong that the Internet was finally opened to cell phones and other devices through the Wireless Web.

Mobile Commerce and WAP

Since the introduction of wireless access to the Internet, various e-commerce service providers have looked at cell phones as one more means of performing online transactions and started introducing m-commerce (mobile-commerce) services.

For customers, m-commerce services are attractive because the only thing you must have to be able to shop online is a WAP-enabled cell phone. Since introduction of m-commerce services, WAP phones have become more than just e-mail clients and micro browsers.

To name just a few, typical m-commerce applications of the Wireless Web could be

- Ordering theatre tickets
- Feeding a parking meter
- Paying your electric bill
- Obtaining stock quotes
- And many, many more

Wireless Web and WAP

Just as the Internet would be impossible without HTTP, the Wireless Web requires some special protocol for transferring data. The HTTP is a monster for wireless applications because of the hardware limitations. That is why the Wireless Application Protocol has been developed by the WAP Forum. Like HTTP, WAP provides the means for wireless devices to communicate with other devices or servers. However, it generally isn't necessary to understand how the Wireless Application Protocol works to develop applications for mobile devices. Most developers will work within the *Wireless Application Environment (WAE)*, which provides the user environment for interacting with applications and the set of tools that developers use to build them. An important part of the WAE is the markup languages, *XHTML Mobile Profile (XHTMLMP)* and *Wireless Markup Language (WML)*.

WML: Simplicity and Power

WML is analogous to and is based on HTML: The only difference is that WML has been specially adopted for mobile devices. It's simple for parsing by the software that can be fit into a small device with limited computational resources.

50000 Feet View on WML

WML is an XML-based markup language designed specially for mobile devices as a result of the joined efforts of the WAP Forum (founded by Nokia, Phone.com, Motorola, and Ericsson) and the W3C Consortium.

In this chapter, we discuss WML version 2.0 (WML2), which became an approved specification in January 2002. The WML2 is based on an entire family of technologies and specifications, such as

- WML 1.3—A markup language optimized for mobile devices
- XHTML Basic—An XML based descendant of HTML4
- CSSMP—CSS Mobile Profile

Why Not HTML?

HTML, which is so good for the World Wide Web, is not suitable for wireless applications for one very simple reason. It was not designed with any mobile applications in mind. The differences between the hardware on which HTML pages are usually accessed and mobile devices are so huge that there is no way to use either HTML as a wireless markup protocol or HTTP as a data transfer protocol in mobile devices.

Here are just a few reasons why HTML is not suitable:

- Memory of mobile devices is extremely low. Not only will the HTML parser not fit into the memory of most mobile devices, but also loading an HTML page could be problematic.
- Most cell phones can display just a few lines and simple icons on screen. Most HTML pages simply cannot be displayed on a mobile device.
- There is no 101-key keyboard or mouse, just a numeric keypad. Navigating lengthy HTML pages could be extremely difficult.

WML2 IN DETAILS

SCHEMA FOR WML2

Because the WML2 specification is based on XML, a *Document Type Definition (DTD)* is defined for WML2 documents. The DTD is available at the WAP Forum Web site, and any WML2 document should conform to this definition.

The full version of the WML2 DTD containing definitions of all the modules is located at the following URL:

`http://www.wapforum.org/dtd/wml20-flat.dtd`

For those interested in the previous version, WML 1.3, a DTD is available here:

`http://www.wapforum.org/DTD/wml13.dtd`

WML2 TAGS

The WML2 specification is based on the XHTML Basic 1.0 and `Modularization of XHTML` W3C Recommendations, and it defines additional WAP-specific extensions and WML1 compatible tags.

Depending on their meaning, the WML tags are grouped into different modules:

- Structure
- Text
- Hypertext
- Image
- Tables
- Lists
- Forms
- Metainformation
- Link
- Base
- Object
- Style Sheet
- Presentation
- Events
- Content and Navigation

Each of the modules defines a set of tags and their attributes. Let's discuss the modules in more detail.

DOCUMENT STRUCTURE

This module defines elements that form the structure of a document. The WML2 specification gives two options in implementing WML documents. It is up to a WML developer to choose either the XHTML style defining the document body within the `<body>` tag or use a deck/card paradigm with the `<wml:card>` element. Table 22.1 summarizes elements of the document structure module.

Caution

Do not be confused with the name of the WML2 document root element, which is *<html>*, not *<wml>* as it was in WML 1.0 or WML 1.1.

TABLE 22.1 TAGS DEFINED IN THE DOCUMENT STRUCTURE MODULE

Name	Attributes	Description
html	Required: None Optional: *xmlns*, *xmlns:wml*, *version*, *xml:lang*, *wml:onenterforward*, *wml:onenterbackward*, *wml:ontimer*, *wml:use-xml-fragments*	This element should be the first element of the WML2 document, and its namespace specification (if one is specified) should point to the WML namespace located at the following URL: `http://www.wapforum.org/2001/wml`. An example of the minimal empty WML2 document is demonstrated in Listing 22.1. Optional tags, such as *wml:onenterforward*, *wml:onenterbackward*, and *wml:ontimer* can be used to specify event-handling behavior, which is discussed later in this chapter.
head	Required: None Optional: *xml:lang*, *profile*	The `<head></head>` tag goes just after the root element of a document and marks the header of the document. The definition of the element in the WML2 specification refers to the W3C HTML4 recommendation.
title	Required: None Optional: *xml:lang*	This element should be located within the `<head>` element. It is used to define the title of the document.
body	Required: None Optional: *id*, *class*, *title*, *style*, *xml:lang*,	If a developer chooses to use the document paradigm as opposed to deck/card, the document content should be defined within this tag. Attributes of the `body` tag allow defining styles for the document, event handling rules, browser behavior on loading the document, and so on.

TABLE 22.1 CONTINUED

Name	Attributes	Description
	wml:newcontext, *wml:onenterforward*, *wml:onenterbackward*, *wml:ontimer*	Only one <body></body> element should appear in the single document.
wml:card	Required: None Optional: id, class, title, style, xml:lang, wml:newcontext, *wml:onenterforward*, *wml:onenterbackward*, *wml:ontimer*	This element provides another way of defining a document body. It has pretty much the same set of attributes. The difference between it and the <body> tag is that a single document can have multiple cards. The *<wml:card>* can contain an entire body of the document or just a fragment. Note that it is not allowed to define both the <body> and the *<wml:card>* within the same document.

Certain requirements should be met in order to make sure that the WML2 document is processed properly. Listing 22.1 demonstrates an example of a minimal WML2 document.

LISTING 22.1 MINIMAL WML2 DOCUMENT

```
<!DOCTYPE html PUBLIC"-//WAPFORUM//DTD WML 2.0//EN"
    "http://www.wapforum.org/wml20.dtd">
<html xmlns="http://www.w3.org/1999/xhtml"
    xmlns:wml="http://www.wapforum.org/2001/wml">
    <!-- The document goes here -->
</html>
```

The first line of the document is the standard definition of the XML document type.

Similar to other XML documents, there is a reference to the default namespace, which is XHTML, and to the WML namespace (second line).

The WML document itself should be located within the root element tags <html> and </html>.

TEXT MODULE

Most of the elements of the Text Module are defined according to the W3C HTML4 Recommendation. Elements of the text module are responsible for formatting text within the document body. Table 22.2 describes tags that are included in the Text Module.

Table 22.2 Tags Defined in the Text Module

Name	Attributes	Description
abbr	Required: None Optional: *id*, *class*, *title*, *style*, *xml:lang*	This tag marks an abbreviation. In most cases, it doesn't affect the way a browser will display the text. But for a spellchecker or a Web crawler, it will give enough information to process it according to the rules that apply for abbreviations.
acronym	Required: None Optional: *id*, *class*, *title*, *style*, *xml:lang*	Just as the `<abbr>` tag defines an abbreviation, the `<acronym>` tag marks an acronym used in the body of a document.
address	Required: None Optional: *id*, *class*, *title*, *style*, *xml:lang*	The `<address>` tag marks a section of a document where the contact information is given.
blockquote	Required: None Optional: *id*, *class*, *title*, *style*, *xml:lang*, *cite*	To mark a long quotation that requires a sepa rate paragraph in the text, the `<blockquote>` tag is used. The *cite* attribute can be specified to refer to the source of the quotation by its URI.
br	Required: None Optional: *id*, *class*, *title*, *style*	The ` ` element forces an agent to break a line of text.
cite	Required: None Optional: *id*, *class*, *title*, *style*, *xml:lang*	The `<cite>` element usually references a source of a quotation, but it doesn't allow it to specify a URI of the source, which would have been logical.

TABLE 22.2 CONTINUED

Name	Attributes	Description
code	Required: None Optional: *id*, *class*, *title*, *style*, *xml:lang*	A code example can be formatted by a browser in some special way, so this tag can be used to mark a code fragment in the text of the document.
dfn	Required: None Optional: *id*, *class*, *title*, *style*, *xml:lang*	The `<dfn>` element marks the definition of a term.
div	Required: None Optional: *id*, *class*, *title*, *style*, *xml:lang*	In most cases, the `<div>` tag is used together with style sheets to define the way a part of a document is presented to a user.
em	Required: None Optional: *id*, *class*, *title*, *style*, *xml:lang*	The `<em>` tag emphasizes the text enclosed between the opening and closing tags.
h1, h2, h3, h4, h5, h6	Required: None Optional: *id*, *class*, *title*, *style*, *xml:lang*	These six elements are used to mark different levels of headings within a document. The `<h1>` is the highest level in the hierarchy, whereas the `<h6>` is the lowest one.
kbd	Required: None Optional: *id*, *class*, *title*, *style*, *xml:lang*	The `<kbd>` element indicates that a user should enter text from the keyboard.

TABLE 22.2 CONTINUED

Name	Attributes	Description
p	Required: None Optional: *id*, *class*, *title*, *style*, *xml:lang*, *wml:mode*, *align*	Paragraphs of text are marked with the <p> element. The <p> tags cannot be nested into one another. The styling attributes *align* and *wml:mode* are deprecated in WML2, and the developers should use the WCSS properties *text-align* and *white-space* instead.
pre	Required: None Optional: *id*, *class*, *title*, *style*, *xml:lang*, *xml:space*	The <pre> tag indicates that the text within the element is preformatted and therefore should be presented as it appears in the text of a document.
q	Required: None Optional: *id*, *class*, *title*, *style*, *xml:lang*, *cite*	Another way to mark a quotation is using the <q> element, which is treated almost like the <blockquote>, but is not presented in a separate paragraph. Usually this tag marks short inline quotations.
samp	Required: None Optional: *id*, *class*, *title*, *style*, *xml:lang*	Documents can include samples of program output, and the <samp> element can be used in conjunction with style sheets to format them properly.
span	Required: None Optional: *id*, *class*, *title*, *style*, *xml:lang*	The <span> tag marks a section of a document just like the <div> does: The only difference is that the <span> is an inline section.

TABLE 22.2 CONTINUED

Name	Attributes	Description
strong	Required: None Optional: *id*, *class*, *title*, *style*, *xml:lang*	The <strong> element emphasizes the text enclosed within it. The emphasis is stronger than with the <em> tag.
var	Required: None Optional: *id*, *class*, *title*, *style*, *xml:lang*	This tag marks a variable. Usually it does not make any sense for a browser, but it can be used to give a hint to a spellchecker, a search engine, and so on.

HYPERTEXT

The Hypertext module defines only one tag, the anchor element <a>, which is used to specify a hypertext anchor within the body of a WML document.

An anchor can associate a text fragment with a link to another site, such as in this example:

```
More on foo: <a href="wap://www.foo.com/bar.wml">bar</a>
```

The preceding code associates the word *bar* with a URL pointing to a WAP site `wap://www.foo.com/bar.wml`.

Or it can be used by WML developers to associate a label within the document that can be accessed from another location within or outside the document:

```
<a id = "foo" name = "foo">
Here you can find a complete collection of links to sites about foo
</a>
```

Assuming that this fragment of code is a part of the document located at the URL `wap://www.foo.com/bar.wml`, we can navigate directly to a part of the document starting with this anchor using the following URL: `wap://www.foo.com/bar.wml`**`#foo`**.

Note

The preceding example uses both the `id` and `name` attributes. The `name` attribute is used for compatibility, but it is preferred to specify the `id` attribute in XHTML and hence, in WML. Refer to Chapter 21, "The Future of the Web: XHTML," for more details on this.

Table 22.3 summarizes attributes of the anchor element.

TABLE 22.3 TAGS DEFINED IN THE HYPERTEXT MODULE

Name	Attributes	Description
a	Required: None Optional: *id*, *class*, *title*, *style*, *xml:lang*, *href*, *charset*, *type*, *hreflang*, *rel*, *rev*, *accesskey*, *tabindex*	A hypertext anchor within the body of a WML document In most cases, it is used in conjunction with *href* or *name* attributes. The href attribute provides a link to another document through its URI. The *name* attribute puts an anchor into the text so that other sections of the document or other documents can refer to the section starting with this anchor element. Other attributes can be used to associate some additional information with the anchor, such as the language of the referred document.

IMAGE

The <img> tag, defined in the Image module is used whenever it is needed to insert an image into a WML document. Its attributes allow specifying the dimensions of the image, its source, description, and so on.

The attributes of the <img> element are listed in Table 22.4.

TABLE 22.4 TAGS DEFINED IN THE IMAGE MODULE

Name	Attributes	Description
img	Required: *src*, alt Optional: *id*, class, title, style, *xml:lang*, *longdesc*, *height*, *width*, *wml:localsrc*, *wml:type*, *vspace*, *hspace*, *align*	The <img> tag marks an image embedded within a document. The *src* attribute is a URI of the image source. The alt attribute defines an alternative text that briefly describes the image. This text can be used by a browser when it cannot display the image. The *wml:localsrc* attribute specifies the alternative local source that the image should be loaded from. The *src* attribute is ignored if the image can be loaded from the local source. The *wml:type* attribute can be used to tell the browser about the media type of the image. Other attributes can be used to pre-format the image; that is, force its size to specified dimensions, define its alignment and spacing, and so on.

TABLES

The Tables module describes WML2 elements responsible for formatting and displaying tables. A typical table consists of a header, caption, rows, and columns. The formatting options for tables could be alignment, spacing, and so on, and can be applied to any element of the table.

Tables or separate cells can be associated with style sheets, thus making it possible to create unique representations of tables. Table 22.5 summarizes the elements of the WML2 Tables module and their attributes.

TABLE 22.5 TAGS DEFINED IN THE TABLES MODULE

Name	Attributes	Description
`caption`	Required: None Optional: *id*, *class*, *title*, *style*, *xml:lang*	This element should be specified immediately after the opening `<table>` tag. It is used by browsers to provide a user with a brief description of the table. The `<caption>` element is optional, but sometimes it is a useful hint, which can save a user time.
`table`	Required: None Optional: *id*, *class*, *title*, *style*, *xml:lang*, *summary*, *wml:columns*, *wml:align*	The `<table>` tag defines a table in the body of a WML document. To make tables more accessible for disabled users, an attribute *summary* is often used by special browsers that render the information to speech engines or other special accessibility tools. It is usually helpful to specify the number of columns in the table using the *wml:columns* attribute. This will give the browser a hint about the table so that it can start displaying the table before the closing `</table>` tag gets to the parser. The *wml:align* attribute is deprecated, and it is not recommended to use it. The WML specification encourages using WCSS style properties.
`tr`	Required: None Optional: *id*, *class*, *title*, *style*, *xml:lang*, *align*, *valign*	The `<tr>` element describes a row in a table. This element encapsulates table cells `<td>` and cell headers `<th>`.

TABLE 22.5 CONTINUED

Name	Attributes	Description
`td`	Required: None Optional: *id*, *class*, *title*, *style*, *xml:lang*, *abbr*, *axis*, *headers*, *scope*, *rowspan*, *colspan*, *align*, *valign*	The table data is located within cells described with the `<td>` element. The specification allows developers to categorize table cells using the *axis* attribute. A browser then can display just a part of the table based on the category chosen by a user. The *headers* and *scope* attributes establish associations between data cells and headers describing data in the cells. The *rowspan* and *colspan* attributes define the number of rows and columns, respectfully, spanned by the data cell. The data in the cell can be aligned horizontally and vertically using the *align* and *valign* attributes. Just like most of the elements in WML2, the `td` can be associated with style sheets.
`th`	Required: None Optional: *id*, *class*, *title*, *style*, *xml:lang*, *abbr*, *axis*, *headers*, *scope*, *rowspan*, *colspan*, *align*, *valign*	The `<th>` element is used to define column headers for tables. The attributes are used with this element the same way as with the `<td>` element.

Listing 22.2 illustrates the use of the Tables Module tags to define a simple table.

LISTING 22.2 EXAMPLE OF THE TABLE DEFINITION

```
<table summary="This table describes our services and latest prices.">
    <caption>Pricelist</caption>
    <tr>
        <th>Ref. number</th>
        <th>Title</th>
        <th>Summary</th>
        <th>Availability</th>
```

LISTING 22.2 CONTINUED

```
        <th>Price</th>
    </tr>
    <tr>
        <td>0001</td>
        <td>Pizzas on-line</td>
        <td>Choose from more then twenty varieties of pizza now!</td>
        <td>Available</td>
        <td>7.50 EUR</td>
    </tr>
    <tr>
        <td>0002</td>
        <td>Holiday offers</td>
        <td>Think about your holiday now and book it on-line!</td>
        <td>Limited</td>
        <td>From 300 EUR</td>
    </tr>
</table>
```

The table described in this example consists of the caption, column headers, two rows, and five columns. The table summary provides additional information about the table that can be useful for disabled users accessing the WML page with a non-visual device.

LISTS

WML2 provides the developers with a number of special tags that can be used to organize information into lists of items. Three types of lists are defined in WML:

- Ordered
- Unordered
- Definition

For each type of lists, special tags are defined. Table 22.6 describes each of them in alphabetical order.

TABLE 22.6 TAGS DEFINED IN THE LISTS MODULE

Name	Attributes	Description
`dt`	Required: None Optional: *id*, *class*, *title*, *style*, *xml:lang*	The `<dt>` tag marks the term in the definition list. It is used in conjunction with `<dd>` and `<dl>` tags. It is assumed that the definition of the term marked with the `<dt>` tag goes next to it and is enclosed into one or multiple `<dd>` elements. One term can be associated with multiple definitions, or multiple terms can be associated with one definition.

TABLE 22.6 CONTINUED

Name	Attributes	Description
`dd`	Required: None Optional: *id*, *class*, *title*, *style*, *xml:lang*	The definition of the term is enclosed within the `<dd>` tag.
`dl`	Required: None Optional: *id*, *class*, *title*, *style*, *xml:lang*	The `<dl>` tag marks the definition list. The elements of the list are marked with the `<dd>` and `<dt>` tags. This type of list can be used for more than definitions. It can also be used for listing phone numbers, marking dialogues, and so on.
`ol`	Required: None Optional: *id*, *class*, *title*, *style*, *xml:lang*, *start*	The `<ol>` tag marks an ordered list of information items. Ordered list items are numbered by user agents.
`ul`	Required: None Optional: *id*, *class*, *title*, *style*, *xml:lang*	The `<ul>` tag marks unordered list of items. User agents usually display unordered lists as bulleted lists.
`li`	Required: None Optional: *id*, *class*, *title*, *style*, *xml:lang*, *value*	The `<li>` tag marks a list item. It can be used in conjunction with ordered and unordered lists, but not with definition lists.

22

LISTING 22.3 EXAMPLE OF THE DEFINITION LIST

```
<dl>
    <dt xml:lang="en-US">Theater
    <dt xml:lang="en-UK">Theatre
    <dd xml:lang="en">A building or an outdoor area where plays and
        similar types of entertainment are performed.
    <dd xml:lang="en-US">Same as cinema
    <dd xml:lang="en">Plays considered as entertainment
    <dd>The work of writing, producing and acting in plays.
    <dd xml:lang="en-UK">Same as operating theatre.
    <dd xml:lang="en">The place in which the war or fighting takes place.

    <dt>Cinema
    <dd xml:lang="en-UK">A building in which films or movies are shown.
</dl>
```

Listing 22.3 illustrates the use of definition list tags to define the meaning of words theatre, theater, and cinema. (Descriptions of these terms have been taken from the *Oxford Advanced Learner's Dictionary*.)

FORMS

The interactive content of WML pages is usually based on forms, which allow end users to submit information required by a WAP application. The Forms module describes the tags and attributes that make possible the interaction between users and servers. These tags and their attributes are listed in Table 22.7.

TABLE 22.7 TAGS DEFINED IN THE FORMS MODULE

Name	Attributes	Description
form	Required: *action* Optional: *id*, *class*, *title*, *style*, *xml:lang*, *method*, *enctype*	The <form> tag marks the beginning of the form. This element is a container for all the form's controls and text. The important attributes of this element are *method*, which defines how the data submitted by the user will be transmitted to the server and *action*, which is a URI of the agent that should receive and process the data submitted by the user.
input	Required: None Optional: *id*, *class*, *title*, *style*, *xml:lang*, *type*, *name*, *value*,	The <input> tag defines a control that expects a user to enter some information. There are quite a lot of pre-defined control types, and the behavior of the control depends on its type. For example, if the type is password, a control is a single-line text box, which hides the text entered by a user with asterisks or some other symbol. Most of the attributes of the <input> element are defined according to the XHTML specification and allow initializing the value and initial state of the control, its dimensions, format, and so on.

TABLE 22.7 CONTINUED

Name	Attributes	Description
	checked, *size*, *maxlength*, *src*, *tabindex*, *accesskey*, *wml:format*, *wml:emptyok*, *wml:name*	The WML specific attributes are *wml:name*, which specifies the name of the control and has higher priority than the XHTML *name* attribute. *wml:format* and *wml:emptyok*, which describe the input mask for the control value. Input controls can be associated with style sheets.
`select`	Required: None Optional: *id*, *class*, *title*, *style*, *xml:lang*, *name*, *size*, *multiple*, *tabindex*, *wml:iname*, *wml:value*, *wml:ivalue*, *wml:name*	The `<select>` is another type of control, and it represents a menu. The choices of the menu are defined and organized using the `<option>` and `<optgroup>` tags. The WML specific attributes of this element are The *wml:name* and *wml:value*, which specify the name and value of the control variable. The *wml:iname* and *wml:ivalue*, which set the control's index variable.
`option`	Required: None Optional: *id*, *class*, *title*, *style*, *xml:lang*, *selected*, *value*, *wml:onpick*	The `<option>` tag marks a choice of the menu. The *wml:onpick* attribute allows associating an event handler with the control, which is executed when the option is picked. All other attributes are the XHTML legacy attributes.
`label`	Required: None Optional: *id*, *class*, *title*, *style*, *xml:lang*, *for*, *accesskey*	The `<label>` element associates a label with a control. The value of the *for* attribute should be the same as the value of the *id* attribute of the control. Only one label can be associated with a control.

TABLE 22.7 CONTINUED

Name	Attributes	Description
`textarea`	Required: *rows*, *cols* Optional: *id*, *class*, *title*, *style*, *xml:lang*, *name*, *tabindex*, *accesskey*, *wml:format*, *wml:emptyok*, *wml:name*	The `<textarea>` tag defines a multiline text input box. It is required to specify the dimensions of the area using the *rows* and *cols* attributes. The WML specific attributes of the element are *wml:name*, which specifies the name of the control and has higher priority than the XHTML *name* attribute. *wml:format* and *wml:emptyok*, which describe the input mask for the control value.
`optgroup`	Required: *label* Optional: *id*, *class*, *title*, *style*, *xml:lang*	The `<optgroup>` element allows authors to create groups of options within the menu. The element is used in conjunction with the `<select>` and `<option>` elements.
`fieldset`	Required: None Optional: *id*, *class*, *title*, *style*, *xml:lang*	It is often necessary to group controls to make the form more intuitive to use. The `<fieldset>` tag can be used to group form controls that logically relate one to another.

METAINFORMATION

WML developers use metainformation to specify "data about data"—properties describing a document, its contents, authors, keywords, and so on.

Metadata is specified as name = value pairs using the `meta` keyword described in Table 22.8.

TABLE 22.8 TAGS DEFINED IN THE METAINFORMATION MODULE

Name	Attributes	Description
`meta`	Required: *`content`* Optional: *`xml:lang`*, *`http-equiv`*, *`name`*, *`scheme`*, *`wml:forua`*	The `<meta>` element defines a property of a document. The *`name`* attribute defines the property name. The *`content`* attribute defines its value. The *`http-equiv`* attribute can be used instead of *`name`* when it is necessary for this property to be a part of the WAP header. The *`wml:forua`* is deprecated. If used, it tells the user agent or intermediate agent whether to deliver the metatag (true) or ignore it (false).

LINK

The Links module defines just one tag described in Table 22.9, which can be used to establish relationships of the document with other resources on the Web.

TABLE 22.9 TAGS DEFINED IN THE LINK MODULE

Name	Attributes	Description
`link`	Required: None Optional: *`id`*, *`class`*, *`title`*, *`style`*, *`xml:lang`*, *`charset`*, *`href`*, *`hreflang`*, *`type`*, *`rel`*, *`rev`*, *`media`*	The `<link>` element describes a link to another document that can be used by a user agent in some special way—for example, displayed in the menu or in a toolbar. The element can only appear within the `<head>` section, and thus is not the same as the anchor element `<a>`.

BASE

The Base module and its only element, `<base>`, describe the base URI of the document, allowing user agents to resolve relative URIs used in the document properly. The element is described in Table 22.10.

TABLE 22.10 TAGS DEFINED IN THE BASE MODULE

Name	Attributes	Description
base	Required: *href* Optional: None	Specifies the base URI to be used with the document.

OBJECT

The Object Module deals with elements that are used to handle embedded data types not supported by browsers internally, but that can be understood by external programs. These elements and their attributes are described in Table 22.11.

TABLE 22.11 TAGS DEFINED IN THE OBJECT MODULE

Name	Attributes	Description
object	Required: None Optional: *id*, *class*, *title*, *style*, *xml:lang*, *declare*, *classid*, *codebase*, *data*, *type*, *codetype*, *archive*, *standby*, *height*, *width*, *name*, *tabindex*	The `<object>` tag defines an embedded object. For example, if the mobile device supports Java, it can be a java applet. Most of the attributes describe the object in different ways. The *classid* attribute specifies a URL from where the code can be downloaded. The *data* attribute points to the location of the object data.
param	Required: *name* Optional: *id*, *value*, *valuetype*, *type*	To initialize objects with runtime data, the `<param>` tag is used. Each `<param>` tag contains a name=value pair. Note that the use of the closing tag is forbidden.

STYLESHEET

The only tag of the Stylesheet module is used to define internal style sheets within the WML documents. The tag is described in Table 22.12.

TABLE 22.12 TAGS DEFINED IN THE STYLESHEET MODULE

Name	Attributes	Description
`style`	Required: *type* Optional: *title*, *xml:lang*, *media*, *xml:space*	The `<style>` tag can be used within the `<head>` section of the WML document, and it defines an internal style sheet rule.

The following example illustrates the use of the `<style>` tag. The result of this internal style definition is that all the anchor elements in the document will be displayed using small letters.

```
<head>
    <style>
        a {font-variant:small-caps}
    </style>
</head>
```

PRESENTATION

The Presentation module defines tags that change the look of the text. Most of them are deprecated. The developers are advised to use WCSS styles instead. The tags are listed in Table 22.13.

TABLE 22.13 TAGS DEFINED IN THE PRESENTATION MODULE

Name	Attributes	Description
`b`	Required: None Optional: *id*, *class*, *title*, *style*, *xml:lang*	The text within the opening `<b>` and closing `</b>` tags will be displayed as bold. Note: The tag is deprecated.
`i`	Required: None Optional: *id*, *class*, *title*, *style*, *xml:lang*	The text within the opening `<i>` and closing `</i>` tags will be displayed in italics. Note: The tag is deprecated.

TABLE 22.13 CONTINUED

Name	Attributes	Description
`small`	Required: None Optional: *id*, *class*, *title*, *style*, *xml:lang*	The text within the opening `<small>` and closing `</small>` tags will be displayed using small font. Note: The tag is deprecated.
`big`	Required: None Optional: *id*, *class*, *title*, *style*, *xml:lang*	The text within the opening `<big>` and closing `</big>` tags will be displayed using big font. Note: The tag is deprecated.
`u`	Required: None Optional: *id*, *class*, *title*, *style*, *xml:lang*	The text within the opening `<u>` and closing `</u>` tags will be underlined. Note: The tag is deprecated.
`hr`	Required: None Optional: *id*, *class*, *title*, *style*, *xml:lang*	The `<hr>` tag adds a horizontal rule to the document.

EVENTS

Before proceeding to the discussion of the elements defined in the Events, Context, and Navigation modules, we need to take a quick look at the event handling mechanisms of WML.

Many of the XHTML and WML elements allow events to be associated with different kinds of user actions. It is also possible that an event might come from some external source. These events should also be treated properly by documents.

There are two kinds of events in WML:

- *Intrinsic events*, generated by the user agent.
- *Extrinsic events*, originated from an external source.

The events defined in the specification are all intrinsic events—in particular they are *timer*, *enterforward*, *enterbackward*, and *pick*. Different *tasks*, which are navigational directives, can be associated with events. The tasks are *go*, *refresh*, *noop*, and *prev*.

The WML allows associating special tasks with different kinds of events, such as expiration of timer, and so on. One of the ways of doing this is to use the `wml:onevent` tag described in Table 22.14.

TABLE 22.14 TAGS DEFINED IN THE EVENTS MODULE

Name	Attributes	Description
`wml:onevent`	Required: *type* Optional: *id*, *class*, *title*, *style*	The `<wml:onevent>` tag binds an event with a task The required attribute *type* supplies the name of the event type.

CONTEXT AND NAVIGATION MODULE

The use of the `wml:onevent` tag is not the only way of dealing with events in WML2. A special set of WML-specific tags, listed in Table 22.14, takes care of the user agent context and behavior and allows associating different tasks with different kinds of events.

The user agent context usually comprises two major components:

- *Navigation history*—A stack of resources the user navigated to prior to getting to the current resource
- *WML variables*—a set of name/value pairs, which can be defined by documents or referenced by documents at runtime.

These tags defined in the Context and Navigation module are compatible with WML 1.

Table 22.15 briefly describes Context and Navigation module tags.

TABLE 22.15 TAGS DEFINED IN THE PRESENTATION MODULE

Name	Attributes	Description
wml:anchor	Required: None Optional: *id*, *class*, *title*, *style*, *xml:lang*, *accesskey*	The *wml:anchor* element defines a hyperlink just like the a element does—with the exception that the destination anchor is a task, such as *wml:go*. The specified task is executed by the user agent whenever a user clicks the element. The *id*, *class*, *title*, *style* and *xml:lang* attributes are standard attributes that can be found in almost any XHTML tag. The *accesskey* attribute specifies an access key to the element, but the WML 2 specification recommends using the WCSS wap-accesskey property instead of this attribute.
wml:access	Required: None Optional: *id*, *class*, *title*, *style*, *domain*, *path*	The *wml:access* tag defines the access rules that apply to the document. Only one *wml:access* element can be present in the document. The *domain* and *path* attributes are used to define the locations of other documents that are allowed to access this document. If the attributes are present, there will be no access to the document from any locations other than the one specified.
wml:do	Required: None Optional: *id*, *class*, *title*, *style*, *xml:lang*, *role*	The *wml:do* tag associates a task, which will be executed when a user activates the element. The actual task is defined by the *role* attribute, which can have predefined values such as *accept* or *reset*.
wml:go	Required: *href* Optional: *id*, *class*, *title*, *style*, *sendreferer*, *method*, *enctype*, *accept-charset*, *cache-control*, *type*	The *wml:go* task forces the user agent to navigate to a URL specified in the *href* attribute. The *sendreferer* attribute tells the browser whether to send a URI of the referring document to the server. The *method* attribute is an HTTP request method, such as GET, PUT, or POST.

22

TABLE 22.15 CONTINUED

Name	Attributes	Description
wml:noop	Required: None Optional: *id*, *class*, *title*, *style*	This element is an empty task: "do nothing."
wml:prev	Required: None Optional: *id*, *class*, *title*, *style*	This element specifies a task of navigating to the previous URI in the history list.
wml:refresh	Required: None Optional: *id*, *class*, *title*, *style*	The task declared by means of this element refreshes the browser context.
wml:postfield	Required: *name*, *value* Optional: *id*, *class*, *title*, *style*	When a URI is requested, this element can be used to set parameters that should be attached to the server request.
wml:setvar	Required: *name*, *value* Optional: *id*, *class*, *title*, *style*	Sets the variable in the current user agent context.
wml:getvar	Required: *name* Optional: *id*, *class*, *title*, *style*, *conversion*	Retrieves the value of the variable defined in the current user agent context. The value is substituted to the text of the document.

TABLE 22.15 CONTINUED

Name	Attributes	Description
`wml:timer`	Required: `value` Optional: `id`, `name`, `class`, `title`, `style`	The `wml:timer` element declares a timer and initializes it with the value specified in the `value` attribute. The timer can be used, for example, to measure inactivity intervals and perform some actions if a user is idle for too long.

FUTURE WIRELESS DIRECTIONS

The evolution of mobile phones and especially of the online services available to wireless devices was probably not as fast as expected during the last several years.

The main reason is that it usually takes more time to prepare people's mentality to accept something new than to create new devices with powerful features.

However, it now seems that people are starting to accept the possibility of performing online transactions using the cell phone. That is why e-commerce service providers started their fight for mobile customers. There are certain implications of using mobile services for conducting complex commercial transactions, such as high operational costs, lack of trust, and so on, but m-commerce has already become a part of people's everyday life in Japan and Europe.

It is certain that one of the most common applications of the WML will be m-commerce.

WML AND M-COMMERCE

At the moment, all the technologies required to facilitate m-commerce services are available to most phones.

The WML is a powerful, yet simple, markup language that allows building pages for mobile phones with small screens and limited resources.

There are security protocols, such as WTLS, that can facilitate secure transactions.

However, there are some disadvantages or limitations of WML.

LIMITATIONS OF WML

The main limitation of WML is the environment in which it is used. Most of the phones not only have very little memory and slow simple processors, but they also have small screens and tiny keypads. WML developers should always keep the average WAP customer in mind.

You will never be able to create a successful WAP service if your WML pages are overloaded with fancy images and lots of text information.

The number of screens to go through and the amount of information requested from the customer should also be minimized so that the customer does not spend 10 minutes trying to order a pizza.

If you follow these simple rules, you will get happy customers and successful service, and you will always say that WML is powerful and easy to use.

ADDITIONAL RESOURCES

- Wap Forum (`http://www.wapforum.org`)—The official site of the WAP Forum, where all the latest news and specifications on WAP and WML can be found.
- The home site of the World Wide Web Consortium (`http://www.w3c.org`)—The latest information related to the consortium activity and all of its documentation is located here.
- WML 2 Document Type Definition (`http://www.wapforum.org/dtd/wml20-flat.dtd`)—The full version of the WML 2 DTD, containing definitions of all the modules.
- WML 1.3 DTD (`http://www.wapforum.org/DTD/wml13.dtd`)—For those interested in the formal definition of the previous version, the WML 1.3, this is a place to look.

ROADMAP

Now that you've learned how content can be marked up and presented using XHTML and how customers on mobile devices can benefit from access to WAP pages and services by means of WML, it's time to find out how the XML can help extend the functionality of your Web services even further.

Chapter 23, "Scalable Vector Graphics," will introduce you to the world of vector graphics. SVG is an XML-based language that allows defining dynamic and interactive images, shapes, and texts in a standard way compatible with other Web services that rely on XML technologies.

CHAPTER 23

SCALABLE VECTOR GRAPHICS

In this chapter

by Andrew Watt

Scalable Vector Graphics (SVG) is one of the most exciting of the new XML-based specifications to emerge from the W3C. Many of the other XML specifications can be pretty abstract at times, but SVG is very visual. As you improve your skills in how to create SVG, you will have the pleasure of easily seeing your increasing control of the technology right in front of your eyes.

SVG provides an XML-based vector graphics format that was intended by the *World Wide Web Consortium (W3C)* to replace many uses of bitmap graphics in Web pages. It can be used for many situations in which you might currently use GIFs, including animated GIFs. It can also be used to create complex animations that can compete with Macromedia Flash and add subtle transitions that Flash, being frame-based, is less suited to produce. In addition, SVG has enormous potential for the creation of maps and technical diagrams in which the ability to zoom in to and out of a map or diagram can be of enormous practical benefit.

A graphics format must be visual, so straightaway we will create a visual example—although we won't examine the syntax in detail at this point. Let's suppose that you want to create a graphics rollover using conventional technologies. You might use two bitmap graphics, perhaps produced in an expensive proprietary graphics editor, together with some JavaScript to create the rollover. Using SVG, you can create rollovers simply by declaring what you want to happen.

Listing 23.1 is a fairly straightforward piece of SVG that creates a rollover button. Don't worry about the detail of the code just now: We will discuss it later. The code describes an SVG button and its behavior in response to particular mouse events. When the button is unmoused, it contains a gradient that has a bright green top and bottom with a quiet pink center and dark blue text. When the graphic is moused, the gradient changes to a red center with pale green edges while at the same time the color of the text changes to white. Figures 23.1 and 23.2 show the appearance onscreen when the graphic is unmoused and moused.

Listing 23.1 A Rollover Button Animation in SVG (RolloverButton.svg)

```
<?xml version="1.0" standalone="no"?>
<!DOCTYPE svg PUBLIC "-//W3C//DTD SVG 20010904//EN"
"http://www.w3.org/TR/2001/REC-SVG-20010904/DTD/svg10.dtd">
<svg width="300" height="250">
<defs>
<linearGradient id="MyGradient" gradientUnits="objectBoundingBox"
  x1="0%" y1="0%" x2="0%" y2="100%">
<stop offset="1%" style="stop-color:#00FF00"/>
<stop offset="50%" style="stop-color:#FF9999"/>
<stop offset="100%" style="stop-color:#00FF00"/>
</linearGradient>
<linearGradient id="MySecondGradient" gradientUnits="objectBoundingBox"
  x1="0%" y1="0%" x2="0%" y2="100%">
<stop offset="1%" style="stop-color:#CCFFCC"/>
```

Listing 23.1 Continued

```
<stop offset="50%" style="stop-color:#FF0000"/>
<stop offset="100%" style="stop-color:#CCFFCC"/>
</linearGradient>
</defs>
<rect id="MyRect" x="20" y="20" rx="10" ry="10"
 width="130" height="45" style="fill:url(#MyGradient); stroke:none">
<set attributeName="fill" begin="mouseover"
 end="mouseout" to="url(#MySecondGradient)"/>
</rect>
<text x="30" y="47" style="fill:#000099; stroke:none;
➥font-family:Arial, sans-serif; font-size:16" pointer-events="none">
<set attributeName="fill" begin="MyRect.mouseover"
 end="MyRect.mouseout" to="white"/>
SE Using XML</text>
</svg>
```


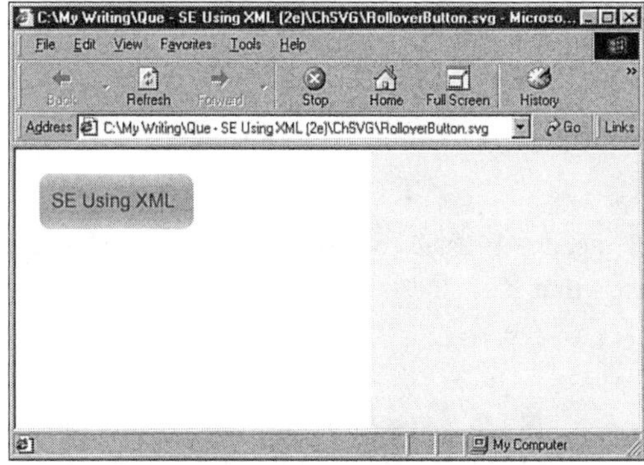

Figure 23.1 The SVG button when not moused.

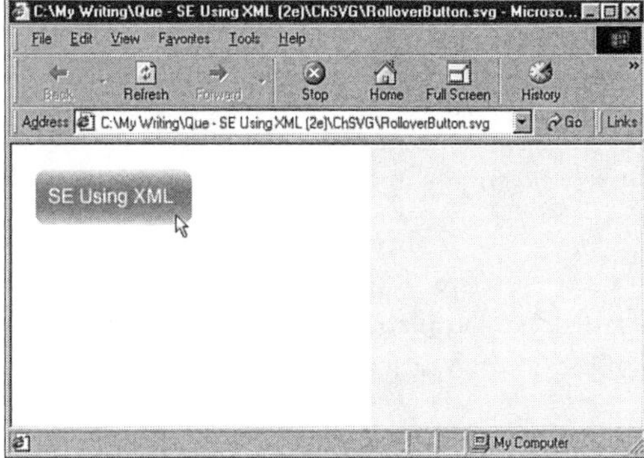

Figure 23.2 The SVG button when moused. Notice the change in color of the background and the text in response to the `mouseover` event.

To produce, without using SVG, a visual effect similar to that produced by Listing 23.1, you would typically have to use two bitmap graphics and a little straightforward JavaScript. In SVG, you simply describe the appearance of the button at rest, as it were, and also describe the animation that is to take place when the rectangle is moused. Assuming that you have the syntax correct, the rest is handled by the SVG rendering engine. SVG makes such animations delightfully simple.

Vector Graphics Overview

Vector graphics, whether based on proprietary or open standards, describe shapes in terms of drawing instructions. When a vector image is scaled up or down, the shapes can be redrawn and allow the quality of an image to be maintained in a way that is impossible with pixel-based bitmap graphics, without returning to the server to download a different copy of the graphic.

The facility for vector images to be re-drawn on the client side allows for functionality such as animations, and allows for interactivity with responsiveness to the user far better than if it were necessary to return to the server to download a new image. SVG has a *Document Object Model (DOM)* based on the W3C DOM, but extended to accommodate specific functionality in SVG. This allows us to script SVG documents on the client side using, for example, JavaScript (ECMAScript). Later in the chapter, we will examine some straightforward JavaScript code to manipulate the SVG DOM.

SVG Tools

To make use of SVG, you need two basic tools—a tool to create SVG and a rendering engine (also called a *viewer*) that will enable you to see the SVG onscreen.

Tools to Create SVG

To create SVG, you can use a simple text editor, an XML-aware editor, or one of the more traditional vector graphics drawing programs such as Corel Draw 10 or Adobe Illustrator 10. One SVG-oriented graphics tool that is of particular interest is Jasc WebDraw, which allows you to create graphics visually, to edit the code within the same program, and also to create SVG animations using a timeline. Further information is available from `http://www.jasc.com/products/WebDraw/`.

Which tool you use is entirely up to you and might depend on the tools you already have.

Tools to View SVG

Several viewers for SVG are already available, but some, at the time of writing, more fully implement the SVG specification than others.

Probably the most complete implementation, although it still has some gaps, is the Adobe SVG Viewer. We will use Adobe SVG Viewer version 3.0 to view most of the SVG examples in this chapter. To obtain the Adobe SVG Viewer, go to `http://www.adobe.com/svg/` and follow the links to the download page.

If you want to program SVG and view your work with Adobe's SVG Viewer, there is also documentation about the SVG Viewer available for download that describes which parts of the SVG specification are already implemented and which have yet to be implemented.

The Adobe SVG Viewer is available for Internet Explorer and Netscape 4 on the PC and the Mac. On the PC, simply double-click on the download, and it will install without further intervention.

Note

The Adobe SVG Viewer can work with Netscape 6, Mozilla, and Opera 5 on the PC. To achieve that, you must first install the viewer for a supported browser. If you install for Internet Explorer, a file NPSVG3.dll (for version 3.0 of the Adobe Viewer) will be located in `C:\Windows\System\Adobe\SVG Viewer 3.0\`. On Windows 98, it will be at `c:\winnt\system32\Adobe\SVG Viewer 3.0` on Windows NT version 4 (or similar). If you are using Netscape 4, NPSVG3.dll will be in the plug-ins directory. To add SVG functionality to Netscape 6, Mozilla, or Opera, copy NPSVG3.dll to the plug-ins directory of the desired Web browser(s). You might need to specify a Helper Application for media type `"image/svg+xml"`. You will likely need to re-start the browser for the new settings to take effect.

The Adobe Viewer currently implements far more of SVG's animation capabilities than any of the other SVG viewers. It also allows extensive scripting of SVG using JavaScript. Because of these capabilities and the ease of installation in many common Web browsers, we will be using Adobe SVG Viewer 3 in most of this chapter.

Caution

Netscape 6.01 was significantly less reliable in displaying SVG using the Adobe Viewer than was the original Netscape 6.0. Netscape 6.1 was an improvement, but reliability seems better in Netscape 6.2. If you plan to use Netscape 6 with SVG, Netscape 6.01 is a version to avoid. You might benefit from improved stability by upgrading to Netscape 6.2.

If you are not using Windows or the Mac, you might want to explore the Batik SVG Viewer, which is part of a Java-based SVG toolkit. For further information, visit `http://xml.apache.org/Batik/`. Batik is very limited in support for animation or JavaScript.

Adobe has recently issued a beta version of the Adobe SVG Viewer for Linux. Further information is available at `http://www.adobe.com/svg/viewer/install/old.html`. Look under the "English" heading for Linux versions.

A further option is the X-Smiles browser, which can display several XML technologies including SVG, XSL-FO, XForms, and SMIL. Further details can be obtained from the X-Smiles Web site at `http://www.xsmiles.org/`. The X-Smiles browser can be downloaded without charge. In a separate download, a range of files using several of the XML technologies just mentioned can be obtained. X-Smiles is very limited in support for animation or JavaScript.

COMPARING MACROMEDIA FLASH AND SVG

For some potential users of SVG, an important question is how SVG compares with Macromedia Flash. A detailed comparison chart is available online at `http://www.carto.net/papers/svg/comparison_flash_svg.html`.

You will likely have or intend to develop an XML tool set and an XML skill set. Because SVG is an XML application language, many parts of the tool set and the skill set can be applied directly to SVG. For example, if you have an XML-aware editor, you can use that to create SVG. If you have skills in programming XML using the DOM, for example, many of those skills will be transferable to programming the SVG DOM. Similarly SVG, being XML, works naturally with XSLT for dynamic server-side generation and can be displayed with other XML namespaces in the same browser, as was mentioned for X-Smiles a little earlier.

Scripting of Flash uses ActionScript, a Macromedia variant of ECMAScript. SVG can be scripted without relying on proprietary variants.

SVG should provide, at least, strong competition to Flash in many application areas. However, many Flash developers will not be keen to learn yet another technology and will continue with Flash. However, as XML becomes the foundation of the Web over the next few years, the fact that XML will have to be "bolted on" to the Flash's proprietary core is likely to provide limitations in some areas. Being an XML application, SVG will not be as restricting.

The frame-based approach to Flash animations might benefit certain types of animation. SVG's approach is to provide multiple renderings of animations, which will produce visually superior output. However, it might pose a significant load on a slower CPU on a client machine.

However, SVG's use of SMIL Animation elements provides the potential for many types of animation that are likely less suitable for production with Flash.

VECTOR GRAPHICS ON THE WEB

SVG will, in time, replace many uses of bitmap graphics on the Web. One crucial practical factor that will determine the rate of movement to SVG is how fast SVG viewers become widespread.

Microsoft, at the time of writing, has given no indication that SVG will be supported natively in Internet Explorer. Microsoft has developed its own standard, the *Vector Markup Language (VML)*, to perform the same kind of functions. The Mozilla project, associated with the Netscape 6 browser, is developing native SVG capabilities. However, for some time at least, the spread of the Adobe SVG Viewer is likely to be an important determining factor in the adoption of SVG.

Adobe is making the Adobe SVG Viewer available with its graphic products, such as Adobe Illustrator, as well as other Adobe products such as Adobe Acrobat. In addition, Adobe is intending to distribute the Adobe SVG Viewer in association with Real Player. A stated aim was to distribute 100 million copies of the Adobe SVG Viewer by April 2002. If those receiving the viewer take the minimal time required to install it, critical mass can be reached fairly quickly.

In certain sectors, such as online mapping, SVG offers such huge and immediate technical advantages (such as zooming in or out and selectively showing or revealing parts of the map) over maps displayed using bitmap technology that the enthusiasm for SVG is already gathering important momentum. Similarly, the use of SVG in technical diagrams and in online teaching will likely raise awareness in parts of the Web community where content developers would not naturally think of themselves as graphic designers.

And, finally, SVG can be used as a solo technology to create Web pages. A prototype site demonstrating some simple SVG Web pages can be viewed at `http://www.svgspider.com/default.svg`.

Taken together, these factors bode well for the future of SVG. Interest in SVG is likely to increase, perhaps in the same way interest in HTML exploded in the mid 1990s—but, of course, prediction is difficult, particularly with respect to the future.

Zooming in SVG

One reason that a growth in the use of SVG can be expected is that it provides superior functionality to that available using bitmap graphics, such as allowing the zooming of diagrams or maps.

The precise technique to achieve zooming varies between SVG viewers. In the Adobe SVG Viewer, you simply right-click on the image and a menu appears. The top two choices are Zoom In and Zoom Out. The third choice, Original View, is grayed out when you first access the menu. But after you have zoomed in or out, you can use it to restore the original zoom factor.

It is also possible to control the zoom factor programmatically using JavaScript. You will see an example of how to do that in Listing 23.2.

Panning in SVG

In SVG, it is possible to pan around an image. This is possible because the part of the SVG image that you see in a browser window is only part of a potentially infinite SVG canvas. Listing 23.2 is a simple representation in SVG of the SVG canvas. The point at which the horizontal and vertical lines cross can be viewed as the point (0, 0) on the SVG canvas.

LISTING 23.2 A SIMPLE REPRESENTATION OF THE POTENTIALLY INFINITE SVG CANVAS (SVGCANVAS.SVG)

```
<?xml version="1.0" standalone="no"?>
<!DOCTYPE svg PUBLIC "-//W3C//DTD SVG 20010904//EN"
"http://www.w3.org/TR/2001/REC-SVG-20010904/DTD/svg10.dtd">
<svg width="500" height="500">
```

LISTING 23.2 CONTINUED

```
<line x1="250" y1="0" x2="250" y2="500"
 style="stroke-width:0.5; stroke:black; opacity:0.5"/>
<line x1="0" y1="250" x2="500" y2="250"
 style="stroke-width:0.5; stroke:black; opacity:0.5"/>
<circle cx="300" cy="290" r="25" style="fill:red;"/>
<rect x="250" y="250" width="102.4" height="76.8"
 style="stroke:black; stroke-width:1.5; fill:black; fill-opacity:0.2"/>
<circle cx="200" cy="290" r="25" style="fill:green;"/>
<circle cx="200" cy="190" r="25" style="fill:yellow;"/>
<circle cx="300" cy="190" r="25" style="fill:blue;"/>
</svg>
```

Figure 23.3 shows the result in a browser window.

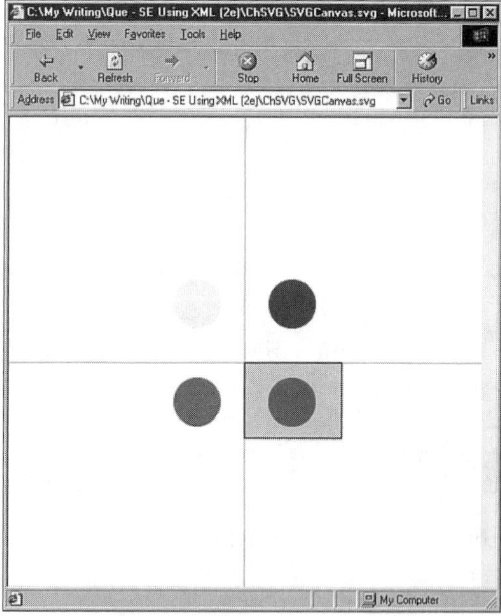

Figure 23.3
A representation of the infinite-sized SVG canvas, with the shaded rectangle representing a browser window giving a view on to the canvas.

The whole image in Figure 23.3 represents the infinite SVG canvas. The four circles represent different parts of an SVG image on the canvas. The light gray rectangle represents the part of the SVG canvas that can be viewed at any one time in a browser window. One of the four circles is viewable in the browser, but there is much more graphical information out of sight. The light gray rectangle can be moved around the canvas to bring the other information into sight. One example might be to follow a road on a map until you reach the map for a particular town or other feature.

Listing 23.3 is a simulation of what you might see when panning around the SVG canvas.

LISTING 23.3 A SIMULATION IN SVG OF PANNING AROUND THE SVG CANVAS (SVGCANVAS02.SVG)

```
<?xml version="1.0" standalone="no"?>
<!DOCTYPE svg PUBLIC "-//W3C//DTD SVG 20010904//EN"
"http://www.w3.org/TR/2001/REC-SVG-20010904/DTD/svg10.dtd">
<svg width="500" height="500">
<line x1="250" y1="0" x2="250" y2="500" style="stroke-width:0.5; stroke:black;
opacity:0.5"/>
<line x1="0" y1="250" x2="500" y2="250" style="stroke-width:0.5; stroke:black;
opacity:0.5"/>
<circle cx="300" cy="290" r="25" style="fill:red;"/>
<circle cx="200" cy="290" r="25" style="fill:green;"/>
<circle cx="200" cy="190" r="25" style="fill:yellow;"/>
<circle cx="300" cy="190" r="25" style="fill:blue;"/>
<rect x="250" y="250" width="102.4" height="76.8" style="stroke:black;
stroke-width:1.5; fill:black; fill-opacity:0.2">
<animate id="Anim1" attributeName="y" from="250" to="150"
 begin="4s" dur="5s" fill="freeze" />
<animate id="Anim2" attributeName="x" from="250" to="150"
 begin="Anim1.end+4s" dur="5s" fill="freeze" />
<animate id="Anim3" attributeName="y" from="150" to="250"
 begin="Anim2.end+4s" dur="5s" fill="freeze" />
<animate id="Anim4" attributeName="x" from="150" to="250"
 begin="Anim3.end+4s" dur="5s" fill="freeze" />
</rect>
</svg>
```

To get an impression of the process, either download and run the code or view it online at `http://www.AndrewWatt.com/SEUsingXML2e/SVGCanvas02.svg`.

The simulation pans, successively, up, left, down, and right. Watch how the content of the gray rectangle changes as it "pans"—simulating how your view of the SVG canvas changes as you pan upward, in the first instance. As you pan up, the red circle moves out of view and the blue circle progressively becomes visible at the top of the screen.

In the Adobe SVG Viewer, on the PC you pan an image by holding down the ALT key and the left mouse button and moving the mouse in the direction in which you want to travel. It is possible to pan in any direction you choose, including diagonally.

SCROLLING

The SVG specification refers to a scrolling functionality—but if you open a sizeable SVG image in a Web browser, you will be struck by the absence of scrollbars at the side of the browser window. Adobe decided to omit scrollbar functionality when creating the SVG Viewer. Of course, you can pan within the image. But in some circumstances, panning is a poor second to having the linear control of vertical or horizontal scrolling.

Fortunately, there is a fairly straightforward way to create scrollbars for a large SVG image—simply embed it in an HTML/XHTML Web page.

The "official" way to embed an SVG image or any other object in an HTML/XHTML Web page is to use the `<object>` element. Unfortunately, there is one practical difficulty—if you attempt to use the `<object>` element, you do not get cross-browser code. For the moment at least, to be confident that Web pages containing SVG images will be viewable across conventional Web browser platforms, you need to use the `<embed>` tag.

If we wanted to display a simple rollover button similar to the one that we created earlier in the chapter (see Listing 23.1) in an HTML Web page, we could use Listing 23.4.

LISTING 23.4 EMBEDDING AN SVG IMAGE IN AN HTML/XHTML WEB PAGE (SIMPLEEMBEDDING.HTML)

```
<!DOCTYPE html
PUBLIC "-//W3C//DTD XHTML 1.0 Transitional//EN"
"http://www.w3.org/TR/xhtml1/DTD/xhtml1-transitional.dtd">
<html>
<head>
<title>Embedding an SVG image in an HTML/XHTML Web page</title>
</head>
<body>
<h3>The image shown below is an SVG image which is embedded
 using the &lt;embed&gt; tag.</h3>
<embed src="RolloverButtonwithBorder.svg"
 width="300px" height="200px" type="image/svg+xml" />
</body>
</html>
```

Note

In Chapter 21 "The Future of the Web: XHTML," you learned that the `embed` tag is deprecated. Using the `object` tag, as recommended, the source would look like

```
<object type="image/svg+xml"
data="./RolloverButton.svg"
NAME="RollOverButtonwithBorder" width="200px"
height="200px" ></object>
```

However, the `<object>` element doesn't work cross browser though. Surprisingly, it handles SVG differently from "ordinary" graphics.

The appearance in the Opera 5.12 browser is shown in Figure 23.4. Notice, if you run the listing and view it onscreen, that I have added a blue border around the SVG image so that you can see that the whole SVG image is visible and displayed correctly when nested within the XHTML page.

If the SVG image is larger in either the horizontal or vertical dimension than the current size of the browser window, scrollbars are added automatically, just as they are for any other HTML or XHTML Web page.

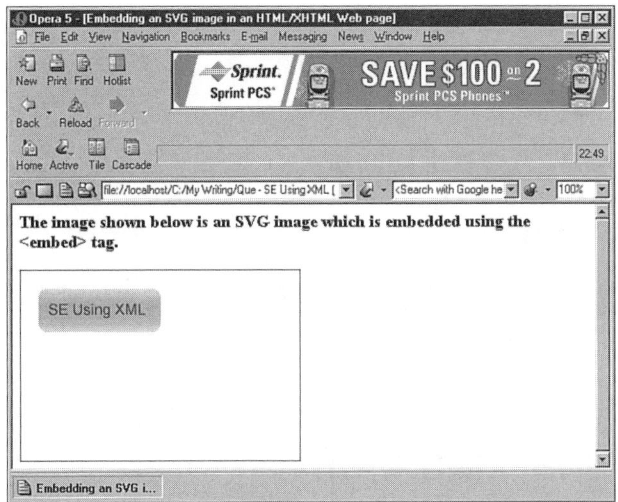

Figure 23.4 An SVG image displayed in an XHTML Web page using the `<embed>` tag. The thin blue rectangle is part of the SVG image.

Thus, to embed an SVG image that is larger than the browser window, you can use code such as Listing 23.4 and be sure that you will be able to scroll—as well as pan or zoom—the image.

Listing 23.5 shows a large, but simple, SVG rectangle.

LISTING 23.5 AN SVG RECTANGLE WITH TWO SIMPLE MESSAGES (BIGRECT.SVG)

```
<?xml version="1.0" standalone="no"?>
<!DOCTYPE svg PUBLIC "-//W3C//DTD SVG 20010904//EN"
"http://www.w3.org/TR/2001/REC-SVG-20010904/DTD/svg10.dtd">
<svg width="1500" height="1000">
<rect x="0" y="0" width="1500" height="1000"
style="stroke:#000099; stroke-width:4; fill:black; fill-opacity:0.15"/>
<text x="20" y="40"
style="font-family:Arial, sans-serif; font-size:30; stroke:#000099; fill:none">
You are near the top left.</text>
<text x="1060" y="950"
style="font-family:Arial, sans-serif; font-size:30; stroke:#000099; fill:none">
You are near the bottom right.</text>
</svg>
```

If you display the SVG file alone—that is, without embedding it in HTML/XHTML—no scrollbars appear despite the fact that the image is bigger than most user's monitors are likely to be able to display. However, if you insert the SVG image into an HTML/XHMTL "shell" of the type shown in Listing 23.6, you will be able to scroll easily to the bottom right and see the second message.

Listing 23.6 Embedding SVG in an Empty XHTML Web Page to Obtain Scrollbars in the Browser Window (InEmpty.html)

```
<!DOCTYPE html
PUBLIC "-//W3C//DTD XHTML 1.0 Transitional//EN"
"http://www.w3.org/TR/xhtml1/DTD/xhtml1-transitional.dtd">
<html>
<head>
<title>Adding scroll bars for an SVG image or Web page</title>
</head>
<body leftmargin="0" marginwidth="0" topmargin="0" marginheight="0">
<embed src="BigRect.svg" width="1500px" height="1000px" type="image/svg+xml" />
</body>
</html>
```

The SVG Rendering Model

Understanding the SVG Rendering model is important so that you can create images that display the parts of an SVG image that you want to be visible.

The SVG rendering model is referred to as the Painter's Model, indicating that it resembles the way in which oil paint is applied and seen on a canvas. The first brush stroke is covered up by subsequent brush strokes. Similarly in SVG an element that occurs early in the document—which overlaps with an element that occurs later in the document—will be covered over by the later element to a degree, depending on the later element's opacity. If the later element is fully opaque, it completely covers the part of the earlier element that it overlaps. If, however, the later element is partly transparent, the color and shape of the earlier element might be seen through the later element.

Listing 23.7 illustrates this in practice. The onscreen appearance is shown in Figure 23.5.

Listing 23.7 The Effect of the SVG Painter's Model (PaintersModel.svg)

```
<?xml version="1.0" standalone="no"?>
<!DOCTYPE svg PUBLIC "-//W3C//DTD SVG 20010904//EN"
"http://www.w3.org/TR/2001/REC-SVG-20010904/DTD/svg10.dtd">
<svg width="500" height="200">
<rect x="10" y="10" width="100" height="75" style="fill:black"/>
<rect x="80" y="20" width="100" height="75" style="fill:red"/>
<rect x="140" y="30" width="100" height="75"
 style="fill:yellow; fill-opacity:0.6"/>
</svg>
```

The red (middle) rectangle, where it overlaps the black (top left) rectangle, completely conceals that part of the black rectangle. It has painted over the black rectangle with completely opaque red paint. However, the yellow (bottom right) rectangle is partly transparent. Therefore, where it overlaps the red rectangle, part of the red rectangle shows through, yielding an orange color.

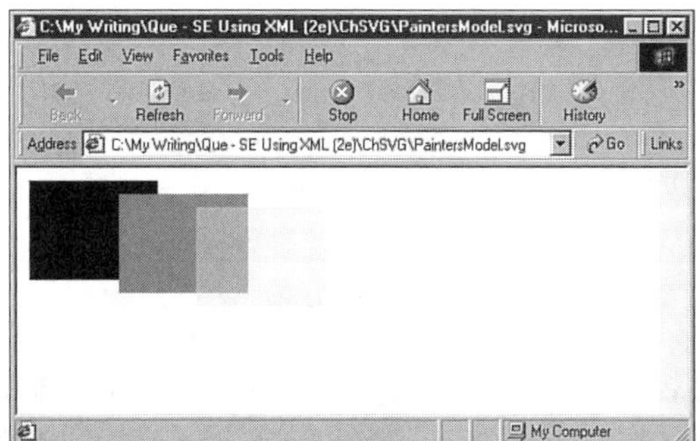

Figure 23.5 The effect of the SVG Painter's Model when opaque and semi-transparent paint is applied later in an SVG document.

SVG Document Structure

An SVG document is also an XML document: Therefore, an SVG document begins with an optional XML declaration. It also, optionally, begins with a DOCTYPE declaration.

The <svg> Element

All SVG documents have, as the root element, an <svg> element. The width and height attributes of the <svg> element define the size of the SVG image. The SVG element also has other attributes such as x and y, which are used to position an SVG graphics element. However, on an <svg> element that is the root element, any x or y attribute has no effect.

A skeleton SVG document is shown in Listing 23.8. The DOCTYPE shown is that for the SVG 1.0 Recommendation of September 2001.

Listing 23.8 A Skeleton SVG Document (SkeletonSVG.svg)

```
<?xml version="1.0" standalone="no"?>
<!DOCTYPE svg PUBLIC "-//W3C//DTD SVG 20010904//EN"
"http://www.w3.org/TR/2001/REC-SVG-20010904/DTD/svg10.dtd">
<svg width="300px" height="100px">

</svg>
```

In Listing 23.8, the width and height are specified in pixels. You can omit any units. In which case, this will produce the same size SVG viewport on screen as in our original example—the default unit of measurement is the pixel. You can specify sizes in cm, in, or pt if you prefer.

Note

The part of the notionally infinite SVG canvas that the <svg> root element of an SVG document contains is called the *"initial viewport"*. It is just a rectangular part of the SVG canvas, similar to that modeled by the gray rectangle in Listing 23.3.

COORDINATE SYSTEMS

If you specify the size of an SVG image in some unit of measurement, such as cm, you are still free to specify the size of parts of an SVG image in user units, as will be demonstrated and explained below. In the `<svg>` root element, you would typically add a `viewBox` attribute.

Listing 23.9 shows a simple SVG document. Notice that we use absolute units for the `width` and `height` attributes on the `<svg>` element. The `viewBox` attribute has four values within it. The first two represent the starting point of the viewbox. The coordinates are (0, 0), which is the top left of the initial viewport. The third and fourth values represent the width and height of the viewbox. These values define the user units for the objects that are contained within this SVG element.

LISTING 23.9 USING A VIEWBOX (VIEWBOX01.SVG)

```
<?xml version="1.0" standalone="no"?>
<!DOCTYPE svg PUBLIC "-//W3C//DTD SVG 20010904//EN"
"http://www.w3.org/TR/2001/REC-SVG-20010904/DTD/svg10.dtd">
<svg width="10cm" height="7cm" viewBox="0 0 1000 700">
<rect x="50" y="50" width="400" height="250" style="fill:#FF66CC;
stroke:#990066; stroke-width:10; stroke-opacity:1"/>
</svg>
```

The `viewBox` attribute functions as a scale, similar to that on a map. In the viewbox, `10cm` (the absolute width) corresponds to `1000` user units; that is, a scale of `100` user units to `1cm`. Similarly, in the vertical direction, a height of `7cm` corresponds to `700` user units; that is again a scale of `100` user units to `1cm`.

Figure 23.6 shows the visual appearance of Listing 23.9.

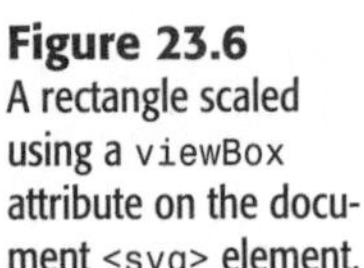

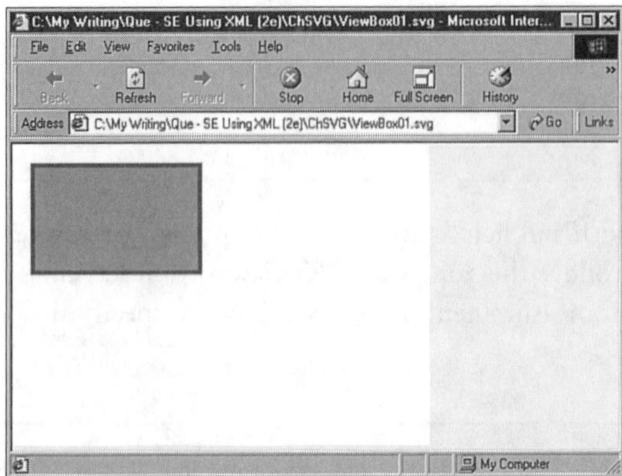

Figure 23.6
A rectangle scaled using a `viewBox` attribute on the document `<svg>` element.

If we change the third and fourth values of the `viewBox` attribute, we effectively change the scale of drawing. Listing 23.10 shows the modified listing in which the rectangle is now twice as large as that produced by Listing 23.9.

Listing 23.10 The Rectangle Doubles in Size Due to Modification of the Values in the viewBox Attribute (ViewBox02.svg)

```
<?xml version="1.0" standalone="no"?>
<!DOCTYPE svg PUBLIC "-//W3C//DTD SVG 20010904//EN"
"http://www.w3.org/TR/2001/REC-SVG-20010904/DTD/svg10.dtd">
<svg width="10cm" height="7cm" viewBox="0 0 500 350">
<rect x="50" y="50" width="400" height="250"
style="fill:#FF66CC; stroke:#990066; stroke-width:10; stroke-opacity:1"/>
</svg>
```


In Listing 23.10, the third value in the `viewBox` attribute, `500` arbitrary units, corresponds to `10cm`—that is, `100` units is now `2cm`, compared to `1cm` for `100` units in the previous listing. In other words, the rectangle doubles in size because it is the same number of units in dimension, and each unit is now 0.02 cm rather than 0.01 cm as it was previously. Figure 23.7 shows the re-scaled rectangle.

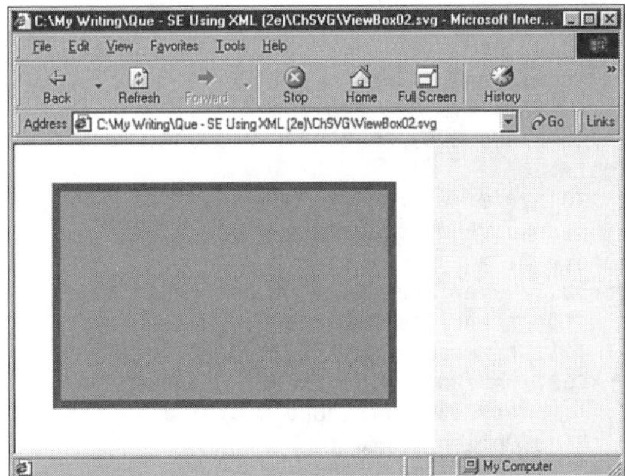

Figure 23.7
The rectangle doubles in size by changing the third and fourth values in the `viewBox` attribute of the `<svg>` element.

Caution

Be careful that the scale is the same for the vertical and horizontal axes. If, for example, you make a mistake and have `viewBox` (`0 0 1000 1000`) for a rectangle rendered as an SVG image 10 cm wide by 7 cm high, the scales for the two axes will be different. You might find that the rectangle is placed around the middle of the image, which preserves its shape but misleads about its position. More than likely, you will end up confused as you try to figure out what is going on. SVG does provide a way to take control of what happens by means of the preserve aspect ratio facilities, but that is beyond the scope of this chapter. Unless you understand how to control aspect ratios in SVG, the simplest thing is to make sure that you keep the vertical and horizontal scales the same for all your SVG images.

X and Y Coordinates

In SVG, the x and y coordinates are determined in relation to the top left of the screen. When an SVG image first loads, the coordinates (0, 0) are at the top left of the screen. As you increase the value of the x coordinate (reflected in the value of the x attribute of the <svg> element or shapes such as the <rect> element), you move to the right. As the value of the y coordinate (reflected in the y attribute) increases, you move down.

If you pan up a significant distance, the top left of the screen will still have an x coordinate—and, therefore, an x attribute of about zero—but will now have a negative value for the y coordinate and y attribute.

You can store unused graphics shapes off screen (but still on the SVG canvas) by giving them a significantly negative value for the y attribute. Listing 23.11 shows a simple example of this. A red rectangle is visible onscreen, and a blue one is hidden off screen. The code uses a time animation to animate the blue rectangle down to cover the red rectangle. More complex versions of such animations that respond to user events can be used to create dynamic menus.

LISTING 23.11 MOVING AN SVG OBJECT FROM A POSITION OFF SCREEN ON TO THE VIEWPORT (OFFSCREEN01.SVG)

```
<?xml version="1.0" standalone="no"?>
<!DOCTYPE svg PUBLIC "-//W3C//DTD SVG 20010904//EN"
"http://www.w3.org/TR/2001/REC-SVG-20010904/DTD/svg10.dtd">
<svg width="600" height="300">
<rect id="RedRect" x="50" y="0" width="200" height="50"
 style="fill:#FFCCCC; stroke:#FF0000; stroke-width:3;"/>
<g transform="translate(0 0)">
<animateTransform attributeName="transform" type="translate"
 from="translate(0,0)" to="translate(0, 205)
" begin="4s" dur="2s" fill="freeze"/>
<rect id="BlueRect" x="50" y="-205" width="200" height="200"
 style="fill:#CCCCFF; stroke:#000099; stroke-width:3;"/>
<text x="60" y="-175">Menu Option 1</text>
<line x1="50" y1="-155" x2="250" y2="-155"
 style="stroke:#000099; stroke-width:3"/>
<text x="60" y="-125">Menu Option 2</text>
<line x1="50" y1="-105" x2="250" y2="-105"
 style="stroke:#000099; stroke-width:3"/>
<text x="60" y="-75">Menu Option 3</text>
<line x1="50" y1="-55" x2="250" y2="-55"
 style="stroke:#000099; stroke-width:3"/>
<text x="60" y="-25">Menu Option 4</text>
</g>
</svg>
```

SVG BASIC SHAPES

SVG provides a number of basic graphic shapes. In earlier examples, you have seen some of these in use—but without any explanation. In this section, each of the basic SVG graphics shapes is introduced.

The <rect> Element

The SVG `<rect>` element, not surprisingly, creates a rectangular shape. A rectangle has a width and a height, which are described by the `width` and `height` attributes on the `<rect>` element. The rectangle also must have a defined position on the screen: Otherwise, the SVG rendering engine has no way of knowing where on the screen the rectangle should be displayed. The position of a rectangle is defined by the `x` and `y` attributes. With those four attributes defined, the SVG rendering engine can display a basic rectangle.

Typically, we might want to control the style to be applied to the rectangle. We can do this using style properties. SVG offers several ways of defining style properties. One option is to use a `style` attribute within which we list style properties separated by semicolons, using a syntax similar to that in a CSS style sheet.

The code in Listing 23.12 creates a simple rectangle with a blue outline, called the "*stroke*" in SVG jargon, and a pale blue semi-transparent fill. Behind that rectangle is a plain green rectangle that is partly covered by the blue one. You can see in Figure 23.8 that the blue rectangle is semi-transparent.

Listing 23.12 An Image Containing Two Rectangles (TwoRectangles.svg)

```
<?xml version="1.0" standalone="no"?>
<!DOCTYPE svg PUBLIC "-//W3C//DTD SVG 20010904//EN"
"http://www.w3.org/TR/2001/REC-SVG-20010904/DTD/svg10.dtd">
<svg width="400" height="350">
<rect x="100" y="50" width="200" height="110"
 style="fill:#009900; stroke:none;"/>
<rect x="80" y="110" width="200" height="150"
 style="fill:#CCCCFF; fill-opacity:0.5; stroke:#000099; stroke-width:3"/>
</svg>
```

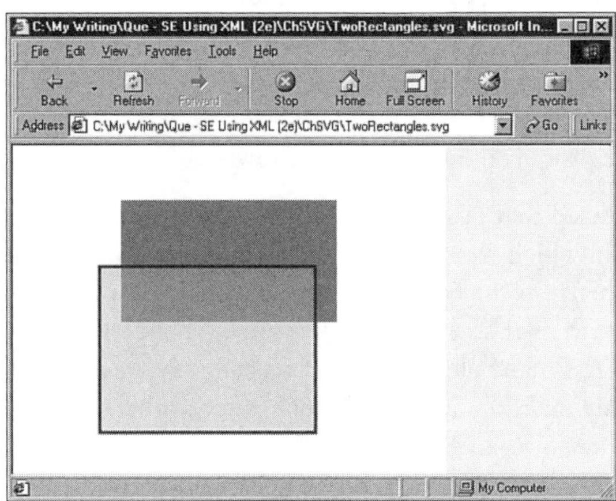

Figure 23.8
A semi-transparent rectangle placed in front of an opaque green rectangle.

THE <line> ELEMENT

The SVG <line> element is used to create straight lines. We can use <line> elements to create, for example, the axes for a graph, as well as including scale marks within the graph. The <line> element has x1 and y1 attributes that define the location of one end of the line and x2 and y2 attributes that indicate the location of the other end. A <line> element might take a style attribute within which you can define the stroke color and stroke width, for example. Listing 23.13 shows a simple skeleton for a graph in SVG, which was created using <line> elements.

LISTING 23.13 A SKELETON FOR A GRAPH CREATED USING SVG <line> ELEMENTS (GRAPHSKELETON.SVG)

```
<?xml version="1.0" standalone="no"?>
<!DOCTYPE svg PUBLIC "-//W3C//DTD SVG 20010904//EN"
"http://www.w3.org/TR/2001/REC-SVG-20010904/DTD/svg10.dtd">
<svg width="750" height="500">
<style type="text/css">
<![CDATA[
.axes {stroke:black; stroke-width:2}
.faint {stroke:#CCCCCC; stroke-width:0.05; opacity:0.4;}
]]>
</style>
<rect x="0" y="0" width="750" height="500" style="fill:#DDDDDD"/>
<line x1="50" y1="100" x2="700" y2="100" class="faint"/>
<line x1="50" y1="200" x2="700" y2="200" class="faint"/>
<line x1="50" y1="300" x2="700" y2="300" class="faint"/>
<line x1="150" y1="50" x2="150" y2="400" class="faint"/>
<line x1="250" y1="50" x2="250" y2="400" class="faint"/>
<line x1="350" y1="50" x2="350" y2="400" class="faint"/>
<line x1="450" y1="50" x2="450" y2="400" class="faint"/>
<line x1="550" y1="50" x2="550" y2="400" class="faint"/>
<line x1="650" y1="50" x2="650" y2="400" class="faint"/>
<line x1="50" y1="50" x2="50" y2="400" class="axes"/>
<line x1="50" y1="400" x2="700" y2="400" class="axes"/>
</svg>
```

The visual appearance produced by the code is shown in Figure 23.9.

You probably have noticed that in Listing 23.13 we used a different way to express style—a <style> element within which we defined styles to be applied to certain classes of elements. Thus, the <line> elements in the code have a class attribute with a value of either "axes" or "faint". The use of the <style> element is more efficient when you want to alter some aspect of style that affects many elements. If you use a <style> element rather than a style attribute, you need only make any changes in one place, rather than in each separate style attribute.

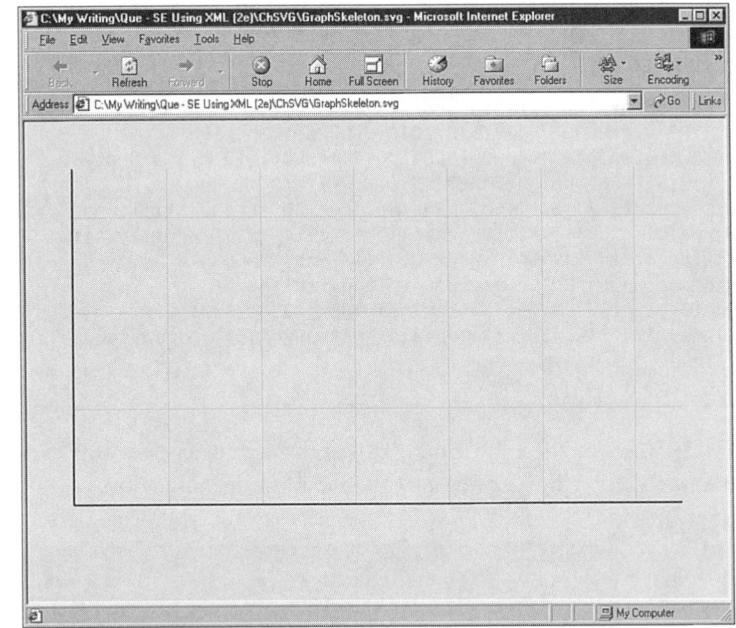

Figure 23.9
A skeleton for a graph with the axes and a background grid produced using SVG `<line>` elements.

The `<circle>` Element

The SVG `<circle>` element defines a circle. We need to know the position of the center of the circle and its radius. The x coordinate for the position of the center is contained in the `cx` attribute, and the y coordinate is contained in the `cy` attribute. The radius is defined by the `r` attribute. In addition, we might style both the fill and the stroke of the circle. Listing 23.14 shows a simple circle.

Listing 23.14 A Circle in SVG (Circle01.svg)

```
<?xml version="1.0" standalone="no"?>
<!DOCTYPE svg PUBLIC "-//W3C//DTD SVG 20010904//EN"
"http://www.w3.org/TR/2001/REC-SVG-20010904/DTD/svg10.dtd">
<svg width="400" height="250">
<circle cx="200" cy="125" r="70"
style="fill:red; fill-opacity:0.3; stroke:red; stroke-width:3;"/>
</svg>
```

The `<ellipse>` Element

An `<ellipse>` element describes an ellipse shape. Like a circle, an ellipse has a center—the position of which is described by `cx` and `cy` attributes. An ellipse has two radii—an x radius described by an `rx` attribute and a y radius described by an `ry` attribute. Listing 23.15 shows two ellipses—one of which is white to match the background, showing how overlapping ellipses can create interesting curved graphic shapes.

LISTING 23.15 TWO OVERLAPPING ELLIPSES—ONE OF WHICH IS ANIMATED (TWOELLIPSES.SVG)

```
<?xml version="1.0" standalone="no"?>
<!DOCTYPE svg PUBLIC "-//W3C//DTD SVG 20010904//EN"
"http://www.w3.org/TR/2001/REC-SVG-20010904/DTD/svg10.dtd">
<svg width="600" height="300">
<ellipse cx="300" cy="150" rx="130" ry="50" style="fill:red;"/>
<ellipse cx="300" cy="150" rx="110" ry="50" style="fill:white;">
<animate attributeName="rx" from="110" to="125"
 begin="0s" dur="5s" repeatCount="indefinite"/>
<animate attributeName="cx" values="300; 280; 300; 290"
 keyTimes="0s; 4s; 7s; 11s" begin="0s" dur="15s" repeatCount="indefinite"/>
</ellipse>
</svg>
```

Figure 23.10 shows the animation part way through its cycle with a curved shape, resulting from how the two ellipses overlap at that point in the animation.

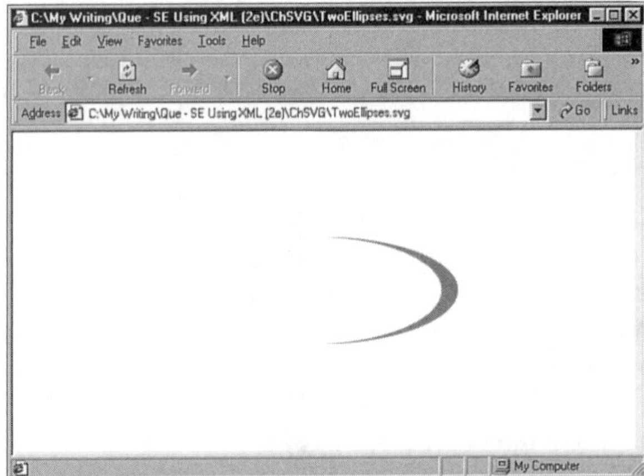

Figure 23.10
A point during an animation involving two ellipses using two `<ellipse>` elements and an SVG animation.

THE <polyline> ELEMENT

A `<polyline>` element is used to draw shapes that consist of more than one straight line. Listing 23.16 shows a `<polyline>` element used to create a shape similar to a letter "*v*".

LISTING 23.16 USING THE <polyline> ELEMENT TO CREATE A V SHAPE (POLYLINE.SVG)

```
<?xml version="1.0" standalone="no"?>
<!DOCTYPE svg PUBLIC "-//W3C//DTD SVG 20010904//EN"
"http://www.w3.org/TR/2001/REC-SVG-20010904/DTD/svg10.dtd">
<svg width="300" height="200">
<polyline style="fill:red; fill-opacity:0.4; stroke:red; stroke-width:2"
  points="50,50 70,150 90,50"/>
</svg>
```

Figure 23.11 shows the appearance produced onscreen. Notice how the space between the two lines is filled by a fill specified in the `style` attribute. If you omit mention of the fill, the default is black. To create a polyline shape with no fill, include within the `style` attribute `"fill:none;"`.

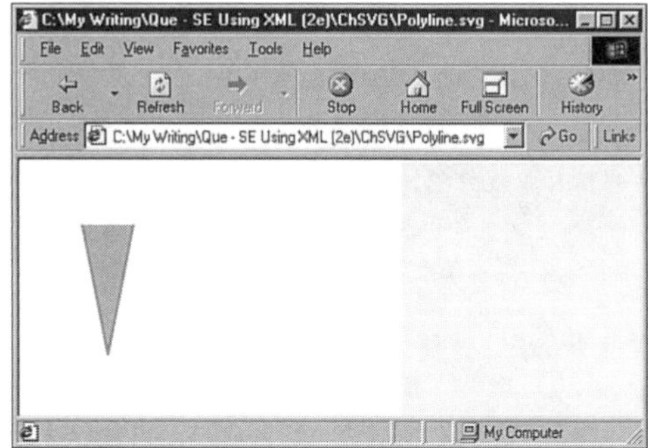

Figure 23.11
A polyline shape with a specified fill.

THE <polygon> ELEMENT

A `<polygon>` element is used to produce regular shapes with straight sides. To produce a hexagon, for example, you could use code like that in Listing 23.17.

LISTING 23.17 USING THE SVG <polygon> ELEMENT TO PRODUCE A HEXAGON SHAPE (POLYGON01.SVG)

```
<?xml version="1.0" standalone="no"?>
<!DOCTYPE svg PUBLIC "-//W3C//DTD SVG 20010904//EN"
"http://www.w3.org/TR/2001/REC-SVG-20010904/DTD/svg10.dtd">
<svg width="500" height="300">
<polygon style="fill:#CCCCFF; stroke:#0000CC; stroke-width:3"
  points="175,75 300,75 375,137.5 300,200 175,200 100,137.5 175,75"/>
</svg>
```

The hexagon has a blue outline and a pale blue fill.

PATHS IN SVG

The shapes that you have seen so far are all very regular shapes—but many shapes used in drawings, diagrams, or maps are not simple shapes such as those. All the shapes you have seen so far can be described using the SVG `<path>` element, although the syntax shown earlier provides a convenient shortcut to create certain shapes.

THE <path> ELEMENT

Perhaps the easiest way to visualize what the `<path>` element does is to think of drawing using a pen on a sheet of graph paper. If you were being instructed how to draw, you might be told where to move the pen, when to apply it to the graph paper, what coordinate to draw to, and whether to use a straight line or a curve.

The <path> element has a complex set of options that we won't cover in full here. We will look at how to draw a square using the <path> element. Listing 23.18 shows how that is done.

LISTING 23.18 CREATING A SQUARE USING THE SVG <path> ELEMENT (PATH01.SVG)

```
<?xml version="1.0" standalone="no"?>
<!DOCTYPE svg PUBLIC "-//W3C//DTD SVG 20010904//EN"
"http://www.w3.org/TR/2001/REC-SVG-20010904/DTD/svg10.dtd">
<svg width="400" height="250">
<path style="stroke:red; stroke-width:2; fill:#FFFF00"
  d="M30,30 L230,30 L230,230 L30,230 z"/>
</svg>
```

Let's look closely at the syntax in the <path> element's d attribute. The first part is "M30,30". The uppercase "M" means move to an absolute position. The "30,30" means that this is 30 units to the right and 30 units down. The "L230,30" means "draw a line from the starting point (30, 30) to the absolute position (230, 30)". The uppercase "L" is what signifies that a line is drawn to an absolute position. Then a line is drawn vertically downward to (230, 230), a line is drawn to the left to (30, 230). Finally, "z" means "connect that position back to the starting point of the shape."

Sometimes it might be more convenient to use relative positions when describing movements or line drawing. Listing 23.19 uses the relative position syntax within the d attribute to produce the same rectangle as produced by Listing 23.18.

LISTING 23.19 USING RELATIVE SYNTAX IN THE d ATTRIBUTE OF THE <path> ELEMENT (PATH02.SVG)

```
<?xml version="1.0" standalone="no"?>
<!DOCTYPE svg PUBLIC "-//W3C//DTD SVG 20010904//EN"
"http://www.w3.org/TR/2001/REC-SVG-20010904/DTD/svg10.dtd">
<svg width="400" height="250">
<path style="stroke:red; stroke-width:2; fill:#FFFF00"
  d="m30,30 l200,0 0,200 -200,0 z"/>
</svg>
```

Again, let's look closely at what is contained in the value of the d attribute. The first part, "m30,30", uses a lowercase "m", meaning that a relative movement is used. The default starting point is (0, 0), which is the upper left corner of the screen. So we move 30 units to the right and 30 units down from there. The next part, "l200,0", begins with a lowercase "l" (letter L), which means "draw a line relative to the starting point." The "200,0" means that the line is drawn 200 units horizontally to the right with no change in the y position. The next part is "0,200". You might imagine that I have made a mistake in the syntax because I have omitted the "l" at the beginning. However, SVG assumes that if you don't add a new letter, the previous one (in this situation, a lowercase "l") again is to be used. Thus "0,200" means "draw a line relative to the starting position 200 units vertically downward." Then "-200,0" means that we draw a horizontal line 200 units to the left. Finally, the "z" means that we connect to the first starting point for the shape. The result is shown in Figure 23.12. Visually, the output is identical to that from Listing 23.18 when we used absolute coordinates.

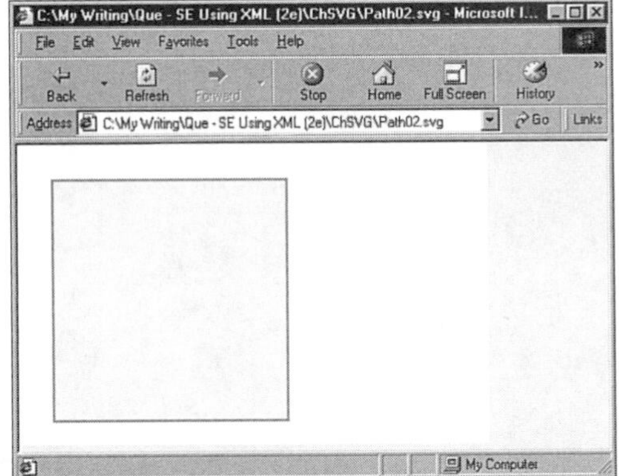

Figure 23.12
A square drawn with the SVG `<path>` element using relative syntax in the `d` attribute.

You have seen how to create shapes with the `<path>` element using straight lines. But how do we use it to create curved lines? Listing 23.20 shows an example.

LISTING 23.20 CREATING A CURVED LINE USING THE SVG `<path>` ELEMENT (PATH03.SVG)

```
<?xml version="1.0" standalone="no"?>
<!DOCTYPE svg PUBLIC "-//W3C//DTD SVG 20010904//EN"
"http://www.w3.org/TR/2001/REC-SVG-20010904/DTD/svg10.dtd">
<svg width="800" height="400">
<path style="stroke:#990066; stroke-width:5; fill:none;"
  d="M50,50
     c 150 200 300 0 400 80
     c 600 250 250 600 400 100"/>
</svg>
```

The curve produced by Listing 23.20 is shown in Figure 23.13.

Let's look at the content of the `d` attribute of the `<path>` element. We first move absolute to (50, 50): Thereafter, we use commands that use a lowercase "`c`". That refers to a cubic Bezier curve. The numbers that follow include pairs which indicate the position of "*control points*" for parts of the line: A notion you might be familiar with if you use vector graphics drawing programs to create curves. A detailed explanation of how to use cubic Bezier or other curves is beyond the scope of this chapter. In practice, you are likely to create complex curves using a drawing program that can export SVG rather than hand code them.

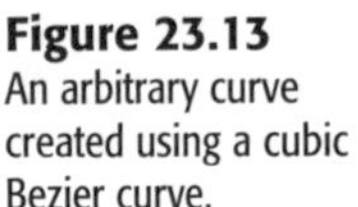
Figure 23.13
An arbitrary curve created using a cubic Bezier curve.

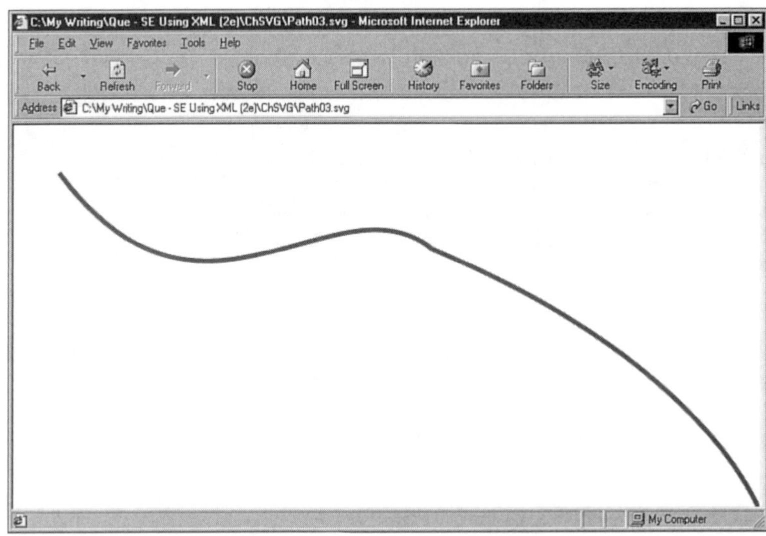

TEXT HANDLING IN SVG

Text handling in SVG is carried out with three elements—<text>, which is always used when laying out text, and, optionally, <tspan> and <tref> elements.

THE <text> ELEMENT

To lay out text, the SVG rendering engine needs to know, in addition to what characters to render, where to place the text, what font and font size to use, and so on. You saw in Listing 23.1, the rollover button example, how text is used with a rollover button.

It is important to notice the difference in how the x and y attributes of <rect> and <text> elements are used. Listing 23.21 illustrates the difference in usage.

LISTING 23.21 THE DIFFERENCE IN USAGE OF x AND y ATTRIBUTES IN <text> AND <rect> ELEMENTS (DIFFTEXTRECT.SVG)

```
<?xml version="1.0" standalone="no"?>
<!DOCTYPE svg PUBLIC "-//W3C//DTD SVG 20010904//EN"
"http://www.w3.org/TR/2001/REC-SVG-20010904/DTD/svg10.dtd">
<svg width="700" height="350">
<text x="20" y="50" style="font-size:20;
➥font-family:Arial, sans-serif; fill:#990066; stroke:none">
The text and rectangle below are both positioned at x="50" y="120"
</text>
<rect x="50" y="120" width="200" height="150"
 style="fill:#CCFFCC; stroke:#009900;"/>
<text x="50" y="120" style="font-size:20;
➥font-family:Arial, sans-serif; fill:#009900; stroke:none">
Positioned at x="50" y="120"
</text>
</svg>
```

Figure 23.14 shows how this appears when rendered.

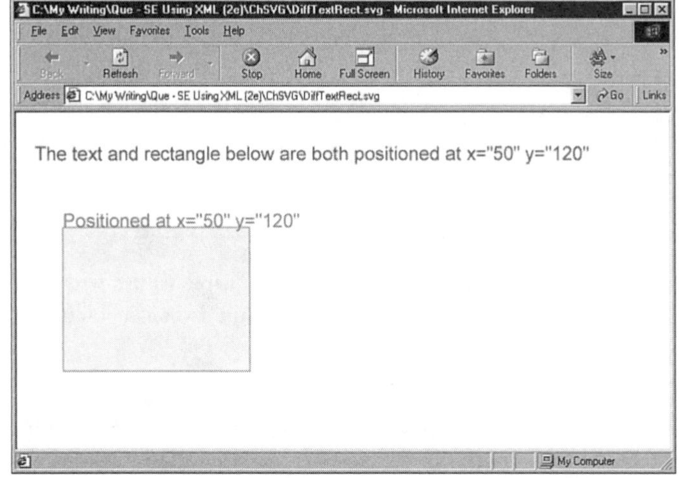

Figure 23.14
This shows the difference in the positioning of text and a rectangle with identical x and y attributes.

You can see that x="50" y="120" for the text refers to the bottom left of the text—in contrast to the rectangle, which refers to the top left of the rectangle. This difference in positioning means that you need to place text carefully on background rectangles if you are hand coding the text.

When you want to copy and paste text from an SVG image or Web page, you will find that you cannot highlight and therefore cannot copy across more than a single `<text>` element. Thus for accessibility reasons and other reasons that we will return to later, it makes sense to use `<tspan>` elements nested within `<text>` elements. This type of fiddling with details of text layout in SVG might come as something of a shock if you are used to just typing `<p>` elements in HTML and XHMLT and then expecting the browser to flow the content as needed according to the browser window size.

Note

It is likely that some form of automatic text flowing will be added to the SVG 1.1 specification currently under development at W3C. Visit `http://www.w3.org/TR/SVG11` to view the latest version of the SVG 1.1 specification.

THE <tspan> ELEMENT

The `<tspan>` element can only be used nested within a `<text>` element. A `<tspan>` element can have its position determined in absolute terms using `x` and `y` attributes in the way you have already seen. Another option is to use `dx` or `dy` attributes that express its position relative to either its parent `<text>` element or the `<tspan>` element that precedes it in document order.

Let's look at the use of absolute positioning. This is shown in Listing 23.22.

LISTING 23.22 ABSOLUTE POSITIONING OF A <tspan> ELEMENT (TSPAN01.SVG)

```
<?xml version="1.0" standalone="no"?>
<!DOCTYPE svg PUBLIC "-//W3C//DTD SVG 20010904//EN"
"http://www.w3.org/TR/2001/REC-SVG-20010904/DTD/svg10.dtd">
<svg width="600" height="350">
<text>
<tspan x="10" y="30"
style="font-family:Arial, sans-serif; font-size:20; fill:#990066; stroke:none;">
ABC</tspan>
</text>
</svg>
```

The <tspan> element also allows us to include multiple values within either an x or y attribute and individually position characters within a <tspan> element. Listing 23.23 shows an example.

LISTING 23.23 ABSOLUTE POSITIONING OF INDIVIDUAL CHARACTERS IN A <tspan> ELEMENT (TSPAN02.SVG)

```
<?xml version="1.0" standalone="no"?>
<!DOCTYPE svg PUBLIC "-//W3C//DTD SVG 20010904//EN"
"http://www.w3.org/TR/2001/REC-SVG-20010904/DTD/svg10.dtd">
<svg width="600" height="350">
<text>
<tspan x="10 100 500" y="30" style="font-family:Arial, sans-serif;
font-size:20; fill:#990066; stroke:none;">ABC</tspan>
</text>
</svg>
```

The characters are individually positioned according to the individual values shown within the value of the x attribute. Of course, to gain appropriate control of each character, the number of values within the x attribute should match the number of characters in the <tspan> element. We will look at a couple of examples that animate SVG characters using this technique later in the chapter.

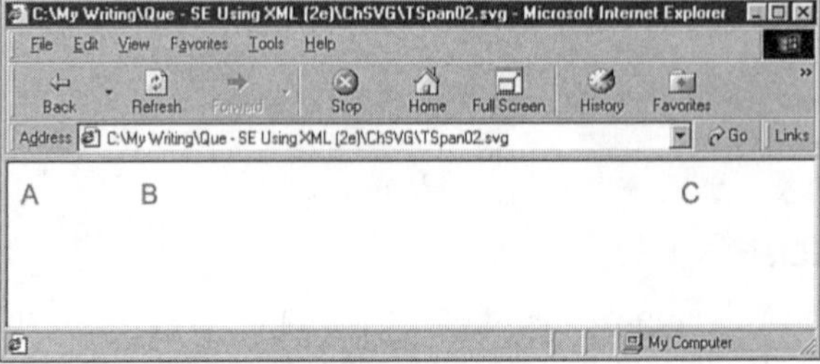

Figure 23.15 Individual characters within a <tspan> element can be positioned individually onscreen in absolute positions.

THE <tref> ELEMENT

The <tref> element allows reuse of sections of text that are used repeatedly. The text to be repeated is defined within the <defs> section of an SVG document using a <text> element with an id attribute. Each time that that text is to be used in the document, a <tref> element is used. The <tref> element possesses an xlink:href attribute with a value corresponding to the id attribute of the <text> element in the definitions section of the document.

One scenario in which a <tref> might be useful is in a newsfeed scenario—where two or three lines of text on running stories each have a link to the full story. Listing 23.23 shows an SVG file that produces a scrolling window of news headlines—each of which accesses, using a <tref> element, a standard text for hyperlinks.

LISTING 23.23 USING A <tref> ELEMENT IN A NEWSFEED SCENARIO (NEWSFEED.SVG)

```
<?xml version="1.0" standalone="no"?>
<!DOCTYPE svg PUBLIC "-//W3C//DTD SVG 20010904//EN"
"http://www.w3.org/TR/2001/REC-SVG-20010904/DTD/svg10.dtd">
<svg width="400" height="300">
<defs>
<text id="Click">Click here for the full story</text>
<style type="text/css">
tref {fill:#0000CC;
      font-size:12;
      font-decoration:underline;
      }

tspan {fill:#000000;
       font-size:12;
       }

tspan.head { fill:#FF0000;
             font-size:14;
             font-weight:bold;
           }
</style>
</defs>
<text>
<tspan class="head" x="10" y="80">
<animate attributeName="y" begin="0s" dur="15s"
 from="80" to="-230" repeatCount="indefinite"/>
Tragic Events in New York and Washington</tspan>
<tspan x="10" dy="1.5em">
Today tragic events occurred in New York and Washington. The twin
</tspan>
<tspan x="10" dy="1.5em">
towers of the World Trade Center are ablaze. An explosion is
</tspan>
<tspan x="10" dy="1.5em">
reported to have occurred at the Pentagon.
```

LISTING 23.23 CONTINUED

```
</tspan>
<a xlink:href="NS012345.svg">
<tref x="10" dy="1.5em" xlink:href="#Click"/>
</a>
<tspan class="head" x="10" dy="2em">
Mayor Giuliani at site of explosions
</tspan>
<tspan x="10" dy="1.5em">
Mayor Rudolf Giuliani is reported to have visited the site of
</tspan>
<tspan x="10" dy="1.5em">
the explosions at the World Trade Center.
</tspan>
<a xlink:href="NS0123456.svg">
<tref x="10" dy="1.5em" xlink:href="#Click"/>
</a>
<tspan class="head" x="10" dy="2em">
President Bush in Nebraska
</tspan>
<tspan x="10" dy="1.5em">
In a surprise move President George Bush is reported to be
</tspan>
<tspan x="10" dy="1.5em">
in Nebraska. Earlier he was reported to be returning to
</tspan>
<tspan x="10" dy="1.5em">
Washington.
</tspan>
<a xlink:href="NS234567.svg">
<tref x="10" dy="1.5em" xlink:href="#Click"/>
</a>
<tspan class="head" x="10" dy="2em">
Many other stories would be placed here.
</tspan>
</text>
</svg>
```

Notice in the preceding code that I start the content of each `<tspan>` element on a fresh line. When hand coding, that is a useful technique to minimize the intrusion caused by SVG's limitations in reflowing text. If you carefully check how many characters fit into the width of a window, you can make the first text line fit the window. Thereafter, you can stop typing on one line and start a new line by visually comparing the length of the line you are typing with one you know fits the window. It isn't a sophisticated technique, but it saves time.

Figure 23.16 shows the onscreen output of running Listing 23.23.

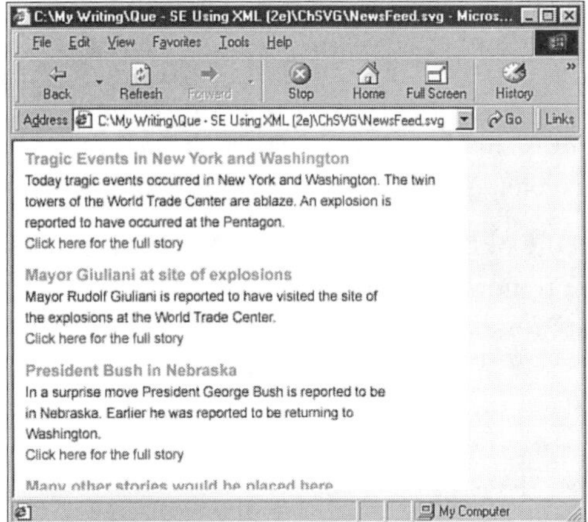

Figure 23.16
A scrolling news feed that reuses text by means of a `<tref>` element. The scroll was paused for the screenshot.

Gradients in SVG

SVG provides us with a technique to create gradients within vector graphics shapes. As with so many other parts of SVG, we simply state how we want the gradient to look. The gradient is defined in the definitions section of an SVG document and is then referenced later in the document when the gradient is being applied to a particular shape.

SVG provides two types of gradients—linear and radial. Let's look at using linear gradients.

Linear Gradients

The rollover button example you saw in Listing 23.1 shows the use of a vertical gradient. But you can also create horizontal gradients. Listing 23.25 shows a vertical bar that you might use as a side decoration on a Web page or as a separator between columns.

Listing 23.25 Using a Horizontal Linear Gradient in a Vertical Piece of Page Furniture (LinGradient01.svg)

```
<?xml version="1.0" standalone="no"?>
<!DOCTYPE svg PUBLIC "-//W3C//DTD SVG 20010904//EN"
"http://www.w3.org/TR/2001/REC-SVG-20010904/DTD/svg10.dtd">
<svg width="20" height="400">
<defs>
<linearGradient id="MyGradient" gradientUnits="objectBoundingBox"
  x1="0%" y1="0%" x2="100%" y2="0%">
<stop offset="1%" style="stop-color:#99FF99"/>
<stop offset="50%" style="stop-color:#6666FF"/>
<stop offset="100%" style="stop-color:#00FF00"/>
</linearGradient>
</defs>
<rect x="0" y="0" width="20" height="400" style="fill:url(#MyGradient)"/>
</svg>
```

You might wonder how I know that the linear gradient is a horizontal one. Look at the x1 and x2 attribute pair and the y1 and y2 attribute pair. The x1 and x2 pair differ, so it is in the x direction that the gradient changes. In other words, it is a horizontal gradient.

Creating a diagonal gradient is simple—you make sure that x1 differs from x2 and that y1 differs from y2, and so a diagonal gradient is created.

Notice that the width attribute of the <svg> element is only 20. At first, that might seem odd. By doing this, we have removed any blank space around the vertical bar. This means that we can use it as a separation bar in other SVG images or Web pages and place it precisely in the image or in an SVG Web page. If we want space around it, we can position elements appropriately. Equally, if we want elements next to each other, the absence of space allows us to do that too. Listing 23.26 shows how this can be done in a simple SVG Web page using the SVG <image> element.

LISTING 23.26 USING THE SVG <image> ELEMENT TO IMPORT OTHER SVG FILES TO MAKE UP AN SVG WEB PAGE (SIMPLEWEBPAGE.SVG)

```
<?xml version="1.0" standalone="no"?>
<!DOCTYPE svg PUBLIC "-//W3C//DTD SVG 20010904//EN"
"http://www.w3.org/TR/2001/REC-SVG-20010904/DTD/svg10.dtd">
<svg width="800" height="400">
<defs>
<style type="text/css">
<![CDATA[
tspan {
      font-size:12;
      fill:black;
      stroke:none;
      }

tspan.head {
      font-family:Arial, sans-serif;
      fill:#FF0000;
      font-size:14;
      }
]]>
</style>
</defs>
<a xlink:href="SomeImportantPage.svg">
<image xlink:href="RolloverButtonTrimmed.svg"
 x="20" y="20" width="140" height="50"/>
</a>
<image xlink:href="LinGradient01.svg" x="160" y="0" width="20" height="400"/>
<text>
<tspan class="head" x="200" y="50">
Visual components in SVG
</tspan>
<tspan x="200" dy="2em">
SVG allows you to re-use what I call "visual components".
 In this simple Web page the rollover
</tspan>
<tspan x="200" dy="1.5em">
```

Listing 23.26 continued

```
button on the left of the screen and the
vertical bar exist in separate SVG files and are
</tspan>
<tspan x="200" dy="1.5em">
imported into this Web page using the SVG &lt;image&gt; element.
</tspan>
</text>
</svg>
```


To use the `<image>` element, we need to specify where on the screen the imported image is to be displayed, what its width and height are, and which image is to be imported.

The SVG `<image>` element has an `xlink:href` attribute, the value of which contains the URL for the SVG (or other graphics) file that is to be imported. Using the SVG `<image>` element, we can import small SVG components within a Web page or SVG image. When creating complex SVG images or pages, labor can be split between members of a team—with each responsible for creating his own part of the overall final product.

Unfortunately, at present the Adobe SVG Viewer will import static SVG graphics only. So the rollover button we imported in SimpleWebPage.svg has lost its rollover functionality. However, it is expected that full `<image>` element functionality will be added in the future, opening up the opportunity to componentize SVG images or Web pages.

Caution

When you want to include the name of an SVG element as I did in SimpleWebPage.svg, you must "*escape*" the opening and closing angled brackets of the tag. So you write `<image>` rather than `<image>`. Depending on the tag name you use, you might get an error such as "mismatched tag" because the SVG rendering engine looks for the matching `</image>` end tag.

Radial Gradients

Radial gradients, as the name implies, are used to create gradients that change along a vector which is similar to the radius of a circle. The color changes equally depending on the distance from a center point. SVG uses a `<radialGradient>` element to define a radial gradient. That radial gradient is then referenced in the fill or stroke of an SVG element within the main part of the image.

Listing 23.27 shows a straightforward radial gradient to which I have added an animation to make it visually a little more interesting. You will need to view this onscreen to get the full effect.

LISTING 23.27 A RADIAL GRADIENT WITH ONE OF THE STOP COLORS ANIMATED (RADIALGRADIENTANIM.SVG)

```
<?xml version="1.0" standalone="no"?>
<!DOCTYPE svg PUBLIC "-//W3C//DTD SVG 20010904//EN"
"http://www.w3.org/TR/2001/REC-SVG-20010904/DTD/svg10.dtd">
<svg width="400" height="250">
<defs>
<radialGradient id="MyRadialGradient" gradientUnits="userSpaceOnUse"
cx="150" cy="150" r="150" fx="100" fy="100">
<stop offset="20%" style="stop-color:#00FF00"/>
<stop offset="70%" style="stop-color:#FF0000">
<animate attributeName="offset" values="70%; 21%; 99%; 21%; 70%"
 begin="2s" dur="5s" repeatCount="indefinite"/>
</stop>
<stop offset="100%" style="stop-color:#FFFFFF"/>
</radialGradient>
</defs>
<circle style="fill:url(#MyRadialGradient); stroke:none"
cx="150" cy="150" r="200"/>
</svg>
```

The animation gives a pulsing circle of changing proportions of green, red, and white. Unfortunately, in only one chapter, it is impossible to teach you in detail all aspects of radial gradients. However, this should get you started. Try things such as changing the radius of either the r attribute of the circle or the r attribute of the radial gradient itself to gain an overview of some of the visual effects that are possible. Figure 23.17 shows the radial gradient part way through its animation.

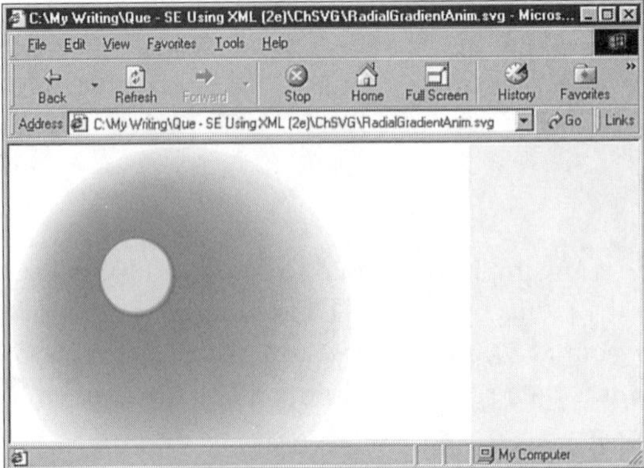

Figure 23.17
An animated radial gradient contained in a `<circle>` element part way through a pulsing animation.

DECLARATIVE SVG ANIMATIONS

You have already seen in this chapter several SVG animations. In this section, I will give you some more examples that will more fully illustrate some of the options available to you.

In SVG animations, you "*declare*" what you want to happen. You say which attribute you want to change, when you want the animation to start, how long it should take, what its starting value should be, what it's completion value should be, whether it repeats, and whether—when the animation has completed—the animated value is held or the original visual appearance is resumed.

So, suppose that we had code like the following:

```
<animate attributeName="x" begin="2s" dur="5s"
from="50" to="800" repeatCount="5" fill="freeze"/>
```

We declare that the attribute we want to animate is the x attribute. The animation should begin at 2 seconds (after the SVG loads), having a duration of 5 seconds. The x attribute starts at a value of 50 and is animated (over 5 seconds) to a value of 800. It then repeats four more times (five in all). When it finishes the animation, it holds the animated position onscreen.

Caution

Be careful to distinguish the fill attribute of elements such as the <rect> or <circle> elements from the fill attribute of an animation element. For the animation element, the fill attribute doesn't, as you might expect, define the appearance of the inside of a shape. It tells the SVG rendering engine whether or not to hold the animated shape. When you see fill="freeze", it means that the animated value is to be maintained (frozen) onscreen when the animation completes.

THE <animate> ELEMENT

The <animate> element is the general purpose animation element in SVG. With the exception of some transformation animations that can only be performed using the <animateTransform> element, the <animate> element can produce almost any SVG declarative animation. For some animations, the <animateColor> or <set> elements provide more specific or succinct syntax.

Let's look at some animations that are possible using text. It is possible to use the <animate> element to animate several values within the x attribute of a <tspan> element at one time. Listing 23.28 shows code to do this.

LISTING 23.28 ANIMATING INDEPENDENTLY MULTIPLE VALUES WITHIN AN ATTRIBUTE VALUE (TSPANANIMATION.SVG)

```
<?xml version="1.0" standalone="no"?>
<!DOCTYPE svg PUBLIC "-//W3C//DTD SVG 20010904//EN"
"http://www.w3.org/TR/2001/REC-SVG-20010904/DTD/svg10.dtd">
<svg width="600" height="350">
<text>
<tspan x="10 20 30" y="30" style="font-family:Arial, sans-serif; font-size:20;
fill:#990066; stroke:none;">
<animate attributeName="x" begin="3s" dur="5s" from="10 20 30" to="10 100 500"
fill="freeze"/>
ABC</tspan>
</text>
</svg>
```

The same technique can be extended to produce attractive character-based animations. Listing 23.29 shows such a character-based animation.

LISTING 23.29 AN ANIMATION BASED ON ANIMATING MULTIPLE VALUES WITHIN <tspan> ATTRIBUTES (TSPANANIMATION02.SVG)

```
<?xml version="1.0" standalone="no"?>
<!DOCTYPE svg PUBLIC "-//W3C//DTD SVG 20010904//EN"
"http://www.w3.org/TR/2001/REC-SVG-20010904/DTD/svg10.dtd">
<svg width="600" height="350">
<text>
<tspan x="-100 130 130 600" y="80 -40 80 80"
style="font-family:Arial, sans-serif; font-size:30; fill:#990066; stroke:none;">
<animate id="Horiz1" attributeName="x" begin="1s" dur="2s"
 from="-100 130 130 600" to="110 130 130 155" fill="freeze"/>
<animate id="Vert3" attributeName="y" begin="Vert2.end" dur="2s"
 from="80 -40 80 80" to="80 80 80 80" fill="freeze"/>
<animate id="Horiz3" attributeName="x" begin="Vert2.end" dur="2s"
 from="110 105 130 155" to="85 105 130 155" fill="freeze"/>
XMML</tspan>
<tspan x="170" y="500" style="fill:#FF6600; font-size:48;">
<animate id="Vert1" attributeName="y" begin="Horiz1.end"
 dur="2s" from="500" to="80" fill="freeze"/>
.
</tspan>
<tspan x="0 195 605" y="400 -100 80"
style="fill:#990066; stroke:none; font-size:23">
<animate id="Vert2" attributeName="y" begin="Vert1.end"
 dur="2s" from="400 -100 80" to="80 80 80" fill="freeze"/>
<animate id="Horiz2" attributeName="x" begin="Vert1.end"
 dur="2s" from="0 190 605" to="180 195 210" fill="freeze"/>
com
</tspan>
</text>
</svg>
```

Figure 23.18 shows the onscreen appearance when you run Listing 23.29.

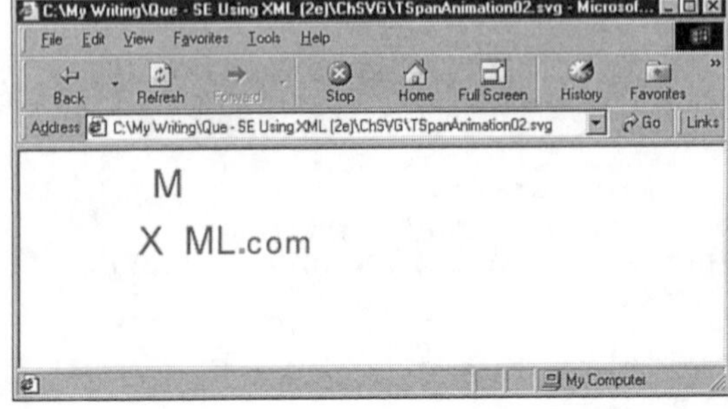

Figure 23.18
A snapshot of an animation where individual characters are progressively positioned onscreen to create a logo for a domain name.

The <animate> element can be used, for example, to change the color (fill or stroke), opacity, position, or size of a shape. In Listing 23.30, we will carry out all those types of animation one after the other. Notice that each of the <animate> elements possesses an id attribute, and the name of the id attribute is made use of within the value of the begin attribute of later <animate> elements. We will add the animations to the circle you saw earlier in Listing 23.14.

Listing 23.30 An Animation that Animates the Fill, Opacity, Position and Size of a Circle (CircleAnimations.svg)

```
<?xml version="1.0" standalone="no"?>
<!DOCTYPE svg PUBLIC "-//W3C//DTD SVG 20010904//EN"
"http://www.w3.org/TR/2001/REC-SVG-20010904/DTD/svg10.dtd">
<svg width="600" height="250">
<rect x="0" y="0" width="600" height="250" style="fill:#00FF00"/>
<circle cx="200" cy="125" r="70" style="fill:red; fill-opacity:1; stroke:blue;
stroke-width:3;">
<animate id="Anim1" attributeName="fill" begin="2s"
 dur="5s" from="red" to="white" repeatCount="2"/>
<animate id="Anim2" attributeName="opacity"
begin="Anim1.end+1s" dur="5s" from="1" to="0" repeatCount="2"/>
<animate id="Anim3" attributeName="cx" begin="Anim2.end+1s"
 dur="5s" from="200" to="600" repeatCount="2"/>
<animate id="Anim4" attributeName="r" begin="Anim3.end+1s"
 dur="5s" from="70" to="200" repeatCount="2"/>
</circle>
</svg>
```

I have set the circle against a green background, so you can see the difference between the change of fill color in the first animation and the change of opacity in the second.

The <animateColor> Element

In Listing 23.30, you saw that the <animate> element can be used to animate a change in color. However, the <animateColor> is dedicated to that purpose. Listing 23.31 shows a simple example using the <animateColor> element.

Listing 23.31 Using the <animateColor> Element to Alter the Appearance of a Rectangle (AnimateColor.svg)

```
<?xml version="1.0" standalone="no"?>
<!DOCTYPE svg PUBLIC "-//W3C//DTD SVG 20010904//EN"
"http://www.w3.org/TR/2001/REC-SVG-20010904/DTD/svg10.dtd">
<svg width="800" height="400">
<ellipse cx="200" cy="150" rx="180" ry="120"
 style="fill:white; stroke:red; stroke-width:5;">
<animateColor attributeName="fill" attributeType="CSS" begin="2s" dur="10s"
 values="white; red; blue; yellow; green; white; yellow"
 repeatCount="indefinite"/>
<animateColor attributeName="stroke" begin="2s" dur="8s"
 values="red; #FF00FF; white; red; blue; yellow; green; white; yellow"
 repeatCount="indefinite"/>
</ellipse>
</svg>
```

Caution

Be careful when creating a list of values within a `value` attribute similar to that shown in Listing 23.34. Be sure not to leave a "trailing semicolon" at the end of the list. Adobe SVG Viewer 3 interprets that as a "bad CSS descriptor" and issues an error message accordingly in the browser status bar.

THE <animateTransform> ELEMENT

SVG transformations can be pretty complex to grasp fully. In this section, I will show you simple examples of the four types of SVG transformation—translate, rotate, scale, and skew. It is possible to use transformations without the `<animateTransform>` element, but that won't be explained here. In some of the animated transformations that follow, we will create and animate a `<g>` (grouping) element.

Let's look at the *translate* transformation. Listing 23.32 shows the source code that will move the rectangle to a new position.

LISTING 23.32 A TRANSLATE ANIMATED TRANSFORMATION (TRANSFORMTRANSLATE.SVG)

```
<?xml version="1.0" standalone="no"?>
<!DOCTYPE svg PUBLIC "-//W3C//DTD SVG 20010904//EN"
"http://www.w3.org/TR/2001/REC-SVG-20010904/DTD/svg10.dtd">
<svg width="600" height="400">
<g>
<animateTransform attributeName="transform" type="translate" begin="2s" dur="5s"
values="0 0; 100 100"/>
<rect  x="150" y="150" width="150" height="75" style="stroke:#009900;
fill:#CCFFCC;">
</rect>
</g>
</svg>
```

Note that the `<animateTransform>` element has a `type` attribute, which in this case has the value of `"translate"`. Notice too the syntax of the `values` attribute—the first pair of numbers is the initial translation (in this case, 0 across and 0 down) and the second pair of coordinates is the final translation (100 to the right and 100 down). The two pairs of coordinates are separated by a semicolon.

Listing 23.33 *rotates* the rectangle clockwise around its center by 360 degrees.

LISTING 23.33 AN <animateTransform> ELEMENT ROTATES A RECTANGLE AROUND A SET OF COORDINATES (TRANSFORMROTATE.SVG)

```
<?xml version="1.0" standalone="no"?>
<!DOCTYPE svg PUBLIC "-//W3C//DTD SVG 20010904//EN"
"http://www.w3.org/TR/2001/REC-SVG-20010904/DTD/svg10.dtd">
<svg width="600" height="400">
<rect x="150" y="150" width="150" height="75"
```

Listing 23.33 continued

```
 style="stroke:#009900; fill:#CCFFCC;">
<animateTransform attributeName="transform" type="rotate"
 begin="2s" dur="5s" from="0 225 187.5" to="360 225 187.5"/>
</rect>
</svg>
```

Listing 23.34 shows the use of an <animateTransform> element to *scale* the rectangle to 1.5 times its initial size.

Listing 23.34 Scaling the Rectangle to 1.5 Times Its Original Size (TransformScale.svg)

```
<?xml version="1.0" standalone="no"?>
<!DOCTYPE svg PUBLIC "-//W3C//DTD SVG 20010904//EN"
"http://www.w3.org/TR/2001/REC-SVG-20010904/DTD/svg10.dtd">
<svg width="600" height="400">
<g >
<animateTransform attributeName="transform" type="scale" begin="2s" dur="5s"
values="1.0; 1.5"/>
<rect  x="150" y="150" width="150" height="75" style="stroke:#009900;
fill:#CCFFCC;">
</rect>
</g>
</svg>
```

When the animation starts, the rectangle moves down and to the right and also, at the same time, grows in size. When a scale transformation happens, all aspects of the rectangle change in relation to the top left corner of the initial viewport.

Finally let's look at a *skew* transformation (see Listing 23.35).

Listing 23.35 An Example of a Skew Transformation (TransformSkewX.svg)

```
<?xml version="1.0" standalone="no"?>
<!DOCTYPE svg PUBLIC "-//W3C//DTD SVG 20010904//EN"
"http://www.w3.org/TR/2001/REC-SVG-20010904/DTD/svg10.dtd">
<svg width="600" height="400">
<g >
<animateTransform attributeName="transform" type="skewX" begin="2s" dur="5s"
values="0; 30"/>
<rect  x="150" y="150" width="150" height="75" style="stroke:#009900;
fill:#CCFFCC;">
</rect>
</g>
</svg>
```

The transformation in Listing 23.35 changes the shape of the rectangle, seemingly pulling the lower edge to the right relative to the upper edge.

THE <set> ELEMENT

You saw the <set> element in the first example in this chapter. By using the <set> element, you can save writing two <animate> elements to achieve the same visual effect (see Listing 23.36).

LISTING 23.36 COMPARING THE USE OF <set> AND <animate> IN INTERACTIVE ANIMATIONS (ROLLOVERSETANIMATE.SVG)

```
<?xml version="1.0" standalone="no"?>
<!DOCTYPE svg PUBLIC "-//W3C//DTD SVG 20010904//EN"
"http://www.w3.org/TR/2001/REC-SVG-20010904/DTD/svg10.dtd">
<svg width="300" height="250">
<defs>
<linearGradient id="MyGradient" gradientUnits="objectBoundingBox"
  x1="0%" y1="0%" x2="0%" y2="100%">
<stop offset="1%" style="stop-color:#00FF00"/>
<stop offset="50%" style="stop-color:#FF9999"/>
<stop offset="100%" style="stop-color:#00FF00"/>
</linearGradient>
<linearGradient id="MySecondGradient" gradientUnits="objectBoundingBox"
  x1="0%" y1="0%" x2="0%" y2="100%">
<stop offset="1%" style="stop-color:#CCFFCC"/>
<stop offset="50%" style="stop-color:#FF0000"/>
<stop offset="100%" style="stop-color:#CCFFCC"/>
</linearGradient>
</defs>

<rect id="MyRect" x="20" y="20" rx="10" ry="10" width="130" height="45"
style="fill:url(#MyGradient); stroke:none">
<set attributeName="fill" begin="mouseover" end="mouseout"
to="url(#MySecondGradient)"/>
</rect>
<text x="30" y="47" style="fill:#000099; stroke:none; font-family:Arial,
sans-serif; font-size:16" pointer-events="none">
<set attributeName="fill" begin="MyRect.mouseover" end="MyRect.mouseout"
to="white"/>
SE Using XML</text>

<rect id="MyRect2" x="20" y="120" rx="10" ry="10" width="130" height="45"
style="fill:url(#MyGradient); stroke:none">
<animate attributeName="fill" begin="MyRect2.mouseover"
 dur="0.01s" from="url(#MyGradient)"
to="url(#MySecondGradient)" fill="freeze"/>
<animate attributeName="fill" begin="MyRect2.mouseout"
 dur="0.01s" from="url(#MySecondGradient)"
 to="url(#MyGradient)" fill="freeze"/>
</rect>
<text x="30" y="147" style="fill:#000099; stroke:none; font-family:Arial,
sans-serif; font-size:16" pointer-events="none">
<animate attributeName="fill" begin="MyRect2.mouseover"
 dur="0.01s" from="#000099"
to="white" fill="freeze"/>
<animate attributeName="fill" begin="MyRect2.mouseout" dur="0.01s" from="white"
to="#000099" fill="freeze"/>
SE Using XML</text>
</svg>
```

The top and bottom buttons show very similar visual effects. The top button uses a single `<set>` element, and the bottom uses two `<animate>` elements to produce the change in the fill. Notice that when you use `<animate>`, you need to create separate animations for the `mouseover` event and the `mouseout` event. Also, you must add a `dur` attribute and a `fill` attribute with value of `"freeze"` to maintain the animated visual state. The advantage of the `<set>` element is that only one animation element is needed. You simply define the event that causes it to start using the `begin` attribute and the event that finishes the animation using the `end` attribute.

SCRIPTING SVG

You have seen how SVG declarative animation can produce visual effects that would require JavaScript if you tried to create the effects using HTML. But JavaScript is still important for use with SVG—for example, when you want to include decision logic about when particular actions are to be carried out. In this section, you will be introduced to some basic JavaScript techniques that you can use with SVG.

THE DOCUMENT OBJECT MODEL

The W3C Document Object Model, often simply called the DOM, is a specification that describes HTML and XML documents as hierarchies of objects. The DOM is essentially an *Application Programming Interface (API)* to the elements in an HTML or XML document. JavaScript is one of the scripting languages that can work with the HTML DOM.

THE SVG DOM

SVG documents also have a document object model. The DOM for SVG images is, of course, different from the W3C DOM because many aspects of an SVG image are distinct from either an HTML Web page or a generic XML document.

ADDING ELEMENTS

Let's look at using JavaScript to add an element to an SVG image (see Listing 23.37).

LISTING 23.37 ADDING AN ELLIPSE USING JAVASCRIPT (ADDELLIPSE.SVG)

```
<?xml version="1.0" standalone="no"?>
<!DOCTYPE svg PUBLIC "-//W3C//DTD SVG 20010904//EN"
"http://www.w3.org/TR/2001/REC-SVG-20010904/DTD/svg10.dtd">
<svg width="400" height="300">
<script type="text/javascript">
<![CDATA[
var SVGDoc;
var SVGRoot;
var MyEllipse;
function CreateEllipse(evt){
SVGDoc = evt.getTarget().getOwnerDocument();
SVGRoot = SVGDoc.getDocumentElement();
```

LISTING 23.37 CONTINUED

```
MyEllipse = SVGDoc.createElement("ellipse");
MyEllipse.setAttribute("cx", 100);
MyEllipse.setAttribute("cy", 150);
MyEllipse.setAttribute("rx", 50);
MyEllipse.setAttribute("ry", 25);
MyEllipse.setAttribute("style", "fill:white; stroke:red; stroke-width:3");

SVGRoot.appendChild(MyEllipse);
}
]]>
</script>
<text id="MyText" x="50" y="50" onclick="CreateEllipse(evt)">
Click here to create an ellipse.
</text>
</svg>
```

SVG has a `<script>` element. You must add a `type` attribute, which can take values such as `"javascript"` or `"ecmascript"`. JavaScript code is not XML: Therefore, you need to hide the content of your script from the SVG rendering engine, or it will try to process the JavaScript as XML/SVG and raise an error. So the JavaScript code is nested within a `CDATA` section.

In Listing 23.37, I have declared three global variables, `SVGDoc`, `SVGRoot`, and `MyEllipse`. It isn't necessary to declare global variables in this example, but in more complex scripts it is good to have variables such as these available to all functions in the script.

Within the `CreateEllipse()` function, we assign a value to the `SVGDoc` variable using the `getOwnerDocument()` method of the object returned by `getTarget()`. This is the document we are working with. We obtain the root element of that document and store a reference to it in the `SVGRoot` variable using the `getDocumentElement()` method of the `SVGDoc` object.

We create a new SVG element by creating an element with the `createElement()` method of the `SVGDoc object`. We then proceed to set the values of individual attributes of the `<ellipse>` element that we are in the process of creating.

To complete our function, we append the `<ellipse>` element as a child to the root element pointed to by the `SVGRoot` variable, which is equivalent to nesting an `<ellipse>` element within an `<svg>` element.

Looking at the `<text>` element, you can see that the `onclick` attribute defines which function is called when the text is clicked. If you run the code, you will see only the text when the SVG loads. When you click the text, an ellipse will be added to the SVG document and displayed on screen.

REMOVING ELEMENTS

You might also want to remove elements from an SVG document using JavaScript. Listing 23.38 shows a method of doing that.

Listing 23.38 Removing an Ellipse from an SVG Document Using JavaScript (RemoveEllipse.svg)

```
<?xml version="1.0" standalone="no"?>
<!DOCTYPE svg PUBLIC "-//W3C//DTD SVG 20010904//EN"
"http://www.w3.org/TR/2001/REC-SVG-20010904/DTD/svg10.dtd">
<svg width="500" height="300">
<script type="text/javascript">
<![CDATA[
var SVGDoc;
var SVGRoot;
var MyEllipse;
function RemoveEllipse(evt){
SVGDoc = evt.getTarget().getOwnerDocument();
SVGRoot = SVGDoc.getDocumentElement();
MyEllipse = SVGDoc.getElementById("TheEllipse");
SVGRoot.removeChild(MyEllipse);
}
]]>
</script>

<ellipse id="TheEllipse" cx="150" cy="150" rx="50"
 ry="25" style="fill:#99FF99; stroke:#33FF33;"/>
<text id="MyText" x="50" y="50" onclick="RemoveEllipse(evt)">
Click here to remove an ellipse.
</text>
</svg>
```

Again, we use the `onclick` attribute of the text to call a JavaScript function. The `RemoveEllipse()` function, not surprisingly, is used to remove the ellipse from the document in response to a user-initiated event.

Again, we create `SVGDoc` and `SVGRoot` variables and assign values to them. The `MyEllipse` variable is assigned a value by using the `getElementById()` method of the document object stored in the `SVGDoc` variable. This method uses the `id` attribute on the `<ellipse>` element to get a reference to the `ellipse` object. Finally, the `removeChild()` method of the root element object is used to delete the `ellipse` element from the SVG DOM tree.

When we click on the text, the `RemoveEllipse()` function is called and the ellipse is removed from the document.

Altering Attributes

We can also use JavaScript to alter the values of attributes within an SVG document. Listing 23.39 shows how we can use text to alter the visibility of an ellipse.

Listing 23.39 Using JavaScript to Make an Ellipse Visible or Hidden (HideAndShowEllipse.svg)

```
<?xml version="1.0" standalone="no"?>
<!DOCTYPE svg PUBLIC "-//W3C//DTD SVG 20010904//EN"
"http://www.w3.org/TR/2001/REC-SVG-20010904/DTD/svg10.dtd">
```

LISTING 23.39 CONTINUED

```
<svg width="500" height="300">
<script type="text/javascript">
<![CDATA[
var SVGDoc;
var SVGRoot;
var MyEllipse;
function HideEllipse(evt){
SVGDoc = evt.getTarget().getOwnerDocument();
SVGRoot = SVGDoc.getDocumentElement();
MyEllipse=SVGRoot.getElementById("TheEllipse");
MyEllipse.setAttribute("visibility", "hidden");
} // end HideEllipse() function

function ShowEllipse(evt){
SVGDoc = evt.getTarget().getOwnerDocument();
SVGRoot = SVGDoc.getDocumentElement();
MyEllipse=SVGRoot.getElementById("TheEllipse");
if (MyEllipse.getAttribute("visibility")=="visible")
{}
else {
MyEllipse.setAttribute("visibility", "visible");
} // end ShowEllipse() function
}
]]>
</script>

<ellipse id="TheEllipse" cx="150" cy="150" rx="50" ry="25"
 style="fill:#99FF99; stroke:#33FF33;"/>
<text id="MyText" x="50" y="50" onclick="HideEllipse(evt)">
Click here to hide the ellipse.
</text>

<text id="MyText" x="50" y="250" onclick="ShowEllipse(evt)">
Click here to show the ellipse.
</text>
</svg>
```

In Listing 23.39, we have two pieces of text—one to make the ellipse hidden and another to make it visible.

The top text, "`Click here to hide the ellipse`", has an `onclick` attribute that calls the `HideEllipse()` function. Within the `HideEllipse()` function, we use `getElementById()` in the same way we did before. Then we use the `setAttribute()` method of the `ellipse` element to cause the ellipse to be hidden.

Note

Causing the ellipse to be hidden is not the same as removing the ellipse. In both cases, the ellipse is not rendered onscreen. When the ellipse is hidden, we can set its `visibility` attribute to have a value of `"visible"`–this will reveal the ellipse. When the ellipse has been removed, it has gone from the SVG DOM and we would need to create a new `<ellipse>` element to replace it.

The lower piece of text onscreen uses the `ShowEllipse()` function, which is associated with the `onclick` attribute in order to change the `visibility` attribute of the ellipse back to visible again. Note the `if` statement within the function—if the `visibility` attribute already has a value of `"visible"`, the `ShowEllipse()` function does nothing.

ZOOMING THE IMAGE USING JAVASCRIPT

Listing 23.40 shows a simple SVG image that includes JavaScript which can change the zoom factor of the SVG image in response to a click event. It works by modifying the value of the `currentScale` property of the object corresponding to the document element.

LISTING 23.40 ZOOMING OF AN SVG IMAGE UNDER JAVASCRIPT CONTROL (DYNAMICZOOMTEXT.SVG)

```
<?xml version="1.0" standalone="no"?>
<!DOCTYPE svg PUBLIC "-//W3C//DTD SVG 20010904//EN"
"http://www.w3.org/TR/2001/REC-SVG-20010904/DTD/svg10.dtd">
<svg id="SVG" width="" height="" onload="Initialize(evt)">
<script type="text/javascript">
<![CDATA[
var SVGRoot;
var MyRect;
var OriginalText;
var GrowingText;
var ShrinkingText;
var SVGDoc;
var ZoomFactor = 1.5;
var InitialStatus = true;
var Growing = true;
window.status = ZoomFactor;

function Initialize(evt){
SVGDoc = evt.getTarget().getOwnerDocument();
SVGRoot = SVGDoc.getDocumentElement();
MyRect = SVGDoc.getElementById("MyRect");
OriginalText = SVGDoc.getElementById("BaseText");
GrowingText = SVGDoc.getElementById("Grow2");
ShrinkingText = SVGDoc.getElementById("Shrink2");
SVGDoc.getElementById("SVG").addEventListener("click", ZoomOnClick, false);
InitialStatus = false;
}

function ZoomOnClick(evt){

if (SVGRoot.currentScale > 3)
{ Growing = false;
 } // end if
else if (SVGRoot.currentScale < 0.2 )
 {
 Growing = true;
 } // end else

if (Growing == true){
ZoomFactor = ZoomFactor * 1.5}
```

LISTING 23.40 CONTINUED

```
else
{ ZoomFactor = ZoomFactor * 0.5;
}

if (Growing == true && InitialStatus == false){
OriginalText.setAttribute("visibility", "hidden");
GrowingText.setAttribute("visibility", "visible");
ShrinkingText.setAttribute("visibility", "hidden");
}
else if (Growing == false){
GrowingText.setAttribute("visibility", "hidden");
ShrinkingText.setAttribute("visibility", "visible");
}

SVGRoot.setCurrentScale(ZoomFactor);
window.status = SVGRoot.currentScale;

} // End function ZoomOnClick()
]]>
</script>
<text id="BaseText" x="20" y="20"
style="font-family:Arial, sans-serif; fill:red;
stroke:none" visibility="visible">
Click this text or the rectangle and watch our size change
</text>
<text id="Grow2" x="20" y="20" style="font-family:Arial, sans-serif; fill:red;
stroke:none" visibility="hidden">
Now I am getting bigger
</text>
<text id="Shrink2" x="20" y="20" style="font-family:Arial, sans-serif; fill:red;
stroke:none" visibility="hidden">
Now I am getting smaller
</text>
<rect id="MyRect" x="75" y="75" width="300" height="50" style="fill:red;
opacity:0.4"/>
</svg>
```

In this section, you have been introduced to the basic use of JavaScript with SVG. There is so much more that can be done. It is possible to create powerful interactive SVG components with more complex logic. Although the creation of these is outside the scope of this chapter, you now understand enough to get started.

LINKING IN SVG

You have seen some use of linking in SVG already. Let's take a moment to look in a little more detail at linking in SVG.

XLINK IN SVG

Linking in SVG is founded on the XML Linking Language, XLink, to which you were introduced in Chapter 13, "Linking Information: XLink, XBase, and XInclude." In SVG, only simple XLink links are used.

THE <a> ELEMENT

The <a> element in SVG differs from the <a> element in HTML or XHTML in the detail of how links are expressed. An <a> element in SVG uses an `xlink:href` attribute to contain the value of the linked Web page or other resource.

We can add a rollover button (like the one we started the chapter with) to an <a> element by nesting the SVG button within it. If we assign the value of `"SimpleWebPage.svg"` to the `xlink:href` attribute, we can cause a click on the button to link to a new SVG Web page. Listing 23.41 shows code to do this.

LISTING 23.41 ADDING A HYPERLINK TO AN SVG BUTTON (ROLLOVERLINK.SVG)

```
<?xml version="1.0" standalone="no"?>
<!DOCTYPE svg PUBLIC "-//W3C//DTD SVG 20010904//EN"
"http://www.w3.org/TR/2001/REC-SVG-20010904/DTD/svg10.dtd">
<svg width="300" height="250">
  <defs>
    <linearGradient id="MyGradient" gradientUnits="objectBoundingBox"
         x1="0%" y1="0%" x2="0%" y2="100%">
      <stop offset="1%" style="stop-color:#00FF00"/>
      <stop offset="50%" style="stop-color:#FF9999"/>
      <stop offset="100%" style="stop-color:#00FF00"/>
    </linearGradient>
    <linearGradient id="MySecondGradient" gradientUnits="objectBoundingBox"
        x1="0%" y1="0%" x2="0%" y2="100%">
      <stop offset="1%" style="stop-color:#CCFFCC"/>
      <stop offset="50%" style="stop-color:#FF0000"/>
      <stop offset="100%" style="stop-color:#CCFFCC"/>
    </linearGradient>
  </defs>
  <a xlink:href="SimpleWebPage.svg">
    <rect id="MyRect" x="20" y="20" rx="10" ry="10" width="130" height="45"
        style="fill:url(#MyGradient); stroke:none">
      <set attributeName="fill" begin="mouseover" end="mouseout"
        to="url(#MySecondGradient)"/>
    </rect>
    <text x="30" y="47" style="fill:#000099; stroke:none; font-family:Arial,
        sans-serif; font-size:16" pointer-events="none">
         <set attributeName="fill" begin="MyRect.mouseover" end="MyRect.mouseout"
            to="white"/>SE Using XML
    </text>
  </a>
</svg>
```

Notice the <a> element, which encloses both the `<rect>` and `<text>` elements. The `xlink:href` attribute of the <a> element links to SimpleWebPage.svg.

If you run the code and click on the rollover button, you will open the SimpleWebPage.svg SVG Web page in the browser window. If you click the Back button of the browser, you will be returned to RolloverLink.svg. In other words, hyperlinks between SVG images, or Web pages, allow us to create complete Web sites using SVG alone. A demonstration all-SVG Web site is online at `http://www.svgspider.com/default.svg`.

XPOINTER IN SVG

The XML Pointer Language, XPointer, is used in a simple way in SVG. Earlier, you saw the syntax `fill:url(#MyGradient)`. The part of the syntax enclosed in parentheses is a "bare names" XPointer that is one technique for linking to a fragment of an XML, or in this case SVG, document. This syntax makes use of the `id` attribute on the SVG element being linked to. If you review the code shown earlier, you will see that the linear gradient has an `id` attribute with a value of `"MyGradient"`.

ADDITIONAL RESOURCES

A number of additional resources are available on the Web for learning about SVG. Here are a few of the best ones to consult:

- SVG 1.0 Recommendation (`http://www.w3.org/TR/SVG`)—The SVG 1.0 Recommendation from the W3C is the final word on SVG.
- SVG 1.1 and Mobile SVG specifications (`http://www.w3.org/Graphics/SVG/`)—An updated SVG specification and profiles for mobile devices are under development at the W3C. This Web site has more information.
- SVG-Developers mailing list (`http://www.yahoogroups.com/group/SVG-Developers`)—The SVG-Developers mailing list on YahooGroups.com is the most active discussion forum for users of SVG.

ROADMAP

From here, we will progress to take a look at the Synchronized Multimedia Integration Language, SMIL, which allows us to control the presentation of multimedia using an XML-based vocabulary.

CHAPTER 24

XML and Multimedia: SMIL—The Synchronized Multimedia Integration Language

In this chapter

by *Andrew Watt*

The *Synchronized Multimedia Integration Language (SMIL)* is the XML-based application language that allows the assembly and integration of multimedia components.

This chapter focuses primarily on SMIL version 2.0, which became a W3C Recommendation in August 2001. The full text of the recommendation can be accessed at `http://www.w3.org/TR/2001/REC-smil20-20010807/`. SMIL 2.0 built on the foundations laid in the SMIL version 1 Recommendation of 1998 (see `http://www.w3.org/TR/1998/REC-smil-19980615`).

The fundamental abilities required of a language to integrate and control multimedia presentations are

- Timing relationships of different parts of the presentation
- Placing multimedia components onscreen
- Providing user interactivity to allow linking between components of the presentation

SMIL provides each of these three foundational capabilities. As well as being able to integrate multimedia components of various technologies, SMIL is designed to be integrated with other XML languages. To facilitate that integration with other XML application languages, SMIL 2.0 is defined in terms of *modules*. A SMIL module aggregates related parts of SMIL functionality. SMIL modules can be grouped together and, optionally, combined with modules from other XML languages to form SMIL *profiles*. SMIL profiles allow the SMIL functionality available on a particular platform, among the growing numbers of user agents, to be tailored to the capabilities that are available on the platform.

SMIL 2.0 includes 45 modules, some of which are dependent on other modules. We will look briefly at many of these modules later in the chapter. A detailed description of the dependencies between modules is found in the SMIL 2.0 Recommendation. Of course, the SMIL modules are in the same namespace. A profile can be created by combining modules from the SMIL namespace or combining a subset of the available modules with elements from another namespace. When the modules are all from one namespace, that is the SMIL 2.0 namespace, the Structure Module must be included because it contains the document element, the `smil` element, for all SMIL documents.

SMIL is, of course, an XML application language. It therefore conforms to the requirements of the *Document Object Model (DOM)* Levels 1 and 2 Core specification. At some future date, a SMIL-specific DOM specification is likely. However, for the present the programmer can treat nodes representing SMIL elements in the generic way provided by the DOM specifications.

A First SMIL Document

In this section, you will see a short SMIL document to introduce you to the type of code you need to create to produce a basic SMIL document. Let's look at a suitable SMIL viewer, which is available as a free download.

Note

In the examples in this chapter, all the multimedia files used will be SVG images because they can be created as short, self-contained files that are useful to illustrate principles of how to use SMIL. Of course, many other multimedia objects–such as video, audio, or images can also be used.

The X-Smiles Browser

Throughout this chapter, we will use the X-Smiles XML browser to contain the SMIL documents that we create. The X-Smiles browser can be downloaded free from `http://www.x-smiles.org/`.

Caution

If you try to access the X-Smiles.org Web site from a corporate location, you might find that access is blocked. There is an unrelated adult site, with a URL that is similar, that might be blocked by the administrator at your organization. You might need to explain that x-smiles.org is a legitimate XML browser developer site.

X-Smiles is, at the time of writing, only at version 0.5 and therefore is very much a tool in the process of development. However, it is already capable of displaying several XML presentation technologies, including SMIL. Because the X-Smiles browser is under ongoing development, it is likely that its capabilities or speed will have improved by the time you read this. Version 0.5 can be slow.

In addition to the X-Smiles browser executable that can be downloaded, there is also an extensive set of demo code, including SMIL code listings. If you have a dial-up connection to the Internet, you will find it more practical to download the zip files of demo code and run code from your own hard drive—some of the SMIL files and their associated images are very slow to download interactively on a dial-up connection.

A Brief SMIL Listing

Listing 24.1 is a brief SMIL listing that will create a pale green background. Displayed against that background is a simple *Scalable Vector Graphics (SVG)* file—a red triangle on a white background—and a short text message.

Listing 24.1 A Short SMIL Document That Displays an SVG Image and a Short Text Message (FirstSMIL.smil)

```
<smil>
 <head>
  <meta name="title" content="*** A First SMIL Document ***"/>
   <layout>
    <root-layout title="First SMIL Demo" id="SMIL Demo"
width="800" height="600" background-color="#CCFFCC"/>
     <region title="image1" height="100" id="image1"
```

LISTING 24.1 CONTINUED

```
top="50" z-index="1" width="100" left="25%"/>
    <region title="image2" height="100" id="image2"
top="176" z-index="1" width="160" left="25%"/>
  </layout>
</head>
<body>
 <par id="MyLayout">
  <a href="http://www.xmml.com/default.svg">
   <img region="image1" id="triangle" src="triangle.svg"
type="image/svg+xml" dur="indefinite" z-index="1"/>
  </a>
  <text id="content_1_1" type="text/plain" region="image2"
src="data:,If the X-Smiles browser was working faster you
would see a triangle straight away. Be patient it will arrive
in time." dur="indefinite"/>
 </par>
</body>
</smil>
```

Note

Be sure to read `http://www.x-smiles.org/xsmiles_faq.html` if you are having problems running the X-Smiles browser. For example, some users using J2SE 1.4 have problems running X-Smiles 0.5.

All SMIL documents have a `smil` element as the document element. The `smil` element must be written in all lowercase characters because SMIL, like other XML languages, is case sensitive. Within the `smil` element, the `head` element contains meta information—such as the document title and authorship, together with layout information—and a `body` element that contains timing elements such as the `par` element, which you can see in the example listing.

Figure 24.1 shows the visual appearance produced in version 0.5 of the X-Smiles browser.

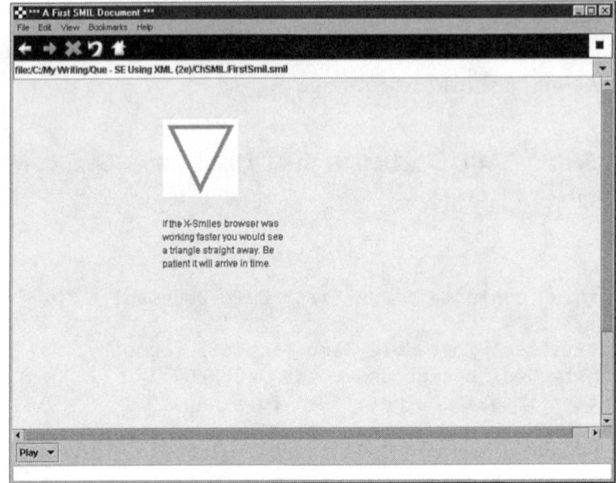

Figure 24.1
The positioning of the triangle and the text shown in the X-Smiles browser correspond to the `layout` elements in the head of the SMIL code.

If you look at the figure and the content of the `layout` element, you should be able to work out the basics of what is being rendered on screen.

```
<layout>
 <root-layout title="First SMIL Demo" id="SMIL Demo"
width="800" height="600" background-color="#CCFFCC"/>
  <region title="image1" height="100" id="image1"
top="50" z-index="1" width="100" left="25%"/>
  <region title="image2" height="100" id="image2"
top="176" z-index="1" width="160" left="25%"/>
</layout>
```

The `layout` element is a child of the `head` element. It has, as a nested element, a `root-layout` element that defines the dimensions of the screen area on which the SMIL presentation is to be presented. Within that overall area, further areas for specific uses are defined within `region` elements.

Multimedia and XML

An XML application language might not seem, at first sight, to be an appropriate choice to support multimedia because many formats, such as video and audio files, are binary in nature. However, SMIL does not attempt to create or define the underlying binary files. It simply aims to provide a way to say which parts of a multimedia presentation are to be presented—depending on a variety of circumstances—and to define the timing and screen placement of those media components.

SMIL and Internationalization

One of the benefits of XML is the way in which it supports internationalization of data contained in XML documents or documents created in XML application languages.

SMIL is no exception. One useful localization technique using SMIL is the use of SMIL's `switch` element. If, for example, visitors to your SMIL Web site were German or Spanish speaking, you could use the `switch` element to provide content appropriate to users with those language preferences.

SMIL Modules

After reading earlier chapters, you are now familiar with the modularization of XHTML and the benefits that modularization is anticipated to bring as the nature of the Web changes. SMIL 1.0, like XHTML 1.0, was created as a single, monolithic language. SMIL 2.0 has been defined in terms of modules. By modularizing SMIL, it enables user agents, browsers, or multimedia players to implement parts of the SMIL recommendation that are relevant to a particular use.

The description of SMIL that follows is based on these modules. Modules are not to be divided—either all the function in a module should be implemented or none of it.

THE STRUCTURE MODULE

The SMIL Structure module defines the basic structure of a SMIL 2.0 document. It is a mandatory module in all SMIL profiles.

As you saw in Listing 24.1, each SMIL document, or document fragment, is nested within a `smil` element. A `smil` element has a number of permitted attributes. The `id` attribute provides a way to uniquely identify the `smil` element. The `class` attribute is new in SMIL 2.0 and allows one or more class names to be assigned to the `smil` element. The `xml:lang` attribute defines the language of the content of the `smil` element. The `title` attribute provides a description of the element and might, optionally, be used by a user agent (such as the X-Smiles browser) to display the value of the `title` attribute. As in other XML elements, there is also an `xmlns` attribute.

Caution

Be careful to distinguish the `xml:lang` attribute used in the `smil` and other elements from the system language. The latter provides a description of a current system setting. The `xml:lang` attribute defines the language used to express the content of one or more elements.

The `smil` element is permitted to have only two elements as its child elements—the `head` element and the `body` element.

THE head ELEMENT

The `head` element has content that is not related to the timing of a SMIL presentation. Thus, it might contain layout information, as you saw in Listing 24.1, meta information (typically contained in a `meta` element), or author-defined content control. For further information on content control in SMIL, see the "Content Control Modules" section later in this chapter.

The `head` element can possess `id`, `title`, `class`, and `xml:lang` attributes but not an `xmlns` attribute. The definitions for the four permitted attributes are the same as for the `smil` element.

THE body ELEMENT

The `body` element can possess `id`, `title`, `class`, and `xml:lang` attributes but not an `xmlns` attribute. The definitions for the four permitted attributes are the same as for the `smil` element.

The `body` element contains elements that define the media objects to be used in a presentation and the timing of their use.

TIMING AND SYNCHRONIZATION

Accurate and predictable timing and synchronization are critically important to a multimedia integration technology. Any presentation in which the synchronization of a video clip and its accompanying speech or on-screen text were out of synchronization would appear very amateurish at best. In order to succeed in synchronizing different parts of a multimedia presentation, it is necessary to have an accurate timing mechanism so that related parts of a presentation can be timed to start together or at various times to produce a synchronized presentation.

Essentially two (or more) multimedia objects can be played at the same time (in parallel), or they can be played one after the other (in sequence). In SMIL, parallel play of multimedia objects is supported by the `par` element, and a sequence of multimedia objects is supported by the `seq` element. Of course, in all but the simplest multimedia presentations, we will need to use both `par` and `seq` elements in potentially complex, deeply nested combinations.

THE par ELEMENT

The `par` element allows us to display multimedia objects in parallel. For example, we might want to display a graphic and its descriptive text at the same time and typically on different parts of the screen. Listing 24.2 shows an example which uses the `par` element.

LISTING 24.2 A DEMO OF USING THE SMIL par ELEMENT (PARALLELDEMO.SMIL)

```
<smil>
 <head>
  <meta name="title" content="*** Displaying objects in parallel ***"/>
   <layout>
    <root-layout title="Parallel Objects Demo" id="Parallel Demo" width="400"
height="400" background-color="#CCFFCC"/>
     <region title="image" height="100" id="image"
 top="50" z-index="1" width="100" left="25%"/>
     <region title="caption" height="100" id="caption"
 top="176" z-index="1" width="160" left="25%"/>
   </layout>
 </head>
 <body>
  <par id="MySimpleSlideshow">
   <a href="http://www.xmml.com/default.svg">
    <img region="image" id="circle" src="circle.svg"
 type="image/svg+xml" dur="indefinite" z-index="1"/>
   </a>
   <text id="content_1_l" type="text/plain"
 region="caption" src="ParallelDemo.txt"/>
  </par>
 </body>
</smil>
```

Listing 24.2 refers to two files—ParallelDemo.txt and Circle.svg. They are shown in Listings 24.3 and 24.4.

LISTING 24.3 THE TEXT REFERENCED BY PARALLELDEMO.SMIL (PARALLELDEMO.TXT)

```
The shape shown is a circle.
```

LISTING 24.4 THE SVG SHAPE REFERENCED BY PARALLELDEMO.SMIL (CIRCLE.SVG)

```
<?xml version="1.0" standalone="no"?>
<!DOCTYPE svg PUBLIC "-//W3C//DTD SVG 20010904//EN"
"http://www.w3.org/TR/2001/REC-SVG-20010904/DTD/svg10.dtd">
<svg width="100" height="100">
<circle cx="50" cy="50" r="35" style="stroke:red; stroke-width:5; fill:none"/>
</svg>
```

As you can see, when we create multimedia presentations—even very simple ones like showing a shape and a separate caption—we often start dealing with multiple files. It is important that you have an understandable system for storing files you use in multimedia presentations. The exact structure you choose isn't too important. But it is vital that you are consistent. Also, all developers involved in creating a multimedia application should understand the directory structure so that the paths to files presented, for example, in the `src` attribute of the `text` element are correct.

THE `seq` ELEMENT

The `seq` element allows you to present multimedia objects one after the other: that is, in a sequence.

We can, for example, use the `seq` element to display a sequence of SVG shapes, each accompanied by its own caption. Because you saw in the preceding section that we keep a shape and its associated text synchronized using the `par` element, we will need to nest a `par` element for each shape and text within the `seq` element. Listing 24.5 shows how we can create a simple slide presentation of shapes and associated captions.

LISTING 24.5 USING THE SMIL `seq` ELEMENT TO CREATE A SIMPLE SLIDE SHOW (SLIDESHOW.SMIL)

```
<smil>
 <head>
  <meta name="title" content="*** Displaying objects in sequence ***"/>
   <layout>
    <root-layout title="Sequence Objects Demo" id="Sequence Demo" width="400"
height="400" background-color="#CCCCFF"/>
     <region title="image" height="100" id="image" top="50" z-index="1"
width="100" left="25%"/>
     <region title="caption" height="100" id="caption" top="176" z-index="1"
width="160" left="25%"/>
   </layout>
 </head>
 <body>
  <seq id="MySlideshow">
   <par dur="15s">
    <a href="http://www.xmml.com/default.svg">
```

LISTING 24.5 CONTINUED

```
    <img region="image" id="circle" src="circle.svg"
type="image/svg+xml" dur="10s" z-index="1"/>
   </a>
   <text id="content_1_l" type="text/plain"
region="caption" src="ParallelDemo.txt"/>
  </par>
  <par>
   <a href="http://www.edititwrite.com/default.svg">
    <img region="image" id="circle" src="triangle.svg"
type="image/svg+xml" dur="indefinite" z-index="1"/>
   </a>
   <text id="content_1_l" type="text/plain"
region="caption" src="ParallelDemo2.txt"/>
  </par>
 </seq>
</body>
</smil>
```


Notice that nested within the `body` element is a `seq` element. The `seq` element defines the sequence of the presentation. In this example, we display a simple sequence of two shapes: each with its caption. To coordinate the presentation of the shape and its caption, we use `par` elements as before. For brevity we will reuse the circle.svg and triangle.svg files you saw previously and will add a second external text file, ParallelDemo2.txt, shown in Listing 24.6.

LISTING 24.6 THE TEXT FILE CONTAINING THE CAPTION FOR THE SECOND "SLIDE" IN THE SLIDE SHOW

```
And this is a triangle.
```

Figure 24.2 shows the final appearance after running Listing 24.2. As mentioned earlier with version 0.5 of X-Smiles, there is a substantial delay in rendering the SVG files.

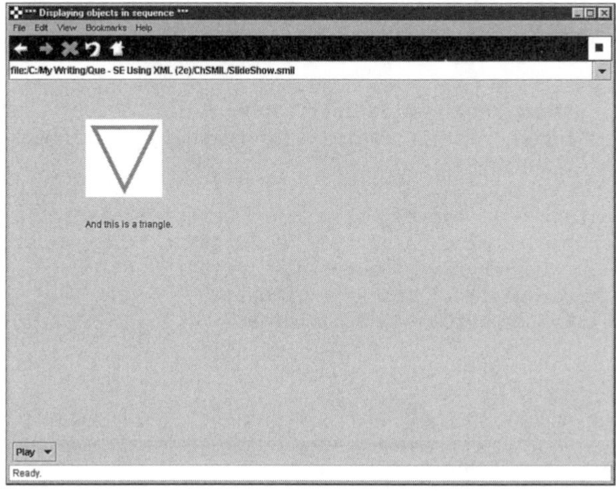

Figure 24.2
The final appearance of the slide show with the shape in triangle.svg and text in ParallelDemo2.txt displayed.

The SMIL 2.0 Timing modules go far beyond the relatively simple functionality described for the `par` and `seq` elements. Further information is to be found in the SMIL 2.0 Recommendation.

THE ANIMATION MODULES

SMIL 2.0 supports animation functionality and splits the animation modules into a `BasicAnimation` module and a `SplineAnimation` module. The two modules contain elements and attributes that define how an animation is to be incorporated on a timeline. As you can probably anticipate, the animation modules are included only in language profiles that require animation functionality.

Animation depends on the `BasicInlineTiming` module, which is one of the `Timing` modules.

THE `BasicAnimation` MODULE

Listing 24.7 shows a simple animation using a SMIL 2.0 animation element within a referenced SVG image.

LISTING 24.7 INCORPORATING AN SVG IMAGE THAT USES A SMIL ANIMATION ELEMENT (ANIMTEST.SMIL)

```
<smil>
 <head>
  <meta name="title" content="*** A First SMIL Document with Animation ***"/>
   <layout>
    <root-layout title="First SMIL Animation Demo"
 id="SMIL Animation Demo" width="800"
height="600" background-color="#FFCCCC"/>
     <region title="image1" height="100" id="image1" top="50" z-index="1"
width="200" left="25%"/>
     <region title="image2" height="100" id="image2" top="176" z-index="1"
width="160" left="25%"/>
   </layout>
 </head>
 <body>
  <par id="MyLayout">
   <a href="http://www.xmml.com/default.svg">
    <img region="image1" id="triangle" src="triangle2.svg" type="image/svg+xml"
dur="indefinite" z-index="1"/>
   </a>
   <text id="content_1_1" type="text/plain" region="image2" src="data:,If the
X-Smiles browser was working faster you would see a triangle straight away. Be
patient it will arrive in time." dur="indefinite">
 <animate attributeName="top" from="176" to="190"
 begin="0s" dur="3s" repeatCount="indefinite"/>
 </text>
  </par>
 </body>
</smil>
```

Listing 24.7 references an SVG file, Triangle2.svg, which incorporates an `animate` element that belongs to SMIL 2.0. Listing 24.8 shows the SVG file with the animated triangle.

LISTING 24.8 AN SVG FILE USING A SMIL 2.0 `animate` ELEMENT TO MOVE A TRIANGLE (TRIANGLE2.SVG)

```
<?xml version="1.0" standalone="no"?>
<!DOCTYPE svg PUBLIC "-//W3C//DTD SVG 20010904//EN"
"http://www.w3.org/TR/2001/REC-SVG-20010904/DTD/svg10.dtd">
<svg width="200" height="100">
<svg x="0" y="0">
<animate attributeName="x" from="0" to="50"
 begin="0s" dur="5s" repeatCount="indefinite"/>
<polygon points="10,10 90,10 50,90" style="stroke:red; stroke-width:5;
fill:none"/>
</svg>
</svg>
```


If you run the SVG file with the Adobe SVG Viewer discussed in Chapter 25, "Using XML to Create Forms: XForms," you will see that the triangle is animated toward the right of the screen. Unfortunately, at the time of writing, although X-Smiles will correctly load the animated SVG image, the X-Smiles SVG functionality does not yet implement the animation.

The `animate` element in Listing 24.8 is one of the SMIL animation elements in the `BasicAnimation` module. The other elements in the module are `set`, `animateColor`, and `animateMotion`. The `set` element provides functionality to change the value of a specified attribute stepwise to a specified value. The `animateColor` element specifies color changes with time. The `animateMotion` element defines motion on a path.

As shown in Listing 24.8, an `animate` element, or other animation elements, can be nested within the element targeted for animation. In our example, the `svg` element is animated because the `animate` element is nested within the `svg` element. However, animation elements need not be nested within their target elements. If the target element possesses an `id` attribute and the animation element possesses a matching `targetElement` attribute, the animation element can be written in any suitable part of the code. Some SVG developers group all the animation elements in one part of the SVG code so that they are easily found. An alternative approach is to use the `href` attribute of an animation element to reference the element to be animated.

The target element can have several attributes capable of being animated. The attribute that is to be animated is specified in the `attributeName` attribute of the SMIL animation element. For example, if we want to animate the `width` attribute of an SVG `rect` element, we specify `attributeName="width"` on the appropriate animation element.

Similarly, we define when an animation is to begin by using a `begin` attribute with values typically expressed in seconds. Thus, to start an animation five seconds after a document loads, we would include `begin="5s"`. For many animations, it is meaningful to express how long it lasts (its duration). We specify this using a `dur` attribute. If we wanted an animation to last eight seconds, we would write `dur="8s"`.

We might want an animation to repeat more than once, and we can use a `repeatCount` attribute to control that. To create an endlessly repeating animation, we could use `repeatCount="indefinite"`. To create an animation that repeats exactly five times, we would use `repeatCount="5"`.

At the completion of an animation, we might want to maintain the animated value or return to the original value. To return to the original value again, we don't need to do anything because the default is to restore the original value. To maintain the animated value, we add the code `fill="freeze"` to the animation element.

The way SMIL specifies that an animation is "frozen" at the end value is potentially confusing. In SVG, for example, it is possible to animate the value of the `fill` attribute of a shape (such as a `rect` element) and also specify that the animated value is to be preserved by using a different `fill` attribute on an animation element. Although the attributes belong to different elements, this can still throw developers off.

The SMIL animation elements provide syntax to create sophisticated animations. Details of the syntax are beyond the scope of this chapter.

Note

Host languages are free to add further animation elements to fulfill any particular purpose. *Scalable Vector Graphics (SVG)* adds an `animateTransform` element to allow animation of transformations in SVG graphic images.

The `SplineAnimation` Module

The `SplineAnimation` module adds attributes to those defined in the `BasicAnimation` module to allow the creation of animations that do not occur linearly in time. The `SplineAnimation` module attributes can be applied to the `animate`, `animateColor`, and `animateMotion` elements only.

The `calcMode` attribute of an animation element is permitted to have an addition value, `spline`. Further relevant values would typically be defined in `keyTimes` and `keySplines` attributes on the animation element.

The `SplineAnimation` module can only be used in a host language that also implements the `BasicAnimation` module. See the SMIL 2.0 specification for further information.

Content Control Modules

Four content control modules allow runtime content choices or the optimization of content delivery. They are `BasicContentControl`, `CustomTestAttributes`, `PrefetchControl`, and `SkipContentControl`. If the `CustomTestAttributes` module is to be used in a profile, the `BasicContentControl` module must also be implemented. The `PrefetchControl` and `SkipContentControl` modules have no prerequisites.

THE `BasicContentControl` MODULE

SMIL 2.0 has several *system test attributes*, some of which are new to SMIL 2.0. These attributes contain information about the host system such as the system language or system screen size. Having such properties available means that a SMIL author can provide alternative presentations of media, depending on the capabilities of the user's system.

The `switch` element allows choices to be made between content options. You might want to present a commentary in a user's language (as determined by the system language) or provide default commentary in English. The `switch` element can be used to do this in the following way.

```
<switch>
<audio src="Bonjour.aiff" systemLanguage="fr" .../>
<audio src="GutenTag.aiff" systemLanguage="de" .../>
<audio src="Hello.aiff" .../>
</switch>
```


A diagram that is to be included in a presentation might have three optional audio tracks to accompany it, depending on the capabilities of the user's Internet connection.

```
<par>
 <img src="TechDiagram.svg" ... />
 <switch>
  <audio src="HighQualDesc.aiff" systemBitrate="56000" ... />
  <audio src="MedQualDesc.aiff" systemBitrate="28800" ... />
  <audio src="LowQualDesc.aiff" ... />
 </switch>
</par>
```

The `par` element indicates that the displaying of the SVG image and the playing of the sound file, contained in the `switch` element, take place in parallel. Depending on the value of the `systemBitrate` attribute of the `audio` element, the `switch` element allows a SMIL player to present a file that is compatible with the user agent's capabilities. The final of the three audio elements shown is presented if the system bit rate is less than 28,800.

The `switch` element has several possible attributes, a number of which are described later, that allow a large number of options to be offered if the SMIL author desires. The `systemAudioDesc` attribute specifies whether audio descriptions are to be rendered. The `systemBitrate` attribute evaluates to true if the user's system bitrate is equal to or greater than the value of the `systemBitrate` attribute. The `systemCaptions` attribute allows an author to determine if a text equivalent of audio is to be displayed. This might be used when a text equivalent is to be made available to deaf users. The `systemCPU` attribute allows a test of the user's system CPU, but must support an option of `unknown` if the user has chosen to conceal the CPU nature. The `systemLanguage` attribute allows appropriate language content to be displayed. The `systemOperatingSystem` attribute allows customized content for a particular operating system to be rendered. Again, the user might choose to conceal this, and a value of `unknown` must be supported. The `systemScreenDepth` attribute evaluates to true if the system is capable of supporting content of a specified color depth. The `systemScreenSize` attribute evaluates to true if the system is capable of displaying visual content of specified dimensions.

THE `CustomTestAttributes` MODULE

The `CustomTestAttributes` module allows author-defined test attributes to be added to those defined in the `BasicContentControl` module. Custom test attributes allow the author of a SMIL presentation to define additional test attributes for use in a particular presentation.

Custom tests are created within the head element of a SMIL document. A `CustomAttributes` element has nested within it one or more `CustomTest` elements, each of which defines the nature of the custom test.

THE `PrefetchControl` MODULE

From the viewpoint of the viewer or listener to a multimedia presentation, it is desirable to avoid or minimize delays between parts of a presentation being made available to watch. The SMIL `PrefetchControl` module provides functionality to control how and when parts of a SMIL presentation are downloaded from the server.

Let's suppose that we used SMIL to control a number of SVG documents as part of a presentation. We might first want to present some introductory text, which we could expect the user to take perhaps 15 seconds to read through. Therefore, while she was reading that, this would be a good time to download some SVG animation that would illustrate a later part of the presentation. The following code shows how that could be done:

```
<smil xmlns="http://www.w3.org/2001/SMIL20">
 <head>
  <!-- Head content goes here. -->
 </head>
 <body>
  <seq>
   <par>
     <prefetch id="SVGAnimation" src="http://www.XMML.com/AnimSVG.svg"/>
     <img id="SVGIntroduction"
src="http://www.XMML.com/Introduction.svg" fill="freeze"/>
   </par>
   <img src="http://www.XMML.com/Introduction.svg" dur="15s"/>
   <img id="mainAnimation" src="http://www.XMML.com/AnimSVG.svg"/>
  </seq>
 </body>
</smil>
```

Notice the content of the `par` element. While the `img` element for the SVG Introduction is loading, the `prefetch` element is also operating in parallel. A `prefetch` element is likely only to be used in this way when the object takes substantially longer to download than the element being presented in parallel. In this example, the `prefetch` continues its work during the 15 seconds that the SVG Introduction is being displayed.

Caution

When using `prefetch`, you must be careful to avoid inconsistencies in the data prefetched. If, for example, you have dynamically created data that is prefetched, it is possible that, where that data is rapidly changing, the prefetched data might no longer reflect the live values of the data. If the user requires up-to-date data, the prefetched data might be misleading.

The `prefetch` element can optionally take three attributes. The `mediaSize` attribute defines the percentage of the file size of the multimedia object that is to be prefetched. The default is 100%. The `mediaTime` attribute defines the percentage of the duration of the object that is to be prefetched. Again the default is 100%. If both a `mediaSize` and a `mediaTime` attribute are defined, the `mediaSize` attribute is used and the `mediaTime` attribute is ignored. The `bandwidth` attribute defines how much of the available bandwidth can be used for prefetch. The value of the `bandwidth` attribute can be expressed as a bitrate or a percentage. The default is 100%.

Note

SMIL players are not required to support prefetch. Therefore, when you design a presentation, you should give some thought to how the presentation will appear in a SMIL player without prefetch support.

THE `SkipContentControl` MODULE

The `SkipContentControl` module has no element definitions. In SMIL 2.0, it contains a single attribute, `skip-content`, which determines whether the element on which the `skip-content` attribute is placed is evaluated or not. The `skip-content` attribute can take the values of `true` or `false`.

The `skip-content` attribute is intended to allow future extensibility of SMIL. For example, if the permitted content of a SMIL element changes, the `skip-content` attribute could be used to determine how that changed content is processed.

THE LAYOUT MODULES

SMIL 2.0 provides four layout modules—a `BasicLayout` module, an `AudioLayout` module, a `MultiWindowLayout` module, and a `HierarchicalLayout` module. The latter three modules build on the functionality of the `BasicLayout` module. The modules are used to control positioning of visual output onscreen and to control the volume of audio output. If a host language has sufficient layout control, it need not implement any of the SMIL layout modules.

THE `BasicLayout` MODULE

The `BasicLayout` module uses the `layout` element contained within the `head` element of a SMIL document. The `BasicLayout` module uses a visual rendering model consistent with that in version 2 of the *Cascading Style Sheets (CSS2)* specification.

A layout element can have a type attribute that specifies the layout language used in the layout. If a user agent does not understand that language, it should skip the layout element and all its content. If the type attribute has the value "text/smil-basic-layout", the layout element can contain region and root-layout elements.

Within the layout element, a number of region elements can be used to divide screen real estate into regions. Media elements contained within the body element of a SMIL document use a region attribute to reference a region element in the head of the document. Thus, for example, a video object could be defined as being in a particular region when its region attribute matches the id attribute of a region element in the document head.

```
<smil>
<head>
<layout>
...
<region id="Main" top="50" left="50" width="500" height="400" ... />
</layout>
</head>
<body>
...
<video region="Main" .... />
</body>
</smil>
```

It is possible to define multiple possible layouts for a document and to define which layout is used by means of the switch element described in the "Content Control Modules" section of this chapter.

When both a root-layout element and one or more region elements are present as children of a layout element, the positions onscreen, defined by the top and left attributes of a region element, are specified relative to the dimensions of the root-layout element. The width and height attributes of a region element can be expressed as percentage values: In which case, the percentages are relative to the dimensions of the sibling root-layout element.

A root-layout element can have backgroundColor, height, and width attributes.

A region element can have backgroundColor, bottom, fit, height, left, regionName, right, showBackground, top, width, and z-index attributes.

Note

The background-color attribute that was permitted on region and root-layout elements in SMIL 1.0 is now deprecated on both elements.

The effect of user-initiated events, such as a mouse click, might depend on the z-index of the object and whether it is transparent. A z-index is an indication of whether an object is toward the front or the back of a stack of objects on screen. Non-transparent objects capture events, whereas transparent objects allow events to percolate through to objects behind it in the stacking order.

THE AudioLayout MODULE

The AudioLayout module requires that the BasicLayout module also be implemented. The AudioLayout module provides a way to control audio volume in presentations.

A soundLevel attribute can be added to a region element to define the sound volume that applies to content related to that region.

THE MultiWindowLayout MODULE

The MultiWindowLayout module provides elements and attributes to define how multi-window SMIL presentations are to be presented. The BasicLayout module is a required prerequisite.

In SMIL 1.0 and in the SMIL 2.0 BasicLayout module, a multimedia presentation is presented in a single window. The MultiWindowLayout module modifies the permitted content of the layout element of a SMIL document to allow more than one window to be used. For example, if we wanted to make use of two windows side by side, each 800 pixels high and 400 pixels wide, we could use code like this:

```
<layout>
 <topLayout id="LeftWindow" title="Diagrams" width="400" height="800"/>
  <region id="diagrams" title="Diagrams" height="100%" fit="meet"/>
 </topLayout>
 <topLayout id="RightWindow" title="Descriptive Text" width="400" height="800">
  <region id="captions" title="explanatory text"
 width="100%" height="100%" fit="meet"/>
 </topLayout>
</layout>
```

As you can see from the example code, each topLayout element might have nested within it one or more region elements. By adding multiple region elements to each topLayout element, you can create multi-window presentations of arbitrary complexity.

A topLayout element can have backgroundColor, close, height, open, and width attributes. The MultiWindowLayout module also adds two new events—the topLayoutOpenEvent and the topLayoutCloseEvent.

THE HierarchicalLayout MODULE

The HierarchicalLayout module adds functionality to allow precise author control of onscreen layout.

The definition of the content of the region element is extended. A regPoint element is also added, which defines a *registration point*. Positioning of media objects that reference the region which contains the registration point can be positioned relative to the registration point. Media objects can have a regPoint attribute and regAlign attribute that define how they are to be positioned relative to a registration point. Additional attributes, top, bottom, left, and right, permit precise positioning within a sub-region.

THE LINKING MODULES

Web-related technologies now have almost an excess of linking technologies, including those in HTML and XHTML and the newer XLink and XPointer. So how does SMIL linking relate to these technologies?

Linking into a particular fragment of a SMIL document might be useful to allow access to a presentation from a particular time within the presentation. XPointer allows addressing of parts of an XML document without the need explicitly to add unique identifiers such as `id` attributes or named anchors. SMIL 2.0 allows support for XPointer, but does not require support for it. Additionally, linking to a named anchor can be expressed in SMIL documents but does require write access to the SMIL document in order to create an anchor at the desired point in the code.

In principle, with sufficient understanding of the document structure, an XPointer link can link to a fragment of the targeted SMIL code without the need for write access to that code. Linking in this way should correspond to the behavior of a video when the user has fast forwarded to a desired part of the presentation. For a variety of reasons, a link to a fragment might fail. In that case, a SMIL player should start the presentation from the beginning.

Caution

At the time of writing, a lively debate is ongoing about what should or should not be included in version 1.0 of the XPointer specification. XPointer is currently at Candidate Recommendation stage, but might yet change significantly in its scope.

SMIL linking constructs have attribute names and values corresponding to those of XLink constructs. However, the SMIL syntax is in the SMIL 2.0 namespace, not in the XLink namespace. A similar situation arises with respect to XHTML linking elements in which SMIL 2.0 again has element and attribute names the same as XHTML constructs, where possible. The namespaces of the XHTML elements and attributes and the SMIL 2.0 elements and attributes are, of course, different. The similarities with XLink and XHTML seem well intentioned but are potentially confusing. A document author might need to be aware of which namespace a particular element or attribute is in, in order to ensure the desired behavior.

The existence of SMIL profiles means that SMIL documents might be embedded in documents of other namespaces, and that such documents might, on the contrary, be embedded in SMIL documents. This raises issues about linking behavior. Where a SMIL document is embedded in another document, the effect of the link in a SMIL 2.0 document is limited to that part of the containing document taken up by the SMIL document. Similarly, where a document is embedded in a SMIL 2.0 document, the effect of a link in the contained document is limited to the part of the visual rendering surface in which it is contained. The SMIL 2.0 Recommendation indicates that this linking behavior might change in future versions, but the constraints just described apply in SMIL 2.0.

SMIL 2.0 has three linking modules—`LinkingAttributes`, `BasicLinking`, and `ObjectLinking`.

The `LinkingAttributes` Module

The `LinkingAttributes` module contains attributes that provide linking functionality on linking elements from non-SMIL namespaces if permitted on particular elements by the applicable language profile.

The `sourceLevel` attribute allows control of the sound volume of a linked resource similar to that described for the `soundLevel` attribute of the layout modules. The `sourceLevel` attribute is combined with any audio level set in the *source* SMIL presentation. The `destinationLevel` attribute is similar to the the `sourceLevel` attribute except that the `destinationLevel` attribute is combined with any sound level settings in the *destination* document from the link.

The `sourcePlayState` attribute determines what happens in the presentation from which the link was made. The `sourcePlayState` attribute can take values of `play`, `pause`, or `stop`. If the link provided detailed background information for part of a presentation, it might be appropriate to set the value of the `sourcePlayState` attribute to `pause`.

The `destinationPlayState` attribute is applicable when the destination of a link is a media object that changes over time. The `destinationPlayState` attribute can take values of `play` or `pause`. If, for example, the destination media object had a text explanation that was the reason for traversing the link, it might be appropriate to set the value of the `destinationPlayState` attribute to `pause` to allow the user to digest the target information at her leisure.

The `show` attribute determines where the target of the link is to be displayed. The approved values of the `show` attribute are `new` and `replace`. A value of `pause` for the `show` attribute is deprecated—the approved method is to set the `show` attribute to a value of `new` and the `sourcePlayState` attribute to a value of `pause`.

The `external` attribute determines whether the target of the link is opened by an external application. The `actuate` attribute determines when traversal of the link is initiated.

The `alt`, `accesskey`, `tabindex`, and `target` attributes behave as they do in HTML or XHTML.

The `BasicLinking` Module

The `BasicLinking` module provides the SMIL linking elements themselves.

The `a` element has similar functionality to the `a` element in HTML 4. The SMIL `a` element must have an `href` attribute that contains the URI of the destination of the link.

In addition, the a element can possess the following attributes whose meanings have been described earlier in the description of the `LinkingAttributes` module—`sourceLevel`, `destinationLevel`, `sourcePlayState`, `destinationPlayState`, `alt`, `show`, `accesskey`, `tabindex`, `target`, `external`, and `actuate`. The permitted content of an a element is defined in the relevant language profile. In general, it is likely that the permitted content will be animation and timing elements.

The a element links to a whole media object. SMIL 2.0 also provides an `area` linking element that is similar to the `area` element in HTML 4 and allows linking from a defined area of the visual rendering surface on which a SMIL presentation is displayed. The `coords` attribute of the `area` element defines the area that is active in terms of initiating the link. The `shape` attribute is used in conjunction with the `coords` attribute to define the active area. In SMIL, the semantics of the `area` element go beyond those of the equivalent HTML element and allow time-based selections to be made using the `begin` and `end` attributes to define the active time period. The area element also has attributes as just described for the `a` element.

THE `ObjectLinking` MODULE

The `ObjectLinking` module adds a `fragment` attribute to the permitted attributes on the `area` element. The value of the `fragment` attribute must be recognizable by the processor within which a language profile is defined. For example, if the referenced media object is an HTML file, the value of the `fragment` attribute will correspond to a named anchor in the HTML document.

THE MEDIA OBJECTS MODULES

There are seven media objects modules. The `BasicMedia` module, as its name implies, provides the basic functionality. The additional modules are `MediaClipping`, `MediaClipMarkers`, `MediaParam`, `MediaAccessibility`, `MediaDescription`, and `BrushMedia`.

THE `BasicMedia` MODULE

The `BasicMedia` module provides a number of elements that, perhaps surprisingly, are semantically identical. A SMIL player gets the necessary information about the type of a media object not from the name of the media elements (which will be described in a moment) but from the value of the `type` attribute of the element, from information communicated by the server that serves the media object, or by some other means. The element type name does not define the type of the media object, contrary to what you might expect.

The elements defined by the `BasicMedia` module are the `ref`, `animation`, `audio`, `img`, `text`, `textstream`, and `video` elements.

As just mentioned, any of these elements could be used to reference any media object, assuming that the relevant `type` attribute had the appropriate value. However, it would be perverse to use an element inappropriate to the known media type of the media object. In order to assist readability and maintenance of code, the following is the suggested use of the available elements:

- The `ref` element is intended to be used when the type of the referenced media object is uncertain or unknown.
- The `animation` element is intended for use with animated vector graphics or some other animated format.
- The `audio` element is intended to reference an audio file.
- The `img` element is used for images such as GIFs and JPEGs.
- The `text` element is used to reference a text file, or it might refer to a string specified within the element.
- The `textstream` element is to be used to refer to streaming text.
- The `video` element is intended for use with video files.

Caution

Be careful not to confuse the `animation` element that is part of the `BasicMedia` module and the animation elements—`animate`, `animateColor`, `animateMotion` and `set`—that are elements in the SMIL animation modules.

Which attributes are permitted on SMIL media elements depends on the language profile within which it might be included. The `src` attribute defines the source of the referenced media object, and the `type` attribute defines the media type of the object.

THE `MediaClipping` MODULE

The `MediaClipping` module adds attributes that can define the beginning and end of the part of a referenced media object which is to be presented. There are two attributes—`clipBegin` and `clipEnd`.

THE `MediaClipMarkers` MODULE

The `MediaClipMarkers` module has the `BasicMedia` and `MediaClipping` modules as prerequisites. The module allows named parts of a media object to be used and referenced by the `clipBegin` and `clipEnd` attributes defined in the `MediaClipping` module.

THE `MediaParam` MODULE

The `MediaParam` module adds a `param` element that can contain parameters required at run-time. The `MediaParam` module has the `BasicMedia` module as a prerequisite.

A `param` element has a `name` attribute that contains the name of the parameter. There is a corresponding `value` attribute for each `name` attribute and, of course, the value of the `value` attribute is the value of the parameter specified in the `name` attribute. The `valuetype` attribute specifies the type of the value and can take values of `data`, `ref`, and `object`. When the value of the `valuetype` attribute is set to `ref`, a `type` attribute specifies the content type of the referenced resource.

The `MediaParam` module also adds attributes to all the basic media elements. The `erase` attribute controls when a media object is removed and can take values of `never` and `whenDone`. The `mediaRepeat` attribute can be used to modify the intrinsic repeat behavior of the relevant media object. The `mediaRepeat` attribute can take values of `preserve` (which is the default) and `strip`. Using the `strip` value would, for example, allow the SMIL author to modify the behavior of an otherwise endlessly repeating animation. The `sensitivity` attribute modifies the sensitivity of media objects to user interface events. The `sensitivity` attribute can take the value of `opaque`, `transparent`, or a percentage value.

THE `MediaAccessibility` MODULE

The `MediaAccessibility` module adds attributes related to accessibility.

The `alt` attribute defines alternative or additional text to be displayed if the user agent cannot render the preferred media object. The `longdesc` attribute specifies a URI that contains a long description of the relevant media object. The `readIndex` attribute specifies the order in which an assistive device should read out any `title`, `alt`, or `longdesc` information.

THE `MediaDescription` MODULE

The `MediaDescription` module adds attributes that provide additional descriptive information about media objects.

The `abstract` attribute contains information about the media object and its content that might be used, for example, when a table of contents is generated for a SMIL presentation. Unlike the `alt` attribute described in the `MediaAccessibility` module, the content of the `abstract` attribute is not typically rendered. In SMIL 2.0, the `abstract` attribute is deprecated in favor of expressing metadata in RDF, the Resource Description Framework, which is described in Chapter 26.

The `author` attribute contains information about the author of the media object that possesses the attribute. The `copyright` attribute contains copyright information. The `title` attribute, specified in the structure module, is desirable to provide a title for each media object. The `xml:lang` attribute specifies the language of the content of the media object.

THE `BrushMedia` MODULE

The `BrushMedia` module adds a `brush` element. The `brush` element allows a color or pattern to be painted onscreen in place of a media object. The `src` attribute is ignored if it is present on a `brush` element.

THE TRANSITIONS MODULES

In a traditional slide show using film slides, the transition from one slide to another is sudden. SMIL 1.0 was incapable of creating any other type of transition. However, users of the Web and other consumers of multimedia presentations have become used to much more sophisticated or subtle transitions from one part of a multimedia presentation to another.

SMIL 2.0 adds, in SMIL syntax, significant capabilities to produce attractive transitions from one part of the presentation to another.

The use of SMIL transitions depends on the language profiles in which it is implemented. However, it is likely that the transitions will be nested within the `head` element.

SMIL 2.0 provides three transitions modules—the `BasicTransitions` module, the `InlineTransitions` module, and the `TransitionModifiers` module.

Four transition types are defined in SMIL 2.0—`barWipe`, `irisWipe`, `clockWipe`, and `snakeWipe`.

THE `BasicTransitions` MODULE

The `BasicTransitions` module defines the behavior of the `transition` and `param` elements.

The `transition` element must have a `type` attribute whose permitted value is one of the four types of transitions just mentioned. An optional `subtype` attribute, if present, more closely defines the precise type of transition to be carried out. A `dur` attribute defines the duration of the transition. It is possible, using `startProgress` and `endProgress` attributes, to start or finish the transition part way through. A `direction` attribute can be used to reverse the geometry of the transition effect, but the transition still takes place from the first object to the second.

For example, to use a left to right wipe transition, we could use code like this:

```
<transition type="barWipe" subtype="leftToRight" .../>
```

To reverse the direction of the wipe—that is, cause it to occur from right to left—we could use code like this:

```
<transition type="barWipe" subtype="leftToRight" direction="reverse".../>
```

A `fadeColor` attribute is used when fading from a media object to a plain color. Thus if we wanted to fade to a blue background, we could use the following code:

```
<transition type="fade" subtype="fadeToColor" fadeColor="#0000FF" .../>
```

The `transition` element can have a `param` element child element. A language profile that includes SMIL transitions might choose to define its own transition types and subtypes. The `param` element is intended to allow the passing of parameters to such transitions.

A `transIn` or `transOut` attribute can be added to media objects that implement the `BasicTransitions` module. The `transIn` attribute can be used to begin a transition at the start of the presentation of that media object. The `transOut` attribute is used to end a transition at the end of the presentation of the relevant object. The default value of both attributes is the empty string.

Within the `head` element of the SMIL presentation, a `transition` element will have an `id` attribute. To make use of that transition definition, we can set a `transIn` or `transOut` attribute to contain the name of the transition.

THE `InlineTransitions` MODULE

The `InlineTransitions` module allows transitions to be expressed inline. Rather than using a `transition` element in the `head` of a SMIL document and referencing it using `transIn` or `transOut` attributes, the `InlineTransitions` module adds a `transitionfilter` element to define transitions inline. The `transitionfilter` element shares most of the same attributes of the `transition` element.

The `transitionfilter` element can have a `param` element child.

THE `TransitionModifiers` MODULE

The `TransitionModifiers` module gives additional options for transitions. See the SMIL 2.0 specification for details.

THE `Metainformation` MODULE

The `Metainformation` module is a single module that contains information about a SMIL resource.

The `meta` element is an empty element. A single `meta` element specifies a name/value pair. Each `meta` element has a `name` attribute and a `content` attribute that provides the name/value pair for that element. In the earlier examples in this chapter, you saw how the `meta` element can be used.

The `metadata` element can also contain metadata about a SMIL document. Typically, the child elements of a `metadata` element would be from the *Resource Description Framework (RDF)*.

SMIL TOOLS

In this chapter, we have looked at the X-Smiles browser as a tool to display SMIL presentations. This is only one of several available tools. The Real.com players also have significant SMIL playing capabilities. Other SMIL players are likely to be available by the time you read this.

> **Caution**
>
> Be aware, when using different SMIL players to test code, that RealPlayer leaves a task running in the background. This can cause problems for other applications attempting to access SMIL files or the files referenced by those SMIL files that you ran earlier using RealPlayer.

The tools to create a SMIL presentation can be as simple as an XML-aware text editor or can be expensive custom SMIL design tools like the GRiNS editor.

In this chapter, you have seen a few of the features that SMIL 2.0 provides. The power of SMIL results from the enormous flexibility with which its elements and attributes can be combined. SMIL, particularly in its modularized incarnation, is not a simple technology. But its functionality is likely to be one that you will come to use often because its acceptance by Real.com is likely to give SMIL a sizeable role behind the scenes in the future of the multimedia-based Web.

Additional Resources

SMIL is, partly because of its size and complexity, penetrating the multimedia market fairly slowly. SMIL resources remain relatively few. Here are a few:

- The SMIL home page on the W3C Web site (`http://www.w3.org/AudioVideo/`) is updated on an ongoing basis and will keep you up to date with available tools, and so on.
- The RealOne Player (`http://www.realnetworks.com/solutions/ecosystem/realone.html?src=rnhmfs`) is a multimedia player built on SMIL.
- The GRiNs SMIL 2.0 Editor (`http://www.oratrix.com/Products/G2R`) is a powerful, but not cheap, SMIL tool.

Roadmap

Chapter 25 introduces you to the Resource Description Framework, RDF, and how it is used to structure metadata in XML syntax.

CHAPTER 25

Using XML to Create Forms: XForms

In this chapter

by Andrew Watt

XForms is a specification under development by the W3C to provide XML-based forms functionality for the Web. XForms makes use of a number of XML technologies that you have seen in earlier chapters: For example, XML Namespaces, XPath, and W3C XML Schema are all used.

In this chapter, we will look at why XForms are needed and how they can improve on the functionality available from HTML/XHTML forms. Later, we will create some example XForms code according to the current W3C XForms working draft.

Note

This chapter has been written on the basis of the December 2001 XForms Working Draft located at `http://www.w3.org/TR/2001/WD-xforms-20011207/`. A further Working Draft is expected before XForms progresses to Candidate Recommendation, and so on. Therefore, be aware that details of the final XForms syntax might change from that described in this chapter. The most up-to-date version of the XForms specification will be located at `http://www.w3.org/TR/xforms/`. If it contains a version later than the December 2001 version, take note of changes (typically listed in an Appendix or in a diff-marked version, which shows the changes made since the previous version).

Let's consider why XForms are needed.

WHY XFORMS ARE NEEDED

As a reader of this book, you are aware of the increased importance of XML as the widely accepted emerging basis for today's and tomorrow's Web.

HTML forms were created long before XML first reached W3C Recommendation status in 1998. Therefore, HTML forms are not designed with the needs of XML and the XML application languages in mind. It is possible for HTML forms to be extended to accommodate some needs of an XML-based Web through custom programming, but achieving that can significantly increase the burden on Web developers.

As data is increasingly exchanged between applications as XML, the lack of any standard way to easily convert data entered into HTML forms to a standard XML format for transmission is becoming a more visible deficiency of the current forms technology.

HTML/XHTML FORMS AND THEIR LIMITATIONS

The use of forms on the Web dates back to their appearance in HTML in 1993. Until that time, HTML Web pages had simply been a tool for the one-way communication of information. The addition of forms to allow data collection was a major step forward in making the Web the interactive medium that we know today.

At the time that HTML forms were first introduced, they simply collected data and transmitted that data unchecked to the server for processing. Server-side processing was typically carried out using scripting languages and was often considered uncomfortably complex for many Web developers. If there was an error in the data submitted to the server, the user would need to be informed that the data entered into a form was incomplete or in error. Because Internet connections were typically slow and all the processing occurred on the server side, the whole process of forms-based interaction with the user could be very slow and tedious.

As the Web developed, client-side scripting languages (of which JavaScript is possibly most widely used) were combined with HTML Web pages to add intelligence within the Web pages to allow at least some data validation on the client side. The use of scripting languages allowed simple problems with data—for example, the omission of a required piece of data—to be identified using a client-side script. An alert describing the problem could be promptly displayed to the user.

By moving initial data validation to the client side, the validation of form data became significantly more responsive to the user.

It would, in principle, be possible for client-side scripters to write code to package data collected from a user into an XML-based format for transmission to the server. To do that, the client-scripter would need a good understanding of the data structure to be created, as well as a good understanding of how to script the XML Document Object Model for the XML to be created. Although all this is possible, it adds yet another burden to often hard-pressed Web developers. It makes better sense for a forms processor to carry out that conversion automatically—but this is not possible with current HTML browsers.

In addition to the factors just mentioned, the fragmentation of the Web into a number of different platforms (including but not limited to the traditional desktop Web browser) raises further issues to be considered in the next section.

Separating Presentation from Data Model

When the only platform to view Web content was the desktop Web browser, if we wanted to collect data from users, it was a fairly straightforward choice to use HTML forms. As the number of platforms has increased, the tight coupling between HTML code and the data model that it represents is becoming more of a problem.

The number of ways that users can interface with the Web is likely to increase even more over the next few years. Not only are different types of visual browsers likely to be common, but also aural browsers might be used in situations in which the user is not able to view visual data. This could be because the user has a permanent or temporary visual impairment or because the user is accessing information when it is unsafe to visually study the presented data: for example, when driving a car.

If you view the Web only using a desktop browser, this emerging variety of browsers might not seem directly relevant to you. However, corporations that need to present their products or services to the largest audience possible are actively exploring the use of these novel browsers. It is inefficient to create entirely separate applications to present a form on each of several types of browsers, and maintenance is unnecessarily expensive. The collected information is likely to be the same on all the platforms, or there might be two formats—for example, full data and abbreviated data. In either case, the data stored in the Web application's back end is likely to be the same. Thus, the need is to find a mechanism to store data in a uniform way but to present that data, or the form to collect it, in a variety of ways appropriate to the user's browser choice.

When, for example, you use an HTML `input` element, you basically know how it will appear when it is produced onscreen. So the HTML `input` element is tightly coupled to its appearance. It's not possible to reuse this same element with an aural browser. (What would you do with the `onclick` attribute, for example?)

Another disadvantage of HTML forms is that the data to be entered into an input element can be almost anything. So, when you use HTML or XHTML alone, you have no way of ensuring on the client side that the data is an appropriate type or value. To validate the data entered by a user, you would need to use a client-side scripting language such as JavaScript, which is likely backed up by server-side validation.

For XML data, the W3C XML Schema specification, which is sometimes called *XSD (XML Schema Definition)* Schema, provides powerful XML-based type checking facilities. If you want data entered into a particular part of a form to correspond to a specific data type, you simply specify the XSD Schema data type that you want it to be. The process of validation need not be carried out by using JavaScript and, for example, complex regular expression code.

So we see that HTML/XHTML forms are poor at providing data validation and are poor at providing flexibility of presentation because the form elements are tightly coupled to the visual appearance produced.

XForms has been designed to address problems such as those mentioned. Let's move on to look at how it handles them.

XFORMS CONCEPTS

In this section, I will introduce you to the concepts that underlie XForms and allow data to be separated from its presentation.

XForms divides the underlying form data and its presentation into separate layers. For example, XForms has an `xforms:input` *form control* that accepts data. It is similar to an HTML/XHTML `input` element. However, the presentation of the `xforms:input` form control is not fixed—its presentation is determined by the *user interface* of individual platforms. It can be presented on a desktop browser with an appearance similar or identical to that of the HTML input element. However, on a mobile browser, it might be presented in a simpler fashion—perhaps just a label, a colon, and a flashing cursor at the position for the entry of text. In addition, the `xforms:input` form control can, on an aural browser, be presented entirely verbally with no visual presentation at all.

In addition, the XForms processor automatically packs up the data collected from the user into an appropriate XML-based format for transmission. Assigning that task to the XForms processor can save the Web developer a lot of time writing custom code.

Data entered into an XForms form is *bound* to *instance data*. Later, we will look at how this is done. Data is entered by using a *form control*. Each form control is bound to part of the instance data. In an application, an `xforms:selectOne` form control can be presented in several ways on different platforms, but the control will be bound to the same part of the instance data in each case. For example, the user might want to indicate which age group he is in during an online survey. The `xforms:selectOne` form control could be presented on a desktop browser as a radio control or audibly in an aural browser. In both cases, the data entered will be bound to instance data of the same structure.

XFORMS MODEL

The XForms model and what the form does are defined in the `xforms:model` element. The XForms model contains information about where and how data collected from the user is to be submitted and also contains the default instance data for the form.

In an XForms application with a single XForms form, the XForms model can be represented simply by code such as the following:

```
<xforms:model>
 <xforms:submitInfo action="http://www.xmml.com/" id="submit" method="post"/>
</xforms:model>
```

25

The `xforms:submitInfo` element has an `action` attribute defining the destination for data submitted. A `method` attribute defines the method used to submit the data to the destination defined in the `action` attribute.

In a more complex application, where more than one `xforms:model` element exists, the `xforms:model` element(s) other than the first must have an `id` attribute to allow them to be referenced unambiguously. Thus, a second `xforms:model` element in the application would be written using code such as the following:

```
<xforms:model id="SecondModel">
 <xforms:submitInfo action="http://www.xmml.com/survey/"
 id="OnlineSurveySubmit" method="post"/>
</xforms:model>
```

In addition to the `xforms:submitInfo` element, the `xforms:model` element contains the instance data for the XForms form and might optionally contain an `xforms:schema` element.

Caution

Be sure to avoid confusing the `xforms:schema` element, from the XForms Namespace, with the `xsd:schema` element from the W3C XML Schema Namespace.

INSTANCE DATA

The default instance data of an XForms form can be contained within the XForms Model, or it can be contained in an external file referenced from an `xforms:instance` element nested within the `xforms:model` element.

Listing 25.1 creates a very simple XForms form embedded in an XSL-FO document. At the time of writing, there is no implementation of the December 2001 XForms Working Draft. The XSL-FO code is fairly lengthy. Look for elements with an `xforms` namespace prefix to see how XForms elements can be used.

Caution

The namespace URI used in the following code was an internal one used by the X-Smiles development team during development of the December 2001 XForms Working Draft. Be sure to check the latest version of the XForms specification for the current namespace URI.

LISTING 25.1 A SIMPLE XFORMS FORM COLLECTING NAME DATA (SIMPLEFORM.FO)

```
<?xml version="1.0" encoding="UTF-8"?>
<!-- XSL-FO page definitions -->
<fo:root font-family="Arial" font-size="12pt" text-align="justify"
xmlns:fo="http://www.w3.org/1999/XSL/Format"
xmlns:xforms="01/11/xforms-editors-copy02/01/xforms">

<fo:layout-master-set>
  <fo:simple-page-master master-name="right" page-height="{/*/@height}"
margin-top="5pt" margin-bottom="5pt" margin-left="50pt" margin-right="50pt"
page-width="900pt">
   <fo:region-body margin-bottom="50pt"/>
   <fo:region-after extent="25pt"/>
  </fo:simple-page-master>

  <fo:page-sequence-master master-name="OddEven">
   <fo:repeatable-page-master-alternatives>
    <fo:conditional-page-master-reference
 master-name="right" page-position="first"/>
   </fo:repeatable-page-master-alternatives>
  </fo:page-sequence-master>
</fo:layout-master-set>

<fo:page-sequence id="SimpleForm" master-name="OddEven">
  <fo:static-content flow-name="xsl-region-after">
   <fo:block text-align-last="center" font-size="10pt">
    <fo:page-number/>
   </fo:block>
  </fo:static-content>
  <fo:flow flow-name="xsl-region-body">
   <fo:instream-foreign-object>
    <xforms:model>
     <xforms:submitInfo id="submit1" method2="postxml"
 localfile="temp2.xml" target2="http://www.xmml.com/"/>
     <xforms:schema/>
     <xforms:instance href="Name.xml"/>
```

Listing 25.1 continued

```
    <!-- The above attribute should be xlink:href
but that is not yet implemented. -->
    <xforms:bind ref="Name/FirstName" type="xsd:string"/>
   </xforms:model>
  </fo:instream-foreign-object>
  <fo:block font-size="20pt" background-color="white"
color="red" font-weight="bold">XMML.com simple XForms form
  </fo:block>
  <fo:block font-size="15pt" space-before="15pt">
  A very simple XForms form using only three
xforms:input elements and a submit button.
  </fo:block>
  <fo:block font-size="15pt" space-before="15pt">
  The form is embedded in an XSL-FO document.
  </fo:block>
  <fo:table space-before="10mm">
   <fo:table-column column-width="60mm"/>
   <fo:table-column column-width="60mm"/>
   <fo:table-column column-width="60mm"/>
   <fo:table-body>
    <!-- TABLE HEADER -->
    <fo:table-row space-before="10pt" font-weight="bold">
     <fo:table-cell>
      <fo:block>
       <fo:instream-foreign-object>
        <xforms:input ref="Name/FirstName" cols="8"
style="font-weight:bold;width:80px">
         <xforms:caption style="font-weight:bold;">First Name</xforms:caption>
         <xforms:hint>Enter your first name here.</xforms:hint>
        </xforms:input>
       </fo:instream-foreign-object>
      </fo:block>
     </fo:table-cell>

     <fo:table-cell>
      <fo:block>
       <fo:instream-foreign-object>
        <xforms:input ref="Name/MiddleInitials" cols="18"
style="font-weight:bold;width:80px">
         <xforms:caption style="font-weight:bold;">
Middle Initial(s)</xforms:caption>
         <xforms:hint>Enter your middle initial or initials
here, if you have one or more middle names.</xforms:hint>
        </xforms:input>
       </fo:instream-foreign-object>
      </fo:block>
     </fo:table-cell>

     <fo:table-cell>
      <fo:block>
       <fo:instream-foreign-object>
        <xforms:input ref="Name/LastName" cols="10"
style="font-weight:bold;color:red;width:100px">
         <xforms:caption style="font-weight:bold;">Last Name</xforms:caption>
         <xforms:hint>Enter your surname here.</xforms:hint>
        </xforms:input>
       </fo:instream-foreign-object>
```

25

Listing 25.1 Continued

```
        </fo:block>
       </fo:table-cell>
      </fo:table-row>
     </fo:table-body>
    </fo:table>

    <!-- SUBMIT BUTTON -->
    <fo:block space-before="10pt">
    <fo:instream-foreign-object>
     <xforms:submit name="Submit" ref="test" to="submit1">""
      <xforms:caption>Submit!</xforms:caption>
      <xforms:hint>Click to submit</xforms:hint>
     </xforms:submit>
    </fo:instream-foreign-object>
    </fo:block>
   </fo:flow>
  </fo:page-sequence>
</fo:root>
```

Default instance data is referenced using the `xforms:instance` element nested within the `xforms:model` element. The Name.xml file that contains the default instance data is shown in Listing 25.2.

Listing 25.2 Simple Instance Data Used in Listing 25.1.

```
<?xml version='1.0'?>
<Name>
<FirstName>Fred</FirstName>
<MiddleInitials>Q</MiddleInitials>
<LastName>Samora</LastName>
</Name>
```

Figure 25.1 shows the appearance produced by the preceding code in the X-Smiles XML browser.

Notice how the data from Listing 25.2 is displayed as default values for the `xforms:input` form controls. Notice too that the content of an `xforms:hint` element is displayed as a ToolTip for the `xforms:input` form control that is moused. The cursor appears as an I-bar because it is mousing a form control that accepts text input.

To download the current version of the X-Smiles browser, visit `http://www.xsmiles.org` and follow the download links.

Note

> If you are trying to access `http://www.x-smiles.org` from a corporate base and find that access is blocked, a system administrator might have erroneously blocked access believing that the URL is an "adult" site. The X-Smiles browser is unrelated to that site.

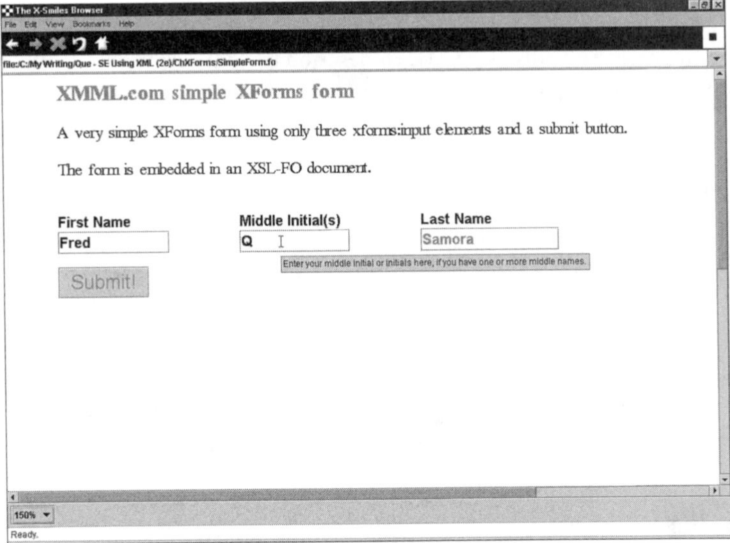

Figure 25.1
A simple XForms form embedded in an XSL-FO document and displayed at 150%.

BINDING

XForms has an `xforms:bind` element that might also be nested within the `xforms:model` element. The purpose of the `xforms:bind` element is to apply a constraint to a selected part of the instance data. Additionally, an `id` attribute within the part of the instance data allows a shorthand reference to that data.

In Listing 25.1, from which the following code is extracted, you can see a simple use of the `xforms:bind` element.

```
<xforms:model>
 <xforms:submitInfo id="submit1" method2="postxml"
 localfile="temp2.xml" target2="http://www.xmml.com/"/>
 <xforms:schema/>
 <xforms:instance href="Name.xml"/>
 <xforms:bind ref="Name/FirstName" type="xsd:string"/>
</xforms:model>
```

The `xsd:bind` element has a `ref` attribute that indicates the part of the instance data which is subject to the constraint. The `type` attribute of the `xforms:bind` element indicates the type of constraint that is being placed on the referenced node-set. In the preceding example, the `type` attribute has a value which indicates that any data of type `xsd:string` is permitted. The `type` attribute could be used, for example, to constrain the entry to `xsd:nonNegativeInteger` values if the associated `xforms:input` form control is intended to accept the number of items to be purchased.

Note

If you are unfamiliar with the W3C XML Schema data types, refer to Chapter 5, "Defining XML Document Structures with XML Schemas," for further information.

XFORMS FORM CONTROLS

XForms form controls use XML to describe the purpose or functionality of the XForms form controls. The attributes of a form control element allow the refinement of its appearance, including a `class` attribute that can be used in conjunction with Cascading Style Sheets to give selected form controls a coordinated look and feel. The form controls within an XForms form are bound to instance data.

A basic notion of the XForms form controls is that they describe a function, but do not indicate directly how the form control is to be presented. For example, the `xforms:selectOne` control is used to pick one or more items from a set. It is possible to use `xforms:selectOne` on a conventional desktop browser, on one of the many forms of mobile browsers, or to avoid a visual presentation altogether using Aural Cascading Style Sheets. In fact, all XForms form controls are suitable for styling using Aural CSS. The behavior of form controls is defined by XForms actions, which are described later in this chapter.

Note

If you are interested in Aural style sheets, further information is available at `http://www.w3.org/TR/REC-CSS2/aural.html`.

XForms form controls also have a number of common attributes that are described following the description of the individual form controls.

Note

In the XForms form controls descriptions that follow, all are described with a namespace prefix present; for example, `xforms:input`. This helps to distinguish the XForms form controls from similarly named HTML/XHTML constructs.

THE INPUT FORM CONTROL

The XForms `xforms:input` form control is intended for the entry of brief free-form textual data. It might be used, for example, to ask for the entry of a name, some brief comments, or some other short message in an unstructured format.

For example, an input form control might be used to record special delivery instructions for an online order.

```
<xforms:input ref="order/shipTo/instructions" class="BlueForm">
<xforms:caption>Delivery instructions</xforms:caption>
<xforms:hint>Describe briefly any special instructions to
 aid efficient delivery of your order</xforms:hint>
</xforms:input>
```

Notice the `ref` attribute on the `xforms:input` element. The value of the `ref` attribute is an XPath location path that indicates with which part of the instance data the form control is associated.

Note

The value held in the instance data might not be identical to the form entered by the user. For example, a purchaser in Germany might enter a number using local conventions for thousands separator (period) and decimal separator (comma), but the data might be stored, for example, using English conventions.

The `xforms:input` form control can bind to any XML Schema `simpleType` data type, excluding `xsd:base64Binary` or `xsd:hexBinary` or types derived from them.

An `xforms:input` form control must enable the entry of a lexical value of the bound data type.

Depending on the type of data to which it is bound, it might take the appearance of a slider to allow numerical data, a calendar to allow date information, or a simple box into which text can be typed in the conventional way.

The `input` form control can have an `inputMode` attribute. The `inputMode` attribute provides a hint to the user agent about how text can best be entered—in contrast to binding to a W3C XML Schema `simpleType`, which is restricted by facets that provide a strict constraint on allowable text.

THE `textarea` FORM CONTROL

25

The `xforms:textarea` form control is intended for the entry of multiline free-form data. It might be used, for example, to contain the body of an e-mail message or for some narrative text that is likely to be multiline in length.

We could use the `textarea` form control to accept delivery instructions in a way similar to that shown for the `xforms:input` form control.

```
<xforms:textarea ref="order/shipTo/instructions" class="BlueForm">
<xforms:caption>Delivery instructions</xforms:caption>
<xforms:hint>Describe any special instructions to aid efficient
delivery of your order. Please be sure to include sufficient
information for the driver.</xforms:hint>
</xforms:textarea>
```

The `xforms:textarea` form control can bind to data of type `xsd:string` or any type derived from it.

THE SECRET FORM CONTROL

The `xforms:secret` form control is the rather unusual name chosen to name the XForms form control that is intended for the input of sensitive information such as passwords. Any information entered into an `xforms:secret` form control is not echoed back to the browser, whether that is a conventional desktop browser or an aural browser.

The `xforms:secret` form control could be used to enter a login password using code such as this:

```
<xforms:secret ref="login/password">
<xforms:caption>Enter your password here</xforms:caption>
```

```
<xforms:hint>Your password won't be visible as letters when
 you enter it - simply as a sequence of  asterisks.</xforms:hint>
</xforms:secret>
```

Notice the `ref` attribute on the `xforms:secret` element, which binds the data entered to a specific part of the form's instance data.

The Output Form Control

The `xforms:output` form control is intended for use to display read-only values. The user is not permitted to alter the value displayed.

The `xforms:output` form control might, for example, be used to display calculated sales tax (assuming that the Web page knew the appropriate rate for the user's locality) and the total price to be charged to a customer. Code might appear as follows, assuming that the XForms form is placed in an XHTML page:

```
<tr>
<td>Sales tax is:</td>
<td><xforms:output ref="Order/SalesTax"/>
</tr>
<tr>
<td>Total cost is:</td>
<td><xforms:output ref="Order/TotalCost"/></td>
</tr>
```

The format in which a number, for example, is stored in the instance data might not be identical to the format used for display. That situation could occur when orders are being accepted from countries that use a decimal separator different from that in which W3C XML Schema numbers are stored. Thus in the instance data, the figure of 1,000.00 might be stored, but the figure displayed to a customer in Germany would be displayed as 1.000,00.

The Upload Form Control

The `xforms:upload` form control allows a user to upload a file from the local file system to that of the Web site, which provides the form control, or to upload input from devices such as pens or digital cameras.

To enable the upload of an image, you would use code such as the following:

```
<xforms:upload ref="Upload/Image" mediaType="image/*">
<xforms:caption>Upload an image to our server.</xforms:caption>
<xforms:hint>Please be careful to select only an image file.</xforms:hint>
</xforms:upload>
```

A graphical browser might render the `xforms:upload` form control as a drop-down menu that, when appropriate, includes an option to browse the local file system to select an appropriate file for upload to the server.

The `xforms:upload` form control can be bound only to the data types `xsd:base64Binary` or `xsd:hexBinary` or data types derived by restriction of those types.

In a system with a file system, the mediaType attribute of the xforms:upload element will determine the options offered to the user for upload. Thus if, for example, the mediaType attribute were used to specify audio files, audio files should be the offered option. For systems with pen hardware, a "scribble" option should be offered.

THE RANGE FORM CONTROL

The xforms:range form control allows the display and input of a range of numerical values with prespecified steps.

The xforms:range form control could be used, for example, to constrain the number of items that a user could order for a special offer of a particular item.

```
<xforms:range ref="SpecialOffer/Widgets" start="0" end="5" stepSize="1">
<xforms:caption>Number of Widgets:</xforms:caption>
<xforms:hint>For this special offer the maximum
number you can order is 5.</xforms:hint>
</xforms:range>
```

The preceding code would create a form control that could accept values from zero to five for the number of widgets to be ordered. The start attribute defines the minimum allowed number, and the end attribute defines the maximum allowed number.

The xforms:range form control can only be applied to scalar types. Thus, the permitted data types to which a range form control can be bound are xsd:float, xsd:decimal, xsd:double, xsd:duration, xsd:date, xsd:time, xsd:dateTime, xsd:gYearMonth, xsd:gYear, xsd:gDay, and xsd:gMonth or data types derived by restriction from the stated types.

THE BUTTON FORM CONTROL

The xforms:button form control, not surprisingly, provides graphical browsers a button for a user to click. In a typical implementation, the caption would be rendered on the face of the button. Using CSS, it is possible to use an image as the button.

An xforms:button form control cannot be bound to instance data and therefore has no ref, model or bind attribute, unlike many of the other XForms form controls. Buttons are used to generate events. The caption provides a label for the button, and a hint can also be provided.

```
<xforms:button>
<xforms:caption>Click here!</xforms:caption>
<xforms:hint>This will perform a stated action</xforms:hint>
</xforms:button>
```

THE SUBMIT FORM CONTROL

The xforms:submit form control initiates submission of all or part of the XForms information. When the submit button, in a graphical browser, is clicked, an xforms:submit event is sent to an xforms:submitInfo element. The target xforms:submitInfo element is indicated by a submitInfo attribute on the xforms:submit element, or—in the absence of such an attribute—the first xforms:submitInfo element in document order is targeted.

The code to represent an `xforms:submit` form control is similar to the following:

```
<xforms:submit submitInfo="Order">
<xforms:caption>Click to submit your order</xforms:caption>
<xforms:hint>This is the final step. Be sure all information
 shown is accurate before submitting it.</xforms:hint>
</xforms:submit>
```

THE selectOne FORM CONTROL

The `xforms:selectOne form` control allows a user to make a single choice from among a number of choices. The `xforms:selectOne` form control can bind to any type of simple content.

For example, if in an online pizza delivery service a number of mutually exclusive choices of toppings were offered, we could use code such as the following:

```
<xforms:selectOne ref="Order/Pizza/Topping">
<xforms:caption>Select one topping</xforms:caption>
<xforms:item>
<xforms:caption>Pepperoni</xforms:caption>

<xforms:value>pepperoni</xforms:value>
<xforms:hint>This selection selects pepperoni topping.</xforms:hint>
</xforms:item>
<xforms:item>
<xforms:caption>Ham and Tomato</xforms:caption>

<xforms:value>HamAndTom</xforms:value>
<xforms:hint>This selection selects ham and tomato topping.</xforms:hint>
</xforms:item>
<xforms:item>
<xforms:caption>Chicken and pineapple</xforms:caption>

<xforms:value>ChickAndPin</xforms:value>
<xforms:hint>This selection selects chicken and pineapple topping.</xforms:hint>
</xforms:item>
</xforms:selectOne>
```

The `xforms:selectOne` form control stores the chosen value in the part of the instance data defined by the value of the `ref` attribute on the `xforms:selectOne` element. In this case, the user would be able to select "`pepperoni`," "`ham and tomato topping`," or "`chicken and pineapple`." These are defined within the `xforms:item` elements. After selecting one, the data instance element identified by the expression "`Order/Pizza/Topping`" would have a value of "`pepperoni`," "`HamAndTom`," or "`ChickAndPin`."

The `xforms:selectOne` form control can have *closed* data entry of the type shown earlier—that is, all the possible choices are defined. Another option is for *open* data entry, with the acceptable data type being `xsd:string`. Free entry of text is handled similar to the `xforms:input` form control. The mode of entry is determined by the `selection` attribute, which might take values of "`closed`" or "`open`," with the default being "`closed`." In addition, a `selectUI` attribute allows selection of the user interface to be used for graphical browsers, with allowed values of "`radio`," "`menu`," or "`listbox`."

Note

The December 2001 Working Draft allows a further "checkbox" option for a value of the selectUI attribute. Because that interface is contrary to the norms of HTML Web forms, it is possible that the option will be removed as the XForms specification is finalized.

THE selectMany FORM CONTROL

The xforms:selectMany form control allows multiple choices to be made from a range of zero or more choices offered. A user can, however, choose only one choice if preferred.

If our fictional online pizza operation is a little more generous and allows two toppings, rather than only one, we could use the xforms:selectMany form control to express that in XForms code.

```
<xforms:selectMany selectUI="checkbox" ref="Order/Pizza/Toppings">
<xforms:caption>Choose Toppings</xforms:caption>
<xforms:hint>You may choose up to two toppings.</xforms:hint>
<xforms:item>
<xforms:caption>Pepperoni</xforms:caption>

<xforms:value>Pepperoni</xforms:value>
<xforms:hint>This selection selects pepperoni topping.</xforms:hint>
</xforms:item>
<xforms:item>
<xforms:caption>Ham and Tomato</xforms:caption>

<xforms:value>HamAndTom</xforms:value>
<xforms:hint>This selection selects ham and tomato topping.</xforms:hint>
</xforms:item>
<xforms:item>
<xforms:caption>Chicken and pineapple</xforms:caption>
<xforms:value>ChickAndPin</xforms:value>
<xforms:hint>This selection selects chicken and pineapple topping.</xforms:hint>
</xforms:item>
</xforms:selectMany>
```

Values permitted for the selectUI attribute in the December 2001 Working Draft are "checkbox," "menu," "listbox," and "radio."

Caution

Although "radio" is a permitted value for the selectUI attribute, it makes no sense to use a radio button interface (which selects only one) in conjunction with a selectMany form control.

COMMON ATTRIBUTES

Many form controls have a number of common attributes that are described here.

The xml:lang attribute is an optional attribute that defines a human language for the data to be entered into a form control on which the xml:lang attribute is present. The permitted content of the xml:lang attribute is of type xsd:language.

The `class` attribute associates a particular presentation style with the form control element on which it is present. The permitted content of the `class` attribute is a space separated list of CSS classes.

The `navIndex` attribute defines the position in tabbing order of the form control element on which the attribute is present. The allowed values of the `navIndex` attribute are of type `xsd:nonNegativeInteger`.

The `accessKey` attribute is an optional attribute that defines a shortcut to place focus on the form control. The value of the `accessKey` attribute must be of data type `xsd:token`.

CREATING CHOICES AT RUNTIME

The examples of the use of form controls that you have seen define the available choices statically—that is, the available choices are hard-coded within the form control itself. XForms also provides the opportunity to define the available selections at runtime using the `xforms:itemset` element.

We could use the `xforms:itemset` element to dynamically create a selection of pizza toppings similar to that we created earlier for the `xforms:selectMany` form control using code similar to the following. The code, could, of course, be augmented to provide choices of pizza size, different bases, and so on.

```
<xforms:model id="Pizza">
<xforms:instance>
<my:pizza>
<my:toppings/>
</my:pizza>
<!-- Other instance data could go here. -->
</xforms:instance>
</xforms:model>

<xforms:model id="toppings">
<xforms:instance>
<my:toppings>
<my:topping type="pepperoni">
<my:description>Pepperoni</my:description>
<my:hint>This selection selects pepperoni topping.</my:hint>
</my:topping>
<my:topping type="HamAndTom">
<my:description>Ham and Tomato</my:description>
<my:hint>This selection selects ham and tomato topping.</my:hint>
</my:topping>
<my:topping type="ChickAndPin">
<my:description>Chicken And Pineapple</my:description>
<my:hint>This selection selects chicken and pineapple topping.</my:hint>
</my:topping>
</my:toppings>
</xforms:instance>
</xforms:model>

<!-- Other XForms markup could go here. -->
<xforms:selectMany model="Pizza" ref="my:pizza/my:toppings">
<xforms:caption>Available Toppings</xforms:caption>
```

```
<xforms:itemset model="toppings"  nodeset="my:toppings/my:topping">
<xforms:caption ref="my:description"/>
<xforms:hint ref="my:hint"/>
<xforms:value ref="@type"/>
</xforms:itemset>
</xforms:selectMany>
<!-- Other XForms markup could go here. -->
```

Notice that the code has two `xforms:model` elements. The `xforms:model` elements can be reliably distinguished in the code because each has an `id` attribute. The `xforms:selectMany` element binds to the `Pizza` model and `my:toppings` instance element of that model. Similarly, the `xforms:itemset` element binds to the `toppings` model and, more precisely, to the node-set that holds the available choices by means of its `nodeset` attribute. The XPath expressions in the `ref` attributes of the `xforms:caption`, `xforms:hint`, and `xforms:value` elements are interpreted relative to the context provided by the value of the `ref` attribute of the containing `xforms:itemset` element.

The example code illustrates "single node binding attributes" and "nodeset binding attributes." The `ref` attribute of the `xforms:selectMany` element binds to a single node. The `nodeset` attribute on the `xforms:itemset` element is used to bind to a node-set. In this case, it binds to the `nodeset` produced by the XPath expression `"my:toppings/my:topping,"` which yields all the `my:topping` elements that are children of the toppings element contained in the toppings model.

25

COMMON CHILD ELEMENTS FOR FORM CONTROLS

In the example code demonstrating the XForms form controls, you have already seen several of these child elements in use.

The `xforms:caption` element is a required child element for all form controls. The `xforms:caption` element provides a label for containing XForms form control. Typically, the `xforms:caption` element will contain the text that constitutes the caption. But, it can optionally take an `xlink:href` attribute to reference an external definition of the caption or one of the binding attributes to reference a caption definition in instance data.

Optionally, a form control can have `xforms:help` or `xforms:hint` child elements. Each of these elements provides information intended to be helpful to the user.

Optionally, a form control can have a nested `xforms:alert` element to express some warning or error message related to the form control. As with other common child elements, the message can be the text content of the `xforms:alert` element—referenced from within the same document using a `ref` attribute or referenced from an external document using an `xlink:href` attribute.

A further optional element permitted within form controls is the `xforms:extension` element. The `xforms:extension` element can be used to contain application-specific extension elements. One possible application is as a container for metadata as the following example adapted from the working draft indicates:

```
<xforms:input ref="dataset/user/email" id="email-input">
<xforms:caption>Enter your email address</xforms:caption>
<xforms:extension>
<rdf:RDF xmlns:rdf="http://www.w3.org/1999/02/22-rdf-syntax-ns#">
<rdf:Description about="#email-input">
<my:addressBook>personal</my:addressBook>
</rdf:Description>
</rdf:RDF>
</xforms:extension>
</xforms:input>
```

The chosen metadata format is the W3C's Resource Description Framework. In principle, any other appropriate XML application language could be used in conjunction with the `xforms:extension` element.

XFORMS ACTIONS

XForms form controls do not intrinsically have behavior, but the XForms specification provides mechanisms for developers to define behaviors for XForms form controls by using XForms *Actions*. Event handling in XForms is defined in terms of the XML Events specification at the W3C. The current working draft for XML Events is located at `http://www.w3.org/TR/xml-events`.

XForms form controls can use attributes from the XML Events Namespace on XForms elements. Thus, assuming that the XML Events Namespace URI had been declared in another part of the code and that the namespace prefix `ev` had been declared with the XML Events Namespace URI, a reset button in XForms could be created using code similar to the following:

```
<xforms:button>
<xforms:caption>Reset</xforms:caption>
<xforms:resetInstance ev:event="xforms:activate"/>
</xforms:button>
```

Caution

Because both the XForms and XML Events specifications are subject to change, details describing XForms actions might be particularly subject to change.

In the following parts of this section, we will look briefly at each of the XForms actions.

THE `dispatch` ACTION

The `xforms:dispatch` action dispatches an XForms event to a target element. The `target` attribute of this element identifies the element that will receive the event. The `xforms:dispatch` element will additionally have a `name` attribute whose value contains the name of the event to be dispatched. Other attributes include an optional `bubbles` attribute, whose value indicates whether the event bubbles, and an optional `cancellable` attribute, whose value indicates, whether the event is cancellable. Bubbling and cancellation are defined in the Document Object Model Level 2 Events Specification.

The refresh Action

The `xforms:refresh` action causes the XForms form's display to be refreshed.

The recalculate Action

The `xforms:recalculate` action causes an XForms recalculate event to be dispatched and might be used when the number of items ordered is altered and the calculated cost, determined by the number of items ordered, needs to be recalculated.

The revalidate Action

The `xforms:revalidate` action causes an XForms revalidate event to be dispatched. This might be used when a user-entered value was invalid with respect to the applicable schema. After the user enters a new or amended value, there is a need for that new value to be validated against the schema.

The setFocus Action

The `xforms:setFocus` action sets the focus on a particular form control. This, of course, is useful to the user if the focus is set on the form control that logically is to be filled in first. Avoiding the need for a mouse click is a small, but significant, improvement in usability of a form.

For example, if we wanted the focus to be on an `xforms:input` form control for the entry of the user's first name, we could use code such as this for the form control:

```
<xforms:input id="firstName"/>
```

The `xforms:setFocus` action could be applied as follows:

```
<xforms:setFocus idref="firstName"/>
```

The loadURI Action

The `xforms:loadURI` action causes an XLink to be traversed. XForms supports only simple type XLinks. To open the linked resource in a new browser window (or an equivalent in non-graphical browsers), we could use code such as the following:

```
<xforms:loadURI xlink:href="http://www.xmml.com"
xlink:show="new"/>
```

Equally, if there was a desire to load a resource into the current XForms form, code similar to the following could be used:

```
<xforms:loadURI xlink:href="http://www.xmml.com/someResource.xml"
xlink:show="replace"/>
```

The setValue Action

The `xforms:setValue` action explicitly sets the value of a specified node in the instance data of a form. The `setValue` element has an optional `value` attribute whose value is an XPath expression. If there is no `value` attribute, the content of the `xforms:setValue` element is the value to be applied. If there is no `value` attribute nor any text content in the `xforms:setValue` element, the specified node is allocated the value of the empty string.

To set the value of the node with an `id` attribute value of "validOrNot" to a value of "invalid," we could use the following code:

```
<xforms:setValue bind="validOrNot">
invalid
</xforms:setValue>
```

THE submitInstance ACTION

The `xforms:submitInstance` action can be used to explicitly submit instance data. The `xforms:submitInstance` element can optionally have a `submitInfo` attribute whose value is of type `xsd:IDREF`. This attribute associates the action with an `xforms:submitInfo` element.

THE resetInstance ACTION

The `xforms:resetInstance` action explicitly resets instance data. The `xforms:resetInstance` element has a `model` attribute whose value defines the XForms model whose instance data is to be reset.

For example, if an XForms form contained two `xforms:model` elements with `id` attributes `"first"` and `"second,"` the following code could be used to reset the instance data in the second `xforms:model` element:

```
<xforms:resetInstance model="second"/>
```

THE setRepeatCursor ACTION

The `xforms:setRepeatCursor` action sets as current a particular item in a repeating sequence.

THE insert ACTION

The `xforms:insert` action is used to insert nodes into the instance data.

Usually, `xforms:insert` is used to add a new item into a collection, such as a shopping cart. The collection, a part of the instance data, is identified through the use of *nodeset binding attributes*, which include the `xforms:nodeset`, `xforms:model`, and `xforms:bind` attributes. You learned how to use these attributes earlier when we discussed the `xforms:itemset` element. The value of the `xforms:nodeset` attribute is a *binding expression* that selects the collection to which we want to add. A binding expression is simply a limited XPath expression. The `at` attribute of the `xforms:insert` element is evaluated to determine an index into the node-set, which is used to select a specific node in the node-set. Finally, the `position` attribute defines whether the new node is to be inserted before or after the node defined in the `at` attribute. The `xforms:insert` action is used with code similar to the following:

```
<xforms:insert nodeset="/ShoppingCart/Items/item"
at="item[last()]" position="after"/>
```

In this example, a new item would be inserted into the instance data following the last item element.

THE delete ACTION

The `xforms:delete` action deletes nodes in the instance data. The `xforms:delete` element can have a `nodeset` attribute whose value defines the node-set from which a node will be deleted. Similar to the `xforms:insert` element, this element has an `at` attribute that determines which node within the node-set will be deleted.

Adding or deleting nodes dispatches events so that the user interface and other form elements can adjust to the changes appropriately. For example, an input that is bound to a deleted node will be removed from the user interface.

THE toggle ACTION

The `xforms:toggle` action is used when a user interface is constructed conditionally. The `xforms:toggle` element can have a `case` attribute whose value is of type `xsd:IDREF` and references a case element that forms part of the logic used to create the interface presented to the user. The toggle action causes the state of the form to change by selecting a different case.

THE script ACTION

The `xforms:script` action is used to invoke some scripting code. The `xforms:script` element must take a `type` attribute whose value identifies the mime type of the scripting code.

Thus, if we have some JavaScript code in an XForms form, we could use the `xforms:script` element as follows:

```
<xforms:script type="text/javascript">
<!-- The JavaScript code would go here. -->
</xforms:script>
```

THE message ACTION

The `xforms:message` action can be used to display a message to the user. The `xforms:message` element must have a `level` attribute that can take the values of "ephemeral," "modeless," or "modal." The working draft does not clearly distinguish the precise roles of these values. But, the `ephemeral` level seems to correspond closely to the usage of the `xforms:hint` element, producing a brief message when, in a graphical browser, a form control is moused.

The `xforms:message` action can reference an external message by means of an optional `xlink:href` attribute on the `xforms:message` element.

THE action ACTION

The `xforms:action` action can be used to bind XForms actions to form controls and group them in association with a common event handler.

XFORMS FUNCTIONS

XForms processors support the full function library that is included with XPath 1.0. The XPath function library includes functions to handle XPath's four data types—node-set, number, string, and Boolean. You might want to refer to Chapter 11, "Locating Components in XML Documents with XPath," to refresh your memory on the XPath function library.

BOOLEAN FUNCTIONS

XForms provides two Boolean functions—`boolean-from-string()` and `if()` function.

The `boolean-from-string()` function takes a single string argument. The function returns the Boolean value `true` when the argument is the string literal "true" and `false` if the argument is "false." If, when using a comparison that isn't case sensitive, the string matches neither "true" nor "false," an error occurs, causing processing to stop. You might find the `boolean-from-string()` function useful when referencing an `xsd:boolean` data type in an XPath expression. The need for the function arises from the use of both XPath 1.0 and W3C XML Schema data types within XForms.

The `if()` function takes three arguments—a Boolean and two string values. The first argument must evaluate to a Boolean value. If the first argument evaluates to `true`, the first of the two string arguments is returned: Otherwise, the second of the two string arguments is returned.

Thus, the `if()` function might resemble this:

```
if (5>4, "This is correct," "This is misleading")
```

Note that the arguments are separated by commas.

NUMBER FUNCTIONS

XForms provides five number functions—`avg()`, `min()`, `max()`, `count-non-empty()`, and `cursor()`—to augment the number functions provided by XPath.

The `avg()` function takes a single argument, which is a node-set. The function returns the arithmetic average of the values in each node in the node-set. The string value of each node is converted to a number. The numeric values are summed and divided by the number of nodes in the node-set.

The `min()` function takes a single argument, which is a node-set. The function returns the numeric value that is the lowest value found in the node-set after converting the string value of each node to a numeric value.

The `max()` function takes a single argument, which is a node-set. The function returns the numeric value that is the highest value found in the node-set after converting the string value of each node to a numeric value.

The `count-non-empty()`function takes a single argument, which is a node-set. The function returns a numeric value equal to the number of nodes in the argument node-set that have a string value of greater than zero.

The `cursor()` function takes a string, which is the value of an `idref` attribute of an `xforms:repeat` element (see later) and returns the position of the `xforms:repeat` cursor.

STRING FUNCTIONS

XForms provides two string functions—`property()` and `now()`.

The `property()` function takes a single string argument. The argument string can take the values of either "version" or "conformance-level." The `property()` function returns a value corresponding to the property used in the string argument. For XForms version 1, the function

```
property(version)
```

returns the string "1.0."

The `now()` function takes no argument and returns the current system date and time (including any available time zone information).

THE XFORMS USER INTERFACE

XForms can be used on a variety of platforms. Whatever the interface used, the data model that underlies it remains the same for any XForms form.

Because XForms forms can be displayed on graphical user devices from a desktop PC to a palmtop and possibly a mobile phone, the way in which the user interface is constructed can be particularly relevant on some platforms.

GROUPING FORM CONTROLS

The XForms form controls that were described earlier in the chapter can be treated as separate units. However, often there will be a logical relationship among a number of form controls within an XForms form. For example, if we are collecting address information, we are likely to want to treat instance data nodes that might be named `Street1`, `Street2`, `City`, and `PostalCode` as inherently related. Consequently, we will also likely want to keep the corresponding form controls in some relationship with each other. We can group related form controls using the `xforms:group` element.

If the address information just mentioned were part of a shipping address, we could nest the relevant form controls within an `xforms:group` element as in the following code:

```
<xforms:group>
<xforms:input ref="ShippingAddress/Street1">
<xforms:caption>First line of street address.</xforms:caption>
</xforms:input>
<xforms:input ref="ShippingAddress/Street2">
<xforms:caption>Second line of street address.</xforms:caption>
<xforms:hint>Include the name of a village or small town here.</xforms:hint>
</xforms:input>
<xforms:input ref="ShippingAddress/City">
<xforms:caption>Enter the city name here.</xforms:caption>
<xforms:hint>If the address is not in a city enter the
name of the nearest city which the postal authorities
```

```
use to reference the address.</xforms:hint>
</xforms:input>
<xforms:input ref="ShippingAddress/PostalCode">
<xforms:caption>Postal Code</xforms:caption>
<xforms:hint>For United States addressses use the
extended form of the Zip Code, if known.</xforms:hint>
</xforms:input>
</xforms:group>
```

By grouping XForms elements in this way, we signal to the XForms processor that there is a semantic relationship among this group of form controls. If focus is set on the group, it will, by default, set focus on the `first` form control in tabbing order. Tabbing order will correspond to the document order of the XForms form control elements within the group.

Conditional Construction of User Interfaces

XForms is flexible when creating a user interface. The precise format of a user interface can be related to some value within the instance data.

For example, if we expected a user to enter his name into a form, we could adjust the display according to whether the user had entered his name. After a name had been entered, we could change the appearance of the form to greet the user by name. The following code illustrates how this could be done using the `xforms:switch` element, assuming that the document used XForms in conjunction with Scalable Vector Graphics elements, which are represented in the code by the namespace prefix `svg`.

```
<xforms:switch id="NameDisplay">
<xforms:case id="default">
<xforms:input ref="Name/FirstName">
<xforms:caption>Please enter your name</xforms:caption>
</xforms:input>
</xforms:case>
<xforms:case id="nameKnown">
<svg:text x="20" y="40" class="NormalText">Hello
<xforms:output ref="Name/FirstName"/>.
</svg:text>
</xforms:case>
</xforms:switch>
```

The `xforms:toggle` action could be used to affect the `xforms:switch` construct. The `xforms:toggle` action might be activated when the user shifts focus away from the `xforms:input` form control where the first name would be entered.

Repeating Structures in XForms Forms

Forms commonly use repeating structures. For example, in a purchase order, there are places to enter many items. The need for repeating structure is obvious. Equally, we would not typically want to restrict a user as to how many items he can enter. So, we need a way to express a repeating structure that can grow as needed in response to user actions.

We can use the `xforms:repeat` element to create the basic structure of a repeating structure. Assuming that an XForms form was contained in an XHTML document and we wanted each of a set of repeating `xforms:input` form controls to be separated by a new line, we could use code such as the following:

```
<xforms:repeat nodeset="/order/items/item">
<input ref=."" .../><html:br/>
</xforms:repeat>
```

However, if we want the number of available `xforms:input` elements to grow, we need to provide a mechanism to create new `xforms:input` form controls when they are needed.

We could have an XForms model defined as follows:

```
<xforms:model>
<xforms:instance>
<my:lines>
<my:line name="Widget">
<my:price>3.00</my:price>
</my:line>
<my:line name="Hoodja">
<my:price>32.25</my:price>
</my:line>
<my:line name="SomethingElse">
<my:price>132.99</my:price>
</my:line>
</my:lines>
</xforms:instance>
</xforms:model>
```

Elsewhere in the form, we would create a construct that would create a new `xforms:input` form control in response to the user clicking on a button.

```
<xforms:repeat id="lineset" nodeset="my:lines/my:line">
<xforms:input ref="my:price">
<xforms:caption>Line Item Price</xforms:caption>
</xforms:input>
<xforms:input ref="@name">
<xforms:caption>Name of line item</xforms:caption>
</xforms:input>
</xforms:repeat>
<xforms:button>
<xforms:caption>
 Insert a new item after the current one
</xforms:caption>
<xforms:action ev:event="ev:activate">
<xforms:insert nodeset="my:lines/my:line"
 at="cursor('lineset')" position="after"/>
<xforms:setValue ref="my:lines/my:line[cursor('lineset')]/@name">
 New Item
</xforms:setValue>
<xforms:setValue ref="my:lines/my:line[cursor('lineset')]/my:price">
 0.00
</xforms:setValue>
</xforms:action>
</xforms:button>
```

The `xforms:repeat` element ensures that all line items in the XForms model are displayed. The `xforms:button` element is linked to an `xforms:insert` action, which causes a node to be added to the instance data and `xforms:setValue` actions.

Depending on the capabilities of a user agent, only part of a collection of line items might be presented at any one time. Thus the line items might be presented as a scrollable table whose size might depend on detecting the capabilities of the user agent being used to display the form.

ANOTHER XFORMS EXAMPLE

As you will probably have appreciated from the descriptions of the components of XForms throughout this chapter, XForms is a substantial and potentially complex XML application language. Additionally, many new concepts have been introduced. This section shows some of the functionality of a fairly long piece of working XForms code.

Caution

Because the code shown relates to a namespace that was available to the XForms Working Group editors, note that the namespace URI is not one you should use in your own code. Likely, the XForms Working Group will define a new namespace URI in association with a final version of the XForms specification.

The following code is used with the permission of Mikko Honkala and demonstrates some of the XForms functionality implemented at the time that the December 2001 XForms Working Draft became available.

At first sight, the length of the code might be fairly intimidating. Keep your eyes open for `fo:foreign-object` elements because the XForms code will be nested within those.

Listing 25.3 shows the XSL-FO document with embedded XForms functionality.

LISTING 25.3 AN XSL-FO PURCHASE FORM USING XFORMS TO CREATE AN INTERFACE THAT RESPONDS TO USER CHOICES

```
<?xml version="1.0" encoding="UTF-8"?>
<!-- basic FO page definition stuff -->
<fo:root font-family="Times Roman" font-size="12pt" text-align="justify"
xmlns:fo="http://www.w3.org/1999/XSL/Format"
xmlns:xforms="http://www.w3.org/2001/11/xforms-editors-copy">
 <fo:layout-master-set>
  <fo:simple-page-master master-name="right" page-height="{/*/@height}"
margin-top="5pt" margin-bottom="5pt" margin-left="50pt" margin-right="50pt"
page-width="900pt">
   <fo:region-body margin-bottom="50pt"/>
   <fo:region-after extent="25pt"/>
  </fo:simple-page-master>
  <fo:page-sequence-master master-name="psmOddEven">
   <fo:repeatable-page-master-alternatives>
    <fo:conditional-page-master-reference master-name="right"
page-position="first"/>
   </fo:repeatable-page-master-alternatives>
  </fo:page-sequence-master>
 </fo:layout-master-set>
```

LISTING 25.3 CONTINUED

```
<fo:page-sequence id="N2528" master-name="psmOddEven">
 <fo:static-content flow-name="xsl-region-after">
  <fo:block text-align-last="center" font-size="10pt">
   <fo:page-number/>
  </fo:block>
 </fo:static-content>
 <fo:flow flow-name="xsl-region-body">
  <!-- XForms prolog, copy from xml file -->
  <fo:instream-foreign-object>
   <xforms:model>
    <xforms:submitInfo id="submit1" method2="postxml" localfile="temp2.xml"
target2="http://www.hut.fi/"/>
    <xforms:schema/>
    <xforms:instance href="purchaseOrder.xml"/>
    <xforms:bind ref="purchaseOrder/items/item/units" isValid=." &gt; 0"
readOnly=." &gt; 19"/>
    <xforms:bind ref="purchaseOrder/totals/subtotal"
calculate="sum(../../items/item/total)"/>
    <xforms:bind ref="purchaseOrder/totals/tax" calculate="round(../subtotal *
../../info/tax)"/>
    <xforms:bind ref="purchaseOrder/totals/total" calculate=."./subtotal +
../tax"/>
    <xforms:bind ref="purchaseOrder/totals/rowcount"
calculate="count(/purchaseOrder/items/item)"/>
    <xforms:bind ref="purchaseOrder/items/item/total" calculate=."./units *
../price - ((../units * ../price)>1000)*(../units * ../price * 0.1)"
relevant=."./units &gt; 0"/>
    <xforms:bind ref="purchaseOrder/payment/as"
relevant="/purchaseOrder/totals/rowcount &gt; 0"/>
    <xforms:bind ref="purchaseOrder/payment/cc" relevant=."./as='credit'"/>
    <xforms:bind ref="purchaseOrder/payment/exp" relevant=."./as='credit'"/>
   </xforms:model>
  </fo:instream-foreign-object>
  <fo:block font-size="24pt" background-color="blue" color="white"
font-weight="bold">
  XForms constraints and repeating structures.
  </fo:block>
  <fo:block font-size="15pt" space-before="15pt">This example demonstrates the
use of XForms constraints, such as calculate, isValid and readonly. Try moving
the sliders to zero or full. The line items are created using XForms 'repeat'
construct.
  </fo:block>
  <fo:table space-before="10mm">
   <fo:table-column column-width="60mm"/>
   <fo:table-column column-width="60mm"/>
   <fo:table-column column-width="100mm"/>
   <fo:table-body>
    <!-- TABLE HEADER -->
    <fo:table-row space-before="5pt" font-weight="bold">
     <fo:table-cell>
      <!-- SUBTOTAL -->
      <fo:block>
       <fo:instream-foreign-object>
        <xforms:output ref="purchaseOrder/totals/subtotal" cols="8"
style="font-weight:bold;width:80px">
         <xforms:caption style="font-weight:bold;">Subtotal</xforms:caption>
         <xforms:hint>Subtotal</xforms:hint>
```

LISTING 25.3 CONTINUED

```
        </xforms:output>
       </fo:instream-foreign-object>
      </fo:block>
     </fo:table-cell>
     <fo:table-cell>
      <!-- PURCHASE ORDER TOTALS-->
      <fo:block>
       <fo:instream-foreign-object>
        <xforms:output ref="purchaseOrder/totals/tax"
cols="18" style="font-weight:bold;width:80px">
         <xforms:caption style="font-weight:bold;">Tax</xforms:caption>
         <xforms:hint>Tax</xforms:hint>
        </xforms:output>
       </fo:instream-foreign-object>
      </fo:block>
     </fo:table-cell>
     <fo:table-cell>
      <!-- PURCHASE ORDER TOTALS-->
      <fo:block>
       <fo:instream-foreign-object>
        <xforms:output ref="purchaseOrder/totals/total"
cols="10" style="font-weight:bold;color:red;font-size:18px;width:180px">
         <xforms:caption style="font-weight:bold;">Total</xforms:caption>
         <xforms:hint>Total</xforms:hint>
        </xforms:output>
       </fo:instream-foreign-object>
      </fo:block>
     </fo:table-cell>
    </fo:table-row>
    <fo:table-row>
     <fo:table-cell>
      <fo:block>
       <!-- INSERT BUTTON -->
       <fo:instream-foreign-object>
        <xforms:button id="insertbutton">
         <xforms:caption>Insert</xforms:caption>
         <xforms:action>
          <xforms:insert repeat="repeat1"/>
         </xforms:action>
        </xforms:button>
       </fo:instream-foreign-object>
      </fo:block>
     </fo:table-cell>
     <fo:table-cell>
      <fo:block>
       <!-- DELETE BUTTON -->
       <fo:instream-foreign-object>
        <xforms:button id="delete">
        <xforms:caption>Delete</xforms:caption>
         <xforms:action>
          <xforms:delete repeat="repeat1"/>
         </xforms:action>
        </xforms:button>
       </fo:instream-foreign-object>
      </fo:block>
     </fo:table-cell>
```

LISTING 25.3 CONTINUED

```
      <fo:table-cell>
       <fo:block>
        <fo:instream-foreign-object>
         <xforms:output ref="/purchaseOrder/totals/rowcount">
          <xforms:caption>Item count:</xforms:caption>
         </xforms:output>
        </fo:instream-foreign-object>
       </fo:block>
      </fo:table-cell>
     </fo:table-row>
    </fo:table-body>
   </fo:table>
   <!-- TABLE -->
   <fo:table space-before="10mm">
    <fo:table-column column-width="90mm"/>
    <fo:table-column column-width="80mm"/>
    <fo:table-column column-width="20mm"/>
    <fo:table-column column-width="40mm"/>
    <fo:table-body>
     <!-- TABLE HEADER -->
     <fo:table-row space-before="5pt" font-weight="bold">
      <fo:table-cell>
       <fo:block>Units</fo:block>
      </fo:table-cell>
      <fo:table-cell>
       <fo:block>Name</fo:block>
      </fo:table-cell>
      <fo:table-cell>
       <fo:block>Price</fo:block>
      </fo:table-cell>
      <fo:table-cell>
       <fo:block>Total</fo:block>
      </fo:table-cell>
     </fo:table-row>
     <!-- TABLE ROW USING REPEAT-->
     <xforms:repeat ref="purchaseOrder/items/item"
id="repeat1" x-number="4" x-startIndex="1">
      <!-- REPEAT START -->
      <fo:table-row space-before="5pt">
       <fo:table-cell>
        <fo:instream-foreign-object>
         <xforms:range start="0" end="20" stepsize="1" ref="units">
          <xforms:hint>The units of this item</xforms:hint>
         </xforms:range>
        </fo:instream-foreign-object>
       </fo:table-cell>
       <fo:table-cell>
        <fo:instream-foreign-object>
         <xforms:input ref="name" style="width:150px">
          <!--<xforms:caption style="caption-side:left"></xforms:caption>-->
          <xforms:hint>The name of this item</xforms:hint>
         </xforms:input>
        </fo:instream-foreign-object>
       </fo:table-cell>
       <fo:table-cell>
        <fo:instream-foreign-object>
         <xforms:input cols="3" ref="price" style="width:40px">
```

25

Listing 25.3 Continued

```
          <xforms:hint>The price of this item</xforms:hint>
         </xforms:input>
        </fo:instream-foreign-object>
       </fo:table-cell>
       <fo:table-cell>
        <fo:instream-foreign-object>
         <xforms:output cols="6" ref="total" style="width:40px">
          <xforms:hint>The total value of this item</xforms:hint>
         </xforms:output>
        </fo:instream-foreign-object>
       </fo:table-cell>
      </fo:table-row>
     </xforms:repeat>
     <!-- REPEAT END -->
    </fo:table-body>
   </fo:table>
   <!-- Payment method -->
   <fo:table space-before="10mm">
    <fo:table-column column-width="60mm"/>
    <fo:table-column column-width="65mm"/>
    <fo:table-column column-width="80mm"/>
    <fo:table-body>
     <!-- TABLE HEADER -->
     <fo:table-row space-before="5pt" font-weight="bold">
      <fo:table-cell>
       <fo:block>
        <fo:instream-foreign-object>
         <xforms:selectOne ref="purchaseOrder/payment/as"
 style="list-ui:checkbox">
          <xforms:caption style="font-weight:bold;">
Select payment method</xforms:caption>
          <xforms:item value="credit">Credit card</xforms:item>
          <xforms:item value="cash">Cash</xforms:item>
         </xforms:selectOne>
        </fo:instream-foreign-object>
       </fo:block>
      </fo:table-cell>
      <fo:table-cell>
       <fo:block space-before="0mm">
        <fo:instream-foreign-object>
         <xforms:input ref="purchaseOrder/payment/cc" style="width:130px">
          <xforms:caption style="font-weight:bold;">
Credit card number</xforms:caption>
         </xforms:input>
        </fo:instream-foreign-object>
       </fo:block>
      </fo:table-cell>
      <fo:table-cell>
       <fo:block space-after="5mm">
        <fo:instream-foreign-object>
         <xforms:input ref="purchaseOrder/payment/exp" style="width:80px">
          <xforms:caption style="font-weight:bold;">
Expiration date</xforms:caption>
         </xforms:input>
        </fo:instream-foreign-object>
       </fo:block>
      </fo:table-cell>
```

LISTING 25.3 CONTINUED

```
      </fo:table-row>
     </fo:table-body>
    </fo:table>
    <!-- SUBMIT BUTTON -->
    <fo:instream-foreign-object>
     <xforms:submit name="Submit" ref="test" to="submit1"
  style="font-family: Arial; font-size: 20px; font-style: bold; color: red">
      <xforms:hint>Click to submit</xforms:hint>
      <xforms:caption>Buy!</xforms:caption>
     </xforms:submit>
    </fo:instream-foreign-object>
   </fo:flow>
  </fo:page-sequence>
</fo:root>
```

The appearance of the form when first loaded is shown in Figure 25.2.

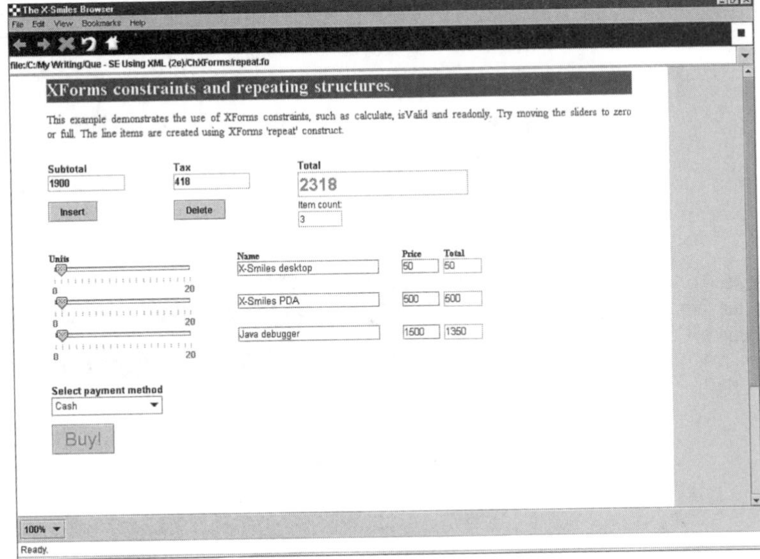

Figure 25.2
The purchase form when first loaded in the X-Smiles browser.

Notice that even before we start entering any data, default values have been provided in several XForms form controls. For example, each of the slide controls has been set to a default value of `1`. The name and price for the three available items is loaded from an associated file by means of the `ref` attribute on the `xforms:instance` element nested within the `xforms:model` element.

When we mouse a form control, a ToolTip is displayed as shown in Figure 25.3.

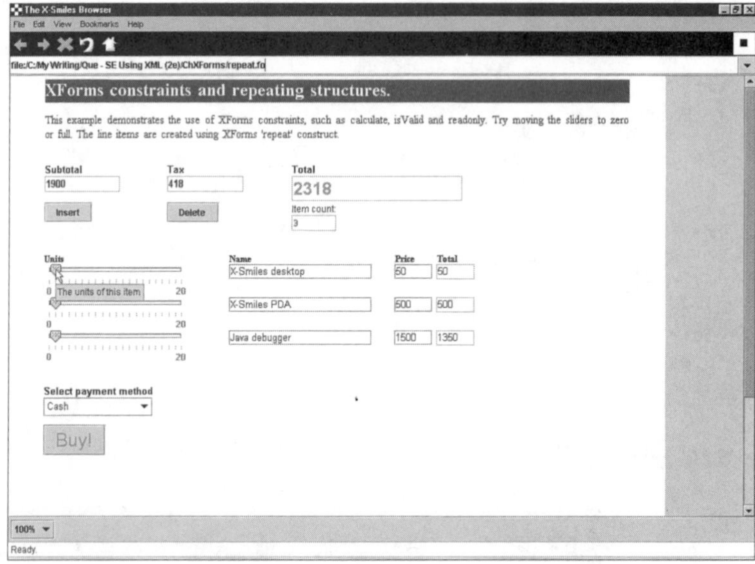

Figure 25.3
The `xforms:hint` element provides ToolTips when form controls are moused.

Once we have selected a form control by clicking on it, its background color changes to yellow in this example. Also if we move the slide control, the value of the order for that item automatically adjusts. That adjusted value is reflected in an updated total value for the order as you can see in Figure 25.4.

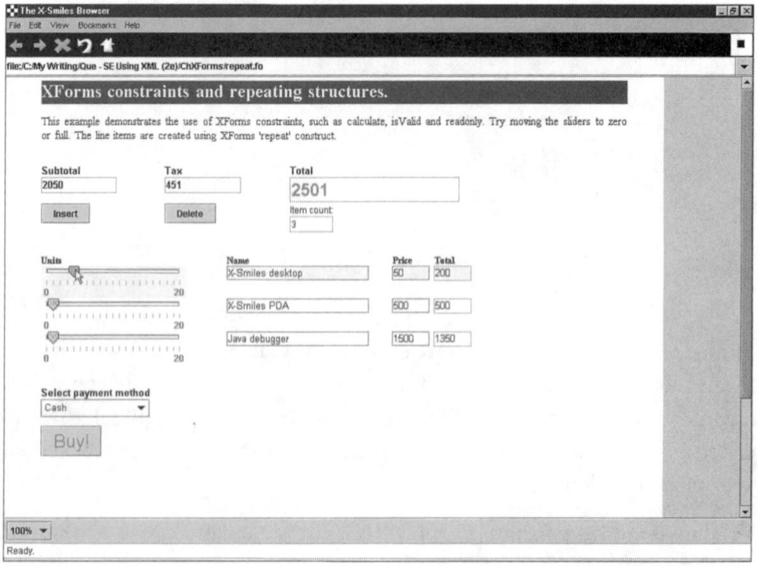

Figure 25.4
Values in the form are automatically updated to reflect the value entered by means of a slide control.

Notice, too, that the ToolTip disappears if the cursor is held over a form control for a lengthy period of time.

If we select to pay by credit card, additional information is needed—the credit card number and the expiration date. This becomes relevant when the credit card option is chosen and is then displayed for user input. Figure 25.5 shows that.

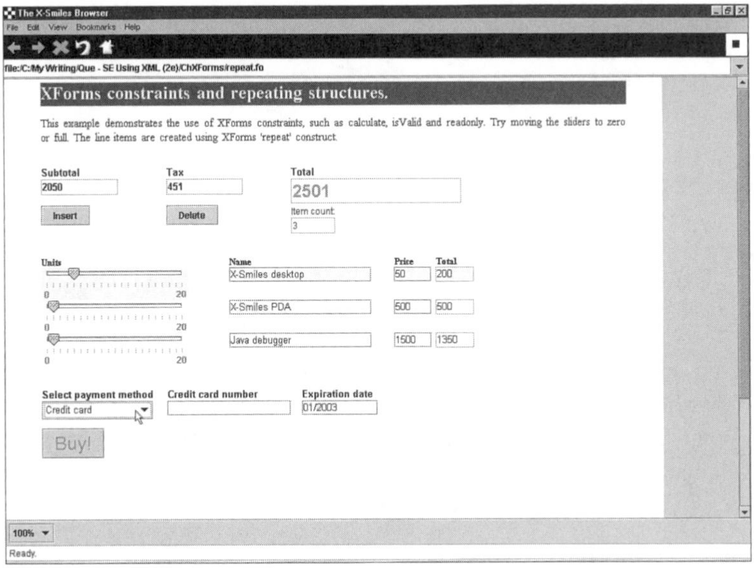

Figure 25.5
Form controls can be selectively displayed only when they are relevant.

Listing 25.4 shows the PurchaseOrder.xml file, which supplies the default instance data.

LISTING 25.4 DEFAULT INSTANCE DATA FOR LISTING 25.3 (PURCHASEORDER.XML)

```
<?xml version="1.0" encoding="ISO-8859-1"?>
<!-- edited with XML Spy v4.0 beta 2 build Jul 26 2001 (http://www.xmlspy.com)
by Mikko Honkala (W3C XForms Working Group) -->
<purchaseOrder xmlns="">
    <items>
        <item>
            <name>X-Smiles desktop</name>
            <units>1</units>
            <price>50</price>
            <total>0</total>
        </item>
        <item>
            <name>X-Smiles PDA</name>
            <units>1</units>
            <price>500</price>
            <total>0</total>
        </item>
        <item>
            <name>Java debugger</name>
            <units>1</units>
```

LISTING 25.4 CONTINUED

```
            <price>1500</price>
            <total>0</total>
        </item>
    </items>
    <totals>
        <subtotal>0</subtotal>
        <tax>0</tax>
        <total>0</total>
        <rowcount>0</rowcount>
    </totals>
    <info>
        <tax>0.22</tax>
    </info>
    <payment>
        <as>cash</as>
        <cc/>
        <exp>01/2003</exp>
    </payment>
</purchaseOrder>
```

In this example, we have seen a snapshot in the development of the XForms technology at a time when the detail of code, and therefore of implementations, have been undergoing rapid change. By the time you read this, XForms will likely have changed at least a little; but you will hopefully have understood the principles on which it is based and will be able to adapt code to any subsequent detailed changes.

Future version of X-Smiles will implement XForms in XHTML. Other tools, likely to include those from Cardiff.com and Mozquito.com, will also implement XForms in XHTML and in other XML-based application languages such as SVG. In addition, there is significant XForms functionality being built into the Mozilla browser. This chapter gives you only a glimpse into a technology that will play an important part in an interactive XML-based Web which will be part of our future.

ADDITIONAL RESOURCES

The primary source of information about emerging XForms implementations and other news is shown here:

- The XForms 1.0 specification at the W3C. The latest version of the XForms 1.0 specification will be located at `http://www.w3.org/tr/xforms`.
- Information about XForms implementations is updated on an ongoing basis at `http://www.w3.org/MarkUp/Forms/`.
- An archive of discussion about the XForms specification is located at `http://lists.w3.org/Archives/Public/www-forms/`.
- Information about an XForms mailing list and how to subscribe to it is located at `http://www.yahoogroups.com/group/XForms`.

ROADMAP

Chapter 26, "Future Directions and Technologies," will introduce you to several other emerging XML-based technologies.

CHAPTER 26

Future Directions and Technologies

In this chapter

by Earl Bingham

XML has come a long way and is still growing in many directions. Currently, a number of major vendors are building enterprise-computing frameworks that use Supply Chain, Enterprise Computing, and Web Service solutions. These areas are still evolving and maturing with technology and business models to accompany their growth. Also, many standards are being introduced and ratified that will make the Internet a more complex and interactive medium to work with. This chapter discusses these issues as well as a few of the major technologies in this area relating to Web Services—ebXML and BizTalk.

WEB SERVICES—INTRODUCTION

As Internet technology and development tools mature so that products for the Internet are easily built, companies must either partner or perish in today's global economy. This concept has been often referred to as "collaborative enterprise." One technology that will help make integration much less difficult is Web Services. This technology is still maturing and evolving, with some companies stating that Web Services will "make integration as easy as plugging an appliance into the electrical grid."[1] Companies that do not support these new industry standards will be isolated from Web Services and will not be fully interoperable.

Here we define a *service* as a value-added task provided by a person or company so that you don't have to do it yourself. A Web Service is a value-added task that is provided to you over the Internet, freeing you up from having to manually build or execute the task.

Many Web sites and portals provide a suite of services to customers that have taken a long time to develop. And as the number of services and amount of information grows, the work to integrate all these services isn't cost effective. Many companies have attempted to build proprietary communication systems that allow services to be exchanged, but these are often too complex and expensive to be adopted by the general community. In addition, problems arise because of the structure of security systems on the Internet. Many systems have difficulty transferring data across firewalls, which are designed to stop unauthorized traffic.

The large software corporations are developing solutions to solve these problems. Currently, IBM, BEA, Microsoft, and Sun are stating that Web Services, and the provider chosen, will dictate how companies do business. This is a large statement to make about Web Services.

WHAT ARE WEB SERVICES AND HOW WILL THEY BENEFIT THE INTERNET MARKET?

A Web Service relies on the popularity of the HTTP protocol, the standard protocol for Internet communication. Web Services also use XML to send commands and move data to and from objects residing on one server. The applications that use the data and send the commands can be written in any language, for any computer architecture, and they can be simple or complex. All the applications need to know is the Web Service's location.

Web Services are the next level of computing. Developers can assemble a group of Web Services from completely different locations and use them in their own applications. Collectively, these features provide the potential to have completely different platforms communicate effectively. A Web Service thus provides an infrastructure to have disparate systems around the world be tied together.

The normal example used to describe Web Services demonstrates how other Internet applications can use Web Services. For example, an e-commerce site calculates shipping charges for customers ordering products on its Web site. This site would normally have to maintain an up-to-date table for calculating shipping costs based on the shipper, the shipping location, the priority, and so on. With Web Services, the site can place a "call" to the shipping company directly, using an XML command, and it receives the quotes instantly. Thus, the e-commerce Web site can dynamically use various Web Services based on shipping companies, providing a service that could allow for shipping companies to be removed or added dynamically.

A Web Service is defined as an endpoint for communication that uses standard high-level Internet communication protocols like Hypertext Transfer Protocol (HTTP) or Simple Mail Transfer Protocol (SMTP). The Web Service transfers data using XML messages, describing its message types using a portable type of system that is both language and platform neutral. And finally, a Web Service also provides a way to access metadata describing the messages.

The XML messaging that takes place to facilitate this is associated with some specific XML standards. These standards are still changing and being enhanced. The first standard is SOAP (Simple Object Access Protocol) messaging—these XML messages provide the communication mechanism used to invoke Remote Procedure Calls (RPC) operations. The second standard is XML Schema (XSD), which is a mechanism for defining the contracts between Web Services and their corresponding clients. The third is Web Service Description Language (WSDL) that models the characteristics of Web Services, making information services available over the Web in a transport-independent fashion. WSDL is an XML format for describing network services as a set of endpoints operating on messages containing either document-oriented or procedure-oriented information. The fourth is Universal Description, Discovery, and Integration (UDDI). This standard is a project to help create a platform-independent, open framework for describing services, discovering businesses, and integrating business services using the Internet, as well as an operational registry that is available today. The UDDI Project operates a global public registry called the UDDI Business Registry.

Each of these XML standards for Web Service communication can be further described, taking up a whole book for each standard. This section simply dives in to a few specific examples, using software from industry leading software vendors.

With Web Services, a number of XML standards are being proposed or are commonly used. These Web Service standards are broken up into various groups. These groups include XML-based messaging, service description, service discovery, service publication, and service integration or service workflow. Other standards are being used across the Web Service stack for transaction management, quality of service, and security. I will discuss briefly the most common Web Service standards for XML-based messaging, service description, and service discovery and publication.

The most common XML-based messaging standard is SOAP. SOAP is considered a *wire* protocol for remote procedure calling communication. It has many benefits over previous wire protocols that were used for network enabled applications. SOAP messaging provides a framework for how business applications can communicate over the Internet. Please view the SOAP technical specification at `http://www.w3.org/TR/SOAP/` for more information.

SOAP defines a messaging framework, encoding rules, and a binding to a specific network protocol, such as the HTTP protocol. Yet with SOAP messaging, other protocols could be used, such as SMTP. It is up to the developer to choose which protocol binding he wants his SOAP communication to use.

SOAP is defined in essentially four XML elements:

`env:Envelope`—It is the root of the SOAP request. At the minimum, it defines a SOAP namespace.

`env:Header`—It contains auxiliary information. Examples include information on authentication or a transaction identifier.

`env:Body`—It contains the main information of the SOAP document.

`env:Fault`—It is a special block that indicates protocol-level errors.

Here is an example of a SOAP request

```
POST /soap/servlet/rpcrouter HTTP/1.0
Host: frodo.righton.com
Content-Type: text/xml; charset=utf-8
Content-Length: 551
SOAPAction: "http://www.righton.com/2002/soapaction"

<?xml version='1.0' encoding='UTF-8'?>
<SOAP-ENV:Envelope xmlns:xsd="http://www.w3.org/2001/XMLSchema"
xmlns:SOAP-ENV="http://schemas.xmlsoap.org/soap/envelope/"
xmlns:xsi="http://www.w3.org/2001/XMLSchema-instance">
<SOAP-ENV:Body>
<ns1:getFreeResourcesOn xmlns:ns1="http://www.righton.com/2002/resourceful"
SOAP-ENV:encodingStyle="http://schemas.xmlsoap.org/soap/encoding/">
<start xsi:type="xsd:timeInstant">2002-04-01T00:00:00Z</start>
<end xsi:type="xsd:timeInstant">2002-04-01T00:00:00Z</end>
</ns1:getFreeResourcesOn>
</SOAP-ENV:Body>
</SOAP-ENV:Envelope>
```

Here is an example of a SOAP response:

```
HTTP/1.0 200 OK
Content-Type: text/xml; charset=utf-8
Content-Length: 682

<?xml version='1.0' encoding='UTF-8'?>
<env:Envelope xmlns:xsd="http://www.w3.org/2001/XMLSchema"
     xmlns:env="http://schemas.xmlsoap.org/soap/envelope/"
     xmlns:xsi="http://www.w3.org/2001/XMLSchema-instance">
<env:Body>
<ns1:getFreeResourcesOnResponse
     xmlns:ns1="http://www.righton.com/2002/resourceful"
     env:encodingStyle="http://schemas.xmlsoap.org/soap/encoding/">
<return xmlns:ns2="http://schemas.xmlsoap.org/soap/encoding/"
        xsi:type="ns2:Array" ns2:arrayType="ns1:String[2]">
<item xsi:type="xsd:string">John Smith</item>
<item xsi:type="xsd:string">Jane Doe</item>
</return>
```

```
</ns1:getFreeResourcesOnResponse>
</env:Body>
</env:Envelope>
```

SOAP is similar to other protocols such as the IIOP for CORBA, ORPC for DCOM, or Java Remote Method Protocol (JRMP) for Java Remote Method Invocation (RMI). With SOAP, you have a number of benefits over these previous wire protocols, namely the ability to have SOAP messages run through firewalls. SOAP is also easier to debug because the messages are in text format versus binary format. SOAP is vendor agnostic so that you can have Java and Microsoft applications communicate with each other.

UDDI provides a database of businesses searchable by the type of business. A typical search uses a business taxonomy such as the North American Industry Classification System (NAICS) or the Standard Industrial Classification (SIC). Searching can also be by business name or geographical location. UDDI is an industry effort started in September 2000 by Ariba, IBM, Microsoft, and 33 other companies. Today, UDDI has more than 200 community members. Microsoft and other companies have UDDI SDKs that can be used to publish the Web Services your company provides. To learn more information about UDDI and Microsoft's implementation, check out the Microsoft UDDI SDK `http://www.microsoft.com/downloads/release.asp?ReleaseID=24822` and Microsoft's test UDDI node `http://test.uddi.microsoft.com/register.asp`.

When you do a search, you could search on a specific type of business. For example, with NAICS you could do a search on category NAICS code 3341, which corresponds to computer manufacturers. This search would return a list of companies that are registered with UDDI.

Each business registered with UDDI lists all its services and gives each of these services a type. This service type has a unique identifier and comes from a pool of well-known service types that are registered with UDDI. These service types are called *tModels* in UDDI speak. Each tModel has a name, description, and a unique identifier. This unique identifier is a UUID and is called the `tModelKey`. The primary advantage of UDDI is having a pool of well-known service types. UDDI makes it possible to find out how to do electronic business with a company.

26

Here is an example of a UDDI Binding Template:

```
<bindingTemplate serviceKey="SK12345">
  <description xml:lang="en">My Home Page</description>
  <!-- URL of the MyCo home page is in the accessPoint -->
  <accessPoint URLType="http">http://www.myco.example/index.html</accessPoint>
  <tModelInstanceDetails>
    <tModelInstanceInfo tModelKey="UUID:4A4567-1F68-4B23-8CB7-8BAA1234589"/>
  </tModelInstanceDetails>
</bindingTemplate>
```

This is a typical `bindingTemplate` that contains a tModel home page. The design goal for the tModel home page is to standardize a discovery mechanism of home pages within UDDI. Inquiries can be performed to find business home pages.

A UDDI registry contains categorized information about businesses and the services that they offer, and it associates those services with technical specifications of the Web Service. These technical specifications are usually defined using WSDL. WSDL describes what a Web Service does, how it communicates, and where it lives. A Web Service consumer queries the UDDI registry to find the WSDL descriptions to determine how to use the Web Service. The UDDI Web site, `http://www.uddi.org`, contains additional information about this useful and interesting service.

The third Web Service standard is WSDL. WSDL is used to define Web Services and describe how to access them, normally by a server. This XML format can be used to create a file that identifies the services provided by the server and the set of operations within each service that the server supports. For each of the operations, the WSDL file also describes the format that the client must follow in requesting an operation. Refer to the Web site on WSDL for more information: `http://xml.coverpages.org/wsdl.html`.

A WSDL file is required to set up both the server and the client. These files are the contracts between the two. The server agrees to provide certain services only if the client sends a properly formatted SOAP request.

To illustrate, suppose that a WSDL file defines a service called `GetAddressService`. This service describes operations such as `GetLastAddressAdded` and `GetAddressOfName`. You place this file on the server. A client who wants to send a SOAP request to the server first obtains a copy of this WSDL file from the server. The client then uses the information in this file to format a SOAP request. The client sends this request to the server. The server executes the requested operation and sends the resulting address back to the client as a SOAP response.

Here is an example WSDL document from a Web Service example for the GLUE Web Service framework:

```
<?xml version='1.0' encoding='UTF-8'?>
<!--generated by GLUE on Mon Jan 14 12:20:39 PST 2002-->
<definitions name='myexamples.Example'
targetNamespace='http://www.themindelectric.com/wsdl/myexamples.Example/'
xmlns:tns='http://www.themindelectric.com/wsdl/myexamples.Example/'
xmlns:electric='http://www.themindelectric.com/'
➥xmlns:soap='http://schemas.xmlsoap.org/wsdl/soap/'
➥xmlns:http='http://schemas.xmlsoap.org/wsdl/http/'
➥xmlns:mime='http://schemas.xmlsoap.org/wsdl/mime/'
➥xmlns:xsd='http://www.w3.org/2001/XMLSchema'
➥xmlns:soapenc='http://schemas.xmlsoap.org/soap/encoding/'
➥xmlns:wsdl='http://schemas.xmlsoap.org/wsdl/'
➥xmlns='http://schemas.xmlsoap.org/wsdl/'>
  <message name='getTitle0SoapIn'/>
  <message name='getTitle0SoapOut'>
    <part name='Result' type='xsd:string'/>
  </message>
  <message name='setTitle1SoapIn'>
    <part name='arg0' type='xsd:string'/>
  </message>
```

```
 <message name='setTitle1SoapOut'/>
 <portType name='myexamples.ExampleSoap'>
   <operation name='getTitle' parameterOrder=''>
     <input name='getTitle0SoapIn' message='tns:getTitle0SoapIn'/>
     <output name='getTitle0SoapOut' message='tns:getTitle0SoapOut'/>
   </operation>
   <operation name='setTitle' parameterOrder='arg0'>
     <input name='setTitle1SoapIn' message='tns:setTitle1SoapIn'/>
     <output name='setTitle1SoapOut' message='tns:setTitle1SoapOut'/>
   </operation>
 </portType>
 <binding name='myexamples.ExampleSoap' type='tns:myexamples.ExampleSoap'>
   <soap:binding style='rpc' transport='http://schemas.xmlsoap.org/soap/http'/>
   <operation name='getTitle'>
     <soap:operation soapAction='getTitle' style='rpc'/>
     <input name='getTitle0SoapIn'>
       <soap:body use='encoded'
       ➥namespace='http://tempuri.org/myexamples.Example'
encodingStyle='http://schemas.xmlsoap.org/soap/encoding/'/>
     </input>
     <output name='getTitle0SoapOut'>
       <soap:body use='encoded'
       ➥namespace='http://tempuri.org/myexamples.Example'
encodingStyle='http://schemas.xmlsoap.org/soap/encoding/'/>
     </output>
   </operation>
   <operation name='setTitle'>
     <soap:operation soapAction='setTitle' style='rpc'/>
     <input name='setTitle1SoapIn'>
       <soap:body use='encoded'
       ➥namespace='http://tempuri.org/myexamples.Example'
encodingStyle='http://schemas.xmlsoap.org/soap/encoding/'/>
     </input>
     <output name='setTitle1SoapOut'>
       <soap:body use='encoded'
       ➥namespace='http://tempuri.org/myexamples.Example'
encodingStyle='http://schemas.xmlsoap.org/soap/encoding/'/>
     </output>
   </operation>
 </binding>
 <service name='myexamples.Example'>
   <port name='myexamples.ExampleSoap' binding='tns:myexamples.ExampleSoap'>
     <soap:address location='http://192.168.0.157:8004/glue/urn:example'/>
   </port>
 </service>
</definitions>
```

MICROSOFT .NET

Microsoft's .NET technologies are associated with three products or product suites: the .NET Framework, .NET Enterprise Servers, and XML Web Services. In this section, I will briefly discuss each component and their relationships to each other. Then examples will be included that relate to the specific information.

26

Table 26.1. List of Products and Description from Microsoft for Web Services Platform

Product	Description
.NET Class Libraries	Class libraries used for developing and deploying Web Services.
.NET Languages	C#, VisualBasic .NET, Jscript .NET, and Extensions to C++ and Visual J.
ASP.NET	Web application scripting framework.
ADO.NET	Database access services.
SOAP, WSDL, UDDI, WS-Security, WS-License, WS-Routing, WS-Referral	XML Standard communication languages used for messaging between network systems.
COM+	COM components for transaction processing, queued components, object pooling, role-based security, and so on.
Visual Studio .NET	Integrated Development Environment for creating .NET applications.
Windows 2000 Servers	The operating system will become a .NET framework platform that will have .NET framework as its foundation.
.NET Enterprise Servers	These include the BizTalk Server, Commerce Server, SQL Server, Sharepoint Portal Server, and so on.

The .NET Framework is a platform for building, deploying, and running XML Web Services and applications. This includes the Common Language Runtime and all the .NET Framework class libraries. To build .NET Framework applications, you need either the .NET Framework Software Development Kit (SDK) or Visual Studio .NET. The difference between the two is that the Visual Studio .NET is an integrated development environment and is the recommended platform for development when using the .NET Compact Framework and Smart Device Extensions. In addition, the Microsoft SDK only includes the C# compiler. The .NET Compact Framework is a subset of the .NET Framework that brings managed code and XML Web Services to small, resource-constrained devices. The release of .NET Compact Framework will support Pocket PC devices. The .NET Smart Device Extensions allow developers who write desktop or server applications to easily write applications for devices, without having to re-train or learn unfamiliar concepts.

Microsoft .NET Enterprise Servers are used to integrate, manage, and Web-enable an enterprise architecture built on the Microsoft platform. Designed to use XML, these servers are built to provide interoperability with an existing infrastructure investment and for scalability to meet Internet demands. The servers that are .NET Enterprise Servers include, but are not limited to, SQL Server 2000, Microsoft Exchange Server, and Microsoft BizTalk Server.

SQL Server 2000 is a relational database product that works with the .NET Framework. This product has a number of XML APIs that were discussed in previous chapters. The MSDN Web site has a number of associated links to components of .NET Enterprise Servers and SQL Server 2000. Refer to the resource links at the end of this chapter.

Microsoft Exchange Server has the capability to be used with Web Services. Microsoft, on the MSDN Web site, provides source code to develop applications for a Web storage system and for Outlook Web Access. This includes a suite of methods using XML and HTTP to manipulate data on the server.

The Microsoft BizTalk Server is an infrastructure for allowing enterprise systems to quickly integrate, manage, and automate business processes. This is done by exchanging business documents among applications within or across organizational boundaries. The server comes with a set of tools used for "business process orchestration"—meaning that BizTalk Server helps you build processes that span more than just applications, but also businesses over the Internet. Included are a set of graphical tools to make it easier for business analysts and developers to implement solutions. BizTalk Server also includes a set of plug-in components for specific markets that are called BizTalk Accelerators. In addition, it includes adapters that enable the server to work with other industry leading platforms, including SAP and IBM's MQSeries.

Microsoft also has a set of XML Web Services development tools to allow developers to build messaging systems that use XML standards that are associated with the Web Services framework. Included in this suite of software products is the SOAP Toolkit 2.0. The toolkit provides documentation and a set of examples that allow developers to quickly learn how to implement SOAP messaging communication between various systems in a network, as well as have them work with a database or other application. The suite also includes an API to the Microsoft Messenger product, the Passport product and its SDK, the .NET My Services SDK, the Microsoft UDDI initiative, XML Core (including parsers and support for XSL, and so on), and an XML Specification for multilanguage support.

Although these products are paving the way for markets to be Web Service enabled, there still is a long way to go. Architecture components such as security, operational management, transactions, and reliable messaging need further enhancement and development. All these components are associated with the notion of a Global XML Web Services Architecture. Microsoft's goal for this architecture is to help take XML Web Services to the next level by providing a coherent, general purpose model for adding new advanced capabilities to XML Web Services that are modular and extensible.

Another point of note is the work Microsoft is doing for security with Web Services. There are two modules for security: WS-Security, which defines a complete encryption system, and WS-License, which defines techniques for guaranteeing the identity of the caller and ensuring that only authorized users can use a Web Service. WS-Security and WS-License are part of the specifications in the Global Web Services Architecture (GWSA).

Operational management needs, such as routing messages among many servers and configuring those servers dynamically for processing, are also part of the GWSA. They are addressed by the WS-Routing and the WS-Referral specifications. As the Global Web Services Architecture grows, specifications for these and other needs will be introduced.

Finally, WS-Inspection is a new specification for assisting in the inspection of a site for available services. It is also a collection of rules for how inspection-related information should be made available for consumption. A WS-Inspection document provides a means for aggregating references to pre-existing service description documents that have been authored in any number of formats. These inspection documents are then made available at the point-of-offering of the services as well as through references, which can be placed within a content medium such as HTML.

ADDITIONAL WEB SERVICE PROVIDERS

Sun and IBM have also been working hard on their Web Service solutions.

Sun has constructed a package of XML related products for Web Services into the Java Web Services Developer Pack. It includes the Java XML Pack (JAX). This bundle includes the early access versions of the following packages:

- Java API for XML Messaging (JAXM)—This package enables developers to send and receive XML messages based on SOAP 1.1 with attachments specification. Included is a set of profiles for industry standard XML protocols—namely ebXML TR&P and WS-Routing.
- Java API for XML Processing (JAXP)—This package enables developers to process XML documents by providing support for the XML processing standards SAX, DOM, and XSLT.
- Java API for XML Registries (JAXR)—This package provides a uniform and standard Java API for interacting with XML registries such as UDDI and ebXML Registry/Repository.
- Java API for XML-based RPC (JAX-RPC)—This package enables developers to build web-based applications and web services that incorporate XML-based remote procedure call (RPC) functionality based on the Simple Object Access Protocol (SOAP) 1.1 specification. By using JAX-RPC, Java developers can rapidly achieve Web services interoperability based on widely adopted standards and protocols.
- Then finally, a future release will include Java Architecture for XML Binding (JAXB). This is a runtime framework to support a two-way mapping between XML documents and Java objects. JAXB includes a schema compiler that translates XML DTDs into one or more Java classes. These classes contain automatically-generated code to perform error and validity checking of incoming and outgoing XML documents, thereby ensuring that only valid, error-free messages are accepted, processed, and generated by a system.

The Java Developer Web Service Pack is intended for enterprise developers building J2EE applications. The Web Services pack is designed for major tool vendors who will incorporate the standards-based technology into future versions of their Java toolkits—toolkits such as Sun's Forte and Borland Software Corp.'s JBuilder.

IBM currently has the Web Services Toolkit, which is a software development kit that includes a runtime environment, a demo, and examples to aid in designing and executing

Web Service applications that can automatically find one another and collaborate in business transactions without additional programming or human intervention. Simple examples of Web Services are provided, as well as demonstrations of how some of the emerging technology standards, such as SOAP, UDDI, and WSDL, work together.

OPEN SOURCE TECHNOLOGY—SYSTINET AND THE MIND ELECTRIC

One company that provides a free version (BSD Open Source License) of a Web Services implementation is Systinet. The product line includes a Web Service application server (WASP) that allows Java or C++ developers to create Web Services.

Systinet's WASP product line includes a high-performance runtime framework designed to support the rigors of enterprise computing. The environment supports comprehensive security options, rich data type mapping, full J2EE integration, and a browser-based administration console. The modular architecture of the framework supports an extensive set of plug-in capabilities to accommodate multiple configurations and requirements. WASP Server for Java can support any servlet engine, any EJB container, and any communications protocol, as well as custom datatypes, custom encodings, custom serialization modules, and custom authentication and authorization mechanisms.

Also, Systinet includes a suite of productive development tools that automate the construction and deployment of Web Services, generating WSDL from existing Java classes or client stubs and server skeletons from WSDL descriptions. These tools are available as integrated plug-ins to popular Java IDEs, such as NetBeans, Sun's Forte for Java, and Borland JBuilder.

Another product is the WASP UDDI that supports the UDDI V2 specification, as defined by the UDDI Project. The WASP UDDI is available in two editions; Standard Edition is essentially a reference implementation of the UDDI V2 specification that is suitable for deployment as either a public or private registry, although it doesn't provide additional security controls. Enterprise Edition extends the UDDI V2 specification, providing enhanced security and usability features that more closely match the requirements of a private enterprise or community.

Another interesting company that freely provides its Web Service product line is The Mind Electric. It has a product named GLUE, which is a platform that simplifies and unifies traditional distributed computing with the emerging world of Web Services. It is based completely on open standards including XML, HTTP, SOAP, WSDL, UDDI, and WAP. You can also download the Electric XML, which is a Java toolkit for parsing and manipulating XML documents. It is simple, small (46K JAR file), fast, and comprehensive, with support for namespaces, XPATH, and multiple encoding schemes.

The Electric XML also has some interesting development tools: the first provides the ability to work with the XML parser for transparent, bidirectional, XML serialization; then there is a set of command-line tools for generating Java from XML schema and XML schema from Java. It also has a unique annotated schema system that allows default mappings to be overridden without coding and a fast transactional persistence for storing Java objects as XML documents.

The Mind Electric's product, GLUE, is a Web Services platform that includes useful features such as an XML/Java mapping system, an XML storage system, SSL, authentication, a browser-based management console, EJB integration, JMS integration, JBuilder plug-in, Web server, servlet engine, and Electric XML+ (a high performance toolkit for parsing and manipulating XML). GLUE standard edition ships as a single 480K JAR file and can be used standalone or within a third-party servlet engine such as Apache Tomcat or BEA WebLogic.

We will use The Mind Electric's GLUE to demonstrate how easily Web Services can be built. The following example sends an instance of the `Example` class between a client and a server.

The code for the `Example` class is shown Listing 26.1. This class is a value object that is used to contain a title.

Here is an example using the GLUE standard edition development kit. In this example, I use the electric.registry package. This package provides a `Register` class that exposes static methods for publishing, binding, and invoking services. In this example, I show two files. The first is `Publish.java`, which includes a main method used to start a Web server and publish the class that I want to expose as a service named `Double`. `Double.java` is the simple method used to show how a class can be exposed. A Web Service client will be able to discover and use this simple service.

LISTING 26.1 `Example` **CLASS**

```
// myexamples/Publish.java
package myexamples.register;

import electric.registry.Registry;
import electric.server.http.HTTP;

public class Publish
  {
  public static void main( String[] args )
    throws Exception
    {
    // start a web server on port 8004, accept messages via /glue
    HTTP.startup( "http://localhost:8004/glue" );

    // publish an instance of Double method
    Registry.publish( "double", new Double() );
    }
  }

// myexamples/Double.java
package myexamples;

public class Double
  {
  public int double( int value )
    {
    return value*2;
    }
  }
```

To run the example, ensure that you have gone through the documentation associated with the GLUE installation, taking care to set up your CLASSPATH environment variable appropriately. Type the following command to start the service:

```
> java myexamples.Publish
GLUE 2.0 (c) 2001 The Mind Electric
startup HTTP server on http://192.168.1.107:8004/glue
```

Another interesting function of GLUE is the ability to see the associated WSDL document associated with the Web Service that was just constructed.

You would need to run the ExampleServer and then open a Web browser on http://localhost:8004/glue/example.wsdl.

To learn more information about The Mind Electric's products, go to the company's Web site at www.themindelectric.com.

THE FUTURE OF WEB SERVICES

The enterprise, which is already running plenty of Unix or Linux boxes and has attained a level of comfort with Java, probably will tilt toward J2EE as the platform to use for Web Services. It's a proven tool for extending legacy systems and applications into Web Services. Conversely, a business that is Microsoft-centric—particularly one that's looking to extend the desktop into Web Service—will probably want to give .NET a hard look. These are starting points for arriving at a decision for which platform to use for your Web Services product development.

Another note is that the current XML standards for Web Services do not address the need for dynamic discovery of new Web Services, transaction models, security, or integration with object or workflow-based programming models. These topics have become very popular recently, and vendors are working hard on the solutions they will have to provide to address these issues. Some industry analysts are stating that Web Services are still an immature technology and a lot of vendor hype. They are recommending that firms use Web Services today for simple, read-only activities and set an agenda to tackle more complex efforts later on. Many reports indicate that the market will continue to develop until the end of 2002. However, right now many companies are selling Web Service frameworks that you can download and evaluate today.

THE VOICEXML MARKUP LANGUAGE

VoiceXML is a Web-based markup language similar to HTML for representing human-computer dialogs. Whereas HTML assumes a graphical Web browser, with display, keyboard, and mouse, VoiceXML assumes a voice browser with audio input and output. VoiceXML leverages the Internet for voice application development and delivery, greatly simplifying these difficult tasks and creating new opportunities.

VoiceXML is a specification of the VoiceXML Forum, an industry consortium of more than 300 companies. The Forum is active in conformance testing, educating, and marketing of

VoiceXML, and has been given control over further language development to the World Wide Web Consortium (W3C). Because it is a specification, applications that work on one conformant VoiceXML platform will work on others as well.

The ordinary phone has been very important in the development of VoiceXML, although VoiceXML's appeal is more general. The typical VoiceXML voice browser of today runs on a specialized voice gateway node that is connected both to the public switched telephone network and to the Internet. The VoiceXML technology works directly with any kind of phone.

Two speech technologies that need to be understood are automated speech recognition (ASR) systems and text-to-speech (TTS) synthesis.

ASR systems constructed with VoiceXML use the VoiceXML markup language (VXML) and grammar specifications (GRXML, GSL, and TellMe's grammar markup language). The grammar specifications define what words or phrases can be expected as input to the application. An application can then incorporate a number of VoiceXML documents and grammar sets to construct integrated voice recognition applications.

TTS systems used to sound like stupid robots, being difficult to listen to or understand. Now waveform concatenation speech synthesis is being deployed. With this technique, speech is assembled from libraries of prerecorded waveforms.

VoiceXML can be used without ASR or TTS. VoiceXML is often used for users to listen to recorded audio and press keys in response. Speech technology makes applications more powerful and pleasant to use, but VoiceXML brings the advantages of Web development and deployment to older styles of computer telephony applications.

EXAMPLE OF VOICEXML

This example shows how a user can create a simple application that handles an event caused by the calling user. Applications in VoiceXML are based on a collection of VoiceXML documents and grammars. When the conversation takes place, the caller is continuously in a specific dialog state. Each dialog state is assembled using a form element that handles the discrete logic of a conversation that the caller has with the application. Associated with each form is a grammar that defines the accepted input words from the caller. Here is an example grammar:

```
LIB_YES_NO [
  [ yes yeah yup sure okay correct right
    ( you got it )
    ( yes i do )
  ] {return("yes")}
  [ no nope incorrect
    ( no way )
    ( no it isn't )
    ( ?no it isn't )
  ] {return("no")}
]
```

Here is an example VoiceXML Application constructed using Nuance's V-Builder that allows a user to become verified and then execute a simple program. Figure 26.1 shows the diagram flow of the application.

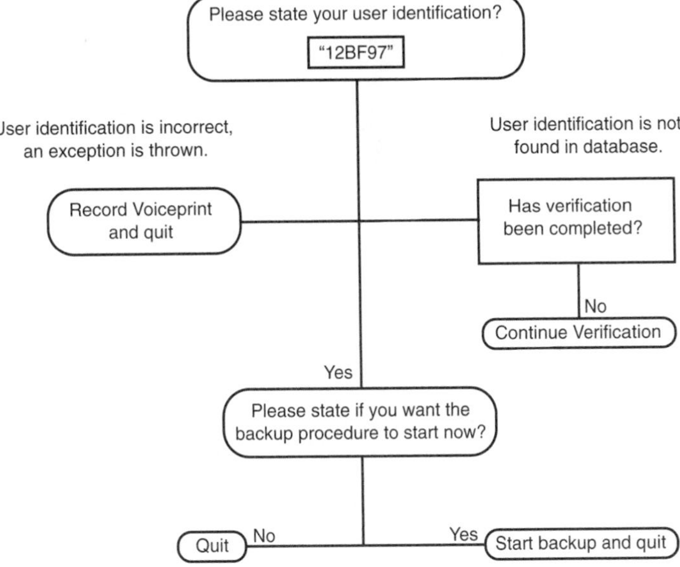

Figure 26.1
A simple VoiceXML application flow diagram.

This diagram shows a simple application that allows an IT manager to phone the application and then start a backup operation to back up a database server. The dialog contains three states. The first state is the `StartVerification` that prompts the user for user identification. The second state is a reject state that tells the caller that the phone is going to be terminated and then hangs up. The third state is an accept state that then allows the user to say Yes or No. Then a final message is given to the caller and the application hangs up.

Here is the VXML documents that define this logic:

```
<?xml version="1.0" encoding="ISO-8859-1"?>
<!DOCTYPE vxml PUBLIC '-//Nuance/DTD VoiceXML 1.0//EN'
'http://voicexml.nuance.com/dtd/nuancevoicexml-1-2.dtd'>
<vxml version="1.0">

  <meta name="Generator" content="V-Builder 1.2.26"/>

  <form id="StartVerification">
    <field modal="false" name="phone" type="phone" voiceprint="buffer">
      <audio src="../prompts/welcome.wav" />
      <filled>
        <vscreate type="verification" expr="'svdb:?key='+phone" />
        <vsimport />
        <vbdestroy />
        <if cond="lastResult$.verification.decision=='accepted'">
          <goto next="#accepted" />
```

```
          <elseif cond="lastResult$.verification.decision=='rejected'" />
          <goto next="#rejected" />
          <else />
          <goto next="#rejected" />
        </if>
      </filled>
      <catch event="error.badfetch">
        <vscreate type="recordbaduserid" expr="'svdb:?key='+phone" />
        <vsimport />
        <vbdestroy />
        <goto next="#rejected" />
      </catch>
    </field>
  </form>

  <form id="accepted">
    <field modal="false" name="pin" type="digits?length=6" voiceprint="session">
      <audio src="../prompts/more_info_pin.wav" />
      <filled mode="any">
        <if cond="lastResult$.verification.decision=='accepted'">
          <vscreate type="startbackup" expr="'svdb:?key='+entry" />
      <vsimport />
          <goto next="#rejected" />
          <elseif cond="lastResult$.verification.decision=='rejected'" />
          <goto next="#rejected" />
        </if>
      </filled>
    </field>
    <block name="block2">
      <vsdestroy complete="true" />
      <audio src="../prompts/verified.wav" />
    </block>
  </form>

  <form id="rejected">
    <block name="block3">
      <vsdestroy complete="true" />
      <audio src="../prompts/rejected.wav" />
    </block>
  </form>

</vxml>
```

VoiceXML has done well because of the growth of the WWW and of its capabilities. Also, there have been great improvements in computer-based speech recognition and text-to-speech synthesis. With the spread of the WWW beyond the desktop computer, VoiceXML has spread to the phone with an analogous user interface.

As the Internet infrastructure improves in performance, bandwidth, and quality of service, VoiceXML strongly benefits from the ability to move audio data efficiently across the Web.

VoiceXML is a complement to the notion of the ubiquitous Web. As speech technology improves, there will become a very natural and powerful interface for Web devices. Microphones are much smaller than keyboards and keypads. Speakers for cell phones are smaller than the computer screens on PDA devices. Future Web devices will have on-board speech recognition to potentially voice-activate universal remotes that talk to the devices in our immediate surroundings. The future will bring even more Web devices: networked MP3 portables, vending machines that reorder supplies when running low, wall displays that download artwork, Web-based stereos and televisions, and so on.

XML AND SECURITY

The W3C has done a lot of development of various standards associated with encrypting documents for Internet messaging. The first interesting standard is XML Signature. This standard is an evolving standard for digital signatures that addresses the special requirements that XML presents for digitally signing business operations while using XML syntax. XML Signature provides authentication, data integrity, and support for non-repudation. Here is an example of XML Signature:

```
<?xml version="1.0" encoding="UTF-8"?>
<Signature xmlns="http://www.w3.org/2000/09/xmldsig#">
<SignedInfo Id="example">
<CanonicalizationMethod
  Algorithm="http://www.w3.org/TR/2001/REC-xml-c14n-20010315"/>
<SignatureMethod
  Algorithm="http://www.w3.org/2000/09/xmldsig#dsa-sha1" />
<Reference URI="http://www.examplecompany.com/news/2002/05_12_06.htm">
<DigestMethod Algorithm="http://www.w3.org/2000/09/xmldsig#sha1" />
<DigestValue>j6lwx3rvEPO0vKtMup4NbeVu8nk=</DigestValue>
</Reference>
<Reference
  URI="http://www.w3.org/TR/2000/WD-xmldsig-core-20000228/
  Âsignature-example.xml">
<DigestMethod Algorithm="http://www.w3.org/2000/09/xmldsig#sha1"/>
<DigestValue>UrXLOGERVskoV5hkGK78KJHWE467=</DigestValue>
</Reference>
</SignedInfo>
<SignatureValue>MC0E~LE=</SignatureValue>
<KeyInfo>
<X509Data>
<X509SubjectName>CN=John Smith,O=Righton Inc.,ST=LOS ALTOS,
ÂC=CA</X509SubjectName>
<X509Certificate>
MIID5jCCA0+gA...lVN
</X509Certificate>
</X509Data>
</KeyInfo>
</Signature>
```

Another standard associated. with security is XML Encryption. .XML Encryption is a standard that facilitates the ability to encrypt a set of XML data with a number of different encryption schemes. The important item about the XML Encryption standard is the ability to only encrypt sections of the XML document that you want to encrypt. It is easy to encrypt an entire document, but the ability to encrypt only sections allows developers to streamline the document creation and maintenance.

26

This section discusses one implementation, XSS4J, that can be easily downloaded and tested from the IBM alphaworks Web site. In this example, we have a sensitive XML document, `bookorder.xml`, that needs to be encrypted before being sent out:

```
<?xml version="1.0" encoding="UTF-8" ?>
<Invoice>
  <bookorder>
    <item>
      <title>XML and Java</title>
      <quantity>1</quantity>
      <price>100.0</price>
    </item>
  </bookorder>
  <payment type="card">
    <issuer>A Card Company</issuer>
    <amount>100.0</amount>
    <due>10/10/1999</due>
  </payment>
  <cardinfo>
    <name>Your Name</name>
    <expiration>04/2001</expiration>
    <number>5283 8304 6232 0010</number>
  </cardinfo>
</Invoice>
```

In this example, the `cardinfo` element will be encrypted using `template.xml`:

```
<?xml version="1.0" encoding="UTF-8" ?>
<EncryptedData Id="ed1" Type="http://www.w3.org/2001/04/xmlenc#Element"
➥                           xmlns="http://www.w3.org/2001/04/xmlenc#">
  <EncryptionMethod Algorithm=
  ➥"http://www.w3.org/2001/04/xmlenc#tripledes-cbc" />
  <KeyInfo xmlns="http://www.w3.org/2000/09/xmldsig#">
    <EncryptedKey xmlns="http://www.w3.org/2001/04/xmlenc#">
      <EncryptionMethod Algorithm="http://www.w3.org/2001/04/xmlenc#rsa-1_5" />
      <KeyInfo xmlns="http://www.w3.org/2000/09/xmldsig#">
        <KeyName>John</KeyName>
      </KeyInfo>
      <CipherData>
        <CipherValue />
      </CipherData>
    </EncryptedKey>
  </KeyInfo>
  <CipherData>
    <CipherValue />
  </CipherData>
</EncryptedData>
```

`template.xml` specifies that triple-DES will be used to encrypt the data, using a randomly generated key. The key itself is encrypted using John's key obtained from the key store specified in the `keyinfo.xml`:

```
<?xml version="1.0" encoding="UTF-8" ?>
<!--
 This is a sample keyinfo containing information on a key store
 named "keystore" in the same directory.
```

```
  -->
  <keyinfo>
  <keystore>
  <name>keystore</name>
  <password>storepass</password>
        </keystore>
  <keys>
    <key>
      <alias>John</alias>
      <password>keypass</password>
    </key>
    <key>
      <alias>Jane</alias>
      <password>keypass</password>
    </key>
  </keys>
</keyinfo>
```

After encrypting `bookorder.xml` using XSS4J, the resulting document looks like this:

```
<?xml version="1.0" encoding="UTF-8"?>
<!-- This is a sample document. --><Invoice>
  <bookorder>
    <item>
      <title>XML and Java</title>
      <quantity>1</quantity>
      <price>100.0</price>
    </item>
  </bookorder>
  <payment type="card">
    <issuer>A Card Company</issuer>
    <amount>100.0</amount>
    <due>10/10/1999</due>
  </payment>
  <EncryptedData xmlns="http://www.w3.org/2001/04/xmlenc#"
    Id="ed1" Type="http://www.w3.org/2001/04/xmlenc#Element">
  <EncryptionMethod Algorithm=
  ➥"http://www.w3.org/2001/04/xmlenc#tripledes-cbc"/>
  <KeyInfo xmlns="http://www.w3.org/2000/09/xmldsig#">
    <EncryptedKey xmlns="http://www.w3.org/2001/04/xmlenc#">
      <EncryptionMethod Algorithm=
      ➥"http://www.w3.org/2001/04/xmlenc#rsa-1_5"/>
      <KeyInfo xmlns="http://www.w3.org/2000/09/xmldsig#">
        <KeyName>John</KeyName>
      </KeyInfo>
      <CipherData>
        <CipherValue/>
      </CipherData>
    </EncryptedKey>
  </KeyInfo>
  <CipherData>  <CipherValue>QkUEXSHO3skH0yO+Hb5nI3sJxK3YEf6+x0/
➥ysYg+SNkWpYshUYa0Hpf12NS2flECdVjUw5YeATzL7gIukC65Ng7D9LgSDOo1Dl41
➥XzVwGdvm1++e+SnBv2vYEY6kkPqnw7XbBWI3H7B4f7P6tyfRHofoWR2XPHk2DxPl6
➥Iw1IHtLA2PQVXkNCEmBKkeHzH8C</CipherValue>
  </CipherData>
</EncryptedData>
</Invoice>
```

As you can see, the `cardinfo` element has been encrypted. This example uses the W3C's standard for encrypting XML documents and represents the resulting information in XML. The data can be arbitrary data, including an XML document, an XML element, or XML element content. The result of encrypting data is an XML Encryption element that contains or references the cipher data. To execute this example, there is code that comes with this chapter that should be available for download.

Another XML security standard of note is the Security Assertion Markup Language (SAML), which is an XML security standard for exchanging authentication and authorization information. SAML is being developed within the OASIS XML-Based Security Services Technical Committee (SSTC). The purpose of SSTC is to define an XML framework for exchanging authentication and authorization information.

SAML tries to solve security problems associated with integrating security features that reside on different systems and use security data differently. Also, there is the need to cross network domains more easily with a potential XML messaging framework. For example, users of a particular Web site might want to access content on another Web site without having to log in to both sites.

Here is an example SAML authorization request that contains username, password, and response requirements:

```
<samlp:Request MajorVersion="1" MinorVersion="0"
  RequestID="1falEwoDa2XSqpN++/LcFpBmZWrQg=">
  <samlp:RespondWith>AuthenticationStatement</samlp:RespondWith>
    <samlp:AuthenticationQuery>
      <saml:Subject>
        <saml:NameIdentifier Name="test"/>
        <saml:SubjectConfirmation>
          <saml:ConfirmationMethod>
            http://www.oasis-open.org/committies/security/docs/
            ➥draft-sstc-core-25/password
          </saml:ConfirmationMethod>
          <saml:SubjectConfirmationData>
            cGFzc3dvcmQ=
          </saml:SubjectConfirmationData>
        </saml:SubjectConfirmation>
      </saml:Subject>
    </samlp:AuthenticationQuery>
</samlp:Request>
```

What follows is the response to the request. This verifies that the authentication assertion is signed. The next step from the calling application is to do a proof of origin check.

```
<samlp:Response InResponseTo="1fgtTGzMXSqpN++/LcFpBmZWrQg="
  MajorVersion="1" MinorVersion="0"
  ResponseID="upuSGdmqx7ov01mExYlt+6bDCWE=">
  <samlp:Status>
    <samlp:StatusCode Value="samlp:Success"/>
  </samlp:Status>
  <saml:Assertion AssertionID="+1UyxJDasea+ao+LqMrE98wmhAI="
    IssueInstant="2002-05-12T14:33:58.456" Issuer="WASPCard"
    MajorVersion="1" MinorVersion="0">
```

```
    <saml:Conditions NotBefore="2002-05-12T14:33:58.466"
      NotOnOrAfter="2002-05-12T15:03:58.466"/>
      <saml:AuthenticationStatement
        AuthenticationInstant="2002-05-12T14:33:55.201"
        AuthenticationMethod="http://www.oasis-open.org/committies/security/
        ➥docs/draft-sstc-core-25/password">
          <saml:Subject>
            <saml:NameIdentifier Name="test" SecurityDomain="card:SQLDatabase"/>
            <saml:SubjectConfirmation>
              <saml:ConfirmationMethod>
                http://www.oasis-open.org/committies/security/docs/
                ➥draft-sstc-core-25/password
              </saml:ConfirmationMethod>
            </saml:SubjectConfirmation>
          </saml:Subject>
        </saml:AuthenticationStatement>
  </saml:Assertion>
</samlp:Response>
```

SAML is very flexible and provides several functions for authenticating and authorizing users between systems. It is sure to be a significant standard. For additional information about SAML, see the "Additional Resources" section of this chapter for several good pointers.

W3/OASIS STANDARD DEVELOPMENT AND MIGRATION

W3C creates Web standards. W3C's mission is to lead the Web to its full potential, supporting the development of specifications, guidelines, software, and tools. These components create a forum for information, commerce, inspiration, independent thought, and collective understanding.

One of W3C's primary goals is to make these benefits available to all people, whatever their hardware, software, network infrastructure, native language, culture, geographical location, or physical or mental ability. By enabling Internet users to solve problems that they find tedious—such as helping us quickly find what we're looking for: medical information, a movie review, a book purchase order, and so on—they are helping build a "Web of Trust" that offers confidentiality, instills confidence, and makes it possible for people to take responsibility for what they publish on the Web.

The consortium is a vendor-neutral organization that promotes interoperability by designing and promoting open computer languages and protocols that avoid the market fragmentation of the past. The W3C helps build a Web that can easily evolve into an even better Web, without disrupting what already works. Finally, the W3C is helping build a suite of interactive and rich media for the Web. This includes resizable images, quality sound, video, 3D effects, and animation standards.

OASIS ORGANIZATION

OASIS, the Organization for the Advancement of Structured Information Standards, is a non-profit, international consortium that creates interoperable industry specifications based on public standards such as XML and SGML, as well as others that are related to structured information processing. OASIS is a group of specialists who use specific technologies as well as provide specific solutions that implement these technologies. Their responsibilities include providing structured information standards that will potentially work in practice. The members include those who have a deep stake in XML and SGML.

Each standard includes a group of the OASIS members who disseminate information that describes the technology and its implementation. OASIS creates an open forum for the members of these groups to recommend the guidelines for the interoperability of product development. These then, in turn, formulate the development of strategies for how others will be able to use the technology and standards. The groups are focused on the application of structured information standards, but not on creating more standards that are unused or that burden already overly complex standards in which they try to achieve industry consensus that will support the standards they are trying to help formulate.

With these characteristics, they provide synergy within various marketplaces to help ensure the strength of XML-related technologies and standards.

Example of How Specific Standards Are Developed and Then Become a Recommendation

Standards are developed by technical committees that are organized within the OASIS group. These technical committees are formed from a group of companies that want to work together to produce a specific standard or the evolution of an existing specification that requires additional development and refinement. Many technical companies have provided markup language specifications to OASIS. OASIS then starts the process to formulate a technical committee from other technical companies or groups within that specific industry. A number of Web organizations have moved to OASIS. Some include topicmaps.org, authxml.org, and so on.

One interesting example of a recommendation that has recently been introduced is the RELAX NG standard for XML schema design. This was originally two standards on which different groups were working—TREX and RELAX. A technical group of developers was assembled, and they then combined the two standards to produce RELAX NG. On December 3, 2001, they released Version 1.0 of the specification, and then provided a number of mechanisms for community involvement—including mailing lists and tutorials for others to learn about the standard.

Additional Resources

A number of very good additional resources are available. Here are a few of the best ones to consult:

- A list of UDDI standards can be found at `http://www.census.gov/epcd/www/naics.html`.
- XML Signature Working Group Homepage (`http://www.w3.org/Signature/`)

- The Cover Page on SAML (http://xml.coverpages.org/saml.html)
- Microsoft and Security (http://www.microsoft.com/security/)
- Netegrities JSAML product (http://www.netegrity.com/products/index.cfm?leveltwo=JSAML)

ROADMAP

This chapter provided a number of implementations of XML and its power to help in various ways with technology. From here you can now learn more about XML with more focused books that go into explicit detail on specific technologies.

CHAPTER 27

The Semantic Web and W3C Activities

In this chapter

by Alexander Kachur

WHAT IS THE SEMANTIC WEB?

Did you ever think about the Internet as more than a global directory of resources—as a common place to process knowledge that has meaning to both humans and machines? Unfortunately, today's World Wide Web is not suitable for the complex automated processing of information. This chapter discusses a new vision of the Web—the concept of the Semantic Web where knowledge can be represented in a structurized way by means of combining information with sets of predefined rules and descriptive data.

The term *semantics* describes the study of meaning.

The same item can be seen in multiple ways depending on the viewpoint of the person. For instance, the entity "water" can be described by a chemist as a molecule that is comprised of two atoms of hydrogen and one atom of oxygen. The same word will sound different to the ear of the physicist, who might first point out that water is a liquid substance. In this case, the chemist's interest in water is different from that of the physicist.

Regardless of the viewpoint, the semantics of the concept "water" is the same and it includes all known properties of water. However, it is a challenging task to describe the concept properly so that the chemist and physicist from our example can share information that is meaningful to each other.

If the chemist or physicist in our example was to go to the Web and search for "`water`," he would probably be frustrated by the results. He would get thousands of links to pages containing this word. To retrieve the results he desired, he would need to have a search engine capable of finding and counting words in documents and also extracting the meaning of words. The result of a search in the Semantic Web could look somewhat similar to this:

```
Semantic Search: water
Found: 38 properties, 5468 documents:

* Sites describing chemical properties of water:
*     Chemistry for dummies
*     On-line chemical encyclopedia

* Sites describing electrical properties of water:
...
```

Incredible, isn't it? This can be achieved by structuring information and describing it's semantics in such a way that a machine can understand.

The Semantic Web is an information space that combines the decentralized fashion of the modern World Wide Web with structured, machine-understandable representations of knowledge.

In other words, the Semantic Web is an environment in which computers and humans "speak the same language."

Need for the Semantic Web

Imagine a Stone Age human seeking a stone suitable for making a primitive knife. After a long search, he finds a piece of iron ore, but he just throws it away because it is not suitable for his purposes. He doesn't know yet that he can make a better tool with this ore. If he spoke some language, he would be able to describe the look of this piece of ore to his tribesmen. He might even counsel them to avoid a pit full of the useless stones.

Now imagine that another tribesman accidentally threw a similar piece of ore into a fire and after some time found some sharp solid pieces of iron. After a few experiments, he already knows that there is a better use to this rock than throwing it at somebody. He uses the language to share his new knowledge with his fellows. During the conversation, the first caveman points out that a lot of stones like this are in a pit a half day's walk from the cave, thus establishing a relationship between the new and the existing knowledge. The knowledge then spreads among the people, establishing new complex relations—that was probably how the Stone Age ended.

For a computer, the information accumulated in the modern World Wide Web is something similar to holding a rock in your hands without knowing how to use it. A computer can search the Internet following links on Web pages or by using keywords, but it doesn't have full power. The Semantic Web will represent knowledge properly for the machines to understand it and perform automated reasoning.

WWW and Semantic Web

The World Wide Web is a decentralized information space. In most cases, it is used by humans to communicate with humans. (Name it H2H communication). The machines are only a means of this communication and nothing more.

The Semantic Web will expand the modern World Wide Web by introducing new kinds of communication or even collaboration: *human to machine (H2M)* and *machine to machine (M2M)*. For the first time in the history of human beings, thousands of machines will participate in communication as partners capable of searching, collecting, processing, and even using information based on the needs of humans or other computers participating in communication (compare Figures 27.1 and 27.2).

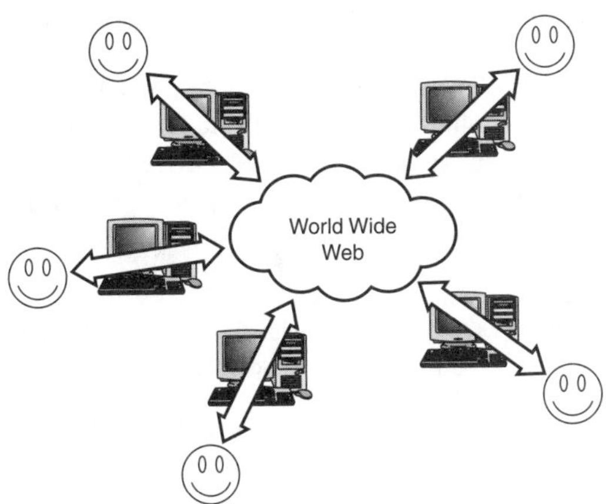

Figure 27.1
Relationship between a human and a computer in the World Wide Web.

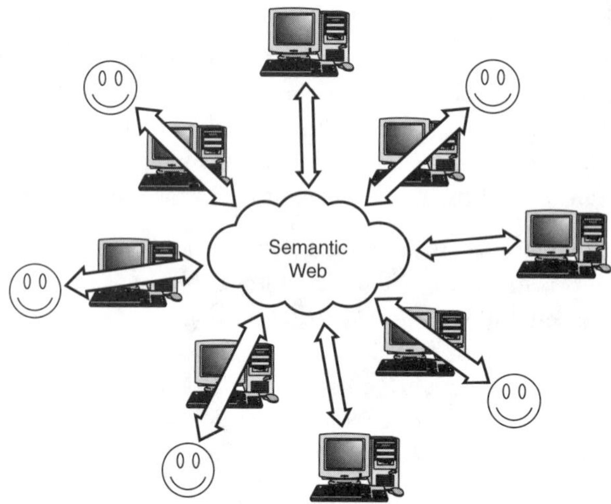

Figure 27.2
Relationship between a human and a computer in the Semantic Web.

Separating Knowledge and Semantics

In the modern World Wide Web, the most common practices of putting data online imply separating data and its representation. The Semantic Web allows us to make a further step forward by qualifying data with its meaning so that the computer that parses a Web page is able to comprehend the statement `"The book costs 49.99 USD"` based on a few tags hidden inside the Semantic Web page file, which annotate the knowledge represented on that Semantic Web page.

Note, however, that the comprehension is achieved not by the means of any sophisticated AI system—a computer still doesn't understand a single word of English. The meaning of the statement or preceding *literal* has already been extracted by somebody else (a human or an intelligent annotation program) and translated into the language of *subjects* and *predicates*. The page has already been annotated with special XML tags, and a dictionary or *ontology* has already been created in order to make the semantics comprehendable by a computer. Tim Berners-Lee, the godfather of the Semantic Web, described machine-understandable documents as a concept that "…relies solely on a machine's ability to solve well-defined problems by performing well-defined operations on well-defined data."

The Semantic Web is based on the Predicate Calculus as a mechanism of describing such "well-defined problems," "well-defined operations," and "well-defined data." We will discuss the Predicate Calculus and in particular the First Order Predicate Logic (FOPL)—on which the Semantic Web is based—in the next section, and you will see that there is no magic at all in automated comprehension.

Subject in the first order predicate logic represents an individual item, such as "John Doe." Anything that represents a class of individual items and can be split into individual items is not a subject.

Predicate is a class of items. Predicates are used to associate an attribute with a subject or express relations between subjects. For example, the subject "John Doe" belongs to the predicate a "human."

PREDICATE CALCULUS AND AI SYSTEMS

The Predicate Calculus operates with literals, which consist of subjects and predicates. For example, the literal `"John Doe is a human"` will be represented with the following simple formula:

Aa,

where symbol "`A`" represents a predicate `"is a human"` and symbol "`a`" represents a human individual whose name is John Doe.

The following, more complex example of the literal represents a statement `"Some people are genius"`:

`∃x (Ax & Bx),`

where predicate `A` means "`is a human`" and predicate `B` means "`is genius`." The formula above reads: "Exists x such that x '`is a human`' and x '`is genius`.'" Or, in other words, "Some people are genius."

Literal in the Predicate Calculus is an atomic statement built from a single predicate, its subjects, and other literals.

Although Predicate Calculus helps to express a knowledge base, the quality of computer comprehension is in direct relation to the quality of the annotation obtained as a result of work spent to extract semantics from knowledge and establish proper relationships between items of knowledge. In other words, the quality of comprehension is a function of how well data are defined. Let's use a simple example to prove this.

For the computer, two statements like `"The book costs 49.99 USD"` and `"The book costs 0.8 tod"` could be equally valid literals and might even have the same meaning depending on the annotation and definitions of terms in the dictionary or ontology used.

As used in the Semantic Web, *ontology* is a conceptualization of a domain of knowledge. It expresses the set of terms and relations between them for a particular knowledge base. It is similar to a dictionary defining a joined terminology that is used to carry knowledge from one member of an application domain to another. The word "*member*" here means both humans and automated agents.

Returning to the example about genius, depending on the definition of the predicate `A`, the same formula can say "Some cows are genius." If we define predicate B as `"is stupid,"` the formula will be translated as "Some people are stupid." As you see, it is not enough only to write a formula; a terminology is also needed to make formal representation of the semantics fully comprehendable because computers can only operate with "well-defined data." That is why annotation that represents knowledge in the Semantic Web is supported by means of ontologies, which provide structure and vocabulary relevant to a domain of knowledge.

So, as you can see, the Semantic Web is based on a very strong theoretical basis, which is the same as the basis on which AI systems are built.

Note

Though the theoretical bases for the Semantic Web and AI Systems are the same, the Semantic Web *is not* an Artificial Intelligence system. It is an environment–a virtual space in which computers running intelligent programs are able to exchange knowledge with humans and each other.

SEMANTICS OF HUMAN LANGUAGES

Probably the best way to teach a computer to comprehend knowledge is to copy and adopt algorithms that are programmed in a human brain. Unfortunately, we cannot connect our brains to an Ethernet network and download the software to a computer.

However, science is able to give answers to difficult questions even if only indirect data or facts are available. Linguists can say a lot about the mechanisms of human comprehension by comparing different human languages.

For instance, despite the huge differences between the English and Russian languages, they are absolutely the same in the sense of using nouns, verbs, pronouns, adjectives, and so on to describe different kinds of entities, relations, and properties.

Note

All the human languages use the same set of entity types to describe the semantics of their knowledge: nouns, verbs, adjectives, and so on.

DESCRIBING SEMANTICS

To describe semantics and to carry knowledge from one human brain to another, we use words that describe objects, subjects, properties, and relations.

For example, to be able to share our knowledge about the temperature of water in a pool, we need to specify the name of the entity, which is "`water`," the name of one of its properties, which is "`temperature`," and its value, which is "`cold`." In order to do this, we construct a sentence composed of a noun, verb, and adjective.

UNDERSTANDING SEMANTICS

The process of comprehension is similar to this, but everything is upside down. When we hear a statement such as `"The water is cold,"` we understand (based on the entity types) that the object `"water"` has a property `"temperature,"` which has a value of `"cold."`

Parsing this statement further, we search for our own definitions of the terms `"water,"` `"temperature,"` and `"cold,"` which are associated with some memories, experiences, and knowledge. Memories could be something like a picture of a sunny day on a seashore. Experience reminds us how it was when we felt cold and knowledge establishes further links with other entities so that we can probably think that if the water is cold, the weather might not be pleasant outside.

The Semantic Web will provide computer systems with access to a huge network of data that defines terms and establishes links between them. The entire system will in some sense "live" its own life. It will be autonomous, like the modern Internet. Knowledge will evolve. Automated systems will use the semantic Web not only to operate with existing knowledge, but also to generate new logical models, and hence new knowledge based on the existing knowledge.

KNOWLEDGE AND THE SEMANTIC WEB

After a bit of theory, it's a good time to move into the more practical things. Let's look at the technologies that will help a computer to do so many exciting things with knowledge.

To put any data online, it is enough to build a very simple HTML file or to create something more complex with the use of dynamic scripts, and so on. However, to make knowledge accessible for computers, something more is required.

Even if somebody annotates information with XML tags as in Listing 27.1, it is not enough to make the data comprehendable.

LISTING 27.1 USELESS ANNOTATED DATA CONTAINING INFORMATION ABOUT A LATE TRAVEL AGENCY OFFER

```
<late-offer>
    <location>
        <region>Mediterranean</region>
        <country>Cyprus</country>
        <city>Limassol</city>
    </location>
    <hotel>
        <name>Amathus</name>
        <class-stars>5</class-stars>
    </hotel>
    <dates>
        <check-in>05/05/2002</check-in>
        <check-out>05/15/2002</check-out>
    </dates>
    <accommodation>
        <room>double</room>
        <view>sea</view>
        <terms>half board</terms>
    </accommodation>
    <agency>
        <name>Foo Travel</name>
```

LISTING 27.1 CONTINUED

```
        <phone>(000) 000-00-00</phone>
        <fax>(000) 000-00-01</fax>
        <url>http://www.footravel.com</url>
    </agency>
    <pricing>Per person</pricing>
    <price>Call!</price>
</late-offer>
```

The problem with this annotation is that a computer doesn't know what the XML tags such as `<dates>` mean, unless it is explicitly specified somewhere. Or, even if it is properly specified, what if somebody else uses the same tag to define something completely different? Humans can guess based on the context, but computers cannot.

There are many possible approaches to solving these problems. The least efficient is to use hard-coded predefined values for the tag names and their meaning, which significantly reduces usefulness of publishing data on the network.

Imagine a tourist looking for available tours to Cyprus. He might look for the tour himself, or he might use a travel agency, which might need to interact with other agencies to book the tour. In either case, the tourist or the agency will probably use the Internet to find and arrange the tour. Within a small group of agencies, the XML markup presented in Listing 27.1 might have meaning, but from the global perspective, it's 100% useless.

What if agencies and tourists had an efficient way of finding one another using automated agents who search the Semantic Web for specific data about available tours, based on the information that stands behind the words chosen to describe it rather than particular keywords? A tourist could find an agency that offers what he needs, or an agency could find another agency for the customer and at least get commissions.

To solve these and many other problems efficiently, the Semantic Web provides a framework or model to handle knowledge. This model consists of *metadata*, *ontologies*, and *agents*.

Metadata is used to annotate information. Metadata is data about data, and you've already seen an example of metadata in Listing 27.1. In that example, the tags are descriptive of the data contained in the element.

Metadata **is "data about data." In the Semantic Web terminology, metadata means special tags in the Web page that describe the information it contains.**

In the Semantic Web, metadata are used in conjunction with ontologies, which are conceptualizations of domains of knowledge. In other words, an ontology is a taxonomy describing concepts and terms combined with axioms related to an information domain. We have already defined the term ontology earlier in this chapter. Now it's time to give a more precise definition.

An ontology is a taxonomy of *explicitly* defined terms, concepts, and relations between terms. An ontology also defines a set of axioms–basic rules–that are cornerstones of the domain of knowledge.

The creation of ontologies requires a huge amount of effort. Currently, several ontologies are available in different domains of knowledge. For example, there is an ontology for the Human Resources sector of business or the Tourist Business ontology. There will be more ontologies available in the future, and every domain of knowledge will be covered by a number of ontologies.

Note

If you are interested in further details regarding existing ontologies, you can refer to the "Additional Resources" section of this chapter. It suggests several sites that define ontologies and provide ontology creation tools.

METADATA

As we discussed earlier, ontologies comprise definitions of terms or concepts and relations between them. These terms are used to represent knowledge thus making it available to a computer. In order to create a machine-understandable document, it needs to be annotated with metadata based on the terms that belong to a chosen ontology.

DATA ABOUT DATA

Metadata is data about any information contained in a Semantic Web page. An example of metadata could be descriptions of goods and their prices in the online retail shop.

Metadata has already been used for a while in the Internet. However, without a standard approach to defining metadata in a document, it is almost impossible to use it Web wide.

For metadata to be useful, there must be a standard to define the structure and properties of metadata. For that purpose, a special XML-based language has been proposed by the World Wide Web Consortium. It is the *Resource Description Framework (RDF)*.

RDF

RDF is a result of joint efforts of many communities interested in defining a standard way of metadata description and interchange. The W3C's RDF Model and Syntax Specification document refers to these communities:

- Web standardization community
- Library community
- Structured document community
- Knowledge representation community

With such a broad consideration and participation, the RDF is one of the most universal approaches of describing information accumulated in Web resources.

The newest version of the RDF specification can be found in full at the following URL: `http://www.w3.org/TR/REC-rdf-syntax`.

Although the Predicate Calculus, and especially the FOPL were considered when RDF was designed, the RDF is not a "computer language" representation of FOPL. Instead, the RDF is based on "well-established principles from various data representation communities" as the RDF Model and Syntax Specification states, and the best of FOPL has been taken into account and implemented in the RDF.

Similar to Predicate Calculus (which operates with subjects, predicates, and literals), the Resource Description Framework uses three types of objects: *resources*, *properties*, and *statements*.

RDF Objects

A resource in RDF corresponds to the subject in the Predicate Calculus, and it can be anything that can be described with a URI. It can even be an entity that doesn't belong or is not accessible from the Web—a hotel, a CD, a barrel of crude oil, and so on. That RDF is a framework for describing resources is clear from its name.

Resource in RDF means anything that can be described with a *Universal Resource Identifier (URI)*.

Every resource has a set of properties. A book has its authors, publisher, title, and page count, as well as a lot of other properties. Some of them might be useful for everybody, whereas some of them might only make sense for a professional working in the publishing industry.

In RDF, the term *property* maps to a predicate in the Predicate Calculus. Our earlier travel agency example contains several resources and properties, and a bit later we will translate its semantics into the RDF notation.

A *property* in RDF means anything that characterizes a resource from a certain point of view.

The specification of a resource and its properties forms a statement, which can be expressed as a literal in the Predicate Calculus. A resource can be a property of another resource—in other words, a statement can contain other statements inside.

The specification of a resource and its properties forms a *Statement*.

Turning back to our example, in the statement "Amathus is located in Limassol," "`Amathus`" is a resource, and "`location`" is its property, which has a value of "`Limassol`." However, "`Limassol`" will be a resource in the statement "Limassol is located in Cyprus."

As you see, both statements use the same property, "`location`." However, the subjects (Amathus and Limassol) are different. The common property, "`location`," describes a class of entities that have a location. To further distinguish between resources, more properties are needed. More complex statements, with additional properties, can make the specification of a resource unique.

Consider the difference:

- The Amathus is located in Limassol.
- The Amathus is a hotel, and it is located in Limassol.
- The Amathus is a hotel, and it is located in Limassol, which is located in Cyprus.
- The Amathus is a hotel, and it is located in Limassol, which is a town located in Cyprus.
- The Amathus is a five-star hotel, and it is located in Limassol, which is a town located in Cyprus.
- The Amathus is a five-star hotel, and it is located in Limassol, which is a town located in Cyprus, which is located in the Mediterranean.
- The Amathus is a five-star hotel and it is located in Limassol, which is a town located in Cyprus, which is located in the Mediterranean, which is a region.

The last statement consists of several other statements that describe four resources—"`Amathus`," "`Limassol`," "`Cyprus`," and "`Mediterranean`." The sixth statement mentions the entity "`Mediterranean`" but doesn't define it—it is implied that those who parse the statement will at least know the meaning of this word.

The last statement describes the semantics of the entity "`Mediterranean`" by means of another entity, which is "`region`." However, the term "`region`" is still undefined. There is no end—it is impossible to explicitly define absolutely everything, but the difference between the first and seventh statements is huge.

It is very important to be able to find a good balance between the amount of semantics extracted from knowledge, the volume of data to be parsed by a computer, and the cost of translating knowledge into "semantic" languages. In the early stages of the Semantic Web, the amount of semantics will be very low, but it will become something huge within just a few years.

So, although the seventh statement doesn't provide complete information about all the resources, it is enough. A Semantic Web search engine could give the correct answer to the question "Where is the Amathus hotel?" or answer the request "Give me a list of five-star hotels in Limassol."

RDF GRAMMAR

Listing 27.2 demonstrates how RDF can be used to extract and describe the semantics of the statement "The Amathus is a five-star hotel, and it is located in Limassol, which is a town located in Cyprus, which is located in the Mediterranean region."

The XML code from Listing 27.2 can be inserted into a Web page of a tourist agency, which might contain an article about the accommodation options available in the region.

At the very beginning of the code are references to two namespaces. The first one, `xmlns:rdf`, is the formal specification of the version of RDF syntax used. The second namespace, `xmlns:t`, defines terms that are specific to the tourist business. The second namespace doesn't correlate to any real schema. It is just for the purpose of this example. Let's assume that it defines the terminology of tourist agencies.

Listing 27.2 An Example of RDF Notation

```
<?xml version="1.0"?>

<rdf:RDF
    xmlns:rdf="http://www.w3.org/1999/02/22-rdf-syntax-ns#"
    xmlns:t="http://www.foo-schemas.org/schemas/tourbusiness">

    <rdf:Description about="http://www.foo-schemas.org/
        resources/tourbusiness#Amathus">
        <t:Type>hotel</t:Type>
        <t:Location rdf:Resource="http://www.foo-schemas.org/
            resources/tourbusiness#Limassol" />
        <t:Class>5-star</t:Class>
    </rdf:Description>

    <rdf:Description about="http://www.foo-schemas.org/resources/
        tourbusiness#Limassol">
        <t:Type>town</t:Type>
        <t:Location rdf:Resource="http://www.foo-schemas.org/
            resources/tourbusiness#Cyprus" />
    </rdf:Description>

    <rdf:Description about="http://www.foo-schemas.org/resources/
        tourbusiness#Cyprus">
        <t:Type>Country</t:Type>
        <t:Type>Island</t:Type>
        <t:Location rdf:Resource="http://www.foo-schemas.org/
            resources/tourbusiness#Mediterranean" />
    </rdf:Description>

    <rdf:Description about="http://www.foo-schemas.org/resources/
        tourbusiness#Mediterranean">
        <t:Type rdf:Resource="http://www.foo-schemas.org/resources/
            tourbusiness#Region" />
    </rdf:Description>

</rdf:RDF>
```

The XML code used in the example is quite readable (this is a great advantage of XML!), and you can see that it describes one resource using another as a property establishing relations between different kinds of entities such as hotel, town, country, region. In this description, the "`terminal`" resource is "`region,`" which is used to describe the resource "`Mediterranean`" that is not defined in the code. Note that RDF requires resources to be identified by means of URIs (see the `rdf:resource` tag), and it's a common practice to use URLs for that purpose. However, there aren't any requirements whatsoever to the actual contents of documents located at given URLs.

RDF SCHEMA

The Resource Description Framework Model discussed earlier is a very simple and effective mechanism for describing resources, their properties, and the relationships between resources.

However, it does not define any means of declaring properties or defining relations between resources and their properties. For example, it could be nice to have some standard way to say that the property "`Author`" cannot be used with any resources of type "`Hotel`," or that the resource "`MySecureDocument`" should have the property "`TimestampID`" among the others.

The World Wide Web Consortium proposed a special framework to declare such relationships between properties and resources. This framework is the RDFS, or RDF Schema. The full text of the RDFS specification is located at `http://www.w3.org/TR/rdf-schema`.

Caution

Note that the RDF Schema specification used and discussed in this chapter has a status of W3C Candidate Recommendation at the time of writing–meaning that it can change when it moves to a W3C Recommendation phase.

The RDFS provides a designer with a simple mechanism to create machine-understandable definitions of properties and resources. RDFS is a schema system designed to permit a user to define languages for RDF. An RDF schema defines the basic types that can be used and how they can be used together. It also provides a means to validate RDF instance documents.

The RDFS has been proposed to be used in conjunction with RDF as a namespace that can be referenced inside an RDF element.

As an example of using RDFS, the RDFS code represented in Listing 27.3 defines a simple set of resource classes and their properties that can be used within the tourist business and links the schema with the earlier example in Listing 27.2.

27

LISTING 27.3 AN EXAMPLE OF THE RDF SCHEMA SPECIFICATION FOR THE TOURIST BUSINESS

```
<?xml version="1.0"?>

<rdf:RDF
    xmlns:rdf="http://www.w3.org/1999/02/22-rdf-syntax-ns#"
    xmlns:rdfs="http://www.w3.org/2000/01/rdf-schema#">

    <rdfs:Class rdf:ID = "hotel">
        <rdfs:comment>The class of hotels</rdfs:comment>
        <rdfs:label xml:lang="en">Hotel</rdfs:label>
        <rdfs:label xml:lang="fr">Hôtel</rdfs:label>
```

Listing 27.3 Continued

```
        <rdfs:subClassOf rdf:resource = "http://www.foo.org/
            tourbusiness/2001/12/Classes#Resort"/>
    </rdfs:Class>

    <rdf:Property ID="Location">
        <rdfs:domain rdf:resource="#hotel"/>
        <rdfs:label xml:lang="en">Location</rdfs:label>
        <rdfs:label xml:lang="fr">Emplacement</rdfs:label>
        <rdfs:range rdf:resource="http://www.foo.org/geography/2001/10/
            Classes#PlaceOnEarth"/>
    </rdf:Property>

    <rdf:Property ID="Class">
        <rdfs:domain rdf:resource="#hotel"/>
        <rdfs:range rdf:resource="#HotelClass"/>
        <rdfs:label xml:lang="en">Class of the hotel</rdfs:label>
        <rdfs:label xml:lang="fr">Classe d'hôtel</rdfs:label>
    </rdf:Property>

    <rdfs:Class rdf:ID = "HotelClass"/>
    <HotelClass rdf:ID = "1-star"/>
    <HotelClass rdf:ID = "2-star"/>
    <HotelClass rdf:ID = "3-star"/>
    <HotelClass rdf:ID = "4-star"/>
    <HotelClass rdf:ID = "5-star"/>


<!--Here goes the definition of other classes and properties ➥
...

</rdf:RDF>
```

Let's go through Listing 27.3 and try to understand each of the lines.

The schema starts with a standard XML prologue and an RDF element that references the namespaces used.

To describe this sample schema, we are using two namespaces—RDF and RDFS:

```
<?xml version="1.0"?>

<rdf:RDF
    xmlns:rdf="http://www.w3.org/1999/02/22-rdf-syntax-ns#"
    xmlns:rdfs="http://www.w3.org/2000/01/rdf-schema#">
```

Then, the schema defines one of the classes we used in Listing 27.2.

```
    <rdfs:Class rdf:ID = "hotel">
        <rdfs:comment>The class of hotels</rdfs:comment>
        <rdfs:label xml:lang="en">Hotel</rdfs:label>
        <rdfs:label xml:lang="fr">Hôtel</rdfs:label>
        <rdfs:subClassOf rdf:resource = "http://www.foo.org/
            tourbusiness/2001/12/Classes#Resort"/>
    </rdfs:Class>
```

In this code, the text given within the `rdfs:comment` tag contains a human-readable description of the class being defined. The `rdfs:label` tag gives a human-readable name of the class, in two languages in our example. The keyword `rdfs:subClassOf` establishes the inheritance relationship between two classes, and, finally, the tag `rdf:resource` identifies the class that participates in the relationship.

The class ID is "`hotel`," and now our RDF instance document can use the type "`hotel`" when referring to "`Amathus`" as a resource. Because we have defined a vocabulary for our application, a computer can now "understand" the statement "Amathus is a hotel." In the scope of our example, the word "understand" means exactly the following:

- A computer will know that the Amathus is a hotel.
- A computer will know that the Amathus is a resort because a hotel is a subclass of resort.
- A computer will also be able to "say" that Amathus is a hotel in two languages—English and French.

When we have the resource "`hotel`" defined, we need to specify a set of properties that can be used with it and the range of values that are valid for the properties. The property `"Location"` is defined as follows:

```
<rdf:Property ID="Location">
    <rdfs:domain rdf:resource="#Hotel"/>
    <rdfs:label xml:lang="en">Location</rdfs:label>
    <rdfs:label xml:lang="fr">Emplacement"</rdfs:label>
    <rdfs:range rdf:resource="http://www.foo.org/geography/
        2001/10/Classes#PlaceOnEarth"/>
</rdf:Property>
```

This code declares that the location is a property of a resource of class `hotel`, and that the location can be any "`PlaceOnEarth`," which is defined in some geographic schema referenced by a URI.

An additional property is defined in almost the same way as the `"Location"` property. The only difference is that we have provided a list of valid values for the property instead of referencing a definition that exists somewhere else:

```
<rdf:Class rdf:ID = "HotelClass"/>

<HotelClass rdf:ID = "1-star"/>
<HotelClass rdf:ID = "2-star"/>
<HotelClass rdf:ID = "3-star"/>
<HotelClass rdf:ID = "4-star"/>
<HotelClass rdf:ID = "5-star"/>
```

We didn't define all the classes and properties used in Listing 27.2, but as an exercise, you can try creating a full RDF Schema.

Finally, after defining all the classes of resources and their properties, we can put the RDF Schema somewhere on the network. So the link to the second namespace in Listing 27.2 points to this schema.

```
<?xml version="1.0"?>

<rdf:RDF
    xmlns:rdf="http://www.w3.org/1999/02/22-rdf-syntax-ns#"
    xmlns:t="http://www.foo-schemas.org/schemas/tourbusinness">

    <rdf:Description about="Amathus">
        <t:Type>hotel</t:Type>
        <t:Location rdf:Resource="Limassol" />
        <t:Class>5-star</t:Class>
    </rdf:Description>

...
</rdf>
```

AGENTS

Metadata, RDF annotations, RDF Schemas, and ontologies altogether create a solid foundation for agents—special programs that are capable of understanding the semantics described with metadata and ontologies.

In the Semantic Web, an agent is a program capable of comprehending data described with metadata based on ontologies and communicating with each other using joint ontologies.

Figure 27.3 represents a conceptual schematic diagram of the Semantic Web, its components, and interrelationships between them.

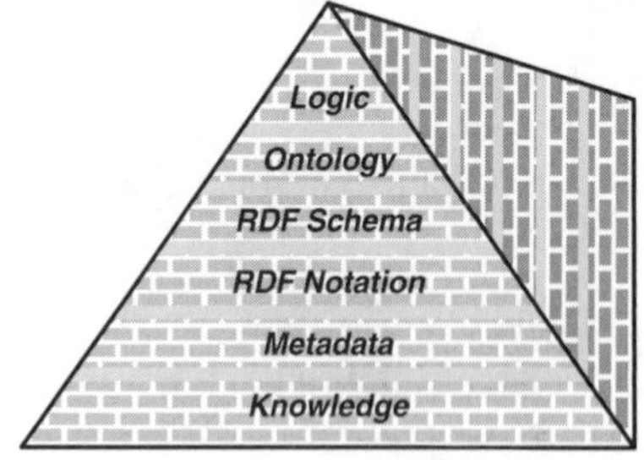

Figure 27.3
Conceptual components of the Semantic Web.

The foundation of the pyramid on this diagram is Data or Information, which is described by means of metadata. Metadata is represented with RDF and RDF Schema, which defines types and relationships in terms of classes of resources and properties they can have. On top of this, there is an ontology layer—a conceptualization of a domain of knowledge. On the very top of the pyramid, there is a logic layer—a layer that machines can use to reason with.

The logic layer is represented by computer programs—agents capable of doing useful things with knowledge. Agents benefit from all the layers of the pyramid down to the very bottom and can talk to each other in the same common language even if they were not specially designed with the other agents in mind.

FUTURE DIRECTIONS AND THE SEMANTIC WEB

The Semantic Web activity is run by the *World Wide Web Consortium (W3C)* and is the W3C's current view on the future development of the World Wide Web. This section discusses some possible directions of the technology and its impact on everyday life.

W3C SEMANTIC WEB ACTIVITY

W3C puts a lot of effort in the development of common standards, open protocols, and shared vocabularies, which will then become a foundation for the Semantic Web.

Currently, several interest and working groups are involved in the Semantic Web activity. They are

- RDF Interest group—A forum designated to a discussion of RDF issues, applications, and so on. Both W3C members and nonmembers participate in this group.
- RDF Core working group—This is a working group charted to the further development of the RDF/RDFS.
- Web Ontology working group—The goal of this group is the development of the ontology language on top of the RDF/RDFS, which will provide different Web communities with a standard way of interchanging semantic data.
- The W3C Semantic Web Activity is also in alliance with the DAML project run by the DARPA.

SEMANTIC WEB APPLICATIONS

It is obvious that the Semantic Web will be a perfect basis for future development of knowledge processing applications. To mention just a few possible directions in which the technology might evolve, there are

- Inference engines
- Intelligent search engines
- Cataloging and classifying knowledge
- Knowledge Exchange and Accumulation Agents
- Expansion of e-commerce applications

Let's have a quick look at each of these.

INFERENCE ENGINES

Inference engines might be one of the most incredible applications of the Semantic Web. The amount of knowledge currently accumulated by mankind is so tremendously huge that the brain of even the most intelligent individual is unable to remember any significant portion of it.

When knowledge becomes available for computers, it will be possible to build a system capable of processing the existing knowledge and generating new ideas. You might be asking yourself "How is it possible?"

When you prove a theorem, you create a logical chain of axioms and statements that have already been proven. Using Predicate Calculus, the result of this chain is either true or false. If the result is true, the statement is correct. Otherwise, it is wrong. Using the Semantic Web, machines can construct logical chains using the existing knowledge and determine for themselves if something is correct.

An *inference engine* is an agent application running in the Semantic Web, which processes the existing knowledge and *creates* new ideas based on predefined inference rules.

Intelligent Search Engines

A common problem with even the most powerful search engines is that it takes too long to find what you are actually looking for. Often, you have to navigate through large amounts of irrelevant Web pages that contain the same set of keywords as your query but semantically do not correlate to your question.

One application of the Semantic Web produces a substantial increase of the power of search engines. New search engines will be capable of performing semantically meaningful searches. Web crawlers that gather data for search engines will not only find words, but will also parse the RDF formatted metadata of Web pages to index pages in accordance with their semantics.

Cataloging and Classifying Knowledge

Another astonishing application of the Semantic Web is the classification of knowledge. Imagine that you have thousands of documents related to different domains of knowledge and you just need a few of them—perhaps documents that are about eighteenth century music. Today, it's impossible to find what you need in a reasonable amount of time.

However, if the documents are marked up properly with RDF, it's easy for an agent application to classify the documents and build a tree structure in which leaves represent documents and nodes represent domains of knowledge. Back to our example, an agent could build a document tree, which would have a node "`Music`" with a subnode "`Eighteenth Century`" and so on, and this would be a result of automated processing.

Knowledge Exchange and Accumulation Agents

Knowledge is only useful when it can be exchanged between people and/or computers and accumulated. Let's have a look at a very simple example.

John knows a lot about Verdi who is the author of *Aida*. He wants to see this opera in the local theatre, but he doesn't want to waste his time if the performance is bad. Helen has heard this opera in the local theatre—she liked it, and she would like to know if there is anything else by Verdi as good as *Aida*.

John and Helen both have special knowledge exchange agents installed on their computers, so they use their agents to find out if anybody can answer their questions. The agents find each other in the Semantic Web and share their knowledge so that now the agents know everything John and Helen need.

John and Helen obtain reports from their agents. Because Helen was really excited with the opera, John's agent decided to book a ticket for John, so it communicated with John's Calendar Agent to find out the most appropriate time. Helen's agent was not so lucky—there was nothing else by Verdi being staged. But because John recommended a few other masterpieces, Helen's agent communicated with the online music store and ordered some MP3s for her.

Although this is a simple example of knowledge exchange powered by the Semantic Web, the application is exciting and highlights its usefulness. Real-world applications will naturally be much more complicated. They will have to deal with many real-world issues, such as security and trust, intellectual property, and so on. However, as we have seen, the vision of the Semantic Web includes plans to address some of these issues.

EXPANSION OF E-COMMERCE APPLICATIONS

The Semantic Web will boost the development of e-commerce in the near future and will make intellectual property a valuable commodity.

It will also dramatically increase profits of the companies that will be brave enough to decide to make the Semantic Web their main platform for information sharing and exchange.

The Semantic Web will destroy the barriers that prevent modern e-commerce from growing and becoming a part of everyday life. Imagine a computer agent that browses the Semantic Web searching for the best offer on a two-week holiday in Cyprus. Now imagine that it was you who asked the agent to do this job for you sparing you from hours of conversations with travel agents.

Or, imagine an agent run by a restaurant—an agent, which maintains the stock of food products and does necessary arrangements with wholesalers' agents when any of the items gets too low in stock.

In both cases, the savings realized will make e-commerce even more attractive than it is today.

WILL IT CHANGE OUR LIVES?

Today it's difficult to imagine the world without personal computers, but a couple of decades ago there were no PCs.

In the early 1980s it was impossible to predict the impact of the PC on our lives.

It's difficult to imagine the world without the Internet, but HTTP was invented just about a decade ago.

In the early 1990s it was impossible to predict the impact of the WWW on our lives.

Now it is impossible to predict how we will live when the Semantic Web becomes an everyday reality.

We can think about how it might affect us, but history says that imagination is usually far beyond reality when this reality becomes history.

Yes, it will change our lives.

How? Let's return to this question a few years later.

Additional Resources

This chapter was intended to give an overview of the Semantic Web. If you intend to become more acquainted with the technologies discussed here or would like to find out more, it might be useful to read some additional documentation. Here is a list of resources that might help you:

- XML 1.0 Recommendation. (`http://www.w3.org/TR/REC-xml`). The XML 1.0 Recommendation (Second Edition) from the W3C is the final word on XML. If you have a question about a technical aspect of XML, this should be the first source you consult.
- The World Wide Web Consortium Web site (`http://www.w3c.org`). Here you can find information about all the WWW standards, recommendations, and specifications, as well as the most recent information about the W3C activity.
- The W3C's Semantic Web Activity Web site (`http://www.w3c.org/2001/sw`). This site is dedicated to the Semantic Web activity and contains links to RDF and RDFS specifications, as well as other information concerning the Semantic Web.
- Another site dedicated to the Semantic Web (`http://www.semanticweb.org`). The semantic Web Community Portal contains a lot of useful links and documentation.
- If you are interested in the W3C Metadata activity, the best place to go is `http://www.w3c.org/Metadata`.
- If you are interested in the Dublin Core Initiative, their Web address is `http://dublincore.org`.
- One more interesting place to go is the Web site of the DARPA Agent Markup Language and Ontology Interchange Language projects (DAML+OIL): `http://www.daml.org`.
- SENSUS (`http://www.isi.edu/natural-language/projects/ONTOLOGIES.html`) is a 70,000 node taxonomy containing definitions of English words and various concepts. It was developed by Kevin Knight, Eduard Hovy, and Richard Whitney. The purpose of this ontology is the machine translation.
- OntoWeb (`http://www.ontoweb.org`) Ontology-based information exchange for knowledge management and electronic commerce.

ROADMAP

The Semantic Web represents what is to come from organizations such as the W3C as we move toward the goal of using the Web to truly share information in an organized and efficient manner. However lofty the goals of the Semantic Web, there are still the matters of current information technology and organization that we must tend to in the here and now. That is the goal of XML—to bring structured documents to the Web now. That is also the goal of this book—to provide you with all the tools you need to bring XML to your projects and make informed decisions about how you will work with XML now and, hopefully, for many years to come.

Throughout this book, we have tried to concentrate on presenting you with a balanced view of each member of the XML family so that you have an understanding of the technology on a conceptual, as well as a practical, level. All theory and no practice doesn't help in real-world applications, while at the same time, no theory would put you at a distinct disadvantage when faced with difficult choices. We hope that you have struck some balance, and that with the treatment of each of the XML technologies in the book, you now have an understanding of XML, XSL, XSLT, XPath, XPointer, and so on, so that you know how these technologies work together and how to get started putting them into practice in your daily work. Of course you are not going to come away an expert on all XML has to offer from an overview text such as this, but what we hope to have provided in addition to some nitty-gritty code examples is perspective. This insight should prove valuable to you as you begin to narrow down the field of the specific XML technologies that are right for your project, and dive into becoming an expert in the appropriate area with the appropriate resources.

Appendixes

APPENDIX

Recommendation Pointers

In this appendix

The topics covered in this book are all either directly related to Recommendations from the World Wide Web Consortium or are very closely related to the W3C's activities. Because the W3C is the de facto standards group for the World Wide Web (in spite of having no formal standards granting authority), the W3C is the best place to turn when you have specific questions regarding the implementation of a Web-based technology.

A list of the technologies discussed in this book follows, as well as the links to the appropriate resources (where possible) on the W3C Web site. When the technology is not a W3C technology, the link to the appropriate governing body is given.

XML 1.0

At the core of all the technologies discussed in this book is the Extensible Markup Language recommendation from the W3C. Here are links to the general XML page at the W3C, as well as a direct link to the XML 1.0 Recommendation:

Extensible Markup Language (XML)

`http://www.w3.org/XML/`

Extensible Markup Language (XML) 1.0 (Second Edition)

`http://www.w3.org/TR/REC-xml`

These pages should serve as an excellent general resource for any of the other technologies discussed here. Because the other technologies presented are either derived from XML or developed to support XML, a thorough understanding of XML is essential for understanding the entire range of technologies it supports.

XML SCHEMAS

The XML Schemas Recommendations exist as a support mechanism for XML. Defining schemas allows you to validate XML documents. Here are links to the W3C XML Schema site, as well as links to the three individual recommendations that compose the entire set of XML Schema:

XML Schema

`http://www.w3.org/XML/Schema`

XML Schema Part 0: Primer

`http://www.w3.org/TR/xmlschema-0/`

XML Schema Part 1: Structures

`http://www.w3.org/TR/xmlschema-1/`

XML Schema Part 2: Datatypes

`http://www.w3.org/TR/xmlschema-2/`

The Part 0: Primer, is actually a Recommendation, although it serves as a tutorial rather than a formal definition. Part 1: Structures, deals with the syntax and physical structures of XML Schema, whereas Part 2: Datatypes deals with the mechanisms for specifying data types in XML Schema.

Namespaces

The XML Namespaces recommendation is closely related to both the XML 1.0 Recommendation and XML Schema. The latest version of the Recommendation can be found at

Namespaces in XML

`http://www.w3.org/TR/REC-xml-names/`

CSS

Although Cascading Style Sheets are not explicitly an XML-based or related technology, it is possible to use CSS in conjunction with XML documents for display on the World Wide Web. Therefore, you might want to familiarize yourself with the Recommendations that define CSS:

Cascading Style Sheets

`http://www.w3.org/Style/CSS/`

Cascading Style Sheets, Level 1

`http://www.w3.org/TR/REC-CSS1`

Cascading Style Sheets, Level 2

`http://www.w3.org/TR/REC-CSS2/`

Since the introduction of CSS Level 1, a number of changes have been introduced, resulting in the more robust CSS Level 2. At the time of publication, CSS Level 2 (or CSS2) was the most recent version of CSS. However, you can check the general CSS activity page for more information on the current changes in CSS.

XSL

The Extensible Stylesheet Language (XSL) provides a more natural interface to creating stylesheets for XML. XSL was designed to work with XML and is also XML derived. The general XSL activities and the first Recommendation can be found here:

The Extensible Stylesheet Language (XSL)

`http://www.w3.org/Style/XSL/`

Extensible Stylesheet Language (XSL) Version 1.0

`http://www.w3.org/TR/xsl/`

The XSL Recommendation encompasses the general XSL syntax and processing information, as well as the XSL Formatting Objects (XSL:FO) section for producing more robust layout and printed materials as well.

XSLT

In addition to providing formatting abilities, XSL Transformations provides the ability to manipulate the content of XML documents dynamically. The XSLT Recommendation can be found at

XSL Transformations (XSLT) Version 1.0

`http://www.w3.org/TR/xslt`

The W3C is also in active development on the next version of XSLT, which is currently a Working Draft that can be found at

XSL Transformations (XSLT) Version 2.0 (Working Draft)

`http://www.w3.org/TR/xslt20/`

XPath

The XPath Recommendation provides a mechanism for locating elements and attributes within an XML document. The Recommendation can be found at

XML Path Language (XPath) Version 1.0

`http://www.w3.org/TR/xpath`

In addition to adding functionality for XML processing, XPath is essential in enabling technologies such as XSLT by providing the mechanism to locate specific areas within an XML document with a high degree of granularity. XPath 2.0 is also currently in development, and it has been released as a Working Draft that can be found at

XML Path Language (XPath) Version 2.0 (Working Draft)

`http://www.w3.org/TR/xpath20/`

XML Pointer, XML Base, and XML Linking

XML Pointer, XML Base, and XML Link are all closely related technologies that allow interconnectivity among XML documents and the ability to use and reference subsections of larger documents. The W3C general activity page for the three technologies can be found at

XML Pointer, XML Base and XML Linking

`http://www.w3.org/XML/Linking`

In addition, each of the individual technologies has a site with their respective Recommendations.

XLink

XLink is a final Recommendation, which can be found here:

XML Linking Language (XLink) Version 1.0

`http://www.w3.org/TR/xlink/`

XLink provides a mechanism for inserting links into XML documents to link documents together, such as with hyperlinks in HTML.

XBase

XBase is also a Recommendation, and it provides the mechanism for creating base URIs for XML documents. The XBase Recommendation can be found at

XML Base

`http://www.w3.org/TR/xmlbase/`

XPointer

XPointer provides a mechanism for pointing to XML document fragments, which can be useful in assembling larger documents from smaller fragments:

XML Pointer Language (XPointer) Version 1.0

`http://www.w3.org/TR/xptr/`

Although at the time of press, XPointer was only a Candidate Recommendation, the preceding link should point to the proper resource when the XPointer Recommendation is adopted in its final version.

XInclude

The XInclude Recommendation provides the mechanism for including XML infosets together into a single document. The Recommendation can be found at

XML Inclusions (XInclude) Version 1.0

`http://www.w3.org/TR/xinclude/`

At the time of press, the XInclude Recommendation was still a Working Draft, the preceding link should be an appropriate resource as it moves into the Candidate Recommendation and Final Recommendation stages.

DOM

The Document Object Model is a very important Recommendation that identifies the structure of documents, and it is the basis for Web-based document processing. The activities of the W3C as related to the DOM can be found at

Document Object Model

`http://www.w3.org/DOM/`

The DOM is in a constant state of evolution, and the current incarnation is DOM Level 2. However, DOM Level 3 is currently in active development and promises new features as well.

DOM Level 1

The first release of the Document Object Model can be found at

Document Object Model (DOM) Level 1 Specification

`http://www.w3.org/TR/REC-DOM-Level-1/`

There are still software packages that only support DOM functionality at this level. DOM Level 1 provided the base functionality for XML.

DOM Level 2

The current set of Recommendations that comprise DOM Level 2 can be found at the following locations:

Document Object Model (DOM) Level 2 Core Specification

`http://www.w3.org/TR/DOM-Level-2-Core/`

Document Object Model (DOM) Level 2 Views Specification

`http://www.w3.org/TR/DOM-Level-2-Views/`

Document Object Model (DOM) Level 2 Events Specification

`http://www.w3.org/TR/DOM-Level-2-Events/`

Document Object Model (DOM) Level 2 Style Specification

`http://www.w3.org/TR/DOM-Level-2-Style/`

Document Object Model (DOM) Level 2 Traversal and Range Specification

`http://www.w3.org/TR/DOM-Level-2-Traversal-Range/`

These Recommendations define various aspects of the Document Object Model, including how documents are structured, displayed, parsed, and navigated.

DOM Level 3

The next phase of activity with the Document Object Model is represented by a number of Recommendations that collectively serve to describe DOM Level 3:

Document Object Model (DOM) Level 3 Core Specification

`http://www.w3.org/TR/DOM-Level-3-Core/`

Document Object Model (DOM) Level 3 Abstract Schemas and Load and Save Specification

`http://www.w3.org/TR/DOM-Level-3-ASLS/`

Document Object Model (DOM) Level 3 Events Specification

`http://www.w3.org/TR/DOM-Level-3-Events/`

Document Object Model (DOM) Level 3 XPath Specification

`http://www.w3.org/TR/DOM-Level-3-XPath/`

These recommendations are still in the Working Draft phase; however, they do represent the future direction for the DOM.

SAX

In addition to the Document Object Model, the Simple API for XML provides an event-based model for parsing XML documents. Information about SAX can be found at

Simple API for XML

`http://www.saxproject.org/`

SAX is not a Recommendation of the W3C. However, because it is widely used by members of the XML development community, it is important to recognize SAX as an alternative to the DOM when parsing XML documents.

XQuery

The XQuery activities at the W3C are still in the Working Group stages, and as yet there are no formal Recommendations. However, general activity in XQuery can be tracked at

XML Query Activity

`http://www.w3.org/XML/Query`

The goal of XQuery is to provide a query language that can be used with XML documents for searching and locating data within XML infosets.

XML INFOSET

The XML Infoset Recommendation is a very high level and abstract recommendation, which can be found at

XML Information Set

`http://www.w3.org/TR/xml-infoset/`

The Infoset recommendation serves to define a data set for XML documents, which is critical for operations such as XQuery. However, the Infoset establishes guidelines that are primarily used by other XML Recommendations, not by XML authors directly.

BIZTALK

BizTalk is not a Recommendation from the W3C; in fact, BizTalk is not a single XML technology at all. BizTalk is an effort by Microsoft to promote the use of XML based applications and vocabularies for business communications. The BizTalk effort can be followed at

BizTalk.org

`http://www.biztalk.org/home/default.asp`

The goal of BizTalk is to produce a body of standards for business, with Microsoft's interests also at hand.

EBXML

Similar to BizTalk, ebXML is an effort to coordinate a group of XML-related standards for use in business communications. The ebXML efforts can be tracked at

ebXML.org

`http://www.ebxml.org/`

Unlike BizTalk, the ebXML effort is an open source community effort, not sponsored by a single vendor.

CANONICAL XML

Canonical XML was created to provide a method for differentiating between XML documents that have the same logical structure, but might differ in content. The two Recommendations related to Canonical XML can be found at

Canonical 1.0

`http://www.w3.org/TR/xml-c14n`

Exclusive XML Canonicalization Version 1.0

http://www.w3.org/TR/xml-exc-c14n

The first of these Recommendations deals with straightforward Canonical XML, whereas the Exclusive XML Canonicalization Recommendation deals with documents that have special needs, such as those with XML Signatures.

XML Signatures

The XML Signature effort is still in the early stages of development, and the activity of the Working Group can be found here:

XML Signature Working Group

http://www.w3.org/Signature/

The goal of the group is to provide a mechanism for computing and verifying signatures of Web resources in XML documents. However, this should not be confused with encryption efforts or digital signatures for security purposes.

XML Encryption

The XML Encryption effort is also in the Working Group stage of development:

XML Encryption Working Group

http://www.w3.org/Encryption/2001/

The goal of XML Encryption is to produce a means of encryption for documents and, more importantly, an XML syntax to represent the encrypted data and information for decryption.

XHTML

The most fundamental Recommendation for the World Wide Web is the HTML Recommendation that defines the Hypertext Markup Language. The most recent change in HTML is the effort to make it compatible with XML, and the result is XHTML. Efforts concerning HTML and XHTML can be found at

Hypertext Markup Language

http://www.w3.org/MarkUp/

XHTML 1.0: The Extensible Hypertext Markup Language

http://www.w3.org/TR/xhtml1/

XHTML is a reworking of HTML, within the rules of XML, to provide greater compatibility and extensibility.

WML

The Wireless Markup Language is an XML-based technology for wireless communication. Information regarding XML and wireless technologies can be found at

Mobile Access Interest Group

`http://www.w3.org/2001/di/Mobile/`

WAP Forum

`http://www.wapforum.org/what/technical.htm`

The Mobile Access Interest Group is the W3C working group developing wireless Web standards. The WAP Forum is an independent group that is also developing wireless standards, including WAP and WML.

SVG

The Scalable Vector Graphics recommendation is designed to allow the use of vector graphics in browser context. Information regarding SVG can be found at

Scalable Vector Graphics (SVG)

`http://www.w3.org/Graphics/SVG/Overview.htm8`

Scalable Vector Graphics (SVG) Version 1.1

`http://www.w3.org/TR/SVG11/`

Although SVG is still in the Working Draft stage, it promises to be one of the more glamorous applications of XML.

SMIL

The Synchronized Multimedia Integration Language is designed for authoring complex multimedia presentations that incorporate multiple type of media, such as audio or video. Information regarding SMIL can be found at

Synchronized Multimedia

`http://www.w3.org/AudioVideo/`

Synchronized Multimedia Integration Language (SMIL) 1.0 Specification

`http://www.w3.org/TR/REC-smil/`

Synchronized Multimedia Integration Language (SMIL 2.0)

`http://www.w3.org/TR/smil20/`

The current version of SMIL is 2.0. However, the link to 1.0 is provided here for historical purposes and because there might still be software packages that only offer support for v.1.0.

RDF

The Resource Description Framework is a set of Recommendations that can be used to describe resources on the Web in a common format to facilitate the exchange of information:

Resource Description Framework

`http://www.w3.org/RDF/`

Resource Description Framework (RDF) Model and Syntax Specification

`http://www.w3.org/TR/REC-rdf-syntax/`

Resource Description Framework (RDF) Schema Specification 1.0

`http://www.w3.org/TR/rdf-schema/`

RDF Model Theory

`http://www.w3.org/TR/rdf-mt/`

At the time of press, the RDF Model and Syntax Specification was the only final Recommendation. The RDF Schema Specification was a Candidate Recommendation, whereas the RDF Model Theory was still a Working Draft. However, updates to the status of these recommendations can still be tracked through the generic RDF site.

XFORMS

XForms represents the next generation of forms for the World Wide Web, based on XML, so that the forms are not limited to use on the Web:

XForms

`http://www.w3.org/MarkUp/Forms/`

XForms 1.0

`http://www.w3.org/TR/xforms/`

At the time of press, XForms 1.0 was in the Working Draft stage of development. However the preceding links should point to the proper resources to track XForms as it moves to the final Recommendation stage.

SEMANTIC WEB

The Semantic Web represents the further efforts of the W3C to refine the way the Web functions—specifically to develop mechanisms that provide meaning to information disseminated via the Web. The activities of the W3C in relation to the Semantic Web can be found at

Semantic Web

`http://www.w3.org/2001/sw/`

Although the Semantic Web is still very much in the early stages of development, it promises to be one of the more ambitious undertakings of the W3C in years to come.

APPENDIX 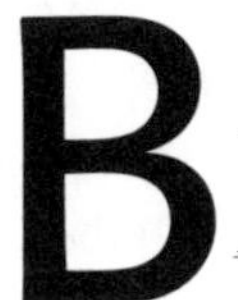

GUIDE TO READING THE XML RECOMMENDATION

In this appendix

In order for a new technology to succeed widely, it needs to achieve a critical mass of users. If the technology fails to achieve enough supporters to keep the technology going, slowly, but surely, it will die off.

One of the mechanisms that can be employed to aid in adoption is standardization. By adopting a standard for implementing new technologies, businesses can be assured that they are using technology correctly, and that their implementations of a technology will be compatible with other vendors and clients.

Implementing standards can be an arduous process. It involves bringing together experts in a technology, representatives from industry in some type of committee, and then reaching a consensus about how a technology should be defined.

And as if that were not trouble enough, there is also the matter of defining the technology in a clear and concise language. The standard that is eventually adopted needs to be as clear as possible to avoid differing interpretations of the standard, which would result in incompatibilities.

Unfortunately, if standards are not your core business, keeping up with them can be a chore. Not only can waiting for a standard cause delays in your implementation, but they can also be difficult to read.

That is why I have included this appendix: to give you an overview of how the XML Recommendation (and related standards) is created, how you can best work with them, and how to read and implement the final standard. You might be able to work with XML for a long time without ever looking at the XML Recommendation. But if you do need to consult the recommendation, hopefully this will help you make sense of it.

Why Reference Is Important

Establishing standards have been an important part of our interactions as humans for a very long time. The necessity of standard weights and measures comes from the need to standardize trade; and the need to standardize XML is really no different.

The idea behind XML, after all, is to be able to exchange information independent of applications and systems. If you have an XML-based application and a document with a DTD, you can exchange that document with any other system capable of handling XML. You can do that because of the XML v.1.0 Recommendation from the W3C. If we didn't have that recommendation to base our XML documents on, we would quickly encounter incompatibilities.

For example, let's take a quick look at end tags. If we are basing our tag structure on something we are familiar with, such as HTML, our tag pairs will always look something like this:

```
<TAG></TAG>
```

So, we have a beginning tag, and then use the slash (/) to denote an ending tag. But HTML also includes some tags that do not have ending tags:

```
<BR>
<P>
```

Because HTML (and SGML) allows for the omission of end tags, in certain circumstances, there is an opportunity for confusion. In XML, only empty elements do not require end tags, and even those tags use a special syntax:

```
<empty/>
```

In the XML format, a tag that is empty has the slash appended, which denotes that it is empty. Specifying this type of information is exactly what a standard is for; to eliminate confusion and to ensure that everyone uses the same conventions in their documents.

THE W3C RECOMMENDATION PROCESS

The W3C is the body that issues standards for the World Wide Web. As a matter of fact, the W3C has no formal power as a standards body. In fact, SGML is not a W3C Recommendation: It is an ISO standard.

That is why the standard documents that are formally published by the W3C are called *Recommendations*. They are adopted as standards by the Web community through a consensus. That is, manufacturers, authors, and users agree to abide by the recommendations of the W3C, even though none are formally required to do so.

Note

There are numerous examples of deviations from W3C standards. The best examples are browser *extensions* to HTML, such as the dreaded `<BLINK>` tag. Both Microsoft and Netscape have strayed from W3C recommendations in the past to extend the functionality of their browsers. The cost, however, is that Web authors using these extended features limited their audiences to users of certain browsers, defeating the purpose of HTML.

The XML Recommendation's origins began with the SGML Editorial Review Board. This board, working in conjunction with the SGML Working Group, was working toward adapting SGML to uses with the World Wide Web.

In 1996, the XML Working Group was formed to develop XML into a formal recommendation. Building on the work of people such as James Clark, Jon Bosak, and Dan Connolly, the final version was authored by Tim Bray, Jean Paoli, and C. M. Sperberg-McQueen. It became an official W3C Recommendation on February 10, 1998, and the final version can be found at the official XML 1.0 Recommendation Web site: `http://www.w3.org/TR/1998/REC-xml-19980210`.

STANDARDS RELATIONSHIPS

The XML Standard depends on a number of other standards that are used as building blocks for the XML Recommendation. These supplementary standards include

- SGML (ISO 8879:1986)—The SGML standard is defined by the International Standards Organization, and it is the basis for XML. XML is actually a limited subset of the SGML standard, and, therefore, changes in the SGML standard might influence changes in the XML Recommendation.
- ISO/IEC 10646 and Unicode—These standards are used to define the character sets and encoding that are used to represent character data with XML documents.
- IETF RFC 1738 and RFC 1808—These Requests for Comments from the Internet Engineering Task Force are the standards that define the syntax for Universal Resource Locators (URLs). Because URLs are the common addressing form on the Web, they are also used in XML to represent paths to data.

Because XML relies on these specifications, as they change, XML might also change. This is one more reason why keeping up on the current standard is beneficial to anyone using XML.

XML DESIGN GOALS

There were a number of design goals that the authors of the XML specification kept in mind as they were designing XML. These goals are designed to keep XML well focused, and to ensure that the standard meets the needs of those who will be using XML in real-world applications. These goals include

- XML shall be straightforwardly usable over the Internet.

  This goal is rooted in the need to adapt SGML for use in conjunction with the World Wide Web. Although the SGML specification doesn't limit uses to traditional publishing or electronic documentation, many have felt that it is too broad and confusing to easily adapt to Internet-related technologies. SGML will always have a place for building complex documents and document sets. However, by adapting XML specifically for electronic use over the Internet, the XML standard will fill the need for a majority of users without the complexity of SGML.
- XML shall support a wide variety of applications.

  XML is not limited to marking up any one kind of data. It can be used for everything from the expression of mathematical formulas to creating a new language for vector graphics markup to real estate listings. By making XML easier than SGML, it opens the door to an unlimited number of new applications that can be limited to an individual, a company, or even standardized by an industry.

- XML shall be compatible with SGML.

  Because XML is based on the SGML standard, and many SGML users might want to implement limited XML solutions in conjunction with SGML, the two languages strive for compatibility, so XML is a subset of SGML.

- It shall be easy to write programs that process XML documents.

  In spite of how it might look at first glance, the XML specification is actually quite simple. At just more than 40 pages, it is one of the shortest of the W3C's Recommendations. XML achieves its power through simplicity. By only specifying that which is absolutely essential, XML is robust and still simple to implement in a variety of settings.

- The number of optional features in XML is to be kept to an absolute minimum, ideally zero.

  The inclusion of optional functions allows different application developers to write applications with potential incompatibilities. Having incompatible versions of XML defeats the purpose of XML, and therefore the WG has to strive to keep optional features at a bare minimum.

- XML documents should be human-legible and reasonably clear.

  XML documents are based in text, and the tags can be formed with words that have clear meanings to human beings. Because of this, and the highly organized structure of XML documents, a human can simply look at an XML file, and more than likely make sense of that file's content. Unlike a graphics file format, like a JPEG, an XML file can be read by a human and still hold value, thus freeing the document from cumbersome overhead for processing.

- The XML design should be prepared quickly.

  The XML Recommendation was authored and adopted by the W3C in less than two years, and it continues to evolve at a lightening quick pace. The pace of Internet development is clearly reflected in the development of Internet standards such as XML.

- The XML design shall be formal and concise.

  The XML Recommendation is concise: limited to about 40 pages. It is also quite formal, which is why we have dedicated this appendix to the reading of the recommendation. If you are unfamiliar with the formal semantics and syntax used in the recommendation, it can be very confusing to read.

- XML documents shall be easy to create.

  XML documents are very easy to create. They can be edited in any editor capable of reading ASCII text files. An XML document can be as simple as

  ```
  <? XML version="1.0"?>
  <DOCUMENT/>
  ```

and need not consist of anything else. Of course, a document this simple might not be of much use, but it's clear that XML does not *need* to be complex, even though it can be.

- Terseness in XML is of minimal importance.

  One thing that makes SGML confusing is that in order to save data overhead, you can eliminate things like those pesky end tags. However, that can lead to confusion, and adding end tags to your document isn't going to take up a ton of time or file space. So XML is not concerned with sacrificing clarity and structure for terseness. Be as long winded as you like with XML.

These design goals are what guided the XML Working Group to create the XML 1.0 Recommendation. Keeping these goals in mind, they have succeeded in creating a very simple, yet powerful language for creating data markup that is usable across a variety of electronic applications. Even now, in its infancy, it is easy to see the potential for XML. And as the standard continues to evolve, it will continue to adapt to future technologies.

READING THE SPECIFICATION

For all the effort that went into developing the draft of the 1.0 Recommendation, not much effort went into explaining the Recommendation to the lay person. That really is not the fault of the working group. They created a recommendation that is very concise, clear, and well-defined, leaving very little room for interpretation.

This is the sign of a well-constructed recommendation. It is clearly and formally defined so that anyone implementing XML does so with the same understanding of how XML documents are created and defined. This is the very core of what makes a successful standard.

However, that is not very comforting as you sit down to look at the XML 1.0 Recommendation, and you can't make any sense of it. If you don't understand the specification, you cannot implement it correctly, nor can you come to understand it very easily.

In the next section, we will take a look at how the recommendation is written so that you can gain a better understanding of the vocabulary and, therefore, have an easier time following the spec.

TERMS

Many terms are used in the XML Recommendation that have very specific meanings, as outlined by the recommendation's authors. The meaning of some of these terms will be obvious, but some might be interpreted slightly differently from what you would expect. So take a few minutes to familiarize yourself with the terminology used in the specification.

may—We warned you that some of these terms would be obvious. However, when referring to the recommendation, this means that XML data and applications "are permitted to but need not behave as described."

must—This means that the data or applications are required to exhibit the specified behavior.

error—An error occurs when the rules of the recommendation are violated. The error is generated by a processing application, which can deal with the error appropriately.

fatal error—A fatal error is an error in which the application processing the XML data is required to generate an error and to cease parsing the XML document. This is reserved for errors that cause some kind of violation of the XML recommendation, serious enough to be corrected immediately before continuing.

validity constraint—A validity constraint is a rule in the recommendation applying to any XML document that is to be considered valid. A violation of a validity constraint must cause an error to be generated by validating XML processors.

well-formedness constraint—All XML must be well-formed. Therefore, an XML document that violates a well-formedness constraint must cause the XML processor to generate a fatal error.

at user option—This phrase means that any software conforming to the XML Recommendation needs to implement the ability to enable or disable this functionality as a user option.

case-folding—Case-folding is a process in which all characters in a character set are specified as "non-uppercase" into their uppercase equivalents. So, for example,

```
ThIs Is A sENtenCE witH MiXEd case.
```

would become

```
THIS IS A SENTENCE WITH MIXED CASE.
```

This is done to facilitate matching in character sets regardless of case sensitivity.

match—A match in the recommendation can mean one of several things. It can refer to a match of strings or names, which is not a case-sensitive match that occurs after the items being compared have been case-folded. For example,

`<Element>` matches `<ELEMENT>`.

A match can also refer to content and content models. In which case, a match occurs "if the content is `Mixed` and consists of character data and elements whose names match names in the content model, or if the content model matches the rule for `elements`, and the sequence of child elements belongs to the language generated by the regular expression in the content model." Got it?

This is not quite as easy to follow as may and must, but let's break it down to see what it really means. Say that we have an element defined in our DTD called `<STORY>`, and `<STORY>` must contain `<TITLE>` and `<AUTHOR>`.

If we have some XML that looks like this,

```
<STORY>
<TITLE>The Little Coder Who Could</TITLE>
<AUTHOR>Jim Causey</AUTHOR>
</STORY>
```

we have a match because our `<STORY>` element matches the requirements of our content model.

exact match—An exact match is simple: when two strings match and they are case sensitive. Thus,

`<Element>` does **not** match `<ELEMENT>`.

`<ElEmEnT>` **does** match `<ElEmEnT>`.

for compatibility—This term applies to XML features that are included solely for the purpose of remaining compatible with SGML.

for interoperability—This term applies to features that are recommended to help XML remain compatible with existing SGML processors. However, implementation of these features is not required to conform to the recommendation.

Notation

In addition to these terms, a number of special notations are also used within the XML specification. You might be familiar with some of these notations from other specifications or programming languages. However, understanding what type of information these notations describe is critical to correctly following the XML Recommendation.

At the heart of the grammar used for XML is a simple Extended Backus-Naur Form (EBNR) notation. It is really pretty straightforward:

```
symbol ::= expression
```

This just means that a `symbol` is defined by an `expression`. For example, let's say that we were using this notation to define `Pi` as a literal value of 3.14. Our rule would look like this:

```
Pi ::= "3.14"
```

Of course, this is an oversimplification, but it gets the point across.

The symbol portion of this rule can either begin with an uppercase letter, as in our example, which means that the symbol is defined by a simple regular expression. Or it can begin with a lowercase letter, which indicates that a recursive grammar is used to define the symbol. We'll take a look at some examples a little later.

The expression on the right side of a rule can consist of several different notations. These notations include

`#xN`

In this notation, `N` is a hexadecimal integer, and the expression represents the corresponding character in the ISO/IEC 10646 specification.

`[a-zA-Z], [#xN-#xN]`

These expressions represent any character with a value in the range specified, inclusive. So `[l-pL-P]` would include any letters from *l* to *p*, including the *l* and the *p* in both lower and uppercase.

`[^a-z], [^#xN-#xN]`

These expressions represent any character with a value outside the range given. The caret symbol (`^`) means *not*, so `[^a-q]` would exclude any letter in the alphabet up to, and including *q*, which would make the set of characters defined consist of *r* through *z*.

`[^abc], [^#xN#xN#xN]`

This expression represents any character except those given. So `[^abcdefghijknopqrstuvwyz]` would be a very long way to represent `xml`.

`"string" or 'string'`

Any string within quotation marks represents that string, literally. So `"XML"` is `"XML"` is `'XML'`.

`a b`

This means that the symbol is defined as *a* followed by *b*.

`a | b`

This means that the symbol can be defined by *a* or by *b*, but not both.

`a - b`

This means that any strings are represented by *a* but not by *b*.

`a?`

This means that the symbol might contain *a*, but it is not required to contain *a*.

`a+`

This means that the symbol must contain at least one *a*, but it might contain more.

`a*`

This means that the symbol might contain zero *a*s or more.

`%a`

The `%` sign signifies that the represented data can be replaced by a parameter entity reference within the external Document Type Declaration.

`(expression)`

This simply means that the entire expression contained within the parentheses is to be treated as one unit. Any of the notations that apply to a single unit can then be applied to the expression, such as the `?`, `+`, or `*` suffix operators.

`/* ... */`

These are used to denote comments.

`[WFC: ... ]`

The Well-Formedness Check (WFC) identifies any check for well-formedness associated with a rule.

`[VC: ... ]`

The Validity Check (VC) identifies any check for validity that is associated with a rule.

DISCUSSION OF XML 1.0 RECOMMENDATION

Now that you have an idea of how to read some of the information used in the XML Recommendation to define the components of XML, let's take a look at some actual definitions that are found in the specification.

First, we will look at how the specification defines whitespace.

You are probably familiar with whitespace in many shapes and forms. In fact, there is whitespace in between each of the words in this sentence. Whitespace in XML is denoted in the specification by an `S`. Whitespace can also consist of several different types of input. For example, a space (created with your spacebar), a tab, and a carriage return all produce whitespace in XML.

So, here's a look at the formal declaration for whitespace:

```
S ::= (#x20 | #x9 | #xd | #xa)+
```

This defines our symbol, `S` to be equal to the expression contained in the parentheses. Inside the parentheses, we have a series of characters that are defined by their ISO/IEC 10646 Representation. The expression simply says that we can have a space, a carriage return, a line feed, or a tab.

Finally, the + suffix operator is used to apply to the whole expression, which means that whitespace might consist of "one or more occurrences" of each of the characters that are legal whitespace.

This is a pretty simple rule, but it illustrates many of the grammatical constructs that we have been looking at, which will come in handy when reviewing the XML specification.

Let's take a look at a few more rules from the specification, to get a feel for reading how they are constructed.

One of the most commonly used elements in XML is parsed character data (PCData). PCData is the information that is contained between your start and end tags in an element, and most of your document will likely take the form of PCData. Here is how PCData is defined according to the specification:

```
PCData ::= [^<&]*
```

This is a very simple rule. It means that the PCData symbol is defined as being any character, except a less than (<) or an ampersand (`&`).

These two characters cannot be used in character data because the less than sign is used to denote the start of a new tag and the ampersand is used to denote the start of an entity. If these two symbols were used in your PCData, they might confuse a parser that assumed they were part of the markup. Remember that PCData is Parsed Character Data.

Now, here is how start and end tags are defined:

```
STag ::= '<' Name (S Attribute)* S? '>'
ETag ::= "</" Name S? '>'
```

By now, you should have a pretty good idea how to read these two rules. So give it a try before you continue on with the explanations. You might be surprised at how something that once looked like gibberish is beginning to become clearer.

Okay, we will begin with the rule for the start tag:

```
STag ::= '<' Name (S Attribute)* S? '>'
```

Here we begin with the symbol for the start tag `STag`. Now, the first thing that we have in a start tag is the less than sign, which is represented as a literal character, contained in single quotes. Next comes the *`Name`* of the tag (which is defined elsewhere in the spec).

Now, the next section,

```
    (S Attribute)*
```

is treated as a single expression because of the parentheses. The `S` represents a whitespace character, followed by an attribute. The `*` suffix operator on the expression indicates that there might or might not be an attribute in the tag. Finally, the tag is closed with a greater than symbol.

So our final construct for a start tag consists of a `'<'`, a tag name, maybe an attribute, and then a final `'>'`. Thus, any of the following are valid start tags:

```
<START>
<START What="Attribute">
<Title Author="me">
```

However, none of the following would be valid tags:

```
>START<
<Start
Start>
```

The rule for constructing end tags is very similar:

```
ETag ::= "</" Name S? '>'
```

The major differences are that end tags require the slash `/` character following the less than sign (`'<'`), and they do not allow for attributes.

Armed with the knowledge from this appendix, you should be able to make out much of the full XML 1.0 Recommendation. In addition, some other resources are available to help you understand the information contained in the XML Specification, including one of the best XML resources available on the Net: the Annotated XML Recommendation.

The Annotated XML Recommendation (`http://www.xml.com/axml/testaxml.htm`) is written by Tim Bray, one of the XML 1.0 Recommendation authors, and it is an excellent resource for XML beginners. If you have questions about the recommendation, consult this resource first. Chances are good that it will contain an answer for you.

APPENDIX C

XML Resources

In this appendix

Many of the technologies covered in this book are extensive enough for books to be written about them: In fact, many of them do. Other technologies are new enough that they are changing too rapidly to have books out currently, but will likely as they mature.

The goal of this book is to show you all the different possibilities for XML solutions and how they fit together, and then to present the technology with enough detail to get you started on development. As you build more advanced solutions however, you might encounter some stumbling blocks or progress beyond the scope of this book. To help you in your efforts to master all these technologies, here are some additional resources to help you learn more. Keep in mind that some of these technologies might not have many resources available, simply because they are new and not widely implemented yet.

XML

The following general resources are for learning more about well-formed XML, as defined in the XML 1.0 Recommendation. These resources are a good springboard for learning about XML and the technologies that are related to XML.

- XML-DEV (xml-dev@xml.org)—This is the mailing list for XML developers. The topics of discussion run the gamut from simple to complex XML topics, sometimes with heated debate.
- comp.text.xml—The USENET Newsgroup for the discussion of XML-related issues. As with XML-DEV, the topics of discussion cover a wide range of skills and subjects.
- xml.com (`http://www.xml.com`)—XML.com is a site dedicated to following and reporting on developments with XML. It is a commercial site, although the content tends to be fairly neutral.
- xml.org (`http://www.xml.org`)—XML.org bills itself as the industry portal for XML. Here, you can find links to a number of XML-related resources.
- XML-FAQ (`http://www.ucc.ie/xml/`)—The XML Frequently Asked Questions covers a range of questions dealing with XML.
- XML in 10 Points (`http://www.w3.org/XML/1999/XML-in-10-points`)—This note from the W3C, written by Bert Bos, addresses some of the design considerations for XML.
- Annotated XML (`http://www.xml.com/pub/a/axml/axmlintro.html`)—The Annotated XML is a version of the 1.0 Recommendation, complete with annotations from Tim Bray, one of the Recommendations editors.
- James Clark XML Resources (`http://www.jclark.com/xml/`)—James Clark is an established figure in the structured document world, and he is also the editor of a number of XML-related Recommendations. This page on his site contains pointers to a number of XML resources.
- The Cover Pages (`http://www.oasis-open.org/cover/`)—The Cover Pages serve as a resource for various XML-related topics. The site is maintained by Robin Cover and includes links to other sites as well as important postings to the XML-DEV list.

- IBM Developer Works (`http://www.ibm.com/developerworks/xml/`)—IBM hosts the Developer Work site as a resource and forum for developers of many technologies, including XML. This is the XML section of the site, and contains great resources for XML developers, including articles, code samples and downloads.
- XML 101 (`http://xml101.com/`)—XML 101 is a site that features introductory articles and tutorials. This can be a good site for learning about the basics of XML authoring.
- Perfect XML (`http://www.perfectxml.com/default.asp`)—Perfect XML is an XML Portal that features news related to XML advances and information about general XML events.
- XML Papers (`http://www.rpbourret.com/xml/index.htm`)—This site is Rob Bourret's page, which lists several papers on XML and related technologies.
- W3 Schools (`http://www.w3schools.com/`)—The W3 Schools site contains a number of free tutorials on Web technologies, from HTML, to CSS, to XML. Topics range from general XML to XSL and Schemas. It is a good resource for free tutorials.
- XML Pitstop (`http://www.xmlpitstop.com/`)—The XML Pitstop is another portal site, linking to resources around the Web. Of particular interest on the Pitstop site is the library of XSL stylesheets, which can be downloaded for use.
- ZVON Org (`http://www.zvon.org/index.php`)—ZVON is a site that offers tutorials on XML technologies, presented using XML technologies.
- Web Developer (`http://www.webdeveloper.com/xml/`)—Web Developer is a general resource for Web development. This links to the XML section of the site.
- XML Hack (`http://www.xmlhack.com`)—XML Hack, founded by Simon St.Laurent, is essentially a Web log that tracks news and events related to the XML community. It's a great resource for keeping up with announcements from many different areas, all related to XML.

DTDs

Because DTDs aren't actually a separate recommendation, but a part of the XML 1.0 Recommendation, there aren't very many DTD specific resources available. However, there are a few places where you can turn to learn more about Document Type Definitions.

- XML's DTD (`http://www.w3.org/XML/1998/06/xmlspec.dtd`)—This is the DTD that describes XML itself. Although you probably won't have a need to consult this DTD, it can be interesting to see how the DTD is structured.
- Converting an SGML DTD to XML (`http://www.xml.com/pub/a/98/07/dtd/index.html`)—This article can be helpful if you have an SGML DTD that you need to convert to XML. Because SGML is a much older technology, a number of DTDs are available for different uses in SGML.
- XML 101 DTDs (`http://www.xml101.com/dtd/default.asp`)—This site contains a number of tutorials for using DTDs.

XML SCHEMAS

There is a great deal of discussion about XML Schemas on the various XML lists and newsgroups. However, because XML Schemas are a new technology, there aren't many resources formally dedicated to information about them. In addition to the Recommendation itself, here are a few sites that contain information about XML Schemas:

- XML Schema Part 0: Primer (`http://www.w3.org/TR/xmlschema-0/`)—Although this is part of the XML Schema Recommendation, it is non-normative, and is really a tutorial on how to work with XML Schemas.
- XML Schema in Context (`http://www.ascc.net/~ricko/XMLSchemaInContext.html`)—This article by Rick Jelliffe discusses XML Schemas in relation to well-formed XML and Document Type Definitions.
- Cover Pages Schema Section (`http://www.oasis-open.org/cover/schemas.html`)—This section of the Cover Pages is dedicated specifically to XML Schemas.
- Using XML Schemas (`http://www.xml.com/pub/a/2000/11/29/schemas/part1.html`)—This XML. com article is a tutorial for working with XML Schemas.
- Schema.net (`http://www.schema.net`)—This site started out as James Tauber's site, and it has since become a repository for various types of schemas.

XML NAMESPACES

The XML Namespaces Recommendation is one of the most simple and still most misunderstood Recommendations in the XML family. Here are some resources you can use to learn more about Namespaces, as well as the issues surrounding namespaces and their uses:

- XML Namespaces FAQ (`http://www.rpbourret.com/xml/NamespacesFAQ.htm`)—This is the Frequently Asked Questions document for XML Namespaces.
- James Clark on Namespaces (`http://www.jclark.com/xml/xmlns.htm`)—This article from James Clark attempts to clarify some of the confusion surrounding Namespaces.
- 19 Short Questions About Namespaces (`http://www.megginson.com/docs/namespaces/namespace-questions.html`)—This article addresses some commonly asked questions about namespaces, written by David Megginson, the author of SAX.
- Namespaces by Example (`http://www.xml.com/pub/a/1999/01/namespaces.html`)—This XML.com article by Tim Bray (one of the authors of the Namespaces Recommendation) is a simple namespaces tutorial.

XML AND CSS

A number of resources are available on the Web dedicated to the issues surrounding the use of XML and Cascading Stylesheets. It just so happens that most of them are hosted by the W3C. These are some great resources that address the use of CSS and XML.

- CSS and XML, Which Should I Use? (`http://www.w3.org/Style/CSS-vs-XSL`)—This document hosted by the W3C deals with the choice between using CSS or XSL in order to display the contents of your XML documents.
- Using XSL and CSS Together (`http://www.w3.org/TR/NOTE-XSL-and-CSS`)—This document deals with using both CSS and XSL together as display technologies for XML.
- CSS Properties, XML Attributes, Cascading and Inheritance (`http://www.w3.org/TR/1999/WD-SVG-19990211/attrib.html`)—This W3C document addresses issues of structure when working with CSS and XML Documents.
- Associating Stylesheets with XML (`http://www.w3.org/TR/xml-stylesheet/`)—This is the W3C Recommendation that defines how to associate XML documents with style sheets.

XSL

The Extensible Stylesheet Language has a number of resources available for learning how and when to use XSL. Here are some sites that discuss XSL in general or offer tutorial information:

- XSL-List (`http://www.mulberrytech.com/xsl/xsl-list/`)—This is a mailing list for the discussion of XSL issues.
- XSL FAQ (`http://www.dpawson.co.uk/xsl/xslfaq.html`)—This is the Frequently Asked Questions page for XSL.
- What is XSL? (`http://www.w3.org/Style/XSL/WhatIsXSL.html`)—This document serves as an introduction to XSL from the W3C.
- Hands On XSL (`http://www-106.ibm.com/developerworks/library/hands-on-xsl/`)—This is a hands-on XSL tutorial from the IBM Developerworks site.
- XSL Cover Pages (`http://www.oasis-open.org/cover/xsl.html`)—This is the section of the Cover Pages that is dedicated to following XSL.
- XSL Info (`http://www.xslinfo.com`)—This XSL site is from the authors of schema.net, and serves as a general portal to other XSL resources in print and on the Net.

XSLT

Although very closely related to XSL, XSLT is actually a separate Recommendation. As such, there are a few resources that deal with XSLT specifically.

- xslt.com (`http://www.xslt.com/`)—This is a portal dedicated specifically to XSLT. Here, you can find links to XSLT News, Software, and Tutorials.
- XSLT Cheat Sheet (`http://www.ejim.co.uk/module/overview/xsl.htm`)—This site provides some links to XSLT Resources and also allows you to test your XSL style sheets with your XML documents.

- exslt.org (http://www.exslt.org)—This XSLT site is a collection of extensions for XSLT contributed by the development community at large.
- Jeni's XSL Site (http://www.jenitennison.com/xslt/index.html)—This site contains tutorial information regarding XSL and XSLT.

XSL-FO

Although the XSL Formatting Objects are part of the XSL Recommendation, we've treated them separately because most developers deal with XSL-FO separately from other aspects of style sheet authoring. XSL-FO is currently being implemented in many tools, so the resources available to learn about XSL-FO are certain to increase. In the meantime, here are some resources to consult for XSL-FO information:

- W3C XSL-FO List (http://lists.w3.org/Archives/Public/www-xsl-fo/)—This is an archive of the W3C Mailing list dedicated to the discussion of XSL-FO.
- XSL-FO List (http://groups.yahoo.com/group/xsl-fo/)—This site is another mailing list for the discussion of XSL-FO.
- XSL-FO Reference (http://zvon.org/xxl/xslfoReference/Output/index.html)—This reference site for XSL-FO provides a quick and easy way to look up Formatting Objects and their syntax.

XPath and XPointer

Because XPath and XPointer are both new and highly specialized XML technologies, virtually no resources on the Web address them specifically. The best resource for both XPath and XPointer is the official Recommendations. (URLs for the Recommendations can be found in Appendix A.) However, there is one site to turn to as an XPath resource.

- XPath Cheat Sheet (http://www.ejim.co.uk/module/overview/xpath.htm)—This site contains links to XPath resources, and it also features an innovative graphical "cheat" for learning about XPath terms.

XLink, XBase, and XInclude

The XLink, XBase, and XInclude Recommendations also have specialized applications, and therefore not many resources deal with using them. The best resources for these technologies is the W3C, although there are a few other sites to consult as well.

- What is XLink (http://www.xml.com/pub/a/2000/09/xlink/index.html)—This W3C publication introduces XLink.
- XInclude.net (http://www.xinclude.net/xi/)—This is a free command line resource for processing XInclude elements.

DOM AND SAX

SAX and DOM are both subjects for advanced XML development, specifically for the development of applications or automated XML solutions. A number of online resources exist for learning more about SAX and DOM. Here is a selection of sites:

- SAX Project.org (`http://www.saxproject.org/`)—This is the main site for SAX, and it contains project news and updates.
- SAX FAQ (`http://www.saxproject.org/?selected=faq`)—This is the Frequently Asked Questions document for SAX.
- W3C DOM Site (`http://www.w3.org/DOM/`)—This is the W3C site for maintaining information regarding the development of the Document Object Model.
- DOM Cover Pages (`http://www.oasis-open.org/cover/dom.html`)—The Cover Pages area is dedicated to tracking information regarding DOM.
- DMOZ DOM Directory (`http://dmoz.org/Computers/Programming/Internet/W3C_DOM/`)—This portal site contains links to a number of DOM-related sites.

C

XML, JAVA, AND .NET

If you aren't developing applications, you probably won't need to consult additional resources to learn more about XML and Java or XML and .NET. However, there are a few sites you can check out to learn more if you are interested in pursuing Java or .NET development with XML.

- JDOM (`http://www.jdom.org/`)—This is the main site for the JDOM project, which is an effort to develop a Java-based set of tools that are DOM compliant.
- Apache Xerces (`http://xml.apache.org/xerces2-j/index.html`)—This is the Apache Xerces XML Parser main site.
- SAX Quickstart (`http://www.saxproject.org/?selected=quickstart`)—This is a tutorial for getting started using SAX.
- Microsoft .NET (`http://www.microsoft.com/net/`)—This is the Microsoft site for news and information regarding .NET.
- Sun's site for Java technology and XML (`http://java.sun.com/xml/` and `http://www.sun.com/xml/`)—An early sponsor of the development of XML, Sun has created these sites to provide access to its technologies related to Java and XML.

XML AND PERL

XML documents are text, and Perl is a scripting language with excellent features for dealing with text. Therefore, the fit between XML and Perl is very good. The following sites contain more information on using XML with Perl:

- Perl and XML FAQ (http://www.perlxml.com/faq/perl-xml-faq.html)—This is the FAQ for using XML with Perl.
- Perl.com (http://www.perl.com/pub/a/1998/06/perl-xml.html)—This article outlines working with Perl and XML.
- XML.com (http://www.xml.com/pub/q/perlxml)—This is the XML.com site area dedicated to working with Perl and XML.

XML Databases and Document Repositories

In addition to XML support built in to a number of existing relational databases, a number of specialized databases are also designed specifically for working with XML. The same holds true for document repositories. There are a number of document management solutions that were based on SGML but have been retrofitted to deal with XML. We will list a number of these products in Appendix D, "XML Software and Applications." However, the following resources deal with the subject of data management and XML in general, not vendor specific solutions:

- XML and DBMS (http://www.25hoursaday.com/StoringAndQueryingXML.html)—This article discusses the use of XML and Databases on a broad level.
- Introduction to XML Native Databases (http://www.xml.com/pub/a/2001/10/31/nativexmldb.html)—This article introduces using databases that are designed for use with XML.

XQuery

XQuery is still in the development stage and isn't yet a finished Recommendation. Therefore, not many resources exist for learning more about XQuery, and there likely won't be until XQuery matures. However, there are some sites that discuss various aspects of XQuery.

- XML.com (http://www.xml.com/pub/rg/XQuery)—This is a summary of articles on XML.com that are related to the development of XQuery.
- IBM Developer Works (http://www-106.ibm.com/developerworks/xml/library/x-xquery.html)—This is the IBM site for developers working with XQuery and Java.

XHTML

Because XHTML is HTML rewritten using XML, if you are familiar with HTML, mastering XHTML shouldn't be difficult. There are a few resources you can consult to review the details and differences between HTML and XHTML, but chances are you won't need them.

- HTML Home Page (`http://www.w3.org/MarkUp/`)—This is the main W3C Home page for Hypertext Markup Languages.
- XHTML Overview (`http://hotwired.lycos.com/webmonkey/00/50/index2a.html`)—This is an introduction to XHTML from the Webmonkey site.
- Introducing XHTML (`http://www.wdvl.com/Authoring/Languages/XML/XHTML/`)—This is a simple XHTML Tutorial.

WML

Wireless Technologies are becoming more and more popular. However, because of limitations in wireless hardware, the solutions possible with WML still aren't very mature. These resources are for organizations that are working to develop wireless technologies.

- WML Programmers (`http://groups.yahoo.com/group/wmlprogramming/`)—This is a mailing list and discussion group for developers working with WML.
- The WAP Forum (`http://www.wapforum.org`)—The WAPForum is a consortium of vendors working with wireless technologies, including WAP and WML.
- The Wireless FAQ (`http://www.allnetdevices.com/faq/`)—This FAQ addresses issues with Wireless technologies, from hardware to software, including WAP and WML.
- WAP Tutorial (`http://www.w3schools.com/wap/default.asp`)—This site contains a step-by-step tutorial for working with WAP.

SVG

Scalable Vector Graphics offer one of the most promising XML vocabularies for the future of graphics and the Web. One company with a very big vested interest in SVG and its success is Adobe. The graphics powerhouse has been a longtime supporter of SVG, and it is also one of the best resources for software and information.

- W3C SVG Site (`http://www.w3.org/Graphics/SVG/`)—This is the W3C site for SVG activity.
- Adobe SVG Zone (`http://www.adobe.com/svg/main.html`)—This is Adobe's site for SVG, which includes many resources, such as software.

SMIL

SMIL could potentially bring multimedia to the Web in a vendor neutral format, and as SMIL matures, the possibilities are promising. However, the lack of widespread browser support has prevented SMIL from becoming an overwhelming success. The best resource for SMIL remains the W3C:

- W3C SMIL Home Page (`http://www.w3.org/AudioVideo/`)—This is the W3C site for SMIL activity.

RDF

The RDF Recommendation from the W3C is a complex and controversial recommendation. There are a few resources for tracking what the W3C is doing with RDF and the future activities related to the development of the Semantic Web.

- W3C RDF Home Page (`http://www.w3.org/RDF/`)—This is the W3C page for RDF activity.
- RDF Resource Guide (`http://www.ilrt.bris.ac.uk/discovery/rdf/resources/`)—This site is a guide to various RDF resources available on the Web.
- W3C Semantic Web (`http://www.w3.org/2001/sw/`)—This is the W3C Page for activity related to the Semantic Web. The Semantic Web and RDF are closely related initiatives.

XFORMS

Because XForms are new, resources aren't currently dedicated to XForm development. The best resource for XForms remains the W3C.

- W3C XForms (`http://www.w3.org/MarkUp/Forms/`)

APPENDIX D

XML Software and Applications

In this appendix

XML

XML has now been around long enough for a body of software supporting XML to have begun to mature into applications which are stable and useable. However, because the technologies related to XML are still in a constant state of flux, many software packages still do not offer robust support for everything that is possible with XML. There are a few Web sites that are good resources to consult when looking for XML software:

- `http://www.xmlsoftware.com/`
- `http://www.garshol.priv.no/download/xmltools/`
- `http://www.alphaworks.ibm.com/xml`

Each of these sites can assist you in your search to find XML tools for your specific project.

With that said, a number of packages have been developed for specialized uses, and you might be able to find what you need. Similarly, you might find that you can build your own solutions by piecing together a few different components.

This appendix is by no means a complete list of software packages available for XML. Some packages out there—whether they are freeware, shareware, or commercial products—are only supported by individuals, and they might not be very far along in development. Or they might be based on older versions of a Recommendation. For example, many applications are compatible with SMIL 1.0, but only a few have been updated for SMIL 2.0. Finally, some applications claim XML support; however, the support is slightly dubious. For example, Microsoft Office uses XML. However, that doesn't mean you can edit XSL in Word. It simply means that the file formats (.doc, .xls, and so on) are based on XML.

What we have assembled here is a list of applications offering the best current support in their categories. For the most current versions and information, you should always consult the individual vendor sites.

XML Capable Browsers

XML was designed for use with the World Wide Web. However, when XML was first released, Web browsers could only display XML as a text file. Since that time, however, browsers have integrated a great deal of XML support. There is still much to be accomplished, such as adding support for XSL Stylesheets. However, a number of options are now available for XML browsers.

- Amaya (`http://www.w3.org/Amaya/`)—Amaya is the W3C reference browser. In addition to supporting XML, it is also one of the few products to support a wide range of XML technologies, including XML, DTDs, XHTML, and SVG. Amaya is also an open source project that features an easy-to-use WYSIWYG interface.
- Internet Explorer (`http://www.microsoft.com/windows/ie/default.asp`)—Internet Explorer was the first commercial browser to support XML. IE supports the display of well-formed XML (as a tree), as well as the display of valid XML in tree form. IE also

supports the display of XML documents using CSS and some levels of XSL. IE makes use of the MSXML Parser and .NET to provide robust XML support. With version 6.0, IE offers support for SMIL 2.0 as well.

- Netscape (`http://home.netscape.com/browsers/6/index.html?cp=dju6xpod`)—Netscape has been very slow to adopt XML, but has recently made up for lost time with version 6.1. Version 6.1 and higher of Netscape supports XML, DTDs, XHTML, and XSL. In fact, version 6.0 of the browser features an interface written using XUL, or the XML User-Interface Language.
- X-Smiles (`http://www.x-smiles.org/`)—X-Smiles is an early development Open Source XML browser, which is designed to be used with a variety of XML technologies. Although the User Interface isn't as advanced as the commercial browsers, X-Smiles does feature support for XML, XSLT, XForms, SVG, and SMIL 2.0.

XML Editors

XML files are simply text files, and, as such, they can be edited in any application that is capable of reading a text file. However, that doesn't allow for much flexibility, such as seeing the relationship between elements and attributes easily or validating the document against a DTD or XML Schema. Here are a few editors that are designed specifically to work with XML, and they offer some features that allow you to manipulate XML files with ease.

- XMetal (`http://www.softquad.com`)—XMetal is a very advanced XML editor that allows users to edit XML documents in a natural document interface (similar to a word processor). XMetal also has features to allow for collaborative authoring and database integration. XMetal is also one of the few XML tools to offer SGML support for backward compatibility.
- XML Pro (`http://www.vervet.com`)—XML Pro is a lightweight editor developed in Java, which is designed for data-centric XML editing. XML Pro offers a convenient GUI for editing documents based on their tree structure, and also features full validation against DTDs.
- XML Spy (`http://www.xmlspy.com`)—XML Spy is also an XML editor with a GUI interface, which allows you to edit documents with a natural document interface. XML Spy has actually matured into a suite of applications designed to allow you to edit XML documents, as well as DTDs and XML Schemas.
- Excelon Stylus Studio (`http://www.stylusstudio.com/`)—Stylus Studio is an XML development environment that includes full featured XML, XSLT, and Java editors, as well as the ability to graphically create schema documents, execute Xpath Queries, and debug XSLT style sheets. Stylus Studio is another very powerful tool that can help with many aspects of XML development.
- XML Cooktop (`http://www.xmlcooktop.com/`)—XML Cooktop is a free development environment for authoring, editing, and testing XSLT style sheets, XML documents, DTDs, and XPATHs. It works with all versions of Windows.

- ActiveState Komodo (`http://www.activestate.com/Products/Komodo/`)—Komodo is a multifunction, cross-platform IDE for programming in more than 24 languages, including XML, XSLT, C++, C#, JavaScript, Perl, PHP, Python, and Tcl. It includes full syntax checking and autocompletion. In addition, it provides XSLT, Perl, Python, and PHP debugging.

DTDs

Although XML editors allow for the editing of XML documents, they do not necessarily support the authoring of Document Type Definitions. The following applications allow you to edit DTDs so that you can use them with your XML instance documents to create well-formed XML.

- Near and Far Designer (`http://www.opentext.com/near_and_far/`)—Near and Far Designer features multifunction, cross platform IDE for programming a GUI that allows users to design DTDs visually, and then export an XML-compliant DTD for use with XML instance documents.
- TurboXML (`http://www.tibco.com/products/extensibility/index.html`)—TurboXML allows you to edit DTDs using a GUI, and in fact offers support for a number of different Schema formats, not just limited to DTDs and XML Schemas.
- XML Spy (`http://www.xmlspy.com`)—XML Spy allows the editing of DTDs, using a text-based interface. Although this allows you to edit DTDs, it doesn't offer some of the GUI features of various other DTD products.

XML Schemas

XML Schemas are relatively new, and as such the editors that currently support DTD editing do not all support XML Schemas at this time. That will likely change as XML Schemas Recommendation matures. However, two of the editors mentioned previously allow XML Schema editing and creating:

- TurboXML
- Stylus Studio

XML and CSS

The ability to display XML using CSS for presentation purposes is a feature that is actually supported in the browsers. No special software packages exist specifically for designing CSS sheets with XML. However, the following browsers support XML and CSS:

- Internet Explorer
- Netscape

- Amaya
- X-Smile

XSL

Support for XSL can be broken down into a couple of categories. The first category is the ability to display XML in conjunction with XSL Stylesheets. That functionality is provided by the Web browsers used to display XML. Currently, Internet Explorer offers limited XSL support, as do Netscape, Amaya, and X-Smile. As XSL matures, the browser support will progress rapidly as well.

The second category involves designing and editing the XSL Stylesheets themselves. This category breaks down into applications that deal with XSLT and applications that deal with Formatting Objects.

XSLT

The following software packages are for working with XSL Transformation style sheets. Some of these applications are designed for processing XSLT, whereas some are for designing the style sheets themselves.

- XSL Transform (`http://www.tibco.com/products/extensibility/index.html`)—XSL Transform is a product for designing and working with XSLT. It features a graphical interface that allows you to map XSLT files for transforming XSL to XML or into HTML.
- XSLT Designer (`http://www.xmlspy.com/products_xsl.html`)—XSLT Designer is also a GUI-based tool that allows the end user to design XSLT Stylesheets.
- SAXON (`http://saxon.sourceforge.net/`)—Saxon is a command line XSLT Processor written in Java that allows you to apply XSLT Stylesheets to your XML documents and then have the output written to a file.
- XT (`http://www.jclark.com/xml/xt.html`)—XT is an XML Parser that allows for the parsing of XSLT style sheets. Written in Java, this isn't a basic end-user application.
- Visual XSLT (`http://aspn.activestate.com/ASPN/Downloads/VisualXSLT/`)—Visual XSLT is an add-on package for processing XSLT Stylesheets and is designed to work with .NET development.
- Excelon Stylus Studio (`http://www.stylusstudio.com/`)—In addition to editing XML documents and Schemas, Stylus Studio also has a competent XSLT editor, which includes previewing the results and XSLT debugging.
- XML Cooktop (`http://www.xmlcooktop.com/`)—As mentioned earlier, XML Cooktop is a free development environment for authoring, editing, and testing XSLT style sheets. With it, you can easily substitute XSLT processors from the menu, making it particularly suitable for compatibility testing.

XSL-FO

XSL Formatting Objects are more complicated to implement than XSLT because they involve the graphical rendering of the formatting objects themselves. They are

- FOP (`http://xml.apache.org/fop/index.html`)—This is the Apache Project home page for FOP, which is their open-source XSL-FO processor, written and implemented in Java.
- XSLFast (`http://www.xslfast.com/`)—XSLFast is a GUI-based XSL-FO editor for designing XSL-FO style sheets. It also includes the ability to export data for use with QuarkXPress and Framemaker.
- XEP (`http://www.renderx.com/`)—XEP is a commercially available XSL-FO processor that allows you to apply XSL-FO style sheets to XML documents in order to produce rendered output in either PDF or PostScript format.
- XSL Formatter (`http://www.antennahouse.com/axf20/AXF20topEN.htm`)—XSL Formatter is another XSL-FO processor that allows you to apply XSL-FO style sheets to documents for output into various formats.

DOM AND SAX

Support for DOM and SAX really isn't applicable to general XML software, but is more appropriate for development level software, such as XML parsers and processing applications. Here are two examples of DOM/SAX software:

- Xerces (`http://xml.apache.org/xerces2-j/index.html`)—The Xerces XML Parser from the Apache Project is a Java-compliant, DOM-based XML Processor.
- SAX (`http://www.saxproject.org`)—SAX is the Simple API for XML, and the site features a Java-based parser based on SAX.

XML, JAVA, AND .NET

Software related to XML, Java, and .NET is mostly development software that is specific to application programming. The following shows a few examples of XML parsers that can be used for this purpose. But, if you are interested in working with XML and Java or .NET, you should consult the appropriate developer resources for your language.

- Xerces (`http://xml.apache.org/xerces2-j/index.html`)—Xerces is an open source, Java, DOM-compliant XML Parser from the Apache Project.
- Xalan (`http://xml.apache.org/xalan-j/index.html`)—Xalan is an open source, Java-based XSLT Parser from the Apache Project.
- Java XML Pack (`http://java.sun.com/xml/javaxmlpack.html`)—Includes packages for processing XML and using XML for Web Services.

- MSXML 4.0 (http://www.microsoft.com/xml)—MSXML is Microsoft's XML Parser that includes support for Sax, DOM, and XSLT processing.

XML and Perl

A number of XML Perl modules are available for working with XML. These include some XML Parsers that have been implemented in Perl as well as some that serve as Perl interfaces to other XML applications. Here is a selection of XML-related Perl tools:

- XML::XPath (http://xml.sergeant.org/xpath.xml)—This is a Perl module that allows for the processing of XPath information.
- XML::Parser (http://wwwx.netheaven.com/~coopercc/xmlparser/intro.html)—XML::Parser is a Perl extension module that serves as an interface to the expat parser from James Clark.
- Xerces Perl (http://xml.apache.org/xerces-p/index.html)—This is a Perl implementation of the Apache Project's open source XML parser, Xerces.
- XT (http://www.jclark.com/xml/xt.html)—This is a Perl implementation of the XT parser from James Clark.

D

XML Databases

Although many vendors are now building XML support into their database offerings, some databases are currently on the market that have been developed natively with XML. The following databases are designed to work with XML:

- X-Hive (http://www.x-hive.com/)
- Excelon (http://www.exceloncorp.com/)
- TEXTML (http://www.ixiasoft.com/)

Also, a few open source databases support XML natively:

- Xindice (http://www.dbxml.org/)
- eXist (http://exist.sourceforge.net/)

Document Repositories

Although XML can be used for data centric applications, XML can also be used for documents. These document repositories are designed to work with XML documents natively, to support complex document management features:

- XML Canon/Developer (http://www.tibco.com/products/extensibility/index.html)
- OpenText BASIS (http://www.opentext.com/basis/)

- Documentum (`http://www.documentum.com/`)
- FormBridge (`http://www.texcel.com/`)

XHTML

Because XHTML is simply an implementation of HTML with some of XML's restrictions, most software that supports HTML will support XHTML. Internet Explorer, Netscape, Amaya, and X-Smile all support XHTML. And many of the current HTML editors on the market, such as Macromedia Homesite, also have support for XHTML.

SVG

SVG represents a great leap forward in graphics for the Web. However, the revolution can't occur until the Web browsers support SVG natively. Currently, the browsers that support SVG are Amaya and X-Smile. However, that will certainly change in the future. In the meantime, a number of standalone viewers are available for SVG, as well as graphics packages that are capable of exporting SVG.

- SVG Viewer (`http://www.adobe.com/svg/overview/whatsnew.html`)—This is an SVG viewer from the graphics powerhouse, Adobe.
- Batik (`http://xml.apache.org/batik/svgviewer.html`)—Batik is an open source SVG viewer from the Apache Project.
- Illustrator 10 (`www.adobe.com`)—This popular graphics program allows the creation of vector graphics and supports the export of those graphics in SVG.
- CorelDraw 10 (`www.corel.com`)—This is another popular graphics product that also supports the export of graphics in SVG.

SMIL

Similarly to SVG, SMIL applications can't really take off until there is widespread browser support. Currently, Internet Explorer offers the best support for SMIL, although other browsers are progressing. Also, a number of editors exist that allow you to work with SMIL documents. However, there aren't any WYSIWYG editors that currently support SMIL 2.0.

- Internet Explorer 5.5 and 6.0—Internet Explorer offers support for SMIL starting with 5.5 and with 6.0 IE support for SMIL 2.0.
- RealOne Platform (`http://www.realnetworks.com/solutions/ecosystem/realone.html?src=rnhmfs`)—The RealOne Platform offers support for playing SMIL presentations and animations.
- X-Smiles (only SMIL 1.0)—The X-Smiles browser offers some SMIL support, but only for version 1.0.

- SMILGen (`http://www.smilgen.org/`)—SMILGen is a Java-based SMIL editor that allows you to author SMIL files with a GUI. It should be noted, however, that SMILGen is not a purely WYSIWYG application.
- Homesite (`http://www.macromedia.com/software/homesite/`)—Adobe's Homesite also offers support for SMIL without being a full WYSIWYG SMIL editor.

Not all the technologies covered in this book have software packages available: some because they are so new. But most of the technologies not covered in this appendix are technologies such as XLink, for which there really is no software necessary. Instead, XLink would be supported by an XML browser.

Visiting the manufacturer's page is the best way to learn about these applications and to see what level of XML support they currently offer.

INDEX

A

F

I

J-K

L

M

O

Q

R

S

T

U

V

W

X-Y

Z